# HUMAN
# SEXUALITY

*To Mark, for his support and patience during this challenging and exciting project, and to my parents; my sister, Janice; my brothers, Brad and Dick; and their families, who have all provided me with such tremendous love and have always believed in me*

# HUMAN SEXUALITY

## Personality and Social Psychological Perspectives

# Craig A. Hill

*Indiana University-Purdue University Fort Wayne*

**SAGE Publications**

Los Angeles • London • New Delhi • Singapore

*For information:*

Sage Publications, Inc.
2455 Teller Road
Thousand Oaks, California 91320
E-mail: order@sagepub.com

Sage Publications Ltd.
1 Oliver's Yard
55 City Road
London EC1Y 1SP
United Kingdom

Sage Publications India Pvt. Ltd.
B 1/I 1 Mohan Cooperative Industrial Area
Mathura Road, New Delhi 110 044
India

Sage Publications Asia-Pacific Pte. Ltd.
33 Pekin Street #02–01
Far East Square
Singapore 048763

Printed in the United States of America.

*Library of Congress Cataloging-in-Publication Data*

Hill, Craig A.
Human sexuality: Personality and social psychological perspectives / Craig A. Hill.
    p. cm.
Includes bibliographical references and index.
ISBN 978-1-4129-0483-4 (pbk.)
  1. Sex. 2. Sex (Psychology) 3. Personality and cognition. 4. Social psychology. 5. Developmental psychology. I. Title.

HQ21.H4563 2008
306.7—dc22                            2007005880

This book is printed on acid-free paper.

05  06  07  08  09  10  9  8  7  6  5  4  3  2  1

| | |
|---|---|
| *Acquiring Editor:* | Cheri Dellelo |
| *Associate Editor:* | Deya Saoud |
| *Editorial Assistant:* | Anna Marie Mesick |
| *Marketing Associate:* | Amberlyn Erzinger |
| *Production Editor:* | Veronica Stapleton |
| *Copy Editor:* | Edward Meidenbauer |
| *Typesetter:* | C&M Digitals (P) Ltd. |
| *Proofreader:* | Joyce Li |
| *Indexer:* | Rick Hurd |
| *Graphic Designer:* | Edgar Abarca |

# PHOTOGRAPH CREDITS

Images reprinted with permission.

## Chapter 1

Images on pp. 2, 5, 8, 18, 19 (right), ©Jupiter Images

Images, p. 3: Center ©iStockphoto.com/Tyler Stalman; clockwise from top: ©iStockphoto.com/Lisa F. Young; ©iStockphoto.com/ShellyPerry; ©iStockphoto.com/BonnieSchupp; ©iStockphoto.com/Jelani Memory

Images, p. 11: (left) ©iStockphoto.com/Marcin Balcerzak; (right) ©Corbis

Images, p. 17: ©Corbis

Image, p. 19: (left) ©iStockphoto.com/Amanda Rohde

## Chapter 2

Image, p. 29 (right): ©iStockphoto.com/Alison Stieglitz

Image, p. 46: ©AP Photos.

Images, pp. 50, 52, 77: ©The Kinsey Institute for Research in Sex, Gender, and Reproduction

Image, p. 53: ©iStockphoto.com/Alex Slobodkin

Image, p. 75: ©Bettman/Corbis

## Chapter 3

Images, pp. 66, 68: ©The Kinsey Institute for Research in Sex, Gender, and Reproduction

Image, pp. 82 (top): ©The Kinsey Institute for Research in Sex, Gender, and Reproduction. Photograph by William Dellenback

Images, p. 73 (bottom),79, 80, 81: ©Bettman/Corbis

Image, p. 82 (bottom): ©Steven Clevenger/Corbis

Image, p. 84: ©Ted Streshinsky/CORBIS

Image, p. 85: ©Henry Diltz/CORBIS

## Chapter 4

Image, p. 95: ©iStockphoto.com/Matej Pribelsky

Image, p. 96: ©iStockphoto.com/James Pauls

Images, pp. 101, 102 (bottom), 110, 111, 117: ©Jupiter Images.

Image, p. 102 (top): ©iStockphoto.com/Darren Baker

Images, p. 107: ©iStockphoto.com/Libby Chapman

## Chapter 5

Image, p. 130: ©iStockphoto.com/Cristal Goodman

Images, pp. 139 (left), 140, 142 (top left), 142 (bottom left), 142 (bottom right), 146, 148, 170: ©Jupiter Images

Images, p. 135: ©iStockphoto.com/Anna Bryukhanova

Image, p. 139 (right): ©iStockphoto.com/Jennifer Trenchard

Images, p. 142 (top right): ©iStockphoto.com/Tyler Stalman

Image, p. 144: ©Douglas Engle/Corbis

Images, p. 354 (left): ©iStockphoto.com/Kevin Russ; (middle): ©iStockphoto.com/Steven Robertson; (right): ©iStockphoto.com/Kevin Russ

## Chapter 12

Image, p. 372: ©iStockphoto.com/Stephen Sweet

Images, pp. 387, 392, 395: ©Jupiter Images

## Chapter 13

Images, pp. 406 (top), 411, 412, 419, 434: ©Jupiter Images

Image, p. 406 (bottom): ©iStockphoto.com/Felix Thiang

Image, p. 408: ©iStockphoto.com/Tomaz Levstek

Images, p. 421 (right): ©iStockphoto.com/Thomas Gordon; (middle): ©iStockphoto.com/Eileen Hart; (left): ©iStockphoto.com/Ivar Teunissen

Images, p. 424 (right): ©iStockphoto.com/Nicholas Monu; (left): ©iStockphoto.com/Chandra Widjaja

Image, p. 427: ©iStockphoto.com/Dawn Liljenquist

Image, p. 431: ©iStockphoto.com/Ivar Teunissen

Images, p. 436 (right): ©iStockphoto.com/Pattie Steib; (left): ©iStockphoto.com/Stephanie Phillips

## Chapter 14

Images, p. 446 (top): ©iStockphoto.com/Tyler Stalman; (bottom): ©iStockphoto.com/Libby Chapman

Images, pp. 449, 462, 466, 469, 473 (top left); 473 (bottom right), 475: ©Jupiter Images

Image, p. 452: ©iStockphoto.com/Kevin Russ

Image, p. 455 (top): ©Andrea Gingerich

Images, pp. 456, 457 (top): ©Cervical Barrier Advancement Society

Image, p. 457 (bottom): ©Peter Andrews/Corbis

Image, p. 464: ©A. Inden/zefa/Corbis

Images, p. 473 (top right): ©iStockphoto.com/ Maartje van Caspel; (bottom left): ©iStockphoto .com/Cliff Parnell

# BRIEF CONTENTS

# Detailed Contents

# ACKNOWLEDGMENTS

I am immensely grateful to Sage Publications for the tremendous opportunity to write this book, an opportunity provided initially by Editor Jim Brace-Thompson and Associate Editor Katja Fried, and then Editor Cheri Dellelo and Associate Editor Deya Saoud. Their openness to new perspectives and approaches in the study of human sexuality has allowed me to realize my goal of presenting a largely psychological view of the field. I am immensely grateful for this opportunity, and for their invaluable conceptual and intellectual contributions.

Second, I am truly gratified by the substantial contributions of the reviewers of this book, who have profoundly enriched it through their many creative, inspiring suggestions. This project has been an invigorating, uplifting learning experience for me as a result. I can only hope that the students who read this book come away with the same knowledge and appreciation as I have received as a result of the reviewers' many offerings.

I would also like to thank my colleagues in the Psychology Department at Indiana University—Purdue University Fort Wayne (IPFW) for providing me with such a supportive, encouraging intellectual environment. I appreciate the opportunity to have grown professionally through their collegiality and friendship. Although all of them are important colleagues and friends, I would especially like to thank Elaine Blakemore, who has contributed to my professional and intellectual development in a myriad of ways since coming to IPFW. Carol Lawton has likewise been an outstanding scholar and friend who has provided invaluable advice and insight throughout my research program. I am also very grateful for the top-notch secretarial assistance that Christina Rockwell provided, as well as that of Jessie Todd and Hope Peters.

Finally, I want to acknowledge June Machover Reinisch, Director Emerita, and Stephanie A. Sanders, Associate Director, of The Kinsey Institute for Research in Sex, Gender, and Reproduction. By bringing me onto their research team at the world-renowned Kinsey Institute from 1987 to 1991, I was given the opportunity to launch my research program on human sexuality. I will always value the incredible experience, knowledge, and insight I gained from these exceptional scholars and scientists. More than that, I will always cherish their tremendous friendship and counsel.

Sage Publications would like to thank the following peer reviewers for their editorial insight and guidance:

Margit I. Berman, University of Minnesota

Linda L. Black, University of Northern Colorado

Anne E. Fisher, University of South Florida at Sarasota/Manatee

Irene Hanson Frieze, University of Pittsburgh

Jenny Gessler, Webster University

George Spilich, Washington College

Susan Sprecher, Illinois State University

Gabie E. Smith, Elon University

Tami Eggleston, McKendree College

# PREFACE

A good number of human sexuality textbooks are currently available to instructors who are looking for one to best suit their particular students' needs. Many cover a wide range of standard topics. Typically, they have an early chapter on female anatomy and physiology, followed by one on male anatomy and physiology, one on gender, and others on intimacy, sexuality across the life span, communication, specific sexual behaviors and sexual positions, and sexual diversity. Later topics might include atypical sexual behaviors, contraception, childbirth, sexually transmitted diseases, and sexual problems and therapy.

It is also the case that most textbooks focus in only a minor way on psychological aspects of sexuality. A great number of topics deal almost entirely with biological or physical health issues, barely or superficially addressing psychological factors, if at all. Prime examples where this tends to be true include chapters on sexual arousal and response, contraception, pregnancy and childbirth, sexually transmitted diseases, and even sexual dysfunction.

Where textbooks do focus on issues approaching the psychological, often little empirical research has been conducted on the topics that are discussed. Professional wisdom, intuition, or even folklore frequently fill in where formal theory and science are not available. On the other hand, when information is grounded in actual empirical research, the discussion may involve simply laying out a series of "facts," rather than presenting information in a theoretical context and information based on theoretically driven research.

Furthermore, when research is brought to bear, the focus may be on what are actually more demographic factors, such as gender and age, rather than psychological processes that might provide a richer understanding of the reasons for behavior. In such cases, the good news is that the information presented has been obtained using scientific methods. The shortcoming often is that "the facts" are not discussed in terms of a larger theoretical perspective, a larger psychological perspective. That is, psychological theory often does not drive the presentation of information, and therefore much of the information is not really extremely relevant to an understanding of the psychology of sexuality.

Don't get me wrong. Of course, biological and physical health information is extremely valuable and important, but it is not more important in a psychology class than is psychological information. A predominant focus on biology and physical sexual health is especially important and justified in a biology or health class on sexuality. It is also very important for all people, maybe especially young people, to be informed about the physical aspects of sexuality.

The problem for me as an instructor has been that the course I teach is a psychology course, and so many sexuality textbooks do not seem to be psychology textbooks. I have long hoped for a book that focused on the psychology of sexuality. Ironically, it was the feedback of students that helped me to come to terms with what was so dissatisfying about the textbook and the course structure I built around the book. A number of students in my classes have told me that the course was very different from what they had expected of a psychology course. Many have said that they have already covered so much of the sexual anatomy and physiology in high school classes and in other settings several times, and they expected more information from a psychological perspective, bearing on behavior and psychological processes. (As it turns out, students often don't always remember the biological and health information they received well, and they need to have their memories refreshed or even completely redirected. However, this misses the larger point that a focus on the physical and biological seems to overwhelm the psychological.)

Moreover, to a personality and social psychologist, even psychological issues that are addressed in many sexuality textbooks are not very satisfying in their treatment. Again, the focus tends to lack a theoretical (meaning a conceptual) depth that is often the concern in personality and social psychology research and courses. This is more than simply an arcane, stuffy argument about differences in world views among disciplines, or subfields within disciplines. The point is that students are not really challenged to engage in true critical thinking related to sexuality, particularly from a scientific perspective. That is one aspect of the dissatisfying nature of many presentations about sexuality in textbooks—little challenge to students to adopt a problem-solving, hypothesis-testing strategy in dealing with issues. The course that I teach at my university is a 400-level, advanced undergraduate course that fulfills the highest level of requirement for our general education policy. This general education category is called *inquiry and analysis,* and classes that fulfill this requirement have the goals of helping students to develop their ability to "gather, evaluate, select, organize, and synthesize" information and their ability to "think critically and solve problems by applying knowledge and skills."

The purpose of inquiry and analysis courses is to help students develop these abilities using the methods and perspectives of a particular discipline; in the case of the course I teach, the methods are those of science and the perspective is based on the theories and concepts of psychology. For this reason, the first chapter places the study of sexuality within the context of the meta-theory of science, including its assumptions, perspectives, and methods of gathering information. In addition, an entire chapter is devoted to the methods of science, while also keeping in mind that many nonmajors may take the sexuality course. A substantial focus on the scientific method of gathering information proves to be essential to the goal of inquiry and analysis. It is also vital to students as they write term papers analyzing psychological research published in scientific journals, as they are required to do for the course I teach.

The current textbook is intended to present information at a higher level of challenge and analysis than is true for many textbooks designed for this course. Nonetheless, many students who take the course are not psychology majors, and so additional background information is often provided for these students. Because the primary concern is the psychology of sexuality, psychological theory and concepts drive the organization of the book, as well as the topics and information that are presented.

For example, the issue of the self and identity are central concepts of personality and social psychology, leading to an entire chapter devoted to the issue. In addition, formal theoretical frameworks are central organizing features of many chapters, such as the one on arousal and attraction, and the chapter on love and intimacy. Issues related to anatomy and physiology are cast within the larger issue of the attributes associated with sex and gender, providing a theoretical and psychological perspective on their importance. Biological factors influencing sexuality, as they are important to behavior, are also addressed from a psychological perspective in an entire chapter on the biopsychology of sexuality.

Furthermore, because the overarching perspective of this book is that of personality and social psychology, the predominant focus is that of basic science. The concern is to examine the scientific evidence that is available related to the causes underlying, and the factors influencing, sexual behavior.

The substantial departure from the primary focus on scientific evidence in this book is the inclusion of chapters on religion and history. In keeping with the desire to provide a meta-theoretical context about the assumptions and the cultural backdrop influencing our scientific world view, it is essential to understand where our ideas come from. Many students have little idea what the basis for their values and beliefs is, or at least they are not able to articulate them very well. Religion profoundly influences most people's understanding of sexuality, determining to a great extent what they are able to accept even when trying to assume a scientific perspective about the issues. By considering an overview of how ideas and values have developed in Western civilization, students may become more open to what science has to offer at this point in history.

Issues related to sexual orientation are integrated throughout the textbook, to convey the sense that concerns about identity, intimacy, relationships, and development are universal to all individuals. Nonetheless, topics important within psychology, such as the self and identity (chapter 7), and biological factors affecting behavior (chapter 12), have focused especially intensely on sexual orientation. Consequently, these two chapters address sexual orientation in particularly great detail.

An absolutely mandatory component in many textbooks today is a focus on diversity. Many texts attempt to cover various ethnic and cultural groups in every chapter. Rather than resorting to this approach, this book gathers together issues of race, ethnicity, and culture in one chapter. Critics will argue that treating race, ethnicity, and culture in a separate chapter marginalizes these important perspectives and issues. However, I think it is important to point out that there has been very little scientific research conducted on the relationship of race and ethnicity to sexuality, or even within psychology to love, intimacy, and romance. This is particularly true with respect to research that is genuinely based on theory and formal hypotheses testing. Because of this tremendous void in our body of empirical knowledge, it is generally necessary in sexuality textbooks to paste together bits and pieces of scattered information to be able to address race, ethnicity, and culture throughout an entire book. I believe it is worse to pretend that there is enough supporting scientific research when there is not; it glosses over the problem that exists and trivializes the issues.

The strategy of incorporating an entire chapter on race, ethnicity, and culture is an attempt to confront reasons for the amazing silence of science with respect to diversity. The desire is to confront it at the meta-theoretical level, with the goal of identifying the value-laden assumptions and historical factors that have left this void in research. Addressing these types of issues in a critical and analytic way will advance the understanding of students, as well as scientists, to a far greater extent than constructing the impression that we have a legitimate body of information on diversity and sexuality. The chapter is meant to provoke critical analysis and possibly inspire students to want to engage in research to eliminate the unfortunate void.

Finally, this book has been an all-consuming, absorbing life project for me, but ultimately a highly rewarding one. The final outcome is far different from what I had anticipated because it took shape based on the available theory and research as I encountered them. My hope is that students learn as much from the knowledge they encounter in the book as I have in writing it.

## The Instructor's Resource Manual (on CD-ROM)

An Instructor's Resource CD provides PowerPoint presentations; chapter study material; classroom handouts; and suggestions for course projects, discussion questions, and Internet exercises. Also included is a Computerized Test Bank that allows for easy test creation with multiple-choice, true/false, and essay questions.

## Companion Study Site

To further enhance students' understanding of and interest in the material, we have created a student Web site to accompany the text. This Web site includes e-Flashcards, self-quizzes, Web exercises, *Learning From Journal Articles* (which includes original research from Sage journal articles accompanied by critical thinking questions), and a link to the author's blog, where students can post comments and correspond with other students using this text. Go to www.sagepub.com/hillhsstudy to view the site.

# Chapter 1

## THE STUDY OF SEXUALITY

For most people, sexuality is an aspect of life that is quite challenging to make sense of and place into some type of meaningful perspective. We receive a multitude of messages about sexuality from virtually every source imaginable, including very explicit ones from movies, television, music, magazines, and books. The media may often provide a very explicit source of information, as illustrated in this personal account of finding out about the pleasure associated with sexuality:

*I am a 17 year old girl who has just discovered masturbation about a year ago. I was surfing this [Web] site, aware of the concept of touching oneself, but mostly ignorant to the technique or ability to orgasm. I never even really had understood what an orgasm was [before reading about it on the Web site]. I had touched myself before, but never in an attempt to make myself come or to do anything besides explore the feelings. I remember once being in a hotel room and watching a late night show about a sexual encounter and becoming very aroused and getting throbbing sensations in my vagina and clitoris. I didn't know, at that time, what was happening, but I realized the sensations felt good. I may have even had an orgasm, because I remember feeling an extreme pleasure. (The Experience of Desire, On-line forum, retrieved July 22, 2006, from The-clitoris.com. Reprinted with permission of The-clitoris.com. The words in brackets were added.)*

We may also receive messages from our family, friends, and even teachers and clergy. Messages from these particular sources possibly come to us in very subtle, disguised forms, because of the sensitive or delicate nature of the topic for many people in U.S. society (Tiefer, 2001). Often the vagueness of the information conveyed may be more bewildering than it is helpful, as in the following example:

*One girl in my [sex education] class asked about masturbation, and the teacher said, "If a girl touches herself 'down there' she could become very excited." And that was IT! I got excited watching the Richard Simmons show. It didn't mean I want to marry the exercise guru! What was she talking about? I got excited watching the dance number before the Oscars. I didn't think this had anything to do with my "unmentionable." The idea that my "fun spot" and babies had any connection was beyond me. I was desperately waiting for SOMEONE to tell me I wasn't the only one who possessed one of these things [a clitoris]. (Helen, mother of an 8-year-old stepdaughter, talking about her own experience as a school girl; The Experience of Desire, On-line forum, retrieved July 22, 2006, from The-clitoris.com. Reprinted with permission of The-clitoris.com. The words in brackets were added.)*

In fact, the very meaning of sexuality has long been guarded by **allegory**, which refers to the use of fictional figures or actions to represent the truth. In the past, sex, pregnancy, and the birth of children were explained to youngsters using such allegories as *the birds and the bees, the cabbage patch,* and *delivery by the stork.* Sexuality has likewise been obscured by **euphemism**, which is the use of a more pleasant phrase in place of a concept that is perceived as unpleasant or offensive. Euphemisms that have been popular, at least in the past, were such phrases as *making love, deflowering, petting,* and *in the family way.* More recently, euphemisms seem to have given way to slang phrases that do not disguise sexuality in pleasant symbols, but rather are intended to shock and sensationalize it; this may be a way of downplaying the potential for intimacy and tender feelings within sexuality, or even avoiding them altogether.

The woman in the above passage suggests that she was accustomed to the common use of euphemisms while she was growing up. The teacher used the euphemism "down there" to refer to female genitals, whereas Helen herself used the terms "unmentionable" and "fun spot," although in a rather sarcastic way. The sarcasm reflects her unhappiness and frustration with being kept in the dark about sexuality.

In addition to negative attitudes about sexuality, another reason that sexuality may be difficult to conceptualize for many people is the lack of clarity and directness in discussions of it typically found even in more intellectual or academic forums. One woman notes, "Throughout my childhood I read many books on sexuality, and found them to be interesting and entertaining but never as honest as I'd hoped for." (Rachael; The Experience of Desire, On-line forum, retrieved July 22, 2006, from The-clitoris.com.) You might notice that many books on sexuality, whether strictly academic references or more popular sources, never really define the concept explicitly; it is often assumed that it is implicitly understood what *sexuality* means. To be fair, it has in fact been difficult to construct even a simple definition, especially one that captures all of the different meanings of sexuality associated with the various people who make up our society.

Children receive messages very early in life that lay the groundwork for later sexual attitudes. *What are your earliest memories of learning about sexuality or pregnancy? Were they largely positive, or was there an element of secrecy, or even negativity?*

Even looking to a dictionary does not provide much of a satisfactory definition, because the goal of dictionary editors is to be exceptionally succinct. For example, *Webster's 10th Collegiate Dictionary* (Merriam-Webster, 2004) defines sexuality as "the quality or state of being sexual," "the condition of having sex," and "expression of sexual receptivity or interest especially when excessive." Yet such definitions gloss over many aspects of sexuality important to human beings. Rather than using only a few words to describe an aspect of human experience that has a myriad of meanings, a more detailed definition is needed.

Sexuality may have a variety of meanings for individuals in a society, depending on their unique backgrounds and characteristics.

**Human sexuality** refers to all emotional, cognitive, behavioral, and physical experiences of humans related to their sexual nature. Figure 1.1 provides examples of each of these types of experiences related to sexuality. Sexuality has as its starting point the system of the body necessary for reproduction of human life. However, sexual feelings and sexual expression extend vastly beyond the body parts and behaviors directly involved in reproduction of the species. Individuals are very capable of transforming many aspects of their lives—even though they are not really related to reproduction—into erotic, sexually arousing stimuli.

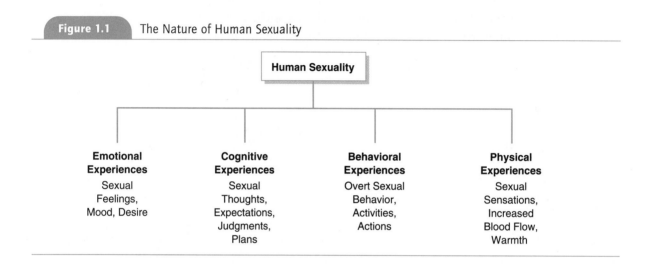

**Figure 1.1**    The Nature of Human Sexuality

People may react to human characteristics, such as the tone of a person's voice or the person's type of smile, with sexual attraction. Yet these features essentially have nothing to do with reproduction directly. In fact, nonhuman objects can arouse strong feelings of sexual desire for some individuals, as if they are like an actual sexual human being. Objects that might excite sexual feelings for some include shoes of a particular style, or a piece of clothing, such as lacy underwear or a negligee. Through personal experience and the way we come to understand those experiences, all sorts of aspects of our lives and other people take on an erotic allure. Yet profound differences among individuals result as well. Whereas one person finds stiletto high-heel shoes maddeningly attractive, others may react to these shoes in a ho-hum way, or may even find them disgusting.

For humans, sexuality most importantly involves *the subjective desire to experience sexual arousal* and possibly to engage in *overt expression of that desire*. In many instances, the sexual desire involves the motivation to engage in sexual contact with another human being. However, in some instances, the desire may focus on oneself, in terms of interest in self-stimulation or fantasy, or it may focus on nonhuman targets, such as clothing or animals. **Sexual contact** may involve actual bodily contact, ranging from gentle touches and caresses of any part of the object of desire to stimulation of genitals with hands, mouth, or another individual's genitals. In other instances, the desire for sexual "contact" may involve imagining, fantasizing, or observing erotically stimulating situations rather than direct physical contact with a body or object.

The single most important aspect of a situation that causes it to be sexually relevant or arousing for individuals is their **understanding** and **interpretation** of the situation, not the presence or absence of overt sexual behavior. In other words, for humans, emotional and cognitive activities that lead individuals to identify situations as sexual, that lead to motivation to engage in sexual expression, or that lead to physical arousal are the criteria that define sexuality. For this reason, personality and social psychological factors are at the heart of human sexuality, and distinguish human sexuality from the reproductive tendencies of lower animals in very fundamental ways.

In other words, our abilities and interests go far beyond a primitive urge that drives virtually all other animal species. For this reason, human sexuality involves not only basic biological features such as reproductive organs, hormonal influences, and neural pathways. Sexual nature in humans refers as well to characteristics developed through life experiences, learning processes, cognitive development, intellectual capabilities, relationships with others, societal expectations, cultural conventions, religious values, and historical trends.

As with all other human qualities, the factors influencing development and expression of sexuality are tremendously complex and intricate. Many of these factors will be examined in the chapters that follow. Anatomical issues related to sexuality will be presented later in chapter 6 on gender and sexuality, while biological factors affecting sexual development and sexual behaviors will be presented in chapter 12 on the biopsychology of sexuality. Issues central to psychological aspects of sexuality are considered first because the primary concern of this book is psychological functioning. However, those who would like to refresh their memories about basic sexual anatomy and the terms traditionally used to talk about sexual organs may skim those sections in advance (see pages 191–199).

How you personally understand a particular situation will determine whether you respond sexually, and how you respond. *Would you find this particular situation arousing or not? How would you react?*

## The Need for the Scholarly Study of Sexuality

Our images of perfection come from magazines, books, movies, television, which are themselves fantasies. How many of us have seen our movie screen idols up close? If you have, you know that most of the time they do not meet their screen images of perfection. Somehow we forget about tricks of makeup, photography, editing, brushovers, and all kinds of techniques that make us look different from reality. Yet these figures of make-believe become our sexual icons. (Brown, 2000, p. 40)

Few topics require as little convincing about their value and interest as sexuality. A surge of popular books dealing with sex, romance, attraction, and relationships within the last several decades drives home how interested many people are in the topic. Likewise, rental of erotic videos currently makes up a huge portion of all video rentals. Sex-related issues are a frequent focus on TV and radio talk shows, reality shows, soap operas, and movies. Moreover, in recent times, among the most profitable Internet Web sites are those that offer erotic images, stories, services, and products.

Popular media often present sexuality in provocative and entertaining ways. Think about what you've seen on television or in magazines recently. *What is your reaction to the sexual images and content you have seen?*

Given the availability of such a rich goldmine of tantalizing, colorful, and seemingly informative sources, why would anyone need, or *want,* to take a course on human sexuality? For example, on the topic of giving oral–genital sex to men, the "Bedroom Baroness" tells her readers in *Cosmopolitan,* "The advice was unanimous among my male friends: Simply put, guys like when you like doing it. Your enthusiasm for the oral act is 80 percent of the game, so take that hot tamale in your mouth as if it were your favorite treat in the universe" (Deborchgrave, Sheri, 2001, *The Bedroom Baroness gives advice on oral sex.* Retrieved January 5, 2001, from cosmo.women.com/ cos/love/ baroness/b0expr11.htm). She also recommends ample eye contact during the performance, as well as various techniques for squeezing the penis with lips, hands, and tongue. For an extra special treat, she suggests that the woman should have two Altoid mints in her mouth during the episode.

"The Playboy Advisor," however, proposes that the male oral-sex recipient consume artichoke before the sexual encounter because research has found that artichoke improves the flavor of whatever follows it. Other flavor enhancers mentioned are garnishing the penis with brandy or flavored liqueur, or topping with whipped cream, to increase the allure. Beyond taste considerations, The Advisor suggests slowness and sensitivity in letting the oral-sex provider control the pace and extent of inserting the penis in her mouth. "[D]ouble your effort to reassure her. (It can be lonely down there.) Moan. Stroke her hair. Tell her how good she makes you feel. Don't whine for more when she's had enough. You'll probably find that once she's overcome her initial reluctance, you won't have to ask a second time" (The Playboy Advisor, 2001, *My partner doesn't like giving oral sex. What should I do?* Retrieved January 5, 2001, from www.playboy.com/sex/columns/advisor/faq/oral.html).

Typical topics covered in these advice columns are preventing premature ejaculation, lack of sexual interest or compatibility, and lack of orgasm for women during sexual intercourse (usually meaning penile-vaginal intercourse). With respect to the "inability" of women to experience orgasm during sexual intercourse, The Playboy Advisor recommends that "the cure for lack of orgasm is simple: self-help. Your girlfriend should teach herself to climax—via vibrators, or shower massage units or her own hand." The key here is apparently learning how to orgasm and becoming accustomed to it. However, he points to another potential problem— poor vaginal muscles, according to one study. Isometric exercises are the answer in this case, and The Advisor finishes the advice with, "There's no explanation for the relation between fitness and fun, but if it gets results, who cares?" In contrast, the Bedroom Baroness focuses on couples engaging in a "surefire tactic" called the coital alignment technique to provide more effective stimulation of the clitoris. The technique involves positioning the couple's bodies in a particular way and rocking rather than thrusting. She also recommends that women may increase their capability for orgasm through masturbation.

For most people, the difficulty presented by these myriad books, magazines, videos, and talk shows is being able to determine how scientific and accurate the information is, in addition to how appropriate or relevant the question is. The typical person has little or no formal training in the fundamentals of scientific methodology, let alone its technicalities and intricacies.

How is a person to know whether the information offered by advice columnists is worthy of one's faith, given that the information could affect such important aspects of the person's life as sexual pleasure, self-esteem, and the quality of intimate relationships? How are people to know whether they are receiving extremely biased information from individuals or groups with hidden agendas? How is an individual to decide whether recommendations offered by people with titles behind or in front of their names (i.e., PhD, MD, Bedroom Baroness) are grounded in scientific research? Or, how is one to know if the advice is instead entirely based on anecdotes (which are stories or examples involving particular individuals that are meant to convey a message) or on professional common wisdom (i.e., "expert folklore")?

Does one high-quality study lend sufficient confidence to the results and conclusions drawn by the researchers? So, what's the answer to the "problem" of lack of orgasm by women during penile–vaginal intercourse: proper body positions and motion, tightening vaginal muscles through exercises, increased masturbation on the part of women? Is "lack of orgasm" even the best way to frame the question, or is it even the way that *you* personally would frame it?

Discussion of sexuality in the popular media such as in magazine advice columns is substantially lacking in several ways. The topics are typically selected because they are sensational and entertaining, intended to excite readers' sexual interest. The purpose of such articles is largely to provide pleasure in order to lead readers to want to buy the magazine in the future. The underlying intent is revealed in the entertaining, comical style used to discuss the topic, such as referring to the penis as a "tamale" and describing the masturbation technique to enhance orgasms as "self-help." Enjoying information that one is reading is a worthy goal; however, if that is the primary intent of an article, the information may have been selected largely *because* it is entertaining, not because it is important.

---

**Box 1.1**                                             **An Eye Toward Research**

### How Do the Media Present Gender and Sexuality?

Prompted by comments from its readers around the world, the Web site, *girls, women + media project . . . what are* you *looking at?* surveyed a sampling of studies related to the way that gender and sexuality are presented by the media. The viewers of their Web site expressed outrage and frustration at the superficial and demeaning presentation of images and information about women and sex. Here are a number of findings they highlight on their site:

- Teens are deluged with portrayals of sex. They are exposed to 14,000 references to sex per year on TV. Teens say that television, movies, and other media are their top source of information about sex and sexuality.
- Only 165 of the references to sex focus on abstinence, delaying sex, birth control, risk of pregnancy, or sexually transmitted disease.
- A favorite television channel of girls aged 11–19 is MTV, which typically presents females as sex objects. Women artists are seldom featured on the channel. Males are seldom presented largely as sex objects. When men are presented in the background, they are usually fully clothed. Women are usually presented in a way that exposes or focuses on their breasts and buttocks

*(Continued)*

(Continued)

- Very few video games feature females as central characters. When they do, the characters wear revealing clothes and have exaggerated features, such as extremely large breasts and tiny waists (Girls and Gaming, Children Now; 2000).
- Research on advertising found that women were portrayed wearing very few clothes or wearing bikinis or underwear quite frequently. White women were presented this way in 62% of ads, with Black women presented this way in 53% of ads. Only a quarter of advertisements present men in revealing outfits.
- Women are represented primarily as underweight and with idealized figures.
- Many actresses and models are dramatically underweight, and diet and smoke to keep their weight down.
- Research indicates that many college women feel worse about themselves after looking at magazines, and approximately 50% of teen girls read fashion magazines.
- Plastic surgery for teens has increased 50% from 1996–1998, most of which is performed on girls.

Adapted from *girls, women + media project . . . what are* you *looking at?*, 2006, Retrieved June 2006, from http://www.mediaandwomen.org/problem.html

Topics in popular magazines are in fact often selected for their entertainment value, not for their practical or scientific value. The focus is often on **sexual techniques**, such as how to provide "good" oral sex. Yet the specific technique a sexual partner uses for stimulating one's sexual organs is not likely to be as important for many people in overall sexual enjoyment as are other issues. Instead, an individual's attitudes and comfort with oral–genital sex in general may be more of a deciding factor in whether they enjoy oral stimulation. Maybe even more important is a person's happiness with the relationship he or she is involved in. Many people may be quite satisfied with the sexual aspects of their relationship in large part because they are happy and comfortable overall with the relationship. Emotional intimacy and comfort are often very powerful factors in sexual happiness. On the other hand, if major conflict exists in the relationship, sexual interaction may be less desirable in general.

This means that popular media may focus on relatively unimportant issues and provide a distorted view of significant factors affecting sexuality. Another example of distortion or incomplete information is provided by discussions about lack of orgasm for women during penile–vaginal intercourse. The fact that some women do not experience orgasm may be related much more to satisfactory stimulation of the clitoris during penile–vaginal intercourse than learning to orgasm in general through masturbation. Substantial numbers of women may not be sufficiently stimulated by the penis during intercourse to experience pleasure and orgasm. The coital alignment technique that was mentioned by the Playboy Advisor was in fact designed to increase the

Happiness with a relationship in general may be one of the most powerful influences on sexual satisfaction. Substantial conflict for a couple can reduce their experience of sexual satisfaction.

amount of stimulation that women experience during intercourse. The point of all of this is that popular media may focus on factors that are less important in affecting sexuality because of the concern with presenting entertaining, very simple solutions to problems.

Such concerns illustrate the value of a course on human sexuality. To help sort through all of the issues, this text is intended to guide students through the potentially mystifying, and even overwhelming, task of evaluating information about sexuality. One goal of this book is to help with the development of a more formal and complete understanding of not only what we know about sexuality, but also the process of *obtaining* information and *evaluating* its quality. In this way, students are encouraged to become good "consumers" of information about sexuality—that is, students are encouraged (a) to learn to judge the quality of the logic and methods of research, (b) to be able to draw their own informed conclusions so they can evaluate the accuracy of expert conclusions, and (c) to decide on the usefulness or limitations of the information.

## The Predominant Views Used in This Book

### The Scientific Perspective of Sexuality

One major view predominating in this book is that the field of science is capable of providing high-quality information about sexuality in terms of how verifiable and how objective the information is. **Science** is defined as a systematically organized body of knowledge obtained through the scientific method. Therefore, the tools used to obtain and understand information about sexuality in this textbook are those primarily of the **scientific method**. Scientific methodology is actually only one of several means of acquiring systematic, formal knowledge. However, a major advantage of the scientific method is the great concern it has with objectivity.

The logic guiding the scientific method, in the ideal, requires scientists to openly recognize the bias that is inherent in all knowledge. Moreover, the scientific method provides established procedures to try to limit such bias. Whether scientists have actually followed through with effectively evaluating bias is also a question that will be addressed throughout the book. Because of the complex and profound ways in which views of sexuality have been influenced by historical, cultural, and political factors, these factors will be examined first. This will provide a conceptual context in which to understand contemporary scientific information (White, Bondurant, & Travis, 2000).

Knowledge, even scientific knowledge, is not gathered in a vacuum. It is not completely removed from social and political forces that operate at a particular point in history. Scientists create theories as a way of attempting to understand issues in which they are interested. Yet theories are always based to some extent on assumptions, albeit assumptions grounded in logic and reason; nonetheless, they are informed speculation about likely causes of behavior, because scientists seldom have preexisting knowledge that even comes close to a complete understanding. Consequently, they must fill in the gaps in knowledge with speculation about factors affecting the issue. Of course, in the case of psychologists interested in sexuality, the knowledge and assumptions concern emotions, thoughts, and behaviors related to sex.

Although a high-quality theory builds its assumptions on reasoning provided by formal philosophy, all understanding is influenced by the ways of thinking that prevail in a given society at a specific point in time. Particular ways of thinking tend to be favored by philosophers and scientists during a particular historical period for a variety of reasons; the prevalent way of thinking is referred to as the *Zeitgeist*, a German term meaning "the spirit of the time."

Consequently, it is important to examine the various theories that scientists use to conceptualize and make sense of the information they have available. After an initial examination of the general scientific views embraced within this book—those of personality and social psychology—the nature of the development of theories in science will be discussed.

## Personality and Social Psychological Perspectives of Sexuality

Another major focus of this book is the role of personal characteristics and social influences in the development and expression of sexuality. This type of focus draws heavily upon the theory and research of the fields of **personality psychology** and **social psychology**. More generally, **psychology** is the scientific study of affect, cognition, and behavior, largely in humans, although some areas of psychology examine animal behavior as a means of drawing inferences about human behavior. **Affect** refers to emotions, feelings, and mood—the private, subjective experiences of individuals related to pleasure, displeasure, happiness, sadness, love, and hate, to name a few types of emotions. **Cognition** refers to covert (unobservable) intellectual activities, including thinking, understanding, planning, perceiving, interpreting, and problem-solving. In psychology, **behavior** refers specifically to overt (observable) actions, easily verifiable movements such as walking, talking, writing, gesturing, facial expressions—and sexual behaviors such as touching, kissing, and genital stimulation.

Because of the expanded definition of sexuality discussed in the first several paragraphs of the book, a thorough overview requires much more than simply an understanding of the physical aspects of sexual development and functioning (e.g., those aspects related to the genitals, brain, and nervous system). A complete understanding also concerns the psychological, social, and cultural aspects of sexuality. The specific areas of psychology, personality psychology and social psychology, provide precisely the type of scientific information bearing on these fundamental components of sexuality. **Personality psychology** is the scientific study of the individual; more specifically, **personality** refers to the patterns of affect, cognition, and behavior that *characterize* individuals across a number of situations and across time. That is, personality psychology is concerned with processes occurring within the individual that cause the person to behave in relatively consistent ways. Many personality theorists currently view this behavioral consistency as resulting from traits or attributes that have developed gradually over time, although such a view was extremely controversial in earlier times.

A field highly related to personality psychology in its focus on the psychological experiences of the individual is social psychology. **Social psychology** is the scientific study of the influence of human beings on the affect, cognition, and behavior of the individual. Both personality and social psychology are interested in the functioning of the individual. However, several important differences distinguish the two areas of psychology. First, personality psychology is concerned with the totality of factors that influence the development and expression of the psychological tendencies of the individual (including biological), whereas social psychology is largely concerned with interpersonal or social influences on the development and expression of psychological tendencies.

Second, personality psychology also tends to focus more on the existence of differences among individuals, the ways in which individuals react differently to the same situations. Social psychology concentrates more on the ways that individuals in general, or on average, react in a given situation; that is, social psychology tends to treat individuals as if they are very similar, with few important differences. Finally, social psychology historically has focused on the role of the external social environment in individual behavior rather than on factors internal to the individual himself or herself, such as idiosyncratic emotional or intellectual reactions or biological factors; personality psychology has tended to focus on factors internal to the individual. A comparison of the focus of the two areas of psychology is presented in Table 1.1.

**TABLE 1.1**    Comparison of Personality Psychology and Social Psychology

| Theoretical Issue | Personality Psychology | Social Psychology |
| --- | --- | --- |
| 1. Level of focus | Functioning of the individual | Functioning of the individual |
| 2. Breadth of focus | Totality of factors influencing the individual | Interpersonal influences |
| 3. Emphasis on difference or sameness | Differences among individuals | Similarity of individuals |
| 4. Emphasized influence on behavior | Psychological processes within the individual | External factors in the environment |

Actually, sexuality historically has been examined by a variety of different disciplines: primarily biology, medicine, psychology, sociology, anthropology, history, philosophy, and theology. In this sense, **sexology**—the formal, academic study of sexuality—has been multidisciplinary all along. Each discipline has focused on its own somewhat unique type of questions, using its own methodology to collect information to answer these questions.

Again, it is not assumed that one approach is more appropriate or more accurate than the others; rather, each discipline provides valuable information suited for addressing issues particular to that discipline. As Geer and O'Donohue (1987) have noted, individuals who are not religious, or who are atheist, are likely to discount the usefulness of considering religious values or morality. Those who are devoutly and intensely religious, on the other hand, may be more likely to be skeptical of, or disinterested in, scientific explanations of sexuality. Yet theologians will not be able to provide objective, empirical answers about personality traits or social factors that influence sexuality. Likewise, scientists are not able to provide answers to morality in terms of the goodness or badness of a particular course of action on the basis of a belief in a supreme being. In the realm of sexuality, however, issues of religious morality have dominated the types of perceptions, emotional reactions, and decisions about sexual behavior that have influenced individuals for centuries. Both types of factors are important and must be taken into account.

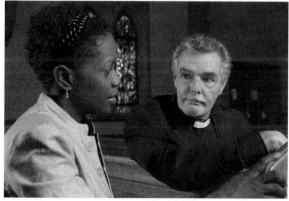

Scientists deal with issues that may be examined objectively, whereas clergy and theologians concern themselves with subjective matters of faith.

# *The Nature of Theory and Understanding in Science*

When most people look to science, it is usually because they simply want the best solution to a specific question, such as one frequently addressed in sex advice columns presented earlier: What is the best way to overcome the problem of lack of orgasm in a woman? The general answer to this type of question is that the solution is most likely to be found if the cause of the problem is known. Without knowing what causes a problem behavior (or lack of behavior), all attempts to remedy the problem are essentially "shots in the dark," and any successful remedy is likely to be an accident or based on an informal guess.

Remember all of the suggested solutions for lack of orgasm: practice with stimulating the clitoris, isometric exercises to tone vaginal muscles, and achieving the correct position during sexual intercourse? Furthermore, recall the statement by the Playboy Advisor: "There's no explanation for the relation between fitness and fun, but if it gets results, who cares?" The problem with this type of lucky solution is that it may not be effective for other types of behaviors and problems, and the reason for its lack of success with other problems may not be at all apparent without understanding the reason that the remedy "works" for lack of orgasm. Is muscle fitness relevant to all sexual experiences and behaviors? Other limitations may arise even with respect to the orgasm problem, such as if it is effective for some women and not for others, or worse, if the isometric exercises actually causes pain or other problems for some women. Another limitation that may crop up is that the inability to experience orgasm may return after a while. Again, no explanation for this may be evident, and the problem-solver will have no understanding to fall back on to explain the development or to recommend an additional remedy. The remedy may have been bogus, an ineffective solution that just seemed to work when it was first developed; on the other hand, it may simply be based on *one* of a number of factors affecting the experience of orgasm. However, one has no way of knowing what the situation is in this case.

## Basic Science Versus Applied Science

To avoid the limitations of hit-and-miss solutions or "band-aid," "let's-only-worry-about-fixing-this-problem" answers to questions, scholars typically are more interested in acquiring a broad reservoir of knowledge, organized according to some meaningful system; this more expansive, conceptual focus in science is known as **basic science**. Even scientists concerned about solving real-world problems, such as clinicians, consultants, and those involved in **applied science**, recognize the importance of collecting basic information. Basic science therefore is conducted, not with specific problems in mind, but for the purpose of simply understanding phenomena and the ways in which they are related. These relationships provide a network of meaning that may eventually allow applied scientists to conceptualize more effective solutions to real-world problems; applied science is concerned with using theory and empirical knowledge to solve practical, real-world problems.

Therefore, a broad body of knowledge and related conceptualizations are the most effective tools scientists can develop. Such conceptualizations are what scientists mean by theory. As Kurt Lewin, a noted social psychologist, observed, "There is nothing as practical as a good theory" (Lewin, 1999, p. 336). High-quality, basic science is driven by theory, and the most effective applied science is based on theory that has been substantiated by basic science.

## A Definition of Theory

In science, a **theory** is a set of (a) **assumptions**, (b) **rules**, and (c) **principles** that is used to understand and explain a phenomenon; theory is also used to guide the collection of new information, through the development of logical, specific predictions, called **hypotheses**, about what will occur during research. Because complete knowledge of any phenomenon is not possible, **assumptions** are necessary as a starting point, to provide an initial foundation for developing a theory. In psychology, common fundamental assumptions involve the view that mental processes and behavior are determined by biological factors or by environmental factors; this has historically been called the *nature versus nurture* controversy. The **rules** of a theory are grounded in the logic and reasoning derived from philosophy that allow theorists to draw conclusions and make predictions consistent with what is known about the world. With respect to the last aspect of a theory, **principles** refer to evidence that has been repeatedly and validly obtained through objective (empirical) research, ultimately providing a solid bedrock of confidence in the accuracy of a theory.

## Logical Positivism

The predominant philosophical position that has guided science virtually from its beginning is **logical positivism**, or simply positivism (Weis, 1998). Positivism has exerted an enormous influence on the development of scientific theory, establishing four fundamental components as essential to the quality of theory; these are summarized in Table 1.2. First, theory must be subjected to empirical testing, meaning the collection of data through observation, measurement, and the use of experiments. Second, theories are built on concepts; a **concept** ". . . is an abstract, symbolic representation of an idea or phenomenon" (Weis, 1998, p. 2). The definition of concepts that constitute theories must be agreed upon by experts in the area. Moreover, concepts must be capable of being measured and tested in order to consider them adequate.

| **TABLE 1.2** Characteristics Essential to the Quality of a Theory |
| --- |
| 1. A theory must be testable, capable of being subjected to empirical testing. |
| 2. Theory is built on concepts whose definitions are agreed upon by experts. |
| 3. Concepts are related to one another by propositions. |
| 4. A theory must explain a specific set of phenomena, not all aspects of existence. |

Third, concepts making up a theory must be related to one another within a given theory by **propositions**, logical statements that specify exactly how one concept is associated with other concepts. Assumptions are broad, general statements about human nature that often go largely untested because it is not possible to measure such expansive ideas; an example is that of early learning theories, which assumed that human behavioral tendencies develop largely through contact with the environment and such tendencies may be modified in virtually limitless ways. Assumptions may underlie the premise of propositions, but ultimately the propositions derived from assumptions must be testable themselves.

A final component of high-quality scientific theories is that they are designed to explain a specific set of phenomena, rather than being created to explain all aspects of existence. Limiting theories to a prescribed, definable group of events and behaviors prevents the explanation from becoming too complex; extreme complexity can lead to confusion in understanding it, as well as to vagueness in the propositions created.

Because theory incorporates principles established by empirical research, scientific theory is not viewed in the way that nonscientists use the term *theory*, as in "it is only a theory." For scientists, the issue is the degree of empirical support for a given theory; some theories have accumulated greater support than other theories. A theory is not "just a theory" if it has been supported by an ample body of research. As greater evidence accumulates to validate a theory, it will receive a broad basis of acceptance and recognition among scientists.

In fact, every theory that receives substantial empirical support must be considered legitimate, even when two well-supported theories seem to contradict one another. Despite the desire of many people for one absolute, best answer, the reality is that a multitude of forces may be involved in causing any particular event or phenomenon. Within psychology, seemingly opposing theories may seek to explain, for example, gender differences in desire for certain types of sexual expression. A biologically based theory may propose that differences in brain structure account for men being more interested in some forms of sexual expression than women. Nonetheless, social learning theory may propose that differences in the behavior of role models for girls versus boys account for the gender difference. Although it is tempting to demand to know which of these theories is correct, it is likely that both types of factors are involved in the development of gender differences in sexual interest. They may simply address different aspects of the same process.

Historically, scientists have adopted an overarching viewpoint that the accuracy of information is largely a matter of conscientiously and precisely measuring what is "out there" in the world; this is the **logical positivism view**. This position maintains that an understanding of the nature of reality, including human behavior, will logically and meaningfully follow after enough "hard facts" have been accumulated. The long-standing, predominant view within the philosophy of science has been that objective data about the world will lead scientists to the "true" meaning of the information—that is, facts will eventually reveal the answers that are inherent in them. The perspective dates back thousands of years to arguments made by the Greek philosopher, Aristotle, advocating an inductive logic as the best way to discover the laws of the universe that explain its operation. The period during which Western European society began to accept the scientific method as a legitimate source of information is called *the Modern Era;* the perspective that has begun to question the usefulness of the modernist and logical positivist assumptions has come to be known as **postmodernism**.

Only fairly recently in the history of formal philosophy and science have some scientists and scholars begun to challenge the notion that it is possible to discover perfectly objective information uncontaminated by bias and opinion. It has become increasingly obvious to many scientists that assumptions are *always* at the bottom of attempts to discern the meaning of data that have been collected, even when using methods that have come to be accepted as objective and valid. In the study of sexuality, the traditional scientific perspective based on induction has led to a focus on more easily observable and objectively measurable issues, such as the functioning of the physical body; other issues that are not related to physical sexuality have been ignored and neglected. The factors involved in this rather limited focus of sexology is the subject of the following sections.

Aristotle (384–322 BCE) is considered to have developed the foundations of systematic logic, which has influenced modern philosophical thought for over 2,000 years.

## Social Constructionism

The postmodern position on the nature of knowledge is called *social constructionism*. This perspective maintains that perfectly objective information, completely devoid of bias and interpretation, does not exist. Rather, all information must be interpreted in order for individuals to understand it; all information is placed within a context of meaning as it is communicated or received. The view conceives of all human experience as a product of the interaction of individuals with the external world, which most importantly consists of other people who have their particular perspectives and agendas.

In other words, information is in reality constructed through interaction with the source of that information, rather than simply existing in a pure form "out there" in the real world to be objectively discovered. Because meaning is created, social construction theorists argue that only those interpretations with which the most powerful individuals in a society agree are granted the status of "truth." All other interpretations are ignored or ridiculed and rejected. Consequently, the accumulation of knowledge within a society is essentially a process of one viewpoint exerting dominance over all others (White et al., 2000).

## *Historical Factors in the Scientific Investigation of Sexuality*

The social and political influences on the construction of sexology have seldom been recognized by historians of sexuality, although historical descriptions of sexology have usually assumed what Leonore Tiefer (2000) calls a nativist approach. By this she is referring to the traditional logical positivist view of science, that sexuality is "really . . . out there, just waiting for researchers to come and uncover the facts" (p. 90). Again, this perspective opposes the social constructionist view, which maintains that reality is constantly being created by individuals through their perception and interpretation of events. Social constructionism allows for multiple, equally valid interpretations of the same events and objects.

Logical positivist historians portray the development of sexological knowledge as removed from social and political influences, simply a process of collecting objective facts out there in the world. According to Tiefer (2000), historians of sexology typically provide little or no theoretical analysis or commentary about the context in which research has occurred, but represent the researchers simply as seekers of truth by using the tools of science to "counteract the lies and repressions of the Victorian era. . . . This type of uncritical history, written largely to praise the courage and usefulness of sex researchers, disguises its own role in promoting a nativist view of sexuality" (p. 90). In fact, Tiefer indicates that such historians often condemn scientists who advocate for particular points of view, most especially political ones; according to her analysis, however, logical positivist historians are in fact strongly advocating their perspective of logical positivism.

Social constructionist historians, in contrast, argue that information and understanding are embedded in a multitude of competing forces, requiring active interpretation rather than simple discovery. Tiefer cites the analysis of Irvine (1990) as one that identifies the goal of American sexologists after the 1940s as a "quest for professional legitimacy" and a desire to redress the oppression of women and gays and lesbians. However, by focusing research largely on women's sexual pleasure within heterosexual relationships, early sex researchers actually reinforced the importance of women's dependence on men for satisfaction and health. Furthermore, they ignored or were oblivious to other issues that are as important, and in some cases more important, to well-being than sexual pleasure, such as sexual violence and harassment. Without realizing or acknowledging it, therefore, traditional sex researchers have legitimized certain concepts and issues, while de-legitimizing others.

## The Sexological Model of Sexuality

Sexology over the course of the 20th century has adopted a set of assumptions that may be called the *sexological model of sexuality* (Tiefer, 2000). These assumptions have guided theory development and research pervasively and profoundly, although most sexologists have not explicitly recognized the influence of this viewpoint on their thinking. In fact, Tiefer noted that this sexological model does not explicitly appear in any sexology textbooks (until the current one).

### Sex Is a Universal Natural Force Affecting All People in the Same Way

The overarching assumption of the sexological model, inherited from the traditional scientific philosophy of logical positivism, is that fundamental, essential factors determine all behavior and bodily processes. Human beings are all essentially alike in basic nature because of these universal laws. Therefore, differences among people have often not been the focus of research on human sexuality. This is because, according to the sexological model, the goal of science is to discover these fundamental principles, which will subsequently allow the identification of the factors producing variation among individuals and groups. Eventually, then, a complete knowledge of sexuality would be achieved by discovering the larger causal framework and overlaying the factors producing variation (Tiefer, 2000).

A potential limitation of an exclusive emphasis on searching for universal principles is that the nature of the concepts have historically tended to be more descriptive, operational definitions, stating only what is involved at an observable level. Context is frequently not included, and terms are largely nontheoretical, meaning they are not based on any understanding or connection with what is known beyond the objectively observable. Historical, social, and cultural considerations have often been avoided within this perspective, possibly because they have been assumed to be of relatively minor importance compared with other more general factors. The problem, according to critics, is that very little depth of understanding is provided about the actual complexity of sexuality by focusing only on observable, common factors. Little investigation of the *meaning* of sexual behavior in the lives of individuals has been undertaken (Lewis & Kertzner, 2003; Simon, 1996; Tiefer, 2000; Vance, 1991).

Lack of a historical context in sexuality research often results in ignorance about the ways in which the meaning of sexuality changes, even within the lifetimes of individuals. Lewis and Kertzner (2003) point to the way in which the meaning of the term *homosexuality* has shifted in only several decades "from psychopathology to (relatively) protected cultural identity for many Americans" (p. 387). The oversight is significant because the meaning of sexual behavior and relationships is not only intrinsically important; understanding the meaning of sexuality will enable researchers to better predict patterns of sexual behavior and development.

The difficulties are substantially compounded in research on racial and ethnic minorities; little or no attention has been devoted to establishing that the measurement methods have any accuracy or validity for racial and ethnic minorities (Lewis & Kertzner, 2003). Therefore, assumptions about the applicability of theory and scientific methods led early researchers to ignore issues about how universal their conceptualizations really are. This has resulted in a substantial gap in knowledge about sexuality and leaves wide open the question about how universal conclusions really are.

Even when the focus of investigation has been explicitly on African Americans, such as that dealing with behaviors that place individuals at risk for HIV infection, the scope of the research has been extremely limited conceptually. Concern is usually with factors directly related to HIV risk, and has not been about basic research on African American sexuality. The goal, for example, is to develop ways to get African Americans to

An extreme focus on discovering universal principles may lead scientists to downplay or ignore cultural differences and historical changes in sexuality, as well as people's perceptions of sexuality. *How do you think these people might differ in their views of sexuality and their sexual behavior?*

A wedding celebration in Niger.

An Asian couple.

Couples dancing at a beach party in Ecuador.

use condoms during sexual behavior, a limited **problem-centered perspective**. The purpose has not been **basic knowledge-centered** in nature: That is, it is not concerned with understanding the typical behaviors and feelings of African Americans, or the typical pattern of sexuality development (Lewis & Kertzner, 2003).

The traditional concern with discovering general, universally relevant principles has typically resulted in a neglect of racial and ethnic issues involved in sexuality altogether. Moreover, when race has actually been addressed in research, as in research on African American men, a number of conceptual problems have often plagued the research (Lewis & Kertzner, 2003). In keeping with the desire to develop broadly generalizable principles, members of a given racial minority are all assumed to be identical to one another. For example, the term *Black* is used to characterize all individuals supposed to belong to the racial group, when in fact substantial differences exist among the many ethnic groups subsumed under the racial label; Afro-Caribbeans (those who voluntarily immigrated to the United States from Caribbean nations) view African Americans (whose ancestors were enslaved and involuntarily brought to the United States) as ". . . morally suspect, lazy, and sexually undisciplined . . ." (Lewis & Kertzner, 2003, p. 384). Clearly, identity among all Black individuals is not exactly the same, and is actually quite varied.

Likewise, lower socioeconomic urban African Americans are most often the participants included in sexuality research, such that results are presumed to generalize to middle-class and upper-class African Americans. Moreover, this produces a **confound** in the interpretation of results; a confound is a situation in which it is not possible to tell which of several explanations most accurately accounts for the results obtained. In this case, race and ethnicity are confounded, or confused, with the impoverished social environment in which the poor

Income level may actually explain differences in sexuality among racial and ethnic groups. If scientists do not examine income in their research, differences in sexual behavior may incorrectly be attributed to race itself. *In what ways do you think being wealthy versus having limited financial means might influence sexuality?*

African Americans live. Does race or poverty and deprivation more adequately explain the nature of sexuality for study participants? In these studies, there is no way to tell for sure.

### The Preeminence of Biological Variables

The dominance of the medical view during the early part of the 20th century was responsible for the elevation of a particular scientific perspective to prominence above all others within the sexological model: **biological essentialism**. Biological essentialism maintains that almost all important aspects of human sexuality can be reduced to the operation of physiological processes; all other factors, such as culture and learning, are relatively unimportant, producing only minor variations on the biological programming provided by genes, hormones, and neurological structures (White et al., 2000).

Moreover, the search for the most influential, pervasive causes of sexuality promoted the emphasis on biological factors as the most intuitively primal, elemental "building blocks" of human nature (Tiefer, 2000). This is because they seem to be common to all animals, as well as seeming more substantial and "real" because they are tangible and more easily apparent to human observation than environmental factors. Likewise, gender differences seem to be extremely physical in nature because of the obvious external physical differences between men and women, which contribute to the sense that gender is entirely controlled by biological factors. Other obvious physical differences among people (e.g., skin, eye, and hair color; facial shape, body type) contribute to thinking that those with similar characteristics belong to one biological group (race) and must be similar with respect to all other characteristics, nonphysical as well as physical. Because the physical differences are salient, biological factors have often been assumed to underlie virtually any other difference among groups of people.

Within this view, human sexuality has been seen as resulting largely from, activated by, and driven by biological functioning, starting prenatally in terms of development of basic characteristics, as well as after birth throughout the life span. Prenatally, sexologists have emphasized that hormones are responsible for basic sexual differentiation of brain structure related to maleness and femaleness, in addition to setting up the basic capability for sexual response later in life, including sexual orientation. Increases in hormones at puberty are viewed as a vitally important influence on the onset of sexual interest and arousal. In fact, hormones are cast as a major determinant of patterns of sexual behavior in adulthood, and identified as important factors in health and well-being (Tiefer, 2000).

A danger of an extreme focus on the importance of biological factors is the potential for bias that limits the understanding of human sexuality. For example, theorists adopting other perspectives have observed that the primary focus has been on the seemingly fundamental biological function of sex, procreation; this in turn has contributed to the overwhelming sense that sex, meaning "real sex," essentially consists of only one type of activity: penile–vaginal intercourse. Most other behaviors, according to this narrow view, are really just foreplay leading up to the main act (Tiefer, 2000, 2001).

According to critics of an exclusively biological perspective, a solitary emphasis on biological factors has likewise led to the definition of sexual disorders, or sexual dysfunctions, largely in terms of the malfunctioning of body parts and problems with being able to engage in penile–vaginal intercourse (Tiefer, 2001). Even the term, *sexual dysfunction*, conveys the sense that a part, as in a biological "machine" part, is not functioning or working correctly. The most historically prominent of the disorders include erectile dysfunction (the penis not sustaining an erection) and vaginal pain during intercourse. The result, from the perspective of some theorists, is that human sexuality has become fragmented conceptually, broken down into separate, small parts, like components of a machine. No understanding is provided of the overall picture of human sexual nature, and humans have become objectified, treated as if they are not complete, real humans living in a complex world of relationships, families, stresses, and daily activities (Tiefer, 2000, 2001).

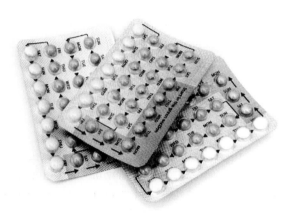

*How important do you think issues such as preventing unwanted teen pregnancy and treating erectile disorder are compared with other sexual concerns that individuals might experience? What questions would you like to see addressed by scientists?*

## The Theoretical View Used in This Book

As stated previously, the two overarching views used in this book are (a) the scientific perspective and (b) a focus on the role of personal characteristics and social influences in the development and expression of sexuality.

### The Scientific Perspective

First, with respect to the value of science in acquiring knowledge, most of the assertions advanced by postmodern theorists are accepted as legitimate statements about knowledge: that the meaning of information is influenced by the values of both the researcher and the consumer of the information, and that truly objective, unbiased data collection is not possible. Personal and cultural values influence (a) the choice of issues to examine, (b) the nature of the hypotheses that are advanced, (c) the methods used to collect information to test the hypotheses, (d) the types of analyses conducted, (e) the manner in which they are interpreted, and (f) the nature of the conclusions drawn from these analyses. The recognition of the effect of values on science, however, does not mean that the scientific method is invalid or useless, because all methods of information-gathering involve some manner of bias and value orientation. The implication for science is that scientists must constantly, explicitly assess and acknowledge the bias that underlies all research that they conduct. This means that scientists must actively communicate possible alternative explanations beyond those tested within the main hypothesis guiding their research.

Furthermore, scientists generally attempt to use techniques that avoid consciously injecting bias into the data they collect; that is, the scientific method involves techniques that attempt to identify bias that undermines their ability to determine whether a particular factor influences behavior. Scientists also use methods that attempt to eliminate these other types of factors that confuse the ability to tell whether the factor of primary interest is related to behavior or not. In the effort to identify relevant influences on behavior, the two most important tools in guiding the conduct of research are logic and theory. The scientific method therefore provides an extremely useful means of keeping track of possible influences on behavior, allowing scientists to rule out with some degree of confidence most others besides the one that is of primary interest.

Because of the scientific processes of prediction, control, and logical evaluation of the accuracy of the data, science offers a very important system for understanding the nature and biases of data collected. Science involves measuring behavior in a way that is **repeatable and accurate**. This means that other individuals using the same measurement technique will be able to obtain very close to the same quantities as the person who obtained the initial measurements. Repeatability and accuracy are the core features of what is meant by scientific **objectivity**. Once the measurements have been taken, the task of understanding and interpreting remains necessary.

However, if theory has been used to guide the research and measurement from the very beginning, the interpretation following data collection is a continuation of thinking about the issues, rather than a disconnected floundering to grasp the meaning of the measurement. Scientists in more recent times have begun to recognize the critical importance of **theory** in knowledge. In fact, the predominant substance of personality psychology and social psychology in their short histories has been the development and testing of theory. The dangers of unacknowledged bias have stemmed from conducting scientific study *without* an explicit, acknowledged theory. This technique has been called **dust bowl empiricism** because it involves collecting measurements that have little meaning; theory did not guide the data collection, such that the information must be interpreted to give the data meaning after they have been collected.

Data collection without theory, in fact, is really a mindless process. Yet high-quality information is more than the product of the procedure used to collect it. The process of collecting high-quality, meaningful information, to use an analogy, is similar to the process of driving a vehicle. Science may be likened to the vehicle, a tool for getting to one's destination. Yet the vehicle must have a knowledgeable driver to operate it to be able to arrive at the destination. The theory created or used by a knowledgeable scientist is therefore similar to the driver of the vehicle. The quality of the route taken to a destination, or even whether the destination will be reached, depends on the quality of the driver's knowledge. Dust bowl empiricism—scientific data collection without theoretical guidance—is analogous to a vehicle that has been set in motion without a driver. Logic is critical and it is the theory that must be placed at the center of the scientific process.

## The Role of Personal Characteristics and Social Influences

The second major view of this book is a focus on the personal characteristics and social influences on sexuality, drawing heavily on the theory and research of personality and social psychology. The adoption of personality and social psychological perspectives directly addresses the two primary limitations of the traditional sexological model identified by the social constructionist theorists in previous sections. The two limitations are viewing sexuality as determined almost exclusively (a) by universal, essential laws that influence all people in virtually the same way and (b) by biological factors, such that experiential, social, and cultural factors are of minor significance (a position called biological essentialism). Such issues have been debated within personality and social psychology since its early origins approximately 100 years ago, with different theories focusing on various levels of explanation of behavior. The various theories have focused on a number of different levels of analysis, much as a microscope is capable of focusing on different levels of a specimen under examination.

A criticism of the traditional sexological model is the tendency to analyze sexuality into the individual functioning of parts of the body and into types of specific sexual behaviors. This type of perspective objectifies human existence into dehumanized segments, with no clear understanding of how the segments relate to the whole person or to the entire sphere of individuals' lives. The goal of many personality theories is to account for the person from a broader perspective, as a whole, integrated individual. Likewise, social psychology is concerned with individuals as interacting with the social environment, influencing others and being influenced by them. Incorporating sexuality within this broader, person-oriented level should provide a more expansive, organized, and realistic understanding of sexuality.

## *Summary*

The study of sexuality is extremely challenging because of the extreme complexity of human sexual nature. Sexuality has been greatly regulated and restricted by religious beliefs for thousands of years, such that in many eras of history, simply alluding to sexual issues has been viewed as embarrassing and shameful.

Human sexuality is defined as all emotional, cognitive, and behavioral experiences, as well as bodily functions, related to the sexual nature of humans. Sexual nature for humans most importantly involves the subjective desire to experience sexual arousal and possibly to engage in overt expression of that desire. Emotional and cognitive activities that lead individuals to identify situations as sexual, that lead to motivation to engage in sexual expression, or that lead to physical arousal are the criteria that define sexuality.

The study of sexuality, a field called sexology, developed in the late 19th century and 20th century when conceptions of sexuality were first dominated by medicine rather than religious philosophy, as it had been for millennia prior to this time. The alignment of sexology with the physical and natural sciences had substantial effects on the types of assumptions and the nature of theories adopted to explain sexuality.

The primary theoretical perspectives adopted within sexology are that sexuality is determined by (a) fundamental, universal principles affecting the sexuality of all

*(Continued)*

(Continued)

individuals in the same way, with little important influence of social or cultural factors, and (b) biological factors, such that experiential, social, and cultural factors are of minor significance (a position called biological essentialism).

As a result of assumptions provided by medical and biological perspectives, certain issues have become the major focus of research and theory on sexuality, to the exclusion of others. The major issues include (a) the biological aspects of sexual arousal and behavior, (b) gender differences in sexual behavior and attitudes, (c) the causes of sexual orientation, and (d) common types of sexual behavior, most especially penile–vaginal intercourse. The issues that have been neglected include viewing individuals as whole persons living in social environments and specific relationships and examining interpersonal and cultural processes involved in the construction of the meaning of sexuality.

Addressing issues of sexuality within the fields of personality and social psychology will help to overcome the limitations of the sexological model inherent in previous conceptions of sexuality. The social psychological field in particular has explored the power differences between women and men as a major area of inquiry for some time. Moreover, to avoid the reduction of human sexuality to the mechanical operation of body parts, personality and social psychological theories typically view humans from the perspective of whole, purposeful, integrated individuals functioning within social situations and relationships.

## Chapter 1 Critical Thinking Exercises

1.  Sources of information about sexuality

    During late childhood and the early teen years, what type of communication about romantic relationships and sexuality took place between you and your parents? Was the communication about sexuality direct and open, or was it couched in subtle, indirect terms? What overall messages do you think you obtained from communication with your parents and family? If you did not receive any, or if you received very little, information, what effect do you think this absence of information had on you?

2.  Theory and understanding in science

    Identify three issues or questions related to sexuality that you find personally interesting and important. Has thinking on these issues changed across time, or has it remained largely the same? What types of social factors might influence thinking about these issues, such as factors related to differences in personal backgrounds?

Visit www.sagepub.com/hillhsstudy.com for online activities, sample tests, and other helpful resources. Select "Chapter 1: The Study of Sexuality" for chapter-specific activities.

# Chapter 2

## SEXUALITY IN A HISTORICAL, RELIGIOUS, AND PHILOSOPHICAL CONTEXT

U nderstanding the monumental influence of religion on sexual values is essential to the study of sexuality because religion, in particular Judaism and Christianity, historically has been at the core of ethics in Western cultures. This is especially true for sexual values, possibly more than any other single factor. Religious values have more than just a vague, general influence on culture at large. They often reach down to shape peoples' lives in a very powerful way, as described in the following passage:

I am a 27-year-old woman, and I was raised in a very religious community in the United States. From an early age, I was taught that self-exploration and feelings of desire were inappropriate and sinful. Abiding by these principles was a constant struggle for me, because I am a very emotional and passionate person. Masturbating seemed so natural, but I was disciplined and punished for doing it! ... There have definitely been times when my upbringing affected my ability to enjoy sex. Even now, I occasionally have difficulty reaching orgasm because I'm so inhibited—it's so hard to let go and simply enjoy the moment. (anonymous; Women's Sexual Experiences, On-line forum, retrieved July 22, 2006, from The-clitoris.com. Reprinted with permission of The-clitoris.com. The words in brackets were added.)

On the other hand, some individuals rebel against the prohibitive influence of religion, and even influence others to change their views:

I am a 26-year-old male, a professional, single, and been around. Met this 21-year-old girl 9 months ago. She was raised in a holy roller church and was a virgin. Led a very sheltered life and had never seen or felt a real ... [penis] before mine. She is a beautiful girl. When I met her, I could sense she was uptight and very horny....She now loves oral sex, giving and receiving....She has now discovered she loves and needs sex, a normal thing for any healthy 21-year-old. Some would say I corrupted her. I say she finally discovered and accepted *her sexuality and is no longer sexually frustrated and afraid of it. I don't know why some churches … [mess] people up and make them feel so guilty about sex. Some churches make people feel like sex is an unforgivable sin. On the other hand, lying and cheating, etc., … well you can be forgiven for those. Sin is sin and none of us are perfect. I rarely lie, don't cheat my fellow man, don't mess with my neighbor's wife and have never injured or killed anyone. Sex is my shortcoming. Again, I am not perfect. I just accept a gift nature gave me without guilt. We are now talking about marriage. Maybe this wasn't such a bad thing after all. (Confession Junkie, 2006a)*

To get an idea of the way in which religion has come to have such a profound effect on sexuality, we will examine the various world religions. However, a good deal of attention will be devoted to Christianity and Judaism because these two religions have had the greatest impact on the largest proportion of people throughout the history of Western society. As an overview, looking back to ancient times, Western religion was greatly affected by highly respected schools of Greek philosophy that were prevalent in Roman culture. However, in a tremendous historic reversal, eventually Christianity came to dominate formal philosophy throughout the Middle Ages in a powerful way; the two fields, theology and philosophy, in fact, were virtually indistinguishable on many issues until the Enlightenment in the 1700s. For this reason, theology, and to some extent philosophy, will be examined as the fundamental basis for attitudes about sexuality into current times.

In the modern era, philosophy and science began to evaluate sexuality using other methodologies besides faith and intuition, which are the tools of religion. Throughout much of history, however, philosophy and science have often explicitly endorsed many of the values pronounced by Christianity, rather than acting as objective fields whose goals are to critically evaluate and empirically examine assumptions about sexuality.

The treatment of sexuality within the five major world religions will be examined initially, along with Native American views of spirituality. Ultimately, however, Christianity became the most pervasively influential religion in Western society. The historical analysis in chapter 3 will then document the rise of Christianity as the predominant influence on views of sexuality, even after the emergence of philosophy and science.

## The Historical Analysis of Sexuality

**History** is an academic discipline that records and explains past events. **Philosophy** is an academic discipline devoted to evaluating the meaning of phenomena. It largely uses **logic**, which contrasts with scientific disciplines that rely upon direct observation to obtain evidence about phenomena. **Logic**, as developed within philosophy, refers to a system of accepted rules for judging the validity or accuracy of conclusions that are drawn (Woolf et al., 1973). History and philosophy overlap and complement one another when history is concerned with the examination of the origin and development of ideas and values. Until recently, historians have been reluctant to examine sexual behavior, and as a result, have often perpetuated inaccurate or completely erroneous beliefs about it (Bullough & Bullough, 1977). This in large part has been due to the fact that attitudes about sexuality have been primarily negative at the societal level throughout Western civilization.

The term, *sexuality,* is actually relatively new. Greek and Medieval Latin languages had no words directly related to modern notions of "sex," "sexual," or "sexuality" (Weisner-Hanks, 2000). The word *sexuality* first appeared in 1836 in a series of writings by the English poet, William Cowper, according to the *Oxford English Dictionary*. In his initial use of sexuality, however, Cowper wrote about the sexuality of plants, and was apparently referring to the fact that plants may be classified as either male or female. The first use, therefore, did not involve the various meanings that have come to be associated with the word in more recent times. Sexuality was used in a few other isolated and somewhat idiosyncratic ways during the 19th century, until it came to refer to types of sexual attraction in the noted writings of Richard von Krafft-Ebing (1937). In this context, the prefixes of *hetero-* and *homo-* were added to indicate attraction for the other sex and for the same sex, respectively. After that point, the terms *heterosexuality* and *homosexuality* made their way into more popular usage, and have gradually taken on additional meanings (Bristow, 1997).

The importance of concerns about the meaning of events and behavior becomes very clear when the nature of historical analysis is taken into account. In most cases, historians must piece together and reconstruct what happened in earlier times on the basis of multiple sources of information; the process of deduction—"filling in the gaps"—is more necessary the earlier the events occurred in history because less was documented in writing in ancient times. The process is similar to that used by a detective who is attempting to reconstruct a crime: collecting and making use of the piecemeal evidence that is available. This process requires speculation and inference—albeit based on education and experience—to fill in the gaps where direct evidence is not available. The process of understanding events that happened to people who are no longer alive, as in the case of ancient cultures, therefore is in very great danger of being seen in ways that are relevant to modern times, but that may have very little to do with earlier times (Weisner-Hanks, 2000).

The concern is that, since the concept of sexuality did not exist prior to the middle 1800s, the meaning of sexual behavior and relationships was likely to be very different in earlier eras. Given the very recent appearance of the words *sexuality, heterosexuality, homosexuality,* and *bisexuality,* some historians have cautioned against interpreting the sexual and reproductive behavior of previous generations and cultures based on our current understanding of sexual behavior (Bristow, 1997). Such historians (Halperin, 1990; Weeks, 1986) argue that it would be wrong to view sexuality as a fundamental, unchanging quality characterizing all humans in the same way throughout history, because the concept has only emerged within the last 150 years.

An implicit premise of this social constructionist perspective is that words and concepts develop when they are needed, either to communicate an idea or to serve some other function as people talk and interact with one another. From this viewpoint, the term, *sexuality,* came into existence only when a particular understanding about sexual behavior and relationships had developed, where this understanding had not existed explicitly prior to that point. Because the concept was not used earlier, it may be that the notions we associate with sexuality would not be relevant to, or involved in, the experiences of earlier generations (Weisner-Hanks, 2000).

A major example of this problem is the meaning of sexual behavior that occurs between same-sex individuals. In more modern times, the stereotype of "homosexuality" is of a relatively stable sexual orientation that is opposite of, and incompatible with, "heterosexuality"; the factors presumed to "cause" homosexuality are often popularly viewed as very different from those that "cause" heterosexuality. The notion of a fixed, established attraction toward individuals of one sex or the other, however, did not exist prior to the modern era (Bristow, 1997; Weeks, 1986). Sexual behavior between individuals of the same sex was viewed largely as an occasional lapse or indulgence (White, 1993); in different eras, same-sex behavior was thought to result from an inability to control primitive impulses, from moral weakness, or from temporary disease. Therefore, the notion of "sexual orientation" may not be entirely appropriate when considering sexual behavior among earlier peoples.

Most historians, however, maintain that it is possible to establish the nature of events as they happened with fairly good accuracy, as well as determining the nature of people's reactions to events. They point out that, in relying on historical documents to obtain this information, historians in more recent times have tended to base their descriptions and conclusions on a wider variety of sources than was true previously, in order to increase the quality of the information obtained. Literature and art are now included as sources of information, which is especially crucial in attempting to understand sexuality; in previous eras, sex was more likely to be addressed in art and literary works than in formal or official documents. With respect to the issue of using modern concepts to understand previous historical periods, historians generally do not view this as a problem unique to the topic of sexuality; it will always be the case that prior events are understood in terms of current knowledge and perspectives (Weisner-Hanks, 2000).

## The Centrality of Religion in Attitudes About Sexuality

Religion has provided the primary basis for the justification of moral and ethical principles across many cultures and eras. The words **morality**, **ethic**, and **values** all refer to the same basic concept, standards of good and bad conduct, providing the criteria for judging whether behavior is acceptable and healthy, or unacceptable and destructive.

Although Judaism and Christianity have had the most pervasive influence on the evolution of values in the United States, the effect has not been completely universal nor have they been the only religious influences. In fact, sociologists typically propose the existence of five "world religions," four others beyond Judaism and Christianity: Confucianism, Hinduism, Buddhism, and Islam. The concept of world religions is based on the distinctiveness of these five religions in comparison to other religions in terms of (a) the numbers of people who are followers of the belief system, (b) the development of an established, formal ethical or moral system, (c) and conceptualization of an overarching supreme power or force governing existence (Sharot, 2001). In addition to the world religions, Native American spiritual traditions will also be presented because of the historical importance of these cultures in the United States and because of a revival of interest among Native Americans in their heritage and identity (Young, 2002). The ethical and moral system of each of these religions has had an impact on cultural understandings of the meaning and role of sexuality in the lives of individuals within their cultures. Therefore, the religions will be examined briefly in terms of their fundamental beliefs and then the nature of the effect of such beliefs on sexual attitudes and behaviors.

### Judaism and Christianity

Despite the influence of a number of different religions in a variety of civilizations, Judaism and Christianity have indisputably had the greatest impact historically in the majority of European countries (Eder, Hall, & Hekma, 1999), as well as being the predominant influence in virtually all modern North, Central, and South American countries:

> Since the fall of the Roman Empire the great common denominator of Western civilization has been the Christian religion. The vast majority of the members of Western society have subscribed even if they have not lived up to its creeds, ideals, and moral standards. Furthermore, the vitality of these creeds, ideals and moral standards has derived, in large measure, from the belief that they are of divine origin and sanction. Indeed, it is difficult to conceive of Western civilization as it has developed thus far without this basic faith at its center. (Harrison & Sullivan, 1971, pp. 503–504)

The foundation for the Judeo-Christian tradition is Judaism, the Jewish religion dating back many centuries before Jesus, the central figure in the Christian religion. Judaism was fairly unique among religions that developed in the eastern area of the Mediterranean region in ancient times, in that it was based on the worship of only one god (it is therefore a *monotheistic* religion; Duling, Perrin, & Ferm, 1994; Weisner-Hanks, 2000). Most other religions in the world at that time believed in the existence of a multitude of deities (*polytheistic* religions), and it was the Judaic insistence on the existence of only one true God, Yahweh, that was a defining feature of Jewish identity and culture.

## The Development of Judeo-Christian Morality About Sexuality

### Judaism

As with morals in general, sexual values in Judaism were believed to be commandments from God. These commandments were passed from one generation to the next verbally over many years, just as were the teachings of Jesus that form the basis of Christianity. Over time, the various accounts of these commandments and the history of the Jewish people were written down, becoming the books of the Hebrew scriptures (later Christians adopted these writings as the Old Testament in the Christian Bible). The books were written in various forms across the ages, some of them over a 1,000-year period, and some of them resulting from combinations of several sources written by different authors. Over a period of time, a portion of the books came to be seen as the true, legitimate commandments of God, whereas others were abandoned or rejected; the accepted ones became known as the Scriptures and, because they were believed to be divine laws, they had **moral authority**: that is, they took on the force of determining what is considered good and moral versus bad and immoral.

### Symbols of Judaism

The Star of David, or the Magen David, meaning the shield of David. This is a relatively modern symbol of Judaism, and is rarely found in ancient Jewish literature. A common sign of good luck in Africa and the Middle East, the Magen David became a popular symbol for identifying Jewish synagogues in the 17th century. David was a great king of Israel for 40 years sometime between 1010 and 970 BCE (from http://www.jewishvirtuallibrary.org/jsource/Judaism/star.html).

The menorah is a candelabrum holding seven candles. The menorah is a symbol of Israel, which serves as "a light unto the nations" (Isaiah 42:6; from http://www.jewishvirtuallibrary.org/jsource/Judaism/menorah.html).

One of the most sacred rituals in Judaism involves the male sexual organ, the penis. The ritual focuses on the circumcision of the penis, in which the foreskin is ceremonially removed with a knife. The ritual is seen as partaking in a covenant of loyalty to God, and therefore is celebrated as a time of great elation and holiness (Sandmel, 1978).

## Regulation of Sexual Behavior to Preserve the Boundaries Established by God

The basic philosophy of Judaism is that the integrity (the distinctive quality) of the different aspects of the universe must be preserved and protected; the basic principles of ancient Judaism are summarized in Table 2.1. God established separate domains within creation and the qualities of the domains need to be maintained as God created them. Establishing and protecting boundaries therefore is considered essential to the order of creation and is at the heart of the laws provided by the Scriptures. This is true for laws regarding sexual interaction, as well as the multitude of laws encompassing more mundane aspects of life. The intense concern for order and structure extends equally to food and its preparation, and to types of cloth worn together. For example, it is an offense to wear linen and wool combinations because one is produced by a plant and the other by an animal, requiring the punishment of death. The blurring of categories resulting from intermingling the two is believed to violate and jeopardize God's system of order and structure (Frymer-Kensky, 1995).

A major issue in maintaining boundaries between domains is separating the holy and divine from the physical world, that which is lowly and profane. In Genesis accounts of the early history of humans, divine beings (e.g., angels) visited humans and even engaged in sex with them. This intermingling was one factor in the wrath of God that led to the Great Flood, after which God established even greater distinctions among categories. To accomplish this, God is believed to have shortened the life span of humans, and divine beings no

**TABLE 2.1**     Basic Principles of Ancient Judaism

| Issue | Principle | Implication of the Principle |
|---|---|---|
| Overarching premise | Preserving the integrity of aspects of the universe (especially separating the holy from the physical world) | Keep different kinds of phenomena separate (e.g., do not wear different kinds of cloth together) |
| Sexuality in general | Sexual behavior is a source of ritual (routine) impurity | Impurity from sexual behavior does not result from sin or evil<br>Engage in ritual bathing<br>Avoid contact with holy aspects of the universe until the day following sex |
| Sexual behavior outside of marriage | Sexual behavior outside of marriage is more than a source of impurity | Specific behaviors are prohibited: a man having sex with a married woman not his wife (adultery)<br>Sex with certain relatives (incest)<br>Sex with animals (bestiality) |

longer engage in sex with humans. God is also believed to have imposed more profound distinctions between humans and animals, which are thought to have been created originally as companions to humans. Commandments were handed down that humans may kill animals for food (but the blood may not be consumed); animals, however, could not kill humans under penalty of death. To complete this separation, sex between humans and animals (bestiality) was not permitted. Bestiality came to be viewed as "improper mixing" (Frymer-Kensky, 1995).

### Sex as a Source of Ritual Impurity

God creating the domains of the universe.

The Jewish commandments related to sexual behavior in general were, therefore, established to preserve the integrity and purity of the separate domains of the sacred and the sexual. Contamination and becoming unclean are considered to be unavoidable, necessary aspects of existence, however, because individuals come into contact with impure elements of the world in daily life. Consequently, becoming impure is not viewed as the result of sin or evil; individuals become contaminated or defiled while engaging in highly honorable and important functions, such as burying the dead. Likewise, negative consequences are not necessarily assumed to result from becoming impure—not illness, nor punishment, nor death—for the impurity can be cleansed with ritual baths, and the contamination disappears after a certain period of time. For a number of types of impurity, the defiled individual is expected to be isolated during the contamination so as not to corrupt anyone or anything else, but most especially the sacred. Unclean individuals are not allowed into the temple nor permitted to engage in sacred ceremonies during this time (Frymer-Kensky, 1995).

Sexual phenomena of any kind are by definition sources of ritual (routine) impurity. Men experiencing the emission of seminal fluid (fluid coming from the reproductive system), even while asleep, or individuals who engage in sexual intercourse are considered impure. The impure state requires bathing, after which the person remains impure until evening (Leviticus 15:16–18; Frymer-Kensky, 1995). The time restriction assures that impurity remains separated from anything holy. Even money from a prostitute is not to be given to the temple as a donation, because that, too, defiles the temple. Moses was told by God to refrain from sexual behavior for three days prior to climbing the mountain where he was believed to have received the Ten Commandments (Frymer-Kensky, 1995).

Priests at one time were required to carefully observe the separation of the sacred from sexual aspects of life, and to represent the ideal of sexually disciplined behavior. Yet, priests did not abstain from sexual behavior entirely; they were simply required to observe the separation in time between sexual behavior and entering into any building or ceremony that was holy. Families of priests were also expected to observe the separation of the sacred from the impure. Priests were required to marry a virgin, never a divorced woman, and his daughters were expected to remain virgins while living with their father. A daughter who violated this requirement was thought to defile her father, and the law requires that she be burned for her unforgivable contamination of the holy priest (Frymer-Kensky, 1995).

## Box 2.1  Analyze This: Looking at Different Perspectives

### *A Value Judgment About Religious Values*

A source of controversy, particularly within Christianity, is the literalness with which the passages in the Scriptures should be understood. The issue at the center of this controversy is the concept of **inspiration**. Most Christians believe that the writings included in the Bible are *inspired,* meaning that God motivated particular individuals to communicate his commandments to other humans; therefore, the writings are actually the writings of God. Some groups of Christians further believe that the inspired writers were merely passive recipients of God's thoughts and that, because the resulting texts are entirely of divine creation, they are perfect and without error. These individuals believe that the passages should be understood by their surface meaning; that is, they should be interpreted literally, and in full, as the word of God. Such Christians have been referred to more recently as **fundamentalists**. Beginning in the early 19th century, advocates of the fundamentalist position assumed a **supernaturalist perspective** in order to be able to explain incredible events and beings, such as miracles, angels, and demons (Perrin, 1974). This position maintains that such phenomena are explainable outside of the realm of rational logic and science, because they actually are produced by divine power or supernatural forces.

Other Christians point to "contradictions, scientific errors, absurd statements, exaggerations, and immature views . . . throughout the Bible" (Bratton, 1959, p. 5). An example of a type of factual contradiction Bratton notes is that, in the book I Samuel, David is said to have killed Goliath, although Elhanan is said to have killed Goliath in II Samuel; later in Chronicles the record is corrected by stating that Elhanan actually killed the *brother* of Goliath. Because of problems of this sort, **nonfundamentalist Christians** argue that the notion of the inspired word does not mean that the passages are the word of God *verbatim*, exactly as they were communicated to the author. Instead, they believe that the words are inspired in the sense that they are based on the *spirit* of the meaning intended by God generally, and that they are inspirational because they communicate a positive message for humans (Bratton, 1959). This understanding of the meaning of God's message is that it has evolved and changed in its form as a result of the historical changes that have occurred through a variety of cultures: "The Bible is not a preordained, supernatural deposit of truth but a record of the experience of man in his long search for that truth" (Bratton, 1959, p. 7). Rather than viewing the Scriptures as an accurate historical record, nonfundamentalists believe that history may be understood, at least in some form, by avoiding an explanation of the incredible and miraculous aspects of the accounts. Such a view is called a **rationalist position** regarding the accuracy of the Bible (Perrin, 1974). Nonfundamentalists generally feel that each book of the Bible must be viewed within the culture and the demands prevailing at the time that the passages were written (Bratton, 1959).

In summary, a substantial degree of controversy exists among different types of Christians regarding the way in which the Bible is to be understood. Fundamentalists argue that the Scriptures are perfect, without flaw, and must be obeyed without exception or failing. Nonfundamentalists maintain that Scriptures represent the general principles conveyed by God through imperfect humans, and that these principles provide guidelines for appropriate behavior; however, they believe that interpretation is involved in applying the principles to specific behaviors and situations. Therefore, a literal understanding of the intent of the writings is not possible, making absolute adherence to the rules likewise impossible.

*Implications of the fundamentalist versus nonfundamentalist debate for sexuality.* Because fundamentalist Christians believe that the Scriptures are literally the commandments of God, violation of these laws are seen as endangering an individual in terms of not being allowed to enter into eternal life with God in Heaven. This belief means, then, that people must not engage in sexual behavior outside of heterosexual marriage, nor violate any of the commandments about sexuality in the Scriptures.

Nonfundamentalist Christians believe that the Scriptures contain communications from God that represent the spirit or general intent of divine will, but are not literal commandments or laws from God. Because they view the Scriptures as communication from God that are interpretations by the human who received the divine messages, the information is influenced by the culture and the nature of understanding available to the individual in the historical context in which they were received. Therefore, the writings are not purely the word of God, but are general representations of it, and involve some degree of interpretation to apply them to the specific situations in each individual's life.

This type of thinking evolved to a great extent during the liberal era of the 1960s with respect to sexuality, in the form of what has been called the **new morality**. During this era of great change in culture and sexual behavior, Christians attempted to reconcile the fact that many people who, along most other dimensions of evaluation seemed to be moral Christians, nonetheless engaged in sexual behavior condemned in the Scriptures. The basic premise of this new morality, also called **situation ethics**, was that each individual must evaluate the implications of a particular situation, and the choices it presents, to determine what the likely implications of those choices are. If a given choice is evaluated to lead largely to good outcomes, then the behavior is moral and good. With respect to sexuality, if individuals engage in sexual behavior out of love for one another, then the behavior is moral, even if it is condemned by traditional morality. For Christians who endorsed this view, not all sex outside of marriage (e.g., premarital sex) is necessarily evil (Allyn, 2000).

## References

Allyn, D. (2000). *The sexual revolution: An unfettered history.* Boston: Little, Brown.

Bratton, F. G. (1959). *A history of the Bible: An introduction to the historical method.* Boston: Beacon Press.

Perrin, N. (1974). *The New Testament, an introduction: Proclamation and parenesis, myth and history.* New York: Harcourt Brace Jovanovich.

Moses descending from the mountain with the Ten Commandments.

Given that sexual behavior is considered a source of ritual impurity, which can be cleansed and isolated, sexuality in general is not considered evil or horrible. In fact, according to Frymer-Kensky (1995), sexuality does not occupy any especially important position in Jewish morality, and is viewed as one of the many aspects of social life that simply requires routine regulation. Sexual behavior is of value because it creates intimate bonds that form the basis of the family. It is viewed as a positive force in the very controlled and regulated context of marital responsibility and obligation. It is a religious duty of Jewish men to have sex with their wives, and women are expected to have sex with their husbands, although it is not a religious requirement for women. The Jewish religion actually looks down upon *celibacy* (refraining from sexual behavior); *chastity* is defined as abstaining from *prohibited* sexual behavior, rather than total abstinence from all sexual behavior (Weisner-Hanks, 2000).

### Sexual Behavior That Is More Than a Source of Ritual Impurity

Outside of the sanctioned context of marriage, sexual interaction is seen as threatening to the order and structure of society. Within Jewish philosophy, unregulated, uncontrolled sexual behavior came to be seen as the epitome of disloyalty and disregard for social obligation. This is particularly true if it involves a married woman, because she is required to give exclusive sexual rights to her husband. In the Hebrew tradition, "free" sexual behavior came to stand as the symbol of evil behavior in general. Over time, the symbolism was used to such a great extent by the ancient prophets that it is virtually impossible to determine whether they were condemning sexual violations, involvement with foreign powers occupying Israel, or involvement with other religions besides Judaism (Frymer-Kensky, 1995).

Commandments regarding sex were not developed according to an extremely systematic, logical set of principles, but rather were established to protect the boundaries among highly selected domains (Frymer-Kensky, 1995). Sexual behavior occurring in some, but not all, contexts other than marriage are more than a source of impurity; these types of sexual behavior are considered abominations and in many instances are punishable by death. Specific abominations included a man having sex with a married woman (adultery), incest (specific relatives were defined as off-limits for sexual behavior), and sex with animals (bestiality; Frymer-Kensky, 1995; Weisner-Hanks, 2000).

Adultery. The boundary that is violated in the case of adultery is the boundary between households; however, adultery is defined specifically as sex with a married woman, not sex with a married man (Frymer-Kensky, 1995). The reason for the double standard in the definition of adultery is because sexuality is cast in the framework of protecting the property of men in building household domains. Women are viewed as belonging to a particular household, and by having sex with a married woman, the man violates the sanctity of another household, using or stealing sacred property from that household (Frymer-Kensky, 1995).

**Sex With Unmarried Women.** The Judaic commandments contain no direct prohibitions against men having sex with unmarried women. However, scriptural law in Exodus 22:15–16 commands that a man who has sex with an unmarried woman must marry her, regardless of whether he wants to do so or not.

**Incest.** In addition to a concern about violation of male authority through inappropriate intermingling among households, commandments also prohibit the crossing of boundaries within households. Laws against incest very specifically indicate that certain relatives are outside the bounds of acceptability regarding sex: parents, stepmothers, one's mother-in-law, father's brothers and their wives, both father's and mother's sisters; one's sisters, and brothers' wives; daughters and sons' wives; and granddaughters. Only in a few instances are men mentioned as off-limits for sexual interaction, specifically one's father and father's brothers; the law is more concerned with restricting heterosexual men than women as potential offenders, although some possibilities for heterosexual women are so offensive that they have to be identified specifically (Frymer-Kensky, 1995).

**Sex With Prostitutes and Slaves.** The Hebrew scriptures prohibit other inappropriate sexual encounters, but not all others. Sex with prostitutes and slaves is not a violation of Judaic law for men (Frymer-Kensky, 1995), but Jewish women are not permitted to engage in prostitution (Weisner-Hanks, 2000). (No consideration is given to the possibility of a woman having sex with a prostitute.) A major reason for the prohibition against prostitution, at least for women, may have been that it was associated with the religious practices of other religions, in which priests and priestesses engaged in sex for money to support the temples of the gods they worshiped (Weisner-Hanks, 2000). Yet, this does not explain why sex with prostitutes is not specifically condemned for men.

**Sex Between Men.** According to long-standing interpretations of the Scriptures, sex between men is more than a source of ritual impurity (Frymer-Kensky, 1995). However, according to Helminiak (2000), interpretations that have developed over time have come to ignore the historical and cultural context in which the prohibition against male–male sexual behavior appeared. See Box 2.2 for an examination of different points of view regarding this issue.

Sexual behavior between women is not specifically prohibited in Jewish law (Frymer-Kensky, 1995). Less attention is generally devoted to sexual offenses by women than men in the Hebrew scriptures, although some behaviors by women are forbidden (e.g., bestiality). Attitudes about women and about the definition of sex may account for the lack of concern with female–female sexual behavior. It was probably viewed as unimportant because it involved only women and, in a sense, is not "really sex" because it does not involve penetration by a sexual organ (i.e., the penis; Frymer-Kensky, 1995).

### Sexual Body Fluids

The Hebrew scriptures likewise present a highly negative view of bodily discharges related to sexuality, because they are thought to be a source of contamination: for example, the discharge of **seminal fluid** (emitted by the male reproductive system during sexual arousal and sexual behavior, and sometimes spontaneously while asleep), **menstrual discharge** (a combination of uterine tissue, mucus, and small amounts of blood expelled by the female body in preparation for the next reproductive cycle), and discharges associated with **childbirth**. Contact with such substances was believed to defile the individual who touched them, and sexual intercourse was therefore prohibited during menstruation (Frymer-Kensky, 1995; Sandmel, 1978; Weisner-Hanks, 2000). The logic is somewhat inconsistent in these restrictions because ejaculation or leakage of semen may occur during sexual intercourse. Given that semen is a source of contamination, concern about contamination

## Box 2.2 Analyze This: Looking at Different Perspectives

### Controversy About What the Scriptures Say About Same-Sex Sexuality

Across the last several thousand years, the view within Judaism and Christianity has been that sex between men is a violation of God's commandments. The traditional basis for this belief is a set of several passages within the holy books of the religions. In the Christian scriptures, five passages focus on sex between men: Leviticus 18:22, Leviticus 20:13, Romans 1:27, 1 Corinthians 6:9, and 1 Timothy 1:10.

As noted in Box 2.1, some scholars, however, have disputed what is now the traditional interpretation of the meaning of these scriptural passages. The heart of the disagreement is whether the biblical statements, such as the prohibition against male–male sexual behavior, should be interpreted literally and the commandments should be followed exactly as they are stated. This viewpoint has been called the fundamentalist position. The opposing, nonfundamentalist perspective is that the Scriptures cannot be interpreted literally because factual errors and contradictions suggest that the writings are not the verbatim statements of God. Instead, the Scriptures convey the spirit of God's intentions, but the writings were influenced by the understandings that prevailed in a particular ancient culture at a particular point in history (Bratton, 1959; Helminiak, 2000).

The nonfundamentalist perspective has evolved to the extent that organizations have formed that are devoted to a belief system that is not grounded in a rigid, traditional understanding of the Scriptures. One example of this is The Center for Progressive Christianity (http://www.tcpc.org/template/index.cfm), an alliance of various churches, organizations, and individuals whose purpose, according to their motto, is to promote "an approach to Christianity that is inclusive, innovative, informed." Their philosophy is summarized in their definition of progressive, "By calling ourselves progressive, we mean we are Christians who . . . invite all people to participate in our community and worship life without insisting that they become like us in order to be acceptable (including but not limited to): believers and agnostics, conventional Christians and questioning skeptics, women and men, those of all sexual orientations and gender identities, those of all races and cultures, those of all classes and abilities, those who hope for a better world and those who have lost hope." Of particular noteworthiness is their explicit embrace of all sexual orientations and gender identities. Their philosophy also states that they "find more grace in the search for understanding than we do in dogmatic certainty—more value in questioning than in absolutes," a reference to the group's rejection of fundamentalism.

A second example of the nonfundamentalist view is the Religious Institute on Sexual Morality, Justice, and Healing. According to their Web site (http://www.religiousinstitute.org/declaration.html), "more than 2,200 religious leaders from more than 35 religious traditions endorse the Religious Declaration" advocated by the organization. Among other objectives, the Religious Institute advocates the "full inclusion of women and sexual minorities in congregational life, including their ordination and the blessing of same-sex unions." Their position is based on the philosophy that "sexuality is God's life-giving and life-fulfilling gift. . . . Our faith traditions celebrate the goodness of creation, including our bodies and our sexuality. We sin when this sacred gift is abused or exploited. However, the great promise of our traditions is love, healing, and restored relationships. . . . It accepts no double standards and applies to all persons, without regard to sex, gender, color, age, bodily condition, marital status, or sexual orientation." Nonfundamentalist faith groups, therefore, do not accept the traditional belief that same-sex sexuality is condemned by God and inherently wrong.

The movement away from a literal, fundamentalist perspective of principles of faith is not restricted to Christianity. In fact, Reform Judaism began at least 100 years before the progressive movement in Christianity. According to the Web site for this tradition (http://rj.org/whatisrj.shtml), "Reform Judaism took root in North America more than 130 years ago under the leadership of Rabbi Isaac Mayer Wise, one of several European rabbis who brought the changes in Judaism occurring in Europe to these shores. Reform Judaism is now the largest Jewish movement in North America, with more than 900 congregations and 1.5 million people." The fundamental perspective of Reform Judaism is that it "affirms the central tenets of Judaism— God, Torah and Israel—even as it acknowledges the diversity of Reform Jewish beliefs and practices. We believe that all human beings are created in the image of God, and that we are God's partners in improving the world. Tikkun olam—repairing the world—is a hallmark of Reform Judaism as we strive to bring peace, freedom, and justice to all people.

The Reform Judaism position is absolute acceptance of nonheterosexual orientations. This is based on the goal of social justice for all: "Reform Jews are committed to the principle of inclusion, not exclusion. Reform Jews are committed to the absolute equality of women in all areas of Jewish life. . . . We were the first movement to ordain women rabbis, invest women cantors, and elect women presidents of our synagogues. . . . Reform Jews are also committed to the full participation of gays and lesbians in synagogue life as well as society at large" (http://rj.org/whatisrj.shtml).

Another type of criticism of the fundamentalist religious belief about same-sex sexuality is based on the historical-critical approach. This approach views the scriptural passages from the perspective of the human authors with respect to their intentions and in the context of the culture of that time. The historical-critical approach has been employed by scholar Daniel Helminiak (2000) to conclude that "The Bible does not condemn gay sex as we understand it today" (p. 131).

An initial issue in this analysis is that a search of the Jewish and Christian scriptures reveals that not a single passage explicitly and indisputably condemns sex between women. Furthermore, Jesus never commented on same-sex sexuality at all. The belief that Sodom was destroyed by God in punishment for sex between men is based on speculation rather than an explicit reference to this as the reason for its destruction. It is also partially the result of a mistaken translation within the King James Bible in referring to "sodomites" in Deuteronomy and First and Second Kings; it is not at all clear that this term should have been used in the translation.

Beyond this, according to Helmniak (2000), the scriptural verses in Leviticus, Romans, 1 Corinthians, and 1 Timothy that are believed to prohibit same-sex sexual behavior have been misinterpreted across the centuries. The misinterpretation is based on an inaccurate blending of issues related to gender with issues related to sexuality, as well as Judaic concerns about impurity resulting from mixing separate domains. In fact, the reference to the impurity of male–male sex in Romans was actually intended to provide an example that would illustrate that Christians were no longer concerned with the impurity issues underlying the Judaic religion. Finally, Helmniak contends that it is not clear that a reference to male–male sexual behavior occurs in 1 Corinthians and 1 Timothy; even if it is interpreted in such a way, the point was to condemn sexual exploitation and abuse, not same-sex behavior itself. In sum, Helmniak disputes the very foundation for the belief that same-sex sexuality is condemned within the Scriptures, particularly the Christian Bible.

## References

Bratton, F. G. (1959). *A history of the Bible: An introduction to the historical method.* Boston: Beacon Press.

Helminiak, D. A. (2000). *What the Bible really says about homosexuality* (Millennium ed.). Tajique, NM: Alamo Square Press.

from menstrual discharge would seem to be a moot issue; both a man and a woman could come into contact with semen during sexual intercourse. If exposure to semen is not viewed as an equivalently extreme contaminant in this context, the law makes an arbitrary distinction between natural (spontaneous) semen emission that occurs at night and semen that is ejaculated during sexual behavior. Moreover, distinguishing seminal fluid from menstrual fluid is an arbitrary distinction and may reflect the difference in power between men and women: male fluid is an acceptable contaminant, but female fluid is not.

### Inconsistent Treatment of Sexuality

Modern scholars have attempted to develop an understanding of the basic philosophy and principles underlying treatment of sexual behavior in the Hebrew scriptures. However, passages addressing it are scattered throughout the Scriptures, often with very little context or explanation of the statements. Moreover, the focus is often on pronouncing restrictions on specific sexual behaviors, rather than attempting to explain and place them in a conceptual framework. The result is a relatively unsystematic, not extremely coherent perspective of sexuality, according to some students of Jewish religious law. At times, sex is treated as an important creative force in building bonds and intimacy—in the context of marriage; yet, at the same time, it is viewed with suspicion and fear as a destabilizing, potentially destructive force. Even in marriage, sex is seen as a source of contamination and defilement, despite the fact that sex is a religiously required behavior. Furthermore, too much interest in it—overindulgence in sex—leads to condemnation, abuse of power (i.e., David and Bathsheba), and retribution by God (i.e., the Great Flood, the fall of Satan). According to some scholars, the Scriptures creates a two-sided image of sex—both positive and negative—instilling a sense of ambivalence about it, without necessarily providing a clear understanding of how to deal with the conflicted feelings (Frymer-Kensky, 1995).

## Christianity

Christians believe that Jesus was resurrected after his death, and ascended to Heaven to become the means through which people may enter into Heaven as well. By having faith in the divinity of Jesus, Christians believe that they may be forgiven for their faults and offenses against God; the basic principles of ancient Christianity are summarized in Table 2.2. For Christians, morality, the set of values about appropriate behavior, is provided by the instructions pronounced by Jesus while he was alive on Earth, which are extensions of the Judaic system of laws. Accounts based on Jesus' life and his teachings were eventually written down and became the Christian scriptures, the various books of the New Testament. Both Judaism and Christianity, then, are identical in that they believe that morality is revealed: that is, communicated by God and divine in origin.

Jesus ascending into Heaven.

As with the books of the Old Testament, the information that was eventually included in the books of the New Testament was told orally, for at least 25 years after the crucifixion of Jesus. The primary reason was that his followers believed that he would return within a very short time after his death, because he was believed to have ascended to Heaven as the Son of God; therefore, no reason existed for having a written record. Eventually, the oral accounts of Jesus' life and teachings were written down and particular writings came to be seen as authoritative. As with the books of the Old Testament, this evolution of specific writings into Scriptures was a long, involved process.

| **TABLE 2.2** | Basic Principles of Ancient Christianity | |

| Issue | Principle | Implication of the Principle |
|---|---|---|
| Overarching premise | Morality is based on following the instructions provided by Jesus | Violations of morality require forgiveness by God |
| Sexuality in general | Jesus did not address sexuality virtually at all Paul advocated that Christians should not engage in sexual behavior at all, if they are strong-willed | Avoid "sexual irregularities" by marrying and having sex only with one's spouse |
| Specifics of sexuality | Augustine cast sexuality as evil and destructive | Abstinence and celibacy are the ultimate ideals Sexual behavior for married couples should occur only for reproduction Pleasure should be avoided in sexual behavior for married couples Penile–vaginal intercourse with the husband on top of the wife is the only moral sexual behavior |

Similar to the Hebrew scriptures, little systematic treatment of sexuality exists in the books of the New Testament (Bullough & Brundage, 1994). Jesus actually said next to nothing about sexuality himself, at least as recorded in the New Testament books. Rather, the ethics pronounced by Paul have formed the cornerstone and foundation for Christian attitudes about sexuality, even through modern times. Statements about sexual issues appear as responses to particular concerns addressed to Paul by early Christian communities.

### Paul

Paul came to be greatly respected and eventually became a preeminent authority in the early Christian communities. Paul advocated that the best course of action would be for Christians not to engage in sexual behavior at all, if they are strong-willed enough to be able to avoid sex. Yet, to prevent succumbing to "sexual irregularities," as a last resort, Christians should marry, with one man having one wife and one woman having one husband. Husbands and wives should engage in sexual behavior with their spouses, unless they agree to be celibate, which should only occur for a limited time (Duling et al., 1994; Sandmel, 1978). Paul also stated that Christians should not separate from their spouses (Sandmel, 1978). Paul declared that adultery, fornication (sex outside the context of marriage), and possibly masturbation (self-stimulation) would prevent individuals from entering the kingdom of God (Bullough & Brundage, 1994).

Paul's proclamations about sexual and gender issues were in keeping with the traditional morality prevailing in the dominant Roman culture during his life. Strong elements of Hellenistic (Greek) beliefs, developing out of a philosophy called **dualism**, are apparent in his statements about sin and virtue, along with evidence of traditional Judaic rules about holy versus unclean behavior. Other aspects of Paul's moral statements reflect the importance of his

PAUL BEFORE THE COUNCIL.

Paul (approximately 10–67 CE), early Christian church leader

belief in the fulfillment of ancient Jewish prophecies about the coming of a savior messiah through the life and death of Jesus. The Messiah, or Christ, was thought to herald the end of the world as it had previously existed. Again, physical and sensual indulgence were considered to detract from spiritual development and the attempt to become more like God in preparation for the return of Jesus. Given this belief, a major factor contributing to the negative attitude toward sensuality and sex, in addition to dualistic thought, was the sense that worldly pleasures and reproduction would not exist with the coming of the Heavenly Kingdom (Duling et al., 1994).

### Greek Philosophical Influences

Along with Judaic legal traditions and Paul's ministries, another major influence on the development of early Christian attitudes were schools of Greek philosophy that were highly revered in ancient times. Among the most prominent ancient Greek philosophers was Plato (428–347 BCE; BCE is identical to time period BC, but means "Before the Common Era"). Plato modified and strongly advocated ancient

**dualistic** views of existence. **Dualism** is the belief that the universe consists of two opposing forces, the spiritual and the physical. The spiritual aspect of human existence is the soul, while the physical aspect is the body. The fundamental position of dualism is that the soul is imprisoned in the human body as punishment, a view possibly based on ancient Greek creation stories, although its origin is not entirely certain. The primary goal of humankind is thought to be the liberation of the soul from its physical prison through spiritual enlightenment and expansion. A focus on physical aspects of existence is believed to detract from the spiritual transcendence of the human body, with sexual behavior representing the conquest of the physical over the spiritual (Bullough & Bullough, 1995).

Plato argued that the nature of the world could not really be known through the senses of the body, but only through intuitive perception using one's soul, the true connection with the divine. The real essence and meaning of existence could only be understood by clearing the mind of body senses, which are distractions, and employing the

PLATO.

Plato (approximately 428–347 BCE), Greek philosopher

soul to search for ultimate meaning. Plato extended this dualistic notion to human relationships and love, asserting that love focusing on the body was destructive and contaminating; love focused on appreciation of a person's mind and character, in contrast, would permit the experience of true happiness (Bullough & Bullough, 1995). Physical, sexual love became known by the Greek word **eros** (pronounced AIR ohs), whereas spiritual, nonphysical love became known as **agape** (pronounced AH gah PAY).

The Platonic dualistic view of human existence influenced successive generations of philosophers, becoming increasingly more negative toward sensuality and sexual pleasure across various offshoots of dualistic thinking. **Stoicism**, developing in the second and first century BCE, maintained that sex in itself was not evil, although extreme indulgence, as with any other bodily activity, was unhealthy. However, later Stoic philosophers argued that sex is acceptable only for reproduction, but is not at all appropriate for the purpose of only experiencing pleasure, even within marriage. Stoic views strongly affected medical literature, and became a pervasive factor in formal thinking during this period (Bullough & Bullough, 1995).

Although these later writers did not have a *direct* influence on the authors of the New Testament books, their writings provide evidence about the type of philosophical and religious climate prevailing at the time. In addition, later church leaders did actually incorporate the principles of the Greek philosophers into their own beliefs and teachings (Bullough & Bullough, 1995).

### Gnosticism

A major factor that pushed Christian thinking in the direction of Hellenistic beliefs was the competition that developed between Christianity and a religious philosophy called Gnosticism. **Gnosticism** developed from Platonic dualism and maintained that humans were born with both good and evil components, the spiritual and the physical.

During this period, the group of orthodox (conventional) Christians, who were the forerunners of modern Christianity, found themselves competing with Gnostic Christians for new converts and for control over Christian philosophy. In many ways, this rivalry led conventional Christians to incorporate increasingly more restrictive, conservative views into their understanding of the Scriptures, so that they would be as concerned about spiritual issues as were the Gnostics. As the Gnostics grew prominent and successful in recruiting followers, Christians began to advocate Gnostic beliefs that were more compatible with the core of their own beliefs and vehemently attacked those aspects that were different. Eventually, the acceptable attitudes within the Orthodox Church consisted only of those at the more "liberal" extreme that tolerated sexual intercourse for purposes of procreation, and those at the other extreme that maintained that Christians should remain celibate throughout their lives (Bullough & Bullough, 1995).

The conventional form of Christianity gradually established greater influence over Christian thinking, probably because of their stronger emphasis on organization and church structure. By the end of the second century CE, the most vocal opponents of Gnosticism within mainstream Christianity had become highly negative toward sex, even within marriage, and one leader, Tertullian, went so far as to question why God had ever created it. Yet, by being tied to the Judaic religion, the mainstream Christians were grudgingly obligated to acknowledge the importance accorded to marriage by the Hebrew scriptures (Bullough & Bullough, 1995).

### Manichaeism and Augustine

The waning influence of Gnosticism did not end the movement toward more negative Christian views about sexual behavior. Another religion, **Manichaeism**, developing during the fourth century CE, took a similarly harsh stance toward sexuality. Manichaeism grew to be very successful at recruiting new followers and therefore became a major rival of Christianity during that time. Nonetheless, some followers of Manichaeism eventually converted to Christianity and, just as converts from Gnosticism injected contemptuous beliefs about sex

into Christian philosophy, so did converts from the new rival religion. One convert in particular, **Augustine** (354–430), towers above all others in his influence on Christian sexual beliefs, possibly second only to Paul in his impact on religious doctrine (Bullough & Bullough, 1995).

Augustine was never able to attain the highest level of religious development during the 11 years that he was a member of Manichaeism. He was unable to free himself from feelings of sexual desire and from sexual behavior, living with a sexual companion during his involvement in the religion. The inability to adhere to the principles of Manichaeism led him eventually to convert to Christianity; he was the Bishop of Hippo from 396 until his death in 430 (Hippo was an ancient city in northern Africa). Yet, his extremely negative feelings about sexual desire and behavior remained deeply entrenched in his personal philosophy and he avidly incorporated them in the doctrines he developed as

Augustine (354–430), early Christian church leader and theologian a Christian leader. Because sex within marriage and reproduction were portrayed as religious obligations in the Hebrew scriptures, Augustine was prevented from applying the Manichaein principles of sexual abstinence entirely. Celibacy (not engaging in sexual behavior, even if one has done so previously) and virginity (never having engaged in sexual behavior at all) remained the ultimate good for Augustine. However, he reluctantly acknowledged that sexual intercourse could be justified within marriage, but only for reproduction, and he believed that sex for the purpose of pleasure was not at all good (Bullough & Bullough, 1995).

For this reason, Augustine established a number of standards for evaluating the acceptability of sexual behavior within marriage. Foreplay (e.g., kissing and caressing to enhance sexual arousal, fondling genitals) was defined as totally unacceptable. He advocated that the only virtuous type of sexual behavior was penile–vaginal intercourse (penis in vagina), with the man on top of the woman, because this was thought to be the most likely to lead to procreation. All other behaviors and positions could only be devoted to the experience of pleasure, and therefore were sinister. The basis for these proclamations was not biblical scripture, but the principles of pagan (Hellenistic) philosophy. Furthermore, the conclusions by Augustine and other early church leaders were not based on a scientific understanding of human nature or sexual physiology. Yet, the contempt and disgust for sex embodied in these principles have become the foundation for Western sexual values through modern times (Bullough & Bullough, 1995), influencing not only religious and individual values, but also legal and judicial thinking.

## The Institutionalization of Christian Values Within Society

**Institutionalization** is the process of establishing a set of beliefs, philosophy, and practices within a formal organization as official policy. The Christian church is one of the first prominent organizations in Western civilization to adopt an official position regarding sex, with governments of Europe and then the United States later adopting the values espoused by the church. Early Christian philosophers initially established the basis for the intensely negative view toward sexual behavior held within much of Western civilization. Beyond what little had been written about Paul's views on sex, church leaders could not find explicit statements in the Scriptures regarding the specific behaviors that should be identified as sinful. The leaders therefore began to appeal more and more to the standard of what is "natural" to formalize prohibitions against most forms of sexual expression. The concept of "natural" originated from Greek philosophy as advanced by Aristotle, who evaluated phenomena using observation of what occurs in nature; applying such criteria, he maintained that he had proven the natural inferiority of women (Bullough & Bullough, 1995).

In a similar way, Christian leaders used analogies from nature to evaluate sexual behavior, comparing it to the sowing of seed in fields by farmers. Natural, therefore, was sexual behavior that "bore fruit"—that is, produced offspring. All else was unnatural. A second criterion was the comparison of human behavior to animal behavior; behavior in which animals engage must be "natural." The intent was to determine what the primary function of body organs is and this function was then deemed the natural one. Vision is the purpose of eyes, hearing is the purpose of ears, and procreation is the purpose of genitals. Yet, another criterion was needed in applying the animal standard: animals seemed to have different structures than humans, so these differences needed to be taken into account. Even to this day, however, philosophers and religious scholars cannot agree what are natural behaviors, and early Christian leaders were highly selective in the examples they used to justify their conclusions (Bullough & Bullough, 1995).

Ultimately, the standards established by Augustine became the final basis for decisions. His primary conclusion was that procreation is the only acceptable purpose of sexual intercourse, and then only within marriage; all else is sinful. Even this standard had exceptions, however, because Augustine acknowledged the right of spouses, especially the husband, to demand sexual intercourse with the partner despite the impossibility of procreation (e.g., due to infertility or old age). He concluded that it was better for an individual to have penile–vaginal intercourse with his or her spouse than to be denied the activity and, overwhelmed by lust, succumb to "unnatural," sinful behaviors with other individuals, or sinful behaviors involving orifices (body openings) other than the vagina, or organs other than a penis (i.e., dildos; Bullough & Bullough, 1995).

The standard of natural versus unnatural sex eventually became incorporated in secular (nonreligious) law. The first law prohibiting sexual behavior not involving rape or adultery was enacted against same-sex sexual behavior in the Roman Empire in 342 CE under co-emperors Constantius and Constans, who were Christians. However, it was not until the sixth century under the Christian emperor, Justinian, that a law used the concept "contrary to nature" to prohibit "diabolical and unlawful lusts" committed by certain men. Later law prohibited a broad range of sexual behavior, essentially criminalizing all behavior that was not directly related to procreation (Bullough & Bullough, 1995).

The principle of allowing only procreative, and therefore apparently natural, sexual behavior was formalized in religious doctrine through the creation of **penitential literature**. The adjective *penitential* derives from *penance,* which means the act of expressing sorrow for sinful behavior. Penitential literature is a body of writing in the Catholic Church describing sin according to standards adopted by the church; the penitentials also prescribed the penance or punishment individuals must perform in order to be forgiven by God for committing each sin. The penitentials were not doctrines formally issued by any pope or church council. They were collections of rules created by local church leaders to govern the behavior of individuals in each region (Tannahill, 1992).

Justinian I (approximately 483–565), Emperor of the Eastern Roman Empire, who enacted law defining sex between men as "contrary to nature."

This literature came to describe sinful sexual behavior in great detail, including insertion of the penis in the anus; thrusting the penis between the thighs (but not in the vagina); masturbation; sexual intercourse in which the penis was withdrawn from the vagina before ejaculation of semen (*coitus interruptus*); bestiality; nocturnal emissions of semen; sex outside of marriage; and many other sexual behaviors. However, different writers advocated different punishments and many did not distinguish between "natural" and "unnatural" sex in providing for punishment. During the 11th century CE, one church scholar, Peter Damian, appealed to Pope Leo IX to institute the maximum punishment for all unnatural sexual behavior, without consideration of any mitigating factors that may have contributed to committing the sin. The pope did not entirely follow Damian's advice, stating that justice must also incorporate the concept of mercy and forgiveness (Bullough & Bullough, 1995).

Among various theological scholars over several centuries, the notion of unnatural sex was formalized even further in the concept of **sins against nature**; see Figure 2.1. Within the treatment of the issue by Thomas Aquinas (1225–1274), the sin of **lust** included nonmarital sex, adultery, seduction, rape, incest, and **acts against nature**. Acts against nature were, in the order of decreasing sinfulness, (a) bestiality, (b) sodomy (sexual behavior between people of the same sex), (c) all sexual intercourse that did not involve penile–vaginal intercourse with the man on top and the woman underneath him, and (d) masturbation, the least sinful of all. The term *sodomy* was derived from the biblical account of the destruction of the ancient cities of Sodom and Gomorrah by God for extremely sinful behavior. The actual nature of the sins that drew God's wrath is disputed among religious scholars; however, throughout much of the history of Christianity, the sins have been designated as the demand by men of Sodom to engage in sexual behavior with male visitors of a Jewish resident, Lot. For a behavior to be identified as a sin against nature, according to Aquinas, ejaculation must occur; otherwise, the sexual behavior involves only the sin of lust, a less offensive category (Bullough & Bullough, 1995).

Aquinas was actually concerned that some "natural" sexual behavior, such as adultery, seduction, and rape, were more serious offenses than some of the "unnatural" types of sexual behavior, because these specific "natural" behaviors harmed others. Yet, he argued that because the ordering of sinfulness had been ordained by God, it could not be disputed or changed.

The term *sodomy* was used in early American law

Thomas Aquinas (approximately 1225–1274), early Christian philosopher and theologian

among the colonies most commonly as a generic concept of criminal sexual behavior. The Puritan colonists employed the term *sodomy* to include all sexual behaviors, including male–female sexual behaviors, that were not for purposes of procreation and that were not specifically prohibited in the Scriptures. Such a usage was based largely on English legal principles and precedents,

**FIGURE 2.1**    The Sin of Lust According to Thomas Aquinas

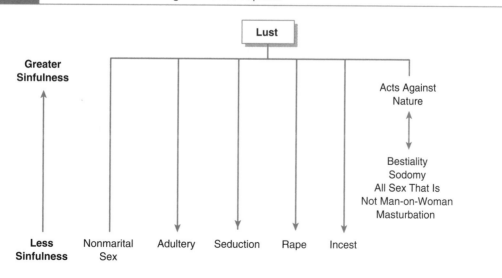

which resulted in the concept of *buggery* also being incorporated in early American law. Many state governments outlawed sexual crimes against nature that were generally called sodomy or buggery without specifying exactly what those behaviors are. In legal cases in 1869 and 1873, courts in Texas ruled that the laws prohibiting sexual crimes against nature were not specific enough to allow prosecution and refused to accept English common-law definitions. To clarify the category, the Texas legislature eventually included many types of sexual behavior under the category, making all of them illegal by enacting new legislation. At the end of the 19th century, English and American lawmakers attempted to identify even further what sexual behaviors constituted crimes, and in many U.S. states, crimes against nature included penile–anal intercourse (penis in the anus or rectum) and oral–genital sex (mouth or tongue on the penis or vulva; Bullough & Bullough, 1995).

Within recent years, many states eliminated the concept of sodomy from their legal codes altogether (Bullough & Bullough, 1995), although all remaining sodomy laws were essentially invalidated by the U.S. Supreme Court ruling on June 26, 2003. In the historic case of *Lawrence and Garner v. Texas* (John Geddes Lawrence and Tyrone Garner v. Texas; U.S. Supreme Court 2003), the Court decided that the Texas statute outlawing sexual conduct between people of the same sex violated the Due Process Clause of the U.S. Constitution.

The justices voting in the 6–3 majority determined that the earlier Supreme Court decision of 1986 *Bowers v. Hardwick* failed to take into account the degree to which fundamental human liberty was harmed by sodomy laws. They further concluded that a more comprehensive examination of historical evidence undermines the belief that the U.S. has a long-standing tradition of laws prohibiting same-gender sexual behavior. Early sodomy laws instead were directed at all nonprocreative sexual behavior, with those outlawing same-gender behavior appearing only within the past 30 years; even then, only nine states enacted such laws. The fundamental basis for the 2003 decision was that decisions made by adults to engage in relationships involving physical intimacy is a freedom protected by the Constitution (John Geddes Lawrence and Tyrone Garner v. Texas; U.S. Supreme Court 2003).

The influence of religious values on sexual attitudes has been immense throughout Western history, possibly dwarfing or subsuming all other factors to the extent of making them virtually irrelevant until very recently. The concept of sins against nature is a pivotal factor in Christian religious thinking. A principle that started out in Greek philosophy as a general way of understanding the nature of the world evolved into a moral standard for determining the sinfulness of sexual behavior in early Christianity. Because civil legal systems looked to Christianity for standards of acceptable behavior, the highly ambiguous moral principle of "sins against nature" was eventually incorporated into laws enacted by government. In this way, sins against nature became *crimes against nature* (Bullough & Bullough, 1995) and punishment for violations of these standards transformed from ritualistic religious penance to imprisonment or death.

Tyron Garner, left, and John Lawrence, right, greet supporters after a rally celebrating their court victory in Houston June 26, 2003. The Supreme Court struck down a ban on same-gender sex, ruling that the law was an unconstitutional violation of privacy. Garner and Lawrence were each fined $200 and spent a night in jail for a misdemeanor sex charge in 1998.

## Native American Spirituality

The name *Native American* is currently considered to be synonymous with *American Indian* and refers to the people who have resided on the North

American continent since before the arrival of Europeans. According to William Young (2002), many writings about Native American spirituality discuss beliefs and traditions in a way that gives the impression that a widely accepted, common tradition is shared among all groups of Native Americans. Although some similarities may be found across the beliefs of the 500 Native American nations, each group of people actually has its own unique spiritual tradition. The term, *religion,* is not typically used to characterize the spiritual beliefs of Native Americans because the concept is in many ways predominantly a European American and European concept; for a number of reasons, the notion of religion mischaracterizes the system of beliefs embraced by American Indians. Therefore, the term *spirituality* is used to refer to Native American beliefs; the basic principles of ancient Native American spirituality are summarized in Table 2.3.

**TABLE 2.3** General Principles of Ancient Native American Spirituality

| Issue | Principle | Implication of the Principle |
|---|---|---|
| Overarching issue | Each of the 500 nations had its own unique spiritual tradition | Impossible to make sweeping generalizations about common beliefs |
| Sexuality in general | Sexuality and nudity are not evil or shameful | Acceptance of sexual exploration by children and adolescents<br>Many native cultures were polygamous<br>Some tribes accepted extramarital sexual behavior<br>Two-spirits were highly revered as possessing greater spiritual powers |

Before the landing of Europeans on the North American continent, Native Americans generally did not regard sexuality or nudity as evil or shameful. In fact, many American Indian cultures were quite accepting of sexual exploration among children and young people, ranging from masturbation to sexual involvement with other youth of either sex. Many Native American cultures were polygamous, meaning that men had more than one wife, although women often enjoyed great freedom to select who would be their sexual partners. Because of the several year period of nursing young children and avoidance of sex during this period to control family size, married men were permitted to engage in sexual behavior with partners outside of the relationship among some tribes. Other cultures, however, did not permit sexual relationships outside of the marriage. Couples who were not able to stay in a marriage often simply ended the relationship with very little resentment, often entering another relationship after the separation. Prostitution did not occur among Native populations, with rape hardly ever occurring until after contact with Europeans (D'Emilio & Freedman, 1997).

Another common aspect of Native culture was the existence of individuals who experienced a spiritual calling to become a two-spirit, or one who is both a woman and a man. The derogatory term *berdache,* meaning sodomite in French (D'Emilio & Freedman, 1997), was used among European Americans in earlier times to refer to two-spirits. Women who felt such a calling were not as common, however, as were men. The individuals were thought to be a third and fourth gender, departing radically from European conceptions of only two genders (Roscoe, 1998). Men would sometimes begin to dress and live as women, even becoming the wife of a man (D'Emilio & Freedman, 1997), although in other cultures they may dress differently from men or women or they may dress like women only on special occasions (Roscoe, 1998). Women two-spirits would often dress in men's clothing primarily when hunting or going to war; some even became chiefs. Often two-spirits were highly esteemed among Native Americans, because it was believed that they were called to the position by gods or spirits. Typically, the move to two-spirit status was prompted by the cross-gender behavior and interests of the individual during childhood. A dream or vision may then confirm the appropriateness of this change. Native Americans usually believe that two-spirits possess greater spiritual powers than most individuals; this belief was particularly prevalent among the Plains Indian cultures (Roscoe, 1998).

Two-spirits who were originally male would sometimes become involved in marriages, usually to men, with the man's gender and sexual status being considered to be identical to other men. In fact, same-sex marriages were fairly common and widely accepted as legitimate. Sometimes, two-spirits would engage in sexual behavior with a number of different people, although the status of two-spirit is not defined on sexual bases; other two-spirits may never engage in sexual behavior or become involved in a marriage (Roscoe, 1998).

## Confucianism and Daoism

Confucianism and Daoism both originated in China, and have existed side-by-side for centuries as relatively similar, compatible religious beliefs. The fundamental principle underlying Confucianism is the belief in **Tian**, or Heaven, as the provider of organization and morality in the universe. This moral organization establishes respect and homage for familial ancestors as its core value; the basic principles of ancient Confucianism and Daoism are summarized in Table 2.4.

A fundamental principle of Chinese philosophy is the organizing forces of **Yin** and **Yang**. Yin is the passive aspect of existence and Yang is the active, which operate in conjunction to produce cycles of growth and change. These forces are believed to determine the functioning of all aspects of the universe, not only physical cycles such as the seasons, and of life (Yang) versus death (Yin), but also historical and social aspects as well. Political stability involves periods of greater Yin, while upheaval occurs during periods of Yang. Furthermore, heterosexual sexual intercourse is viewed as the union of complementary aspects, female (Yin) and male (Yang). Humans are one of the many products of these universal forces, called **qi**, but because humans are capable of influencing these forces, they are conceived of as critical agents in the universe (Feuchtwang, 2002).

The concepts of Yin and Yang include the notion that all aspects of existence consist of both forces, even those that appear to be predominantly influenced by only one. During periods when Yin appears to dominate, for example, as in winter or times of political stability, a small core of the opposite force, Yang, is harbored in the phenomenon in a way that energizes and adds to the power of the dominant influence. This becomes the basis for change and movement toward the opposing aspect during a period of change, such that the other aspect eventually becomes the dominant force operating. The same is believed to be true with respect to human nature, such that with respect to gender, men and women alike are influenced by both Yin

Confucius (551–479 BCE), the originator of a philosophy and set of ethical principles that formed the basis for Confucianism

**TABLE 2.4**    Basic Principles of Ancient Confucianism and Daoism

| Issue | Principle | Implication of the Principle |
|---|---|---|
| Overarching premise | Confucianism: Tian (Heaven) is the source of order and morality<br>Daoism: Maintain balance with the forces of the universe; reestablish balance if disrupted | Confucianism: Morality places respect for ancestors as a core value<br>Daoism: Interaction of Yin and Yang contribute to harmony |
| Sexuality in general | Sexual behavior affects the interaction of Yin and Yang | Chinese religions held a positive view of sexuality throughout its early history |
| Specifics of sexuality | Yin is limitlessly available to women<br>Yang is easily depleted by men | Penile–vaginal intercourse is very important to the well-being of men; it supplies Yin to men that is converted to Yang<br>Too much ejaculation is unhealthy for men<br>Masturbation is not dangerous to women; it is to men<br>Cunnilingus is very desirable to generate Yin essence by women<br>Same-sex behavior was not seen as harmful |

and Yang. While Yin is conceived as determining female characteristics and Yang male characteristics, women also possess some degree of Yang and men possess some degree of Yin (Feuchtwang, 2002).

The concern of Daoism, and to some extent Confucianism, is to maintain harmony and balance with the forces of the universe, and reestablish the harmony when it is upset. The interaction of Yin and Yang help in the quest for harmony, such that sexual intercourse is conceived as a method of facilitating this interaction. The genitals are viewed as obvious indications of the two aspects of existence, the vagina exhibiting the receptive characteristic of Yin and the penis representing the active characteristic of Yang. Beyond this, however, the essence of Yin was thought to be found in the lubricating fluids produced by the vagina, with the essence of Yang in the central component of semen (Tannahill, 1992). Daoism therefore holds that sexuality extends from the natural forces inherent in the universe and that sexual interaction promotes the joining of these forces. Consequently, Chinese philosophy embraced a largely positive stance toward sexuality throughout much of its early history. As noted by Tannahill,

> Just as the European of early medieval times knew, without quite understanding why, that sex was sinful but occasionally permissible, so his contemporary in China knew, without quite understanding why, that sex was a sacred duty and one that he must perform frequently and conscientiously if he was truly to achieve harmony with the Supreme Path, the Way, Tao. (1992, p. 168; Tao is an alternative spelling of Dao)

Because of its great potential to enable individuals to become aligned with the Dao, the Chinese were the first to produce books on instruction about sexuality and sexual behavior. Although Chinese culture has also maintained a long-standing ethic of modesty and restraint in personal issues, including sexual ones, the sex

Picture from a pillow book, instructing couples on sexual techniques to promote alignment with the Dao.

manual represented an acceptable way of communicating explicitly about a highly important topic. By the time of the Han dynasty (207 BCE–220 CE), eight sex instruction manuals were available.

The Chinese instruction manuals were written in an extremely exotic, poetic style because of their association with the beliefs about the cosmic forces of Yin and Yang and the relationship of sexuality to the Dao. The penis was often referred to allegorically as the Jade Stalk (the white type of jade, rather than the green), the Red Bird, and Heavenly Dragon Pillar; the erect penis is the Positive Peak or Vigorous Peak. The vulva was called the Open Peony Blossom, Golden Lotus, or the Cinnabar (Red) Gate, whereas the clitoris was known as the Jewel Terrace. Various sexual positions are also presented, and given highly lyrical, whimsical names, such as the Unicorn's Horn, Bamboos by the Altar, and Gamboling Wild Horses. A number of the positions were believed to provide relief from various ailments, particularly if combined with a magical number of thrusts, such as nine, considered to be a Yang number, and 81, called *complete Yang*. Despite this, the man-on-top-of-woman position was still considered the natural and most important position (Tannahill, 1992). Attitudes about non-penile–vaginal sex were based on their relation to Yin and Yang:

> Anal intercourse and fellatio were quite permissible as long as no *yang* essence was lost by ejaculation, although they did not do much to strengthen a man's *yang*. Cunnilingus was actively approved, as preparing the woman and simultaneously procuring *yin* essence for the man. Masturbation, a matter of indifference where women were concerned, their supplies of *yin* being inexhaustible, was condemned in men for its wastefulness. Particularly worrying was an emission during sleep. The Chinese believed that this often happened as a result of some succubus [a female demon] assuming the guise of a beautiful woman so as to steal a man's *yang* essence by having intercourse with him in his dreams. (Tannahill, 1992, pp. 177–178; the words in brackets are added)

Sexual behavior between people of the same sex was quite acceptable during some periods in Chinese history. Sex between men involved the interaction of two Yang aspects, which was viewed as less constructive than Yin and Yang interaction, but not harmful. Sex between women was seen as squandering precious Yin essence, in that it was not devoted to enhancing Yang in men; however, it was not particularly threatening, given that Yin essence was considered to be relatively inexhaustible in women. The use of dildos was thought to be dangerous, especially if overused because they could damage the tissues in the vagina. Later eras gave rise to more negative attitudes about bisexuality because of the fear that bisexual fathers are likely to produce hermaphroditic children (having both male and female sexual organs; Tannahill, 1992).

In earlier periods, it was not uncommon for men to have a number of wives, although this was more likely for middle-class and wealthy men because peasants could not afford to support many wives. Despite the rather positive view of female sexuality, women have not been accorded equal social and political status throughout much of Chinese history. Men and women often interacted only during meals and at night in bed, with women expected to remain isolated from men, avoiding physical contact altogether. Prostitution was also quite common throughout many periods of history, although men often went to brothels more for fine dining, to enjoy musical entertainment, and to cultivate business transactions, rather than for sex with the prostitutes (Tannahill, 1992).

## Hinduism

According to followers of the Hindu faith, Hinduism is the oldest existing religion, possibly dating as far back as 2500 BCE. Currently, 800 million people are members of Hinduism, such that it is the third largest religion in the world; the basic principles of ancient Hinduism are summarized in Table 2.5.

**TABLE 2.5**  Basic Principles of Ancient Hinduism

| Issue | Principle | Implication of the Principle |
|---|---|---|
| Overarching premise | Four major goals must be pursued, including the pursuit of pleasure and material well-being | Pleasure is desirable, but should not be the most important goal |
| Sexuality in general | Sexuality is a religious obligation, contributing to one's karma | Sexual behavior is desirable and healthy<br>Erotic picture books instructed about techniques for pleasurable sexual behavior |
| Specifics of sexuality | Love is an important aspect of sexuality | Couples who are truly in love will naturally engage in pleasurable sexual behavior |

Four major goals are established for humans by Hinduism, with all four being acceptable goals, although the fourth one leads to removal from the process of rebirth, the highest achievement. The goals are: "(1) sensory gratification (*kama*), (2) material well-being (*artha*); (3) religious behavior (*dharma*), which leads to heaven or higher rebirth; (4) salvation, escape from rebirth (*moksha*)" (Smith, 2002, p. 20). Those of the highest caste tend to concentrate mainly on dharma, attempting to fulfill religious, social, and moral obligations. However, pursuing the goals of pleasure and material well-being are not necessarily viewed as negative, inappropriate, or demeaning; these should simply not be the most important goals for individuals. Nonetheless, sex is viewed as a religious obligation and contributing to one's karma (Tannahill, 1992).

An early form of ritual in one branch of Hinduism involved sexual behavior because of the belief that "Pleasure is liberation (*moksha*)" (Smith, 2002, p. 26). The tantric tradition resulted in sophisticated texts documenting this philosophy, often expressed in the form of dialogue between the gods, Shiva and Shakti; Shakti is the goddess who personifies femininity and is the spouse of Shiva (Smith, 2002). These texts are strong evidence that early Hindu society viewed sexuality as primarily positive and even healthy.

The most prominent example of the erotic texts is the ***Kamasutra*** (believed to have been written by Vatsyayana). It is possible that the *Kamasutra* was influenced by earlier Taoist erotic texts existing in China or by Ovid's *Ars Amatoria* (translated *The Art of Love*). The *Kamasutra* was more than simply a sex manual instructing on various positions in which sexual intercourse might take place, although this type of instruction was a significant aspect of the book. The text presented a spiritual philosophy that included an understanding of love, represented prominently as an important aspect of sexuality. Love was believed to exist in four types: (a) simple love of sexual intercourse, similar to a passion for pleasure and recreation; (b) desire for specific types of sexual behavior, such as touching, kissing, or oral–genital sex; (c) spontaneous, mutual romantic attraction between two people; and (d) adoration of the beauty of someone an individual desires. The philosophy

Picture from the *Kamasutra*, instructing individuals who are not truly in love in techniques to increase their experience of pleasure. *What types of advice columns, magazine articles, self-help books, or Web sites have you read that provide information about relationships and sexuality?*

maintains that individuals who are truly in love are likely to engage in behavior toward one another that is driven purely by natural, instinctive forces; they therefore do not need instruction in the expression of passion (Tannahill, 1992).

More than 30 different positions for sexual intercourse are described, many of them requiring a great deal of limberness and physical versatility. Examples include *The Wife of Indra*, in which the woman is on her back with the man squatting between her legs, her lower legs doubled against her thighs; *The Knee-Elbow*, in which the man has the woman suspended while he is standing holding the woman up against his body with his arms under her knees; and the position in which the woman is lying face down and her lower body is pressed up against the man who is standing, the woman's legs folded back toward her head (Tannahill, 1992).

Further evidence of the high regard with which the early Hindu religion held sexuality is the multitude of erotic art known as *Maithuna* figures found in various parts of India. This art portrays couples or groups of individuals engaged in sexual activity. The art represents a reaction by the lower castes to their exclusion from religious practices by the Brahmins, who devoted themselves to religion through sacrifice and restraint. The lower castes asserted themselves by establishing more personal relationships with the gods, excluding the role of priests. In doing so, they developed cults that were more focused on *kama* and the experience of pleasure through sexuality (Tannahill, 1992).

Traditionality prevails overwhelmingly in India even today. Many Indian youth remain willing to let parents choose their husband or wife for them, and the development of high-quality children continues to be the predominant purpose of marriage. Family forms the bedrock of society as it has throughout Hindu history, with parents cared for by their children in their senior years, living as large extended families. Consequently, divorce is relatively rare in Indian society even today. Women oversee the religious life of their families, maintaining the household shrine to their special deities to ensure the family's well-being. Grandmothers provide the important service of instructing grandchildren in the meaning and rituals of their religion (Smith, 2002).

## Buddhism

Buddhism is the fourth largest religion, with approximately 357 million believers worldwide, and ever-increasing numbers in the West. It is the dominant religion in some countries in Southeast and East Asia, and is on the rise in other Asian countries (Cantwell & Kawanami, 2002). The basic principles of ancient Buddhism are summarized in Table 2.6.

A major goal of Buddhists is to achieve Buddhahood by becoming enlightened and releasing the spirit from worldly concerns. Buddhist monks attempt to accomplish this by entering isolated monasteries and reading Scriptures. However, monks may gain financially and in terms of spiritual credits by reading the Scriptures and performing sacrificial offerings for lay people. Monks serve the special function of tending

| TABLE 2.6 | Basic Principles of Ancient Buddhism |

| Issue | Principle | Implication of the Principle |
|---|---|---|
| Overarching premise | Buddhahood is pursued through enlightenment and releasing oneself from worldly concerns | Rejection of worldly and sensual pleasures promotes spiritual enlightenment |
| Sexuality in general | Indulgence in excessive levels of sexual behavior is detrimental to spiritual growth and enlightenment | Avoid extreme indulgence in sexual behavior |

to the dead, helping them to gain credit, and caring for the forgotten dead (Feuchtwang, 2002). Monks therefore reject sensual pleasure to a great extent, including sexual pleasure, as a means of concentrating on achieving spiritual enlightenment. Such an extreme dedication is not expected of most Buddhist faithful, but excessive indulgence in sensuality is seen as detrimental to spiritual growth and enlightenment. Nonetheless, most types of sexual behavior are considered morally acceptable, including that occurring before marriage, masturbation, and between people of the same sex.

## Islam

The name *Islam* is Arabic and may be translated as the voluntary, committed submission to the will of the one and only God, Allah. The basic principles of ancient Islam are summarized in Table 2.7. Individuals who willingly submit themselves to the will of Allah are called **Muslims**. The term *din* (pronounced *deen*) refers to the tradition of faithfulness to the will of Allah as presented in the Scriptures, called the **Qur'an**. The Qur'an is believed to be the commandments of Allah provided to **Muhammad**, the Prophet (who lived approximately 570–632), in a series of revelations over several decades. The Qur'an is considered to be the actual word of God, and cannot be altered in any

The Mosque of Al Aksa, Temple Mound, Jerusalem Old City. The mosque is a place of worship in the Islamic religion.

way because they are God's commandments for righteous living. Because the revelations occurred in Mecca, Muhammad's birthplace, and then in Medina, the two cities are considered holy sites. A major aspect of the Islamic religion is to travel to Mecca at least once in one's lifetime to worship in Mecca. Currently, more than 1 billion people are Muslims, with Islam being the second largest religion following Christianity. In fact, Islam recognizes many of the leaders and prophets of the Jewish and Christian religions as legitimate prophets of Allah, including Adam, Abraham, Moses, and Jesus. Muhammad is simply seen as the ultimate prophet, representing the final realization of Allah's will (Waines, 2002).

| TABLE 2.7 | Basic Principles of Ancient Islam |

| Issue | Principle | Implication of the Principle |
|---|---|---|
| Overarching premise | Total submission to the will of Allah is required of the faithful | Muslims must follow Allah's commandments for righteous living |
| Sexuality in general | Early views about sexuality were fairly positive<br>Later views have become more conservative | Early Islamic culture had sex instruction manuals reflecting the positive view |
| Specifics of sexuality | Muhammad advocated polygamy (men having several wives)<br>Early Islamic cultures held highly negative views of women based on the curse brought about by the fall of Eve<br>Modern views favor monogamy and more egalitarian views of women | Women were considered property of their husbands or male relatives<br>Women had virtually no civil rights<br>Many modern Islamic cultures have broadened the rights of women |

Attitudes and practices regarding sexuality have changed dramatically across Arabic civilizations, which are largely Islamic in current times. Moreover, early Islamic culture was vastly different from modern Islamic views.

Muhammad supported the practice of polygamy, men taking more than one woman as wives, saying that a maximum of four wives is appropriate. However, the relevant passage in the Qur'an leaves a good deal of room for interpretation regarding this issue. If a man did not feel that he could provide equal love and attention for all wives, then he was advised to have only one wife, as well as a number of concubines. Early Islamic scholars maintained a fairly negative view of women, based on the punishment of Eve resulting from her sin in the Garden of Eden. Women were thought to be subject to Eve's punishment, which includes menstruation; the labors of childbirth; not having legal authority over themselves (this belonged to men—first their father and then their husband); being able to have only one husband; the requirement that they remain secluded in the home; the requirement that they wear veils even in the house; the fact that their husband may divorce them, but they may not divorce their husband; and a host of other religious and legal restrictions. Women were supposed to be segregated from the men in a separate area of the residence, the harem, although for households of little resources this was seldom more than symbolically possible. Wealthier men provided a separate suite of rooms for each wife, or even their own personal residence. Nonetheless, at all economic levels, women were essentially prisoners of their husbands and fathers (Tannahill, 1992).

The effect of the extreme isolation of women gave rise to the development of an intense fascination and allure for these enigmatic women. They became the subject of fantastic stories, poems, and songs, in which the man who longed for a wealthy woman experienced nothing but pure love for her; he was so enamored of her that he did not want to violate her sexually or cause her to engage in adultery. The intent of the love-stricken man was only to devote himself to focusing on his love for the woman from a distance. This concept of pure love evolved into the notion of *ennobling love,* the belief that pure love elevates the man above his crass, carnal nature to that of an inspired spirituality (Tannahill, 1992). Ennobling love captivated European Christians during the many Crusades in which they attempted to wrest the Christian Holy Land of Palestine away from Muslims; this significant cultural export to Europe is discussed as well in chapter 3 (p. 60).

Early Islamic culture had its sex instruction manuals, which were strongly influenced by Hindu manuals such as *Kamasutra.* Titles of the Arabic books included *The Book of Exposition in the Science of Coition* (coition is a word meaning penile–vaginal intercourse) and *The Perfumed Garden for the Soul's Recreation.* Beyond the instructions provided in the *Kamasutra* for various types of sexual positions, the Arabic books included erotic stories to give readers ideas for handling sexual situations and to sexually stimulate men who might have problems with erections (Tannahill, 1992).

In modern times, Islamic scholars have interpreted the Qur'an to call for monogamy, rather than polygamy. Islamic societies have generally eliminated child marriages common in earlier times, curtailed the ability of men to divorce their wife, enhanced the right of women to divorce their husband, and have made divorce settlement regarding children more equitable. Some Muslim cultures have improved conditions for women, supporting greater education of girls and allowing women to enter into employed work. According to Waines (2002),

> Debates about the place of religion in the modern state, the very nature of the state, the place of the family in modern society and the very nature of the family, the role of men and women within life's private and public spheres—all are being conducted along a spectrum ranging from pure secularists [those who are not religious] at one end to advocates of religious purity at the other. . . . At the present juncture it would be rash to speculate on the future course of developments within the richly diverse religious world of Islam. (p. 201; words in brackets added)

## *Summary*

The largely restrictive view of sexuality that has characterized Western societies into modern times originates from moral values resulting predominantly from Christian and Jewish philosophy. Ancient Jewish morality has held that sexual behavior must be separated from the religious aspects of life to avoid contamination of the divine. However, sexuality is not viewed as inherently evil; rather, it is simply an aspect of life that must be regulated and restricted to certain times and to certain people. The primary context for acceptable sexual behavior is marriage. However, complete abstinence from sexual behavior is viewed negatively.

Christian morality has traditionally maintained that sexuality and sexual behavior are corrupting to spiritual purity, jeopardizing one's chances of entering Heaven and attaining eternal life. The major source of this negative view was the Hellenistic (Greek) philosophy of dualism prevalent during the formation of early Christianity. Church philosophers allowed that sexual intercourse was acceptable for purposes of procreation; however, the experience of pleasure must still be minimized. In this belief system, the only acceptable type of sexual behavior occurs within marriage and involves only penile–vaginal intercourse with the man on top of the woman. These beliefs were not, however, based on commandments in the Old or New Testaments.

In contrast to traditional Christian views on morality, early Native American spirituality typically viewed sexuality in more positive, accepting terms. Many early Native American cultures accepted sexual interaction among children and youth before marriage. In some Native cultures, married men were allowed to engage in sexual behavior with partners outside of the relationship. Finally, individuals known as two-spirits were people who assumed the behaviors and characteristics of the other gender. Many Native cultures believe two-spirits are specially chosen by gods or spirits, and therefore often have special spiritual powers.

*(Continued)*

(Continued)

Traditional Chinese conceptions of sexuality grounded in Confucianism and Daoism reflect the belief in supreme controlling forces in the universe, with Yin the passive component and Yang the active. Vaginal fluid is believed to contain the essence of Yin, and semen is thought to consist of the essence of Yang. The view is that for women, Yin is unlimited; however, Yang exists in small supply and is easily depleted for men, although it is essential to their health and well-being. Sexual intercourse is able to resupply Yang, because the Yin of women can be absorbed during sex and converted to Yang by men.

Hinduism, the predominant religion in India, likewise has traditionally held an extremely positive view of sexuality. A fundamental premise of Hinduism is that individuals are reincarnated after death to live a new life; the status of the person in the new life is determined by his or her karma, the quality of spiritual growth in the previous life. The importance of sexuality in promoting religious growth is indicated by the creation of philosophical sex manuals, such as the *Kamasutra,* to provide instruction on love and sexual behavior.

Buddhism has strong elements of asceticism, a philosophy of downplaying the importance of bodily concerns and avoiding sensuality. A major concern within Buddhism is to experience spiritual enlightenment, thereby being released from worldly concerns and achieving salvation. Extreme sensuality is viewed as an impediment to progress toward spiritual enlightenment and salvation.

Islam holds a largely restrictive position toward sexual expression. In recent times, the Qur'an has been interpreted as calling for monogamy, and Islamic cultures are by and large highly conservative and not at all permissive concerning sexuality and sexual expression. Islamic tradition historically has maintained a highly negative view of women; a number of modern Islamic cultures, however, have moved substantially away from this oppressive position.

## Chapter 2 Critical Thinking Exercises

1. Modern religious views of sexuality
   a. Identify two specific religions in which you are interested; one may be the religion of which you are a member. Be very specific in selecting the religion. For example, if you select a Protestant religion, identify a specific denomination, such as the Baptist Church or the Methodist Church. Search the Internet to obtain several documents that present a formal statement by that religion regarding sexuality. You may do this by entering a key phrase such as "Methodist position on sexuality" into a search engine such as Google (www.google.com).
   b. How similar is the current doctrine regarding sexuality of each religion to the view of that religion presented in chapter 2? What differences exist between current doctrine and early views?

2. Select a document from one of those below that are posted on the Internet.

   *Judaism*

   A page written by a student http://www.mc.maricopa.edu/~tomshoemaker/StudentPapers/JewishSexuality.html

   *Christianity*

   Lutheran Church- Missouri Synod report www.lcms.org/graphics/assets/media/CTCR/Human_Sexuality1.pdf

   *Islam*

   The Muslim Women's League site: http://www.mwlusa.org/publications/essays/sexuality.html

   What was the primary message the author or authors intend to convey in the document? Was the message persuasive and convincing? Did you encounter any information in the document that you had not really known previously?

# Chapter 3

## THE HISTORICAL COURSE OF SEXUALITY

C hristianity became the predominant religion throughout Europe after the fall of the Roman Empire, establishing the procreation view of sexuality as the dominant moral system across the continent and into the British Isles. As European explorers charted and then settled the American continents, the Christian religion grew to be the major faith in this area of the world as well, its influence therefore sweeping across vast expanses of the globe. The current chapter will examine the reasons that Christianity came to pervade every aspect of life, including sexuality, for the early Europeans and their descendants into the modern era. The chapter also documents the specific effects that Christian values exerted on sexuality, standing virtually as the solitary dominant influence until challenged by the emerging sciences and secular philosophies of the Age of Enlightenment in the 18th century.

## Western Civilization Prior to the 20th Century

### The Middle Ages (500–1300)

The pathway to current views and trends related to sexuality, of course, was an ongoing, evolving process extending from ancient folk beliefs and formal Christian theology. The current generations did not create contemporary cultural patterns related to sexuality entirely anew. Early concerns by Christian clergy regarding the salvation of their congregations led to the development of informal rules about appropriate sexual behavior, as well as penance (self-punishment to express repentance) that must be performed following violation of these rules. Eventually, these rules were formalized into what is called the **penitential literature** that influenced thinking about sexuality from the early centuries of Christian religion into the High Middle Ages (an era from approximately 1100 to 1300; the various historical periods prior to the 20th century and the sexuality issues prevalent during those periods are presented Table 3.1).

During the late Middle Ages, cultural sexual values were influenced by the Crusades. These were a series of military expeditions conducted by Christian nations to take Palestine, the Holy Land, away from Muslim powers in the 11th, 12th, and 13th centuries. With large numbers of knights from France, England, and Germany away in battle, women began to take over the duties of their husbands and male relatives in

**TABLE 3.1**   Historical Trends in Sexuality Before the 20th Century

| Historical Era | Time Span | Sexuality Issues |
|---|---|---|
| The Middle Ages | 500–1300 | Development of penitential literature to govern appropriate sexual behavior and penance for violations<br><br>Introduction of ennobling love that idealized pure love uncontaminated by sexual lust |
| The Renaissance | 1300–1520 | Development of civic morality that set the standard for marriage, family, and sexuality in Western civilization throughout the modern period<br><br>Civic morality held that the only legitimate purpose of sexual behavior is procreation to produce high-quality offspring |
| The Reformation | 1520–1700 | Development of the view that the need for sex is a fundamental element of human nature and important to well-being<br><br>Love came to be seen as essential in marriage<br><br>Physical pleasure came to be seen as vital within marital sexuality to promote reproduction, although it is a secondary part of a marital relationship<br><br>Extreme harshness of Puritans concerning violations of sexual morality prevailed in New England |
| The Enlightenment | 1700–1820 | Enlightenment philosophy affected English sexuality by making sexual freedom and happiness another aspect of the pursuit of individual rights<br><br>In other countries, negative moral beliefs and prohibitive social and physical factors inhibited the sexuality of the lower classes |
| The Victorian Age | 1820–1910 | Strict, repressive values required guarding against even the suspicion or possibility of an immoral character<br><br>The belief that women are sexually passionless and morally pure required protecting them from even the hint of sensuality or lustfulness<br><br>The belief that men possess strong, overpowering sexual urges required women to help men control their lust |

managing estates, business, and government. This trend allowed women not only to gain more practical knowledge and expertise about the operation of society, but it also gave them more control and visibility. Such events therefore moved women into position to have more influence on the development of cultural values related to sexuality. Literature and song imported into Europe from Arab cultures based on the Hellenistic concept of dualism idealized **ennobling love**. This belief proposes the existence of a pure love uncontaminated by sexual desire, a love that elevates a couple above the vulgar and destructive nature of carnal love (Tannahill, 1992).

Despite the idealization of nonsexual love, values changed to the extent that children born outside of marriage were an accepted phenomenon—at least for men of nobility in France and Germany. Such offspring were raised right alongside children of married couples and bequeathed inheritances of money (but never property). In addition, privately owned prostitution was quite common throughout ancient and medieval Europe, and official attempts to eradicate it were often met with protest and outrage from the citizenry. The belief was that respectable women would not be safe after the elimination of prostitution because of the uncontrollable lust of the multitudes of men whose sexual needs remained unsatiated. In addition to brothels, bath houses sprang up all over Europe during the Middle Ages, as a result of exposure to Arabic bath houses during the Crusades. The baths allowed for public bathing for both women and men, with some pools permitting a number of people to occupy them at a time and others providing more intimate spaces for two. Needless to say, these became places in which individuals could indulge their carnal desires (Tannahill, 1992).

## The Renaissance (1300–1520)

The name *renaissance* is French for "rebirth" and refers to a "rediscovery" of classical Greek and Roman philosophy and art. The development of civic morality during the Renaissance wove the concepts of marriage and family intricately into its philosophy, elevating them to a role of central importance to the success of society. Renaissance moral philosophy set the standard for marriage, family, and sexuality in Western civilization throughout the modern period continuing into current times. Principles established in general terms in the Christian scriptures became more completely expressed in such moral philosophy, and also provided a justification for the structure of government and its relationship to the lives of its citizens (Ruggiero, 1993).

The Renaissance conception of sexual morality was easily integrated with the traditional Augustinian conception that the only legitimate purpose of sexual behavior is procreation. By focusing on marriage and family as the centerpiece of forces that create a stable, healthy society, sexuality was secured within a well-controlled, respectable role. Sexual behavior was viewed as good and proper only in the context of creating high-quality, productive citizens. This position regulated sexuality in order to make it a regimented, stabilizing factor within society, rather than whimsical and unpredictable, as it would be under the influence of the personal passions of the individual. As an exercise of personal pleasure, sexuality was seen as disruptive because pleasure in itself was not considered to provide any structured, systematic service to society (Ruggiero, 1993).

Examination of historical records indicates that society as idealized by Renaissance philosophers did not conform closely to such values in actual life, as commentators at the time often complained. Premarital sexual involvement, rape, adultery, prostitution, and male–male sexual behavior occurred with some frequency. Moralists chastised parents for failing to live up to these exalted standards, and in doing so provided an explanation for the problems society was experiencing. From this perspective, the failures of proper socialization seemed to support the accuracy of the very principles that were violated—if parents only performed their required roles dutifully, the immoral behavior would not occur (Ruggiero, 1993).

A couple experiencing ennobling love, an idealized, spiritual love uncontaminated by sexual desire, in which lovers long for one another from afar.

The painting by Leonardo da Vinci, dating from 1507–1513, entitled the Virgin and Child with St. Anne, reflects the extreme importance placed on the family during the Renaissance. The painting portrays Mary, Jesus, and Jesus' grandmother, Anne.

Although the numerous sexual violations of civic morality appear to have become fairly commonplace by the 1400s, public discussion of these ideals established a framework for solidifying values about sexual behavior. It created an ideal standard against which conduct could be evaluated and prosecuted when violations were observed. By the late 1400s and early 1500s, public sentiment began to object to the aspects of culture that did not conform to the ideals of civic morality. Violations of Christian values that were treated as minor infractions in the Middle Ages became seen as major, heinous transgressions by the end of the Renaissance. A conservative backlash therefore catapulted formal Christian dogma back in the direction of stoic, Manichaean demands for sexual purity and restraint (see pages 42–43 of chapter 2 for more on Manichaeism).

## The Reformation (1520–1700)

By 1700, virtually half of Western Christianity separated from Roman Catholicism to form new churches, resulting in massive wars and devastation over a number of years. Collectively, these movements have become known as Protestantism, a division of Christianity that protested a number of the principles of the Catholic Church (Stipp, Hollister, & Dirrim, 1972). During this time, Christianity split into many different factions because of dissent over the meaning of the very principles and beliefs that defined the religion. The split in the Christian church set the stage for the Modern Era, in that Western culture was no longer dominated by one pervasive worldview. Challenges to the fundamental belief system advocated by the Catholic Church opened the door to the possibility of a number of alternative worldviews. In doing so, the belief that faith in God is the *only* legitimate source of knowledge was undermined, laying the groundwork for the possibility of gaining knowledge through collecting objective information about the world. These dawning beliefs became the foundation for the beginnings of scientific thought and inquiry.

Martin Luther (1483–1546), one of the early critics of Catholic doctrine who broke away to establish one branch of Protestantism, Lutheranism

One effect of the return of Protestant reformers to the original texts of the Scriptures was a somewhat different perspective on sexuality than had developed in the early years of the Christian church. Martin Luther, one of the leaders of the Protestant reformation, was greatly persuaded by the view developed by Augustine that sex is inherently sinful, but he also concluded that the need for sex is a fundamental element of human nature; in his view, sex is as essential to well-being as the need for food or water. His position therefore was that sexual expression was a necessary evil. Despite its sinfulness, it was acceptable in the context of marriage and served the purpose of sustaining the physical being of individuals. Luther referred to sex as having a medicinal effect and being a "hospital for the sick" (Tannahill, 1992).

In addition, because of the more important status accorded to sexuality by the Protestant philosophers, it was thought to be as important for clergy to marry as lay people. Celibacy came to be viewed as undesirable and unhealthy for everyone (D'Emilio & Freedman, 1997; Tannahill, 1992).

For those who were not from the upper class or nobility, love was gradually seen as essential in marriage, such that the experience of feelings of love for a person became one criterion for selecting a marriage partner. The expectation developed during this period that a husband and wife should cultivate emotional intimacy in their relationship, as well as promote affectionate bonds with their offspring. Nonetheless, the experience of physical pleasure was considered to be vital within marital sexuality to promote reproduction (D'Emilio & Freedman, 1997).

The model for Protestant families once again became the structure represented in the Old Testament, with the man established as the ultimate authority, the woman as the completely compliant and subservient wife and mother, and children expected to be entirely obedient and respectful of parents without exception (D'Emilio & Freedman, 1997; Tannahill, 1992). The Puritans of New England, who were Protestant zealot followers of John Calvin's views, took this ideal to unsurpassed heights. The extremity of Puritan views is nowhere as clearly demonstrated as in their harshness toward sexual behavior. Their conception of human nature was that the original sin of Adam and Eve had condemned humans to an existence of fundamental sinfulness and wickedness. They assumed that all humans are capable of great evil, and are generally too weak to resist the temptation of sin; therefore, it was the duty of the church and the community to assure that all members followed God's commandments (D'Emilio & Freedman, 1997).

Those who engaged in sexual intercourse outside of marriage were publicly whipped, were required to confess their sins in church, and were branded or required to wear symbols indicating the nature of their transgressions. Couples whose first child was born fewer than 9 months after their marriage could likewise suffer public humiliation by spending time in the stocks in the town square (Tannahill, 1992). Yet examination of civic records of the time indicates that as many as a third of women in the English colonies by 1750 were pregnant before they were married (D'Emilio & Freedman, 1997).

## The Age of Enlightenment (1700–1820)

*"Madame, you must really be more careful. Suppose it had been someone else who found you like this."*

Duc de Richelieu [18th century], on discovering his wife with her lover (Cassell Publishers Limited, 1993, p. 8)

The period of religious reformation occurring in the 16th and 17th centuries set the stage for the beginning of the Modern Era, in which

A Puritan couple in early New England. *What do you think life would have been like for you if you had been born into a Puritan community? Would your attitudes toward sexuality have been different than those you currently hold?*

"IN THE NAME OF JUSTICE": SOME OLD METHODS OF TORTURE

*How effective do you think the threat of such punishment as public humiliation, whipping, and branding would have been in keeping you from engaging in prohibited sexual behavior?*

Jean-Jacques Rousseau (1712–1778), a French philosopher who advocated for the importance of emotions and passion in human nature, as well as the fundamental goodness of humans in their natural state when they are free from the corrupting influence of society

the Christian church no longer controlled thinking and philosophy with a unified, overpowering force. The rise of such fundamental disagreement about core beliefs created an intellectual and emotional atmosphere that made it safer to question and challenge all aspects of traditional conceptions of the universe and assumptions about the very meaning of existence. Along with religious disagreement, the development of new, scientific methods of studying the world, and the rise of a philosophy that resulted from the new information, coalesced to create what has been called an intellectual revolution, or the Enlightenment (Harrison & Sullivan, 1971).

Despite the call by the philosopher Rousseau for enhancing personal development through the pursuit of happiness, emotional experience, and sexual indulgence, other traditional and practical forces exerted a profound inhibiting influence on the sexual experience of the general populace in the 18th century (Hause & Maltby, 1999; Porter, 1982). The traditionally negative Christian attitudes toward sensuality and pleasure in general, and sexual pleasure in particular, continued to permeate most of European culture. These beliefs generally led many individuals to experience guilt, as well as a fear of eternal damnation, for committing the vast range of sexual acts branded as immoral; horrific divine punishment awaited even private lustful feelings (Porter, 1982).

Based on long-standing philosophical views of the body, medical practitioners believed that body fluid levels determined the health of individuals, and depletion of these fluids resulted in imbalances that led to disease and illness. One ounce of semen, seen as a distillation of life-giving body fluid, was thought to be equivalent to 40 ounces of blood, such that it was believed that expenditure of semen during sexual behavior would debilitate a man's body. For this reason, physicians fanatically warned individuals to limit sex only to that necessary for procreation (Hause & Maltby, 1999). This was also the basis for the extremely negative stance toward masturbation, stimulation of one's own genitals, which was often called "self-abuse." These beliefs were medical, pseudoscientific extrapolations of ancient Christian condemnation of any sexual behavior not solely intended for purposes of reproduction.

However, by the end of the 18th century, in some regions of Europe the birth rate outside of marriage soared as much as five times the rate it was at the beginning of the century (D'Emilio & Freedman, 1997; Hause & Maltby, 1999); in the previous century, birth outside of marriage was virtually nonexistent, especially outside of urban areas. In addition to an apparent increase in nonmarital sexual behavior, the trend was amplified by a lack of effective birth control methods and by Christian prohibitions against birth control. Yet the overall birth rate dropped among the English upper class and in France in general, suggesting the use of some type of birth control techniques.

Despite all of the influences inhibiting sexual expression, according to many historians, the 18th century was nonetheless an era of major sexual revolution, with a greater openness of sexual behavior at least among the wealthy and the nobility. Royalty married for reasons of political advantage, but many of them had lovers, a number of them maintaining entire entourages of what were called euphemistically "favorites." For the upper classes in both England and France, extravagance in sexuality came to be yet another way for them to distinguish themselves from the lower classes, whom they looked down on as unthinking creatures of habit steeped in tradition and magical beliefs.

The greatest effect of the Enlightenment revolution in thought, therefore, was upon the wealthy and the ruling classes. A prevailing view among scholars and the upper classes that developed, called natural philosophy, led to the view that pleasure is inherently good and healthy. This was true regarding sexual pleasure as well. The effect of natural philosophy on English sexuality was to promote a freer expression of sexuality and a movement away from the belief that sexuality exists only for purposes of procreation. That is, sexual freedom and happiness became another aspect of the pursuit of individual rights. Whereas the change was probably concentrated more in the upper classes, evidence suggests that the lower classes also experienced a movement toward greater and more open sexual expression (Porter, 1982).

The one area in which the notion of the essential goodness and healthiness of sexual behavior did not extend was that of same-gender sexual behavior. The fundamental rationale of Enlightenment philosophers held that sexuality is intrinsically good and healthy because it originates from the benevolent laws of Nature. Despite this positive view of sexual expression, perceptions of same-gender behavior continued to be determined predominantly by the age-old concept of acts "contrary to nature"; this was a standard of analysis used by ancient Greek philosophers to decide what the functions of the various aspects of the universe were.

The increase in birthrate outside of marriage, the use of contraception, and the greater freedom of sexual indulgence outside of marriage, point to an untethering of sexuality from marriage. As the birthrate and survival rate into adulthood increased during the Enlightenment, procreation ceased to be the powerfully compelling, singular reason for the importance of sex. Sexuality within marriage was subsequently free to serve other purposes and satisfy other needs: "In short, in eighteenth-century England—the source for most American immigrants and ideas—science, social thought, and family life all reflected a belief in more freedom of individual choice in sexual relations" (D'Emilio & Freedman, 1997, p. 41). As this change took place, interpersonal attraction and the potential to experience personal gratification within romantic and sexual relationships increased in importance.

Although the Enlightenment was a period of intensely positive advocacy of sensuality and sexuality, the English demanded that sexuality be expressed in a cultured, sensible, and respectable manner, following a genteel, polite script (Porter, 1982). The sensitive, romantic view of sexuality dovetailed with the increasing tendency to conceive of affection and love as an integral component of marital relationships, qualities that individuals should come to expect from spouses. Progressively, love came to be seen as a reasonable criterion to judge the acceptability of entering into relationships and marriage, weakening the role of parents in the choice of marriage partner. As love and sexuality moved from the realm of control by the family more into the domain of the individual, parents not only exerted less influence, but governments became progressively less involved in regulation of personal morality; instead, laws focused to a greater extent on oversight of public conduct (D'Emilio & Freedman, 1997).

Ironically, with the migration of control to the personal level, the control did not extend to women, who instead were exposed to greater risks than when oversight by families and communities predominated. Premarital sexual behavior that resulted in pregnancy was less likely to lead to marriage than in previous eras; the danger of young, gullible women being seduced and then abandoned by an immoral man achieved almost mythic status. A factor that decreased the power of women even further was that the sex ratio reversed in America from the first days of the colonies, such that women outnumbered men. Consequently, women were at less of a premium than in the early days because they were no longer a rare, prized commodity. For this reason, it became incumbent on women and society to develop strategies for protecting women from sexual exploitation.

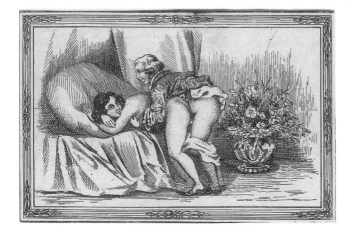

Erotic art from the 1700s. Such art indicates an increasing belief in the value and importance of self-fulfillment and personal gratification through romantic and sexual relationships.

The primary strategy was to call on women to exercise extreme restraint over their sexual feelings, to develop a sense of feminine "modesty," and to preserve their chastity. The view at the end of the Enlightenment did not yet include the belief in the passionlessness of women that developed throughout the Victorian era. The belief expressed in late Enlightenment America that represented a transition to the Victorian era is that women experience love more strongly than men, but feel other passions less intensely than men. In this way, the nature of sexuality became even more conceived of in terms of gender differences, a view that reached its zenith during the following Victorian period (D'Emilio & Freedman, 1997).

## The Victorian Age (1820–1910)

Most historians refer to the 19th century as the age of the Industrial Revolution, because it was the period during which many extremely important mechanical inventions revolutionized commerce and society. The industrialization of the Western world certainly involved monumental advances in technology that propelled society into the late modern era. Yet, from a cultural and moral perspective, the major transformation in values that has lasted throughout the 20th century was the most historic and defining aspect of the era. Because Queen Victoria of Great Britain came to symbolize the strict, repressive values evolving during this period, it is called the Victorian Age in the context of cultural standards for behavior, beliefs, and sexuality.

The core of Victorian morality was concern about respectability. The rising British and American middle class attempted to establish criteria for judging respectability and worthiness, given the lack of tradition for this emerging class of society. The Victorian ethic was to guard against even the suspicion or possibility of an immoral character, avoiding any behavior or feeling that could cause one to fall from goodness and respectability. With the revival of a concern about religion by the middle class, ancient Christian beliefs moved to the forefront as the only acceptable laws for appropriate, respectable sexual behavior. According to these ancient standards, any interest in erotic pleasure was an indication of an evil nature within the person, and the concern of the Victorians was to do whatever was necessary to avoid evil and disrepute. The hallmark of Victorian values then was to avoid *any* behavior or situation that could remotely lead to contamination and corruption—the simple experience of physical or sensual pleasure in any way became the signal of this danger.

### The Victorian Conception of Female Sexuality

In conjunction with this perception of threat, the view of women and children as entirely virtuous, pure, and innocent—completely devoid of any tendencies that are evil and corrupt—was revived from medieval Christian codes of chivalry. The belief derived from the Hellenistic philosophical distinction between spiritual love and carnal love; the two types were seen as opposed to one another, with physical, pleasure-oriented desire distracting from spiritual growth and achievement (see pages 40–43 of chapter 2). Physical, sexual desire was

Queen Victoria with one of her many grandchildren. Victoria became an almost-perfect symbol of intense devotion to marriage and children, as well as morality and purity.

held as the epitome of the worldly, carnal orientation, and with women increasingly being conceived as spiritual and virtuous, they also came to be seen as entirely free of sexual impulses. Women therefore were considered to be generally incapable of impure urges of sensuality and lasciviousness associated with sexual desire. "As late as 1905 an Oxford physician could seriously testify that nine out of ten women disliked sex, and the tenth was invariably a harlot" (Hause & Maltby, 1999, p. 665).

Furthermore, it was thought that women needed to be protected from exposure to even the suggestion or hint of sensuality or lustfulness—in conversation, entertainment, daily experience, and most certainly as objects of sexual attraction; decent women did not incite sexual desire, and men should not debase decent women by lusting after them (Seaman, 1973; White, 1993). Women's natural behavioral urges were thought to originate from maternal instincts and a basic desire to provide nurturance and emotional expressiveness. Consequently, a decent, respectable woman submitted to the sexual advances of her husband entirely out of a desire for children and to fulfill her wifely duties to her husband; in fact, the expected emotional reaction to the obligation was repulsion and disgust because it violated her essential purity and integrity. With mundane, domestic sensibilities replacing erotic, sensual urges in the Victorian image of women, the responsibility for protecting society from the ravages of uncontrolled, abandoned sexual indulgence fell on women; men were thought to possess strong, often overpowering, primitive sexual urges. Therefore, women were expected to help their husbands control, if not entirely suppress, their animalistic drives with the woman's natural feminine repulsion. Women were required to be stridently unresponsive to the appeals or demands of men before marriage in order to preserve the chastity of both; yet wives were to make themselves selflessly, unflinchingly available to their husbands on demand to satiate his primordial passions, and to prevent him from turning to other "outlets," such as prostitutes, mistresses, or affairs.

The Victorian Era was a time of profound contradictions. Despite being a conservative period, fashion eroticized and exaggerated features of women's bodies. Furthermore, erotic photography and literature flourished underground during this time.

On the other hand, women were supposed to take great care not to intentionally, or even inadvertently, arouse and excite their husbands. In the Victorian ideal, sex therefore should occur as infrequently as possible, out of necessity on the part of men and out of duty on the part of women (Seaman, 1973; White, 1993). Furthermore, sexual intercourse should be as brief as possible, with minimal pleasure because of its inherently corrupting nature, and should only occur in the sexual position advocated by Augustine as most likely to result in procreation—penile–vaginal intercourse with the man on top of the woman. The practiced disinterest in, and disdain for, sex cultivated a great sense of guilt and anxiety about sexuality for both women and men, whether by dutifully adhering to Victorian repressiveness or by "slipping" with unacceptable behavior and suffering intense private recrimination for it afterward (Seaman, 1973).

The extremely negative view of sexuality and the view of women as nonsexual combined to produce a highly derogatory, oppressive culture surrounding female sexuality. Even the slightest evidence of sexual desire by women was seen as indicating an abnormal, destructive nature, with the medical field casting the experience of any feminine sexual desire at all as a disorder called *nymphomania*. Consistent with this extremely negative view, society found evidence of female sexuality's vile nature in an easily observable phenomenon that superficially was associated with disease: the release of blood from the genitals during the monthly menstrual cycle. The event reinforced the idea that female sexual functioning was related to a diseased condition, blood flowing from a contaminated wound, and women were thought to be afflicted by an illness once a month. In fact, it was believed that menstruating women could contaminate food simply by touching it, and were required to stay entirely away from food preparation during the time of their menstrual flow (Masters, Johnson, & Kolodny, 1995).

## The Victorian Conception of Male Sexuality

The Victorian emphasis on the development of character on the part of men likewise involved a great demand for morality related to sexual restraint. Men were expected to cultivate a standard of monumental emotional control over primitive sexual urges, to protect both themselves and women from these destructive forces. Men were called upon to be "athletes of continence": that is, to conquer their sexual impulses through training and discipline. Sexual intercourse was supposed to occur only for purposes of reproduction, and indulging in sexual behavior was thought to consume precious energy and body fluids necessary to maintain general health. Therefore, for men as well as women, sexual activity became associated with disease and danger in its very essence. This dangerous expenditure of bodily resources occurred in sex with spouses, as well as with prostitutes or in masturbation; all sexual behavior was considered destructive. Furthermore, a focus on sexuality and pleasure siphoned off energy that could be devoted to achievement, both in business and in community service (White, 1993).

American social commentators, such as Mark Twain, promoted the view that American men had developed a higher moral character than European men because of their greater self-control and sexual restraint.

Americans prided themselves on the way that women were treated with respect and decency by men, strong evidence of male character. Politicians boasted that American women could walk the streets of major cities alone at any time without fear of being harassed, accosted, or raped, unlike European women. This belief was in reality an idealized view, overlooking the ways in which poorer women and prostitutes were treated. Yet, it set a standard toward which men were supposed to aspire, and against which they were judged. Women came to be idealized and idolized by men; men were not supposed to lust after virtuous women, and certainly not to have sex with them before marriage (White, 1993).

## The Victorian Practice of "Calling"

Strict customs developed in the late Victorian period that separated men and women almost completely. It became inappropriate for unmarried men and women to interact at all without a chaperone. The polite practice of "calling" on a young woman by a romantically interested young man predominated in middle- and upper-class society; the purpose was to demonstrate respect for the virtuosity of the woman and to preserve her honorable reputation in the community, meaning that she remained a virgin. Calling on a woman consisted of a gentleman presenting his calling card to an elder family member or a servant at the front door and asking to see the woman. The card was taken to the woman to see if she was interested in receiving the man. If she received him, it indicated that she was interested in him romantically as well; if she refused the request, it communicated that she was not interested in him, protecting her delicate sensibilities from the embarrassing situation. After several times of receiving the calls of a particular man, it was considered appropriate for the couple to go out into public together, but only with a chaperone. All such occasions were required to be very polite and controlled to indicate respect for the woman (White, 1993).

An amazing caveat of the American Victorian tradition of courting was that, after a woman had accepted the calls of a man a number of times, they were often viewed as intensely romantically involved with one another. After this point, the couple was given a fair degree of latitude in terms of what was considered acceptable behavior because the two individuals were perceived to be strongly committed to one another. Deep romantic love not only legitimized physical intimacy, but it was also a natural culmination and expression of emotional intimacy. Preferably, it occurred after marriage, as it did in the vast majority of cases; however, even before matrimony, sexual contact was considered understandable and even impolitely acceptable because it would be a moot issue after the couple was married (White, 1993).

## The Influence of Victorian Sexual Morality on all Aspects of Culture

Concern about avoidance of any behavior or experience that even remotely suggested sensuality or sexual interest reached almost unimaginable heights by the end of the 19$^{th}$ century. An extreme exaggeration of the ethic of covering the human body with extensive, conservative clothing was that the body should not be revealed under most circumstances. Husbands and wives avoided exposing their bodies to one another, and this may have even led many couples to engage in sex while completely clothed, at least dressed in bed clothing (e.g., nightgowns).

Such exaggerated modesty prevented women from seeking medical help because of the need for physicians, who were almost always male, to inquire about the woman's body; this was a violation of Victorian respectability, even if the problem did not involve the reproductive system. Women typically endured as much pain as possible before going to a medical doctor, and then only with a chaperone. Dolls were used to point out where problems with the body were located, rather than a woman identifying them on her own body (Hause & Maltby, 1999). Examination of the sexual organs was avoided entirely, with rare exception in extreme cases.

The obsession with modesty and propriety eventually dominated all aspects of everyday life, as Victorians became vigilant of any lure that would drag individuals toward decadence and corruption. It became offensive to polite sensibilities to refer at all to body parts, even in connection with animals and furniture. Decent people did not refer to a leg or a breast of chicken because it was thought to incite sexual feelings. The legs of furniture were covered to hide their nakedness; piano legs were dressed in crinolines (frilly leggings) and sofa legs were hidden by skirts. The doctrine of decency achieved an astounding extremity in the publication of *Lady Gough's Book of Etiquette,* which included the warning that books by male authors should not be shelved beside books written by female authors, unless the authors were married (Hause & Maltby, 1999).

## Negative Views of Masturbation

> *From age 12, into my early teens, I was extremely paranoid about my parents, doctors, and friends finding out that I masturbated. I thought my parents would walk into my room and catch me so I locked the door. Then I thought that if they tried to open the door and it was locked, they would think I was up to something worse than masturbating. I would have scary dreams that my parents walked in on me. Some were so vivid that I was convinced it really happened the next day. My parents had always been open about sex and sexuality so I didn't think they would punish me. However, they didn't really say much about masturbation so I feared the unknown reaction I would get and the embarrassment I would have from getting caught in the act. I wasn't sure if I would be sent to a sex therapist or have to go to some other kind of rehabilitation. It may sound strange but I believed doctors could tell I was a masturbator from examining me. (Male Masturbation Reality, 2006)*

Exposure to sexuality was considered to be extremely destructive to young children, who were thought of as completely free of any type of sexual nature or desire until after puberty. Yet, in reality, boys naturally experience *spontaneous erections,* arousal of the penis without stimulation or any other apparent cause, as well as *nocturnal emissions,* the release of semen at night from the opening of the penis; both of these occur as a result of the normal physiological maturation of the body and the increased production of hormones around the time of puberty. Victorian folk wisdom, and eventually the medical field as well, came to believe that such phenomena, however, resulted from touching one's genitals and self-stimulation—that is, masturbation. The desire to engage in masturbation was thought to indicate the growth of wickedness in the boys' temperament, or at best, the development of a disorder (Masters et al., 1995). Engaging in masturbation was believed to actually physically damage the nervous system because it created a diseased state in the body, leading to blindness, mental illness, or even death. To protect boys from temptation or accidental stimulation of the genitals, metallic coverings were devised in the shape of the penis and scrotum to cover them at night. Other contraptions included rings made to fit around the base of the penis with spikes extending from the inside; with erection of the penis, the spikes would poke into it as it increased in size—the pain was thought to be an antidote to the erection. Generations of children were raised to believe that masturbation was "self-abuse" and would result in sickliness, wasting, debilitation, and disease (Masters et al., 1995).

### Same-Gender Orientation

Historical evidence suggests the existence of same-gender relationships in the United States, and during the Victorian period, intense same-gender relationships were extremely common. Whether actual genital contact occurred is not always clear in literary and historical accounts, although bodily contact such as hugging and kissing were not at all uncommon between individuals of the same gender. As indicated in chapter 2, concepts of heterosexuality, homosexuality, and bisexuality did not yet exist prior to the late 19th century, such that intimate friendships often blurred with same-gender sexual relationships. Same-gender romantic friendships were universally considered to lack any genital component in times prior to the 20th century. It was not until the appearance of medical writings on sexual proclivities toward the end of the 19th century that the possibility of different stable sexual orientations arose in the cultural mind-set.

Various anecdotal reports from diaries of individuals and literary accounts indicate that relatively long-standing same-gender sexual relationships existed, however. Moreover, tales about the western frontier include accounts of cowboys seeking out and becoming involved in sexual relationships with other men and male prostitutes. It was not at all uncommon for an unmarried White, middle-class woman to become involved in lifelong relationships with another woman. Historically prominent American individuals who reported intimate same-gender relationships, including some explicitly sexual, are Emily Dickinson, Susan B. Anthony, Ralph Waldo Emerson, Herman Melville, Nathaniel Hawthorne, and Walt Whitman (D'Emilio & Freedman, 1997).

### The Incidence of Sexually Transmitted Diseases

The prevalence of sexually transmitted diseases was astoundingly high in the late Victorian period. Infection and death from syphilis in Britain was almost two times higher than that for acquired immunodeficiency syndrome (AIDS) in the late 20th century. Only tuberculosis-related death was greater in France (150,000 per year) than the death rate for syphilis (140,000 per year). Medical estimates in Germany were that 50% of men in that country were infected with gonorrhea and 20% were infected with syphilis (Hause & Maltby, 1999).

## The United States in the 20th Century

By the second decade of the 20th century, the United States and Britain began to shake off the staidness and propriety of the Victorian Era and launched into a period of booming growth and rapid social change. At the dawn of the 20th century, economic and cultural conditions shifted from independent self-employment in small businesses and farming to employment in factories and corporations; consequently, society evolved toward a more urban and cosmopolitan mind-set as never before witnessed in history. With personal identity and motivation based less and less on achievement and gratification through one's work, the focus of much of society came to be on personal fulfillment through leisure and recreational activities (D'Emilio & Freedman, 1997). This set the tone for the 20th century and pleasure became a more legitimate pursuit for individuals. Such a pleasure orientation positioned sexuality as an important aspect of life, vital to health and well-being. The various historical periods of the 20th century and the sexuality issues prevalent during those periods are presented Table 3.2.

**TABLE 3.2**    Historical Trends in Sexuality in the United States During the 20<sup>th</sup> Century

| Historical Era | Decade | Sexuality Issues |
|---|---|---|
| The Progressive Era | 1910–1919 | Emergence of the *New Woman*, characterized by somewhat greater economic, social, and political independence<br><br>Culture, fashion, music, and dance became more flamboyant and risqué |
| The Roaring Twenties | 1920–1929 | Beginning of the first Sexual Revolution in the United States with liberalization of sexual attitudes and increases in sexual behavior<br><br>Development of gender roles in sexuality, with men seen as needing to inspire passion in women<br><br>Sexual orientation came to be seen as an inherent characteristic of individuals, with homosexuality becoming the negative, unhealthy inversion of heterosexuality |
| The Great Depression | 1930–1939 | Dating transformed from a means of evaluating prospective mates to a way to socialize with peers and pursue entertainment |
| World War II | 1940–1949 | Substantial numbers of men engaged in sex while out of the country fighting in World War II<br><br>Some women, known as V-girls, engaged in sex with soldiers out of a sense of patriotic duty |
| The New Traditionalism | 1950–1959 | Many Americans longed for a return to an idealized version of traditional small-town family life and togetherness<br><br>Popular culture reflected greater sexual openness and liberal attitudes |
| The New Frontier | 1960–1969 | A culture of pleasure-seeking arose, embraced especially by those of the counterculture<br><br>The second Sexual Revolution was reflected in more positive attitudes about, and increases in, sexual behavior outside of marriage<br><br>The Stonewall Riots led to the emergence of an increasingly more positive identity for lesbians and gays |
| The Seventies | 1970–1979 | The second Sexual Revolution continued<br><br>The Religious Right began to organize against the prevailing cultural and sexual liberalism, targeting abortion and gay rights most notably<br><br>Cultural feminism turned away from sexual liberation as the core issue related to attaining equality |
| The Conservative Counter-Reaction | 1980 to Recent Times | The New Right increasingly gained political power and took on issues of women's rights, sexual permissiveness, the availability of erotica, gay rights, and abortion |

### The Progressive Era (1910–1919)

The term **New Woman** came to refer to the changes in ever greater numbers of young, 20th century women in terms of self-sufficiency, attitudes, interests, and behavior (Gerhard, 2001; McLaren, 1999; White, 1993). The appearance of the New Woman was made possible by the movement of women into the workplace, providing them with some small degree of economic independence from male relatives and eventually husbands. Women typically found low-paying work in factories or as department store clerks and secretaries, and gave most of their money to their families. Yet their new earning power allowed them to develop more individual lives with friends at work and in leisure pursuits (Gerhard, 2001).

Before World War I, upper- and middle-class society generally harbored negative attitudes toward working-class women who stepped outside of the traditional Victorian role of the passive, proper, demure "lady." Women who sought pleasure in the new world of dance halls and entertainment were scornfully labeled "women adrift" (Petersen, 1999). Likewise, the derisive term "charity girl" was also hurled at women who engaged in sexual touching or other sexual behavior for gifts, access to entertainment or amusements, or even simply for excitement (Gerhard, 2001; Petersen, 1999).

During the 1910s and 1920s, the emergence of dance halls drastically changed the expectations for behavior and fashions for women. Women who would not participate in the new dances, who would not drink alcohol, and who did not dress in flashy clothes had difficulty achieving popularity, and were less likely to receive attention from men. Flamboyant, more risqué styles became fashionable, accentuated by elaborate costume jewelry, high-heeled shoes, and use of facial cosmetics.

Hemlines on dresses rose modestly from the floor to above the ankle in the 1910s, but soared to the knee in the 1920s in racier styles of "flapper" dresses (Gerhard, 2001; Petersen,

A woman working at a shoe factory in Lynn, Massachusetts. *How important do you think the opportunity to earn an income has been to advancing women's rights and social power? If you were a woman in the early 20th century, do you think you would have been one of the trailblazers who joined the workforce?*

Dance halls were a major feature of the dramatic change in culture that exploded during the 1910s and 1920s. Their appearance was a sign that the United States and Britain were discarding the puritanical values of the Victorian Era, at least in urban areas.

1999). More than simply raising the hemline, rebellious young women rolled their stockings down and powdered their naked knees to draw attention to them. Brassieres came into fashion, but rather than accentuating the breasts, they were flattened to accommodate the new, sleek style of dress.

The variety of alcoholic beverages and mixes offered in dance halls and taverns changed during this period to be more appealing to women (Petersen, 1999). Fads—activities, fashions, and phrases attaining great popularity for a short period of time—swept across the United States throughout the decade of the Twenties, including such phenomena as raccoon coats, hip flasks, and the phrases *keen, phooey, the Ritz,* and *making whoopee* (having sex; Petersen, 1999).

## The Roaring Twenties (1920–1929)

### The First Sexual Revolution

Historian Kevin White (1993) has referred to the dramatic changes in sexuality during the years before the 1920s and throughout the following decade as **the First Sexual Revolution.** This title is an allusion to a period of comparably profound changes that occurred during the 1960s, often called **the Sexual Revolution** (see page 83). Actually, these labels take into account only U.S. culture; in fact, a similarly dramatic change swept France and especially England in the 18th century, as a counter-reaction to Puritan restrictiveness and prudery. Nonetheless, substantial departures from Victorian morality and practices did evolve during the second and third decades of the 20th century in the United States, representing a very real cultural and sexual revolution in American society. Changes began most intensely in the largest urban areas, such as New York City and Chicago, but then gradually permeated less-metropolitan regions.

A primary reason that the 1920s represented such a dramatically important era of change was the extent to which the massive White middle class was affected. A number of factors contributed to the change. Foremost among these were the greater commercialization of sexuality, the profound influence of working class and Black music and dance upon the culture of White dance halls, increasing sexual openness in popular literature, the growing prominence of psychological and medical theory in general thought, and the pervasive sense that the moralist purity crusaders of the previous decade were archaic, irrelevant prudes. Such forces propelled sexuality outside the confines of reproduction and marital relationships into the public sphere; at the same time, control over sexuality was cast within the domain of individual rights of fulfillment and pleasure.

These were the beginnings of the set of values that has been called **sexual liberalism,**

> an overlapping set of beliefs that detached sexual activity from the instrumental goal of procreation, affirmed heterosexual pleasure as a value in itself, defined sexual satisfaction as a critical component of personal happiness and successful marriage, and weakened the connections between sexual expression and marriage by providing youth with room for some experimentation as preparation for adult status. (D'Emilio & Freedman, 1997, p. 241)

### Gender Roles Within Sexuality

Apparently as an extension of long-standing beliefs and Victorian values, gender roles related to sexuality evolved during this time. Men were conceived as possessing strong sexual drives and women were considered virtually passionless (Gerhard, 2001; White, 1993). Such gender roles were defined most explicitly in marriage manuals that became very popular during the 1920s. The substance of the belief in gender differences in sexuality was highly similar to the earlier Victorian belief; what changed was the assessment of the meaning and implications of these differences. One writer described the male temperament as influenced primarily by the "sex instinct," with the "paternal instinct" being subsidiary to the sex drive. The reverse was thought to be true for women, with the sex instinct of far lesser importance than the maternal instinct.

**The Male Gender Role.** In the Progressive Era of the 1910s, attitudes toward the strength of male sexuality moved away from the view that the male sex drive needed to be controlled and suppressed. In fact, the earlier Victorian belief in the danger of the male sex drive was cast as the great culprit that had led to an increase in effeminacy among U.S. men, because it had suppressed men's natural male strength. In the Progressive Era mindset, male sexual potency and power came to be enthusiastically celebrated as positive, constructive forces in marriage and society (White, 1993).

Because sexual satisfaction was increasingly seen as essential to individual well-being and marital bliss, social commentators and marriage manual authors conceived of the male sex drive as playing a critical role in marital satisfaction. It was considered to be the impetus necessary to create the great symphony of sexual ecstasy that

During the Progressive Era, men were expected to be natural experts in romantic and sexual matters, given the supposedly "natural" lustiness and aggressiveness associated with masculinity. Women, it was thought, need to have their passion aroused by the skillful overtures of men, because women were viewed as passionless and as having a childlike innocence.

ensures vitality and bonding in a marriage. Given that men were believed to be innately sexual creatures and to have an intuitive sense about factors necessary for sexual pleasure, the overwhelming responsibility for the quality of sexual interaction between men and women was therefore attributed to men. Men were believed to be responsible for igniting and arousing sexual passion in women because women were thought to be devoid of sexual capacity of their own. It was thought that men need to develop techniques that are effective in stimulating a woman's body in order to ignite her sexual interest. Only in this way could women experience sexual pleasure—through the skillful actions of the man (D'Emilio & Freedman, 1997; Gerhard, 2001; White, 1993).

The man became responsible for properly stimulating the woman erotically and "giving" her an orgasm. Because it was believed that men could reach climax at any moment, the man was expected to be able to coordinate his orgasm to occur at exactly the same time as his wife's (D'Emilio & Freedman, 1997; Gerhard, 2001; White, 1993). Marriage manuals referred to this knowledge as aptitude, ability, and skill, rendering sexual pleasuring into a type of masculine competence. Furthermore, this competence was linked at its very essence to the natural virility and masculinity of men; that is, it was believed to spring from their own innate sexual character. During the era of the 1920s, therefore, sexual competence came to be added to the repertoire of abilities men were expected to have or develop. This became another arena in which men would ultimately be judged, not only in their minds by one's wife or sexual partner, but implicitly at least by peers and the generalized audience of society (White, 1993).

In linking sexual competence to intrinsic masculine nature, authors also grounded male aptitude within the core features of masculinity such as power, strength, forcefulness, and even aggressiveness. Masculine forcefulness was thought to be essential to arouse primitive passion in a man's wife, almost against her rational will. Marriage manual authors became the masters of contradiction in advising the man to be "aggressively gentle." This set of contradictory beliefs can be explained by the fact that the authors believed that other prominent male characteristics are strength of will and self-control. Some experts claimed that men had not become accomplished in the art of love if they did not know to proceed with sexual stimulation when their partner asked them to stop, probably representing the foundations of what is currently called the **rape myth belief system**. At the same time, men were cautioned to be tender and sensitive while forging ahead with sex; otherwise lack of compassion would have devastating effects on the woman by physically hurting and frightening her. Therefore, men were called upon by experts to employ their masculine strength to govern their naturally powerful sexual urges (White, 1993).

**The Female Gender Role.**  While placing men in a position of being evaluated according to virtually unattainable, baseless standards of "competence," experts cast women within a conceptualization that was similarly grounded in entirely inaccurate knowledge about female anatomy, physiology, and psychology. To appease concerns about the unknown implications of women being capable of sexual interest and desire, female sexuality was fundamentally linked to heterosexuality and the requirement that men are necessary to ignite the sexual interest. In this capacity, men were placed in an absolutely essential, active role as creator and mentor, whereas women were cast in the dependent, passive role as recipient and novice. Men were supposed to awaken passion in their wives, because of women's inherently nonsexual nature, with love and romance being the sole catalyst that initiates the cascade of passion in women (Gerhard, 2001).

Marriage manual authors wrote in poetic, lyrical styles to assist in romanticizing the tone of thinking for readers, conceiving of sexual intercourse as communion between a man and a woman. Marital compatibility and emotional satisfaction became equated with sexual bliss within what was called "**the companionate marriage**"; in this concept, the husband and wife were equals that were fulfilling different, complementary functions (D'Emilio & Freedman, 1997; Gerhard, 2001). Even the physical health of women became linked to sexual interaction with their husband in that some authors thought that injection with semen protected their mental and physical health (Gerhard, 2001).

## The Culture of Personality and Sensuality

Physical attractiveness, social gracefulness, and suaveness were critical in presenting a convincing performance in social life and romantic attractiveness, evidence of the increasing importance of sexuality in U.S. culture. Moreover, the sensuality of dance halls and the privacy that dates and automobiles afforded promoted sexual exploration. These were also situations in which men acquired the more powerful role because of the necessity to spend money for dates to occur. Because men earned substantially more in wages, they acquired even greater power than in earlier times to influence developing relationships. Consequently, men asserted their own more sexually open values and, whether subtly or otherwise, pressured women for greater sexual intimacy. One prominent indicator of this was that it became more acceptable to speak in sexually explicit ways to women in the context of dates, a frequent complaint of women writing to personal advice columnists (White, 1993).

The negative consequence for men of the need to spend money, despite the power that it gave to them, was that expectations rose about exactly what should constitute a good date. Women began to expect more and tended to base their evaluation of men as attractive romantic partners on the quality of the entertainment provided. As a result, men complained that they could not afford the cost of dating and, by extension, the cost of marriage (Petersen, 1999; White, 1993). Earning power became a criterion against which women judged men as potential spouses to an even greater extent during this time (White, 1993). "**The battle of the sexes**" therefore blossomed in modern times in the context of (a) dating becoming a game of attempting to inspire attraction in the desired partner, (b) men needing to spend money on dates and expecting "thrills" in return, and (c) women expecting to be treated to extremely entertaining times on dates while protecting their virginal honor.

## Increases in Premarital Sexual Behavior and Liberalization of Sexual Attitudes

### Sexual Intercourse

Working-class men came to expect to engage in sexual behavior at earlier ages than men who were college-educated. According to the monumental, groundbreaking research of Alfred Kinsey in the 1930s and 40s (Kinsey, Pomeroy, & Martin, 1948), the frequency of sexual behavior before marriage almost doubled for young men with an eighth-grade education or lower compared with those in the first decade of $20^{th}$ century. Premarital penile–vaginal intercourse by age 15 rose from 34.5% for those born before 1900 to 51.1% for those born after 1900. Corresponding increases were observed among women by age 20, but across all socioeconomic groups: 8% for women born before 1900, 18% for women born between 1900 and 1909, 23% for women born between 1910 and 1919, and 37% for women born between 1920 and 1929 (Kinsey, Pomeroy, Martin, & Gebhard, 1953). One intriguing corollary of the increase in premarital intercourse was that prostitution became less prevalent during the 1910s. Increasingly, American men were obtaining sexual gratification with women who were not prostitutes. Sex with prostitutes among young men of the 1920s dropped by as much as two-thirds of the levels that were found for the previous generation (White, 1993).

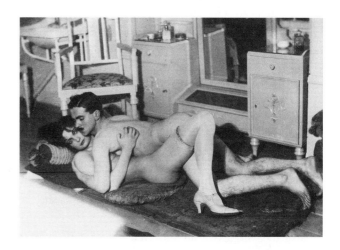

Evidence indicates that rates of premarital penile–vaginal intercourse skyrocketed over the decades around the turn of the 20th century. *What factors do you think contributed to the dramatic change that took place in sexual behavior rates during this time?*

### Petting

The frequency of a type of sexual behavior called *petting* rose even more dramatically. Petting referred to fondling, massaging, and stimulating sexually sensitive parts of the body, especially the genitals and breasts. In the Kinsey research, approximately 80% of women born before 1900 had engaged in petting with a man, with the proportion increasing to 99% of women born after 1900. The differences in proportions are particularly striking when considering the percentage of women who had engaged in petting by the age of 20: 66% for women born before 1900, 81% for women born between 1900 and 1909, 90% for women born between 1910 and 1919, and 94% for women born between 1920 and 1929. By 20 years old, 76% of men born before 1900 had engaged in petting with a woman, while 93% of men born after 1900 had engaged in petting. Likewise, oral–genital sex, both cunnilingus (oral stimulation of female genitals) and fellatio (oral stimulation of male genitals), increased from relatively low proportions among the generation born before 1900 to approximately 25% for both men and women born after 1900. All of these types of sexual behavior occurred at an earlier age for the generation born after 1900.

## The Double Standard

Working-class men held less negative attitudes toward sex before marriage for themselves than for women. This set the stage for the momentous hypocritical conflict in values that was a prominent feature of the 20th century, eventually even among the middle class: **the double standard**. The double standard is the belief that it is acceptable for men to engage in sex before marriage, but it is unacceptable for women.

The distinction between "good women" and "bad women" became less clear during the 1910s and 1920s. Good women were considered to be those who did not engage in sex outside of marriage, whereas bad women were those who did. Middle-class women as a group were perceived to be good women, because it was assumed that they were "respectable" and therefore were not interested in sex outside of marriage. Yet working-class women, it was believed, could be distinguished into the two types, and the distinction grew to be very prominent as a way of judging the quality of women. It also, however, created a discomforting quandary for both heterosexual men and women. It was acceptable for men to want to engage in sex and to indulge this desire, but they also wanted "good women" for wives. In the ideal, the belief was that working-class women who were "good women" (virgins) and who were being courted as a prospective wife were to be treated with the utmost respect; this meant specifically that sexual advances were not supposed to be made toward them before marriage (White, 1993).

## Changes in Conceptions of Sexual Orientation

Progressive Era experts, writing in academic publications and in marriage manuals, subscribed to the traditional view that same-gender behavior was wrong, and incorporated relatively modern concepts to provide further justification for their negative view of it. Furthermore, the concepts of heterosexuality and homosexuality made their way into common thinking during the 1920s. Prior to the Victorian period, sexual orientation was not explicitly included as an aspect of personal identity; **identity** refers to one's self-understanding, the kinds of attributes an individual believes he or she possesses, and the value placed on these attributes. Sexual behavior between people of the same sex was instead viewed prior to this time as the result of a temporary moral lapse or weakness, a sin; however, it was not thought to be caused by a stable characteristic of the individual.

Using knowledge derived from the Victorian underground, sexologists Karl Ulrich, Richard von Krafft-Ebing, and Havelock Ellis formalized same-gender sexual orientation into a type of pathological medical syndrome called **homosexuality**. These authors relegated same-gender orientation into the netherworld of disease for the first time, casting it as a condition that an individual "has" because of some debilitating factors within the person (D'Emilio & Freedman, 1997). In doing so, same-gender attraction became a stable attribute of the person, and by the 1920s, *homosexuality* was the dark, sinister side of sexual orientation, with *heterosexuality* the good, healthy, logical nature. Heterosexuality became an important "natural" aspect of an individual's constitution, and homosexuality was its opposite that could contaminate and corrode that constitution.

Ellis in particular had a profound effect on popular conceptions of sexual attraction and sexual orientation identity. His notion of **inversion** (a reversal of typical conditions) cast sexual attraction within the constellation of traits that constitute masculinity and femininity, or maleness and femaleness; attraction to women was conceived as a fundamentally masculine trait that was inextricably imbedded in the network of other masculine traits. Likewise, attraction to men was perceived as a fundamentally feminine trait, intrinsically a part of all other important feminine traits.

In traditional thinking, masculinity and femininity are considered to be incompatible opposites; an individual is believed to be incapable of possessing both stereotypically masculine and stereotypically feminine characteristics. Furthermore, because masculine attributes are thought to involve strength and power, any behavior or situation that suggests weakness or femininity are believed to diminish masculinity, no matter what the specific nature of the unmasculine behavior is. Therefore, being too gentle or unassertive in social relations in gen-

Conceptions of sexuality changed during the early 1900s as sexual orientation came to be seen as a characteristic of the individual, and "homosexuality" was thought to be caused by gender "inversion." *What do you think this 1920s photograph of New York gay men dressed as pirates says about the accuracy of the inversion theory?*

eral, as well as feeling attraction or desire for virtually any kind for men, were evidence of lack of masculinity and lack of attraction for women (bisexuality does not fit easily into this inversion model).

With the association of same-gender orientation with inferiority, deficiency, and disorder, particularly given psychoanalytic endorsement and religious moral sanction, widespread societal condemnation of gay men and lesbians was a tiny next step. Consistent with the medical disease model, an "infected" individual (meaning a gay man or lesbian) could infect a "clean" person; following from the religious moral model, evil entities (gay men or lesbians) were thought to thrive on the seduction of innocent victims into a life of sin and corruption. Popular moralists (e.g., Schmalhausen, 1931) warned the American people, especially naive, unsuspecting young boys, about the "recruitment" of new members (White, 1993), apparently into some suspected secret society. Such portrayals drew upon Victorian conceptions of male sexuality as animalistic and almost uncontrollable, such that "homosexuality" was characterized as a consuming, out-of-control passion that relentlessly, insatiably required satisfaction with new "victims"—this became the basis for the predator stereotype of same-gender orientation, particularly for males.

### Attitudes About Masturbation

Masturbation generally retained its status as "self-abuse," dangerous to both physical and psychological well-being. Although some experts argued that masturbation was not actually damaging to health, they still believed that it was nasty and immoral, or caused disturbances of some lesser degree. Authorities continued to subscribe to the Victorian belief that masturbation would drain and wither testicles, or cause sickliness and loss of general energy. It was nonetheless relatively more tolerated by some experts than in previous times, who disputed its more radical dangers. In fact, some writers maintained that occasional masturbation may be necessary to avoid marital problems related to disagreement about sexual frequency or to prevent indulgence in nonmarital sex (White, 1993).

## The Great Depression (1930–1939)

Dating evolved dramatically during the 1930s away from its original primary role as a means of evaluating prospective spouses. Instead, it soon became the major basis for socializing with peers and for pursuing entertainment. This trend gradually weakened the link between dating and relationship commitment. The predominant factor contributing to this trend was the acceleration of the emphasis on youth, which began in the 1920s.

Another factor that transformed socializing and dating was the increasing prevalence of automobiles. The desire of adolescents to use the family car to go out on dates grew to be source of conflict with parents. The automobile became a means for young people to assert greater independence from parents because it transported them to places distant from the home where they could escape the vigilance and control of parents. Greater privacy was also afforded by the automobile in that adolescents would park the cars in isolated areas such as country lanes and parks to engage in kissing, fondling, and other types of sexual behavior (Kyvig, 2002).

## World War II and the Atomic Age (1940–1949)

Pin-ups—sexy pictures of famous actresses—became popular adornments on trucks, jeeps, and other vehicles, including bombers, during World War II. Original caption 06/04/1945— Okinawa: Glamorous Dorothy Lamour is the pin-up girl of leatherneck motor transport battalion on Okinawa. Pointing to the film star's photo is PFC Edward M. Szynczak, 27, Pittsburgh, PA; looking on (left to right) are: CPL Theodore Papit, 21, Philadelphia, PA; PFC Pat O. Cerinehe, 24, Lansford, PA; and PVT Albert Servadio, 38, Pittsburgh, PA.

World War II exerted a profound effect on sexuality and sexual attitudes. A number of people engaged in sexual behavior outside of marriage, possibly directly attributable to the massive exodus of millions of men out of the United States. Nonetheless, highly conservative, restrictive attitudes prevailed throughout the decade, even intensifying by the end of the period (Petersen, 1999). Evidence suggests that American men did not entirely refrain from sexual behavior while away at war. American service men defending the shores of Britain developed a reputation for being extremely interested in sex. One survey indicated that 80% of U.S. men who had been shipped out of the country for 2 years or longer had engaged in sex; moreover, half of married men engaged in sex with women while away from home. American men married 50,000 British and 10,000 Australian women during the war. Beyond this, around 300,000 children were born outside of marriage. European women were far less prejudiced against African Americans than were U.S. women, such that involvement of

British women with Black American men caused riots in several British cities as angry White American service men attacked the "offending" Black men (Petersen, 1999).

Women and girls also indulged in short-lived sexual escapades, some in a pattern of regular indulgence. Cast as a form of patriotic support for service men, women would travel to military bases to help entertain them. Such women became known as "**V-girls**" (short for Victory girls because this was seen as contributing to the war effort). Volunteer organizations, such as the Red Cross, the YMCA, and the USO, in addition to providing entertainment by movie and music stars, trained women to become hostesses at parties for service men. Some of these V-girls would engage in sexual behavior with servicemen, interested in the thrill of involvement with men in uniforms, as well as possibly as a means of rewarding them for their service to country (Petersen, 1999).

Rates of sexually transmitted diseases apparently also increased during the war years, although 6% of American men entering the armed forces at the beginning of United States involvement were infected. As many as 10% of service men stationed in France and Italy contracted sexually transmitted diseases, with 15% of all of those stationed overseas being infected by 1945. Yet the rate of infection increased in the United States as well, rising 200% during the war (Petersen, 1999).

## *A Return to the Past: The New Traditionalism (1950–1959)*

The 1950s represented an era of considerable paradox. As Americans longed for an era of peace, stability, and security after World War II, they also dreamed of an idealized version of the quiet, small town family life they believed existed in more innocent times before the war. This idealized value system has been called the **new traditionalism**, a demand for sharply defined and highly distinct gender roles, as well as for "family togetherness" and for regarding the home as a sanctuary of relief from the hostile outside world. However, this romanticized philosophy came into increasing conflict with a greater, more public openness about sex and sensuality that began to appear in American society (Gerhard, 2001).

The Kinsey volumes based on scientific research on human sexuality were highly visible examples of this movement toward greater openness, but other, more pervasive undercurrents in American culture would in fact exert a more profound, longer-lasting influence on society. Popular culture as represented in music, literature, and cinema had weakened the restrictions on sexual openness in previous eras, and the restrictions were no longer successful against the hedonistic trends welling up in American society.

The second volume, *Sexual Behavior in the Human Female*, based on Alfred Kinsey's research was published in 1953, ironically coinciding with the peak in conservative values and concern with an idealized family life. The very fact that the research addressed the sexuality of women at all represented an extreme outrage in the increasingly restrictive sociocultural climate;

Original caption: 12/18/1951—Levittown, NY— Robert Rehm, who fits the census bureau's description of the "average American," takes a walk with his family through his suburban community. Mr. Rehm fits the "average American" classification to a "t." He's a semi-skilled worker, has a wife and two children, and an average income of around $3,000, owns a refrigerator, radio, and telephone, and is still paying on his home. Other members of his family are, left to right: Chris, three months old; Jeff, three years; and his wife Peggy. The family dog rounds out the picture.

Alfred Kinsey and his colleagues at Indiana University in Bloomington conducted pioneering research on the sexual behaviors of Americans by interviewing roughly 12,000 individuals during the 1930s and 40s.

however, the revelation of such sexual behavior as masturbation, premarital sexual experience, and extramarital affairs among women was perceived as an unforgivable, supreme affront to traditional views of women (Petersen, 1999).

Soon after, an incensed Congress formed a special committee to investigate the source of funding for the research conducted by the Kinsey Institute for Sex Research. For a number of years, the private Rockefeller Foundation had funded the research, but given the intensely unfavorable publicity aroused by the publication of the female volume, the foundation withdrew its support. Instead, it granted financial support to Union Theological Seminary, whose leader had been one of the most vitriolic critics of the Kinsey research. Kinsey continued to be attacked both professionally and personally, causing his health to decline dramatically from that point on; he died in 1956 at the age of 62 (Petersen, 1999).

## New Frontiers (1960–1969)

### The Pleasure-Seeking Culture

One of the most defining slogans of the 1960s was "**Sex, drugs, and rock 'n roll**," the three major elements of the culture of pleasure-seeking that arose during this era. This value system was most explicitly, defiantly, and joyously embraced by those of the **counterculture**, those who protested against and worked to change "the Establishment" and, later in the decade, those who totally rejected mainstream society, the "hippies." The liberalization of attitudes toward sexuality was much more complicated than the notion of a decay of general societal standards into irresponsibility and abandonment of duty, as sometimes portrayed in popular accounts of the period. Most people in the protest movements—whether antiwar, civil rights, or generally anti-Establishment—were truly motivated by a desire to address what they perceived to be substantial problems with traditional values and established practices related to daily life and social issues. Moreover, desire

During a Bay Area rock concert, two people share what appears to be a marijuana cigarette, 1969.

for innovative, socially sensitive ways of living, to provide an alternative to the increasingly materialistic world of 1960s middle-class America, began to permeate all segments of youth society in a matter of a few years (Marty, 1997).

## The (Second) Sexual Revolution

The monumental changes in attitudes toward sexuality and changes in the prevalence of sexual behavior outside of marriage has led to the 1960s being virtually universally called the era of **the Sexual Revolution**. The changes that occurred in the 1960s, however, did not mysteriously materialize without any prior antecedents. *Dating* replaced "calling" much earlier in the century, and the liberalizing of conventions related to dating evolved across the intervening decades as well. Gender roles transformed during the 1920s and again in the 1940s prior to the transformations of the 1960s. Erotica was produced during the Victorian era at unprecedented levels, a trend continuing through the Progressive Era. A more recent form of erotica that gained more visibility and acceptability than ever before was the World War II phenomenon, the pin-up, predating the "men's magazines" of the 1950s and 1960s (Allyn, 2000). In fact, because of the progression toward greater sexual openness, some commentators have questioned whether a revolution actually occurred during the 1960s. However, others have argued that evidence suggests a dramatic and unprecedented rise in levels of sexual behavior outside of marriage during this decade. Beyond this, since the 1960s, attitudes have continued to be more positive about sex between unmarried individuals involved in long-term emotional relationships (Hill, 2002; Reiss, 1967; Smigel & Seiden, 1968). The stability of the changed attitude suggests a fundamental restructuring of society, therefore a revolution rather than merely a passing phase in history. Furthermore, the percent of births outside of marriage rose from 4% in 1950 to only 5.3% in 1960, but the rate rose steeply to 14.2% by 1975, despite the increasing availability of the oral contraceptive (the pill) after its introduction in 1960 (Marty, 1997). The term *sexual revolution* has also been aptly applied to the changes in sexual behavior among White, middle-class college women that occurred after the appearance of the pill (Allyn, 2000).

The label *sexual revolution* was additionally reinforced throughout the decade by the extensive rejection of censorship by the U.S. Supreme Court that involved sex-related topics; legal prohibitions against birth control were widely overturned during this time, as well. In addition, college students protested the segregation of men and women into separate dormitories and the strict prohibitions against entertaining the other sex in dorm rooms. Eventually, many universities began to relax or do away with such regulations altogether. Later in the decade, the term *sexual revolution* was employed to characterize the sudden openness prevailing in discussion about sexuality and in the portrayal of nudity and sexuality in magazines, movies, and theater (Allyn, 2000).

The sexual liberalism that had evolved by the 1960s functioned exactly as all other types of sexual liberalism that had come before it, in that it labeled certain behavioral patterns as good and healthy, whereas others were considered bad and unacceptable. Sexual desire and expression came to be viewed positively in general, but only so long as it occurred within a long-term, exclusive heterosexual relationship. Moreover, the expectation was that healthy sexual relationships were headed on a trajectory toward eventual marriage, even though marriage was not a major concern in the short-term. This value system cast same-gender attraction and relationships as lying outside the bounds of acceptability. Likewise, the trend at the time among Black teenagers to have children and remain unmarried violated sexually liberal standards, and was therefore looked down on by those in White liberal society (D'Emilio & Freedman, 1997).

## Gay Liberation

The 1960s witnessed the emergence of the push for tolerance and acceptance of gay men and lesbians. Eventually, this drive would evolve into a campaign for basic civil rights protection in the next several decades. The revolution in gay sexuality came about in a sudden, spontaneous act of rebellion by patrons of a gay bar in Greenwich Village in New York City on June 27, 1969. Police raided the Stonewall Inn, intending to arrest the bartenders and drag queens (men dressed in women's clothing). The outrage of bar patrons evicted onto the street exploded when a police officer struck a patron on the head with a club. The incident escalated into riots throughout the Village during the entire final weekend of June (Allyn, 2000).

A same-sex couple hold each other during the first gay rally, held in Union Square, San Francisco, CA, 1960s. The placard in the background reads, "Take the COURTROOM out of your BEDROOM!"

Subsequently, the **Stonewall Riots** became a rallying point for the anger and loathing that gays and lesbians felt because of the degradation and discrimination they had experienced throughout the years. Yet political activism and a well-organized movement would build only gradually over the next several decades, beginning in the 1970s. The most important immediate change to take place was in emotional terms, with a channeling of anger and resentment into defiance, determination, and a redefinition of identity into that of individuals who deserve fair treatment. This was the first glimmer of a common sense of identity and community among gay men and lesbians—the beginnings of what is now called **gay pride** (Allyn, 2000).

# *The Seventies: The Walls Come Tumbling Down (1970–1979)*

The second Sexual Revolution did not end in the 1960s, instead gathering momentum throughout the 1970s. In a number of important ways, the challenges to traditional values and morality became much more explicit and public during the Seventies; the most vocal proponents of Sexual Liberation and the New Morality were unabashed and unapologetic about their attitudes and goals in confronting mainstream culture, adopting an even bolder and more strident defiance of conventional wisdom.

Yet the greater liberalism and interest in sexual exploration was not confined to the most extreme segments of the counterculture. The walls of traditional values tumbled, with inhibitions against sexual expression crumbling as never before in modern Western civilization (Petersen, 1999). As with the 1960s, most people did not engage in the extreme forms of sexual expression that come to mind when thinking of "the Sexual Revolution." However, adolescents and young adults lived in an age of increasing acceptance of sexual behavior before marriage and decreasingly negative attitudes toward individuals who experienced unwanted outcomes from sex before marriage, such as unplanned pregnancies and sexually transmitted diseases. Large numbers of people headed to nightclubs, discos, bookstores, and theaters, whereas other smaller numbers attended private swinging clubs to get "a piece of the action" for themselves.

## The Rise of the Religious Right

The born-again movement represented one of the first, most noticeable examples of the rise in the 1970s of **evangelism**, the ancient view that individuals must profess belief in Jesus as the Messiah and convince others of the necessity of adopting that belief. **Fundamentalism** quickly dominated evangelism, which advocated a value system of strict adherence to a puritanical, restrictive moral code. Proponents of fundamentalism adopted the position of extreme opposition to the philosophical view called **humanism**; this is a belief in the importance of promoting the quality of human existence and is not explicitly grounded in

The profound changes in attitudes during the 1960s and 70s involved an increasing acceptance of sex before marriage and a greater openness toward discussion, as well as expression, of sexuality.

specific religious principles. According to fundamentalist Christians, the movement toward liberalism, openness, and self-expression embodied in humanism was responsible for elevated levels of sexual experimentation, drug and alcohol use, and rebelliousness (Marty, 1997). Conservative Christians also decried the **1973 U.S. Supreme Court Roe v. Wade decision** declaring restrictions on medical abortion unconstitutional during the first three months of pregnancy; medical abortion is the surgical termination of pregnancy. In addition, the ruling asserted that only a woman and her physician had the right to decide whether an abortion would be performed during the second three months.

Because of their belief that same-gender sexual behavior is immoral, one other defining issue of the Christian conservative movement was opposition to protection of civil rights for gay, lesbian, and bisexual individuals (Marty, 1997). In contrast, in 1973, the American Psychiatric Association (APA) undertook a reevaluation of their categorization of *homosexuality* as a psychological disorder in the *Diagnostic and Statistical Manual of Mental Disorders* (*DSM*). Same-gender sexual orientation had been classified as a sexual disorder, placed within the same general category as fetishism, transvestism, and necrophilia. Approximately 58% of the APA membership voted to support the removal of the classification in 1974, with only 38% voting against.

## Feminism

One important effect of the 1960s feminist movement was the change in philosophy that developed during this time. By the mid-1970s, some feminists had begun to question the extreme focus of the feminist movement on sexual liberation as the key to a broader liberation and as a means of further advancement for women. **Cultural feminist theory** began to gain prominence as a unifying theme among the emerging factions of feminism during this period, a position that downplayed striving for sexual liberation as a means of more universal empowerment. In its place, **cultural feminism** emphasized the importance of maternal attributes and goals, such as a commitment to survival, nurturance, and the promotion of well-being in others. This became a rallying point around which to unify all of the various voices seeking to define feminism at the time (Gerhard, 2001).

# *The Conservative Counter-Reaction (1980 to Recent Times)*

Despite the image of dazzling, intoxicating sensuality, self-indulgence, and abandon that seemed to characterize the 1970s, the seeds of conservative counter-reaction that would burst onto the scene in the 1980s were planted as early as the 1950s. Among some segments of society, the sexual freedom and indulgence of the 1960s and 1970s represented wanton decadence and decay. The outrage and disgust among conservatives in particular would produce a reaction of profound proportions by the end of the 1970s, ushering in a more visible, highly publicized counter-reaction by vocal conservatives, most especially those who were part of the administration, or held sway with newly elected President Reagan.

Social concerns became the compelling forces that reinvigorated the conservative base and transformed it into the **New Right**. Conservatives abandoned their alarmist, relentless anxieties about the communist threat, and focused much more on social trends of the 1960s and 70s that offended the values of the evangelical Christians: the liberal push for women's rights, sexual liberation and its accompanying permissiveness, the availability of erotica, the growing visibility and forcefulness of gays and lesbians, the legalization of abortion, the Supreme Court ruling against organized school prayer, desegregation and school busing, and concern about employment quotas for racial minorities and women (Dunn & Woodard, 1996; McGirr, 2001).

## Trends in the Composition of Families

Domestic life underwent significant changes during the 1980s. Marriage declined by approximately 25% from the 1960s to the 1980s, with the median age of marriage soaring to 25.5 years for men and 23.2 years for women. Another sign of the times, most likely a result of the Sexual Revolution, was the tremendously larger number of unmarried couples living together in the 1980s (D'Emilio & Freedman, 1997); this is called **cohabitation**. The number rose from approximately 500,000 in 1970 to around 2 million in 1985, a fourfold increase, although for people between 25 and 44 years old the number increased by a factor of 12 (Marty, 1997).

Yet marriage became a more satisfying type of relationship during this period compared with what was called the "golden age" of the family in the 1950s. Couples increasingly perceived the relationship as a source of emotional intimacy, support, and mutuality. Gender roles changed ever so slightly as men became somewhat more responsible for certain household tasks compared with earlier times; nonetheless, the bulk of the chores still fell to women, even when they were employed outside of the home (Marty, 1997).

## Changing Attitudes About Sexuality

With the beginning of the new decade of the 1980s, the luster of casual attitudes about sex and the desire for simple sexual recreation began to dim for some segments of society. Surveys of readers of popular magazines such as *Cosmopolitan*, although hardly scientifically representative samples, seemed to indicate that women were upset by the lack of intimacy and romance in relationships that they had heard of, and read about, in days gone by. Other magazines such as *New Yorker, Esquire, Psychology Today,* and *Time* all proclaimed in the early 1980s that the Sexual Revolution was dead and that it had fallen short of its many "promises" (Petersen, 1999).

In hindsight the belief by the popular media that the Sexual Revolution had resulted in extremely lax attitudes toward casual sex was not entirely accurate. Rather, the greatest changes had occurred with respect to beliefs about the appropriateness of engaging in sexual behavior outside of marriage. As will be discussed in later chapters, attitudes had changed such that the appropriateness of sexual behavior was linked to being in an emotionally involved and committed relationship, independent of whether the relationship was formalized through marriage.

# BOX 3.1 AN OPPORTUNITY FOR SELF-REFLECTION

## Sexual Attitudes Throughout History

Western culture has advocated a variety of beliefs about sexuality throughout the ages. Rate your own beliefs related to each of the statements below by selecting the point on the scale that best represents how you feel. Afterward, respond to each of the statements as you believe represents the standard expectation prior to 1900.
1 = Do not agree at all, 2 = Agree slightly, 3 = Agree moderately, 4 = Agree mostly, and 5 = Agree completely.

1. Women should be loved and admired, but feeling great sexual desire for them is wrong and destructive to both women and men.    1 2 3 4 5

2. Penile–vaginal intercourse is the only morally acceptable type of sexual behavior, and married couples should only engage in it when they are trying to have children.    1 2 3 4 5

3. Couples should not get married because they are romantically and sexually attracted to one another, but so that they can have children who will be raised as high-quality, productive citizens.    1 2 3 4 5

4. Sex is inherently evil, but sexual fulfillment is fundamental to a person's well-being.    1 2 3 4 5

5. Feelings of love for a person is an important basis for wanting to marry him or her.    1 2 3 4 5

6. The man should be the supreme head of the family, with his wife and children completely subservient to his will.    1 2 3 4 5

7. It is the duty of the church and the community to constantly monitor individuals' behavior and make sure that they behave morally.    1 2 3 4 5

8. Excessive indulgence in sexual behavior can lead to poor health.    1 2 3 4 5

9. An individual has a right to sexual happiness and to engage in sexual behavior as frequently and with whomever he or she desires.    1 2 3 4 5

10. Sexuality is inherently good and healthy.    1 2 3 4 5

11. Engaging in behavior with another person of the same sex is contrary to nature.    1 2 3 4 5

12. Sexual partners must be treated with kindness, consideration, and sensitivity no matter whether they are spouses, romantic partners, or casual sexual partners.    1 2 3 4 5

13. Women should exercise great control over their sexual feelings and behave in a sexually modest way.    1 2 3 4 5

14. Individuals should show great restraint with respect to sexuality and try to behave as respectably and conservatively as possible.    1 2 3 4 5

15. Men should develop extreme control over their powerful sexual natures and inhibit their sexual impulses as much as possible.    1 2 3 4 5

16. Masturbation is extremely unhealthy and is particularly harmful to children.    1 2 3 4 5

*(Continued)*

(Continued)

17. Women basically have lower sex drives than men, and need to be stimulated and aroused by a man in order for them to become passionate about sex.

    [1]  [2]  [3]  [4]  [5]

18. It is more acceptable for men to engage in sexual behavior outside of marriage or a relationship than it is for women.

    [1]  [2]  [3]  [4]  [5]

19. Attraction to the same sex results from an individual having a personality that is more similar to someone of the opposite sex.

    [1]  [2]  [3]  [4]  [5]

20. Sexual behavior is healthy and perfectly acceptable as long as a couple is involved in a long-term, emotionally intimate relationship, even if they are not married.

    [1]  [2]  [3]  [4]  [5]

To get an idea of the meaning of each rating, responses of "1" or "2" suggest lack of agreement with each of the historical beliefs below discussed in the chapter. Responses of "3" through "5" suggest agreement with the historical beliefs.

| Rating number | Type of belief | Historical era |
|---|---|---|
| 1 | ennobling love | Middle Ages |
| 2 | Christian belief in penitential literature | Middle Ages |
| 3 | civic morality | Renaissance |
| 4 | Protestant belief | Reformation |
| 5 | Protestant belief | Reformation |
| 6 | Puritan belief | Reformation |
| 7 | Puritan belief | Reformation |
| 8 | medical belief | Enlightenment |
| 9 | natural philosophy | Enlightenment |
| 10 | natural philosophy | Enlightenment |
| 11 | natural philosophy | Enlightenment |
| 12 | romantic view | Enlightenment |
| 13 | general belief | late Enlightenment |
| 14 | general belief | Victorian Era |
| 15 | general belief | Victorian Era |
| 16 | general belief | Victorian Era |
| 17 | general belief | 1920s |
| 18 | double standard | 1920s |
| 19 | medical inversion view of homosexuality | 1920s |
| 20 | general belief resulting from the Sexual Revolution | 1960s |

## Conclusions About the
## Historical Course of Sexuality

Over time, sexuality and sexual satisfaction came to be seen as central components to achieving personal growth and happiness. This emerging ethic, of course, was diametrically opposed to the traditional values of restraint and asceticism advocated by Christianity, such that many aspects of established society acted to undermine the trend toward what they saw as self-indulgence. Often the opposing effect was simply that mainstream society continued on with its business of marrying, bearing children, and raising families. The demands of routine life would generally restore the status quo to a great extent, although with each push toward sexual openness and rebellion, society would inch a little more in a liberal direction.

American culture has remained somewhat more sexually open in some ways since the 1960s, such as in the prevalence of sexual behavior outside of marriage and in the availability of erotica in television programming, cinema, magazines, and Internet sites. In a critical way, however, traditional Christian values and Victorian ethics have endured as an underlying bedrock of American culture and individual consciousness. In general, sexual behavior is still evaluated morally in terms of whether it occurs in an established relationship; the vast majority of people eventually marry or become involved in long-term, committed relationships, and view extramarital affairs in extremely negative ways. For the most part, the procreation or love-based philosophies derived from religious ethics discussed in the second chapter continue to influence the fundamental conception of sexuality in the United States.

## Summary

Informal rules regarding sinful sexual behavior and associated religious penalties were developed in early Christianity, known as penitential literature. In the late Middle Ages, cultural thinking idealized and romanticized the concept of pure love uncontaminated by sexual desire in the form of song and literature about ennobling love.

A philosophy arose during the Renaissance based on traditional Christian morals regarding the evil of pleasure and sensuality that cast sexual behavior outside of marriage as destructive to societal well-being.

Nonetheless, rape, sex outside of marriage, and immoral types of sexual behavior occurred with some frequency.

In the late 1500s, Protestant leaders returned to the original scriptural commandments, resulting in a number of changes in religious practices and views of morality. Those who engaged in sexual intercourse outside of marriage were publicly whipped, were required to confess their sins in church, and were branded or required to wear symbols indicating the nature of their transgressions.

*(Continued)*

(Continued)

Commoners during the 1700s continued to embrace traditional Christian views, as well as their negative beliefs about sexuality. These beliefs, along with other more practical factors, inhibited sexual indulgence of the lower classes.

In the 19th century, attitudes became even more profoundly conservative during one of the most sexually repressive periods of modern times, the Victorian Age. Even the slightest hint of pleasure or sensuality was avoided. Women came to be seen as totally devoid of sexual desire due to their essential purity and innocence, needing to be protected from even the suggestion of sensuality. Yet men were viewed as seething with lust in their basic masculine constitutions, although they were expected to develop extreme control over these urges.

During the 20th century, people began to value personal fulfillment, with sexual satisfaction increasingly seen as essential for personal growth and happiness. During the Roaring Twenties and the onset of the First Sexual Revolution, women were conceived as incapable of passion on their own, such that men were believed to "give" women orgasms through their skillful lovemaking. The bliss and emotional satisfaction resulting from sexual interaction was thought to create the companionate marriage. Rates of both sexual intercourse and petting increased substantially during this period. Gay men and lesbians were conceived as possessing traits typical of the other gender, a type of disorder that was labeled homosexuality.

The era of the Great Depression (1930–1939) witnessed the transformation of dating from evaluating prospective mates to a type of entertainment. The period around the time of World War II (1940–1949) involved substantial levels of sexual behavior outside of marriage as millions of American men left to fight the war. The decade of the 1950s was characterized by the "new traditionalism," yet popular culture increasingly reflected greater sexual interest and openness in music, literature, and cinema.

With the onset of the Sexual Revolution during the 1960s, culture moved in a more pleasure-oriented direction. The ultimate nature of the change that occurred was a lasting, more positive view of sex between unmarried individuals involved in emotionally committed relationships. Other aspects of the sexual revolution included rejection by the U.S. Supreme Court of censorship of sexual topics in the media, elimination of legal prohibitions on various medical birth control methods, and a much greater openness toward discussion of sexuality.

The 1970s were characterized by a much increased intensity of expression and openness. However, the decade also saw the rise of the Religious Right, the growing numbers of socially and politically activist Christians. Conservative Christians opposed the legalization of surgical abortions and civil rights protections for gays and lesbians. The movement toward greater conservatism and restrictive morality accelerated in the 1980s and has continued into current times, the era of the Conservative Counter-Reaction.

## Chapter 3 Critical Thinking Exercises

1. The value of a historical perspective of sexuality
   a. What is the value of examining historical trends in sexuality in terms of gaining a better understanding of sexuality in current times?
   b. What insight might a historical view provide about psychological factors involved in sexuality?
   c. What value might there be in examining religion in developing an understanding of psychological aspects of sexuality?

2. Historical trends
   a. Has any particular pattern occurred throughout Western history with respect to the restrictiveness/conservativeness versus permissiveness/liberalness toward sexuality? That is, have Western societies become progressively more liberal into current times, or have societies alternated between periods of conservatism and liberalism?
   b. What has been the nature of attitudes toward sexual pleasure and sensuality across time? Has there been any relationship throughout history between the view that sex is for pleasure and the view that the reason for sex is reproduction?
   c. What has been the relationship between attitudes toward love and attitudes toward sexuality across time in Western societies? What changes have taken place in the relationship between attitudes toward love and sexuality?
   d. What has been the nature of expectations across time concerning appropriate sexual behavior for women and men? What has been the nature of changes in gender expectations?
   e. What specific role has religion played in attitudes toward sexuality and patterns of sexual behavior? What other factors besides religion have been most influential in changes in sexuality that have occurred?
   f. What are the implications of the changes in sexuality that have taken place? Has the nature of sexuality become healthier and more positive, or have the changes largely been for the worse? What predictions would you make for changes in sexuality that will occur in the future?

Visit www.sagepub.com/hillhsstudy.com for online activities, sample tests, and other helpful resources. Select "Chapter 3: The Historical Course of Sexuality" for chapter-specific activities.

# Chapter 4

## THE SCIENTIFIC STUDY OF SEXUALITY

At the very beginning of formal scientific thinking about sexuality, Richard von Krafft-Ebing (1937/1906) wrote "Woman, . . . if physically and mentally normal, and properly educated has but little sensual desire. If it were otherwise, marriage and family life would be empty words. As yet the man who avoids women and the woman who seeks men are sheer anomalies" (p. 14). In late Victorian times, it was believed that women cannot have both a strong maternal drive and a strong sexual drive. Maternal drive—the desire to mother children—was thought to be caused by women's feminine nature, whereas sexual desire was thought to be caused by men's masculine nature. For this reason, almost all women were believed to be feminine and motivated entirely by their maternal drive; because they are not masculine, they cannot experience sexual desire. Thinking of femininity and masculinity as completely opposed to one another led to the conclusion that, if women were to experience sexual desire, they would not want to have children. This was the reason that Krafft-Ebing believed that the very existence of marriage and family life in civilized society depends on women not experiencing sexual desire.

Krafft-Ebing wrote these words with tremendous certainty and confidence. The pronouncement makes it seem as if the almost complete absence of sexual desire in women, and the overwhelming sexual attraction of all men for women are undeniable truths; it is as if everyone recognizes these beliefs as describing the nature of reality for humans without question. What's more, Krafft-Ebing's view carried the weight of the medical profession, because he was a physician; he must have known what he was talking about, because he was a medical doctor, right?

The problem is that scientific research on sexuality was virtually nonexistent at the time that Krafft-Ebing published his observation. Beyond this, the few studies that existed at the time are currently not seen as very high quality by today's scientific standards. Therefore, not a whole lot of confidence can be placed in their results. Even worse, Krafft-Ebing's conclusions were not even based on this small number of studies. His view was grounded in essentially common folk wisdom of the time, and as such his view was really simply a belief or opinion. It was not actually a scientific conclusion. What makes a scientific conclusion different from a belief is that it is based on objective, verifiable information. Beliefs and opinions are often not based on scientifically collected information, but rather largely on personal experience and cultural values prevailing at the time. Scientific conclusions are based on information that is collected according to logical standards; these standards try to get rid of factors that confuse or cover up information that will trick scientists into drawing the wrong conclusion.

To make matters worse, early theorists were very strongly influenced by moral beliefs of the time, and usually were not even aware of how they were being influenced. Often, religious beliefs have shaped—even openly guided—the very essence of scientific views, and also have been used to justify the validity of the views. The effect in early medical texts was that writers made pronouncements as if they were based on scientific investigation, and as if they were indisputable, uncontested facts, despite their lack of grounding in empirical research.

## *Early Scientific Research on Sexuality*

Another problem in early thinking about sexuality was that it was not based on an explicitly stated and formal theory. Proposing a formal theory allows the researcher and other scientists to consciously understand the assumptions upon which information collection is based. It also allows the researcher to carefully and purposefully look at the data and see if the result comes out like the theory predicted it would. This gives scientists additional confidence that their conclusions are accurate.

Despite the central role that theory should play in scientific investigation, early research was not based on any particular formal theory. In fact, the first studies were being conducted at approximately the same time as, if not before, the first formal theories were published by Havelock Ellis, Sigmund Freud, and Richard von Krafft-Ebing. Therefore, research could not have been influenced greatly by the newly developing theoretical writings. The view guiding scientific investigation in the late 19th and early 20th century was based on the general philosophy of logical positivism, discussed in chapter 1. This early view championed a purely **inductive approach**: that is, collect objective facts about behavior and then develop a conceptual understanding that is not colored by values or beliefs. This technique is the opposite of proposing a theory and then seeing if the results of a study turn out like the theory predicted, a strategy called the **deductive approach**.

The Kinsey research, one of the first major scientific projects on sexuality, followed the inductive approach, rather than the theory-testing approach. As Kinsey and his colleagues stated about their own research,

> The present study, then, represents an attempt to accumulate an objectively determined body of fact about sex which strictly avoids social or moral interpretations of the fact. Each person who reads this report will want to make interpretations in accordance with his understanding of moral values and social significances; but that is not part of the scientific method and, indeed, scientists have no special capacities for making such evaluations. (Kinsey, Pomeroy, & Martin, 1948, p. 5)

Since these early days, standards and techniques have been developed within science to assist in avoiding unrecognized biases. Even more importantly, testing formal theoretical positions explicitly allows scientists to openly acknowledge the possibility of bias and to deal with it straightforwardly. This chapter examines the scientific method in greater detail, which is an alternative to the methods of information collected through philosophical and historical analysis.

## *Collecting Scientific Information on Sexuality*

### The Philosophy of Scientific Investigation

Two features of information-gathering that distinguish the scientific method from methods used in history and philosophy are (a) restriction of its focus to testable issues and (b) reliance on systematic empiricism

(Stanovich, 2004). **Restriction to testable issues** is the principle that only issues that may be reliably observed and measured are legitimate to address in science. Reliable observation and measurement of that which is observable is, in fact, **systematic empiricism**. You might remember from chapter 1 that empiricism is the bedrock of science; it is the centerpiece of the philosophy of logical positivism traditionally embraced by scientists.

An issue, for example, that is testable with currently available scientific methods is how often individuals engage in various types of sexual behavior. A related issue that is also testable is the extent to which each type of sexual behavior is viewed as enjoyable or valuable or is considered moral to individuals. Researchers are able to ask people in a questionnaire how often they have engaged in different sexual behaviors. Individuals may also be asked

*What aspects of the couple's experience in this setting do you think are scientifically testable?*

to express how pleasant or how moral they feel sexual behaviors are on a rating scale. An issue, however, that is not empirically testable is whether each type of sexual behavior is *inherently* moral or immoral. This last issue cannot be empirically addressed by scientists, although philosophers and theologians may be willing to address it. This is because no objective source of morality exists to be measured; instead, all sources of morality result from faith in divine revelation or essentially intuitive value judgments.

Stanovich (2004) emphasizes the point that empirical observation must be **systematic**. This means that it must be related to testing a specific explanation of the world in an organized and meaningful way. The most meaningful type of explanation is a formal **theory** that is logically and coherently organized. On this basis, very specific, concrete hypotheses may be advanced from the theory; observation and measurement then will allow a test of whether the **hypotheses** accurately predict the outcomes obtained through the data-collection process. You may want to look back at chapter 1 to refresh your memory about the importance of theory in science.

A third quality of the scientific method noted by Stanovich is that the information obtained must be **evaluated by peers**. For information to be admitted as an acceptable piece of evidence in scientific understanding, it must be submitted in the form of papers or manuscripts to other scientists who are experts in the field. These experts are called upon as **reviewers** for scientific periodical publications, or **journals**, to evaluate the accuracy, credibility, and meaningfulness of the information; the experts determine if the data meet scientific standards to the extent that the information is worthy of being published in a journal. The individuals who oversee the reviewers in their evaluation of manuscripts are **editors**, who themselves are experts in the field and who have been selected by a committee of other experts in the discipline. An editor evaluates the judgments of the reviewers about the quality of the data and makes a decision to accept or reject the manuscript for publication.

## Types of Information About Individuals

Social and personality psychology, as specialty areas in the broader discipline of psychology, are concerned with the measurement of the behavior and mental processes of individuals. They are also concerned with the

Social scientists frequently measure behavior using self-report surveys, in which individuals rate or describe their own behavior. *Do you think that the setting in this picture would be ideal for having individuals disclose information about their sexual attitudes and behavior?*

measurement of aspects of the social and physical environment that are thought to affect behavior. **Measurement** is the process of assigning numbers using a standard scale with specified units or quantities; in the case of psychology, the targets of measurement are behavior, mental processes, and related aspects of the world. For measurement to be empirical or scientific, the behavior or psychological process must be observable and verifiable, for the reasons discussed in the previous section.

The requirement that behavior and processes must be **observable** can be applied even to those experiences taking place within individuals, such as the experience of feelings, emotions, and thoughts. These types of experiences were considered to be completely hidden to scientists at one time. However, it has become widely accepted within psychology that aspects of them can in fact be measured with subjective rating scales; **ratings scales** consist of verbal statements that are evaluated along a dimension that is labeled by specific descriptions at each of its various points. A particular example of the rating process may involve requesting individuals to read the question, "How sexually aroused do you feel at this moment?" (See Table 4.1). Beneath the statement would be a series of numbers ranging from one to five, which are labeled with the descriptors "not at all" under the number one (1), "moderately" under the number three (3), and "extremely" under the number five (5). This is a **subjective measure** because it asks individuals for an intuitive judgment based on their perception of themselves. No objective means exist for others to evaluate a person's subjective experience of sexual arousal and, in this way, come to some type of agreement about the level of arousal. It is not available to others outside of the description provided by the person feeling the sexual arousal.

Another example of a subjective measure is the questionnaire, the Brief Sexual Attitudes Scale, presented in Box 14.1. You may want to respond to the questionnaire yourself to see how your attitudes compare with those of participants in three studies conducted by Hendrick and his colleagues (Hendrick, Hendrick, & Reich, 2006).

| **TABLE 4.1** | Example of a Rating Scale |
| --- | --- |

| How sexually aroused do you feel at this moment? | | | | |
| --- | --- | --- | --- | --- |
| 1 | 2 | 3 | 4 | 5 |
| Not at all | | Moderately | | Extremely |

# BOX 4.1  AN OPPORTUNITY FOR SELF-REFLECTION

## The Brief Sexual Attitudes Scale

Listed below are several statements that reflect different attitudes about sex. For each statement mark the response that indicates how much you agree or disagree with that statement. Some of the items refer to a specific sexual relationship, whereas others refer to general attitudes and beliefs about sex. Whenever possible, answer the questions with your current partner in mind. If you are not currently dating anyone, answer the questions with your most recent partner in mind. If you have never had a sexual relationship, answer in terms of what you think your responses would most likely be. 1 = Strongly agree with the statement, 2 = Moderately agree with the statement, 3 = Neutral—neither agree nor disagree, 4 = Moderately disagree with the statement, 5 = Strongly disagree with the statement

1. I do not need to be committed to a person to have sex with him or her. ☐1 ☐2 ☐3 ☐4 ☐5
2. Casual sex is acceptable. ☐1 ☐2 ☐3 ☐4 ☐5
3. I would like to have sex with many partners. ☐1 ☐2 ☐3 ☐4 ☐5
4. One-night stands are sometimes very enjoyable. ☐1 ☐2 ☐3 ☐4 ☐5
5. It is okay to have ongoing sexual relationships with more than one person at a time. ☐1 ☐2 ☐3 ☐4 ☐5
6. Sex as a simple exchange of favors is okay if both people agree to it. ☐1 ☐2 ☐3 ☐4 ☐5
7. The best sex is with no strings attached. ☐1 ☐2 ☐3 ☐4 ☐5
8. Life would have fewer problems if people could have sex more freely. ☐1 ☐2 ☐3 ☐4 ☐5
9. It is possible to enjoy sex with a person and not like that person very much. ☐1 ☐2 ☐3 ☐4 ☐5
10. It is okay for sex to be just good physical release. ☐1 ☐2 ☐3 ☐4 ☐5
11. Birth control is part of responsible sexuality. ☐1 ☐2 ☐3 ☐4 ☐5
12. A woman should share responsibility for birth control. ☐1 ☐2 ☐3 ☐4 ☐5
13. A man should share responsibility for birth control. ☐1 ☐2 ☐3 ☐4 ☐5
14. Sex is the closest form of communication between two people. ☐1 ☐2 ☐3 ☐4 ☐5
15. A sexual encounter between two people deeply in love is the ultimate human interaction. ☐1 ☐2 ☐3 ☐4 ☐5
16. At its best, sex seems to be the merging of two souls. ☐1 ☐2 ☐3 ☐4 ☐5
17. Sex is a very important part of life. ☐1 ☐2 ☐3 ☐4 ☐5

*(Continued)*

(Continued)

18. Sex is usually an intensive, almost overwhelming experience.  ☐1  ☐2  ☐3  ☐4  ☐5
19. Sex is best when you let yourself go and focus
    on your own pleasure.  ☐1  ☐2  ☐3  ☐4  ☐5
20. Sex is primarily the taking of pleasure from another person.  ☐1  ☐2  ☐3  ☐4  ☐5
21. The main purpose of sex is to enjoy oneself.  ☐1  ☐2  ☐3  ☐4  ☐5
22. Sex is primarily physical.  ☐1  ☐2  ☐3  ☐4  ☐5
23. Sex is primarily a bodily function, like eating.  ☐1  ☐2  ☐3  ☐4  ☐5

There are four separate scales. To calculate your score for the Permissiveness Scale, add together all of the numbers for items 1 through 10, and then divide by 10. For the Birth Control Scale, combine the numbers for items 11 through 13, and divide by 3. For the Communion Scale, combine the values for items 14 through 18, and divide by 5. For the Instrumentality Scale, combine the values for items 19 through 23, and divide by 5. Lower average values indicate **_greater_** endorsement of the attitude dimension. The Permissiveness Scale measures beliefs in the acceptability of casual, impersonal sex. The Birth Control Scale measures beliefs that individuals should use birth control when engaging in sex. The Communion Scale measures beliefs that sexual interaction should be based on love and sharing of emotional intimacy. The Instrumentality Scale measures beliefs that sex serves the purpose of providing pleasure for the individual.

You may want to compare your own scores with the average scores obtained in research by Hendricks and his colleagues. These are presented in the table below separately for women and men, averaged across their three studies:

| Scale | Women | Men |
| --- | --- | --- |
| Permissiveness | 4.41 | 3.35 |
| Birth Control | 1.52 | 1.69 |
| Communion | 2.13 | 2.09 |
| Instrumentality | 3.49 | 3.33 |

The questionnaire was developed by Clyde Hendrick, Susan S. Hendrick, and Darcy A. Reich and appeared in Hendrick, C., Hendrick, S. S., & Reich, D. A. (2006). The Brief Sexual Attitudes Scale. *The Journal of Sex Research, 43,*76–86. Reprinted with permission of the authors and the Society for the Scientific Study of Sexuality.

A more objective measure of sexual arousal may also be used in a given study. An **objective measure** is one that is based on events that can be easily observed and judged by others beyond the person under study. Objective techniques for measuring sexual arousal that are commonly used in research are the **plethysmograph** (pronounced *pluh THIGHS moh graff* ) and **strain gauge**; a plethysmograph is an instrument that measures changes in the size of organs. The penile plethysmograph and strain gauge for men are placed around the penis and measure the extent to which it becomes engorged with blood, that is, the extent to which it becomes larger and more erect. The **vaginal plethysmograph** consists of a small tampon, a cylinder inserted in the vagina, that contains tiny electrical sensing devices; the devices detect changes in blood flow in the walls of the vagina, which increases during sexual arousal. These methods are objective because the readings they produce are observable to others beyond the person experiencing the increased arousal; therefore, the reliability (repeatability) of the measurement can be verified.

Many psychological activities, processes, and characteristics, however, cannot be observed directly and must be inferred; this means they are logically assumed to exist. To take an example from the physical world, gravity cannot be directly observed. Nonetheless, it is assumed to exist, and is widely accepted as real. To demonstrate the existence of unseen forces or happenings, events that are observable and believed to be connected to the unseen processes are often relied upon to provide pieces of evidence for them. To demonstrate the existence of gravity, as a simple type of evidence, a scientist might drop a ball to measure the factor affecting the ball. The scientist may then infer the existence of a force called gravity.

The need for an adequate understanding of unseen factors once again highlights the importance of using theory to understand an internal psychological process. The theoretical explanation must be proposed *before* conducting a study. A specific hypothesis must be stated that predicts the outcome for the study that logically follows from a theory in advance. If the results of the study are largely consistent with the predictions, the researcher may have substantial confidence in the correctness of not only the hypothesis about the difficult-to-observe process, but also increased confidence about the theory from which the hypothesis was drawn.

The procedure is similar to that of a detective who tries to solve a particular crime. A detective seldom witnesses a crime himself or herself. However, the detective must collect whatever observable pieces of evidence are available and link them together logically and plausibly to identify the criminal, the method of committing the crime, and the motive for the crime (Funder, 2004). This job must be completed convincingly enough that a jury will accept it and convict the accused person. In the same way, the psychologist must link the evidence sufficiently to an explanation that it convinces the "jury" of scientific experts of its validity and plausibility. In a criminal investigation, as well as in a scientific investigation, one piece of evidence is not sufficient to be convincing of an explanation. It is the entire body of evidence, and the plausibility of the way that it links together, that provides a convincing argument for the explanation of crime, or the explanation of a cause of behavior.

Four types of data that may be collected as evidence within psychology are Self data (S data), Informant data (I data), Behavioral data (B data), and Life Outcomes data (L data) (Funder, 2004). See Table 4.2.

## Self Data (S Data)

*Self data,* or *S data,* are assessments made by the individual of interest about his or her own psychological activities, outcomes, or characteristics (Funder, 2004). S data are extremely valuable pieces of information because they can provide insight into experiences occurring within the individual that are not directly observable to others. An example of measurement providing this type of information was presented in the previous section in the self-rating, "How sexually aroused do you feel at this moment?" This type of information is one

**TABLE 4.2**    Four Types of Data

| Type of Data | Abbreviated Name | Nature of the Data | Methods for Collecting Data |
|---|---|---|---|
| Self data | S data | Assessments provided by the individual of interest about his or her own psychological activities, outcomes, or characteristics | Self-report questionnaire, interview |
| Informant data | I data | Assessments provided by someone who knows the individual of interest concerning his or her psychological activities, outcomes, or characteristics | Self-report questionnaire, interview |
| Behavioral data | B data | Observations of the behavior of the individual of interest by the researcher | Direct observation of overt behavior, electronic recordings of less overt behavior, diary |
| Life outcomes data | L data | Observable, often formally documented events in the life of the individual of interest (e.g., official records, government registries, hospital records) | Archives of agencies and institutions |

of the most frequently obtained by psychologists because of the value of the insight provided into the individual, as well as the ease of collecting it compared with other types of data.

Series of ratings are often assembled within booklets, and individuals circle the point on each of the rating scales that follows the questions; or they mark their answer on a Scantron sheet that can be machine-read. More recently, questionnaires are presented on computer monitors, and respondents describe themselves by clicking on a point on a rating scale. This method is called a **self-report questionnaire**, because individuals provide information about themselves and record the responses on their own. Another procedure to collect S data is the **interview** method, in which individuals provide information about themselves in response to statements or questions from a trained interviewer; the interviewer also records the information provided by the respondents. The question on sexual arousal therefore could also have been presented as part of an interview.

Ratings such as the one on arousal are entirely standardized in format. A **standardized format** is the presentation of a statement or question that is exactly the same for all respondents; the standardized format also involves providing a response format that is exactly identical across respondents. **Standardization** provides comparability across individuals; that is, comparisons across people are very direct and straightforward, because all aspects of the procedure are precisely the same. Another technique available to researchers is one that is less standardized, in that individuals are simply allowed to talk or write about themselves in an **open format** (Funder, 2004). Typically, this technique is used when a researcher is interested in unique, idiosyncratic aspects of individuals, rather than general aspects common to others. For instance, a researcher may pose the question to respondents, "In what types of situations are you most likely to become sexually aroused?" Respondents would then verbally describe such situations or write about them in their own words.

### Advantages of S Data

*Advantages* refer to the positive aspects of a type of data that increase the likelihood a researcher will decide to collect that type of information. Two advantages have already been mentioned. The first is that Self data provide insight into experiences occurring privately within the individual that are not directly observable by others, and therefore are not directly or easily obtained by other sources. Furthermore, an individual is likely to have the most complete information about himself or herself because the individual is the only one who has been present in all situations of his or her life. No family member or friend is typically present with an individual every moment of his or her life, or even for all psychologically significant events.

Self data have been found to correlate highly with reports provided by other people who are familiar with the person being evaluated (Funder, 1999; Kenrick & Funder, 1988; McCrae, 1982). Self-report data have also been found to correlate strongly with overt behavior measured independently of the self-reports (Kenrick & Funder, 1988). Consequently, Self data may often be considered a good source of valid information.

*Why do you suppose that Self data are such important sources of information?*

### Disadvantages of S Data

*Disadvantages* refer to the negative aspects of a type of data that reduce the likelihood a researcher will decide to collect that particular type of data. One disadvantage to S data is the flipside of the coin to the advantage that an individual has access to the best information available about himself or herself. The problem is that individuals consciously may not want to reveal certain information about themselves that they view as too intimate and revealing, too embarrassing, or too risky for fear of being punished for the behavior (e.g., some sexual behaviors are illegal). It is also possible that individuals are not able to report accurately on certain aspects of their mental processes and behavior. Subtle biases may cause a type of distortion of which the individual is not even aware (Funder, 2004). One potential influence is that of **the social desirability bias**, in which individuals report behavior in a way that is more socially approved than the behavior in which they have actually engaged; for example, people tend to report fewer or more sexual partners depending on what is considered socially desirable for women or men (Alexander & Fisher, 2003; Meston, Heiman, Trapnell, & Paulhus, 1998).

Furthermore, some aspects of psychological functioning are simply **inaccessible to conscious awareness**. It would be futile to ask them questions about such activities because they would not be able to provide any really useful information.

## Informant Data (I Data)

*Informant data,* or *I data,* are assessments made by someone who knows the individual of interest in terms of his or her psychological activities, outcomes, or characteristics (Funder, 2004). The term ***informant*** refers to an individual who has witnessed events that are of concern to a project, and then reports on those events. In order for an informant to be able to report on what has occurred, the events must be **observable**.

*How much have you talked with close friends about your views on relationships, intimacy, and sexuality? Do you think they would be able to provide high-quality information to scientists about your private feelings, interests, and behaviors?*

In psychological functioning, much of what occurs, and possibly much of what is important to humans, is not directly observable. However, humans are capable of making **inferences**, or judgments, about the emotions and thoughts that others are experiencing based on a variety of observable behaviors. Also, in trying to understand the events of their lives, individuals often talk with their friends, romantic partners, or family members about their feelings as events are happening. Such intimate confidants become aware of the private concerns, thoughts, and emotions of their loved ones and friends. Other sources of information about these private processes include facial expressions, eye movements, gestures, posture, and nonverbal sounds, such as sighs.

I data may be obtained using techniques identical to those used to obtain S data. These methods are questionnaires and interviews. However, in the case of I data, people who are knowledgeable about an individual respond to the questionnaires or interviews regarding the behavior or characteristics of the target individual, not the behavior and characteristics of themselves. **Knowledgeability** refers to the fact that informants are sufficiently familiar with the individual they are reporting on that they are able to base judgments about the person on past experience (Funder, 2004). For nonsexual issues, knowledgeable informants might even be acquaintances or coworkers if the behaviors are those that would have been performed in a more public or job-related setting. Such informants might report, for example, on general personality traits, such as friendliness, conscientiousness, and dominance.

*How many of your friends and family would be able to provide high-quality information and intimate details about the dates, private interactions, or sexual behavior you have experienced?* For most people, the number of knowledgeable confidants is probably extremely small.

For sexual issues, knowledgeable informants are likely to be much less plentiful, because sexual issues are generally restricted to only those with whom one is extremely emotionally or physically intimate. This may include very close friends or family members with whom an individual has discussed sexual topics. However, research focusing on I data would need to obtain the information from marital or romantic partners with whom individuals are involved in sexual relationships. Yet very few sexuality studies have in fact collected this type of data.

As noted by Funder (2004), informants typically do not need a great deal of formal psychological expertise because of their familiarity with many aspects of an individual's functioning. In fact, research indicates that informants are generally capable of providing extremely accurate information about individuals for whom they have observed relevant behavior (Funder, 1993; Kenrick & Funder, 1988).

### Advantages of I Data

One of the most valuable advantages of I data is that, similar to S data, they are based on a great wealth of evidence about individuals if the informants are truly **knowledgeable** about the individuals. Friends, family members, and romantic partners typically observe a tremendous quantity and variety of behaviors, emotional reactions, and problem-solving. Again, with respect to sexuality, only those who have intimately discussed sex with an individual, or who have been involved in a sexual relationship with an individual, over a period of time will be able to bring this type of advantage to providing information. A related advantage is that the information offered by informants is based on real-world, or **naturalistic**, experiences with the individual. This produces a higher-quality data than can be obtained from observations of behavior by psychologists themselves in artificial laboratory settings. The data more accurately and confidently reveal how an individual typically behaves in his or her everyday life; the laboratory observation may only be relevant to how individuals behave in artificial settings (Funder, 2004).

### Disadvantages of I Data

A significant disadvantage of I data is that they potentially do not provide the quality of information available from S data. Knowledgeable informants may have a great wealth of information about an individual if they are loved ones or friends of the individual. Nonetheless, even romantic partners and very close friends are not with the individual every single moment of the individual's life, likely missing some instances of behavior relevant to what a scientist is investigating (Funder, 2004). This is particularly true with respect to sexuality. As discussed previously, usually only sexual partners with whom the individual has been involved for some time are likely to be privy to much of the individual's sexual behavior and attitudes.

## Behavioral Data (B Data)

*Behavioral data,* or *B data,* are observations of an individual's behavior by the researcher (Funder, 2004). Observations may be of **overt behavior**, that which is easily observable without special techniques or instrumentation (e.g., electroencephalograph readings of brain wave patterns, measurement of vaginal blood flow). These types of special equipment allow documentation of **less easily observable behavior**. Behavioral data can be collected in two generally different types of settings: in the normal environment in which an individual lives or in a scientific laboratory.

The first setting provides what Funder calls **natural B data**, indicating that the data come from observations in the natural environment in which the individual carries out his or her daily life. An extreme version of collecting natural B data would be to observe, and possibly record, every action that a person takes, such as by following the person around with a video camera. This would be very time-consuming and very expensive in terms of paying a person to do the recording, the cost of the videotape, and then going back to observe the tapes to conduct analyses of them. Even if recording were restricted to situations in which sexual issues would be most likely, this would still involve a great deal of time and expense. Moreover, with sexual interactions, the researcher would need to confront the issue of the ethics of recording individuals involved in every single sexually intimate situation with every partner.

One means of overcoming the expense is to have individuals record information in a **diary**. Such a technique might involve having individuals record information about overt behaviors they perform in the course of their daily lives, and then to have them submit the diaries to the researcher on the day following the data collection. For example, individuals could be asked to record the number of times they engaged in discussions about sexuality, as well as the nature of the discussions. In reality, this is a blending of B data and S data, in that the individual is reporting about his or her own behavior rather than the behavior being directly observed by the researcher.

The second setting in which Behavioral data can be collected is in the experimental laboratory. This type of information is called **laboratory B data** by Funder (2004). Data may be collected in **experiments** in which the environment is manipulated, or varied, for different groups of participants. After manipulating the environment, the researcher then has the participants engage in a specific activity, during which their behavior is recorded in some way. Experiments are designed to see if changes in the environment result in different types of behavior in individuals.

One additional way of obtaining behavioral data in the laboratory is illustrated by the research of Masters and Johnson. In this research, participants engaged in sexual behavior with their marital partner, or masturbated by themselves, as their physiological activities were recorded through various instruments. Physiological measurements included heart rate, blood pressure, and the activity occurring in their genitals. This is *not* an experiment, because no aspect of the environment is varied, or made to be different, for one group of participants compared with another group. The term, *experiment,* is a specific type of scientific study, which will be discussed later in greater detail.

## Advantages of B Data

This type of data is especially important in sexuality research because it provides the researcher with information about real-world behavior—at least in the case of *natural B data*—and little danger exists in generalizing the results of the study to what actually happens in real life. It is therefore said to have strong **external validity**, meaning it is accurate regarding behavior outside or beyond that observed in the study. An advantage of *laboratory* B *data* is that scientists are able to prompt behavior in a highly controlled setting that is specifically relevant to a particular theory and hypothesis; scientists do not have to wait around for the right environmental conditions to occur on their own to take advantage of happenstance. Therefore, this is a much more **efficient procedure** than collecting natural B data. Furthermore, it is possible to test a wider range of theories in the laboratory because of the greater control provided by the laboratory (Funder, 2004).

## Disadvantages of B Data

Behavioral data are pieces of information, or evidence, that **must be interpreted** (Funder, 2004). Facts by themselves do not provide answers; rather, the meaning of facts must be determined after the data are collected. This is likely to be the case more for B data than for S data or I data, because Self and Informant data can result from ratings that require interpretation and judgment on the part of the individuals making the ratings. For example, after interacting with someone for a period of time, individuals may be asked how sexually attracted they are to this interaction partner. A good degree of meaning is inherent in a response to such a request for information. However, the meaning of evidence that individuals look into the eyes of attractive people more frequently than unattractive people must still be interpreted to a great extent.

## Life Outcomes Data (L Data)

*Life outcomes data,* or *L data,* are observable, often formally recorded events in individuals' lives that are relevant to a particular psychological issue. For this reason, Life data may be available from archives, or official records, such as those in government registries, hospital records, academic histories, or even police reports. With respect to sexuality, researchers may be interested in number of marriages, number of children, medical problems, and number of complaints filed, or arrests for, domestic disturbances or sex crimes.

### Advantages of L Data

This type of information is intrinsically relevant to real life, because it is a record of events occurring in real life; it has great **external validity** (Funder, 2004). Therefore, it does not suffer from the possibility that it is relevant only to the behavior performed in the artificial environment of the research laboratory. Life data may also be highly **psychologically significant**, relating to relationship and sexual satisfaction (e.g., number of marriages, number of children), ability to engage in desired sexual behavior (e.g., physical health), and emotional adjustment (e.g., reports of domestic disturbances or sex crimes).

### Disadvantages of L Data

Although some Life outcomes may be relevant to psychologically important issues, **not all life events are meaningful**. For example, an individual's monthly grocery expense is unlikely to be directly related to any important aspects of his or her sexuality, although it may be possible to conceive of some relationships (e.g., health because of the importance of nutrition, attractiveness because of amount of musculature or fat distribution, popularity because of the number of dinners or parties hosted). However, the linkage between food expenditure and sexuality is at best indirect. Other types of data are likely to provide more meaningful relationships with sexuality, such as medical records to measure health, ratings of attractiveness by peers or independent judges, and statements or ratings by others regarding an individual's popularity.

A related problem is that Life data are very often determined or influenced by a range of different factors that have nothing to do with the issue under investigation. This **multidetermination** of Life outcomes (meaning, caused by a variety of factors) also makes it difficult to know exactly which factors have the most influence on the life events. With respect to the size of one's monthly grocery expense, factors such as annual income, family size, number of pets, extravagance of taste in food, and the region of the country in which one lives will all exert an influence. This type of information, therefore, may be too conceptually "messy" to be worth the effort of collecting it. Moreover, many of these factors are essentially irrelevant and uninteresting to the study of sexuality.

## Conclusions About Types of Data

As noted by Funder (2004), an absolutely perfect measure of behavior, psychological process, or sexuality does not exist in the real world; it is a mythical concept like that of the unicorn or the Holy Grail. Empirical data must be viewed as pieces of evidence that provide information in a particular way about a limited aspect of the topic of concern. All four types may be able to provide highly useful and meaningful information, but they nonetheless must be logically interpreted using some type of conceptual and theoretical framework. However, each type has a particular set of disadvantages, limitations, or dangers that can cause a scientist to misinterpret their meaning due to the uncertainty involved in the data (e.g., the meaning of increased heart rate or the psychological importance of the number of children an individual has—do more or fewer children relate to sexual satisfaction or life satisfaction?). Because each type of data has its own set of advantages and disadvantages, the evidence available from each must be linked together theoretically. If all point to essentially the same conclusion about a proposed hypothesis, a scientist may therefore have greater confidence in the hypothesis and related theory.

## *Evaluating the Quality of Measurement*

Because of the recognition that no perfect measure of behavior exists and that each type has its disadvantages, scientists must therefore be concerned about the quality of the data they collect. Consequently, standards have been developed to evaluate the quality of measures with respect to two major dimensions, **reliability** and **validity**.

### Reliability

*Reliability* is the extent to which a measure is accurate in the sense that it can be repeated in subsequent measurements; that is, each additional measurement will produce an outcome that is extremely close to the first measurement. The ability of a measurement instrument to produce very similar values if measuring exactly the same object or event is an indication of the precision of the instrument, one aspect of its goodness.

Consider your bathroom scale, on which you dutifully check your weight each morning. When you step on the scale the first time, imagine that it produces a reading of 125 pounds. You step off of the scale, wait for it to return back to exactly zero, and then step back on. The reading this time is 137 pounds. Horrified, you may step back on a third time, but this time it registers 103 pounds. Now, you may be tempted to stop at this point and accept the final reading as the most accurate. However, you realize that you would probably be deceiving yourself if you believed the last number. Obtaining a different weight every time you step on the scale, you would of course be convinced that the scale was broken; this is because it was unreliable. A **reliable scale** is one that provides very close to the same reading every single time it is used. Nonetheless, even a finely tuned, extremely precise scale will produce some small amount of variation across the different readings that are taken of the same object if the measurement is repeated a number of times. Every measurement involves some degree of fluctuation, which is considered to be error, and is called **measurement error**.

The same standard is used when evaluating psychological measurement. In fact, rating scales and questionnaires are often referred to as *instruments* in technical terminology. Psychologists must establish the extent to which their rating scales and questionnaires provide accurate measures of behavior and psychological processes. Two methods of evaluating reliability are summarized in Table 4.3.

One method of determining the reliability of a rating scale is to have individuals evaluate themselves on the rating scale at one point in time, and then ask them to rate themselves again a second, or even third time, on the scale. A statistic called a **correlation** can be calculated in which the ratings taken the first time for a group of people are compared with the ratings by the same individuals taken at the second time. Correlation values range between zero and one (in absolute value). If the ratings for the two times are very similar, or nearly identical, the number associated with the correlation will be very high, that is close to 1. If the ratings are not very similar, the value for the correlation between the two groups of ratings will be closer to zero; that is they are not correlated. Comparing ratings taken at two different times for the same group of people is evaluating the **test–retest reliability** of a measure.

| **TABLE 4.3** | Methods of Assessing Reliability |
| --- | --- |

| Method | Explanation | Example |
| --- | --- | --- |
| Test-retest reliability | Compare the measurements of the same behavior or psychological process obtained at two different times | Correlate scores on a self-report questionnaire obtained in August with scores on the same questionnaire for the same people obtained in October |
| Internal consistency | Compare the measurements of the same behavior or psychological process obtained by different rating scales or instruments | Correlate scores on one rating of sexual arousal with scores on another rating of sexual arousal within the same questionnaire for the same people |

Test–retest reliability involves measuring the same group of individuals' behavior at two different times. If people are found to behave similarly on the two separate occasions (e.g., expressing physical intimacy, such as kissing), the statistical correlation will be a high value. This means that test–retest reliability is large, and the method of measurement can be considered effective.

When evaluating individuals' level of interest in engaging in sexual behavior, a researcher may use a self-report scale such as "How strong is your interest in engaging in sexual behavior?" Individuals might judge their interest along a rating dimension ranging from 1 (*not at all strong*) to 3 (*moderately strong*) to 5 (*extremely strong*). To examine the reliability of this measure, the researchers would administer the rating to the same individuals again some time later, such as the next week when they come back to the laboratory for the second part of the study. If the rating did not make sense to individuals, or if the rating was not a meaningful type of evaluation, or if respondents were not taking the rating seriously, it would not reflect anything true about them. Consequently, they would be very likely to rate themselves somewhat differently the second time around, or even very differently. This is particularly the case if the rating is part of a large number of other ratings; they will be unlikely to remember exactly how they rated themselves the first time simply as a matter of having memorized it. For this reason, a high test–retest correlation for the rating would provide evidence for the stability or reliability of the scale.

Another strategy for assessing the reliability of measurement is to compare the readings obtained on one instrument with the readings of the same object or event using another instrument. If both instruments—or rating scales—designed to measure the same attribute provide very similar values, it can be concluded that the scales are accurate, or reliable. This is one aspect of the rationale for including more than one rating of a particular feature in questionnaires or interviews. Similar responses to ratings measuring similar features (sexual interest) provide evidence for the reliability of both ratings being compared. Therefore, a second type of reliability that is routinely examined for measures, particularly for S data and I data, is called **internal consistency**; this procedure compares the ratings made on one question or statement in a questionnaire with other ratings in the questionnaire measuring the same concept or behavior. The idea behind this is the same as checking the precision of one machine that measures heart rate with another machine measuring heart rate. Because they are assessing the same activity, they should produce virtually identical readings. A statistic is available to compare more than two ratings with one another at the same time called the **Cronbach's alpha**; this is a measure of **internal consistency** for a group of ratings.

In fact, more precise measurement is provided by having more than one rating of behavior and combining them. This is called **aggregation**, which means adding together. Because most differences in ratings made on one scale by an individual are considered to be accidental or random, these differences are just as likely to result in values higher than the real value of the behavior as they are likely to be lower. This means that if ratings are made on a number of scales, the error involved in them will also produce relatively equal numbers of ratings that are too high and too low. If all of the ratings are combined, the two types of error will average out to a value that is neither too high nor too low, but will be close to the true value; therefore, the high and low errors cancel each other out. Combining measurements then improves the accuracy of the final measurement used. The more ratings or readings made, the more reliable the overall measurement will be. This is the rationale for developing multirating questionnaires measuring the same behavior or process, and then computing a total score by adding ratings together to more adequately measure the behavior or process.

## Validity

The second standard of measurement quality is **validity**. Validity is the extent to which a rating or reading measures what it is intended to measure. If a sexuality researcher uses a machine that measures heart rate, the speed at which blood is pumped is not really the activity of interest in itself. Heart rate is probably measured because it is presumed to correspond to increases in sexual arousal during sexual behavior. Therefore, the validity of the readings as measures of sexual arousal must be verified in some way independently of the machine output. This is because heart rate is related to a multitude of types of responses and activities other than sexual arousal. For the same reason, even self-ratings focused on the experience of sexual arousal, such as "How sexually aroused are you at this moment?", must be validated as truly measuring sexual arousal. Why? Because of the problems associated with S data discussed previously: the possibility of intentional or unintentional distortion of ratings, and inability to detect and report on some bodily and psychological processes. Consequently, even ratings that are self-evident or obvious in their content and wording may not accurately reflect what the researcher intends to measure.

Yet establishing the reliability of the measurement instrument does not by itself speak to the validity of the instrument. In considering the measurement of your body weight, stepping on your bathroom scale does not guarantee that it is providing you with an accurate measure of your weight, even if it gives virtually the same reading every time you step on it (it is reliable). Many people have probably had the experience of stepping on the scale at the doctor's office or at the gym, only to find that it consistently indicates that you are heavier than your bathroom scale. Which measurement is correct, the one in your bathroom or the one at the gym? It is hard to say without comparing the bathroom scale and the gym scale with other scales. This is one strategy for determining the validity of a measurement: compare the instrument that is used in research with other instruments that are intended to measure the same dimension, such as body weight. This is called **convergent validity**. The evidence from similar instruments converges on, or points to, the validity of an instrument that is used in research. This type of validity, as well as another type that will be discussed below, are summarized in Table 4.4.

**TABLE 4.4**    Methods of Assessing Validity

| Method | Explanation | Example |
|--------|-------------|---------|
| Convergent validity | Compare the measurements of the same behavior or psychological process obtained by different questionnaires or instruments | Correlate scores on one questionnaire measuring a sexual attitude with scores on another questionnaire measuring the same sexual attitude for the same people |
| Construct validity | Compare the measurement of a particular behavior or psychological process for a construct (trait or characteristic) with the prediction made about the behavior or process based on theory about the construct before the measurement occurred | Predict that scores on a questionnaire measuring sexual desire will correlate with the frequency of sexual behavior, then compare scores with the number of times individuals engage in sexual behavior to see if a correlation exists |

However, the issue is actually more complicated when measuring behavioral and psychological aspects of individuals. Such attributes are not only less visible, less tangible, and therefore less objective; they are also profoundly more complex and sophisticated than physical characteristics such as heart rate and body weight. Many behaviors and psychological processes are thought to result from higher-level organizing functions within the emotional and intellectual constitution of the individual. These organizing functions are conceived as relating in meaningful ways to the needs, goals, and intentions important to an individual. However, the implication of this is that a single overt behavior or reaction may have a multitude of meanings and may represent a range of motives or goals. The variety of meanings associated with any given overt behavior may be different for different individuals, or a variety of meanings may even exist within the individual, meaning different things at different times for him or her.

An example of the potential for variation in meaning is that sexual arousal may occur for some individuals only with the person with whom they are strongly in love; such individuals may be unlikely to become sexually aroused by overtures from a casual acquaintance or a complete stranger. Simple sensual physical contact with just any person is not sufficient to produce arousal for these individuals. Therefore, intimate caresses and touching of the genitals have different meaning for such individuals in a situation representing love and caring than they do in a situation not characterized as strongly by love. The meaning of the overt behavior, touching genitals, is not necessarily explicit or obvious to an outside observer or a scientist collecting information about genital touching.

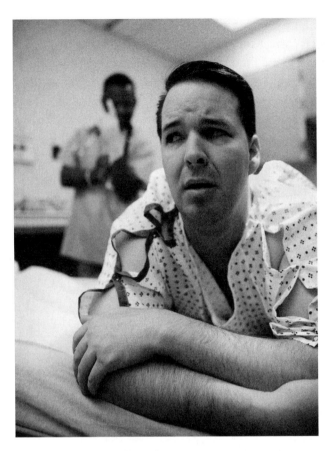

*Do you think that this man will find it sexually arousing to be touched on his buttocks in this setting? Do you think he might be more likely to be sexually aroused by a sexual partner touching and caressing his buttocks in another setting?*

These issues once again demonstrate the importance of having a well-developed **theory** available in advance of collecting empirical data. A theory relating genital arousal, sexual arousal, sexual interest, emotional reactions, and sexual motivation would provide a means of interpreting the data once they are obtained. The supreme importance of theory in validity within measurement was formalized with the publication of standards for validity in 1955 (Cronbach & Meehl, 1955). The standards were a product of the work of a blue-ribbon panel of experts in methodology and measurement appointed by the American Psychological Association. The field that is concerned with measurement of psychological processes is called **psychometrics**. According to these classic standards, all measurement must be cast within the perspective that specific behaviors are indicators of constructs. A **construct** (pronounced CON struct) is a theory created specifically to understand human traits or characteristics; typically, the theory concerns the higher-level organizing functions that traits serve in influencing behavior.

As discussed in chapter 1, the validity of a theory is tested by proposing hypotheses based on the theory that predict behavior in a very precise, concrete way, and then collecting empirical data on the behavior. If the predictions for behavior are supported by the data, the hypotheses are confirmed and support is provided for the theory. This is exactly the same principle underlying **construct validation**. Construct validation is the process of collecting empirical data (measurement) to test the correctness of a proposed construct. Constructs permit the prediction of the behavior measured; therefore, the results of measurement provide support for the accuracy of the construct if they are consistent with what the construct proposes about the behavior. This is summarized in Table 4.4, along with convergent validity.

According to Cronbach and Meehl (1955), evidence can be provided for constructs such as sexual interest by measuring objective expressions or correlates of the subjective experience. Based on a proposed construct of sexual interest, both the experience of sexual arousal and the enlargement of the clitoris or erection of the penis *may* result from, and indicate, sexual interest; however, such physical responses do not necessarily always indicate sexual interest. Erections occur spontaneously under certain conditions, such as during the sleep cycle or because of fluctuations in hormones. Stimulation of the body through caressing or touching may also produce arousal, sometimes without conscious desire to become aroused. Because physical arousal is therefore an imperfect indicator of sexual interest, other behaviors or processes must also be measured.

Construct validation therefore proceeds by measuring as many different correlates as possible that are proposed within the construct (e.g., sexual interest). Other correlates of sexual interest might be time spent looking directly into another person's eyes, physical proximity maintained with the other person, frequency and duration of touching, body posture, suggestive verbal statements made to the other person, and self-reports of being sexually interested in the other person. Another method frequently used to provide support for measures of constructs of higher-level personality characteristics is to administer various self-report questionnaires that are all purported to measure a given construct, such as sexual motivation (Hill & Preston, 1996) or similar constructs. If the measures of the various aspects of the construct are fairly highly correlated with one another, this provides validation for each of the measures as a good indicator of the construct. Moreover, the high correlations of the measures with one another additionally lends further credence to the construct as it is conceptualized. The bottom line for the validity of measurement is verifying that the characteristic a researcher intends to measure is in fact really being measured.

*What behaviors do you think are good indicators of sexual interest? Would you have thought of these behaviors as prime examples? Do you think it would be important to look for other behaviors as well?*

## Methods of Collecting Data

In presenting the four types of data available to scientists, specific methods of data collection were occasionally discussed as well. Typically, certain types of data are more strongly associated with one method than with others. For example, Self data are often obtained through questionnaires and interviews; however, very commonly, Self data are also obtained in experiments (e.g., asking participants to evaluate their feelings on the rating "How sexually aroused are you at this moment?" after being exposed to an erotic video or another type of video). Likewise, Behavioral data are frequently obtained in questionnaires (e.g., "How often did you discuss sexual issues in the last 24 hours?"), despite the fact that Behavioral data have been traditionally associated with experiments (e.g., observing interactions in a laboratory to determine the way in which individuals discuss sexual topics when provided with the opportunity).

### The Reasons for Different Types of Methods

Different methods of collecting data exist in science because each method presents a different set of advantages and disadvantages. The goals of the researcher for a particular research project will determine which type of method the researcher chooses for that project. The two major dimensions along which the four methods vary are *control* and *generalizability*. **Control** is the ability of the researcher to monitor and influence all of the factors that might affect behavior in the study; the ability to account for a wide range of factors increases the confidence of the researcher that he or she has identified the causes of behavior. **Generalizability** is the extent to which the results of the study can be confidently generalized, or extended, to behavior occurring

| TABLE 4.5 | Types of Empirical Studies | |
|---|---|---|
| **Type of Study** | **Procedure Involved** | **Reason for Use** |
| Case method | Obtain information in great detail from a small number of individuals who have a feature in common; analyze using logic and possibly clinical intuition | Allows the study of relatively rare behaviors, events, or conditions that are not easily examined with other methods; useful for the formulation of hypotheses |
| Observational method | Observe and record behavior as it is occurring | Provides B data, which are more objective than S data or I data |
| Survey method | Present a series of questions, or a series of statements, that are rated for the extent to which they describe an individual | Permits the approximate testing of hypotheses by measuring both the proposed causes and affected behaviors; allows assessment of internal, subjective experiences of the individual |
| Experimental method | Present a proposed cause of behavior to one group of individuals but not another group to determine whether the behavior occurs for the group receiving the proposed cause; control all other possible influences on behavior | Permits a very strong test of hypotheses that allows more confident conclusions about causality by directly varying the presence of the proposed cause |

beyond the study. In everyday terms, generalizability refers to the degree to which the results of the study are relevant to real behavior occurring in the real world across all types of people. A study that is conducted in a more real-world, natural setting is often referred to as a **naturalistic study**; naturalistic studies increase some aspects of generalizability, depending on exactly what is done in the study, because the setting is more similar to situations in which "real" behavior usually occurs.

The scientific methods are presented below in order of increasing control, and therefore increasing confidence in the conclusions that may be drawn about the factors affecting behavior. Generalizability is not related to the order of presentation, given that control is not necessarily related to generalizability. Instead, each method can vary in the extent to which the specific research project is generalizable. The four types of empirical studies are summarized in Table 4.5.

## The Case Method

The *case method* is also called the case study or case history method. The procedure involves examining individuals in great detail who have some behavior, characteristic, or experience in common that is relevant to a particular psychological issue of interest. Often, the case method is used to study relatively rare events, such as those related to psychological disorders, physical diseases, traumatic events, or accidents. Fairly small proportions of the general population are likely to be affected by any particular condition or event of this nature. That is, far fewer than 50% of a population tend to experience a particular psychological disorder, such as fetishism (sexual interest in an inanimate object, including clothing or shoes, or parts of the human body, such as feet or hair, to the exclusion of sexual interest in anything else). Another example of a relatively rare condition is dyspareunia (pronounced DIS pah REE nee ah), the experience of pain during penile–vaginal intercourse that interferes on a regular basis with sexual functioning (American Psychiatric Association, 1994).

Because of the relative infrequency of such conditions, a fairly small pool of individuals are available on whom to conduct research. Moreover, individuals with disorders may not seek treatment all that often, preventing them from being identified to participate in research. In fact, because of the negative associations with unusual behavior, particularly involving sexuality, many individuals may even be motivated to conceal their behavior. Those who have engaged in behavior that is illegal, such as rape or violence against sexual minorities, will be even less likely to acknowledge their behavior.

Case studies may involve only one or two individuals in the overall study, and seldom are 10 or more cases presented in a publication. However, small sample sizes can produce results that are fairly low in reliability; this means that similar results may not be obtained if the study were conducted again with another group of individuals. Consequently, virtually all scientists discount studies based on small numbers of individuals as not very useful for making broad statements about human behavior in general. This is also because the results of the case method are essentially intuitive analyses of the causes of behavior—that is, they are largely descriptive, rather than focused on objectively testing a hypothesis on the basis of standard statistical analyses. Case method studies are therefore rarely published in most scientific psychology journals. Historically, the case method has been used within the medical field and within clinical psychology because of their focus on disease and disorder.

After collecting extensive information about the individuals under investigation, a researcher attempts to develop an understanding of factors contributing to behavior by using **logic**, and in some cases **clinical intuition**. However, scientists are most likely to use the case method as a preliminary strategy for **developing hypotheses** in an under-studied area before calling on other methods to test the hypotheses.

## Advantages of the Case Method

The greatest advantage of the case method is that it allows researchers to examine topics that would otherwise not be addressed at all, or that would not be examined well by the other methods. Given the very low numbers of potential participants available related to a disorder, the responses of the few people participating in the study cannot be meaningfully evaluated with formal statistical analyses. Consequently, the structured, formal response format of the survey method or the experiment would provide virtually no usable information. In addition, the case method may be extremely valuable, even for scientists, in that it permits the development of hypotheses in a previously unexplored area.

## Disadvantages

The major problem with the case method is virtually complete **lack of control**. This results in not being able to have confidence in the actual cause–effect relationships proposed in the case analysis. That is, it cannot be determined with any real certainty that the events occurring earlier in life that are identified by the researcher as important really are major causes of the later behavior of interest. The analysis is actually entirely the **subjective opinion** of the researcher, because other factors that he or she did not notice may in fact be the cause of the behavior. The proposed causes of the behavior are not measured directly or manipulated (varied) by the researcher to observe their effect on behavior, as occurs in the experimental method. Beyond this, the relationship between the proposed cause and effect is not even analyzed statistically to verify the reliability or the size of the relationship.

**Box 4.2   Case Study of a Woman With Severe Anxiety About Her Sexual Anatomy**

I am a 43-year-old female, married 22 years to a wonderful man. However, due to personal insecurities with regard to my sexual anatomy, I have always been an extremely backward and shy person sexually, not ever being able to fully open up to my spouse or other lovers because of embarrassment.

Ever since I was old enough to compare and realize differences between other girls/women, I have been mortified, realizing that for some unknown reason, I had been born with a larger than average clitoris. Due to extreme embarrassment, I never asked questions, and my mother never offered explanations or comfort. (I would assume that she was never educated about this.)

In my mid-20s during an exam with a new female gynecologist, I was made a spectacle of. The doctor, upon seeing my clitoris and vulva, literally went running from the room, gathering all the other nurses and even the receptionist to "come and see this!" I live in a very small community and know most all the women who worked in that office, who now are aware of my previously well-kept "secret." Talk about embarrassing!

The doctor asked me dozens of questions, and continued telling me she had never seen or heard of "such a thing." . . . Anyway, by the time I was able to gather my belongings and my composure and leave the office, I was feeling as if I should be running off to join a circus! Unfortunately, this doctor's actions have created a much larger problem for me. As a result of her actions, I have never gone back to her or any other doctor for the necessary pelvic exams and tests that I should be getting for my usual health care . . . .

After this "doctor's appointment from hell," I continued my life, now more self-conscious than ever before—(nearly 20 years now). I so very much wanted answers to my questions; actually, now, I HAD to know—how much of a freak am I, why am I this way, what causes such a freak of nature, etc., but I had no idea who to turn to in order to find my answers. Who could I confide in?

At the risk of being embarrassed again, I decided I would have to find these answers myself. However, all I was able to find was confusing medical terms, clinical studies, stories of horribly disfigured people, some of whom were nothing more than guinea pigs for medical studies and experiments. I was not willing to take a chance on becoming involved like this for my answers—but I just didn't know where I fit into all of this. Was I the freak I felt I was? Were there "others" out in the world like me? How ashamed must my parents be . . . . (Women's Sexual Experiences, On-line forum, retrieved July 22, 2006, from The-clitoris.com. Reprinted with permission of The-clitoris.com.)

*Note.* This woman needlessly suffered a psychological trauma during her examination by a physician. The doctor should have protected her dignity and privacy, as well as being sensitive to her need for answers and comfort. In fact, it is possible that this woman has a clitoris that is within the typical range of size for women in general, although at the larger end of the range. Moreover, even if she has a larger-than-typical clitoris, this should not affect her ability to experience physical pleasure during stimulation. The difficulty lies in perceptions people develop about what is "normal" and the pressure that is placed on individuals to conform to such standards of normality.

What kinds of psychologically important information do you think that scientists and clinicians would obtain from a case study such as this?

Just as problematic is the likelihood of **sampling bias**. Because an *extremely* small number of people are evaluated in the case method, the possibility that the individuals who happen to have been included in the study are different from other people who also display the attribute is very great. At best, the similarity, or **representativeness**, of the study participants to all other individuals exhibiting the behavior or condition is unknown and unverifiable. This type of limitation means that the conclusions based on the case method run the risk of low generalizability, or little applicability to other individuals in the world.

## The Observational Method

A second method of data collection is *observation*. This method involves the researcher being present during the performance of behavior and recording information about it directly. On the other hand, the researcher may not actually be present physically in exactly the same location as the individuals performing the behavior; rather, the behavior may be recorded on videotape or measured with recording devices, such as medical equipment that monitors physiological activities. An example of an observational study is presented in Box 4.3.

---

**Box 4.3**                                    **An Eye Toward Research**

### An Observational Study Focusing on Women With Dyspareunia

An example of an observational study is that by Wouda and colleagues (1998), which involved the collection of both B data and S data. The purpose of the study was to examine differences in sexual reaction for women who suffer from dyspareunia compared with those who do not suffer from the problem. Dyspareunia is the experience of pain during penile–vaginal intercourse that interferes on a regular basis with sexual functioning.

Eighteen women at a hospital sexology outpatient clinic were identified as experiencing dyspareunia and 16 women who did not experience dyspareunia were recruited through a newspaper advertisement to participate in the study. Each woman was shown a series of videos portraying sexual activity while seated alone in a comfortable chair; the sequence of events used in the study was (a) the presentation of a video of individuals engaged in cunnilingus and fellatio, (b) followed by a rest period in which no video was shown, and then (c) videos of cunnilingus were shown, followed by (d) videos of penile–vaginal intercourse.

Sexual reaction was measured by a vaginal plethysmograph, a tampon containing sensors that is inserted in the vagina, during the presentation of the videos. The sensors detect the level of blood flow in the vaginal walls, or vasocongestion, which is a measure of genital arousal. Women also responded to several questionnaires about the extent to which they felt sexually aroused while watching the videos. This study is not an experiment, because the researcher did not treat any of the women differently from any of the other women. In an experiment, participants are assigned randomly to at least two different groups; the two groups of individuals are then exposed to different conditions to determine if the different experiences affect their behavior. Actually, the study is not purely observational either, because the researchers presented a series of stimuli to the women, although again the stimuli were the same for all women.

*(Continued)*

(Continued)

The results of the study were that women prone to dyspareunia generally experienced the same level of vasocongestion throughout the various video presentations as the women who did not experience dyspareunia. This suggests that the problem for the women who are prone to dyspareunia is not inability to experience genital arousal at all, or lack of responsiveness to sexual stimulation. However, the women prone to dyspareunia experienced a decline in vasocongestion while watching the clip of penile–vaginal intercourse, compared with the clips of oral–genital sex; in contrast, the women not prone to dyspareunia experienced *greater* vasocongestion during the video of penile–vaginal intercourse. Interestingly, the two groups of women subjectively reported equivalent levels of sexual arousal, even in the segment portraying penile–vaginal intercourse.

The authors concluded that the experience of dyspareunia results from a nonconscious decrease in vasocongestion associated only with penile–vaginal intercourse; vasocongestion, the accumulation of blood in the vaginal walls, is responsible for the release of fluid into the vagina, which provides the majority of natural lubrication. A hypothesis can be drawn from these results that such women may experience pain during the time when the penis is inserted in the vagina because of a decline in vaginal lubrication; the decrease in lubrication would result in greater friction against the tissues of the vagina, producing the pain. This explanation must be considered a relatively untested hypothesis because vasocongestion was not measured during actual penile–vaginal intercourse for the women in the study.

The study by Wouda and colleagues points to an important function that observational studies may serve in the study of human sexuality. Similar to the case method, observational studies provide evidence that **suggests explanations** and assists in the **development of hypotheses** in studies in which the sexual behavior of concern is not observed directly, as is the case in the Wouda study (Wouda et al., 1998). In studies in which sexual behavior is observed directly (e.g., women engaging in actual penile–vaginal intercourse), the results, of course, can provide evidence for or against a proposed hypothesis. However, very few observational studies of sexual behavior involving two individuals have actually been conducted after the Masters and Johnson research (Masters & Johnson, 1966). Concerns about the ethics, and possibly the propriety, of observing actual sexual behavior may limit this type of research. An even more important reason, however, is most likely that many psychologists are interested in far more complex issues of human sexuality, and issues more theoretically important within psychology, than simply what the body does during sexual behavior.

### References

Masters, W. H., & Johnson, V. E. (1966). *Human sexual response.* Boston: Little, Brown.
Wouda, J. C., Hartman, P. M., Bakker, R. M., Bakker, J. O., van de Wiel, H. B. M., & Weijmar Schultz, W. C. M. (1998). Vaginal plethysmography in women with dyspareunia. *The Journal of Sex Research, 35,* 141–147.

This method provides largely the type of data discussed earlier called Behavioral data, or B data. In fact, the primary purpose of an observational study is to take advantage of the particular strengths of B data; important strengths are greater **objectivity** and the **avoidance of distortion** that may be associated with Self data or Informant data. Nonetheless, self-report data may actually be obtained as well during an observational study to provide convergent validity information for the B data or to provide insight into unobservable emotional and cognitive experiences.

Two important distinctions in types of observational studies may be made in terms of (a) the **setting** in which the study takes place and (b) the extent to which the observation is **known** to the individuals being observed. With regard to setting, a study may be conducted in the controlled setting of the **laboratory**, or it may be conducted in a **naturalistic setting**, in situations that occur in real life.

## Advantages

One of the most significant advantages of the observational method is that it provides **Behavioral data**, which are more objective than Self or Informant data; that is, the data are more objective in the sense that the accuracy of the measurement can be more easily verified. An important advantage of conducting an observational study in a laboratory setting is the great **control** provided by the ability to limit the number of factors that might influence behavior. On the other side of the issue, the researcher can also control factors that *are* present for participants. Control is virtually nonexistent in an observational study conducted in a naturalistic setting, as in the case of the Bartell study (1971) on group sex and swinging. Bartell did not control who was involved in the sexual encounters (other than those he chose to become involved with himself) or exactly what other factors or activities were occurring in the environment at the time.

*Do you think that observation of romantic and sexual behaviors in real-life settings would always, or even frequently, provide the most accurate information? What might be some problems with this technique?*

## Disadvantages

Disadvantages are usually the other side of the advantages provided by a method, and one of the most significant advantages is that observational studies provide objective Behavioral data. The disadvantage is that only observable, overt behavior may be collected in this technique; important emotional and cognitive activities cannot be directly measured. This means that the motivation and intention underlying behavior, its purpose, can only be inferred, without accompanying self-report data. Consequently, a great deal of **inference** and **interpretation** of the meaning of the behavior is required, leaving room for the potential for a degree of error.

The disadvantage of the control afforded by conducting the study in a laboratory setting is the danger that the environment is not at all similar to that existing in individuals' everyday lives. In addition, the behavior observed may be very different from that in which the individual typically engages. Even in the case where sexual behavior is observed, as in the Masters and Johnson research, little can be said about the causes of sexual behavior in naturalistic settings; participants engage in the behavior because they were requested to do so by the researcher, not for the reason that they typically engage in sexual behavior in their daily lives. The behavior could be extraordinarily high quality because of the feeling that the researcher needs to obtain "good data," or the behavior could be negatively affected by anxiety about "performing well."

Another significant problem for the observational technique is that it is not possible to draw extremely confident conclusions about the **causes** of the observed behavior. This is because the factors thought to affect behavior are not varied, that is, presented to some participants and not presented to others. Therefore, judgments about the causes of behavior are really no more than intuitive speculation, not based on the process of examining whether a hypothesis is supported by the presence and the absence of the proposed causal factor.

## The Survey Method

A **survey** is the presentation of a series of questions requesting specific information (e.g., "How frequently do you engage in penile–vaginal intercourse?") or the presentation of a series of statements that respondents are asked to evaluate; evaluation of statements, such as "I believe that engaging in sex outside of marriage is acceptable," is what is meant by "making a rating." The most effective survey is designed to test particular hypotheses, with specific items (questions or ratings) targeting both the proposed causes of behavior and the behavior itself.

The response format for the questions or ratings may be **standardized** or **open-ended**. A **standardized format** presents only a limited number of options for responses, such as *never, several times a year, once a month, several times a week, once a day,* and *more than once a day* for the questions about the frequency of penile–vaginal intercourse. A standardized rating dimension that consists of a number of response options such as this, representing intervals of increasing or decreasing magnitude, permits the assignment of values to each response option. For example, the value of one (1) may be assigned to *never,* the value of two (2) may be assigned to *several times a year,* the value of three (3) may be assigned to *once a month,* and so on. This type of rating format is called a **Likert scale**. The assignment of numbers that have identical meaning across all respondents is absolutely essential to being able to conduct statistical analyses. The standardized format therefore provides an efficient, objective, automatic means of assigning values to behaviors and psychological processes. The **open-ended format** allows respondents to provide information by writing it or speaking about it in their own words, without any constraints upon the content or the style in which it is presented.

A survey may be administered in the form of a **self-report questionnaire** or an **interview**. A self-report questionnaire is presented in the form of a printed booklet that respondents read to themselves and then mark their own answers on the booklet or a separate response form. An interview is presented by a trained individual communicating the questions to respondents one at a time and then recording their responses for them. An example of a self-report questionnaire is presented in Box 4.4.

### Advantages

The survey, particularly the self-report questionnaire, is one of the most widely used methods for collecting information about behavior and psychological processes. The self-report questionnaire and the interview, if inquiring about an individual himself or herself, provide Self data. One very practical reason for its extensive use is its relative **ease of administration**. The self-report questionnaire can be administered to a large number of people in a single session, allowing the collection of a great deal of data in a short period of time with relatively little expense.

A second advantage is that the survey almost always is concerned with behaviors that occur in everyday life or situations that are actually part of individuals' lives; this means that the data collected are directly **generalizable** (relevant) to behavior beyond the research situation.

Finally, both the self-report questionnaire and the interview method have been established as highly reliable methods of collecting data, even for socially sensitive behaviors such as risky sexual behaviors (unprotected from pregnancy or disease). One method of establishing reliability is to look at the similarity of measurements obtained at two different times, which is **test–retest reliability**. A study by Durant and Carey (2000) obtained extremely high test–retest results for both a self-report questionnaire and an interview method, at a level indicating that almost exactly the same results were obtained for all

# BOX 4.4 AN OPPORTUNITY FOR SELF-REFLECTION

**Attitudes Toward Lesbians and Gay Men**

Indicate your feelings about lesbians and gay men by selecting a point on the following scale for each statement below. 1 = Strongly disagree, 5 = Neutral-neither agree nor disagree, 9 = Strongly agree.

1.  Lesbians just can't fit into our society.  ⬚1 ⬚2 ⬚3 ⬚4 ⬚5 ⬚6 ⬚7 ⬚8 ⬚9

2.  A woman's homosexuality should *not* be a cause for job discrimination in any situation.  ⬚1 ⬚2 ⬚3 ⬚4 ⬚5 ⬚6 ⬚7 ⬚8 ⬚9

3.  Female homosexuality is detrimental to society because it breaks down the natural divisions between the sexes.  ⬚1 ⬚2 ⬚3 ⬚4 ⬚5 ⬚6 ⬚7 ⬚8 ⬚9

4.  State laws regulating private, consenting lesbian behavior should be loosened.  ⬚1 ⬚2 ⬚3 ⬚4 ⬚5 ⬚6 ⬚7 ⬚8 ⬚9

5.  Female homosexuality is a sin.  ⬚1 ⬚2 ⬚3 ⬚4 ⬚5 ⬚6 ⬚7 ⬚8 ⬚9

6.  The growing number of lesbians indicates a decline in American morals.  ⬚1 ⬚2 ⬚3 ⬚4 ⬚5 ⬚6 ⬚7 ⬚8 ⬚9

7.  Female homosexuality in itself is no problem, but what society makes of it can be a problem.  ⬚1 ⬚2 ⬚3 ⬚4 ⬚5 ⬚6 ⬚7 ⬚8 ⬚9

8.  Female homosexuality is a threat to many of our basic social institutions.  ⬚1 ⬚2 ⬚3 ⬚4 ⬚5 ⬚6 ⬚7 ⬚8 ⬚9

9.  Female homosexuality is an inferior form of sexuality.  ⬚1 ⬚2 ⬚3 ⬚4 ⬚5 ⬚6 ⬚7 ⬚8 ⬚9

10. Lesbians are sick.  ⬚1 ⬚2 ⬚3 ⬚4 ⬚5 ⬚6 ⬚7 ⬚8 ⬚9

11. Male homosexual couples should be allowed to adopt children the same as heterosexual couples.  ⬚1 ⬚2 ⬚3 ⬚4 ⬚5 ⬚6 ⬚7 ⬚8 ⬚9

12. I think male homosexuals are disgusting.  ⬚1 ⬚2 ⬚3 ⬚4 ⬚5 ⬚6 ⬚7 ⬚8 ⬚9

13. Male homosexuals should *not* be allowed to teach school.  ⬚1 ⬚2 ⬚3 ⬚4 ⬚5 ⬚6 ⬚7 ⬚8 ⬚9

14. Male homosexuality is a perversion.  ⬚1 ⬚2 ⬚3 ⬚4 ⬚5 ⬚6 ⬚7 ⬚8 ⬚9

15. Just as in other species, male homosexuality is a natural expression of sexuality in human men.  ⬚1 ⬚2 ⬚3 ⬚4 ⬚5 ⬚6 ⬚7 ⬚8 ⬚9

16. If a man has homosexual feelings, he should do everything he can to overcome them.  ⬚1 ⬚2 ⬚3 ⬚4 ⬚5 ⬚6 ⬚7 ⬚8 ⬚9

17. I would not be too upset if I learned that my son were a homosexual.  ⬚1 ⬚2 ⬚3 ⬚4 ⬚5 ⬚6 ⬚7 ⬚8 ⬚9

18. Homosexual behavior between two men is just plain wrong.  ⬚1 ⬚2 ⬚3 ⬚4 ⬚5 ⬚6 ⬚7 ⬚8 ⬚9

19. The idea of male homosexual marriages seems ridiculous to me.  ⬚1 ⬚2 ⬚3 ⬚4 ⬚5 ⬚6 ⬚7 ⬚8 ⬚9

20. Male homosexuality is merely a different kind of lifestyle that should be condemned.  ⬚1 ⬚2 ⬚3 ⬚4 ⬚5 ⬚6 ⬚7 ⬚8 ⬚9

*(Continued)*

(Continued)

The two scales were developed to measure the attitudes of heterosexual individuals toward lesbians and gay men, rather than the attitudes of nonheterosexual individuals. A different measure might need to be used to measure attitudes of nonheterosexual individuals.

To calculate your score on the scales, for items 2, 4, 7, 11, 15, 17, and 20, use the following conversion: 1 = 9, 2 = 8, 3 = 7, 4 = 6, 5 = 5, 6 = 4, 7 = 3, 8 = 2, and 9 = 1. There are two separate scales. To calculate your score for the Attitudes Toward Lesbians Scale, add together all of the numbers for items 1 through 10. To calculate your score for the Attitudes Toward Gay Men Scale, add together all of the numbers for items 11 through 20. Lower average values indicate *greater* endorsement of the attitude dimension.

You may want to compare your own scores with the average scores obtained in research by Herek. These are presented in the table below separately for women and men:

| Scale | Women | Men |
|-------|-------|-----|
| Attitudes Toward Lesbians | 43.67 | 40.83 |
| Attitudes Toward Gay Men | 51.54 | 57.96 |

From Herek, G. M. (1988). Heterosexuals' attitudes toward lesbians and gay men: Correlates and gender differences. *Journal of Sex Research, 25*, 451–477. Reprinted with permission of the Society for the Scientific Study of Sexuality.

participants on both measurement occasions. This finding replicated that obtained in another similar study (Kalichman, Kelly, & Stevenson, 1997). Results obtained using both methods to collect retrospective accounts of the frequency of sexual behavior over a 2-month period were also checked for accuracy. This was accomplished by comparing the results for both methods with reports of sexual behavior by the same participants obtained from a diary they kept over the same period. The diary was considered to be the "true" indication of the amount of sexual behavior, because participants recorded instances of sexual behavior each day that they happened.

The discrepancy between interview self-reports and diaries was found to be significantly greater in the interview method than the questionnaire method for some types of behavior. However, both the self-report questionnaire and the interview method prove to be fairly accurate techniques for collecting information about sexual behavior.

### Disadvantages

The primary disadvantage of the survey method is the relative inability to establish **causality**, that is, that the proposed causes of behavior actually are the causes. In the survey method, hypothesized causes are measured by the respondents reporting information about them, such as the level of anxiety felt before engaging in penile–vaginal intercourse. Even if a correlation is found between anxiety and pain during intercourse for women, it is not possible to state with complete certainty that anxiety *causes* pain. This is because the anxiety could have developed *after* repeated experiences with pain during intercourse. Unless the survey is administered over time, and anxiety is measured prior to penile–vaginal intercourse, it is not possible to determine the direction of influence: whether anxiety causes pain, or pain causes anxiety, or they equally influence one another. A survey based on large numbers of respondents and based on specific hypotheses from a strong theory, however, will be able to provide information about the direction of causality with some degree of confidence; this is especially true if anxiety and pain are measured over time during the period when the pain begins to occur.

Particular problems may be associated with the interview method in comparison to the self-report method. **Discomfort**, whether conscious or nonconscious, in revealing intimate and sensitive information may be intensified by the interview method. An interviewer sitting in the presence of respondents, or even talking to them over a telephone, may resemble a situation of admitting or confessing some aspect of oneself that respondents feel may be judged negatively (Alexander & Fisher, 2003). The skill and training of the particular interviewer very likely is important in diminishing such problems. With telephone interviews, an additional concern of the researcher must be the nature of the social environment for the respondent during the interview, meaning whether others are present in the room with the respondent. A person may be less likely to provide accurate responses to questions with others in the room. A problem specific to the self-report questionnaire method is that a researcher is not able to monitor the nature of responding to detect possible confusion or uncertainty by participants. In an interview, the researcher is able to clarify questions and ratings, as well as to address ambiguous responses and prevent or minimize nonresponding by participants.

## The Experimental Method

An *experiment* is a study in which a hypothesized cause of a particular behavior is presented to one group of participants, but is not presented to another group (or, in some cases, presented at different levels). If the factor that is presented is truly a cause of the behavior, those exposed to the factor should engage in the associated behavior; those not exposed to the factor should not engage in the behavior (or engage in significantly lower levels of it). The presentation of the causal factor to one group, but not the other, is called **manipulation** of the causal factor; that is, the level of the causal factor is varied, or changed, for the two research groups. For example, the effect of viewing erotic movies on attitudes toward women may be examined by showing erotic videos to one group of men, but showing a nonsexual movie to another group of men. The causal factor is exposure to erotic movies, and exposure is manipulated by either showing erotic movies or showing another type of movie. Both groups would then respond to a questionnaire measuring attitudes toward women.

Another set of terms is traditionally applied to the two aspects of the experiment as well. The proposed causal factor as presented in the experiment is called the **independent variable**, whereas the behavior that is hypothesized to be affected by the causal factor is called the **dependent variable**. This is because the occurrence of the behavior *depends* upon the presence of the causal factor, the independent variable. The independent variable is independent of, or not controlled by, the participants in the study; it is instead manipulated by the researcher. In the study on the effects of viewing erotic movies, the independent variable is exposure to erotic movies. The dependent behavior is attitudes toward women.

Manipulation of the causal factor creates what are called different **conditions**; the conditions are created by setting up different experiences for different groups of participants. Furthermore, the two types of conditions are given specific names. The condition in which one group of participants is exposed to the proposed causal factor is called the **experimental condition**, whereas the condition in which the group is not exposed to the causal factor is called the **control condition**. The control condition provides a type of control for unforeseen influences on behavior, either due to simply being in the study or due to characteristics of participants that they bring with them into the study. If simply being in the experiment affects behavior, then the effect should be the same for people in both the experimental and control condition.

The control group therefore provides a comparison for the experimental group; this permits the research to show that the behavior of participants in the experimental group is different from that of the control group above and beyond the incidental factors affecting the control group. The behavior of the control group can be seen as "normal," or baseline, behavior, unaffected by the causal factor being examined. Furthermore, the control group accounts for the influences of characteristics that individuals possess prior to participating in the experiment, such as age, family history, education, or—more importantly—attitudes and traits relevant to sexuality. With **random assignment** of individuals to the two conditions, people are placed in either the control group or the experimental group simply by chance. Consequently, equal numbers of people with all types of characteristics will be in both conditions. Differences in such characteristics will not exist across the two conditions, and therefore cannot account for differences in behavior for the two groups. Any difference in behavior between the two groups obtained in the study therefore can only logically be attributed to the experimental manipulation.

A second important aspect of an experiment is **standardization** of all aspects of the environment. As discussed with respect to surveys, standardization means that every aspect of the procedure is exactly the same for all participants. Beyond this, **the environment** in which the study is conducted must also be identical for all participants as well, for both the survey and the experiment: the same general setting or room, the same type of researcher, the same type of people in the setting, as well as standardization of any other aspect of the environment that could possibly influence behavior in a significant way. By making all aspects of the study identical, nothing else can affect behavior, other than the factor that is manipulated or varied by the experimenter. Therefore, if behavior is found to be different for the two conditions, the only valid explanation is that participants were exposed to the different levels of the causal factor (e.g., an erotic video versus no erotic video).

Finally, **measurement** is another means of establishing control in experiments. The behavior of interest (the dependent variable) of course must be measured. However, it is also possible to measure other aspects of the experience that might be related to the behavior and therefore create doubt that the hypothesized causal factor actually accounts for differences between the two research groups. For example, if the researcher were actually concerned that sexual attitudes might not be the same for the two research groups, a self-report measure of sexual attitudes could also be administered as part of the experiment. Sexual attitude scores might then be examined to determine whether they were equal between the two groups. Information itself is a source of control in research.

### Advantages

The major advantage of the experiment is **the extreme level of control** provided by this type of study. Tremendous control results from (a) the manipulation of the causal factor, the independent variable; (b) the standardization of all other aspects of the environment; (c) random assignment of participants to the research conditions; and (d) systematic measurement of behavior (the dependent variable) and other factors that might inadvertently also affect behavior. **Standardization** eliminates all extraneous environmental factors as causes of the behavior, **random assignment** eliminates individual characteristics as causes, and **measurement** of inadvertent factors allows verification that they are not different for the two research conditions. By eliminating all other explanations for differences in behavior between participants in the two research conditions, the only plausible remaining explanation is the presence or absence of the **causal factor**. The experiment therefore is the type of study that provides the strongest and clearest evidence regarding cause and effect—that is, the causes of behavior.

### Disadvantages

The major danger associated with the experiment is that the steps taken to establish the extreme level of control may **diminish the relevance of the findings** for behavior occurring in **everyday life**. The environment created for the experiment may be **highly artificial**, particularly if the experiment is conducted in a laboratory setting as most experiments are. Because of the artificial nature of the environment, the behavior exhibited during the experiment may not correspond to that which is typically exhibited in daily life. For example, in a study on gender differences in reporting about past sexual behavior (Alexander & Fisher, 2003), pressure to conform to societal gender-role expectations was reduced in one condition by leading participants to believe that they were being monitored by a lie-detector machine. The situation of reporting behavior under conditions in which others are able to tell perfectly whether the answers are truthful or not is so unusual that it may not reveal anything valid about naturalistic behavior. Surveys and the case method are much less susceptible to this problem because they inquire about events that *have* happened in respondents' lives; therefore, the conditions and behaviors are by definition relevant to real-world experiences.

A related problem of the experimental method is that it is simply not possible to study some cause and behavior relationships experimentally (Funder, 2004). This is an especially relevant limitation regarding sexuality, because many sexual behaviors may not be easily observed, which of course therefore is also a problem for the observational method. Observation of sexual behavior occurring between spouses or romantic partners in the setting of their own homes is typically not feasible, and presents some degree of ethical problems.

## *Ethics and Scientific Research With Humans*

What ethical problems might be involved in observing the sexual behavior of couples in their own homes? Would there be any ethical problems with observing the sexual behavior of couples in a laboratory setting? Scientists in fact are greatly concerned about the ethics of conducting empirical research, and have developed an extensive set of standards to assure that studies respect the rights and dignity of individuals who participate in them.

As stated in chapter 2, the term, *ethics*, is defined as a set of beliefs about the types of behavior that are considered good, appropriate, and beneficial, as well as the types of behavior that are considered bad, inappropriate, and destructive. A formal set of ethical principles have been advanced by the American Psychological Association (APA; 1992) governing the conduct of research on humans. A fundamental mission of the APA is that of enhancing the well-being and dignity of all human beings. Consequently, researchers must evaluate every aspect of their procedures to ensure that they do not undermine this basic value; they are also required to weigh the benefits to humankind and to individual participants that will result from the research against the negative outcomes or risks. A formal risk analysis is actually required to be submitted to a committee of scientists at each university or agency; the committee is charged with overseeing the ethics of all research conducted at that institution. The committee evaluates whether research proposals are in compliance, not only with APA ethical guidelines, but also with federal regulations on research with humans.

One of the most basic elements involved in human well-being and dignity is the freedom to make informed choices about all aspects of our lives. This ethical principle requires that individuals who participate in research are given adequate, accurate information about the study before they make the decision to participate or to refuse. This principle is called **informed consent**, and requires that potential participants are given enough of a truthful description about the procedure and any aspect that may entail more risk than they typically encounter in their daily lives.

Usually, surveys that protect the anonymity of participants so that their responses cannot be linked to their identity are considered minimal risk. Studies that involve the video recording of participants are considered to involve greater risk because their participation is not anonymous; this procedure requires taking steps to keep information confidential, such as locking materials in secured areas and then destroying them after the study has ended. The decision to participate should also not involve any element of **coercion**, meaning attempts to intimidate, aggressively persuade, or embarrass individuals into taking part in the study.

Some techniques present severe challenges to the ethical treatment of humans within psychological research. This is because they require the violation of the principle of informed consent or because they involve some element of physical risk. Studies may violate the principle of informed consent by the purposeful use of **deception**, or misleading participants about the actual nature of the research. Deception may be necessary for several reasons. Researchers typically do not inform participants about the exact nature of their hypotheses because of the very real, well-documented tendency of people to be influenced by this knowledge. Unintentionally, participants may be biased in the direction of the researcher's expectations, a phenomenon known as **experimental demand**. Scientific research would never provide an accurate picture of behavior if participants were always told exactly what the guiding hypotheses of studies are. In not revealing the exact purpose of the study, the issue is more of a matter of omission, or not providing complete information; however, individuals are still provided with a description of what the specific activities are that they will be asked to perform, in advance of making a decision about whether to participate.

Of even greater concern are studies in which participants are purposely given information that is inaccurate. The justification for this is to create an environment that more realistically resembles real-world situations and experiences. For example, participants might be told, as in a study by Alexander and Fisher (2003), that they are being monitored by a lie-detector machine, which does not actually occur; this deception is used in an attempt to increase the accuracy of self-reports about past sexual behavior. APA principles, however, state that deception is *never* justified if the deception is related to information that would affect the decision of individuals about whether they want to participate. Such issues involve the actual level of risk to which participants will be exposed during the study, whether physical or emotional.

The standard method for attempting to reduce the magnitude of the ethical violation resulting from deception is to provide a completely truthful explanation to participants of everything that actually occurred in the study when the research session is completed. This process is called **debriefing**, and may include discussion of the feelings participants have about being deceived. The purpose is to try to show consideration for participants as individuals, to assure them that virtually all participants believe the deception and that it is not a sign of exceptional gullibility, and to reaffirm the dignity of the participants.

Some prominent scientists, such as David Funder (2004), are not convinced that the ethical problems of deception are adequately reduced by such strategies, or by arguments that justify the necessity of deception. However, other scientists point out that the vast majority of participants experience little distress and have little problem with having been deceived after a sensitive, respectful debriefing (Epley & Huff, 1998; Kimmel, 1998). The ultimate concern of psychologists is that researchers do not harm participants and, as much as possible, contribute to their well-being.

## *Summary*

The overarching philosophy that guides scientific research involves three basic principles: restriction to testable issues, systematic empiricism, and evaluation by peers. Four different types of data are collected in scientific research: Self (S) data, Informant (I) data, Behavioral (B) data, and Life (L) data. The main advantage of S data and I data is that they can provide unique information about private thoughts and emotions directly relevant to motivations. Their disadvantage has to do with verifiability and accuracy, especially for S data. The advantage of B data is that they may be verified for accuracy by comparing them with observations from other raters or measuring instruments. The critical disadvantage of B data is that they must be restricted to explicitly overt events, and exclude internal, subjective experiences such as thoughts and emotions.

The different types of data therefore in a sense compensate for the disadvantages of other types of data. L data are rarely used in research on human sexuality because the theoretical meaning of such data (e.g., number of children, arrests for domestic disturbances) is often not extremely obvious.

The accuracy of data collected is evaluated along two major dimensions: reliability and validity. Reliability is the degree to which measurement is accurate as indicated by how closely an initial measurement is matched by additional measurements. Validity is the extent to which a rating or instrument measures what it is intended to measure. Theoretical proposals guiding the use of specific measures greatly strengthen confidence in conclusions when the obtained results are consistent with the theory.

*(Continued)*

*(Continued)*

Specific methods of collecting data are the case method, the observational method, the survey method, and the experimental method. The case method involves an in-depth examination of a small number of individuals who exhibit a behavior or condition of interest. The case method affords the least amount of control of all of the research methods, and its degree of generalizability is often difficult to establish because of the extremely small number of respondents involved.

The observational method is the recording of specific overt behavior and related events directly by the researcher, rather than relying on self-reports by participants or informants. This method offers a good deal more control than the case method, because the researcher is present when behavior and events occur, recording them directly. Generalizability in observational research is determined by whether the participants are aware of the observation (overt observation) or not aware (covert observation), as well as whether observation takes place in an artificial laboratory setting or in a naturally occurring (naturalistic) setting.

The survey method is the presentation of a series of questions or ratings that request specific information about behavior and events of interest. The survey provides a substantial degree of control in that the information obtained is determined by the researcher in constructing the questions and ratings, as well as by standardization of the procedure.

The experimental method is a strategy of creating different environments for different study participants with regard to the presence or absence of a factor proposed to cause a specific behavior. Creating at least two different environments is called manipulation. The experiment offers the greatest degree of control of any of the research methods, because the researcher creates or determines all relevant aspects of the environment that might influence behavior. The researcher also controls the exact means through which information is collected about behavior as it is occurring in the study.

Scientists must be concerned about ethical considerations in conducting research. Studies must be approved by a committee that oversees the ethics of scientific research. Basic ethical principles involve providing informed consent to potential participants, avoiding coercing individuals to participate, and debriefing participants when the study is completed.

## Chapter 4 Critical Thinking Exercises

1. Collecting information
   a. Refer to the section of the chapter "The Philosophy of Scientific Investigation," which discusses restriction to testable issues. Think of several sexuality issues that *can* be tested scientifically.
   b. Select one of the issues you proposed above. What type of study would you conduct to collect information about the issue? That is, would you conduct a case study, an observational study, a survey, or an experiment? What specific procedures would you use in your study?

2. Ethical concerns

   What ethical problems can you think of on your own that might be associated with the study you propose to conduct?

**Visit www.sagepub.com/hillhsstudy.com for online activities, sample tests, and other helpful resources. Select "Chapter 4: The Scientific Study of Sexuality" for chapter-specific activities.**

# Chapter 5

## THE PERSON
### *Individuality and Sexuality*

## *The Personal Meaning of Sexuality*

**B**y now you have probably gotten the idea that psychologists are passionately invested in using objective methods to collect information about human behavior and psychological functioning. But what does such an extreme emphasis on scientific objectivity mean for the study of the private, subjective experiences of individuals? Does it mean that psychologists are not interested in the personal feelings and thoughts of individuals?

Actually, the answer was basically *yes,* at least in practice, for Alfred Kinsey and his colleagues. You might remember the Kinsey group was the team of early sexuality researchers who pioneered large-scale scientific research in the United States. Their survey focused almost exclusively on the types of sexual behaviors in which individuals engaged. Hardly any attention was devoted to beliefs or feelings about sexuality because they wanted their research to be as objective as possible.

Their lack of faith in the accuracy of subjective experience is captured in a statement about individuals' understanding of their own sexual arousal:

> The subject's awareness of the situation is summed up in his statement that he is "emotionally aroused"; but the . . . [relevant] sources of the emotional disturbances are rarely recognized, either by laymen or by scientists, both of whom are inclined to think in terms of passion, a sexual impulse, a natural drive, or a libido which partakes of the mystic more than it does of solid anatomy and physiologic function. (Kinsey, Pomeroy, & Martin, 1948, p. 158; word in bracket added)

In other words, people's understanding of their own sexual arousal does not accurately reflect the underlying process that is taking place; instead, their understanding is mythical and fantasy-like.

Despite the skepticism of early sexuality researchers, many theorists within psychology today see individuals' personal perceptions and emotions as of the utmost importance. Such experiences are thought to be major, if not the most important, influences on behavior. The personal feelings an individual experiences are thought to lead the person to choose to react and behave in one way or another.

To illustrate the importance of the meaning applied to events, consider the situation in which one student hurries to catch another student as they are walking out after class. The first person compliments the other one for insightful comments she made during the class discussion that day. After a while, the first student asks if they can get together to study for the next exam. If the student being asked understands the proposal as genuinely based on the desire to do well on the next exam, she may respond differently than if she believes that the student is romantically and sexually attracted to her.

Moreover, personality psychologists propose that the characteristics and attitudes the individual possesses strongly influences her understanding of the other person's intentions and her reactions to such intentions. Characteristics such as her own attraction, or lack of attraction, for the other person, her need for sexual gratification, her attitudes toward sexuality, her self-esteem, her need for emotional intimacy, and her religious beliefs, just to name a few, are all likely to determine how she reacts to the situation. In fact, all of these factors will be important to whether the person who was invited to study with the other student even perceives the proposal as relevant to attraction and sexuality. (As a matter of fact, your own personal characteristics probably determine your understanding of both individuals in the example, including whether the student inviting the other one to study is male or female.)

*What do you think each of these individuals is thinking and feeling about their interaction? Are they interested in one another as mere acquaintances, someone to study with, or are they sexually attracted to one another?*

One theoretical perspective on the role that personality plays in behavior is the **dispositional perspective**, which emphasizes the traits and needs of individuals. Needs heighten individuals' attentiveness to aspects of the environment that may satisfy those needs, and influence their understanding of the environment, as well as the meaning they attach to their experiences with the environment. So, if the person invited to study with the other student is strongly interested in sexual pleasure and expression herself, she may be more likely to pick up on cues that indicate sexual interest and willingness than if she has very little motivation for sexual expression.

A second theoretical view of personality is the **social cognitive learning perspective**. This view focuses on the way that individuals interpret information from the environment. Expectations are thought to develop from previous experiences with sexual situations, such as whether the person believes that positive or negative outcomes will result from a specific sexual encounter. Such expectations are thought to affect how one responds to any given situation. For example, whether the student asked to study with the other student will react favorably or unfavorably may depend on whether she believes that the other person is making an overture toward her. Differences among individuals are thought to result from the interpretations and judgments that each individual makes based on the information available to them.

A third perspective is the **phenomenological view**, which in fact epitomizes the emphasis on individual interpretation. According to this perspective, a person's interpretation of events that happen in life plays a central role in how he or she reacts to those events; the word, *phenomenon,* means "an event or happening," and *phenomenology* is the study of individuals' understanding of the events that happen to them. All phenomenological theorists are concerned with the way in which individuals perceive themselves and the events of their lives; it is proposed that their understanding of the events will relate to the choices they make about the types of behavior in which they will engage. Many of these theorists propose that individuals who are aware of their own feelings and needs will choose to engage in behavior that meets those needs.

Consider the person again who was asked to study together with the other student in her class. Her perception of romantic or sexual interest in her by the other person will depend on the kinds of understanding she has developed of the world. An individual's perceptions are organized meaningfully into mental concepts called *constructs* (pronounced CON structs) by some phenomenological theorists. Beyond this, however, the person's choice of whether to become romantically or sexually involved with her fellow student will be related to her awareness of her own needs and values. The extent to which the resulting outcomes—becoming involved, or avoidance of involvement—fulfill her needs and provide happiness will also depend on her awareness of her needs.

One final theoretical view is the **psychoanalytic perspective**, which also emphasizes the importance of the meaning of events and behaviors. However, psychoanalytic theories propose that meaning exists largely at an unconscious level, such that individuals are not aware of the content of the meaning; nonetheless, all behavior reflects deeply seated needs of the individual. The meaning of behavior is symbolic of these needs, rather than a direct expression of them; this is because unconscious personality processes disguise the meaning of behavior to protect the individual from the unacceptable primitive needs the behavior represents. From this perspective, the person invited to study with the other student will react to the other student based on psychological conflicts and unfulfilled needs that have developed during early childhood experiences. Because the person's characteristics are symbolically meaningful of her conflicts and needs, according to this view, she will either be attracted or not depending on the unconscious feelings sparked by the other student. As with the three other perspectives, at a very fundamental level, the interpretation and meaning of specific situations by each individual determines whether the situation is even relevant to sexuality; beyond this, the individual's own personal understanding of the situation is thought to produce the type of specific behaviors that will occur in the situation.

An individual's personal understanding of his or her life seems to be essential to the way that each person behaves. Personality theorists agree. This view is precisely the concern of personality theories, which are among the oldest and most influential traditions in psychology. The nature of individuality and its relationship to sexuality is the focus of this chapter. Formal personality theory gives us a valuable understanding of the private experiences occurring within the person.

## *The Personality Psychology of Sexuality*

As defined in chapter 1, **personality** refers to the patterns of affect, cognition, and behavior that *characterize* individuals across a number of situations and across time. **Personality psychology** is the scientific study of the individual and is concerned with processes occurring within the individual that cause him or her to behave in relatively consistent ways. The notion of behaving in consistent ways recognizes that people have typical ways of interacting with others and going about their daily lives. Consistency is thought of within a number of personality theories in terms of the concept of traits or attributes that develop gradually over time. However, not all theories agree with the notion of long-developing, enduring characteristics that produce consistency in behavior. In fact, the reason that the different theoretical perspectives exist at all is because of fundamental differences in their assumptions and in the concepts they call on to understand individuality.

## Personality Theories

Four or five major theoretical perspectives are often thought to represent the range of different views of personality. These theories focus on reasons that individuals are different from one another in their personality in general. However, several of them have looked at the ways in which personality and sexuality affect one another as well. Two of the traditional positions will be presented in the current chapter: **dispositional** or **trait theory** and **behavioral–cognitive** or **learning theory**. Two other perspectives that were discussed briefly above, **psychoanalytic theory** and **phenomenological** or **humanistic theory**, are also major traditional theories within personality psychology.

However, psychoanalytic theorists historically have not seen the scientific method as capable of providing valid information about what they consider to be important: the unconscious processes they propose are fundamentally involved in personality development. For this reason, they have not attempted to collect empirical evidence in general nor for their proposals related to sexuality in particular. On the other hand, phenomenological approaches have engaged in very little formal theorizing that has translated into scientific research. As a result, much less empirical research has been conducted to test proposals within these theories, compared with the other two approaches. Moreover, hardly any research specifically focused on sexuality has been generated within phenomenological theories. Because of the absence of scientific evidence for these two perspectives, they will not be discussed further in the chapter. Although a fifth perspective is often included among most contemporary discussions of personality theory, this additional approach, the biological position, will be covered in extensive detail in chapter 12.

## The Dispositional Approach

The theoretical perspective that has had one of the largest impacts on research in personality in current times is the *dispositional*, or *trait*, *approach*. A major reason is that the objective measurement of traits is at the very heart of concerns within dispositional theories. Therefore, dispositional theories demand the collection of data to support the theorizing about traits (Funder, 2004).

The terms **disposition** and **trait** refer to the same concept, and therefore are used interchangeably. A disposition or trait is a characteristic of individuals that creates a tendency to behave in specific ways under conditions relevant to the characteristic; because of this tendency to behave in predictable ways, individuals display a regular, consistent pattern of the behavior over extended periods of time. Traits are often characterized as **emotional**, **cognitive**, and **motivational tendencies** that affect important behavior, such as seeking out particular experiences that individuals find enjoyable and behaving in specific ways when interacting with others.

The dispositional approach to personality may be thought of in terms of four fundamental principles (Carver & Scheier, 2000). These principles are summarized in Table 5.1.

| TABLE 5.1 | Fundamental Principles of the Dispositional Approach |
|-----------|------------------------------------------------------|

|  | **Principle** | **Example** |
|---|---|---|
| First principle | A trait produces regularity in behaviors and psychological processes by causing individuals to perceive stimuli and situations in similar ways (relevant to the trait) | An individual with a strong trait of sexual motivation perceives many stimuli as relevant to sexuality; an individual with a less strong trait perceives fewer stimuli as relevant to sexuality |
| Second principle | A trait influences behavior in most situations relevant to that trait. | An individual with a strong trait of sexual motivation becomes very intensely aroused in sexually suggestive situations, but not in sexually irrelevant situations. |
| Third principle | Individuals differ from one another in the level of a particular trait they possess, and therefore engage in different levels of behavior influenced by the trait. | An individual with a strong trait of sexual motivation engages in sexual behavior on a regular basis; an individual with a less strong trait engages in sexual behavior less frequently |
| Fourth principle | Traits are relatively stable and enduring | Individuals possess the same level of sexual motivation relative to other people over a relatively extended period of their lives. |

## The Effect of Traits on Psychological Processes and Behavior

*At one point in my life, I experienced a period when my masturbation had definitely become too much. I had a girlfriend I really didn't like but I was too shy to tell her the truth about my feelings regarding our relationship. I preferred masturbation to real sex at all times. . . . I found that I could masturbate from five to ten times a day if I really tried. . . . When I got past my teenage years, my sex drive was more controllable. However, my libido became more powerful in such a way that it made me realize that masturbation would probably be something that was going to be part of my overall life. I have come to accept that it's simply something that feels like one of the ultimate intimate forms of personal expression. It's probably the only thing in this world that feels good and also won't kill you if you do it too much.* (Male Masturbation Reality, 2006)

**The first fundamental principle** of the trait perspective is that **traits produce regularity** in behaviors and psychological processes (Carver & Scheier, 2000; see Figure 5.1). A founding theorist of the trait approach, Gordon Allport (1937), accounted for this consistency in his definition of the concept of trait, "a . . . neuropsychic system . . . with the capacity to render many stimuli functionally equivalent, and to initiate and guide consistent (equivalent) forms of . . . behavior" (p. 295). By neuropsychic, Allport was referring to the view that traits are both neural (based in neurons in the nervous system) and psychological (meaning that they involve subjective, mental activities and influence behavior). The part of the definition

**FIGURE 5.1**    The First Principle of the Dispositional Approach

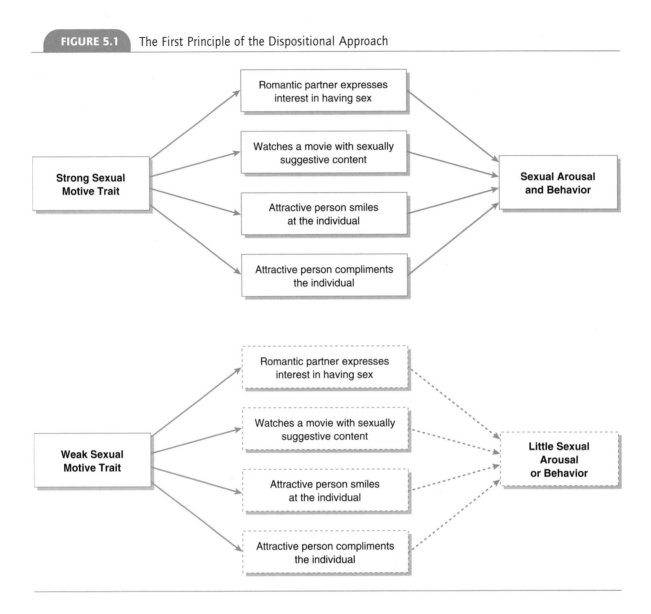

"render many stimuli functionally equivalent" refers to the exact psychological process through which traits are thought to produce behavior. Allport meant that a trait acts like a lens or filter; information from the environment may be thought of as passing through the filter as it enters the nervous system and is acted upon by various psychological processes (e.g., memory and consciousness).

That is, a trait leads individuals to interpret a variety of stimuli and situations in a very similar way, specifically as relevant to that particular trait. For example, the trait of dominance causes individuals to interpret many different social situations as relevant to behaving in a dominant way. An individual understands a range of information in a particular way because of the type of "filter" that he or she possesses.

An individual who is characteristically very interested in sex is more likely to see a wide range of situations as sexually suggestive than someone who is not so typically interested in sex. Even situations of merely working together with another person on a school project may be perceived as nearly as relevant to sexuality as a situation involving touching and caressing.

To others, the different bits of incoming information may seem unrelated or loosely related; however, they may all have a common type of meaning for the individual possessing a strong trait because of the filtering influence of the trait.

For individuals who have a strong trait that is relevant to sexuality (e.g., the person has a strong sex drive), much incoming information is likely to be perceived as having a sexual tone to it. Therefore, statements, compliments, facial expressions, gestures, and actions of others are much more likely to be interpreted as sexually suggestive or indicating attraction, no matter the actual intent of the person. For other individuals who do not have as strong of a sexual trait, the behavior of others will be less likely to be viewed as sexually suggestive or relevant.

The importance of such perceptions is that they are assumed to influence behavior; all sorts of different stimuli function to initiate the same behavior (e.g., engaging in a particular sexual behavior), and so the trait makes the stimuli all functionally equivalent. Because individuals with the strong sexual trait typically see the actions of others as having sexual overtones or signaling sexual interest, they often behave in sexually relevant ways in those situations. Those with a trait that is not as strong will be less likely to respond sexually. In other words, the concept of trait was called upon by Allport to *explain* why behavior occurs (Allport, 1937). The position of many trait theorists in recent times therefore is that traits *cause* behavior.

**The second fundamental principle** of the trait approach is that dispositions influence behavior in **most situations relevant** to the particular disposition (Figure 5.2). Someone with a strong sex drive, a type of trait, will tend to view smiles, compliments, and friendly gestures of others in a wider range of settings as relevant to sexuality compared with someone without such a strong sex drive. The trait leads many different stimuli to be linked to the trait, and therefore to lead to trait-related behavior more often in a number of different settings. Examples of trait-related behaviors might include becoming sexually interested or aroused, or seeking closer contact with someone who is seen as exhibiting sexually enticing behaviors. However, situations that are not perceived as relevant to sexuality will not lead to sexual behavior, even for

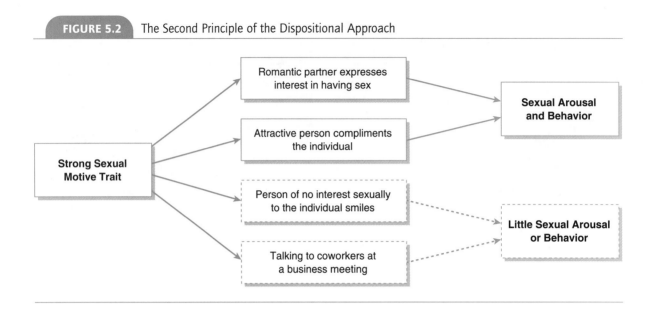

FIGURE 5.2    The Second Principle of the Dispositional Approach

a person with a strong sex drive. Those with a trait that is not quite as strong are not as likely to engage in the trait-related behavior in many situations; they can be said to react in a consistently nonsexual way.

The influence of traits across all relevant situations is the reason for the behavioral consistency focused on in the first principle of the trait approach. The various stimuli a person experiences, such as different people in different settings, are defined as **situations** within psychology. Therefore, the consistency in behavior across a variety of different situations is called **cross-situational consistency**. The second principle of the trait approach is therefore captured within the term, *cross-situational consistency*.

**The third fundamental principle** of the trait perspective is that **individuals differ** from one another in the amount of particular behaviors they typically display (such as behaviors relevant to sexuality). The reason for the behavioral differences is because of differences in the strength of traits that different individuals possess (Figure 5.3). The variation among people produced by the disposition is referred to as **individual differences**. Different individuals are expected to exhibit different levels of trait-related behavior on an ongoing basis (Carver & Scheier, 2000; Funder, 2004). This may mean that some individuals characteristically engage in a particular sexual behavior very frequently, others engage in that same sexual behavior with moderate frequency, and yet others engage in the sexual behavior relatively infrequently or not at all.

The concept of individual differences is used by trait theorists to provide an understanding of the reason for the individuality and uniqueness of humans. The distinctiveness of each person, that is, his or her unique personality, is thought to be produced by the pattern of traits on which he or she is strong and others on which he or she is not strong. In other words, one individual may have very strong tendencies on Trait 1, a low level of Trait 2, and a moderate level of Trait 3; a second individual may possess high levels of all three traits; and yet a third individual may have low levels of Trait 1 and Trait 2, but high levels of Trait 3. It is this variation across individuals that produces individual differences in overall personality and ultimately the uniqueness of each person (Allport, 1937).

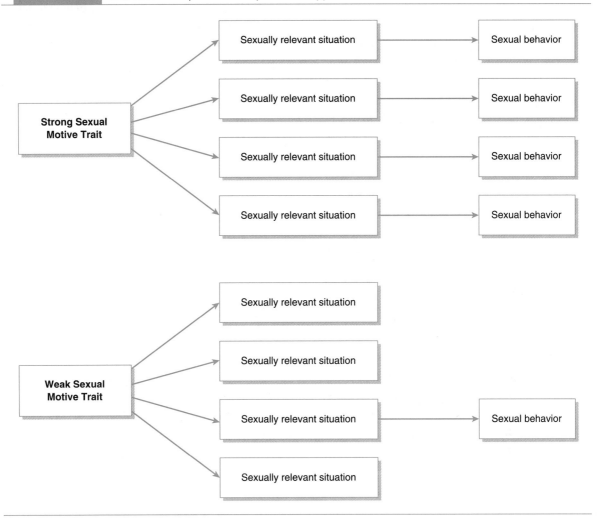

**FIGURE 5.3**    The Third Principle of the Dispositional Approach

*Now in my seventies, I have masturbated ever since I can remember. . . . I married at 19 to a man three years older and he had no problem with the fact that I masturbated regularly. Before we were married we had confessed to one another that we masturbated. If anything, he encouraged me to continue the practice and we often masturbated together. For my 21st birthday he presented me with my first vibrator. It was a very noisy thing but I could really orgasm quickly with it. He would kneel beside me and masturbate watching me. Then we would have sex. . . . Over the years, each of my birthdays brought another "toy" for me and I now have a very extensive collection which I use. He is gone now, but I still enjoy myself on a regular basis. (Women's Sexual Experiences, Online forum, retrieved July 22, 2006, from The-clitoris.com. Reprinted with permission of The-clitoris.com.)*

**A fourth and final fundamental principle** of the trait approach is that dispositions are **relatively stable and enduring** (Carver & Scheier, 2000; Funder, 2004). Traits are proposed to affect behavior across extended periods of individuals' lives, if not throughout their entire lives. This means that the patterns of consistent behavior produced by trait levels will be apparent across the years, creating themes in individuals' lives that become part of the person's reputation. For example, an individual may view himself or herself as a generally very friendly person, or a very meticulous and perfectionistic person, or a very prudish person. A fairly impressive body of research, some of which spans decades of tracking individuals, provides substantial evidence that a number of general traits remain highly constant for individuals across the life span (Block, 1971; Caspi, 1987; Funder & Block, 1989; McCrae & Costa, 1984).

## Identification of Important Psychological Traits

Up to this point, the concept of traits has been presented in a general way, with only brief reference to specific traits. Allport did not talk about the importance of specific traits, nor did he conduct research to identify important ones. His main concern was establishing theoretical guidelines for understanding the notion of traits. Overall, he was more concerned with examining the uniqueness of each individual through analyzing traits that he thought are not common across all individuals. However, other theorists have proposed various groups of traits based on a number of different ways of thinking about them. Funder (2004) has classified these views of traits into four approaches; only the two approaches that focus on the importance of specific traits are presented: the **essential-trait approach** and the **single-trait approach**.

Many trait theorists have attempted to develop a simple, very basic understanding of the organization of personality rather than talking about tens, if not hundreds, of specific traits. The perspective of such theorists has been that traits are expressed in a variety of tendencies and behaviors. Consequently, it may be more meaningful to identify the common themes underlying the huge range of tendencies in order to boil them down into a smaller number of more global traits. Such is the logic of **the essential trait approach** (Funder, 2004). This is one of the most widely agreed upon perspectives and has inspired massive programs of research and theory development.

Within the last several decades, substantial agreement has been reached among trait researchers that **five traits** provide a powerfully accurate understanding of personality. This consensus among researchers is based on the **factor analysis** by various investigators (e.g., Goldberg, 2001; McCrae & Costa, 1987) of considerable numbers of trait questionnaires designed to measure a wide range of dispositional tendencies (McCrae, 1989; for an explanation of factor analysis, see the Big Picture supplement). Because the factor structure with five factors has been repeated numerous times across many studies, the conclusion has gained great credibility and is currently the most prominent perspective on the number of essential traits. The view is called the **Five Factor Model**, or simply **The Big Five**.

The five traits that have been identified are **neuroticism**, **extraversion**, **openness to experience**, **agreeableness**, and **conscientiousness** (see Figure 5.4). **Neuroticism** is a name borrowed from the earlier personality approach of psychoanalytic theory that was described previously; this is the reason the name does not sound intuitively meaningful to those outside of personality theory, as most of the other trait names do. Other names that have been used for this trait are **emotional instability** and **negative affectivity** (negative emotionality), although Watson and Clark (1984) argue that neuroticism is somewhat of a broader concept than negative affectivity. Individuals with high levels of neuroticism tend to experience negative emotions such as feeling anxious, worrying, and nervousness on a regular basis and in reaction to many events. Consequently, they often report feeling insecure, self-conscious, and unhappy, and having emotional and physical problems.

*Why do you think these two couples are responding so differently to one another? Could differences in personality play a role in their reactions?*

---

**FIGURE 5.4**  The Five Factor Model of Personality Traits

| Trait | Low End of the Dimension | | High End of the Dimension |
|---|---|---|---|
| Neuroticism | Calm, secure, happy | ⟷ | Anxious, insecure, unhappy |
| Extraversion | Socially awkward, reserved, low-key | ⟷ | Socially graceful, outgoing, lively |
| Agreeableness | Unconcerned about others, hostile, callous | ⟷ | Interested in others, warm, caring |
| Openness to Experience | Prefers familiarity, unadventurous, traditional | ⟷ | Desires new experiences, curious, creative |
| Conscientiousness | Unreliable, disorganized, unmotivated | ⟷ | Responsible, organized, mastery-oriented |

---

**Extraversion** is the tendency to interact with others in a dominant, outgoing way, and to behave in a socially graceful, self-confident, and comfortable manner; extraversion involves being sociable, friendly, and talkative (McCrae & Costa, 1987). The disposition also includes the tendency to be energetic, lively, and seek stimulation, as well as to be impulsive, or act on a whim (Watson & Clark, 1997). Based on the results of numerous factor analyses, extraversion is an empirically distinct trait from **agreeableness**, another type of interpersonal trait (meaning having to do with the way that people interact with others). Whereas extraversion involves interacting with others in a dominant, forceful, and energetic way, agreeableness involves an interest or motivation in being around others; it also is the tendency to have an intrinsic interest in others for their own sake and in their well-being. It includes such tendencies as being warm, friendly, empathetic, helpful, and caring toward others (Graziano & Eisenberg, 1997). The low, or opposite, end of the dimension is best described in terms of antagonism, hostility, callousness, uncooperativeness, and rudeness (McCrae & Costa, 1987).

**Openness to experience** is a trait that is often difficult for people to understand intuitively when they are first exposed to it. Nonprofessional raters participating in research have been found to possess a fairly different sense of the meaning of "openness." Possibly not surprisingly, therefore, this is the most debated of the five traits in the Five Factor Model. Nonetheless, substantial evidence has accumulated in support of **openness to experience** as a valid and important disposition. Openness is the desire and tendency to seek out a variety of new experiences, to be curious, adventurous, to seek information and understanding for its own sake, to reject that which is traditional and conventional, and to desire creative expression (McCrae & Costa, 1997).

The last remaining trait of the Big Five is **conscientiousness**, which is the tendency to be responsible, dependable, organized, committed to high-quality performance, and committed to moral and ethical standards (McCrae & Costa, 1987). Conscientiousness also involves the ability to adapt effortlessly to authority (Hogan & Ones, 1997).

The value of the Five Factor Model of traits is evident in the vast amount of research demonstrating substantial relationships of the traits to a large group of important, real-life behaviors and outcomes. The five traits have been shown to relate strongly to the well-being of middle-aged adults (Siegler & Brummett, 2000); the ability to cope with a move to a new community (Kling, Ryff, Love, & Essex, 2003); alcohol and marijuana abuse, (Flory, Lynam, Milich, Leukefeld, & Clayton, 2002); the types of emotional reactions individuals experience and their efforts to control emotions (Tobin, Graziano, Vanman, & Tassinary, 2000); the nature of parents' relationship with their 7-month-old infant (Kochanska, Friesenborg, Lange, & Martel, 2004); the amount of support adolescents receive from their families (Branje, van Lieshout, & van Aken, 2004); job satisfaction (Judge, Heller, & Mount, 2002); and leadership ability (Judge, Bono, Ilies, & Gerhardt, 2002). The five traits have also been shown to correlate with grade point average, whether individuals play a musical instrument, frequency of exercising, popularity, dating variety, number of parties attended per month, alcohol consumption, and tobacco consumption (Paunonen, 2003). The influence of the five global traits spans a wide range of domains in everyday life, as well as having an effect on critical aspects of development and coping with stressful life events.

*How might the trait of neuroticism be involved in this situation?*

## The Relationship of the Five Factor Traits to Sexuality

With respect to sexuality and the Five Factor Model, one of the most intriguing lines of research is a study looking at whether aspects of sexuality are related to the Five Factor traits. Schmitt and Buss (2000) used the

**lexical criterion**, one of at least two methods to identify important traits, to discover characteristics related to sexuality (the lexical hypothesis "predicts that the most important dimensions of individual differences are designated by the trait terms found in languages"; Shafer, 2001, p. 314). The lexical criterion for identifying the existence of traits involves obtaining ratings from people regarding how descriptive a series of trait adjectives are of them; in the case of sexuality, examples of trait adjectives used by Schmitt and Buss (2000) are *sexy, provocative, loving, passionate, lewd,* and *prudish.* This procedure also involves using factor analysis to determine which ratings of the adjectives are more similar to one another than are other adjective ratings, as described in the explanation of factor analysis in The Bigger Picture supplement. The technique results in groups of adjectives that as a set can be interpreted to represent some underlying trait.

The groups, or factors, that resulted from this statistical procedure in the study by Schmitt and Buss were labeled as the traits of **sexual attractiveness** (i.e., sexy, stunning, attractive, alluring), **relationship exclusivity** (i.e., faithful, unfaithful, monogamous, devoted, loose), **gender orientation** (i.e., feminine, masculine, womanly, manly), **sexual restraint** (i.e., virginal, celibate, abstinent, chaste), **erotophilic disposition** (*erotophilic* means *positive feelings about erotic experiences;* i.e., obscene, vulgar, lewd, crude), **emotional investment** (i.e., loving, lovable, cuddlesome, romantic), and **sexual orientation** (i.e., homosexual, bisexual, heterosexual). Schmitt and Buss concluded that these seven traits capture the nature of human variation in tendencies related to sexuality.

Beyond this, Schmitt and Buss (2000) were interested in examining whether the seven sexuality traits represented unique characteristics that were truly different from the more general traits of the Big Five. However, the traits of extraversion and agreeableness were found to be fairly strongly correlated with many of the sexuality traits. Several additional statistical evaluations of the relationship of each sexuality trait to the Big Five traits further revealed a large degree of overlap. Schmitt and Buss concluded on this basis that the sexuality traits are essentially **extensions** of the traits identified within the Five Factor Model; again, the sexuality traits were largely specific versions of the traits of **extraversion** and **agreeableness**. In their own words, "Thus, it is our contention that the seven sexuality factors are best viewed as recarving of general personality variation along sex-specific dimensions" (p. 168). This is further evidence of the universal, comprehensive nature of the Big Five traits in explaining human personality, consistent with the large body of previous research on the Five Factor Model.

One other finding of this research that is worth noting involves gender differences. Differences between men and women were found for the sexuality trait dimensions of **relationship exclusivity** (women having higher scores than men), **emotional investment** (women higher than men), and **erotophilic disposition** (men higher than women). These differences are consistent with previous research showing that men, on average, are more favorable toward having greater variety in sexual partners and lower investment in exclusive relationships.

An issue of great concern for some time now has been factors that contribute to the tendency to engage in risky sexual behavior. Risky sexual behavior is that which places an individual at greater risk for infection with disease or unwanted pregnancy (Hoyle, Fejfar, & Miller, 2000). The reason for the heightened concern about risky sexual behavior is the occurrence of more than 19 million cases of sexually transmitted diseases annually in the United States (Centers for Disease Control and Prevention, 2005), the fact that most infection with the human immunodeficiency virus (HIV) occurs through sexual behavior (Centers for Disease Control and Prevention, 1996), and because nearly half of all pregnancies each year in the United States are unplanned (Henshaw, 1998).

The major objective of one review of research on risky sexual behavior (Hoyle et al., 2000) was to determine the extent to which features of "normal personality," in their words, contribute to the tendency of individuals to put themselves at risk. The bulk of research on the topic was conducted before the Five Factor

*Could it be that there is such a thing as a "party animal" personality?* Research on the Five Factor Model would seem to suggest so.

*What traits do you think might be involved in these types of behavior? What evidence exists for particular traits that are involved in the tendency to take risks?*

Model rose to prominence, such that many of the studies were based on psychobiological models of personality. Such models will be considered in later sections. However, Hoyle and his colleagues located five studies that examined the relationship of the Big Five traits to risky sexual behavior. Risky sexual behavior in these studies included having engaged in sex with more than one partner, engaging in unprotected sex (meaning without a condom), or engaging in sex under particularly risky conditions (i.e., after consuming alcohol or drugs, engaging in casual sex outside of a committed relationship).

The analysis across the five studies revealed that only **agreeableness** and **conscientiousness** were reliably related to risky sexual behavior. Individuals with lower levels of agreeableness (those who tend to be hostile, suspicious, and unfriendly) were more likely to engage in all three types of risky behavior. Hoyle and colleagues concluded that the antagonism and hostility associated with low levels of agreeableness translates into a lack of concern for others, which may be involved in willingness to place others at risk. Given that the findings are based on only a few studies, they caution that further research is needed to understand more fully what actually accounts for this relationship. A lower level of conscientiousness (tending to be undependable, not motivated to achieve standards of excellence, and not committed to standards of ethics) was related to a greater likelihood of engaging in unprotected sex. Hoyle and colleagues noted that this finding is consistent with the tendency of low-conscientiousness individuals to fail to plan ahead in general; in particular, such individuals tended to be unprepared for sexual behavior because they did not make sure condoms were available.

In a study on Big Five correlates of condom use that was conducted after the above review was published, Trobst, Herbst, Masters, and Costa (2002) commented that very little previous research has focused on personality variables and condom use at all. Most of the studies examined other traits besides the global traits of the Five Factor Model, and have found little or no relationship with condom use. In a large study of disadvantaged African Americans living in the U.S. South, Trobst and her colleagues looked at the pattern of a number of risky sexual behaviors and sexually transmitted diseases. The risky behaviors included receiving anal sex, sex with a partner who shoots drugs, sex with a partner with AIDS, receiving or giving money or drugs for sex, and sex without condoms. People in the study were classified into three groups on the basis of their reports of risky behavior and condom use: low risk, medium risk, and high risk.

Three traits were found to be associated with risk level: neuroticism, agreeableness, and conscientiousness. In contrast to other research, thrill-seeking traits were not related to risky behavior. The pattern of correlations indicated that "at-risk individuals are anxious, are easily overwhelmed, have difficulties coping, and may engage in risky behaviors to obtain gratification more as temporary relief from their suffering than to increase their arousal levels" (Trobst et al., 2002, p. 128). These conclusions were based on the relationship found for higher neuroticism and lower conscientiousness with risky behavior.

The association of lower agreeableness with risky sexual behavior indicates that lack of sensitivity to others also plays into such behavior, a point also made by Hoyle and his colleagues in the previous review of research. Neuroticism was found to be related to risky behavior in the study of disadvantaged individuals by Trobst and her colleagues, but neuroticism was not identified as a major factor in the review by Hoyle. The difference between the two may be explained by the level of suffering and hardship experienced by the disadvantaged African Americans. It may be that severe stress and anxiety cause those high in neuroticism (anxiety) to react to the negative conditions in risky ways; under conditions of less stress, the way that one responds to stress, which is relevant to the trait of neuroticism, may have little to do with the tendency to act in impulsive, risky ways.

In research on risky behavior among young, predominantly White adults (Miller et al., 2004), however, neuroticism was not associated with risky behavior. Again, low agreeableness was most consistently correlated with high-risk sexual behaviors. As with the previous studies, Miller and his colleagues hypothesized that lack of concern for others, and manipulative, deceitful tendencies lead those low in agreeableness to be unconcerned about the potentially negative effects of the risky sexual behaviors.

## The Eysenck Three-Factor Essential Trait Approach

Hans Eysenck proposed a theory simpler than the Five Factor Model even before the early researchers proposed the Big Five. Eysenck's theory is simpler because it maintains that only three traits are necessary to account for human personality (Eysenck, 1947). Two of the traits have the same names as corresponding traits in the Five Factor Model, specifically **neuroticism** and **extraversion**. The third trait in Eysenck's theory is **psychoticism**, which has been shown to be a dimension that is essentially a combination of the Five Factor Model's **agreeableness** and **conscientiousness** traits, but in the reverse direction (those low in agreeableness and low in conscientiousness tend to be high in psychoticism; Goldberg & Rosolack, 1994).

Goldberg and Rosolack (1994) in fact argue that the psychoticism dimension needs to be separated into the two different traits, for a variety of empirical and statistical reasons. Psychoticism involves the tendency to be hostile, callous, and aggressive, but it also includes an element of impulsiveness and lack of control. Yet, Eysenck's theory has inspired an entire program of research by a large variety of researchers over approximately four decades, providing substantial support for its usefulness. In fact, his theoretical position was the basis for the creation of a scientific journal itself, *Personality and Individual Differences*.

Importantly, Eysenck and his followers have been extremely interested in the relationship between personality and sexuality. Very early on, Eysenck developed a measure of sexual attitudes to explore his hypotheses about the effect of personality on sexual tendencies. Factor analyses of the sexual attitude ratings revealed between 8 and 12 dimensions of attitudes; however, additional analyses demonstrated that it was possible to reduce this number further to two "superfactors," **libido** and **satisfaction** (Eysenck, 1976). Eysenck hypothesized that stronger levels of extraversion relate to more positive attitudes toward sex, a **hedonistic** or **pleasure-oriented view** of sexuality, and greater levels of various kinds of sexual behavior. He also hypothesized that greater neuroticism would be related to more negative attitudes toward sex, sexually inhibited tendencies, and greater levels of sexual problems.

*What type of attitude and what type of trait proposed by Eysenck might this woman possess?*

These hypotheses have received some degree of support, although the evidence is mixed (Barnes, Malamuth, & Check, 1984; Trobst et al., 2002). Interestingly, psychoticism has proven to be reliably related to various aspects of sexuality and sexual behavior across various studies (Trobst et al., 2002), often sexual behavior with potentially negative outcomes. For example, high psychoticism has been shown to relate to unsafe sexual behavior (that which involves the exchange of body fluids) among HIV positive gay or bisexual men (McCown, 1993). This is consistent with the research stemming from the Five Factor Model on the correlates of risky sexual behavior, in which low agreeableness was often shown to relate to greater levels of risky behavior; again, psychoticism has been described as a combination of low agreeableness and low conscientiousness.

## The Single-Trait Approach

In some cases, theorists have concentrated on one trait they view as being exceptionally relevant to topics of particular theoretical or social importance (Funder, 2004). The concern is not about developing as complete an understanding of all aspects of human personality as possible. Rather, the goal is to explore the functioning and role of one particular trait as intensively as possible because it is theorized to have a central role in an area of particular psychological significance.

### Sensation Seeking

One of the most widely studied single-trait personality dimensions with respect to sexual behavior is that of **sensation seeking** (Zuckerman, Eysenck, & Eysenck, 1978). The trait of sensation seeking is the tendency to "seek and engage in activities that provide excitement and risk" (Geen, 1997). It is conceived as consisting of four components: (a) thrill and adventure seeking, (b) experience seeking, (c) disinhibition, and (d) susceptibility to boredom. The Sensation Seeking Scale (Zuckerman et al., 1978) was developed to measure this trait through its four components and is used in a great many studies, particularly for behavior believed to be strongly influenced by physiological factors. Examples of items from the Sensation Seeking Scale are presented in Table 5.2.

**TABLE 5.2**   Sample Items From the Sensation Seeking Scale

| Subscale | Item |
| --- | --- |
| Thrill and adventure seeking | I would like to try parachute jumping. |
| Experience seeking | I have tried marijuana or would like to. |
| Disinhibition | I enjoy watching many of the "sexy" scenes in movies. |
| Boredom susceptibility | When you can predict almost everything a person will do and say, he or she must be a bore. |

In fact, sensation seeking is conceived largely as a trait grounded in the physiological activity of the nervous system. A prominent expert in this area of personality, Russell Geen, has commented that

> Zuckerman's model of the biological basis of sensation-seeking is a good example of an approach that brings together psychometric, behavioral, and biological findings in the service of an evolving theory. For that reason it offers the best explanation for the physiological side of this important personality trait. (1997, p. 403)

Consequently, sensation seeking could as appropriately be covered in the chapter 12 on biological factors involved in the psychology of sexuality as in this chapter; in fact, many theorists do address sensation seeking in chapters on psychophysiological approaches to personality (Geen, 1997). However, the tradition surrounding sensation seeking is one of the most prominent examples of research on *personality traits* related to sexuality; for this reason, it is examined in this chapter. In particular, Geen has noted that the components that have been most frequently examined with respect to physiological functioning have been the **thrill and adventure seeking** and **disinhibition** components.

Research has demonstrated that individuals with high levels of the sensation seeking trait react physiologically to novel stimuli in ways that suggest a more positive response (orienting or attending to it) compared with those low in the trait, who react in ways suggesting that they are startled; these types of responses have been measured in a variety of ways, such as by measuring electrical activity in the skin (electrodermal conductance), heart rate, and brain activity. Although mixed results have actually been obtained, some evidence suggests differences in brain chemicals and neurotransmitter levels for those high versus low in sensation seeking; **neurotransmitters** are chemicals released from cells in the nervous system that allow the transmission of information from one cell to another. The most current thinking on these findings is that high sensation seekers may need higher levels of activity and excitement to compensate for low levels of neurotransmitters and brain activity (Geen, 1997).

Scores on the Sensation Seeking Scale have consistently correlated with both sexual behavior in general and with risky sexual behavior. Heterosexual college students who are high in sensation seeking tend to engage in greater levels of sexual activity, engage in a greater variety of sexual behaviors, and have greater numbers of sexual partners (Zuckerman, Tushup, & Finner, 1976). High sensation-seeking men are more likely to experience greater frequencies of ejaculation, spontaneous erections (those "just happening," not due to masturbation or sexual behavior), and erections due to masturbation (Husted & Edwards, 1976).

Greater levels of sensation seeking have likewise been found to be associated with risky sexual behavior and greater numbers of sexually transmitted diseases (Ripa, Hansen, Mortensen, Sanders, & Reinisch, 2001). Specifically, in several studies, the number of sexual partners in general (Stacy, Newcomb, & Ames, 2000), and the number of sexual partners whom college students had just met were correlated with higher sensation seeking tendencies (Fisher & Misovich, 1990). The sensation seeking trait may lead individuals to engage in risky types of sexual behavior, such as unprotected sex and sex with a variety of partners, because high sensation seekers perceive such risky behaviors to be less dangerous than low sensation seekers (Cohen & Fromme, 2002).

*What trait might these recreational activities have in common?*

Moreover, Kalichman, Heckman, and Kelly (1996) demonstrated that sensation seeking tendencies likely explain the common finding of correlations of drug and alcohol use with risky sexual behavior; the personality scale in this study was a newer measure of sensation seeking, specifically sensation seeking through engaging in sexual behavior. They found that, when controlling for the relationship between sensation seeking and unprotected anal intercourse among gay men, the correlations of drug use and alcohol use with anal intercourse were not significant. This means that drug and alcohol use are associated with risky sexual behavior primarily because high sensation-seeking individuals are more likely to engage in all three types of behavior (drug use, alcohol use, and risky sexual behavior). The finding suggests that drug and alcohol use are not necessarily the primary culprits in dangerous behavior; willingness to engage in risky behaviors in general is the actual issue, because "daredevils" are willing to risk all three types of behaviors.

This finding was replicated for heterosexual men with respect to unprotected sexual behavior and drug use, although alcohol use was in fact not related to frequency of unprotected sex at all (McCoul & Haslam, 2001). Kalichman and his colleagues conclude, "When personality dispositions are accounted for, . . . substance use offered little explanation for sexual risk behavior" (p. 152). This is striking testimony for the importance of personality traits when attempting to understand critical behaviors that affect health and well-being.

### Erotophobia–Erotophilia

*Oral sex with a woman is my favorite of all. I feel a great closeness, a deep intimacy.... I feel that she trusts me fully. I love to look up and see her eyes closed and her face contorted in exquisite agony. (Hite, 2005, p. 86)*

*One weekend my wife sent the kids off to their grandparents' house, and then she told me she had something to tell me. Well, what it was was that she didn't have orgasms the way I thought she did, and that she didn't mean to hurt me, that she had really loved having sex with me all those years, but she just hadn't been honest. I was flabbergasted, I didn't know what to say. We started talking and she told me just how she did orgasm, and then I couldn't believe my eyes, she showed me how she did it. I have never been the same since, I mean for the better. I fell in love with her all over again, or anyway, I got a case of the hots for her that didn't quiet down for about six months. She was much more interested in sex than before.... It was just too much. Bliss. Heaven. I was ready to die. (Hite, 2005, p. 61)*

The term, **erotophobia–erotophilia**, actually describes two extremes of a dispositional dimension; the dimension involves the type of emotional responses individuals have to sex-related issues (White, Fisher, Byrne, & Kingma, 1977). **Erotophobia**, which means revulsion toward erotic stimuli, is the tendency to experience negative emotional reactions (e.g., disgust, discomfort, anxiety) when exposed to sexual situations, information, or images. **Erotophilia**, or a liking for erotic stimuli, is the tendency to experience positive emotional reactions (e.g., pleasure, excitement, enthusiasm) when exposed to sexual situations. Actually, as with all trait dimensions, erotophobia–erotophilia is conceived as a range of positions representing varying degrees of like or dislike for sex-related stimuli. The middle of this range of emotional reactions may be described as neutral or indifferent to erotic stimuli, or neither particularly liking or disliking such stimuli.

The trait was based on a theory dealing with the causes of human sexual behavior, the Sexual Behavior Sequence (Byrne, 1977, 1983a). One factor thought to influence sexual behavior is an individual's tendency to

*How might the trait of erotophobia–erotophilia be involved in these situations?*

respond to sexual cues with typical types of emotions; the term that Byrne used to refer to these typical emotions is *evaluative, attitudinal sets* (because the concept of traits had fallen out of favor in psychology at the time, the concept of *attitudes* was more acceptable; Byrne and his colleagues did refer to the dimension as a "disposition" in a 1988 publication, Fisher, Byrne, White, & Kelley, 1988). The trait of erotophobia–erotophilia was developed by Byrne and his colleagues to measure typical emotional reactions as a component of the Sexual Behavior Sequence. Within the Sexual Behavior Sequence view, emotional reactions to sexual stimuli or situations lead to an evaluation of the stimuli as either negative and undesirable, or positive and desirable. This evaluation is one factor that will influence the nature of the person's response to a stimuli or situation. A self-report questionnaire, the Sexual Opinion Survey, was developed to measure the dimension of erotophobia–erotophilia; this is presented in Box 5.1.

  Scores on the Sexual Opinion Survey are correlated with scores on questionnaires measuring other conceptually related personality traits. Specifically, erotophobia–erotophilia is somewhat correlated with a trait called **authoritarianism** (Adorno, Frenkel-Brunswick, Levison, & Sanford, 1950; Cherry & Byrne, 1977); individuals who are authoritarian are strongly devoted to tradition and maintaining the status quo, they react negatively to behavior that is contrary to accepted standards, and they are intolerant of sexual openness and expression. It makes sense then that authoritarian individuals would be more likely to have negative reactions to sexual stimuli and situations in general; in other words, that they are more erotophobic (Fisher et al., 1988). Erotophobic individuals also score higher on measures of **sex guilt**, a tendency to experience negative feelings about socially unacceptable sexual behavior (Mosher & Cross, 1971) than erotophilic individuals (Fisher et al., 1988).

  What might lead individuals to have more negative or more positive feelings about sexuality as adults? Attitudes of parents and the kinds of messages they give to their children seems like a reasonable possibility. In fact, erotophobia–erotophilia has been found to relate to the nature of the family environment and

# BOX 5.1  AN OPPORTUNITY FOR SELF-REFLECTION

### The Sexual Opinion Survey

Please respond to each item as honestly as you can. There are no right or wrong answers, and your answers will be completely confidential. Use the following scale to indicate your feelings: 1 = I strongly agree and 7 = I strongly disagree.

1. I think it would be very entertaining to look at erotica (e.g., sexually explicit books, movies, etc.).  ① ② ③ ④ ⑤ ⑥ ⑦

2. Erotica (e.g., sexually explicit books, movies, etc.) is obviously filthy and people should not try to describe it as anything else.  ① ② ③ ④ ⑤ ⑥ ⑦

3. Swimming in the nude with a member of the other sex would be an exciting experience.  ① ② ③ ④ ⑤ ⑥ ⑦

4. Masturbation can be an exciting experience.  ① ② ③ ④ ⑤ ⑥ ⑦

5. If I found out that a close friend of mine was a homosexual, it would annoy me.  ① ② ③ ④ ⑤ ⑥ ⑦

6. If people thought I was interested in oral sex, I would be embarrassed.  ① ② ③ ④ ⑤ ⑥ ⑦

7. Engaging in group sex is an entertaining idea.  ① ② ③ ④ ⑤ ⑥ ⑦

8. I personally find that thinking about engaging in sexual intercourse is arousing.  ① ② ③ ④ ⑤ ⑥ ⑦

9. Seeing an erotic (sexually explicit) movie would be sexually arousing to me.  ① ② ③ ④ ⑤ ⑥ ⑦

10. Thoughts that I may have homosexual tendencies would not worry me at all.  ① ② ③ ④ ⑤ ⑥ ⑦

11. The idea of my being physically attracted to members of the same sex is not depressing.  ① ② ③ ④ ⑤ ⑥ ⑦

12. Almost all erotic (sexually explicit) material is nauseating.  ① ② ③ ④ ⑤ ⑥ ⑦

13. It would be emotionally upsetting to me to see someone exposing themselves publicly.  ① ② ③ ④ ⑤ ⑥ ⑦

14. Watching a stripper of the other sex would not be very exciting.  ① ② ③ ④ ⑤ ⑥ ⑦

15. I would not enjoy seeing an erotic (sexually explicit) movie.  ① ② ③ ④ ⑤ ⑥ ⑦

16. When I think about seeing pictures showing someone of the same sex as myself masturbating, it nauseates me.  ① ② ③ ④ ⑤ ⑥ ⑦

17. The thought of engaging in unusual sex practices is highly arousing.  ① ② ③ ④ ⑤ ⑥ ⑦

18. Manipulating my genitals would probably be an arousing experience.  ① ② ③ ④ ⑤ ⑥ ⑦

19. I do not enjoy daydreaming about sexual matters.  ① ② ③ ④ ⑤ ⑥ ⑦

20. I am not curious about erotica (e.g., sexually explicit books, movies, etc.).  ① ② ③ ④ ⑤ ⑥ ⑦

21. The thought of having long-term sexual relations with more than one sex partner is not disgusting to me.  ① ② ③ ④ ⑤ ⑥ ⑦

*(Continued)*

(Continued)

### Scoring the Sexual Opinion Survey

(A) Score responses from 1 = I strongly agree to 7 = I strongly disagree, (B) add scores from items 2, 5, 6, 12, 13, 14, 15, 16, 19, and 20, (C) subtract from this total the sum of items 1, 3, 4, 7, 8, 9, 10, 11, 17, 18, and 21, and (D) add 67 to this quantity. Scores range from 0 (most erotophobic) to 126 (most erotophilic).

You may want to compare your own scores with the average scores obtained in research by Fisher, Byrne, White, and Kelley (1988). These are presented in the table below separately for women and men, averaged across four U.S. and Canadian samples:

| Women | Men |
|---|---|
| 62.24 | 73.30 |

Fisher, W. A., Byrne, D., White, L. A., & Kelley, K. (1988). Erotophobia-erotophilia as a dimension of personality. *The Journal of Sex Research, 25*, 123–151. Reprinted with permission of the Society for the Scientific Study of Sexuality. The wording in some items has been slightly modified.

experiences of individuals during childhood and adolescence. Fisher and his colleagues (1988) described the findings of a retrospective study: "erotophobia is associated with reports of parental strictness about sex, sex-related guilt, fears, inhibitions, and conservative attitudes as well as with avoidance of masturbation, erotica, and (for women, at least) multiple premarital partners" (p. 135). These results were supported by other studies in which erotophobic parents were less likely to give straightforward responses to children's questions about sex (Lemery, 1983) and provide less information about sex to their children (Fisher et al., 1988; Lemery, 1983). Parental erotophobia–erotophilia therefore may influence the development of similar personality tendencies in their children.

Beyond this, erotophobia–erotophilia is linked to the reaction of individuals to their own sexual experiences before the age of 16 years. In one study (Bauserman & Davis, 1996), 61% of early experiences were with peers, who were individuals no more than 3 years different in age at the time. This indicates that most of the early experiences could not have involved molestation or coercion, but were based on sexual curiosity and interest. Those with largely positive feelings about their early experiences had higher scores on erotophilia; this means that they were more erotophilic as adults than individuals with mixed feelings and negative feelings about their early sexual experiences. Those with negative feelings about their early sexual experiences had lower scores than those with mixed feelings; that is, they were more erotophobic as adults.

What about the sexual behavior of adults? Erotophobic women and men have been found to masturbate less frequently (Fisher, Byrne, & White, 1983), have less sexual experience (Fisher, 1984; Semph, 1979), and have fewer sexual partners (Fisher, 1984). Research has even shown that erotophilic individuals believe that merchandise they purchase has helped them to attract sexual partners and to enjoy the experience of sexual behavior, compared with erotophobic individuals. Erotophilic individuals believed that the bed, food, and household decorations and accessories they have chosen have helped them to attract sexual partners. They also felt that their bed, bed furnishings (e.g., sheets), stereo systems, music, food, and sexy clothing all contributed to their enjoyment of sexual behavior much more than erotophobic individuals (Gould, 1995).

The importance of erotophobia–erotophilia is really highlighted in a study looking at sexual satisfaction among a large group of married women. The trait was one of the strongest factors in sexual satisfaction, even when taking into account frequency of sexual behavior, number of orgasms, orgasm consistency, sexual desire, and sexual excitability (Hurlbert, Apt, & Rabehl, 1993). Erotophobia–erotophilia even affects sexuality during pregnancy and in the period after delivery as well. Erotophobic women report less sexual interest, behavior, satisfaction, and experimentation during pregnancy than erotophilic women. Similarly, during the pregnancy of their wives, erotophobic men engage in less frequent masturbation and sexual behavior than erotophilic men; they are also less likely to be present during the delivery of the child. The effect of erotophobia–erotophilia on sexuality is wide-reaching. Erotophobic women delay sexual behavior after the birth of child for a longer period of time, have less interest in sexual behavior, masturbate less frequently, and are less likely to breastfeed their child than erotophilic women (Fisher & Gray, 1988).

Early in the research on erotophobia–erotophilia, erotophobic women were found to use contraception less consistently when they engage in sexual intercourse (Fisher et al., 1979; Kelley, Smeaton, Byrne, Przybyla, & Fisher, 1987). A recent conclusion by leading researchers in the area of personality and contraceptive behavior, Meg Gerrard and Frederick Gibbons (Gerrard, Gibbons, & McCoy, 1993; Smith, Eggleston, Gerrard, & Gibbons, 1996), emphasizes the importance of erotophobia–erotophilia: one of the most consistent findings in research on personality is that the tendency to experience negative emotional reactions regarding issues of sexuality interferes with effective contraception use. As summarized by Smith and colleagues (1996), the negative effects associated with erotophobia include

> a general lack of knowledge about contraception (Fisher, 1980; Gerrard, Kurylo, & Reis, 1991; Goldfarb, Gerrard, Gibbons, & Plante, 1988), discomfort with purchasing birth control devices (Fisher, Fisher, & Byrne, 1977), and . . . the use of ineffective methods of birth control (Fisher et al., 1979; Geis & Gerrard, 1984; Gerrard, 1987). (Smith et al., 1996, p. 88)

Why would negative feelings about sexuality cause problems with using contraception? One reason that has been suggested is that extremely negative emotions interfere with the ability to process information well (Byrne, 1977, 1983b). Support for this explanation comes from a study showing that erotophobic women were less able to recall information presented in scenarios involving sexual moral dilemmas (Lewis, Gibbons, & Gerrard, 1986). The greater discomfort of erotophobic individuals with sexual issues results in poorer analysis of the accuracy of such information, and causes them to become persuaded by illogical or irrelevant factors in making judgments, for example about whether to use condoms or not (Helweg-Larsen & Howell, 2000).

These psychological processes typical of erotophobic individuals led Gerrard and her colleagues to propose the **emotional inhibition hypothesis**. This is the position that negative emotions about sexuality cause lower levels of sexual behavior and contraception; that is, negative feelings about sexual issues inhibit expression of sexuality. Inhibition causes problems when the negative emotions are not strong enough to prevent sexual behavior, yet are strong enough to prevent contraceptive behavior (Gerrard, 1987; Gerrard et al., 1993). Smith and her colleagues (1996) have shown that erotophobic individuals do in fact link sexual concepts more strongly with other negative concepts than erotophilic individuals. Beyond this, erotophobic individuals believe that pregnancy is *less* likely to result from sexual behavior; erotophobic individuals are also less influenced by the negative outcomes thought to result from unplanned pregnancy than are erotophilic individuals. As a whole, these findings indicate that differences in processing information cause erotophobic individuals to believe sexual behavior is less risky than erotophilic individuals, which accounts for the lower rates of using contraception by erotophobic individuals.

Research has also demonstrated that erotophobic individuals react more negatively after viewing various types of erotic material (Kelley, Byrne, Greendlinger, & Murnen, 1997). Erotophobic individuals have been shown to experience greater hostility in a laboratory setting after seeing erotic images in both slides (Kelley, 1985b) and films (Kelley, 1985a). If they were permitted to regulate the amount of time that they looked at explicit erotic slides in a laboratory study, both erotophobic women and men spent less time viewing the slides and made more mistakes in recalling details about the images (Becker & Byrne, 1985). Erotophobic individuals also report that they view erotic materials less frequently in their everyday lives than erotophilic individuals (Fisher, Byrne, & White, 1983).

*Does this type of situation make you uncomfortable?* Your reaction is likely to depend on your standing on the erotophobia–erotophilia dimension.

Such negative reactions to erotic images can even affect health-related behavior. Erotophobic women have been found to examine themselves for breast cancer less frequently and felt less competent when given brochures with pictures of a nude woman demonstrating the technique. In contrast, erotophilic women felt the brochure was more important and that they understood the information better when the nude pictures were present in the brochure (Labranche, Helweg-Larsen, Byrd, & Choquette, 1997). Discomfort with erotic images and situations among erotophobics extends to perceptions of women who breastfeed their infants compared with those who bottlefeed; erotophobic women have even more negative attitudes toward breastfeeding than do erotophobic men (Forbes, Adams-Curtis, Hamm, & White, 2003). The authors of the study comment that these results indicate the extent to which breastfeeding has become sexualized in U.S. society, which accounts for the discomfort of erotophobic individuals with the act.

This body of research demonstrates very convincingly that erotophobia–erotophilia has a substantial influence on many aspects of sexuality. The trait appears to be a highly important and powerful factor in human sexuality.

## Motivational Traits

**Desire** and **wanting** are the central concerns of motivational theories of behavior, which are considered to be the reasons for specific behaviors. Some of the earliest theories in personality psychology, and actually psychology in general, were motivational theories. Emphasizing the central role of motivation in behavior, in fact, has been at the heart of personality psychology over its long tradition and sets it apart: "More than most other fields in the social sciences, personality psychology concerns itself with the internal springs of human action" (McAdams, 1997, p. 6).

One of the greatest early theories focused on motivational traits is that of Henry Murray (1938). According to this view, a **need** is a state within the person involving the lack of something necessary for the person's well-being; the deficiency causes the individual to seek out and obtain resources that will provide what is needed. Activation of a need causes the individual to become sensitive to aspects of the environment that will provide the desired resources or experiences. In other words, a person becomes very aware of, and interested in, opportunities to satisfy the need.

A more recent version of need theory that is specific to sexuality is a **theory of sexual motivation**, which concerns the emotions, cognition, and behavior experienced regarding sexuality (Hill & Preston, 1996). In keeping with traditional personality concepts, **motivation** is defined as increased interest in a particular goal; the desired goal related to sexual motivation is **the experience of satisfaction** through sexual expression and behavior. More specifically, "in operational terms, motivation is the process by which behavior is initiated, energized, maintained, and directed toward a goal (Buck, 1988; Heckhausen, 1991). The process consists of the orientation of cognitive, affective, and motor activities in service of its attainment" (Hill & Preston, 1996, p. 28). Another way of saying this is that, when a person becomes interested in a sexual issue or in sexual expression, his or her thinking, emotions, and behavior all become much more devoted to satisfying that sexual interest. For those who are extremely sexually aroused in a particular situation, that may be the only thing they are able to focus on.

As with the Murray view, environmental factors are thought to play an important part in increasing motivation (Murray gave the name *press* to environmental factors). These environmental factors later came to be known as **incentives**, reflecting the influence of learning theory and behaviorism that dominated psychology in the 1930s, 40s, and 50s. **Incentives** are those aspects of the environment that provide gratification when they are experienced. In the above definition of motivation, the goal that is desired is the incentive. Individuals engage in behavior to obtain the incentives, which when thinking about motivation in general may be tangible or physical resources such as food, water, or money. However, of greater interest in psychology, incentives may also be intangible in nature, such as the experiences that provide gratification of the type Murray discussed—mastering a challenge (an achievement incentive) or having good times with friends (an affiliative incentive). These are more central to human personality than desire for food or water.

In the theory of sexual motivation, eight incentives are proposed to motivate sexual behavior, rather than only one (Hill & Preston, 1996). Previous to this theoretical view, the sole incentive for sexual behavior cited by theorists was the *need for sex*, as proposed by Murray (1938), and an "inborn drive to orgasm" (Masters & Johnson, 1966). Other intuitive proposals for incentives motivating sexual behavior might be a desire to procreate and have children, or to experience physical pleasure. Yet, human beings are often highly complex, such that any given behavior may have a variety of meanings at different times or for different people. Because of this complexity, desire related to sexuality was thought more to involve **social functions** rather than purely biological and physical ones (i.e., orgasm, pleasure, procreation). This complexity was suggested by research that asked individuals about the reasons that they engage in sex, in which they listed a variety of different reasons (Carroll, Volk, & Hyde, 1985; Denney, Field, & Quadagno, 1984; Leigh, 1989).

Therefore, the proposed **eight incentives** spanned a number of reasons for sexual expression:

1. feeling valued by one's partner

2. expressing value for one's partner

3. obtaining relief from stress or negative psychological states

4. providing nurturance to improve a partner's psychological state

5. enhancing feelings of personal power

6. experiencing the power of one's partner

7. experiencing pleasure and physical release

8. procreating

All of these make up a class of incentives that provide the same basic type of gratification related to sexual satisfaction (Atkinson, 1966; Heckhausen, 1991). The concept of **incentive**, like Murray's *press,* concerns environmental factors that motivate behavior. However, unless an individual possesses a personal interest in an incentive, such as an interest in money, the incentive will not motivate behavior to acquire it. For this reason, dispositional **motives** related to sexuality were also thought to be important factors motivating behavior within the theory of sexual motivation (Hill & Preston, 1996). A **dispositional motive** is an enduring interest in a particular type of incentive. Like other motive traits, sexual motives determine the way that individuals will react to incentives available in a situation. Those with a strong motive for a particular sexual incentive, in general, will experience heightened interest in the incentive when it becomes available in a situation; however, those with lower levels of the motive will feel less interest, or no interest, in experiencing the incentive.

Moreover, in keeping with Allport's conception of traits, "dispositional motives also organize perception and emotion around motive-relevant goals, binding together seemingly different behaviors as related to the goals" (Hill & Preston, 1996, p. 28). Therefore, dispositional sexual motives were expected to affect emotional and cognitive reactions to available, relevant incentives. Again, when a person becomes sexually motivated, his or her attention and interests become more strongly devoted to noticing the behavior of others or noticing stimuli that are sexually arousing. This will increase the chances of the person taking direct action to experience the incentives. Finally, differences among people in the strength of these reactions were expected, which is a basic concept involved in the notion of traits.

Because eight different sexual incentives are thought to inspire and heighten sexual interest, the theoretical model proposes the existence of **eight different dispositional sexual motives** that are conceptually and empirically distinct. That is, some individuals will have a strong motive to be valued by their partner through engaging in sexual behavior with them (the **Valued by Partner** sexual motive). Yet, these same individuals may not be interested in one of the other types of sexual incentives, such as expressing one's personal power through sexual behavior (relevant to the **Power** sexual motive). Other individuals may possess a strong motive for **expressing power**, but are not so interested in expressing value and love for a partner through sexual behavior (the **Value for Partner** sexual motive). In other words, individual differences were thought to exist for each of the sexual motives, and differences on one motive dimension were not expected to be highly related to one another. In addition, the sexual motives were considered to be distinct from **sexual desire**, a more generalized experience of sexual interest, similar to the notion of **sex drive**.

Hill and Preston (1996) created a self-report questionnaire, the Affective and Motivational Orientation Related to Erotic Arousal questionnaire (abbreviated AMORE), to measure the proposed dispositional sexual motives. Factor analyses of the ratings of reasons for interest in sex revealed eight factors, or dimensions, suggesting that the reasons fall into eight groups; these eight factors were found again in two additional samples of individuals. The finding of eight groups of reasons for sexual behavior provides support to the theoretical view that eight sexual motives sufficiently account for the occurrence of much sexual behavior.

You might wonder whether women and men are different in terms of their reasons for interest in sex. After all, one of the stereotypes is that men are extremely interested in sex, craving it all of the time, whereas women are less interested; if they do experience any interest, it is thought to be mainly in terms of sharing emotional intimacy and love. Yet differences between men and women on the scale scores created for these eight groups of ratings did not entirely support gender stereotypes. No consistent differences across the three samples of individuals were obtained for interest in sex for reasons of *feeling valued by one's partner, providing nurturance to one's partner, experiencing physical pleasure,* and *procreating.* Women did have higher ratings on the *expressing value for one's partner* dimension, whereas men had higher ratings on the *relief from stress, expressing power,* and *experiencing the power of one's partner* motive dimensions. The desire by men to be dominated by a powerful partner certainly does not fit with traditional expectations for men, nor does the lack of gender differences for sexual motives typically associated with women (feeling valued, nurturing) or with men (physical pleasure).

Men are more likely to express interest in being dominated by a sexual partner than are women. Being the target of sexual forcefulness very likely has different meanings and implications for women.

Do people with greater interest in sexuality actually engage in more sexual behavior than those who express less interest? The sexual motive ratings were correlated with various types of sexual behavior for college students, independently of their ratings of general sexual desire. This means that motive–behavior link went above and beyond any general influence of sex drive. The *Value for Partner, Pleasure,* and *Nurturance* motives were related to greater likelihood of having engaged in sexual behavior in general (i.e., penile–vaginal, oral–genital, or penile–anal intercourse). The *Power* motive was associated with having engaged in penile–vaginal intercourse in the last year; the *Partner Power* motive was related to having engaged in penile–anal intercourse in the last year; and the *Stress Relief* motive was associated with greater frequency of masturbation in the last year, all of these independently of ratings of general sexual desire. Various dispositional sexual motives were likewise correlated with use of different types of contraception or protection techniques, such as use of condoms and the pill.

Other research has demonstrated that the eight dispositional sexual motives are related to ratings of the likelihood of engaging in sexual behavior only in situations specifically relevant to each motive (Hill, 1997). The issue is whether it is any more useful to talk about eight different reasons for engaging in sex, or if instead only one reason—such as general interest or sexual desire—would account for sexual behavior just as well. That is, if ratings for all sexual motives were related to all types of sexual behavior at the same strength, any of the eight motives could explain why the behavior occurred equally well; if this were true, it would not be necessary to deal with eight different motives, but only one. The question is whether it is useful to make so many distinctions among reasons for engaging in sex. One study asked participants to read eight different descriptions of situations and to imagine themselves in each situation as vividly as possible. Each scenario described a situation that was intended to be specifically relevant to only one of the eight motives.

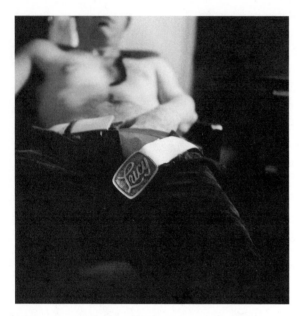

*Why do you think that individuals who have a stronger desire to engage in sex to relieve stress and negative emotions tend to also engage in masturbation more frequently? Why masturbation compared with some other type of sexual behavior?*

For example, one description was of a situation in which a person came to feel immense respect and pride for a romantic partner while talking with him or her; this was intended in advance of conducting the study to be relevant to the motive of wanting to *express value for one's partner*. Another scenario involved an individual coming home from work after a horrible, exhausting day and wanting to unwind and relax; this was intended to be relevant to the motive of *wanting relief from stress*. All eight situations ended by describing events leading up to sexual behavior with the partner. Participants rated the extent to which they would feel aroused, would experience satisfaction, and would want to actually experience such a situation. Ratings on the dispositional sexual motive scales **most relevant to each scenario** were in fact **the most strongly related scale** for that scenario; for example, in the scenario describing feeling great respect and pride for (valuing) the romantic partner, the *Value for Partner* sexual motive scale had the strongest relationship with the scenario ratings.

The exception was the Relief From Stress scenario; in that case, the *Valued by Partner* sexual motive was the most highly correlated with ratings of arousal and satisfaction, although the *Relief From Stress* motive was also significantly correlated. Ratings of the general dimension *Sexual Desire* were independently correlated with only three scenario ratings, but in no case did it have the strongest relationship with the scenario ratings. The dispositional sexual motive scales were, for the most part, uniquely related to feelings about sexuality in the relevant scenario, as predicted within the theoretical model of dispositional sexual motives (Hill, 1997).

A similar set of findings were obtained in another study (Hill, 2002) involving descriptions of scenarios hypothesized to be primarily relevant to only one sexual motive. However, in this study, participants rated the likelihood of engaging in intimate kissing, sexually intimate touching, and having sex. For each scenario, the logically most relevant sexual motive scale was significantly related to combined ratings of the sexual behaviors (e.g., the *Power Scale* was significantly correlated with sexual behavior ratings in the scenario emphasizing the opportunity to express power).

This series of studies supports the theoretical position that it is meaningful and useful to distinguish among eight dispositional sexual motives, rather than only considering a few motives. The perspective focusing on eight motives is also more useful than relying only on the notion of general sexual desire or sex drive. This is because the eight motives for sexual behavior were more strongly related to various ratings of sexual behavior than was the measure of sexual desire.

## The Behavioral–Cognitive Approach

The other approach to personality examined in this chapter after the trait perspective is the *behavioral–cognitive perspective*. This approach is actually a group of theories that represents a chain of evolution from one very basic philosophical perspective—that behavior results from learning about the world through experience with the environment (McConnell, 1985). The approach was partly a reaction against psychoanalytic theory that was prominent in the early years of the 20th century; psychoanalytic theory is concerned with unconscious influences on behavior, factors internal to the individual. **Behaviorism** is the perspective that only **overt behavior** should be studied within scientific psychology. The behavioral approach is based on **learning theory**, the position that focuses on learning. **Learning** is defined as a relatively permanent change in behavior resulting from experience.

The initial view within this approach was **radical behaviorism**. This position advocates that **classical conditioning** is the sole process through which learning occurs, and that only **overt behavior** is the legitimate subject of scientific psychology. *Radical* means *extremist,* and indicates that the initial view within behaviorism was extreme in its views. Radical behaviorist theorists maintain that it is not necessary to deal with emotions and thoughts at all to explain behavior; in fact, they argue that it is scientifically dangerous to focus on internal, private events because such subjective experiences cannot be measured objectively. As McConnell (1985) characterized the position, "For if there is one fundamental tenet of behaviorism, it is this: 'You cannot talk scientifically about anything that you cannot measure objectively'" (p. 687). At that point in history, it was thought to be completely impossible to examine and quantify mental processes.

Because of the limitations of viewing classical conditioning as the solitary learning process, some theorists explored learning that occurs through **operant conditioning**. Eventually, other theorists proposed **observational learning** as another means through which learning occurs. All of these types of learning will be explained in later sections; however, the point to note here is the movement away from radical behaviorism that occurred with the focus on observational learning. Demonstrating that individuals may learn simply by observing the behavior of others (e.g., they can serve as "role models") strongly supports the role of **cognitive processes** in learning; this is because overt behavior is not involved in the initial learning of the observed behaviors.

Research on observational learning led to the development of **social learning theory**, a major factor in the beginning of the cognitive revolution in psychology. **Social cognitive–behaviorism** is currently the most widely embraced perspective within the behavioral approach, which disputes the radical behaviorist view that cognitive processes should not be studied in scientific psychology. In fact, social cognitive–behaviorism places cognitive processes at the center of explanations of behavior; individuals must understand events in the environment and interpret them in order to respond to them. The various types of learning theory are summarized in Table 5.3.

### Radical Behaviorist Theories of Conditioning

#### Classical Conditioning

The terms *classical* and *conditioning,* are not words that have intuitive meaning for most people, and so *classical conditioning* does not convey much of an idea of how learning occurs in this process. The word

| TABLE 5.3 | Types of Learning Theory |
|---|---|

| Theory | Explanation of the Process of Learning | Example |
|---|---|---|
| Classical conditioning | A neutral event that does not produce behavior becomes associated with a stimulus that produces behavior | A sound (e.g., a type of music) becomes associated with a stimulus (e.g., erotic touching) that produces behavior (e.g., sexual arousal) |
| Operant conditioning | A behavior that produces desirable outcomes increases in frequency | A behavior (e.g., providing comfort to one's distressed partner) that results in sexual interest by the partner (an outcome) causes the behavior (providing comfort) to increase |
| Social learning theory | Observing behavior of another person that results in a desirable outcome for that person leads the observer to perform the same behavior | Observing a person compliment someone whom she finds attractive results in her receiving a kiss, causing the observer to compliment an attractive person in order to receive a kiss |
| Social cognitive theory | The conclusion that engaging in a particular behavior will produce a desirable outcome leads a person to engage in the behavior | Interpreting a person's actions as suggestive and alluring leads someone to flirt with the person because he or she expects a positive reaction to the flirting |

*classical* refers to the first major development in a discipline, which is exactly the situation for this type of learning; it launched the area within psychology of learning theory and behaviorism. **Conditioning** is change in behavior that results only from training or experience, rather than due to changes resulting simply from biological maturation and growth. More precisely, **classical conditioning** is the association of a behavior with an aspect of the environment that it was previously not associated with. The aspect of the environment becomes a **stimulus** for the behavior, causing behavior to occur when the stimulus is present in the environment. The linking of the behavior to the new stimulus occurs when **the new stimulus is paired with a stimulus** that already produces the behavior (see Figure 5.5).

To illustrate the process, consider the first research in learning theory that was conducted by **Ivan Pavlov** (1927). Pavlov was not a psychologist, but instead a physiologist studying the role of salivation in digestion. He presented meat powder to dogs to get them to salivate so that he could collect samples of saliva. However, during the research he noticed that they began to salivate to sounds in the laboratory even before the meat powder was given to them. The sounds that caused the unexpected salivation were those that had come to be associated with the meat powder, those occurring just before it was given to them; such sounds included the clanging of metal cabinets and utensils, and the footsteps of assistants coming down the hall to give them the food. Pavlov embarked on a program of research to demonstrate that events such as irrelevant noises can be paired with something such as food, which has a natural response already associated with it. Because the noises of the cabinets and utensils immediately preceded the presentation of the food, they came to signal the upcoming appearance of the food. Therefore, after enough pairings, the noises came to produce the salivation by themselves. Pavlov demonstrated that the sound of metronomes, bells, and lights could all eventually produce salivation in dogs after enough pairings with meat powder.

**FIGURE 5.5**    Learning Theory Explanations of the Causes of Behavior

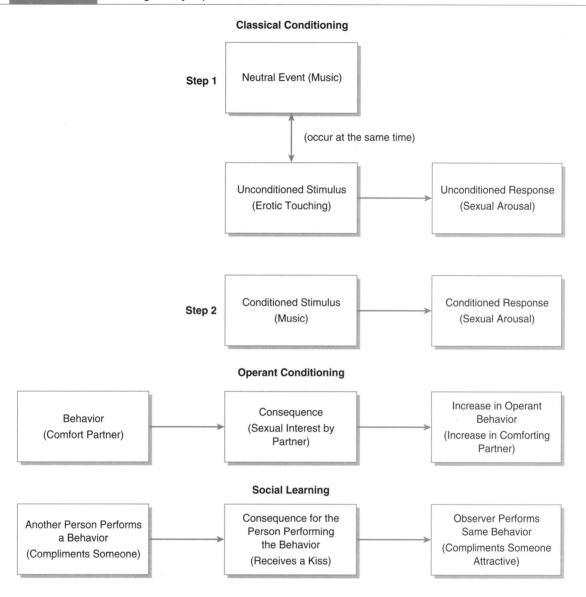

**Classical Conditioning**

Step 1: Neutral Event (Music)

(occur at the same time)

Unconditioned Stimulus (Erotic Touching) → Unconditioned Response (Sexual Arousal)

Step 2: Conditioned Stimulus (Music) → Conditioned Response (Sexual Arousal)

**Operant Conditioning**

Behavior (Comfort Partner) → Consequence (Sexual Interest by Partner) → Increase in Operant Behavior (Increase in Comforting Partner)

**Social Learning**

Another Person Performs a Behavior (Compliments Someone) → Consequence for the Person Performing the Behavior (Receives a Kiss) → Observer Performs Same Behavior (Compliments Someone Attractive)

Technical names were given to each of the aspects of the learning process. The stimulus that already produced the behavior even before conditioning began is called the **unconditioned stimulus**. The behavior that occurs in reaction to the unconditioned stimulus is called the **unconditioned response**. When the paired event, such as the clang of the cabinets, comes to produce the behavior, salivation, the clanging of the cabinet is called the **conditioned stimulus**. The behavior, salivation, when it occurs because of the clanging cabinet and not the appearance of the meat powder, is called the **conditioned response**.

This was the first demonstration that a previously neutral event that is inherently irrelevant to eating, such as a clanging noise, could become a stimulus to eating-related responses; the discovery inspired great enthusiasm and optimism among many scientists at the time. It suggested to learning theorists that human behavior is **highly malleable** and **capable of being shaped**, rather than being driven largely by rigid biological instincts, as established views in science had maintained. Psychological science, therefore, could develop techniques for modifying behavior to promote more adaptive, beneficial tendencies, and improve living generally within human society.

One theorist in particular who took up this perspective stands out as a major champion of behaviorism and learning theory, **John B. Watson**. A famous dictum of his was,

> Give me a dozen healthy infants, well-formed, and my own specified world to bring them up in and I'11 guarantee to take any one at random and train him to become any type of specialist I might select—doctor, lawyer, artist, merchant-chief and, yes, even beggar-man and thief, regardless of his talents, penchants, tendencies, abilities, vocations, and the race of his ancestors. (Watson, 1930, p. 104)

### Operant Conditioning

Not all learning theorists, especially the next generation of theorists, agreed with Watson's stark, simplified view of learning. Rather, even prior to the groundbreaking research of Pavlov, Edward Thorndike (1911) had conducted research on exploratory behavior and learning; this involved behavior that had not been prompted by stimuli immediately preceding it. Continuing with the focus on a more active process of learning, B. F. Skinner (1938) proposed a second type of learning that he called **operant conditioning**. Operant conditioning is the increase in behavior that results from pleasurable consequences that follow the behavior. Alternatively, operant conditioning may involve a *decrease* in behavior if no consequences, or unpleasant consequences, follow the behavior. The individual learns to manipulate or operate upon the environment to obtain desirable outcomes and avoid undesirable ones.

Skinner contrasted this more active type of conditioning with the type studied by Pavlov and Watson, classical conditioning, by referring to classical conditioning as producing **respondent behavior**. The type of behavior that results from operant conditioning is **operant behavior**. The outcome following behavior that *increases* behavior came to be called a **reinforcer**, because it strengthened the behavior and increased its frequency; the process of increasing behavior through the presentation of the reinforcer is called **reinforcement**. An outcome following behavior that *decreases* the behavior is called a **punisher**; the process of decreasing behavior through the presentation of the punisher is called **punishment**.

## Social Cognitive-Behavioral Theories

Two of the most influential approaches that launched the cognitive revolution in psychology are both **social learning theories**, those proposed by Rotter (1954) and by Bandura (1971, 1977). Social learning theory emphasizes the capacity of humans to develop new behavioral tendencies **without direct reinforcement** from the environment, but rather through observing the behavior of others. Humans are capable of understanding the outcomes that result from the behavior performed by another person, as well as the concept that similar outcomes are likely for them as well if they engage in the behavior themselves.

This understanding may motivate an observer to imitate the observed behavior, if positive outcomes result for the observed person; the observer may want to obtain the positive outcomes for himself or herself, too. If negative outcomes result from the behavior, the observer is likely to avoid engaging in the behavior. The social learning approach therefore proposes that people develop **expectancies** about the outcomes of behavior that guide their choice of behavior. The importance placed on concepts of *expectancies* and *choice,* which are *cognitive* concepts, moved behavioral theories virtually completely away from the radical behaviorism of the early 20th century.

Perhaps the ultimate example within the behavioral tradition of the evolution away from the radical behaviorist "black box" perspective is the cognitive approach proposed by Walter Mischel (1999). Mischel proposed the **Cognitive-Affective Personality System**. This theory maintains that behavior results from a number of interacting cognitive systems that influence both a person's interpretations of events and the behavioral choices they make in reaction to these events. This theory and other similar cognitive–behavioral theories are currently among the most prominent approaches within the behavioral perspective; it is therefore safe to say that contemporary behaviorism is no longer dominated by the radical view, but rather by the social cognitive perspective.

## Learning Theory Accounts of Sexuality

The theory and research on sexuality extending from the various learning theory approaches are examined in this section. In actuality, very little research has been conducted to test the ability of learning theory to predict and explain *human* sexual behavior. Much of the research with humans has been in terms of the application of social learning theory principles to produce change in adolescent sexual behavior and in high-risk sexual behavior. Moreover, the greatest proportion of research involving classical and operant conditioning has been conducted on lower animals, rather than on humans.

Before addressing formal theory and research, however, a little known fact of some historical significance is worth noting about **John Watson**, one of the first pioneers of the radical behaviorist perspective. Watson actually also initiated some of the earliest sexuality research in history, most certainly the earliest known research involving direct observation of the physiology of sexual response and arousal. Unfortunately, the research led to Watson's professional downfall as an academic scientist, in large part because the research became evidence against him in a divorce proceeding in 1919. Watson left academia upon being forced out of his position at Johns Hopkins University in disgrace after the ordeal. Based on reports of a confidant of Watson, Lloyd Ring Coleman,

> Watson became enamored of Rosalie Raynor soon after she became a student of his. And, judging from the divorce proceedings . . . , Watson and Raynor did have a love affair prior to the divorce. . . . Mary Ickes (Watson's wife) had intercepted some rather poetic love letters that Watson had sent to Rosalie. . . . (Moreover, ) Watson had become interested in the physiology of the sexual response and . . . he actually "took readings" and "made records" of sexual arousal in his laboratory at Johns Hopkins. Supposedly, Mary Ickes discovered the records and demanded a divorce. Watson agreed—but only if she would return the records to him. According to Coleman, Mary Ickes promised to do so but later broke her word. Instead, she supposedly . . . destroyed the data . . . . (McConnell, 1985, p. 685)

Watson abandoned academic psychology and went to Madison Avenue to enter the profession of advertising. The earliest sexuality research within the learning tradition ended abruptly, and such research would not resume for a number of decades after that.

### Classical and Operant Conditioning of Sexuality

Research on the conditioning of sexual behaviors has become intimately intertwined with biopsychological and neurological research over the course of the 20th century. Scientists interested in the functioning of the brain and nervous system have played a major role in exploring learning, specifically examining neurological changes that occur as a result of behavior changes. Most of this research has been conducted on lower animals, such as rats, voles (mice), and birds, because of the greater control researchers may exert over animals and the less severe ethical problems associated with such research. Learning theorists maintain that substantial similarities in the sexuality of lower animals and humans justify the practice of extending animal research findings to human sexual behavior.

First in this line of reasoning, Ågmo and Ellingsen (2003) argue for the comparability of humans and lower animals such as rats. Both humans and rats engage in **approach behaviors**, seeking closeness and sexual contact with potential partners. For both humans and rats, approach behaviors result from increasing sexual motivation, which is produced by a psychological system that is common to the two species. They cite evidence that sexual motivation in both males and females is dependent on at least minimal levels of hormones, although for some animals (humans and rabbits) the necessary hormones are androgens (male sexual hormones), while in other animals (rats) the hormone is estrogen (a female sex hormone). In addition, Ågmo and Ellingsen note that lower animals engage in sexual behavior with the same sex, another tendency in common with humans.

Finally, they propose that both lower animals and humans engage in sexual behavior because it is pleasurable and intrinsically rewarding. In learning theory terms, "they are attracted to a potential mate because of its unconditioned incentive properties; that is, a potential mate is a stimulus spontaneously activating approach behavior" (Ågmo, 2003, p. 298). Nonetheless, Ågmo and Ellingsen point out that no experimental studies have been conducted to support the assumption that sexuality is an unconditioned (unlearned) stimulus for humans. The overall conclusion based on this evidence, however, is that human sexuality is subject to the same principles of learning as other animals.

In reviewing the scientific studies on conditioning of sexual behavior in animals, Pfaus, Kippin, and Centeno (2001) first define what is meant by sexual behavior, especially because it is hard to distinguish sexual behavior in animals from that which is not sexual. They categorize sexual behavior into three stages: **appetitive**, **precopulatory**, and **consummatory**. Appetitive behaviors are those related to increased sexual interest, consisting of **sexual arousal** and **sexual excitement**. Sexual arousal is defined as increased blood flow to the genitals; sexual excitement is the occurrence of greater levels of activity and movement signaling the expectation of contact with a sexual partner. Appetitive behaviors are those that occur first, and may lead to other types of sexual behavior. Precopulatory behaviors are those that initiate contact with a potential sexual partner (*precopulatory* means "before sexual intercourse"). They include approaching a specific partner and engaging in behaviors that indicate sexual interest in the partner. Consummatory behaviors refer to **mounting** (getting behind the partner and climbing on top) and inserting the penis into the vagina (also called **intromission**).

### Conditioning of Sexual Excitement

Various studies have demonstrated the effectiveness of classical conditioning of male rats and birds in terms of eliciting sexual excitement, increased activity that signals sexual interest. This is accomplished by pairing a neutral aspect of the environment with the presence of a receptive female (one who is in the most fertile phase of the sexual cycle when certain cues indicate greater fertility). The **unconditioned stimulus** (the unlearned one) is the presence of the receptive female and the **unconditioned response** is increased activity approaching and soliciting the female. The presence of the receptive female is paired with such aspects of the environment as a specific compartment in a cage complex or a red light; compartments and red lights do not naturally produce sexual excitement, and so they are not stimuli for sexual excitement. After several experiences with the receptive female and the compartment or red light, the compartment or red light by themselves (without the receptive female) produce increased sexual excitement behavior. The previously neutral compartment and red light become **conditioned stimuli**, or the learned stimuli, producing the **conditioned response**, which is the sexual excitement behavior.

The conditioning effect is less well established for females, although a recent study has reported a definite effect for female quail (Gutierrez & Domjan, 1997). Conditioning effectiveness for females appears to depend on the type of animal (e.g., rat versus hamster), and whether the female is able to control the pace of sexual intercourse (Pfaus et al., 2001); if the male partner is too aggressive and controlling, conditioning is unlikely to occur.

Classical conditioning has even succeeded in overcoming an aversion to a negative aspect of the environment for rats. Male rats were allowed to mate with a receptive female who had been experimentally tainted with an odor that typically repulses rats; such males later eagerly approached a piece of cloth doused in the repulsive odor and handled it. Males who had not had the odor paired with sexual intercourse frantically tried to escape the area with the repulsive odor (Pfaus et al., 2001).

With respect to **operant conditioning**, a substantial body of evidence indicates that animals (often rats) will increase the frequency of a wide variety of behaviors (operant behavior) that are followed by the opportunity to engage in sexual intercourse (reinforcer). Such conditioned behaviors include pressing on a bar in a cage, pecking on an object, going through a hoop, running a maze, climbing a hurdle, running across an electrified grid, and turning a wheel. In the terminology of operant conditioning, the **reinforcer** of the behavior is access to sexual intercourse; the **operant behavior** is the behavior performed to gain access to sexual intercourse (i.e., bar pressing, climbing a hurdle). For male rats, the effect is especially strong when the behavior is followed by sexual intercourse that results in ejaculation; the same level of increase in behavior does not occur if the male is interrupted before ejaculation.

Courtship behaviors, those related to attracting and enticing a partner into sexual intercourse, have also been conditioned after being followed by sexual intercourse. For example, ultrasonic vocalizations ("cries" indicating sexual interest) by male rodents in response to the scent of a receptive female are made by the males only after having already engaged in sexual intercourse (Pfaus et al., 2001).

*Conditioning of Sexual Arousal*

Sexual arousal, as indicated by erection of the penis or increased blood flow in the vagina in studies of humans, may also be affected by conditioning. In fact, this aspect of sexual functioning, sexual arousal, is the area in which most of the research involving humans has been conducted. It is very difficult in practice to measure other aspects of sexual functioning in humans, such as effects of conditioning on sexual behavior and sexual intercourse. This is because of the intrusiveness into typically very private behavior that would be involved, including potential problems with ethics. Monitoring and experimental manipulation of stimuli right before, during, or after sexual behavior with a partner would be necessary to conduct such research. In contrast, measurement of arousal, in terms of erection of the penis or vaginal blood flow, may be very difficult in animals because of the need to attach monitoring devices to these organs. The effect on animals is typically measured in terms of more easily observable behavior, such as sexual excitement (increased behavioral activity) and sexual intercourse.

Classical conditioning of sexual arousal in men has been demonstrated. In these studies, women's boots (Rachman, 1966; Rachman & Hodgson, 1968), or even colored circles and squares (McConaghy,

1970; McConaghy, 1974), were paired with erotic pictures or videotapes. After pairing with the erotic images,presentation of the boots or geometric figures alone succeeded in producing erections in men.

*According to learning theory, how would individuals become classically conditioned to experience arousal to sexually neutral items such as boots and clothing?*

Only one study on classical conditioning has been conducted with women (Pfaus et al., 2001). This study by Letourneau and O'Donohue (1997) did not produce significant conditioning of sexual arousal in response to a previously neutral event, most likely because the women in the study found the unconditioned stimulus, erotic video clips, only moderately arousing.

A later study (Hoffman, Janssen, & Turner, 2004) overcame this problem by using 11 clips from five commercially available erotic videos that had been shown in previous research to be arousing to both women and men. In addition, the manner of pairing the neutral stimulus with the unconditioned stimulus, the erotic videos, was varied in two ways. First, half of the participants were presented the neutral stimulus so quickly (30 milliseconds) that they were not consciously aware of it; this is **subliminal presentation** of the neutral stimulus. For the other half of the participants, the neutral-stimulus presentation was varied in terms of its relevance to sexuality. For half of the participants, the neutral stimulus was a still photo of the abdomen of someone of the other sex (all participants reported that they experienced heterosexual attraction); the neutral stimulus for the other participants was a still photo of a gun pointed at the participant. The control group (comparison group) was presented both types of neutral stimuli (the abdomen and the gun) and the erotic clips in a noticeably random fashion (no pairing of stimuli occurred; see Figure 5.6).

Conditioning occurred for women, such that after the pairing of the neutral stimulus with the erotic videos, the stimulus also produced sexual arousal. However, the specific results depended on the speed of the presentation of the neutral stimulus. The photo of the abdomen produced arousal after conditioning for the **subliminal presentation group**, but not for the **conscious presentation group**. The gun, however, produced arousal for women when it was presented consciously. For men, the overall differences among groups were not significant. Although comparisons between specific groups of men must be treated cautiously because the overall differences were not significant, some expected trends were found. Men tended to experience increased arousal to the picture of a woman's abdomen after its pairing with the erotic videos, regardless of whether the picture was presented subliminally or consciously during conditioning. The expectation of the authors was that the more relevant neutral stimulus, a photo of an abdomen, would be more strongly sexually conditioned than an irrelevant stimulus, a photo of a gun. This was not supported for women because conditioning occurred for both stimuli.

Considering other factors, the effectiveness of associating neutral stimuli with sexual arousal has been shown to be very specific to the particular phase of sexual response in which the neutral stimuli are presented—that is, whether or not arousal is actually experienced **at the time of pairing**. In one study (Kantorowitz, 1978), neutral images were presented to one group of males during masturbation in the period just before orgasm

**Figure 5.6**    Classical Conditioning of Sexual Arousal in Humans

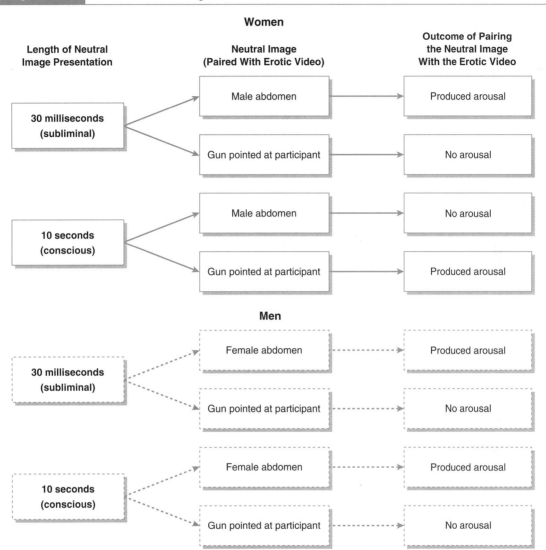

Note that the overall effect for men was not statistically significant. From "Classical Conditioning of Sexual Arousal in Women and Men: Effects of Varying Awareness and Biological Relevance of the Conditioned Stimulus," by H. Hoffman, E. Janssen, & S. L. Turner, 2004, *Archives of Sexual Behavior, 33*, 45–53. Reprinted with permission.

(called the **plateau phase**, involving high arousal); later, when the images were presented by themselves, they successfully did produce penile erection. However, images were presented during the conditioning phase for other males right after orgasm (in the period called the **refractory phase**, a time of extremely low arousal); this pairing actually caused a *decrease* in erection when the images were presented later after the conditioning period. Images paired with the period after the refractory phase during low arousal (called the **resolution phase**) had no effect on penile erection when presented at a later time. The implications of these findings are that, for paired stimuli to have an enhancing effect on sexual arousal, they must be linked with actual pleasurable arousal, rather than simply with any aspect of sexual experience. Pleasurable arousal occurs only right before orgasm, not following orgasm.

The phenomenon of **habituation** that is associated with conditioning has also been demonstrated for sexual stimuli, as well. Habituation is the gradual decline in response to a stimulus with repeated exposure to the stimulus; in a manner of speaking, the stimulus becomes "old" and boring. Continued exposure to the same erotic pictures, audiotapes, or movies results in decreased penile erection or vaginal blood flow over time (Meuwissen & Over, 1990; O'Donohue & Geer, 1985; O'Donohue & Plaud, 1991).

### Conditioning of Sexual Behavior During Sexual Intercourse

No research has been conducted with humans or female animals on the effect of prior sexual experience on sexual behaviors occurring during actual sexual intercourse; however, a number of studies have been conducted with male animals. Males with prior sexual experience specifically involving **intromission** (inserting the penis in the vagina) exhibited less delay in beginning sexual intercourse when a receptive partner was presented compared with males who did not have experience with intromission. The experience with sexual intercourse was the heart of the conditioning process; prior sexual experience that was "rewarded" by inserting the penis in the vagina led to quicker start of sexual behavior—that is, greater learning. The inexperienced males only had earlier experience with mounting a receptive partner (climbing on top of), but not intromission. Whether the males ejaculated or not during the conditioning phase did not make a difference.

In other research, associating a **conditioned stimulus** (being in a particular cage or turning on a light) with the *presence* of a receptive female (the **unconditioned stimulus**), even though sexual intercourse was not permitted, resulted in less time to begin intercourse and to ejaculate than if the conditioned stimulus was not present when the receptive female was made available later. Conditioning can also *inhibit* sexual intercourse; pairing a drug causing nausea with engaging in sexual intercourse tends to inhibit subsequent sexual behavior (Pfaus et al., 2001).

### Conditioning of Preference for Sexual Partners

The selection of sexual partners who possess characteristics associated with previous sexual experiences has been demonstrated across a variety of studies. One line of research has demonstrated that animals that are sexually exclusive at least during one mating season, such as some types of mice and quail, prefer contact with the particular partner that displayed a specific neutral characteristic during sexual intercourse. Such sexually neutral characteristics include odors placed on the partner or attaching brightly colored feathers to the partner. However, conditioning to one particular partner does not occur for animals that are not typically sexually exclusive.

For male animals that are not sexually exclusive, sexual intercourse does not need to occur with the female bearing the neutral stimulus (e.g., an odor or feather). The neutral-stimulus female can be presented immediately after ejaculation with another female, who is then replaced with the neutral-stimulus female. The pleasurable "afterglow" of orgasm results in the conditioning of the previously neutral stimulus; it is not the act of sexual intercourse itself that produces conditioning. Males who have been conditioned even engage in more mounting of an *unreceptive* female bearing the conditioned stimulus than do males who have no experience with the conditioned stimulus; this indicates the behavior is occurring because of the presence of the stimulus and not because of the behavior of the female herself (Pfaus et al., 2001). The effect of conditioned partner preference has also been demonstrated for female rats in one study (Coria, Haley, Manzo, Pacheco, & Pfaus, 2001).

### The Significance of Research on Conditioning of Sexuality

Pfaus and his colleagues conclude that substantial evidence supports the effect of conditioning on all phases of sexual behavior: appetitive, precopulatory, and consummatory. Moreover, research suggests that behaviors traditionally thought to be rigidly controlled by genetically determined biological factors may be affected by conditioning. Pfaus and colleagues (2001) concluded, "By analogy, instinct and hormones appear to 'set the stage' for sexual responding, whereas learning appears to 'write the play,' to determine the kinds of stimuli that animals will respond to and how vigorously such responses will be made" (p. 310). The strongest implication for human sexual behavior, according to Pfaus and colleagues, is that conditioning may account for the development of atypical and disordered sexual behavior, and development of attraction to specific partner characteristics.

### Social Learning Processes Involved in Sexuality

As described previously, social learning theory emphasizes the capacity of humans to modify their behavior without direct reinforcement from the environment. Humans are capable of observing the behavior of others and developing **expectancies** about the likely outcomes of behavior that guide their choices. As with all versions of learning theory, social learning theory assumes that the primary causes of behavior are stimuli from the environment. Many theorists do not accept the conclusion that traits or internal biological drives have very important influences, if at all. Nonetheless, social learning theories have embraced the role of individual differences in cognitive processes that influence learning, in stark contrast to the radical behaviorist view underlying classical and operant conditioning approaches.

Social learning theories also consider behavior on a much broader level than classical and operant approaches. Social learning theorists are often concerned with explaining a range of behaviors occurring in more natural settings, such as modifying various risky behaviors (drug use, unprotected sex); in contrast, the conditioning theories typically focus on modifying one specific behavior, such as erection of the penis or increased vaginal blood flow. Finally, whereas much of the research on conditioning of sexuality has involved animals or has examined therapies aimed at modifying specific disordered behavior in humans, social learning approaches to sexuality have had a much more wide-reaching focus (Hogben & Byrne, 1998).

The earliest research drawing upon the social learning perspective examined imitation of sexual behavior portrayed in the erotica. Because sexual behavior is presented in erotica as always producing pleasurable outcomes, viewing the erotica would be expected to increase the likelihood of observers engaging in similar behavior in hopes of obtaining the pleasurable outcomes. This research is inconclusive, however, demonstrating at most small, brief effects. Furthermore, the research is often difficult to interpret, because measures of expectations about sexual pleasure were not obtained both before and after the erotica viewing (Hogben & Byrne, 1998); expectations are central to the process of learning, according to social learning theory.

Research on adolescent sexuality is among the most common topics examined by social learning theory; this is because of concerns about pregnancy at an age when individuals may not be emotionally and economically capable of caring for offspring (Hogben & Byrne, 1998). Several social learning models have been developed that focus on improving the cognitive processes and behavioral skills necessary to use contraception and use it effectively. An example of such a model was a study by Barth, Fetro, Leland, and Volkan (1992) in which

## Box 5.2 Analyze This: Looking at Different Perspectives

### *Are Abstinence-Only Sex Education Programs More Effective Than Comprehensive Programs?*

Providing education about sexuality to elementary and high school students in public schools is controversial in itself. Generally, individuals who hold conservative views about sexuality object to many forms of information being presented to students at all. In fact, the Kansas Board of Education established a policy that parents must specifically approve the participation of their children in sex education, known as an "opt in" policy. This is virtually unique in the United States, because most state and local education administrations have an "opt out" policy. This means that students will automatically participate in sex education classes unless their parents sign a statement requesting that their children not participate.

Controversial as well is the type of program that is presented to students in states and districts that have sex education. Those holding more conservative views believe that providing information about sexual behavior and contraception use incites sexual interest and promotes permissiveness. Instead, they insist that the function of sex ed programs should be to encourage and motivate young people to abstain completely from sexual behavior; these are called **abstinence-only programs**.

Advocates of **comprehensive education** in the United States argue that, while youth should be encouraged to not engage in sexual behavior, information about contraceptive techniques should be provided as well. Between the ages of 14 and 18, approximately 50% of adolescents have engaged in penile–vaginal intercourse (Blum et al., 2000; Centers for Disease Control and Prevention, 2000). Based on this fact, those who argue for comprehensive education contend that it is dangerous and irresponsible not to give complete sexuality information, including how to protect oneself from unwanted pregnancy and sexually transmitted diseases.

As noted by Santelli and his colleagues (2006), "There is broad support for abstinence as a necessary and appropriate part of sexuality education. Controversy arises when abstinence is provided to adolescents as a sole choice and where health information on other choices is restricted or misrepresented. Although abstinence is theoretically fully effective, in actual practice abstinence often fails to protect against pregnancy and STIs [sexually transmitted infections]" (p. 72; words in brackets added).

An important question, then, for many parents, educators, and policymakers in the United States is whether abstinence-only programs are more effective than comprehensive programs at promoting higher rates of abstinence among adolescents. Another way of asking the question is, do comprehensive programs lead to higher rates of sexual intercourse, as abstinence-only proponents believe?

In a meta-analysis of the 12 available controlled studies comparing the two types of sex education programs, Silva (2002) examined a number of other factors that might be involved in promoting abstinence as well. What did she find?

- The overall influence of sex education programs on promoting abstinence, regardless of type of program, was quite small (specifically, it was .05, meaning it was near zero).

- The type of program, abstinence-only versus comprehensive, had absolutely no effect on rates of abstinence among young people; this means that comprehensive programs do *not* promote participation in sexual behavior more than abstinence-only programs.

- Parental involvement in the sex education programs substantially increases abstinence. However, a huge "but" needs to be emphasized here. Few of the studies involved parental participation because not many programs have been successful in getting parents involved. Consequently, a bid deal cannot really be made out of this finding. Many more studies need to be conducted on this issue.

- Programs that were focused on smaller groups, younger individuals, and those who had not engaged in sexual behavior yet were most effective in producing abstinent behavior.

- Small-scale programs were more effective in promoting abstinence than large-scale. Silva speculated that this may be due to the fact that larger programs often turn to external agencies or companies to deliver the sex education program, such that they are less effective.

- Recent programs tended to be less effective at promoting abstinence than earlier programs. Silva suggested that, because of changing values, it may simply be more difficult in current times to convince adolescents to remain abstinent. Factors that contribute to this may be "an increasing acceptance of premarital sexual intercourse, a proliferation of sexualized messages from the media and increasing opportunities for sexual contact in adolescence" (p. 478).

The bottom line with respect to the controversy between abstinence-only and comprehensive programs is that abstinence-only programs are not more effective at promoting abstinence.

## References

Blum, R. W., Beuhring, T., Shew, M. L., Bearinger, L. H., Sieving, R. E., & Resnick, M. D. (2000). The effects of race/ethnicity, income, and family structure on adolescent risk behaviors. *American Journal of Public Health, 90,* 1879–1884.

Centers for Disease Control and Prevention. (2000). Youth risk behavior surveillance: United States, 1999. *MMWR, 49* (No. SS-5).

Santelli, J., Ott, M. A., Lyon, M., Rogers, J., Summers, D., & Schleifer, R. (2006). Abstinence and abstinence-only education: A review of U.S. policies and programs. *Journal of Adolescent Health, 38,* 72–81.

Silva, M. (2002). Abstinence and abstinence-only education: A review of U.S. policies and programs. *Health Education Research: Theory and Practice, 17,* 471–481.

10th-grade students participated in a series of sessions dealing with contraception. The behavior-change program consisted of information about contraceptive techniques, exposure to role models, and engaging in role playing of appropriate behaviors. The effect was to increase knowledge, intentions, and use of contraception.

*How would social learning theory explain the effects peers might have on increasing knowledge about contraception, strengthening intentions, and promoting contraception use?*

Research by DiBlasio and Benda (Benda & DiBlasio 1994; DiBlasio & Benda, 1990) demonstrated the importance of expectations about the positive outcomes that may result from engaging in sexual behavior. These expectations were found to correlate with frequency of adolescent sexual behavior. Beyond this effect, frequent contact with friends who are sexually active (and therefore serve as role models) was also related to greater frequency of sexual behavior. In other studies, methods developed from social learning principles have been successfully used as strategies to reduce risky sexual behavior. Such strategies include modeling safer behavior, viewing the risk associated with drug use from a new perspective, and providing practice with skills necessary to reduce risky behavior (Hogben & Byrne, 1998).

## Summary

Personality is the pattern of affect, cognition, and behavior that characterizes individuals across situations and across their lifetimes. The trait approach has been one of the most productive theoretical perspectives in the empirical study of sexuality, especially in research involving humans. Traits are emotional, cognitive, and motivational tendencies that create consistency in behavior, especially behavior most importantly related to realizing individuals' personal goals and needs.

One of the most widely endorsed views of the important traits that account for much of human behavior is the Five Factor Model. The five factors are neuroticism, extraversion, agreeableness, conscientiousness, and openness to new experience. Seven traits obtained from factor analyses of ratings specifically focused on sexuality (e.g., *sexy, passionate, lewd*) are largely specific extensions of the Big Five traits, extraversion and agreeableness. The negative extremes of the trait dimensions agreeableness

(hostility, unfriendliness) and conscientiousness (undependability, lack of planning) have been found to relate to risky sexual behavior.

A similar model of human personality traits proposed by Eysenck (1947) identifies three traits, rather than five, as essential to explaining human behavior. Two traits are identical to those in the larger model, neuroticism and extraversion. The third trait is psychoticism, a combination of agreeableness and conscientiousness from the Five Factor Model. Research has tended to support Eysenck's proposal that extraversion is associated with a positive, hedonistic orientation toward sexuality, whereas neuroticism is associated with a negative, inhibited orientation. Psychoticism is consistently related to aspects of sexuality, often risky sexual behavior such as unprotected sexual intercourse.

Single-trait approaches focus on one trait that is thought to have particular significance in determining a range of behaviors of substantial theoretical importance. The trait of sensation seeking is the tendency to seek out experiences involving excitement and risk. Sensation seeking has been shown to correlate reliably with many aspects of sexual behavior in general, as well as the tendency to engage in risky sexual behavior. Research indicates that sensation seeking leads to risky sexual behavior, rather than substance use itself being the sole cause of risky sexual behavior.

Another single-trait approach focuses on the characteristic of erotophobia–erotophilia, the tendency to experience negative or positive emotions in reaction to sexual situations, information, or images. Those who were raised in a family environment of restrictive, inhibited, sex-negative attitudes tend to develop negative attitudes toward sexuality, whereas the reverse is true for those reared in a more open, sex-positive environment. Erotophobia–erotophilia is one of the most extensively investigated characteristics related to sexuality, with research demonstrating relationships with virtually every aspect of sexual expression and behavior.

Motivational factors related to sexuality have also been found to play a role in the tendency to engage in sexual expression. One recent approach proposes that eight separate dispositional sexual motives initiate and direct sexual expression, with individual differences existing for each of the motives. Ratings of the sexual motives have been shown to correlate uniquely with interest in, and likelihood of, engaging in sexual behavior in role-played situations relevant to a particular motive. The motives have likewise been found to correlate with ratings of actual sexual behavior and contraception use.

In addition to the trait approach to personality, the behavioral–cognitive approach has also been applied extensively to the study of sexuality. Research has demonstrated that sexual excitement in animals can be conditioned through both classical conditioning and operant conditioning. The counterpart to sexual excitement in animals is sexual arousal in humans. Arousal has been shown to be influenced by classical conditioning, although no research has been conducted regarding operant conditioning. Conditioning may take different forms for women and men.

Classical conditioning of actual sexual behavior has been demonstrated for animals. The implication for humans is that conditioning may account for atypical or disordered sexual interests, such as sexual arousal to nonhuman objects (e.g., clothing, shoes), because these objects have been paired with sexual arousal over time. The findings also suggest a process through which individuals come to be sexually aroused by particular partner characteristics, such as a color or type of hair, face, and body shape.

Research based on social learning or social cognitive theories has tended to focus on demonstrating that expectations that individuals possess at the time of the study correlate with the types of sexual behaviors in which individuals engage. The types of individuals with whom one has frequent contact, and who consequently are likely to serve as models for engaging in sexual behavior, has also been shown to relate to whether adolescent individuals engage in sexual behavior.

## Chapter 5 Critical Thinking Exercises

1. Think of various people you know who are different from one another in their views and feelings about sexuality.

   In what specific ways are their feelings about sexuality related to their personality in general? Be very specific in drawing connections. That is, think of what these people are like in terms of their personality in general; what specific traits seem to be prominent in what they are like as a person? Do you think these traits have anything to do with what they are like sexually?

2. Select an individual whom you know fairly well in terms of his or her personality and sexuality. Describe what the person is like in terms of each of the following theoretical views:
   a. the Five-Factor Model
   b. sensation-seeking
   c. erotophobia–erotophilia
   d. dispositional sexual motives
   e. behavioral and cognitive approaches to sexuality

Visit www.sagepub.com/hillhsstudy.com for online activities, sample tests, and other helpful resources. Select "Chapter 5: The Person: Individuality and Sexuality" for chapter-specific activities.

# Chapter 6 GENDER AND SEXUALITY

O ne of the first announcements made upon the birth of a new child is whether the infant is a girl or a boy. Of course, parents and family are also intensely concerned about the health of the newborn, and whether he or she has all four limbs and all fingers and toes. However, the label of *girl* or *boy* is central to everyone's understanding of the attributes and interests believed to define and characterize the individual from birth on throughout the rest of a person's life.

Nowhere is the importance of gender brought to mind more clearly than in the situations in which children are born with genitals that are not completely formed as either female-like or male-like (this is known as *intersexuality*, which will be discussed in more detail in a later section). In a relatively small proportion of cases, the external sex organs are neither clearly a penis and scrotum, nor a clitoris and labia. The strategy of medical doctors beginning in the middle part of the last century was to decide very quickly whether to use surgery to "correct" the genitals to be either completely female or, alternatively, completely male. Recent critics of this strategy have concluded that a primary reason for having the surgery soon after birth has been to reduce the anxiety and unhappiness of parents regarding uncertainty about gender (Holmes, 2002; Kessler, 1998). In other words, medical doctors have been so concerned about the stress of having a child with uncertain gender that they have wanted to protect parents through performing reconstructive surgery on their young children. The ethics and wisdom of such a practice are currently under intense debate (Diamond, 1996).

The centrality of gender in perceptions of what individuals are like is true in virtually every culture in the world. The specific qualities and expectations may vary somewhat from culture to culture, but many strong similarities link all of the variations on the main theme that women and men are different in significant ways. Very probably from the moment that others become aware of the person's gender, the individual is treated in different ways, in some ways that are strikingly different, but in many others that are subtle and unrecognized by those who are interacting with the individual.

*"Is it a girl or a boy?"* This is frequently one of the first questions parents of newborns, and their family and friends, ask. Biological sex generally forms the cornerstone of people's conceptions of themselves and others.

Virtually every culture notes distinctions between female and male, although the exact features emphasized and the associated customs may vary substantially across cultures.

The basis for this differential treatment may in fact result from different tendencies of the female or male individual that are present early in life (e.g., those guided by biological factors). However, even before the infant can develop the ability to engage in complex types of behavior, caregivers and other adults may treat baby girls and boys differently.

In the daily life of raising children and interacting with others, behavior is influenced by an extremely complex range of factors involved in being female or male. The difficult task confronting scientists is to untangle all of these various factors to discover their relative importance, as well as how the factors affect one another. Recent theoretical and scientific analyses therefore have evaluated basic assumptions and conclusions at virtually every level, including the most fundamental definitions. Researchers have begun to evaluate the very meaning of words that have traditionally been taken for granted, such as *sex* and *gender*.

## *The Concepts of Sex and Gender*

As a result of an early call by Rhoda Unger (1979) for a clearer understanding in the use of terms, scientists have come to distinguish between the words *sex* and *gender*. Although it is not possible in reality to identify an absolute distinction between the two, psychologists and other academics have designated **sex** as referring to biological distinctions between males and females. In contrast, **gender** refers to the differences between males and females that are not determined largely by biological factors, but that are likely to be influenced strongly by social and cultural forces. Actually, *gender* has evolved into a more widely used concept, because of the difficulty of cleanly separating biological causes from environmental ones. Currently, *gender* is used by many theorists as the term that covers any aspect of maleness and femaleness that is not absolutely and strongly determined by biological factors.

Consequently, in discussing differences between females and males related to such dimensions as personality, interests, roles, and behavior, the term, *gender differences,* is used, rather than the alternate term, *sex differences.* The reason is that it is seldom perfectly clear whether such differences are caused by biological factors or by nonbiological factors. Beyond this, *sex* may be mistakenly interpreted as referring to sexuality or sexual behavior, particularly in a book on sexuality. For this reason, the term *gender* is almost always used to talk about femaleness and maleness rather than the term *sex*. Again, the exception is when considering aspects of biological structure about which much less debate typically occurs as to the primary role.

### Sex

*Sex* is the set of biological attributes that constitute femaleness and maleness (Zucker, 2001). Sex actually consists of two highly related components, *genetic sex* and *anatomical sex* (see Figure 6.1). The typical path of biological development leads to consistency between genetic sex and anatomical sex; however, in a relatively small proportion of cases, a discrepancy may occur between the two. This is the reason that it is important to understand the distinction between these components.

#### Genetic Sex

**Genetic sex** is the type of genetic coding passed along to the individual at the time that the sperm of the biological father fertilizes the egg of the biological mother. Each cell in the human body contains genes, which

**FIGURE 6.1**   Aspects of Sex and Gender

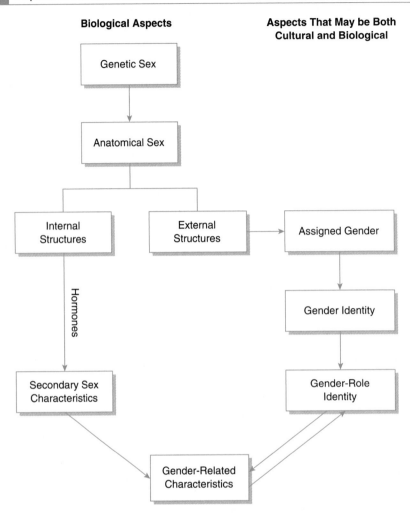

are chemicals that direct the activity and growth of the cell, and ultimately the functioning and development of the body as a whole. Genes are organized into larger strands of many genes; these strands are called chromosomes. Human cells have 46 chromosomes, which are arranged within the cell into pairs. Consequently, there are 23 pairs of chromosomes in each cell, and scientists have labeled each pair with a number to identify them.

The two chromosomes that make up the 23rd pair are responsible for influencing the development of parts of the body that are typically different for males and females; they are therefore called **sex chromosomes**. One type of sex chromosome has the appearance of the letter, X, and is therefore called the **X chromosome**. The other type of chromosome has the appearance of the letter, Y, and has been given the name, **Y chromosome**. Through the process of maturation of the sperm in adult males, only one of these types of chromosomes ends up in any given sperm. The eggs produced by adult females contain only one type of chromosome, the X chromosome.

When a sperm fertilizes an egg, the chromosomes of each are combined within the fertilized egg, which may then develop into an embryo, and later into a fetus. The contribution of an X chromosome by the sperm to the egg results in the presence of two X chromosomes; this usually provides the genetic instructions for the development of female organs. A **genetic female** therefore has two X chromosomes that make up the 23rd pair (the XX configuration). This is illustrated in Figure 6.2. In contrast, the contribution of a Y chromosome by the sperm to the X chromosome of the egg results in the XY configuration that typically leads to the development of male organs. Therefore, a **genetic male** has an XY combination that makes up the 23rd pair of chromosomes.

## Anatomical Sex

**Anatomical sex** refers to the organs of the body that are traditionally considered central to defining sex, specifically the **genitals** and the internal organs associated with the functioning of the genitals. Most often, genes of the sex chromosomes lead to the development of sexual organs characteristic of females when the XX genetic combination is present in the fertilized egg. Sexual organs characteristic of males usually develop when the XY genetic combination is present. The Y chromosome typically results in the production of male sex hormones, which as a group are called **androgens**. Several of these hormones are responsible for the development of certain tissues in the body of the embryo that produce the internal and external organs of the male genitals. Another set of tissues develop in the embryo when the androgens are not present, as in the case of genetic females (the XX combination). These tissues typically lead to the formation of the female internal sexual organs; female external organs form from the same tissue as those of male organs.

In relatively rare situations, the cells of the body of an XY genetic male cannot react to specific androgens that are produced by the body; this results in the development of female external organs in the genetic male, although the internal sex organs, the testicles, are present but infertile (this is called androgen insensitivity syndrome). Internal organs develop through different processes at a different time during pregnancy than do

---

**FIGURE 6.2**  Determination of Genetic Sex During Fertilization of the Egg by the Sperm

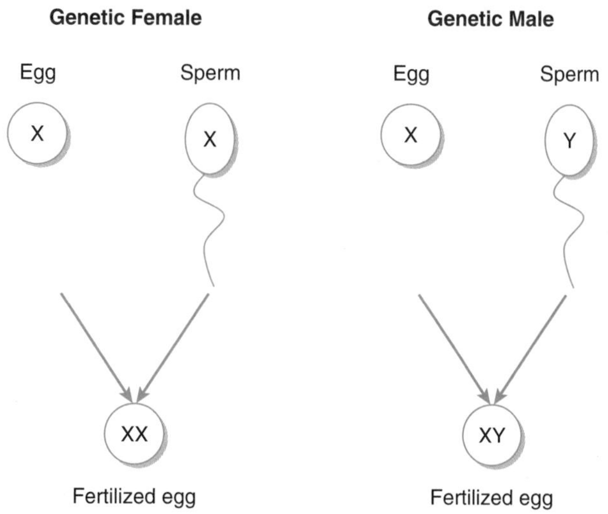

Genetic Female

Egg    Sperm

X       X

XX

Fertilized egg

Genetic Male

Egg    Sperm

X       Y

XY

Fertilized egg

external organs. Other types of rare genetic and hormonal conditions may also result in the development of internal sexual organs of one sex (e.g., female) and the external sexual organs of the other sex (e.g., male). These will be discussed in more detail in a later section.

## Gender

**Gender** refers to the psychological, social, and cultural meanings associated with the existence of maleness and femaleness (Unger, 1979). The specific features and activities assigned to a given gender are strongly determined, in general, by the culture in which one is raised, as revealed in the substantial variability in the ways in which gender is expressed across cultures (Diamond, 2002; Zucker, 2001). Cultural forces therefore assume a central position in the formation of the concept of gender from the very outset of life. **Gender** is the specific concept developed within each culture about the ways that biological sex may be expressed. For this reason alone, gender has proven to be a profoundly complex and challenging domain to investigate.

Gender involves two aspects of psychological importance to individuals, assigned gender and gender identity. **Assigned gender** is the label given to an infant, usually at birth, identifying him or her as either male or female (see Figure 6.1). **Gender identity** is the basic understanding of oneself as being either a girl or a boy that to an extent results from the assigned gender given to a person (evidence also exists indicating that biological factors play a role in the development of gender identity).

For most individuals, the development of one's sense of being female or male takes place in a direct and straightforward way, and being identified as either a girl or boy contributes to this sense. Virtually the only way of identifying maleness or femaleness historically has been to examine the external sexual organs at birth. The presence of a vulva leads those in the delivery room to conclude that the individual is female; the presence of a penis and scrotum leads to the conclusion that the individual is male. These aspects are, of course, the external sexual anatomy of the individual. This decision about the sex of the individual provides the assigned gender. Usually, the presence of a vulva or penis and scrotum accurately reflects the other aspects of biological sex, specifically internal sexual anatomy and genetic sex. However, as discussed previously, sometimes a discrepancy among the aspects of biological sex occurs prenatally (before birth). In these cases, assigned gender does not represent the status of the individual with respect to other features beyond external genitals.

As a child matures after birth and develops more complex cognitive abilities, he or she begins to construct an understanding of himself or herself, in addition to developing an understanding of aspects of the rest of the world. This understanding of oneself is **identity**, a sense of the characteristics and abilities one possesses. In addition to a conceptual understanding, identity also includes an emotional evaluation of one's attributes, most often a positive valuing and deep affection for what one is like. The **self**, a term used in social psychology to refer to this cognitive and affective sense of oneself, takes on a special importance in understanding the world. Individuals typically and frequently use the self and their identity as the frame of reference to evaluate most other aspects of the world.

One of the most fundamental and central aspects of identity very early in life is knowledge of one's own biological sex, usually through the label of assigned gender. Children are verbally identified by others as either a boy or a girl, they are dressed in different ways according to this label, and they are treated differently according to them as well. Given this early experience, children develop an identity strongly incorporating the concept of gender. The basic understanding of oneself as being either a girl or a boy is called gender identity (Zucker, 2001). It is not only the recognition that one is female or male; it also includes a psychological acceptance and embracing of the group membership (Spence, 1985). For many children, the beginnings of such an understanding develop around the age of 2 to 3 years (Deaux & Stewart, 2001), although it is usually not grounded in the knowledge that genitals determine one's gender. The primary sources of evidence about gender are the more readily visible signs. These include clothing, hair length and style, and participation in certain activities, such as playing with particular toys for children and assuming specific occupational roles for adults.

*How can you tell the gender of these children?* We learn from a very early age which characteristics are linked to each gender.

## A Multidimensional Model of the Many Aspects of Gender

The complexity of gender is revealed more fully in what Eckes and Trautner (2000) call the **extended multidimensional matrix of gender issues**. A matrix is a grid framework used to arrange items into categories (see Figure 6.3). A somewhat simpler version was proposed initially by Huston (1983) and then slightly modified by Ruble and Martin (1998).

In this model, gender is thought to be expressed along four dimensions: constructs (concepts), content areas, level of analysis, and time. The dimensions of constructs and content areas are the two major aspects of the model. The first dimension, **constructs**, are the types of psychological processes or behaviors affected by the concept of gender within a given culture. Constructs consist of (a) gender-related concepts or **beliefs** (stereotypes), (b) **identity** or self-perception (one's understanding of what he or she is like), (c) **preferences** (desire to engage in gender-related behaviors), and (d) **behavioral enactment** (the actual overt behaviors typically displayed). Each of these constructs may take a specific form dependent on the various content areas. The **content areas** proposed within this model are (a) biological or categorical sex, (b) activities and interests, (c) personal–social attributes, (d) gender-based social relationships, (e) stylistic and symbolic characteristics, and (f) values. The fact that each of the constructs is expressed across every one of the content areas underscores the extremely complicated nature of what many people consider to be a fairly simple idea, that of sex or gender.

**FIGURE 6.3** The Multidimensional Matrix of Gender Issues

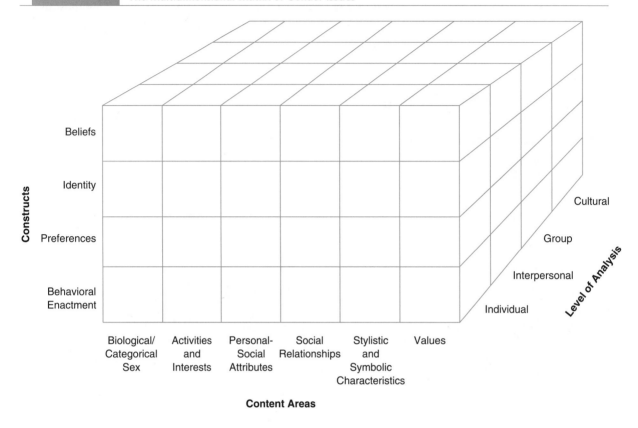

From *Developmental Social Psychology of Gender: An Integrative Framework* by Eckes, T. & Trautner, H. M., copyright © 2000. Reprinted with permission of Lawrence Erlbaum Associates, Inc.

### Beliefs About Gender

> Size—it's a male concern. Who has it, who doesn't have it. Who wants it and who needs it. Who looks and who doesn't (want to) look. Or, to bring it all home, who's not as *much* of a man. . . . All of this tends to get played out in the work landscape, where the matrix of personal ambition intersects with an almost narcissistic phallic preoccupation with winning the game. (Poulsson-Bryant, 2005, p. 23)

The first construct within the extended matrix model, **beliefs**, refers to the knowledge that individuals develop concerning the meaning of gender. In terms of the specific content areas, beliefs may concern **knowledge about biological sex**, which in the multidimensional model includes knowledge of such physical features as the clothing and hair styles assigned to the two sexes. This knowledge involves one of the most fundamental and important concepts underlying many of the others, that of **gender labeling**. Gender labeling therefore is an understanding of the physical and stylistic features that distinguish males from females, and develops fairly early in life, approximately around the age of 2 years. Eventually, the realization occurs that gender assignment is based on anatomical sex, most obviously the external sexual organs of the vulva and the penis and scrotum. This recognition comes much earlier for children whose parents make a point of directly informing them about the anatomical differences, and using names that explicitly distinguish the female and male organs (Eckes & Trautner, 2000). Regarding the other content areas, knowledge and stereotypes also develop for the area of **activities**, the types of play, recreation, work, and chores in which the two genders typically are expected to engage. Individuals likewise develop an understanding of the **attributes** expected of males and females (e.g., dominance for males, being not dominant for females), as well as the **social relationships** expected (e.g., the sex of one's friends, TV or movie idols, and romantic and sexual partners). Beliefs about **styles** concern the facial expressions, gestures, movements, verbal patterns, and ways of participating in activities appropriate for women and men. Beliefs about **values** involve the expectation that individuals will value and demonstrate allegiance to those behaviors and characteristics appropriate for their particular gender (Eckes & Trautner, 2000).

Collectively, these activities, attributes, social relationships, styles, and values that are expected of one gender in contrast to the other gender constitute gender roles. That is, **gender roles** are expectations shared within a culture that females should engage in specific types of behavior and possess specific characteristics, whereas males should engage in other types of behavior and possess other characteristics. Gender roles are based on the types of activities that individuals of each sex perform in occupations and family duties that have been identified as appropriate for a given sex (Eagly, Wood, & Diekman, 2000).

The abilities and traits necessary to successfully carry out these activities become associated with one particular gender for this reason, thereby becoming stereotypes of that gender:

> To the extent that women more than men occupy roles that require predominantly communal [other-oriented] behaviors, domestic behaviors, or subordinate behaviors for successful role performance, such tendencies become stereotypic of women and are incorporated into a female gender role. To the extent that men more than women occupy roles that require predominantly agentic [competent, skillful] behaviors, resource acquisition behaviors, or dominant behaviors for successful role performance, such tendencies become stereotypic of men and are incorporated into a male gender role. These gender roles, which are an important focus of socialization, begin to be acquired early in childhood and are elaborated throughout childhood and adolescence. (Eagly et al., 2000, p. 127; the words in brackets were added)

Furthermore, according to social role theory (Eagly et al., 2000), gender roles are *normative*: That is, they demand that individuals *should* possess the traits and behave in the ways deemed appropriate for their gender. Gender roles, therefore, involve criteria against which individuals are judged. People are evaluated on the extent to which they fulfill these expectations, compared with ideals of being a "real woman" or a "real man." Those who do not measure up are looked down upon in general, and possibly treated negatively by others. This is one reason that people strive to live up to gender roles, which are intensely valued by most societies. In addition, gender role expectations cause others to treat individuals in ways that are consistent with stereotypes, implicitly influencing them to behave in a manner that conforms to gender expectations. For example, men are supposed to be strong, such that others look to men for courage in troubling situations; males consequently respond with bravery and coolness. This is known as expectancy confirmation.

### Identity or Self-Perception Related to Gender

The second construct in the extended matrix model is identity or self-perception. Whereas most individuals develop a very clear knowledge of the expectations a culture has for each gender, not all individuals develop the attributes or engage in the roles that are expected of his or her gender. Individuals' understanding of the extent to which they possess gender-related features is their **gender-role identity**, a term referring to all aspects of identity related to gender (Basow, 1992). Individual gender-role identity varies according to the extent to which an individual feels that he or she possesses the characteristics and engages in the roles associated with maleness and femaleness within a given culture. This is distinguished from a term discussed earlier, **gender identity**, which refers largely to an individual's understanding of whether he or she is male or female, one's biological sex. (The term, *gender-role identity*, is not a widely used term. It is used here to reserve gender identity for the basic, simple recognition that one is male or female. One can be absolutely certain that he or she is male or female, yet not feel extremely masculine or feminine, which is what is being called gender-role identity here. Gender-role identity [masculinity and femininity] is a much more complex issue than simply whether one is male or female.)

**Gender-Role Identity.** In addition to a basic sense of maleness or femaleness, gender-role identity also includes one's perception of the types of gender-linked traits and behaviors that are characteristic of him or her. Another important aspect of gender-role identity is the sense one has of the gender-related ways in which he or she interacts with other people, as well as the gender-related groups to which he or she belongs (Eckes & Trautner, 2000). All of these factors contribute to one's overall sense of being female-like or male-like, a sense of what is most commonly referred to as femininity and masculinity.

However, the perception of one's masculinity and femininity overlaps tremendously with biological sex and gender identity, one's basic sense of maleness and femaleness. Biological sex and gender identity are both defined in an affirmative way, that is, in terms of the *presence* of either male or female sexual anatomy; however, in a sense, they are also defined in a negative way, by the *absence* of the sexual anatomy of the other sex. In earlier times, a rare situation called intersexuality often led to uncertainty about gender labeling and concerns about later gender-role identity because of what seems like the presence of both female and male genitals. Intersexuality is the situation in which an individual has sexual anatomy of both sexes (the condition has also in the past been referred to as hermaphroditism [pronounced HERM afro DĪT ism]; however, the term recently is seen as having negative associations, and is less preferable than intersexuality (Diamond, 2002; Kessler, 1998). Some parents, particularly earlier in history, experience distress about the intersexuality of their child. This is because people often desire and demand certainty about whether the person is male or a female, given that gender is such a fundamental organizing principle in many cultures. The presence of ambiguous genitals makes it unclear whether the individual should be considered a girl or a boy, and how they should be treated. Different perspectives on the implications of intersexuality for the development of gender identity are discussed more fully in Box 6.1.

**The Bipolar Nature of Masculinity–Femininity.** In popular thinking, biological sex and gender identity consist of categories that are mutually exclusive: That is, an individual cannot be both female and male. Femaleness and maleness are thought to be entirely distinct categories. Just as being female is seen as ruling out the possibility of being male, femininity and masculinity are treated as if they are completely distinct, and opposing, categories. That is, in evaluating one's femininity, more than just the presence of feminine characteristics is taken into account by people; the degree to which masculine characteristics are present is also factored into the judgment. Signs of a greater presence of masculine attributes in an individual result in the perception that the individual is less feminine. In the same way, the presence of feminine attributes reduces the perception that an individual is masculine (Deaux, 1987).

## Box 6.1 Analyze This: Looking at Different Perspectives

### *The Development of Gender Identity*

The way in which gender identity develops in children has come to be intensely debated within scientific and clinical circles in recent times. The prevailing perspective among theorists and clinicians in general has been that children's gender identity develops through their experiences after birth and the way they are treated by others. This view is strongly aligned with learning theory (discussed in chapter 5).

Such a learning theory perspective was advocated by one of the earliest, most noted theorists in the area of gender assignment and gender identity, John Money, and his colleagues (Money, 1965; Money & Ehrhardt, 1968; Money & Tucker, 1975). According to this view, gender identity does not exist at all until children learn about gender and its associated meanings through experience early in life, developing only gradually over time. For these reasons, Money and his colleagues concluded that the most acceptable strategy for helping intersex children—those born with genitals that are neither clearly female nor male—was to perform surgery to shape the genitals so that they are female in structure, consisting of a vulva and vagina. This was because female genitals were simpler to construct and medical technology was not able to create a well functioning penis at that point in history. Based on the learning theory assumptions about gender identity development,

it was thought that such children who are assigned to be girls would develop the gender identity of a girl because of being labeled, dressed, and treated by others as girls.

Early examples evaluated by Money and his colleagues included an individual who was misidentified as a boy. He did not undergo surgery to make his genitals more male-like until almost 4 years old. He developed the gender identity of a boy, exhibited masculine behaviors and interests, and was romantically and sexually attracted to females; he also received treatment with male hormones at puberty to produce secondary sex characteristics typical of boys. These cases provided support for the greater role of gender labeling and resulting environmental influences on gender identity; genetic sex and biological influences seemed to have hardly any role at all.

In a particularly well-known case, one brother of a pair of identical twins was surgically reconstructed to have female genitals and had his testicles removed following severe damage to his penis during circumcision (Money & Tucker, 1975). The child received a new female name, Brenda, and was treated as a girl beginning at the point at which the parents decided to have this reconstructive surgery performed. Furthermore, he was regularly administered estrogen beginning at the age of 12 to promote

*(Continued)*

(Continued)

the development of secondary sex characteristics typical of females because he did not have ovaries to produce estrogen himself (Colapinto, 1997).

According to various publications and presentations by John Money, after reassignment as a young girl, David (the name he chose for himself as a teenager) began to behave like a girl and to show interests typical of girls (Money & Tucker, 1975). However, his twin brother and others who knew him personally felt instead that David typically behaved in very unfeminine ways, was interested in boyish activities and play, and resisted treatment with estrogen. Ultimately, David refused to undergo surgery to construct a vagina, completing his transition to being female. Instead, after being told when he was 14 about the gender reassignment as an infant, he decided to have surgery to remove his breasts and begin the process of becoming a male (Colapinto, 1997).

A formal scientific rebuttal to Money's learning theory perspective, partially based on David's case, was eventually published in an article by Diamond and Sigmundson (1997). Their view is that gender identity and sexual orientation are primarily determined by biological factors, whereas childrearing practices and experiences after birth play only a minor role; this is the complete opposite of the position advocated by Money. Diamond and Sigmundson argued that gender reassignment is dangerous, not only for children like David who are born with typical genitals, but also for intersex children who have ambiguous genitals. The danger results from the fact that it is not possible to determine how the gender identity of intersex children will eventually develop (Colapinto, 1997).

Diamond and Sigmundson (1997) contend that surgical alteration of genitals should be delayed until individuals are old enough to have a strong sense of their own gender identity. They have proposed that intersex children may be assigned a gender in infancy to allow them to fit in by being dressed and treated in a way consistent with a particular gender. However, they also argue that the individual should ultimately be involved in decisions about surgical changes that are made to his or her genitals (Colapinto, 1997), a view similar to that of the Intersex Society of North America (ISNA; http://www.isna.org/).

## References

Colapinto, J. (1997, December 11). The true story of John/Joan. *Rolling Stone,* 54–73, 92, 94–97.

Diamond, M., & Sigmundson, H. (1997). Sex reassignment at birth: Long-term review and clinical implications. *Archives of Pediatric and Adolescent Medicine, 151,* 298–304.

Money, J. (1965). Psychosocial differentiation. In J. Money (Ed.), *Sex research, new developments* (pp. 3–23). New York: Holt, Rinehart, & Winston.

Money, J., & Ehrhardt, A. (1968). Prenatal hormonal exposure: Possible effects on behavior in man. In R. P. Michael (Ed.), *Endocrinology and human behaviour: Proceedings of a conference held at the Institute of Psychiatry London, 9 to 11 May 1967* (pp. 32–48). London: Oxford University Press.

Money, J., & Tucker, P. (1975). *Sexual signatures: On being a man or a woman.* Boston: Little, Brown.

Rosenthal, P. (2000, February 24). *Forced crossing: An involuntary traveler across the gender line—And the first man who went under the knife to become a woman.* Retrieved February 23, 2007, from http://archive.salon. com/books/feature/2000/02/24/colapinto_ebershoff/index.html

Common conceptions of femininity and masculinity are based not only on the presence of feminine or masculine characteristics, but also the absence of the "opposite" type of characteristics.

In effect, the gender-role identity dimensions of masculinity and femininity are combined by individuals in a nonconscious, subjective way into a single dimension. Because of this combination process, gender-role identity is treated as a single dimension that has femininity as one extreme pole, or endpoint, and masculinity as the other extreme pole. For this reason, theorists have traditionally referred to masculinity–femininity as a **bipolar opposite dimension**. Bipolar opposite means that it has two endpoints (poles) that are the opposite of one another.

Evidence suggests that the vast majority of individuals possess an overall assessment of themselves as feminine if they are female and masculine if they are male. Similarly, females overwhelmingly tend to feel that they are not extremely masculine, whereas males tend to feel that they are not very feminine. That is, individuals by and large tend to have gender-role identities that are consistent with expectations for their particular biological sex (Spence, 1983, 1985). Such an overlap with biological sex reveals the supreme importance and the centrality of femaleness and maleness to individuals' conceptions of self-worth. This extreme consistency of masculinity–femininity with biological sex and gender identity occurs in spite of substantial variation in the extent to which individuals report that they possess gender-appropriate traits, behavioral tendencies, mannerisms, and gestures.

Apparently, most individuals tend to engage in an idiosyncratic type of analysis in arriving at their sense of masculinity–femininity (see Figure 6.4). Women tend to engage in the process of emphasizing the importance of their feminine characteristics, deemphasizing those they do not possess, and doing the reverse for masculine characteristics. Likewise, generally men greatly emphasize the particular masculine characteristics that they possess, and deemphasize the importance of those that they do not. They also deemphasize the importance of, or completely disregard, feminine characteristics they possess, as well as emphasizing the feminine characteristics that they do not possess (Spence, 1993).

Most women do not perfectly fit the ideal prototype of femininity in terms of traits, behaviors, and mannerisms. Likewise, most men do not perfectly fit the prototype for masculinity. Yet, most women feel that they are very feminine, and most men feel that they are very masculine.

In this way, individuals tend to maintain their sense of gender identity and masculinity–femininity as consistent with their actual biological sex. Gender-role identity really consists of two components: an assessment of actually **possessing specific attributes** in the various gender content areas (i.e., traits, preferences, interaction styles) and one's **overall assessment** of being masculine or feminine. Identity regarding specific attributes corresponds only very loosely to identity regarding overall masculinity–femininity. The overall sense of masculinity–femininity is likely the more important of the two in influencing self-esteem.

Transgenderism. Not all individuals develop a gender-role identity that overlaps perfectly with biological sex, nor do all individuals develop the even more fundamental gender identity that corresponds to their external anatomical sex. Identities that are based substantially on characteristics stereotypically associated with the other sex are transgender identities. Transgenderism is therefore the term used to refer to gender-role identities in which males believe they possess substantial levels of feminine characteristics, and value these characteristics, or in which females believe they possess substantial levels of masculine characteristics, and likewise value these characteristics. The term *transsexualism* has been used in the past by both the medical community and by individuals themselves who have other-sex identities. However, more recently transgenderism has become the accepted term because it is seen as more inclusive of a variety of different types of individuals. These concepts have undergone an often turbulent process of evolution over the past century, a debate that continues well into current times (Bolin, 1998).

Within the range of various transgender identities, historically, transsexual individuals and transvestites have been viewed as two extremes at either end of a continuum, at least from the perspective of transsexuals. **Transsexuals** are individuals who have the deeply held sense that their gender is actually

**FIGURE 6.4**    Cognitive Processes That Maintain the Consistency of Gender-Role Identity With Biological Sex

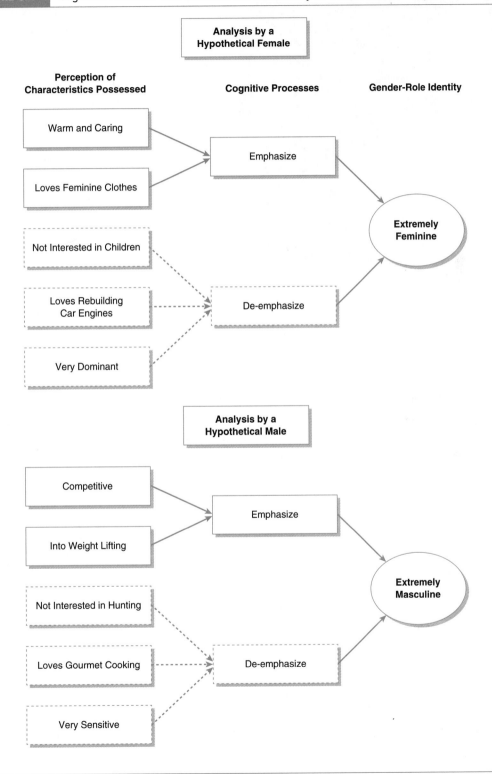

Angela Fernandez, 28, and Angel Romera, 22, step out of the Town Hall where they got married in Igualada near Barcelona, September 9, 2001, in the first transsexual marriage in Spain. Fernandez changed her sex when she was 19, but did not get permission from authorities to get married until years later

that of the other sex; this feeling of being the other sex is so strong that they are dedicated to taking sex hormones and having surgery to reconstruct their genitals in order to actually become the other sex. Individuals born with male genitals who wish to become female are called male-to-female (MTF) transsexuals. Those born with female genitals who want to become male are known as female-to-male (FTM) transsexuals. Transsexualism is not directly related to sexual orientation, with some transsexual individuals attracted to women, some to men, and some to both (Bolin, 1998). The majority of transsexuals are men who feel like they are female, although some transsexuals are women who feel like they are male.

**Transvestites** are individuals who dress in clothing of the other sex because they find it sexually arousing or gratifying (called cross-dressing), or who fantasize about dressing in other-sex clothes in a way that provides sexual pleasure. Cross-dressing fantasy or behavior by heterosexual males that results in clinically significant distress or that interferes with social, occupational, or general functioning is a type of psychological disorder called **transvestic fetishism** (American Psychiatric Association, 1994). Although few large-scale, systematic data exist on the issue, a study by Doctor and Prince (1997) documented that those whose cross-dressing can be labeled transvestic fetishism are largely married heterosexual men. Yet, another study has found that as many as 30% of those who cross-dress identify as nonheterosexual or not sexually active with a partner (Bullough & Bullough, 1997). Nonetheless, transvestism involves an aspect of sexual gratification that does not characterize transsexualism.

The concept of transgenderism has currently come to include more than individuals who desire to have hormone treatment and genital reconstructive surgery (i.e., those who are transsexual). Transgenderism also refers to those who desire to develop and express a social identity of the other sex—for example, men living their lives as women—but who do not want to undergo reconstructive surgery. Some transgender individuals argue that they do not want to be forced into the concepts of gender staunchly promoted within most societies. Instead, the identities of some individuals may be that of women with penises and men with vaginas (Bolin, 1998).

Transgender identity includes those who live part or all of their lives as the other gender to relieve tension due to gender-role strain, to express the feminine or masculine side of their personality, and to develop a cross-sex identity, possibly in preparation for reconstructive surgery. It also includes those who choose to live as a blend of feminine and masculine qualities. Finally, it includes individuals who want to "pass" as a person of the other sex, meaning have others believe that they really are a member of the other sex, as well as those who prefer to be known as a transgender person (Bolin, 1998).

## Gender-Related Preferences

**Preferences** are the types of behaviors and activities in which individuals desire to engage—that is, their personal interests concerning the various possibilities involved in gender (Eckes & Trautner, 2000). Preferences often overlap with identity to a great extent, although individuals may develop some preferences through processes over which they have little awareness or control; these preferences will then not be included in their identity. They may nonetheless be aware that they possess such characteristics.

Preferences span the six gender-related content areas proposed in the extended matrix model. One type of preference is the desire to be the biological sex of either male or female, related to the dimension of gender identity. Preferences in the area of activities and interests include those related to preferred toys for children and pastimes for adults, desired occupation, and the types of household tasks preferred. The other types of preferences concern personality and physical characteristics considered most desirable for oneself; the types of people with whom one is interested in interacting because of their gender or masculine versus feminine characteristics; desire to display specific gestures, postures, speech styles; and endorsement of gender-related values and biases (Eckes & Trautner, 2000).

*What are your favorite pastimes and hobbies? Are these typically thought of in our culture as gender-related, or are they not related to gender? How might your preferences affect your self-concept?*

## Behavioral Enactment

The final area in which factors associated with gender exert an influence is on observable behavior (Eckes & Trautner, 2000). With respect to the first content area in the extended matrix model, overt expressions of gender include the display of bodily characteristics (e.g., facial hair, emphasizing breasts or other body features) and style of clothing. As for the other content areas, behavioral enactment of gender involves the participation in certain recreational and work activities; expressing particular trait-related behaviors; involvement in gender-typed social relationships with friends, colleagues, family, and romantic partners; engaging in particular body movements, gestures, and speech styles; and treating others differently on the basis of their gender (which defines what is meant by discrimination).

# *Aspects of Gender*

Given the profound importance many cultures place on gender, it is critical to examine the relationship of gender to actual behavior, beliefs, attitudes, and feelings of individuals. Several of the content areas proposed within the multidimensional model of gender are considered in order to provide a thorough understanding of the nature of gender differences.

Because of the complexity of the issues involved, two points need to be kept in mind when thinking about evidence of gender differences. The first point is that differences refer to the difference between *groups* of individuals, in this case males and females. Even with a characteristic such as height, for which a very noticeable difference exists between women and men, it is not the case that all women have only one height and all men have only one taller height. If it were true that women had only one height and men had another height, it would match the stereotypical conception of gender differences: "men are from Mars, and women are from Venus" (Lippa, 2002).

Gender difference is indicated by a statistic that compares, for example, the average height of women to the average height of men, taking into account the amount of variability within groups and how much overlap exists for the two groups. The actual difference between the average values for women and men can actually be fairly small, and a good amount of overlap can exist, even though the averages can be *statistically different*.

A **statistically significant difference** means only that such a difference between two averages is unlikely to have occurred by chance or accident. Therefore, if the same measurement of height were obtained for two entirely new, large groups of women and men, it is highly likely that a similar difference in averages for the two groups would be found. In fact, the statistical test informs us that if we were to measure new groups of women and men in 100 different studies, a difference would be found in almost all of these additional studies. However, finding a statistically significant difference in a study tells us very little about *how big* of a difference

The notion of gender differences actually refers to average differences between **groups** of individuals. Yet, not every man has exactly the same height, nor does every woman. Moreover, some women are taller than the average man.

exists between the average height of women and men. Another statistic is needed to give us information about the size of the gender difference.

The statistic was developed by Jacob Cohen (1977) that produces a value called **d**, a number indicating the size of the difference between females and males; it is also called an *effect size*. In the computation of *d*, the average for one gender is subtracted from the average of the other gender. The result is then divided by a number that indicates how much variability exists in the values measured, such as the heights of women and men in the above example.

The **d** statistic is used in meta-analyses of many studies. **Meta-analysis** is the statistical technique of combining the results of different studies to increase the reliability of measurement. Because of the large numbers of studies included in the analyses, and the much larger numbers of participants on which analyses are based, confidence in results is enhanced tremendously.

In a survey of more than 300 effect sizes from a number of meta-analyses on gender differences, Hall (1998) determined that the typical effect was between .36 and .65; these are small to moderate gender differences. Another overview of 15 meta-analyses by Canary and Hause (1993) indicated that *d* values range between .03 and .40. Even considering the higher values reported by Hall, the typical size of gender differences may be labeled as fairly small to medium (LaFrance, Hecht, & Paluck, 2003).

The second issue to keep in mind related to gender differences is that identifying a reliable difference provides absolutely no information about the *cause* of that difference. Knowledge of a difference, therefore, indicates nothing about the factors that are involved in the development of height, and consequently about the causes of the difference in height for women and men. The third issue to keep in mind when considering gender differences is that only those attributes and behaviors for which significant differences have been found are typically discussed. Attributes and behaviors that do not involve gender differences are often barely mentioned or not mentioned at all. This fact can convey the sense that gender differences are numerous when no comparison is made between the number of characteristics for which gender differences have been found and the number for which gender differences have not been found. In many ways, women and men are more similar than they are different, given that we are all human beings.

## Biological and Categorical Attributes

As discussed previously, external sexual anatomy is the first basis for identifying the gender of individuals, usually the result of a decision made by the attending physician at birth. This feature is referred to as **assigned gender**. The genitals and the internal sexual organs are the most extreme aspect of the differences between females and males. This component of gender comes the closest to the conception of gender as categorical—that is, a person has one set of anatomical structures, female or male, but not the other.

### Female Sexual Anatomy

The **external sexual organs** characteristic of females are collectively called the **vulva**, which is Latin meaning "womb" (see Figure 6.5). The vulva includes the mons pubis, the labia majora, the labia minor, and the clitoris. The male counterpart to the vulva is the penis and scrotum, although the vagina is commonly thought to be the counterpart to the penis. The penis, however, is an external organ, while the vagina is an internal structure.

The **mons pubis**, Latin for pubic mound, is the area below the lower abdomen that is padded by layers of fatty tissue. It has a high concentration of nerve endings, making it very sensitive to touch and stimulation in some women. Pubic hair is present over the surface of this area. Another name given to this region is **mons veneris**, Latin for the mound of Venus; Venus was a Greek and Roman goddess believed to be responsible for sexuality.

The **labia** (a Latin word meaning lips, pronounced LAY bee uh) surround the opening to the internal sexual organs, and consist of two sets of folds of skin tissue. The outer folds are called the **labia majora**, which in Latin means "larger lips," or the larger folds. The labia majora extend from the mons pubis to the area of the body in between the two legs, called the **perineum**. The labia majora are also covered by pubic hair and are also highly sensitive to touch and stimulation in many women. The inner folds that are surrounded by the labia majora are called the **labia minora**, in Latin meaning "smaller lips." The labia minora are hairless, and

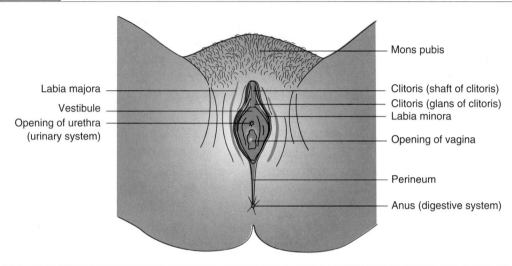

FIGURE 6.5   External Female Sexual Anatomy

extend from above the **clitoris** (pronounced KLIT or us) to the perineum within the labia majora. The labia minora vary a great deal in size and appearance among women, but become filled with blood during sexual arousal and increase in size by as much as two to three times in all women. The area below the clitoris surrounded by the labia is called the **vestibule**, which means entry way or threshold.

The clitoris is a nerve-rich structure at the front of the vulva that often provides pleasurable sensations when touched or stroked. Its external portion is about a quarter of an inch to an inch long, although the size and appearance of clitorises vary greatly from one woman to another. The clitoris might be considered the most important external organ in terms of pleasure, because it is a major source of erotic stimulation for females, and becomes swollen and erect when stimulated. The top of the clitoris is called the **glans**, which contains the highest concentration of nerve endings, and therefore is the most sensitive area to touch and stimulation. The clitoris is covered by an area of tissue that is called the **clitoral hood**. During sexual arousal, the clitoris becomes engorged with blood, causing it to increase in size, primarily in its width rather than length. The internal structures of the clitoris include tissue with spaces, called **corpora cavernosa**, within supporting shafts, called **crura**. The corpora cavernosa are the areas that fill with blood during arousal. Initially, this results in the clitoral hood pulling away to expose the glans of the clitoris. As a woman approaches the peak of sexual stimulation that may result in orgasm, the clitoris retracts again underneath the clitoral hood.

The clitoris develops prenatally from the same tissue as the penis in males, and the internal structures of the penis are essentially the same; however, the clitoris is devoted entirely to the function of stimulation, while the penis also has the urethra extending through it. The urethra is a channel that, in males, transmits semen out of the body during ejaculation, as well as urine from the urinary system during periods when a male is not sexually aroused.

The **internal sexual organs** typical of females include the vagina, uterus, fallopian tubes, and ovaries (see Figure 6.6). The **vagina** (pronounced vuh JI nuh) is the structure whose opening begins at the vestibule, and is a chamber or passageway tilted slightly toward the back of the body inside the abdomen. In women who

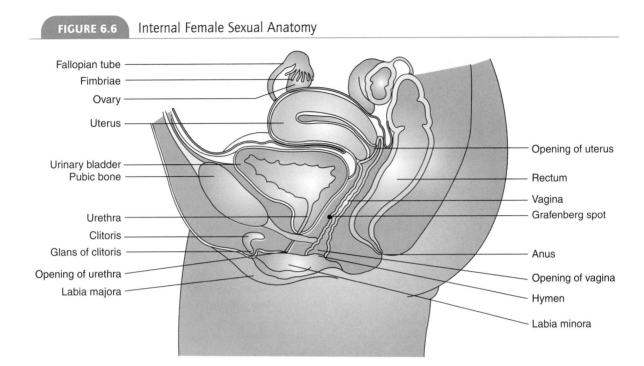

**FIGURE 6.6** | Internal Female Sexual Anatomy

Fallopian tube
Fimbriae
Ovary
Uterus
Urinary bladder
Pubic bone
Urethra
Clitoris
Glans of clitoris
Opening of urethra
Labia majora

Opening of uterus
Rectum
Vagina
Grafenberg spot
Anus
Opening of vagina
Hymen
Labia minora

have never had children, it is approximately three inches long on the back side, and about two-and-a-half inches long on the front side where it joins with the lower part of the uterus, called the cervix; the vagina may be somewhat longer as a result of childbirth. The inner layer of the vagina within the abdomen consists of muscle tissue that can expand. The muscle tissue also engages in contractions during sexual arousal that result in changes in the shape of the vagina as a woman approaches the peak of arousal; the inner two-thirds expands in a process called **tenting**. Contractions within the vagina are additionally involved in childbirth, creating movements that push a baby outside of the body during labor. Virtually no relationship exists between the size of the vagina and the degree of pleasure or comfort experienced when it is penetrated during sexual activity (Masters, Johnson, & Kolodny, 1995).

A great deal of variation appears to exist in the presence and sensitivity of a particular area of the front wall of the vagina, called the **Grafenberg spot** or the **G-spot**. Research suggests that stimulation of this area, which ranges in size from that of a penny to a half-dollar, provides intense pleasure for some women.

The opening of the vagina is typically covered by a thin membrane, called the hymen (pronounced HĪ men), which contains one or several openings itself (see Figure 6.7). These openings allow the passage of tissue and fluid discharged during the menstrual cycle. The hymen has no known biological function, although it may take on a great deal of cultural importance given that it is thought to indicate virginity. Yet, in fact, the hymen may be stretched or even torn early in life because of nonsexual events such that the structure of the hymen typically indicates nothing about the sexual experience of the individual. Furthermore, penetration by a penis may not rupture the hymen, with it stretching instead. Initial sexual intercourse does not always result in pain or bleeding under most circumstances (Masters et al., 1995).

**FIGURE 6.7**  Various Types of Hymens

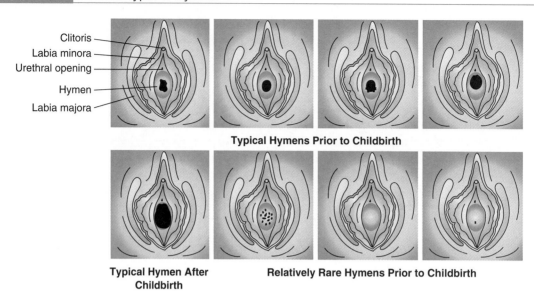

Clitoris
Labia minora
Urethral opening
Hymen
Labia majora

**Typical Hymens Prior to Childbirth**

**Typical Hymen After Childbirth**

**Relatively Rare Hymens Prior to Childbirth**

The **uterus** (pronounced YU tuh rus) joins the front wall of the vagina at its innermost point. The lower end of the uterus that extends into the vagina is called the **cervix** (pronounced SIR vicks), meaning "neck" in Latin. If sperm have been deposited in the vagina, a number of them may travel through the opening in the cervix into the uterus. The uterus is a hollow, pear-shaped organ, usually three inches long and two inches wide, with the wider portion positioned higher in the abdomen. The uterus is the organ in which a fertilized egg usually implants, such that the uterus is responsible for sustaining a pregnancy and providing nourishment to the develop embryo.

This is because the inside lining of the uterus, a layer of tissue called the **endometrium** (pronounced EN doh MEE tree um) thickens and develops a rich network of blood vessels at the midpoint of the menstrual cycle. The midpoint is the time at which an egg typically matures and is released from the ovary into an extremely thin duct called the **fallopian tube**. The upper portion widens into the **infundibulum** (pronounced in FUN di BYOU lum), at a point called the **ampulla** (pronounced AM pyou lah), which is the place at which fertilization of an egg usually occurs. The fallopian tube arches over the ovary with fringes of tissue called **fimbriae** (pronounced FIM bree ee) that do not actually touch the ovary. One fallopian tube leads from each ovary, such that two fallopian tubes join with the upper portion of uterus. Fallopian tubes transport a released egg to the uterus through the action of tiny, hair-like structures that wave the egg through the passage. The release of an egg each month is called **ovulation**. If an egg is not fertilized, it is discharged from the uterus, along with the endometrium, as well as mucus produced by the cervix, and a small amount of blood; this discharge is called **menstrual flow**, also known as **menses**.

The gonads in females are the **ovaries**, two tiny organs positioned near the top of the fallopian tubes above the uterus on either side. The ovaries generate **eggs**, the sex cell involved in reproduction; the technical term for a sex cell is **gamete**. Other names for the egg are **ovum** (plural is **ova**) and **oocyte**. The ovaries produce primitive eggs even before a girl is born, numbering between six and seven million at the outset. However, many of these deteriorate, such that only between 400,000 to 700,000 are present at birth. No additional eggs develop after the prenatal period in which eggs are initially created. Instead, the number continues to decrease throughout the remainder of life (Masters et al., 1995). Each egg is surrounded by a tiny capsule of tissue called a **follicle**.

The ovaries also manufacture female sex hormones, **estrogen** and **progesterone**. These hormones influence the development of the body and produce the changes that occur on a monthly basis within the female sexual system after puberty. **Puberty** is the point at which the body begins to produce dramatically increased levels of the sex hormones. Most relevant to sexuality, these changes include the maturation and growth of the sexual organs, both internal and external. The sexual organs are referred to as the **primary sex characteristics**, because they are central to the process of sexual maturation and functioning. The ovaries gradually develop the capacity to release mature eggs that are capable of being fertilized. They also begin to regulate changes in the uterus that lead to **menstruation**, which is the shedding of the lining of the uterus if fertilization of an egg does not occur. The first menstruation at puberty, and the resulting discharge of menstrual flow through the vagina, is called **menarche**, the beginning of fertility. This occurs on average at about 12.5 years, which is two years after the first noticeable sign of puberty, the initial development of the breasts, called **breast budding** (Brooks-Gunn & Reiter, 1990).

The levels of estrogen and progesterone produced within the body increase at the beginning of each **ovarian cycle**, which encompasses the process of developing a mature egg, a process called **oogenesis** (pronounced OH uh JEN uh sis). The length of the cycle is actually 28 days on average, although it can vary across women from 21 to 40 days. The surge in sex hormones causes one egg to reach full maturation each month, increasing in size to the extent that it ruptures the follicle in which it is housed. This results in the egg being released into the infundibulum of the fallopian tube; the release of the egg is called **ovulation**. The ovaries typically alternate months in releasing an egg, such that one ovary releases an egg one month and the other ovary releases an egg the next month.

The increase in sex hormones, particularly progesterone, not only affects the ovaries; it at the same time causes the inside lining of the uterus, the endometrium, to begin to develop, increasing in thickness and the concentration of blood vessels. This prepares it for the implantation of a fertilized egg in the event that fertilization occurs. The fertilized egg, called an embryo after implantation, receives nourishment and expels wastes through the nearby blood vessels of the mother. The process of affecting the nature of the uterus is called the **menstrual cycle**, which is controlled by the ovulatory cycle; the ovaries produce the bulk of the hormones that cause the changes in the uterus. The embryo produces a hormone, **human chorionic gonadotropin** (pronounced KOR ee ON ik, go NAD oh troh pin; abbreviated HCG), which stimulates the ovaries to produce progesterone, the sex hormone. Progesterone maintains the high quality of the endometrium and the developing embryonic tissues.

If fertilization does not occur, the ovaries are not stimulated to produce progesterone, and the endometrium degenerates, eventually detaching from the uterus and being discharged as part of the menstrual flow. The discharge of the menstrual flow actually occurs at the *beginning* of each menstrual cycle, as hormone levels are at an extreme low from the end of the previous cycle, which is the reason the endometrium has deteriorated. Hormone levels begin to increase on Day 1 of the cycle, even as the menstrual flow makes way for the regeneration of the endometrium for the new cycle.

As discussed previously, the primary sex characteristics develop at puberty as a result of the dramatic surge in sex hormones; these characteristics involve the capacity of the female sexual organs to produce viable sex cells—eggs—that can be fertilized, and to nourish and sustain the resulting embryo. The increase in sex hormones also produces changes in other parts of the female body that are not directly related to the functioning of the sexual organs that are called **secondary sex characteristics**. These characteristics include the enlargement and maturation of the breasts in females, the first noticeable sex-related characteristic beginning at approximately 10.5 years of age in modern times (Brooks-Gunn & Reiter, 1990). As a result of pregnancy and childbirth, breasts become capable of **lactation**, the production of milk to nourish offspring, until the child is weaned from breastfeeding. Other secondary characteristics include the growth of pubic hair, hair in the armpits and on the legs, and increases in layers of fatty tissue around the hips and legs, resulting in a more rounded figure.

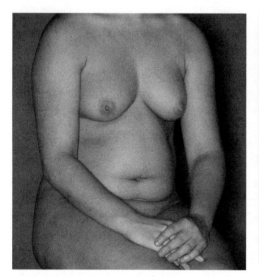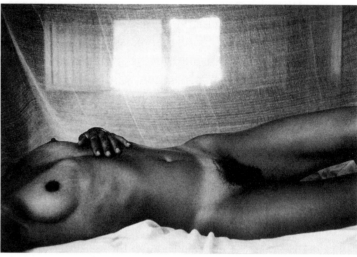

Secondary sex characteristics of women include larger breasts than men, a greater ratio of fat to muscle around the hips and legs than men, and pubic and armpit hair.

## Male Sexual Anatomy

The external sexual organs characteristic of males are the **penis** and the **scrotum** (see Figure 6.8). The penis is the cylindrical organ that extends away from the lower abdomen, on average approximately four to six inches in length in its unaroused condition. The penis, like the clitoris, is nerve-rich, particularly in the tip, called the **glans**. On the underside of the penis is a triangular-shaped area of skin called the **frenulum**, that is the point at which the glans joins with the shaft of the penis; this area has a high concentration of nerve endings as well. Consequently, both the glans and the frenulum provide pleasurable sensations when touched or stroked and are important sources of erotic stimulation for males.

Like the clitoris, the interior of the shaft of the penis on its topside consists of structures called **corpora cavernosa**, meaning "body with chambers," which contain spaces that fill with blood during arousal, causing the penis to enlarge in both length and width. The underneath interior section of the penis consists of a single cylinder, called the **corpus spongiosum**, meaning spongy body. Unlike the clitoris, a channel called the **urethra** extends from the internal sexual organs through the corpus spongiosum. The urethra carries the fluid, **semen**, containing sperm, outside the body during the peak of sexual excitement, called **orgasm**; the expulsion of semen is called **ejaculation**. In addition, during periods when the male is not sexually excited, the urethra transports urine outside the body from the urinary system.

The glans of the penis is covered by a layer of loose skin, called the **foreskin** or **prepuce** (pronounced PREE pyoos) that is a continuation of the skin of the shaft. The foreskin for many men can easily be pulled

**FIGURE 6.8**   External Male Sexual Anatomy

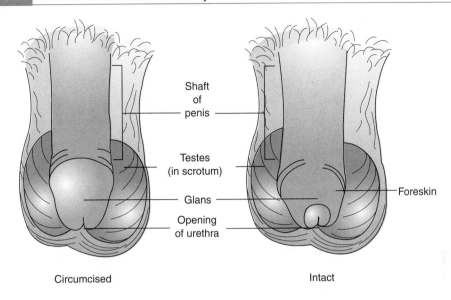

Shaft of penis

Testes (in scrotum)

Glans

Opening of urethra

Foreskin

Circumcised

Intact

back to expose the penis in most cases. During the 20th century, a common practice in the United States came to be removal of the foreskin of young male infants shortly after birth, a process called **circumcision** (pronounced SIR kum SEE shun). This did not become a routine medical practice in other Western industrialized countries, although it may have been justified in the United States as a precaution related to hygiene. The procedure originates out of the Judaic and Islamic religions in which a holy ceremony of foreskin removal is conducted on male infants in honor of a covenant by God with the prophet, Abraham. In recent years, controversy has arisen about the necessity, as well as the benefits, of circumcision.

The size and shape of penises vary widely from one male to another, with size commonly being portrayed as of great concern to many men. Although the average length is four to six inches when it is flaccid (not erect), cold temperatures and negative emotional states typically cause the penis to become smaller.

The **scrotum** is a thin, loose sack of skin hanging behind the penis and away from the abdomen that contains the testicles. It is sparsely covered with pubic hair after puberty. Two layers of muscle inside the scrotum cause it to draw up automatically when the muscles contract. This pulls the testicles closer to the body in colder temperatures, during exercise, or due to sexual stimulation. Under warmer conditions, the muscles relax and allow the testicles to hang away from the body. The response to temperature is important, because it maintains an optimal temperature for the testicles that is necessary for the production of healthy sperm.

The primary male internal sexual organs are the testicles, vas deferens, seminal vesicles, prostate, and Cowper's glands (see Figure 6.9). Two **testicles**, or testes, are contained in the scrotum, which produce **sperm**, the male sex cell involved in reproduction, and male sex hormones. Although they are usually about the same size, on average 1.5 inches long and 1 inch in diameter, one usually hangs lower than the other; often it is the left one that is lower in right-handed men, and the right one is lower in left-handed men. The testicles are extremely sensitive to touch and pressure, such that, for some men, stroking them is sexually arousing. At the back of each testicle is the **epididymis** (pronounced EP ee DID ee mus), a coiled network of tubing folded

Internal Male Sexual Anatomy

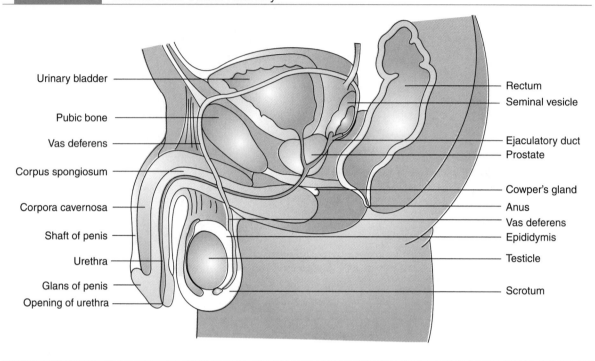

against the testicle; this is the place at which the hundreds of little channels within the testicle, called **semi-niferous tubules,** merge into a warehouse where developing sperm are held while they mature.

The testicles are suspended from the abdomen into the scrotum by spermatic cords, which consist of nerves, blood vessels, and a **vas deferens**. The two vas deferens are tubes about 18 inches long that transport sperm from the testicles along a pathway over the bladder that eventually joins with the urethra. The vas deferens merge with the **ejaculatory duct** within the **prostate,** a structure under the urinary bladder. Here the ejaculatory duct joins the urethra, the passageway eventually extending through the bottom of the penis. The prostate consists of muscular tissue, as well as glandular tissue, which produces a clear fluid that constitutes about 30% of the **seminal fluid,** or **semen,** the liquid that is ejected from the penis during ejaculation. Two **seminal vesicles,** small glands located behind and beneath the urinary bladder, contribute approximately 70% of the seminal fluid. The **Cowper's glands,** or bulbourethral glands, located below the prostrate gland produce a small amount of thick, clear mucus early in sexual arousal before ejaculation occurs.

As noted previously, after puberty, the testicles also produce large amounts of the male sex hormones, **androgens,** one of the most prominent of which is **testosterone**. Testosterone is involved in the development of the body after puberty, as well as being central to the functioning of the male sexual system. The testicles go through cycles of production of sperm at the point at which large levels of testosterone are produced and testosterone accumulates in the seminiferous tubules inside the testicles. As testosterone peaks, signals from the brain shut down the production of testosterone, ceasing the production of sperm; the formation and maturation of sperm is called **spermatogenesis,** a process taking about 64 to 72 days. Every day, a healthy man produces several hundred million new sperm, which are channeled over a 20-day period through the tubules in the testicles and then stored in the epididymis to complete their maturation.

At the height of sexual arousal during ejaculation, the sperm are forced from the epididymis into the vas deferens by muscular contractions in its walls. Muscular contractions in the vas deferens propel the sperm into the ejaculatory duct and then urethra, where they mix with the seminal fluid from the seminal vesicles and prostrate to form semen. The seminal fluid consists of (a) fructose (a sugar associated with fruit) from the seminal vesicles, which provides energy for the sperm; (b) prostaglandins that reduce the thickness of mucus in the cervix of the female; (c) relaxin, a hormone from the prostate that increases the

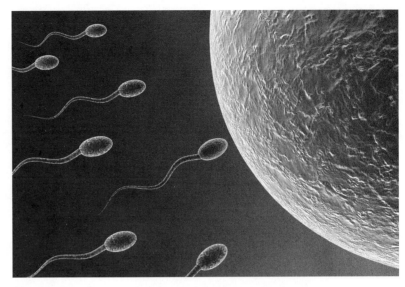

Sperm are the male sex cells, which generally are capable of fertilizing an egg, the female sex cell.

ability of the sperm to move; and (d) seminalplasmin that protects the sperm from bacteria (Masters et al., 1995). After mixing with the seminal fluid, semen is ejected forcefully from the opening at the tip of the penis.

As with females, primary sex characteristics develop at puberty for males, the result of a massive increase in the production of sex hormones. The first sign of puberty in boys is growth of the testicles that occurs on average between 11 and 11.5 years (Brooks-Gunn & Reiter, 1990). The primary sex characteristics involve the enlargement of the genitals and testicles, and the capacity of the testicles to produce viable sex cells (sperm that are able to fertilize eggs). The increase in sex hormones likewise initiates changes in other parts of the male body that are not directly related to the functioning of the sexual organs, the **secondary sex characteristics**. For men, these characteristics include growth of pubic hair, and hair in the armpits, on the face, legs, arms, and torso. The potential for muscle development is also greatly enhanced by the presence of these sex hormones, although the degree of development of course depends on the extent to which they are used or cultivated through weight training. The larynx enlarges, and the voice deepens after puberty.

### Intersexuality

As noted in the earlier section on anatomical sex, a small percentage of individuals develop internal or external sexual organs that are not consistent with their genetic sex. In addition, some individuals develop the internal organs of one gender, but the external organs of the other gender. Still others develop gonads that have tissue of both male and female reproductive organs, in a condition referred to as intersexuality. Whereas sexual anatomy may be the aspect of gender that most completely distinguishes females from males, even this feature is not 100% exclusive to being male or female.

## Personal and Social Attributes

The area of gender differences in personal and social attributes is the domain that is most commonly examined by psychologists interested in gender. Traditionally, the area is separated into cognitive abilities and

 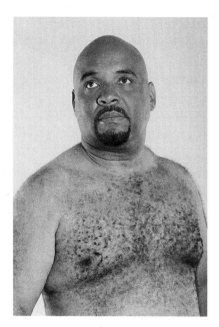

Secondary sex characteristics of men include greater potential for muscle development than women, facial hair, hair on the torso, and, as with women, pubic and armpit hair.

personality traits. Personality traits are characteristics of individuals that produce a tendency toward regular, consistent behavior over extended periods of time in situations relevant to a particular trait. Traits are often characterized as **emotional**, **cognitive**, and **motivational tendencies** that affect important personal and social behavior. Personality characteristics of most concern are those related to the ways in which individuals interact with and affect one another; these are relevant to historically established differences between men and women in terms of power, status, and suitability for domestic and cultural roles.

One area of personality for which substantial gender differences have been found is emotional expressiveness. Men tend to mask the nature of the emotions they experience, and possibly as a consequence experience greater physiological reactions to emotional states. Women are more expressive of their emotions in general, which is likewise supported by meta-analysis ($d = 1.01$; Hall, 1984), indicating that 84% of women are more emotionally expressive than the average man (Lippa, 2002). Women are also more likely to accurately recognize and understand the nonverbal behavior of others ($d = .43$; Hall, 1984), such that 67% of women are more accurate than the average man (Lippa, 2002).

## Stylistic and Symbolic Characteristics

Women and adolescent girls are more likely to smile in general than are men and boys, with a $d$ of .41 reported by LaFrance and her colleagues (2003) and .42 reported by Hall and Halberstadt (1986). The gender difference is even greater when individuals are involved in same-sex interactions, with women smiling more in interacting with women than men do when interacting with men. In a related vein, interacting with a male partner produces a greater gender difference in smiling than interacting with a female partner, with women smiling more than men with a male partner. Males tend not to smile when with other males, possibly because interactions between males involve a great level of dominance striving, and smiling conveys a less dominant

*To smile or not to smile?* That is the question, particularly when talking with a person of the same sex. *What "forbidden" message does smiling seem to convey at least for men talking with other men?*

message. LaFrance and her colleagues also suggest that emotional expressiveness may be less valued by men, such that little motivation exists to promote smiling.

However, it is also possible that smiling is associated substantially with attraction and flirting. Because men tend to interpret social situations in more sexual ways in general than do women, heterosexual men are motivated, whether conscious or not, to avoid giving even the slightest hint of sexual attraction to other men. Therefore, it may be that smiling in reaction to the behavior of other men is uncomfortable, because smiling is strongly associated with attraction in heterosexual interactions.

## Gender Differences in Sexuality and Attraction

The de-eroticizing of the male body shows the priorities of manhood in our society. It can be depicted as a machine, a tool, a weapon, but very rarely as a sexual object. Whereas every aspect of the female body—lips, thighs, breasts, hips, ass—is inscribed with sexual implication, the cock is the only locus of sexuality on the male body. This is why men tend to center their sexuality so heavily around erection, penetration, and ejaculation: the cock is the one part of the male body that we are taught to associate with sex. Everything else—our muscles, hair, nipples—is neutered in the cultural eye. These things have values that can be measured and summed up in mathematical terms, as though they were nothing more than the results of a very sophisticated engineering project. (Hall, 2000, p. 164)

### Sexual Attitudes

Sexual attitudes and behaviors measured across 177 studies were included in a meta-analysis by Oliver and Hyde (1993) to examine whether gender differences exist in sexuality. With respect to attitudes, men held more positive attitudes on a number of issues. These include the acceptability of sexual intercourse outside of marriage between individuals involved in a casual dating relationship or with no emotional commitment ($d = .81$), nonmarital sexual intercourse when involved in a committed relationship ($d = .49$), nonmarital intercourse when engaged to be married ($d = .43$), the acceptability of nonmarital intercourse overall ($d = 37$), sexual permissiveness ($d = .57$), and the acceptability of extramarital behavior ($d = .29$). In contrast, women were slightly more likely to endorse the acceptability of the double standard, the idea that it is more acceptable for men to engage in sex outside of marriage ($d = .29$). Women were also somewhat more likely to report anxiety or guilt about sex ($d = .35$). Differences were not found in attitudes toward lesbians and gays, lesbian and gay civil rights, and masturbation, as well as in reports of sexual satisfaction.

## Sexual Behavior

Small to strong gender differences also occurred in most measures of sexual behavior. The exception is whether individuals had ever kissed, petted, or engaged in oral–genital sex, for which the differences were too small to represent noticeable distinctions in behavior. Males were found to have higher levels for the following aspects of sexuality: having ever masturbated ($d = .96$), age at first intercourse ($d = .38$), having ever engaged in sexual intercourse ($d = .33$), having ever engaged in same-sex behavior ($d = .33$), frequency of sexual intercourse ($d = .31$), and number of sexual partners ($d = .25$).

Age was negatively correlated with gender differences, indicating that the differences between women and men diminished with age. This was particularly the case with attitudes toward sex outside of marriage when engaged, attitudes toward lesbians and gays, number of sexual partners, frequency of sexual intercourse, and ever having masturbated. Oliver and Hyde (1993) noted the limitations of the research on sexuality that is available. Much of the information is based on 18- to 21-year-old individuals, which may not be representative of the sexuality of individuals later in life; it is therefore not possible to examine developmental trends that may provide a more accurate understanding.

In addition, all of the information was based on *self-reports* of sexual behavior, leaving open the possibility that differences in behavior do not actually exist (Oliver & Hyde, 1993). This issue was addressed in chapter 4 on research methods. Although it is important to be cautious about methodological issues related to validity, remember that much of the information available on sexual behavior is necessarily self-report. This has to do with the practical and ethical limitations of researchers or research equipment directly observing sexual behavior. Also, recall that self-reports of personality traits and behaviors often are fairly substantially corroborated by other methods of recording data.

## Sexual Fantasy

Research on the frequency of sexual fantasy has focused almost exclusively on heterosexual respondents, although some research has provided comparisons of the content of fantasies by gays and lesbians with that of heterosexuals. Little information is available for non-White individuals, because most research has included only White respondents. Sexual fantasy is typically examined with respect to three different settings: fantasy occurring during (a) masturbation, (b) sexual intercourse, and (c) nonsexual activities (Leitenberg & Henning, 1995).

Based on 13 studies analyzed by Leitenberg and Henning (1995), 85.9% of men and 68.8% of women reported having fantasized while masturbating. The problem with this comparison is that males tend to masturbate more than females, as well as starting on average at a much earlier age. This provides greater opportunity for males to have ever fantasized during masturbation. With respect to fantasy during sexual intercourse, 76.0% of males and 75.7% of females report fantasizing during sexual intercourse across seven studies that provide percentages for both sexes. These are virtually identical values, suggesting no difference between men and women. The proportions do not appear to have changed across historical periods, given that percentages were similar no matter the year in which the study was published, ranging from 1953 to 1990.

Very few studies have addressed the issue of fantasy during nonsexual activities (e.g., working on a task), and only two have included both males and females (Leitenberg & Henning, 1995). The percentages in the two studies are 97% and 82% for men, and 100% and 81% for women (Knafo & Jaffe, 1984; Davidson, 1985, respectively), indicating virtually identical levels for the sexes. Across the three studies including men, 93.0% of men report fantasizing while engaged in nonsexual activities. Across the five studies including women, 84.8% of women report such fantasizing. Because of the low number of studies on which these data are based, it is probably safest to conclude that very large and highly similar proportions of women and men have fantasized during nonsexual activities.

With respect to frequency of fantasy, a study by Jones and Barlow (1990) had participants record any time they experienced a sexual fantasy or thought, whether during masturbation, other sexual behavior, or nonsexual activities. Women reported on average 4.5 experiences per day, while men reported 7.2 experiences per day. Across all other studies that were based on retrospective self-report (estimating behavior that has occurred in the past), males report more frequent sexual fantasy than females. In fact, males report experiencing at least one sexual fantasy a day, with several studies indicating that males fantasize several times a day about sexual topics. Females typically report experiencing sexual fantasy less than once a day, usually about once per week.

In contrast, women and men report fantasizing during sexual intercourse with fairly equivalent frequency. Approximately, half of women and men report that they do so at least sometimes, if not often. The available evidence also suggests that both men and women who tend to fantasize about sexual issues experience greater levels of sexual arousal to a wider variety of sexual stimulation. Both males and females who fantasize more are also no less likely to be satisfied with their sexual relationships; several studies even suggest that they may be more likely to be sexually satisfied.

## *Summary*

Sex is the term applied to biological distinctions between males and females. Genetic sex is the genetic coding that influences the body to develop female or male features. Gender refers to the psychological, social, and cultural meanings associated with maleness and femaleness.

A recent version of the multifaceted view of gender is the extended multidimensional matrix of gender issues. Gender may be expressed across four specific dimensions: constructs (concepts), content areas, level of analysis, and time. Constructs consist of (a) beliefs or stereotypes, (b) identity, (c) preferences, and (d) behavioral enactment. Within each of these constructs, gender may be expressed in the form of particular content areas, which are (a) biological or categorical sex, (b) activities and interests, (c) personal and social attributes, (d) gender-based social relationships, (e) stylistic and symbolic characteristics, and (f) values.

The extended matrix model indicates that beliefs about gender may concern knowledge about gender. Gender beliefs also include knowledge about activities associated with each gender, attributes typical of each gender, typical social relationships, appropriate styles, and values.

The construct of identity concerns the ways in which one views oneself. Gender-role identity is the overarching sense of the extent to which an individual possesses the

*(Continued)*

(Continued)

characteristics expected of his or her gender. In terms of biological or categorical sex, individuals develop a gender identity, a sense of being either female or male. One's sense of masculinity–femininity typically overlaps almost perfectly with gender identity. Transgenderism is the possession of an identity that is substantially different from one's original anatomical sex or assigned gender.

Using the technique of meta-analysis, the existence of gender differences have been examined for various characteristics and behaviors across large numbers of studies. In quite a few ways, women and men are highly similar, given that we are all human beings.

Sexual anatomy is the most extreme aspect of differences between females and males. Female external sexual anatomy includes the labia majora, labia minora, and clitoris; the clitoris is an important source of stimulation involved in sexual stimulation. The female internal sexual anatomy includes the vagina, uterus, fallopian tubes, and ovaries. The ovaries are the female gonads, the organs that produce the eggs, sex cells that can be fertilized by male sperm to produce offspring. The ovaries also produce female sex hormones, estrogen and progesterone, which both contribute to the maturation and release of an egg and preparation of the uterus to receive a fertilized egg on a monthly basis. The release of the egg is called ovulation; menstruation is the shedding of the endometrium in the uterus to make way for the next build up of the lining. Estrogen is additionally involved in the development of the sexual organs, as well as secondary sex characteristics (e.g., breast maturation, pubic hair), at puberty.

The male external sexual anatomy consists of the penis and scrotum. The penis is the major source of stimulation involved in sexual pleasure for males, becoming erect during sexual arousal. The male internal sexual anatomy includes the testicles, which produce sperm, the male sex cell, as well as male sex hormones, most notably testosterone; testosterone is responsible for the maturation of primitive cells into sperm, as well as for the development of the sexual organs and secondary sex characteristics at puberty. The glands that contribute fluid to the sperm to create semen are the prostate, the seminal vesicles, and the Cowper's glands.

With respect to personal and social attributes, men tend to mask their emotions to a greater extent, whereas women are more emotionally expressive. Females are moderately more likely to smile than males, but even more so in same-sex interactions. Males tend to smile relatively little in interacting with other males.

Concerning gender differences in sexual attitudes, men tend to hold substantially more positive attitudes toward sexual intercourse with little or no emotional commitment and moderately more positive attitudes toward premarital sex and permissiveness in general. Men are substantially more likely to have masturbated, and are only slightly more likely to have engaged in various types of sexual behavior or to have had greater numbers of sexual partners. The differences tend to disappear with age. Regarding fantasy, the vast majority of males and females have engaged in fantasy during sexual intercourse, as well as during nonsexual activities. Engaging in greater levels of fantasy for both women and men is related to greater sexual arousal within all types of sexual stimulation. The tendency to fantasize is most likely not related to satisfaction with sexual relationships, or may even be related to greater satisfaction.

## Chapter 6 Critical Thinking Exercises

1.  Without referring to the information presented in the chapter, consider the following questions: Are women and men more similar than different, or more different than similar, with respect to sexual attitudes? What about with respect to sexual behavior? What about sexual fantasy?

2.  Do any of the research findings presented in the textbook argue against any of your previously held conclusions regarding sexual attitudes, sexual behavior, or sexual fantasy?

3.  What factors might account for the gender differences that were found in sexual attitudes, behavior, and fantasy? What factors might account for areas in which gender differences were not found?

**Visit www.sagepub.com/hillhsstudy.com for online activities, sample tests, and other helpful resources. Select "Chapter 6: Gender and Sexuality" for chapter-specific activities.**

# Chapter 7

## THE SEXUAL SELF AND SEXUAL IDENTITY

*My emotions play an enormous part in sex for me—maybe too much for my liking. I'm too "particular," or selective or delicate—I have to be feeling very intensely, or in love, or overwhelmed by sexual feelings in order to enter a deep sexual encounter. Sometimes I worry about whether the man will expect too much from me, sometimes whether I will expect too much from him. Sometimes I worry about whether I won't feel enough, or will be disappointed afterwards. At times I have gone out to have a totally casual encounter just to avoid these complications. (Hite, 1976, p. 481)*

This self-description is one of a number offered to Shere Hite that were included in an informal examination of female sexuality in the early 1970s. The woman's reflections concerning her feelings and view of herself could just as easily have been written by a young woman of today. She expresses the importance of her feelings in deciding whether to engage in sexual behavior with a romantic partner. She also evaluates her experiences in terms of whether they have met a personal standard she has set for herself. Her self-understanding seems to be based on a private, very personal exploration of her most inner thoughts and feelings, a process known as introspection in social psychology.

Furthermore, the woman engages in behavior based on her assessment of how she is feeling; sometimes she apparently behaves in a way that is opposite of her typical standards, out of frustration at the availability of a man who measures up to her expectations for an ideal romantic partner. Such reasoning is her own unique explanation for engaging in casual sexual encounters, a phenomenon

*What role do you think introspection and self-reflection play in your understanding of your sexuality? Is it an important source of information about who you are, sexually, or are other sources more important?*

that today is called "hooking up" on college campuses; this type of sexual behavior is discussed in detail later in chapter 10.

However, consider the situation in which self-views do not coincide with behavior at all. The description below by J. L. King (2004) is noteworthy because it reveals how individuals are not always aware of their own motivations or tendencies when strong social sanctions condemn and prohibit certain types of sexual relationships; in these situations, introspection and self-evaluation often do not provide a very accurate understanding of oneself. King uses a slang term common among some African Americans to refer to same-sex relationships that are hidden from friends, family, and others in general. Although the focus in this quote is on Black men, this type of secretive experience occurs among all other groups of people:

> I put a face and a name to the behavior. . . . It's called the DL—the down low—brothers who have sex with other brothers. They're not in the closet; they're behind the closet. They are so far removed from attaching themselves and what they do to the homosexual lifestyle that these men do not consider themselves to be gay. (p. 11)

> To these men gay people are over there—far away from them. Gays march in parades, hang out at gay clubs, go to gay beaches. (p. 19)

> These men may be successful. They may be celebrities. They are husbands, boyfriends, lovers, fathers, and grandfathers. . . . I have met many police officers, firemen, and even some serving in all branches of the military who live on the down low. They come in all shapes, sizes, and colors. (p. 18)

> These brothers don't even want to be called DL. They will not openly admit their desires for men. Even if caught in bed with another man, a DL man will deny anything remotely homosexual is going on. He will blame it on drugs, liquor, the lack of sex from his woman, depression, his weakness, or the need for attention—anything but being a homosexual. "Denial" is the operative word. (p. 21; from The Down Low, King, 2004)

Individuals who are on the down low avoid incorporating aspects of their sexual interest and behavior into an awareness of themselves. Such people therefore do not engage in behavior based on a complete understanding of themselves. These issues are considered later in the chapter in covering the development of heterosexual sexual identity.

The view that individuals develop and maintain of themselves has come to be one of the most heavily studied topics in social psychology within the past several decades. The system of beliefs that a person possesses about his or her characteristics, needs, goals, and abilities—called **the self**—affects behavior in pervasive and profound ways. Another name for the sense of self is **identity**, as defined in previous chapters. The self-conceptions that individuals tend to hold regarding sexual characteristics and sexual behavior in particular are collectively referred to as **the sexual self**, and also **sexual identity**.

Historically, the concept of sexual identity has not been treated with a great deal of consistency and has sometimes been confused with gender identity and gender-role identity; these latter two domains were examined in depth in the previous chapter. Sexual identity is in fact related to *gender identity*, one's sense of being female or male in a biological sense; sexual identity is also related to *gender-role identity*, one's sense of possessing characteristics stereotypically associated with the female or male gender. However, **sexual identity** is a distinct concept: the sense of what one is like sexually, in terms of desires, wishes, fantasies, attitudes, traits, and typical patterns of behavior.

## *The Social Nature of the Self*

People with disabilities who have obvious and subtle differences from our movie star fantasies often feel left out in the cold when it comes to looking and feeling sexy. . . . The stereotype of people with disabilities is that we are weak, dependent creatures. Those of us who live with disability know this to be untrue. Indeed the opposite is more often the case. We are strong, fiercely independent beings. We have had to be to survive in this hostile environment in which we find ourselves. This holds true in love and sexuality as well. (Brown, 2000, pp. 40–41)

The self is in great part a product of the interactions that we have with others and the feedback that we receive from them about what we are like. In fact, knowledge about ourselves is provided through four primary means (Aronson, Wilson, & Akert, 2005), three of which are social in nature. The first is simply thinking about what we are like and assessing our own thoughts and feelings, a process called **introspection**; in itself, introspection is not a highly interpersonal process. This is the method that many would intuitively assume is the major source of self-understanding. We are of course capable of monitoring and evaluating a great deal of the important aspects of our behavior, as well as the motives and goals that guide it, as illustrated by the woman's self-description at the beginning of the chapter.

However, research has also demonstrated that we may not always be aware of all of the factors that actually influence our behavior, particularly in any given situation. We are often not particularly accurate at judging the role that other people and the social environment play in determining our feelings and behavior. Moreover, a substantial portion of our own internal psychological activities and processes are simply not accessible by our conscious processes (Nisbett & Ross, 1980; Wilson, 2002). As the passage by J. L. King suggests, individuals may actually protect themselves from certain types of self-knowledge when behaviors and relationships are viewed negatively by society. The only way that we can examine these nonconscious activities is through clever and intricate techniques developed to measure them indirectly in scientific research. Consequently, rather than being able to depend extensively on introspection, we may actually rely more heavily on other sources of information about ourselves.

A second source of knowledge about ourselves comes in the form of **self-perception**, observing how we behave and then inferring what we are like and what our motives are (Bem, 1972). Although we may not have direct access to all of the psychological processes and social influences that affect our behavior, we are of course able to monitor our overt actions. This information may fill in the gaps for when we are not able to directly monitor or keep track of psychological functioning and social factors, or when we have not established our feelings about a particular issue with a great deal of certainty (Andersen, 1984; Andersen & Ross, 1984; Kunda, Fong, Sanitioso, & Reber, 1993).

A third means of obtaining self-knowledge is **reflected appraisal**, which means observing others' reactions to us as we engage in behavior and interact with them. In this sense, observing others' reactions to us is similar to having someone hold a mirror up to us as we behave so that we can see what we are like; for these reasons, earlier theorists referred to this knowledge of ourselves as **the looking glass self** (*looking glass* is an old-fashioned term for *mirror;* Cooley, 1902; Mead, 1934). We are able to directly monitor the way that people respond to our actions and statements, giving us information about our characteristics, such as whether we

How often do we look to others as a comparison to judge our own tendencies and characteristics? When do you think we are most likely to look for this type of information?

are friendly, competent, interesting, or aggressive, among others.

A fourth, related source of self-information is **social comparison** (Festinger, 1954), the process of evaluating our behavior, attributes, abilities, beliefs, and feelings in terms of how they compare with those of others. We watch the actions and behavior of others and use these as a standard to see if we are more or less like them. This is an extensively used method of obtaining an understanding of ourselves, one likely to be used frequently even though we may not be aware of it. However, social comparison is especially likely to occur under conditions in which we are unsure of how we are supposed to react or feel in a particular situation. Therefore, when it is unclear what is expected of us and we experience doubt or ambiguity, we look to others to see what they are doing to get an idea of how we should behave. A young person on his first date may see that other young couples are sitting close to one another, touching and holding hands. He is then likely to move closer to his date and begin to do the same, if he is inclined to engage in sensual behavior. He may then come to see himself as a sensual, sexually assertive person, especially if he learns or believes that relatively few of his peers have engaged in this type of behavior.

Research indicates that individuals are actually much more likely to focus on aspects of themselves that are unique or that distinguish them from others. Characteristics that are relatively rare or infrequent tend to be noticed and may become defining features of one's self-concept. This is known as the **distinctiveness effect**. An individual who has red hair, for example, is more likely to focus on this attribute than are individuals who have black or brown or blond hair, because red hair is a relatively less-common color. Members of minority groups within a given society tend to incorporate their group status into their sense of self, their identity, to a greater extent than members of the majority group. Blacks, Native Americans, Asian Americans, and other ethnic minority individuals often hold their racial or ethnic status as a highly salient aspect of their sense of self-definition (McGuire & McGuire, 1988). This is likely to be equally true with respect to *sexual* group membership for those who are lesbian, gay, bisexual, or asexual (an asexual orientation is one in which an individual does not have a significant sexual interest in either women or men; asexual individuals experience little attraction or arousal to either sex).

## Development of Self-Conceptions About Sexuality

As with all other important or salient aspects of oneself, individuals likewise develop an understanding of their sexuality as well. However, given the significant role that interaction with the social world plays in the development of self-conceptions, the process through which individuals arrive upon an understanding of their sexual feelings, desires, and behaviors is likely to be somewhat different from other aspects of the self. Specifically, the development of sexual self-conceptions may be less direct, limited in substance to a greater extent, or more prone to distortion for two reasons (Garcia & Carrigan, 1998): limited direct sexual contact and negative attitudes about sexuality.

First, because sexuality is considered an extremely private area of one's life, very few people have direct interaction with others in a sexual way, even in terms of discussing issues of sexuality. This limits the influence of the process of **reflected appraisal** (Cooley, 1902; Mead, 1934); again, this is the process through which we obtain information about what we are like on the basis of others' reactions to our behavior. Likewise, the lack of opportunity to observe others in terms of their sexual behavior, or even in terms of discovering their sexual attitudes, greatly restricts our ability to obtain information through social comparison (Festinger, 1954). Even the process of **self-perception** is constrained by the limited opportunity to obtain information in interaction with others, because individuals typically have sexual contact with very few others. In contrast, self-perception is a major source of information for nonsexual types of behavior, such as friendliness, sociability, assertiveness, dominance, and even physical abilities as we see how we perform in recreational activities and sports.

A second reason that the development of sexual self-conceptions may be limited, according to Garcia and Carrigan (1998), is the anxiety, negative beliefs, and guilt typically associated with sexuality in many Western cultures. Negative emotions often cause individuals to avoid topics and situations that produce unpleasant experiences. Consequently, many individuals may be motivated not to think about their sexual feelings, limiting the process of introspection in developing an understanding of what they are like sexually. Sexual self-conceptions may therefore tend to be shallow or very limited, if not virtually nonexistent, or consist of entirely negative evaluations of oneself. One line of research on sexual self-schemas has addressed this possibility of differences in self-conceptions about sexuality, including the possibility that some individuals may have very little sense of themselves in a sexual sense.

## Sexual Self-Schemas and Self-Conceptions

The self is not merely a random assortment of beliefs about oneself. Instead, self-conceptions are meaningfully organized within conceptual networks of related ideas. Especially strongly related features or groupings of information about oneself may be organized within a particular network, which is known as a **self-schema**. A schema is a network of related knowledge, beliefs, feelings, and values concerning a specific aspect of the world that is developed through experience; a self-schema is a specific type of schema, one dealing with information about oneself. Self-schemas are "libraries" of knowledge that are accessed when information from the world or from one's mental processes enters consciousness; self-schemas exist for every feature or aspect of a person of which he or she is aware. They are used to understand the information an individual encounters during their many experiences by matching existing knowledge about oneself with the incoming information.

Well-developed self-schemas lend meaning to the information we come across by serving as a template, or model. Self-schemas allow us to react to situations quickly and with minimal effort, particularly if they are familiar situations. For extremely familiar and important aspects of our lives, we develop highly elaborate self-schemas because they contain a lot of information as we accumulate experiences related to them; such schemas tend to consist of strong, well-defined pieces of information that are easily and quickly available to us. Individuals who have such a well-developed self-schema for a given attribute have been termed **schematic** for that characteristic; those who do not have a highly developed self-schema are called **aschematic** (not having a schema) for the particular characteristic (Markus, 1977).

### A Model of Sexual Self-Schemas

Self-schemas related to sexuality have been called **sexual self-schemas** by Andersen and Cyranowski (1994; Andersen, Cyranowski, & Espindle, 1999; Cyranowski & Andersen, 1998), two of the earliest researchers in the area of the sexual self. As with other self-schemas, sexual self-schemas develop through experience, in this case experience with sexual issues and sexual behavior. They likewise are used to understand current situations and experiences, and they affect behavior through a person's interpretation of those situations. Well-elaborated sexual self-schemas may be expected to exert a stronger influence on perception and overt behavior than less-developed self-schemas.

Andersen and Cyranowski ultimately proposed a two-dimensional model of sexual self-schemas. Specifically, positive and negative views of sexuality are conceived as existing along two separate dimensions that are independent of one another (see Figure 7.1). Consequently, some individuals may possess schemas that consist of high levels of both of these views; such individuals are called **co-schematic**. Other individuals are proposed to have views that have not developed very strongly along either the positive or negative dimensions, and are therefore **aschematic**, which means having very little sense of oneself as sexual at all. In other words, the revised model consists of four possible sexual self-schemas that different individuals may develop: (a) a positive self-schema, (b) a negative self-schema, (c) a co-schematic self-schema, and (d) an aschematic self-schema.

The two sexual self-schema dimensions are measured through a self-report questionnaire that presents 50 trait descriptors that individuals rate according to how characteristic they are of themselves. The positive dimension is measured by adding together traits that are related to being passionate and romantic, as well as open and direct about sexuality. The negative dimension reflects traits of embarrassment and conservatism toward sexuality.

**FIGURE 7.1**    The Two Dimensions of Sexual Self-Schemas

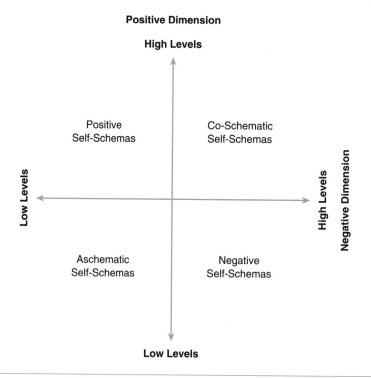

From Andersen, B. L., & Cyranowski, J. M. (1994). Women's sexual self-schema. *Journal of Personality and Social Psychology, 67,* 1079–1100. Copyright © American Psychological Association. Reprinted with permission.

In research by Cyranowski and Andersen (1998), women with largely positive self-schemas were more likely to report that they are extremely passionate about their romantic partner and that they desired greater emotional intimacy. They also have been involved in a greater number of romantic relationships, as well as being more likely to be in a relationship at the time of the study. Women with negative self-schemas reported lower levels of passionate love, greater sexual anxiety, and tended to have an avoidant perspective toward relationships, meaning that they tended to be more distant and fearful of intimacy. Negative self-schema women also reported fewer romantic relationships. Co-schematic women—those possessing both positive and negative views of themselves—tended to report stronger levels of sexual desire and arousal, as well as greater levels of passionate love, desire for emotional intimacy, involvement in relationships, and relationship satisfaction; yet, they also reported greater levels of insecurity about being abandoned or not being loved by their romantic partner. Women who were aschematic were similar to those with negative schemas in having fewer romantic relationships, being less passionate, avoiding emotional intimacy, and being anxious about being abandoned or unloved by their romantic partner, as well as being anxious about sex itself. Finally, they tended to express low levels of sexual desire and arousal.

Women with positive sexual self-schemas express greater passion and desire for emotional intimacy with their romantic partner compared with women with other types of self-schemas. They are also more likely to be involved in romantic relationships.

In later research focused on men, Andersen and her colleagues (Andersen et al., 1999) determined that the sexual self-schemas of men consist of three dimensions that bear some similarities to women, but they also possess striking differences. The dimensions are **passionate–loving**, **powerful–aggressive**, and **open-minded–liberal**. The first dimension, passionate–loving, is very similar to the first dimension identified for women, which is similarly related to romantic, passionate, and tender types of behaviors. The open-minded–liberal dimension is also fairly similar to the negative dimension found for women, but in the direction opposite of conservatism and embarrassment. However, in contrast to women, men who view themselves as more open-minded also tend to engage in greater emotional involvement in relationships. The open-minded–liberal dimension for women was more related to the lack of anxiety among those who are open-minded, whereas those who are less open-minded tend to experience anxiety; this was not the case for men.

The existence of the powerful–aggressive aspect of men's self-schemas, according to Andersen and her colleagues, is consistent with previous evidence related to personality and sexuality for men. The tendencies to be strong and independent have been identified as central aspects of male personality. This self-schema dimension was found to be related to a motivation or interest in sexual activity. As with women, Anderson and her colleagues additionally examined sexual self-schemas of men in terms of a more general positive versus negative dimension. Based on this approach, sexually schematic men may be characterized most accurately as not only passionate, but also warm, compassionate, and loving.

Men with more positive sexual self-schemas are not only more sexually passionate, they also tend to be more loving and affectionate.

Andersen and Cyranowski proposed that one's sexual self-schemas develop as a result of the type of attachment individuals have with their parents in the early years of their lives. Attachment theory (Bowlby, 1969, 1973) views the early parent–child relationship as central in influencing the way that individuals come to represent the world and themselves. Secure, positive attachments are proposed to lead individuals to feel secure in emotional intimacy with others, which generalizes to feelings that develop later in life related to romantic involvement. Individuals who experience rejecting, cold, or inconsistent parenting are hypothesized to develop conceptions of themselves that they are unworthy of love; they have been found to experience insecurity or indifference later in life regarding romantic involvement. Andersen and Cyranowski proposed that these effects extend to the development of feelings regarding sexual intimacy and relationships as well as romantic involvement. Secure attachment early in life may contribute to the development of positive sexual self-schemas, whereas rejecting attachment experiences may contribute to negative self-schemas.

## A Model of Sexual Self-Conceptions

An alternative view advanced by Garcia (1999; Garcia & Carrigan, 1998) proposes that six dimensions are necessary to adequately characterize self-conceptions about sexuality. The dimensions, which can be considered equivalent to the concept of sexual self-schemas, are assessed by combining self-report ratings of 38 traits. The dimensions are (a) extent of **sexual experience**, (b) **sexual deviance** ("kinkiness"), (c) **sexual attitudes** (liberal, permissive), (d) **sexual attractiveness**, (e) **sexual responsiveness** (excitable, orgasmic), and (f) **romanticism** (loving, romantic).

In this research, men viewed themselves as more sexually experienced, more sexually "deviant" or kinky, and more sexually responsive than women viewed themselves. Women may be somewhat more likely to view themselves as sexually attractive and romantic, although gender differences for these two dimensions were not found in the second study (Garcia, 1999). Garcia noted that the gender differences are consistent with traditional beliefs about the nature of women and men, suggesting that individuals tend to assimilate such stereotypes into their self-views.

In addition, reports of sexual behavior were found to correlate with greater levels of all six self-conceptions. Garcia concluded that such a behavior–self-view connection supports the self-perception process of self-schema development discussed previously. To the extent that individuals engage in a certain type of behavior, they will come to perceive themselves as possessing characteristics related to that particular behavior. The strength of an individual's **certainty** about his or her sexual self-conceptions was additionally shown to correlate with ratings of extensiveness of sexual behavior. These results are consistent with the self-perception explanation of self-conceptions; this explanation indicates that people become more certain that they possess specific tendencies because they observe themselves engaging in behaviors related to these tendencies more frequently. The certainty finding is also supportive of the position that feedback from others contributes to the development of self-conceptions. Feedback from others was the source of self-knowledge discussed previously called **reflected appraisals** (Cooley, 1902; Mead, 1934), referring to the reactions others have regarding our characteristics as we interact with them.

Furthermore, certainty about self-conceptions has been shown to relate to the tendency to seek feedback from others and, in particular, feedback that supports one's already established self-conceptions; this tendency to seek information from others about one's self-concept is known as **self-verification** (Swann, 1987). Feedback that confirms one's already existing self-conception would naturally bolster individuals' views of themselves, making firmly held self-views highly stable and resistant to change. Individuals who see themselves, for example, as sexually monogamous, or as sexually attractive or as possessing any other characteristic, may be expected to seek out information that confirms that particular self-conception; for this reason, they are likely to develop more extreme self-views over time. In support of this, extremity of sexual self-conceptions was in fact found to be related to greater certainty about one's self-view (Garcia, 1999). Self-conceptions are likely to be reinforced by further behavior as well, because self-conceptions produce behavior that is consistent with the self-conceptions, and the additional behavior reinforces the self-conception (Breakwell & Millward, 1997).

---

**Box 7.1**                                                    **An Eye Toward Research**

### Adolescent Sexual Self-Conceptions

Another perspective used in investigating the important aspects of sexual self-conceptions is that advanced by Breakwell and Millward (1997). These researchers conducted a study involving a younger sample than in the other two studies that are presented in the main body of the text—474 British adolescents between the ages of 16 and 19 years. Essentially, they asked the question: How are the sexual self-conceptions of young people different from one another? Well, it depends on whether you are a young woman or a young man.

In their study, participants rated themselves on 14 characteristics related to sexuality. Statistical analyses of the ratings were conducted to determine the number of dimensions underlying the group of characteristics. Results of the study suggested that the dimensions at the root of the self-conceptions of males are different than those for females.

The first dimension emerging from the factor analysis for males was labeled the socio-emotional component by Breakwell and Millward (1997); this factor consisted of the traits romantic, passionate, sensitive, eroticism, and faithfulness. The second dimension was the relationship component, comprising the traits unwilling to have sex before marriage, not keen on sexual experimentation, faithfulness, uninterested in sex, unlikely to seduce, and unlikely to exploit the other sex. A more descriptive label for this dimension might be conservativism, given that the first dimension deals with tendencies essential to relationship quality as well; the second factor focuses more on a restrictive attitude toward sexuality in particular.

*(Continued)*

(Continued)

> For females, only one dimension of sexual self-concept was found to be statistically stable. This dimension can be considered a counterpart to the second dimension for males, and represented a sense of liberalism. The female dimension included the traits of keen on sexual experimentation, not interested in sex (scored in the opposite direction), passionate, unwilling to have sex before marriage (scored in the opposite direction), knowledgeable about sex, likely to seduce someone, responsible for contraception, romantic, and in control when sex happens.
>
> Breakwell and Millward (1997) drew two major conclusions from their study. The first is that young women incorporate an element of assertiveness in their self-conception in addition to an interest in sexual expression. This is indicated by the traits of willingness to seduce, being responsible for contraception, and being in control also being a part of the dimension. These findings suggest therefore that the potential for women to be sexually open and adventurous involves a degree of assertiveness and initiative. Similar characteristics do not cluster together as components of male self-conceptions. This may be related to the fact that assertiveness is a standard expectation for males in general and that differences among males for assertiveness are not central to their self-conceptions in this way. However, differences in assertiveness are found for women, and contribute to their sexual self-conceptions.
>
> The other conclusion the researchers drew was that differences in sexual self-conceptions for males involve differences in emotional intimacy. Traits related to emotional intimacy did not fall into a separate, distinct dimension for females as they did for males, indicating that self-conceptions are not organized according to these characteristics for females. Again, this may be due to the fact that being emotionally intimate is a standard expectation for females, such that the tendency is not a central component of their self-conceptions. The separation of emotional intimacy from the degree to which males are sexually open and adventurous is consistent with sexual stereotypes; males tend to be viewed as more willing to engage in sexual behavior that does not involve emotional attachment or commitment. However, some males are more likely to view themselves as experiencing a great deal of emotional intimacy within sexual relationships, as indicated by the emotional intimacy factor that resulted from the factor analysis. This indicates that some males—those who also have a stronger self-conception as sexually liberal—also tend to experience intense emotional intimacy, even as they tend to be sexually adventurous.
>
> **Reference**
>
> Breakwell, G. M., & Millward, L. J. (1997). Sexual self-concept and sexual risk-taking. *Journal of Adolescence, 20,* 29–41.

## *Sexual Identity*

*Sexual identity* is the broad understanding that an individual has of *all* aspects of his or her sexuality, which includes one's *sexual orientation identity.* A self-understanding of being sexually and romantically attracted to males, females, or both, has come to be called **sexual orientation identity** (Mohr, 2002; Worthington, Savoy, Dillon, & Vernaglia, 2002). **Sexual orientation**, in contrast, is typically conceived as a relatively stable tendency to experience emotional, romantic, or sexual attraction to males or females, or both sexes (American Psychological Association, 1998). It is generally conceived of as a characteristic of the individual that may be independent of self-perception.

However, the *understanding* that an individual has of his or her sexual orientation is considered by many theorists to be highly important as well, and according to some theorists (Rust, 1993), more important than "actual" sexual orientation. "Actual" sexual orientation could include occasional fantasy and behavior that is different from the majority of other fantasy and behavior; the occasional experiences however may not be represented in the person's self-understanding about sexual orientation.

Yet, possibly because of the tremendous social, political, and religious issues underlying sexual orientation, most past research has focused on the causes of sexual orientation, rather than on the role of sexual orientation identity, or even on sexual identity in general. The lack of theory and research on the broader dimension of sexual identity has, in fact, been identified as a major weakness of research on sexuality (Worthington et al., 2002).

Why is sexual identity important? It is important not only because the understanding individuals have of themselves influences the types of sexual behavior in which they engage, but it also has effects on a wide range of social behavior, influencing the ways in individuals relate to others and the types of groups with whom they affiliate. An individual who views herself as highly sexual and greatly interested in sex may be exceptionally comfortable addressing issues related to sexuality, and may prefer to have friends who likewise feel comfortable with sexuality. On the other hand, an individual who engages in a great deal of sexual behavior and masturbation, but does not acknowledge the extensiveness of her sexual behaviors within her self-view, may be more willing to associate with those who hold negative beliefs about sexuality. She may also tend to avoid discussions of sexuality, or even actively express negative views of sexuality herself.

*Do you think that this person's sexual attitudes, fantasies, and behaviors are a primary part of her self-concept, even if she engages in sexual behavior frequently? What type of image do you think she presents to her family, friends, and colleagues?*

## A Multidimensional Model of Sexual Identity

A general model of sexual identity and its development—one explicitly encompassing all types of sexual orientation identity—has not yet been advanced within science. Lesbian, gay, and bisexual identities will be considered first because these were the first to be proposed. Several models have been advanced recently, however, that address heterosexual sexual identity. These will be considered after the nonheterosexual identity models. Despite their primary focus on sexual orientation identity, the models also provide the basis for a theory of *sexual* identity, because in fact they deal with a number of possible components beyond sexual orientation identity.

The model of sexual identity presented in this section is an extension of the multidimensional model of heterosexual identity development proposed by Worthington and his colleagues (2002). Sexual identity development may be defined as "the . . . processes by which . . . [individuals] acknowledge and define their sexual needs, values, sexual orientation and preferences for sexual activities, modes of sexual expression, and characteristics of sexual partners" (p. 510). In line with earlier models of racial identity (Cross, 1978) and lesbian identity (McCarn & Fassinger, 1996), Worthington and colleagues propose that sexual identity consists of two components. The first of these components is **individual sexual identity**, which is recognition and acceptance of one's sexual needs, preferences, and tendencies. Sexual identity also involves a sense of belonging to a particular sexual identity group, as well as attitudes toward other sexual orientation groups; this aspect of one's self-concept is called social identity (Worthington et al., 2002), or more accurately **social sexual identity** (see Figure 7.2). Social sexual identity includes not only membership in a particular sexual orientation group (meaning a collection of people sharing an orientation, not a formally organized group); it may also include belonging to a class of people based on other aspects of sexuality, such as being celibate, involvement in a non-monogamous relationship, being nudist, engaging in voyeurism, enjoying role-played sexual dominance and submission, or being sexually conservative and restrictive.

**FIGURE 7.2**    Model of Sexual Identity

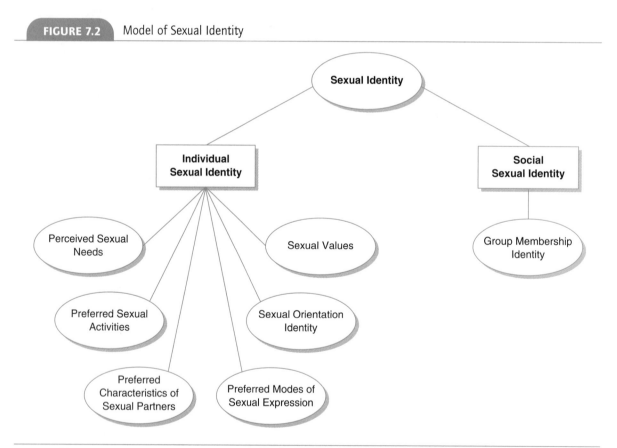

From Worthington, R. L., Savoy, H. B., Dillon, F. R., & Vernaglia, E. R. (2002). Heterosexual identity development: A multidimensional model of individual and social identity. *The Counseling Psychologist, 30,* 496–531. Copyright © Sage Publications, Inc. Reprinted with permission.

Individual sexual identity, according to Worthington and colleagues (2002), consists of a number of specific components:

(a) identification and awareness of one's sexual needs, (b) adoption of personal sexual values, (c) awareness of preferred sexual activities, (d) awareness of preferred characteristics of sexual partners, (e) awareness of preferred modes of sexual expression, and (f) recognition and identification with sexual orientation (i.e., sexual orientation identity). (p. 512)

Worthington and his colleagues define **sexual needs** as largely biologically based feelings of desire and interest; they place sexual orientation in this category, because they presume that it is very strongly determined by biological factors. The issue of the development of sexual orientation is addressed in another section, but it should be noted that, in fact, agreement has not been reached among scientists regarding the primary causes of sexual orientation; evidence does suggest, however, that biological factors play a substantial role.

**Sexual values** are beliefs about the goodness, appropriateness, and desirability of various sexual issues and sexual behavior. An overwhelmingly important basis for sexual values was examined in chapter 2 related to religion and philosophy, and the development of these values was presented in chapter 3 in detailing the history of sexual issues in Western and American cultures.

**Sexual activities** are defined by Worthington and colleagues (2002) as behaviors such as fantasizing, touching, kissing, masturbating, and engaging in penile–vaginal intercourse; other behavior might include oral–genital and penile–anal intercourse. A critical aspect of this definition is that the behaviors are based on sexual attraction or arousal, or the desire for reproduction, because this aspect of identity is defined as one's *preferred* sexual activities. **Preferred characteristics of a sexual partner** involve "any physical, emo-

tional, intellectual, interpersonal, economic, spiritual or other attributes that might be preferred in a potential or current sexual partner" (Worthington et al., 2002, p. 512). **Preferred modes of sexual expression** refer to the types of communication in which an individual engages to define his or her sexuality; the mode may be verbal or involve nonverbal examples listed by Worthington and colleagues such as "flirting, eye contact, touching, vocal quality, compliments, suggestive body movements or postures" (p. 512).

**Sexual orientation identity** is an individual's understanding of his or her sexual orientation, which is the attraction, sexual desire for, and likelihood of engaging in sexual behavior with females or males. One may develop the perception that he or she is (a) sexually oriented exclusively or primarily toward those of the other sex, therefore having a **heterosexual identity**; (b) sexually oriented exclusively or primarily

Individuals have preferred modes of sexual expression, which may include flirting, touching, and eye contact.

toward those of the same sex, therefore possessing a **same-gender sexual orientation identity**, which includes **lesbian identity** and **gay identity**; (c) sexually oriented toward both females and males, therefore having a **bisexual identity**; or (d) a variety of identities representing combinations of identities, or alternatively a **questioning identity** (uncertain of, or uncommitted about, one's interest) or a **pansexual identity** (oriented toward a wide range of sexual partners).

## Theoretical Models of Lesbian, Gay, and Bisexual Sexual Orientation Identity

Theoretical models of lesbian, gay, and bisexual sexual orientation identity were actually developed several decades prior to the models of heterosexual sexual identity, which have only been proposed within the past several years. In fact, the LGB (lesbian, gay, bisexual) identity models were the forerunners of theory about heterosexual identity. Theorists concerned about the well-being of LGB individuals within an oppressive society were anxious to develop LGB identity models early on. The concern was to examine the process through which nonheterosexual individuals develop a healthy, well-grounded identity despite the tremendous challenges and disadvantages they must confront.

Although a recent model of sexual orientation identity advanced by D'Augelli (1994) is intended to be relevant to lesbians, gay men, and bisexual individuals in general, other models have been proposed specifically for the development of identity by lesbian and bisexual women (Chapman & Brannock, 1987; Faderman, 1984; McCarn & Fassinger, 1996; Sophie, 1985–1986). A number of theorists have cited evidence that suggests fundamentally different factors are involved in the sexuality of women compared with men (Baumeister, 2000; Peplau, 2001; Schneider, 2001); specifically, women tend to be much more relationship-focused in their sexuality, as well as to have greater flexibility in its development and expression. Likely because of such differences in the focus and functioning of female sexuality, several studies have provided evidence that identity formation runs a somewhat different course for women and men (Schneider, 2001). Overall, however, little research has been conducted to support or refute many of the identity models. Therefore, both the general model and the more specific model for women advanced most recently by McCarn and Fassinger (1996) are presented in this section. Table 7.1 provides a comparison of the two models.

The D'Augelli model rejects what have been called **essentialist views**, which conceive of identity as an eventual awareness of some "true" nature, some preexisting *essence* or quality within an individual that he or she must discover and come to terms with. In fact, particularly with respect to lesbian and bisexual women, various individuals experience same-gender attraction and identity formation at different points in their lives. In research by Schneider (2001), some women report that they have always felt like they were lesbian from their earliest memories. Other women enjoy an extremely satisfying early life involved in a heterosexual relationship, only becoming interested in women and involved in a same-gender relationship later in life. Yet others experience periods of uncertainty or lack of self-identification as a lesbian, possibly while occasionally or extensively involved in a relationship with a woman. Other women experience a period of "being on hold" in the early part of their life, waiting until later to consider issues of sexuality.

Despite endorsing the view of sexual orientation identity as potentially a fluid process, Schneider (2001) observes that

> it does appear, phenomenologically [subjectively] at least, that some people's sexual orientation is fixed and does not change over the life span. Perhaps, sexual orientation is fixed in some individuals, or it is fixed in everyone, early in life, but with a greater or lesser degree of flexibility that varies from person to person. (p. 78; the word in brackets added)

| TABLE 7.1 | Two Models of Lesbian, Gay, and Bisexual Sexual Orientation Identity Development |
|---|---|

| D'Augelli (1994) Lesbian, Gay, and Bisexual Identity Development | | McCarn and Fassinger (1996) Lesbian Identity Development | |
|---|---|---|---|
| **Steps** | **Psychological Events Involved** | **Phase** | **Psychological Events Involved** |
| | | Awareness phase | Recognition of same-gender attraction |
| | | Exploration phase | Conscious analysis of same-gender identity |
| Exiting heterosexual identity | Adopting a nonheterosexual identity and coming out | | |
| Developing a lesbian-gay-bisexual personal identity status | Modifying one's self-view, heavily based on interaction with others, particularly other lesbians, gays, or bisexuals | Deepening and commitment | Formation of a coherent understanding of one's thoughts, feelings, and desires |
| Developing a lesbian-gay-bisexual social identity | Establishing an association with others who are aware of one's sexual orientation identity and who are supportive and affirming | | |
| Becoming a lesbian-gay-bisexual offspring | Attempting to guide family members beyond simple tolerance toward being affirming of one's nonheterosexual identity | | |
| Developing a lesbian-gay-bisexual intimacy status | Overcoming societal obstacles to forming a satisfying intimate relationship | | |
| Entering a lesbian-gay-bisexual community | Recognition of the societal obstacles involved in a nonheterosexual identity, possibly attempting to overcome them | | |
| | | Internalization and synthesis | Integrating one's desire and love for women into one's self-understanding, and organizing self-conceptions in a meaningful way |

According to D'Augelli (1994), hormonal factors cause sexual identity to become especially relevant at particular times, such as during puberty when secondary sex characteristics begin to develop and sexual interest increases. Yet, social and cultural expectations about adolescent sexuality affect the way in which individuals interpret and react to such changes. A specific outcome in response to such changes is not considered to be preordained and rigidly controlled by biological development. During adolescence, peer influences become more prominent as the influence of the family wanes in its shadow. Peer attitudes typically include strong currents of homophobia—negative attitudes toward gay men, lesbians, and bisexual individuals. Even as adolescents become aware of their same-gender feelings and a lesbian or gay identity may begin to emerge, powerful anti-lesbian and anti-gay beliefs make it very difficult for nonheterosexual individuals to explore such an identity. Adolescents who reveal their lesbian or gay identity sometimes place themselves at great peril.

The D'Augelli model of sexual orientation identity proposes that substantial differences exist across individuals in the process of identity formation, as well as dismissing the traditional notion of only four distinct types of sexual orientation (i.e., lesbian, gay, bisexual, and heterosexual). Instead, it allows for a range of feelings and behavior that may defy these rigid categories, and that may change at different points in a person's life. The model also emphasizes the active role that individuals and their family members have on the evolution of identity, instead of viewing individuals as passive recipients of biological and environmental influences.

## Steps Involved in Lesbian-Gay-Bisexual Identity Development

So, what specifically takes place in the formation of lesbian–gay identity? Rather than thinking of the changes that occur during this process as psychological stages, D'Augelli (1994) refers to them as **steps**, and McCarn and Fassinger (1996) identify them as **phases**. The reason is to avoid the sense that one rigid, uniform pathway exists for all individuals. The problem with the concept of stages is the proposal that all individuals progress uniformly through exactly the same stages in the same order. Central to stage theories in psychology is the concept that one must deal with issues at earlier stages before proceeding on to later stages. A more accurate perspective of identity development is that individuals may return to confront previously examined issues a number of times; self-understanding is more fluid and changeable than conveyed by a stage-theory approach.

D'Augelli (1994) emphasizes a sense of fluidity by defining identity as ongoing, ever changing processes of self-understanding that occur across the course of a person's lifetime. Similarly, McCarn and Fassinger describe the movement to different phases as continuous and circular, meaning that individuals may cycle back to previous phases. Identity is not an end-product in this conceptualization, rather it is a work-in-progress throughout the person's life.

D'Augelli (1994) proposes that individuals may engage in six steps during the process of identity construction: (a) exiting or leaving heterosexual identity, (b) developing a lesbian-gay-bisexual personal identity status, (c) developing a lesbian-gay-bisexual social identity, (d) becoming a lesbian-gay-bisexual offspring, (e) developing a lesbian-gay-bisexual intimacy status, and (f) entering a lesbian-gay-bisexual community. The phases proposed by McCarn and Fassinger (1996) focus less on content and development in specific domains than do the steps proposed by D'Augelli. The four phases identified by McCarn and Fassinger for lesbian identity development are (a) awareness, (b) exploration, (c) deepening/commitment, and (d) internalization/synthesis. The model presented later for heterosexual identity development by Worthington, Savoy, Dillon, and Vernaglia (2002) is based directly on the McCarn–Fassinger model. However, they refer to the various phases as steps, and add one step to their model.

### Awareness (McCarn & Fassinger, 1996)

The **awareness phase** proposed by McCarn and Fassinger in many ways precedes the first step proposed by D'Augelli (1994). This phase involves a recognition that the individual feels different desires and attraction than dictated by heterosexual society. The previously unacknowledged assumptions that all people are naturally attracted to the other sex are examined and possibly questioned, or even challenged. However, growing awareness of sexual feelings that are at odds with powerful societal expectations does not necessarily result in the individual viewing herself or himself as lesbian or gay. This phase is simply the first glimmer of the possibility of experiencing nonheterosexual feelings.

Research increasingly suggests that lesbians tend to come out later in life than do gay men, with women following a great variety of developmental pathways for their identity formation. It appears that, particularly for women, lesbian identity is most accurately viewed as an unfolding, creative process that may begin at virtually any point in their lives (Diamond, 1998; Schneider, 2001). Moreover, Schneider proposes that lesbian development is most accurately viewed within the context of **self-in-relation theory** (Surrey, 1991), which is a perspective that conceives of women's development as an increasing potential for competence in social interactions and relationships. This view acknowledges the absolutely essential role that establishing relationships have in the development of women's sexuality. Involvement in relationships as a means of exploring issues of sexuality may be less central for the development of male sexual identity, because evidence indicates that men are more likely to separate sexuality from relationship intimacy (Schneider, 2001).

The emotional intimacy provided by a romantic relationship is critical to the exploration of sexuality for many lesbians. In contrast, relationship intimacy is less essential to many gay men as a prerequisite for sexual exploration.

What about the formation of the group membership aspect of sexual orientation identity? Group membership identity consists of confronting social attitudes about same-gender sexual desires, as well as one's relationship to sexual orientation groups. McCarn and Fassinger (1996) state that initial conscious awareness of heterosexism is similar to a process within minority identity development in which racist and sexist attitudes are recognized as affecting one's well-being. Awareness is most likely to cause feelings of confusion and bewilderment for lesbians, gays, and bisexual individuals, rather than the rage that is experienced by other minority groups. This is because, by acknowledging same-gender desires, individuals begin to understand the meaning of belonging to a nonheterosexual group; with other minority groups, awareness involves understanding the *pervasiveness* of oppression against the group to which they belong, not its mere existence.

### Exploration (McCarn & Fassinger, 1996)

Based on the description by McCarn and Fassinger (1996) of the second phase of lesbian identity formation, it likewise apparently precedes the first step of the D'Augelli (1994) model. The **exploration phase** consists of conscious, intentional evaluation of the issues originating during the awareness phase. According to McCarn and Fassinger, "For women, it is explicitly hypothesized that this phase involves strong relationships with or feelings about other women or another woman in particular" (p. 522). Although one's private sexual feelings are examined during this phase, the individual may not engage in sexual behavior nor become involved with any partners.

The basis for the formation of group membership identity begins with an active search for information about lesbian, gay, and bisexual people. However, such knowledge may not initially be seen as entirely relevant to oneself, if at all, given that individuals may not consider themselves to really be lesbian, gay, or bisexual; same-gender feelings, or even sexual behavior, may be interpreted as "just a phase," due to intoxication, or a rare, unexplainable event. On the other hand, an individual may begin to develop a more positive image of lesbians and gay men, making later identification with the groups as "my own" possible.

Yet, McCarn and Fassinger (1996) note that one's reassessment of attitudes toward lesbians, gay men, or bisexual individuals may be a highly convoluted, emotionally difficult process for individuals who have strongly internalized the homophobic values promoted by society. The same may be true for individuals who do not have access to other gay men or lesbians. This is most likely the basis for the experience of individuals on the "down low," described by J. L. King at the beginning of the chapter. Because such individuals see themselves as generally good people, but society condemns same-gender sexual behavior, men on the down low cannot bring themselves to identify as gay. Denial and finding other reasons for same-sex sexual behavior helps to protect their sense of worth and self-esteem.

Many people who come to identify as lesbian, gay, or bisexual are likely to react with intense rage and remorse for having participated in the heterosexist system that harms nonheterosexual individuals. "On the other hand, exploring the existence of other lesbians [or gay men] will be likely to produce driving curiosity and exhilarating joy" (McCarn & Fassinger, 1996, p. 525; words in brackets added).

### Exiting Heterosexual Identity (D'Augelli, 1994)

Ultimately, one aspect of the development process is relinquishing the heterosexual identity that many people develop as a result of the compulsory heterosexuality pervading society (D'Augelli, 1994). If the process begins before or during adolescence, sexual identity and sexual orientation identity are likely to be very vague and unorganized for the most part. The process involves an increasing awareness of one's attraction toward the same sex, as well as developing a meaning for the attraction and any same-gender sexual intimacy that may have occurred. For some individuals, this self-examination may involve an explicit decision to adopt a new, nonheterosexual identity; for others, the sense of self may evolve in a less direct way, with a more gradually emerging understanding.

Nonetheless, the process involves discussing one's feelings with others at some point, which becomes an ongoing series of revelations to others called **coming out**. Coming out continues throughout the person's life as one encounters new people who are not familiar with him or her, and includes one's own growing self-awareness of same-gender attractions. The coming out process fades to the extent that the individual becomes more generally identified by others as having a nonheterosexual identity.

**Deepening/Commitment (McCarn & Fassinger, 1996) and Developing a Lesbian-Gay-Bisexual Personal Identity (D'Augelli, 1994).** The two models converge at the point of movement toward developing a same-gender sexual orientation identity. The McCarn–Fassinger (1996) lesbian identity model in particular describes the various outcomes that may result from the exploratory phase; some women may come to feel that involvement with both women and men is desirable, others that male partners are more desirable, and still others that only women are desirable partners. Gradually, the individual begins to understand that intimacy with another person is

*How do you think you would feel if you had to explain and defend your marriage or relationship to every new person you met?* This is the case for many gays, lesbians, and bisexuals throughout much of their lives.

relevant to understanding one's basic nature and who he or she is as an individual. The desire for intimacy and fulfillment eventually wins out over the emotional obstacles that have been erected by a history of exposure to heterosexist and homophobic attitudes common to U.S. culture (McCarn & Fassinger, 1996).

The process of developing an LGB personal identity involves the creation of a relatively coherent understanding of one's thoughts, feelings, desires, and aspirations. Personal identity, as was discussed with respect to self-schemas and self-conceptions, is an organizing structure for individuals; this structure allows them to give meaning to new experiences and guide the decisions that they make about behavior. Within current thinking about identity, LGB personal identity is thought to be highly likely to change as a person continues to evaluate the nature of feelings and goals.

The organizing function of personal identity also affects decisions and goals having to do with interacting with others. As an individual begins to view himself or herself as interested in sexual aspects of the same sex, the person becomes more likely to seek contact with nonheterosexual individuals, those who are similar to oneself. Similar others provide further information about the issues and experiences involved in being lesbian, gay, or bisexual (D'Augelli, 1994). A very important basis for modifying one's self-view is the social interaction that the individual has with others relevant to sexuality and sexual orientation. Information may take the form of discussions with LGB individuals, attending social events or meetings, or sexual interaction with a person of the same sex. Such experiences contribute to a strengthening commitment to the emerging personal identity as a lesbian, gay man, or bisexual individual. This commitment likely leads to a sense of belonging to a lesbian, gay, or bisexual group; this also begins the process of forming a social sexual identity (McCarn & Fassinger, 1996).

A typical function of self-conceptions is to maintain as high a level of regard for oneself as possible, and to protect oneself from undesirable, damaging views of oneself. This self-esteem enhancing function of the self is essential to the general psychological well-being and coping ability of individuals (Armor & Taylor, 1998; Robinson & Ryff, 1999). Therefore, an important aspect of personal identity development accord-

Participation in social events that celebrate the lesbian and gay community, such as gay pride events, is important in the development of one's personal identity. Contact with other gay men and lesbians helps to affirm the person's sense of worth, and strengthens feelings of belonging to a community that values the individual for who he or she is.

ing to D'Augelli (1994) is coming to terms with the negative stereotypes and distorted information that a person has acquired about LGB individuals over the course of his or her life. Myths about same-gender orientation that threaten self-esteem include beliefs that gays and lesbians (a) suffer from problems with gender identity (i.e., they are really people of the "opposite" sex); (b) have a psychological disorder causing their "problem" with sexual orientation; (c) are sexual "predators" (have an uncontrollable lust and "prey on innocent victims"); (d) are dangerous to children; (e) are not able to maintain a satisfying, long-term romantic relationship; (f) are always rejected by their families, friends, and coworkers; and (g) are too weak and unstable to be qualified for positions of responsibility and authority. In addition, contact with individual lesbians, bisexuals, and gay men is often important in helping to dispel and overcome these damaging stereotypes, as is contact with LGB communities in general. In fact, research by Sophie (1985–1986) found that women tend not to identify as lesbian until they have attained a positive view of lesbianism.

Group membership identity intensifies during this phase of deepening and commitment, as individuals come to appreciate the value of others who face the same minority challenges that they do. Friendships and alliances with lesbians and gay men become extremely important, with these communities becoming the new reference groups for individuals forming same-gender identities; **reference groups** consist of those with specific characteristics that make them uniquely relevant as sources of norms and values.

Individuals aligning themselves with a new reference group often become passionate advocates of the norms and values promoted by the group, and they may undergo a substantial revolution in thinking and attitudes. This change may include a rejection of heterosexual values and culture, as well as an immersion in gay and lesbian culture; in fact, models of racial and feminist identity formation refer to this phase as *immersion* and *embeddedness*. Emotions common in this transformation include passion, enthusiasm, and pride on the positive side in relation to lesbian and gay culture; individuals may also experience fury, hostility, and defiance with respect to heterosexual culture. Consequently, the deepening/commitment phase may be an emotionally conflicted time for some individuals (McCarn & Fassinger, 1996).

In the deepening/commitment phase, individuals may become passionate advocates of the values and rights of the lesbian and gay community as they experience increasing commitment and pride.

The two models of same-gender sexual identity diverge in different directions after this point. The lesbian identity model is concerned with the ongoing *process* of becoming more certain of one's orientation and how the sexual identity is integrated into one's overall psychological system; the process is what is involved in the internalization/synthesis phase of the McCarn and Fassinger (1996) model. This is discussed after presenting the remainder of the steps of the D'Augelli (1994) model. In contrast to the lesbian identity model, the D'Augelli model is more concerned with changes that occur in the specific substance and content of sexual orientation identity as a result of becoming more certain about one's orientation, rather than the higher level process involved.

**Developing a Lesbian-Gay-Bisexual Social Identity (D'Augelli, 1994).** Forming an LGB social identity involves establishing a sense of connection and alliance with individuals who are aware of an individual's sexual orientation identity, and who provide a supportive, affirmative environment. An affirmative environment is one in which others reliably and consistently behave toward an LGB individual as bisexual, gay, or lesbian. It also necessarily involves both implicit and explicit messages of acceptance of an individual's sexual orientation as positive and healthy, rather than implying only tolerance, or "putting up with" the issue. Developing a social identity is an ongoing process, as members of the individual's environment continue to embrace all aspects of the person's life; this includes the person becoming involved in romantic relationships and eventually a long-term relationship. Individuals within the person's social environment must also "come out" as well, in terms of acknowledging the person's sexual orientation to others (D'Augelli, 1994).

McCarn and Fassinger (1996), however, comment that even individuals who have formulated a confident, well-integrated personal identity may make choices about their degree of openness in different social settings. The ability of the individual to address the choices and handle them in a way that produces desired outcomes is the primary issue involved in successful integration of life experiences and identity. "That is, a woman may choose to be professionally 'closeted' for important contextual reasons; as long as the choice has been addressed, this woman may be as developmentally integrated as the woman who is professionally open" (p. 523). Nonetheless, they state that it is not very likely that an individual could fully engage in the fourth phase of integration and synthesis without beginning to deal with factors in the social environment that prevent complete openness about one's sexual orientation identity.

*Becoming a Lesbian-Gay-Bisexual Offspring (D'Augelli, 1994).* For many people, parents occupy a central position in the network of significant social relationships, making the maintenance of good relations with parents important to their sense of well-being. Disclosure of a nonheterosexual orientation often involves some degree of adjustment for parents, if not substantial difficulties. This may result in tense interactions, withdrawal, or negative exchanges between parent and offspring (D'Augelli, 1994). Nonetheless, many families are able to come to terms with the disclosure of being lesbian, gay, or bisexual, and successfully reestablish the type of relationships that existed prior to the disclosure, if only after some period of time. Family members respond in different ways to the new information about sexual orientation; however, it is typically the LGB individual who must take the initiative to guide attitudes and behavior away from mere tolerance toward affirmative treatment by family members.

*Developing a Lesbian-Gay-Bisexual Intimacy Status (D'Augelli, 1994).* The process of establishing an intimate, romantic relationship is made tremendously more difficult for LGB individuals by the lack of models available within U.S. culture (D'Augelli, 1994). Beyond the virtual absence of guidance in forming and maintaining same-gender relationships, no formal or easily accessible legal means of sanctioning such relationships exists in many U.S. states. This situation represents a substantial threat to the stability and quality of same-gender relationships because of the additional effort, stress, ambiguity, and disadvantage imposed, economically as well as psychologically. As D'Augelli (1994) notes, "this is a good example of how social structure reinforces heterosexism" (p. 327). The positive feature of the absence of general societal norms for same-gender relationships is that it allows couples to develop their own standards that may better serve individual needs (D'Augelli, 1994).

Despite the ban on lesbian and gay marriage in many U.S. states, some couples choose to have commitment ceremonies. The lack of formal and legal support for same-gender relationships contributes to the psychological and economic disadvantages with which lesbians and gays must cope.

*Entering a Lesbian-Gay-Bisexual Community (D'Augelli, 1994).* This process involves a growing awareness of the extent to which the ability to fully express one's sexual orientation identity is affected by the social and political climate. The recognition is that to be nonheterosexual in an overwhelmingly heterosexually oriented society may often severely limit one's opportunities (D'Augelli, 1994);

limitations include the capability (a) to act openly on feelings of attraction, (b) to safely and spontaneously reveal many aspects of one's personal life in most areas of daily living, and (c) to be able to advance professionally and socially to one's fullest potential, because of outright bias, personal discomfort in social interactions, or difficulty in trying to network with others. Beyond social challenges, disclosure of sexual orientation can result in loss of job, problems with housing, poor quality of medical care, and even danger to physical safety.

Recognition of such disadvantages and dangers may prompt some LGB individuals to become active in community activities, organizations, or politics to attempt to remedy biased and discriminatory practices. According to D'Augelli (1994),

> To be lesbian, gay, or bisexual in the fullest sense—to have a meaningful identity—leads to a consciousness of the history of one's own oppression. It also, generally, leads to an appreciation of how the oppression continues, and a commitment to resisting it. (p. 328)

### Internalization/Synthesis (McCarn & Fassinger, 1996)

McCarn and Fassinger expressed misgivings about characterizing lesbian identity development as a stage-driven process culminating in a final stage of healthy adjustment. Nonetheless, they describe the fourth phase of their model as a process of fully embracing one's lesbian nature and experience. The distinction between the fourth phase of the current model and earlier stage theories of identity development is that McCarn and Fassinger's conceive of the internalization/synthesis phase as an ongoing process, not a final achieved stage; instead, ongoing change in identity is possible. Yet, it appears from McCarn and Fassinger's description that a return to an earlier phase of extreme denial and rejection of one's lesbian nature would be highly unlikely. **Internalization** refers to a process of increasingly integrating more of one's desire and love for women, as well as one's intimate experiences with women, into one's self-understanding. **Synthesis** is the process of organizing these self-conceptions into a meaningful understanding of oneself overall; the result is a growing sense that most aspects of one's life are related and successfully coordinated. An intense desire to remain lesbian, and an unwillingness to change one's sexual identity, often follows from this sense of integration and meaningfulness.

## The Process of Heterosexual Identity Development

Sexual identity, according to the model by Worthington, Savoy, Dillon, and Vernaglia (2002), may develop along a course that takes the form of five different statuses: (a) unexplored commitment, (b) active exploration, (c) diffusion, (d) deepening and commitment, and (e) synthesis (see Figure 7.3). This proposal is based on earlier models of identity development for sexual minorities discussed in the previous sections (Fassinger & Miller, 1996; McCarn & Fassinger, 1996). It also is based on models explaining majority group identity formation, specifically that of White racial identity (Helms, 1995; Rowe, Bennett, & Atkinson, 1994). More recent concerns about the absence of an understanding of the majority heterosexual identity process has led to the proposal of several models of heterosexual identity development (Eliason, 1995; Sullivan, 1998).

For reasons discussed earlier, this perspective assumes that individuals may move from one status to another at various points in their lives, including into statuses in which they had engaged previously. Sexual identity is viewed as potentially dynamic and changing, rather than a straightforward progression with all people advancing through exactly the same sequence.

Model of Heterosexual Identity Development

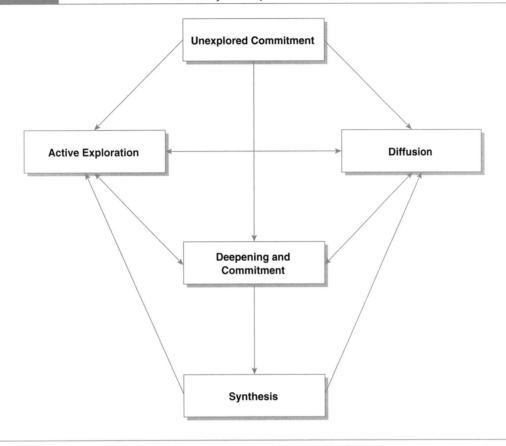

From Worthington, R. L., Savoy, H. B., Dillon, F. R., & Vernaglia, E. R., Heterosexual identity development: A multidimensional model of individual and social identity. *The Counseling Psychologist, 30*, 496–531. Copyright © 2002 Sage Publications, Inc. Reprinted with permission.

Worthington and his colleagues (2002) propose that sexual identity development may occur at both conscious and nonconscious levels in all of the statuses. Exploration is also conceived as occurring both cognitively and behaviorally. This means that individuals may think about and analyze their feelings and desires privately without always acting immediately upon the conclusions they reach. The various aspects of sexual identity (e.g., needs, values, attitudes, activities, orientation) are not likely to all undergo exploration at the same time. Instead, people may typically evaluate the components of sexual identity in an unsystematic, individually unique way.

### Unexplored Commitment Status

**Unexplored commitment** is a status in which an individual has accepted a particular sexual identity with no substantial or meaningful self-exploration. With respect to sexual orientation identity, extreme religious and cultural standards demand the unquestioning development of a heterosexual sexual orientation; this

Societal expectations that all individuals should be heterosexual are promoted and reinforced in a multitude of ways from very early in life, such as through the themes of school dances. Consequently, many individuals never really question that they are heterosexual.

demand has been termed **compulsory hetero-sexuality** (Rich, 1980). The development of heterosexuality is likewise promoted by pervasively negative, anti-erotic attitudes within U.S. society. For many of us, issues related to sexuality in general provoke an automatic, spontaneous response—conscious or not—of discomfort, or even guilt and anxiety. Consequently, we never extensively examine the sexual responses and behaviors that characterize us, let alone explore the motivations and feelings that underlie them.

So what does this mean for sexual identity formation? For the majority of people, heterosexuality is the default orientation, as if no other possible options exist, and very little conscious analysis is devoted to an individual identity as a heterosexual. Therefore, a large group of individuals begin awareness of their sexuality within this status based on little self-examination; some people may never change to another status, at least with respect to sexual orientation identity. Such extreme lack of awareness is not likely to be as true for all aspects of sexuality as it is for sexual orientation identity, because prohibitions against other sexual issues are not as strong as they are for sexual orientation. The development of group membership identity will often result most noticeably in aligning oneself with heterosexuality, for the same reasons discussed for individual sexual identity. The group of people who consider themselves to be heterosexual are seen as the unquestioned healthy comparison group. Heterosexual individuals are thought to possess highly desirable characteristics and to engage in the most acceptable type of behavior. As described by Worthington and his colleagues (2002), "One's status as a member of a privileged, oppressive majority group is either repressed from awareness or accepted without question as normal, understandable, and justifiable" (p. 516). Attitudes toward nonheterosexual groups are generally fairly negative, based on less-than-conscious assumptions about these groups that have not been examined or challenged. Negative beliefs and sentiments toward nonheterosexual individuals is called **heterosexism**. Such beliefs generally view nonheterosexual individuals in a very vague, negatively stereotyped way (Worthington et al., 2002).

### Active Exploration Status

The status of **active exploration** involves intentional, meaningful examination of particular aspects of one's sexual nature. The components of sexuality examined may be in one particular area, or instead several aspects may be evaluated. Remember that the various aspects of sexual identity are sexual needs, values, attitudes, activities, partner characteristics, or orientation. Active exploration is characterized by more than incidental, infrequent, or haphazard episodes in which we engage in unusual sexual behavior or fantasy that has little meaning or impact.

According to Worthington and colleagues (2002), active exploration goes far beyond the type of exploration and self-evaluation typical of individuals for a given context or age. Many of us think about ourselves as a sexual person at particular points in our lives. This occurs most noticeably around the time of puberty as the body changes in its features, and hormonal levels increase the experience of sexual desire. However, active exploration as a specific phase of sexual identity involvement occurs at a time *beyond* the age of puberty, and beyond what is typical for one's age, gender, culture, and religious beliefs.

Because of the overwhelmingly powerful influence of religious and cultural attitudes that devalue, and even condemn, same-gender sexuality, active exploration for most heterosexually identified individuals does not involve sexual orientation. Rather, self-examination and exploration may involve thinking about the attractiveness of new partner characteristics, such as those related to someone from a different socioeconomic background, racial or ethnic group, age, or religion. Other aspects that may be involved in active exploration are experimenting with different sexual behaviors and activities, different types of settings, sexual expression not typical for one's gender, or sexual literature or videos.

*What types of issues do you think heterosexual individuals examine when they engage in active exploration of their sexuality? If you are heterosexual, what types of concerns have you experienced about sexuality beyond those that most people confront during adolescence?*

Some proportion of heterosexually identified individuals may actually explore same-gender behavior, while still ultimately holding onto their heterosexual sexual identity; for many, this is because the privilege that is central to heterosexual status is a powerful incentive to remain identified as heterosexual. However, Worthington and his colleagues propose that those who begin to believe that heterosexual identity does not accurately characterize their feelings and behavior follow an entirely different identity development path than heterosexually identified individuals. The course of identity formation would shift at that point to the process described in the models of same-gender sexual identity development presented in the previous section (D'Augelli, 1994; McCarn & Fassinger, 1996).

Group membership identity, the other major aspect of sexual identity, may also be affected by the active exploration process. A person may either challenge the morality of a system of privilege that gives great advantage to heterosexual individuals, or instead come to wholeheartedly endorse it at a conscious level. The development of group membership identity may likewise be influenced by individual identity experiences; a person who engages in same-gender sexual behavior, but who ultimately decides he or she is heterosexual, may become able to recognize the greater power available to heterosexual groups in comparison to nonheterosexual groups.

Yet others who are heterosexually identified and who experiment with same-gender sexual behavior never identify at all with the oppressed sexual orientation group. Such individuals may continue to embrace heterosexist, derogatory attitudes toward nonheterosexual individuals, and defensively distance themselves to avoid sympathizing with the oppressed. For most individuals who explore same-gender sexual behavior, however, this experience probably does lead to more positive attitudes toward nonheterosexual individuals (Worthington et al., 2002).

## Diffusion Status

Worthington and his colleagues (2002) draw directly upon the pioneering theory of general identity development advanced by Marcia (1987) in defining the status of **diffusion**. Diffusion is the absence of exploration or commitment; it is the lack of alignment and dedication to a particular identity. Behaviors exhibited by those in the diffusion status may appear to be similar to those typical of the active exploration status. This is because individuals in the diffusion status reject many societal expectations for appropriate behavior and consequently may engage in a number of sexual behaviors as an expression of defiance. Such rebellious behavior is different from the sexual experimentation displayed by those within the active exploration status. In the active exploration status, socially prohibited behavior is an attempt to discover the type of identity that best reflects an individual's needs and desires. Those within the diffusion status engage in socially disapproved sexual behavior for the sake of rebellion, and a number of different sexual behaviors may be tried in an almost random, unintentional way.

Often individuals may begin to experiment with socially prohibited sexual behavior as a result of a crisis, an event or realization that disrupts one's sense of identity. For this reason, it is possible for an individual to enter the diffusion status while involved in any of the other identity statuses. However, those within more integrated statuses, such as *deepening and commitment* and *synthesis* (which are discussed in the next sections) are less prone to enter diffusion (Worthington et al., 2002). Not having a sense of identity tends to be directly related to a general absence of self-awareness and self-understanding, often accompanied by various types of psychological distress. According to Worthington and colleagues (2002), active exploration—that is, self-evaluation and questioning—is the only means of moving out of the diffusion status; for some individuals in diffusion status, psychotherapy and professional assistance may be required to initiate the exploration.

*What types of rebellious sexual behaviors do you think individuals experiencing sexual identity diffusion may engage in?*

## Deepening and Commitment Status

This status involves recognition of, and increasing dedication to, the sexual characteristics and tendencies an individual has identified as important for himself or herself. Again, the various aspects of identity include needs, desires, values, activity preferences, attitudes, and sexual orientation. In contrast to Marcia's (1987) identity theory, Worthington and his colleagues (2002) propose that individuals most often move into this commitment status directly from the *unexplored commitment status,* rather than from the *active exploring status.* This is because many individuals begin the process of sexual identity development within the unexplored commitment status, and never consciously examine their sexual needs or characteristics.

The rigid, restrictive standards prevalent in U.S. society, along with generally negative attitudes toward sexuality, lead most individuals to accept vague, stereotypic beliefs about sexuality without analyzing or challenging them to any great extent. As these beliefs and behavior patterns become typical for individuals over time, they increasingly accept them as characteristic of themselves. In other words, commitment to this self-understanding deepens without any meaningful active exploration. Group membership identity likewise may crystallize, with attitudes toward other sexual groups solidifying in a way consistent with the beliefs that have developed over time; attitudes can range from extremely negative to very positive for different individuals. Exiting the deepening and commitment status may result in an individual moving into one of three statuses: the *synthesis status* (presented below), the *active exploration status*, or the *diffusion status*.

---

**Box 7.2**                                                    **An Eye Toward Research**

### Gender Diagnosticity: A New Model of Masculinity–Femininity

Around the beginning of the 20th century, scientists set out to discover the attributes that make up a key aspect of identity, masculinity–femininity, and to develop a way of measuring these attributes. Subsequent research and analysis, however, indicated that the questionnaires created to measure masculinity and femininity do not correlate with individuals' views of how masculine or feminine they feel they are (Lippa, 2002).

A number of decades following this research, Spence and Buckner (1995) maintained that, in fact, masculinity–femininity is nonetheless a concept that is intuitively very meaningful to people in a fundamental way. This suggests that the dimension may be important to individuals in the way they view themselves and others, sexually as well as socially. The fact that researchers have had a difficult time formally conceptualizing it and measuring it does not mean that masculinity–femininity does not exist, nor does it mean that it is a useless concept. As suggested by Lippa (2002), most of us have a very real sense that some women are more feminine than other women, and some men are more masculine than other men. Based on our own personal experience, it just "feels" like masculinity and femininity are real.

Lippa noted that, when people are asked for their own personal definition of masculinity and femininity, they mention a wide variety of attributes, such as **physical features** (dainty, muscular, wears makeup), **roles** (being a mother), **occupations** (truck driver, nurse), **psychological traits** (tough, soft, fragile), **interests** (music, art, sports, work, cars) and, of particular note, **sexual characteristics**, such as virile, seductive, and one's sexual orientation (heterosexual, homosexual, not gay). Consistent with the view that masculinity and femininity are opposite of one another—especially in terms of gender—greater masculinity in women is considered by people in general to be more negative than when it exists in men, and the reverse is true about femininity. Masculine women are believed to be unattractive, overweight, aggressive, and insensitive; feminine men are seen as having a slight build and being weak, fragile, and timid (Helgeson, 1994). Therefore, intuitive conceptions of masculinity–femininity encompass a wide range of different characteristics and features, not simply the psychological traits examined by early psychologists.

Based on a long program of research, Richard Lippa (2002) has proposed that three dimensions are especially central to commonsense notions of masculinity–femininity: (a) gender-related interests, (b) gender-related appearances, and (c) sexuality. **Gender-related interests** concern liking for particular occupations, recreational activities, and mundane tasks. **Gender-related appearances** include style of dress, hairstyle, gestures, mannerisms, and expressions. **Sexuality** specifically refers here to sexual orientation, or the tendency to experience sexual attraction toward individuals of the same sex or the other sex, as well as to engage in sexual behavior with a particular sex.

*(Continued)*

(Continued)

Because gender-related interests are easier to assess in scientific research than the other two dimensions, Lippa has focused solely on interests as an indicator of masculinity–femininity. This conceptualization of masculinity–femininity is called **gender diagnosticity**. *Diagnosticity* refers to the accuracy of a specific characteristic in "diagnosing" or indicating what an individual is really like. Therefore, gender diagnosticity is the degree to which a characteristic is correlated with being female or male. For example, characteristics highly related to gender might include an interest in particular occupations, such as becoming a hairstylist, or interest in specific clothing styles, such as wearing army fatigues and boots as a major component of one's civilian wardrobe. To measure gender diagnosticity, Lippa has advocated employing ratings of interest in 70 occupations for the particular group of individuals under consideration in a given study. In this way, gender norms are established for each group separately, allowing for the use of different standards across cultures and across time.

Each individual in the group receives a gender diagnosticity score on the basis of his or her ratings of interest in the occupations. The score indicates the extent to which the individual's gender can be accurately predicted from the occupational ratings. If someone prefers certain types of occupations, that person is more likely to be a female; however, if the individual prefers other types of occupations, the person is more likely to be a male. Lippa has demonstrated that the dimension at the root of interest in various occupations is a concern with people versus a concern with things. This "People–Things" dimension was identified originally by Prediger (1982) in research on occupational interests.

Therefore, women have been shown to be more likely to be interested in people-oriented occupations; these include professions such as managing, teaching, and counseling. On the other hand, men are more likely to be interested in occupations dealing with inanimate, nonhuman phenomena, such as construction, machine operation, and engineering. These scores do not correlate highly with psychological traits thought to capture the notion of masculinity–femininity by early researchers. However, the scores tend to be related to self-ratings of masculinity–femininity, as well as to judgments by others about how masculine or feminine a given individual is. In other words, Lippa demonstrated that occupational interest taps into the very essence of what a given culture believes is involved in masculinity and femininity.

### References

Helgeson, V. S. (1994). Prototypes and dimensions of masculinity and femininity. *Sex Roles, 31*, 653–682.

Lippa, R. A. (2002). *Gender, nature, and nurture.* Mahwah, NJ: Erlbaum.

Prediger, D. J. (1982). Dimensions underlying Holland's hexagon: Missing link between interests and occupations? *Journal of Vocational Behavior, 21*, 259–287.

Spence, J. T., & Buckner, C. (1995). Masculinity and femininity: Defining the undefinable. In P. J. Kalbfleisch & M. J. Cody (Eds.), *Gender, power, and communication in human relationships. LEA's communication series* (pp. 105–138). Hillsdale, NJ: Erlbaum.

### Synthesis Status

Synthesis refers to the process of integrating and coordinating the various aspects of sexuality into a meaningful understanding. Organizing one's needs, values, activities, partner characteristic preferences, and sexual orientation in a personally relevant way is thought to provide the basis for arriving upon a deeply fulfilling self-understanding. As described by Worthington and colleagues (2002), "Individual sexual identity, group membership identity, and attitudes toward sexual minorities merge into an overall sexual self-concept, which is conscious, congruent, volitional [chosen], and (hopefully) enlightened" (p. 519; the word in brackets was added). Beyond this, many other dimensions of identity are integrated with sexual identity as well. However, Worthington and colleagues state that few people, if any, really ever achieve such a supreme level of integration because of the tremendous emotional and social complexity of the issues involved.

They also propose that only one clear avenue is available through which to progress into the synthesis status—through *deepening and commitment status,* although they speculate it may also be possible through *active exploration.* It is unlikely that individuals would be able to achieve such a level of self-awareness and organization without conscious, intentional self-examination. The model additionally proposes that individuals within the synthesis status become more flexible in their understanding of sexuality; this is likely to lead to more positive attitudes toward other sexual identity groups, such as people with lesbian, gay, and bisexual identities. Individuals may move out of the synthesis status through active exploration or diffusion.

## The Need for Research on the Multidimensional Model of Heterosexual Sexual Identity

Although attention has been increasingly devoted to the development of theory about all aspects of sexual identity, relatively little empirical research has been conducted on the topic. This is particularly true regarding issues that are not related to sexual minority identity, in other words for theory about heterosexual orientation identity. Researchers have been interested for several decades in the ways in which members of highly oppressed minorities—nonheterosexual individuals—develop a self-understanding that promotes healthy psychological functioning in the face of pervasive bias, persecution, and attack. As noted by Worthington and colleagues (2002), "Although our model is founded on existing literature on minority/majority identity development, a sufficient empirical foundation from which to assess the validity of the model is not immediately available" (p. 520). This is likely to be an area of exciting, important research in the near future.

## *Summary*

One area of theory and research within social psychology is the *self:* the individual's understanding of his or her characteristics, needs, goals, and abilities. The term, *identity,* is also used to describe this self-understanding. The self-conceptions that individuals have of their sexual characteristics and sexual behavior are called the sexual self and sexual identity. Sexual identity is a different concept than gender identity and gender-role identity, although the three types of identity are related in some ways.

Knowledge of the self comes from at least four sources: introspection, self-perception, reflected appraisal, and social comparison. Contrary to common sense and intuition, introspection is probably not the most accurate and useful source of information about oneself, because individuals are not always aware of all of the factors that influence their behavior, especially in any given situation. Consequently, individuals typically must rely on the more social sources of information about the self.

*(Continued)*

(Continued)

Identity is typically conceived in terms of personal identity and social identity. Characteristics or group membership that are unique or fairly different from other individuals are especially likely to be central in an individual's self-concept because of their salience. Therefore, being a member of a racial or ethnic minority, or of a sexual orientation minority (i.e., lesbian, gay, or bisexual), figures prominently in the identity of many individuals.

A sexual self-schema is one's conceptual understanding of one's sexual characteristics, feelings, and tendencies. Research has provided support for the existence of two general dimensions underlying sexual self-schemas, positive and negative (Andersen & Cyranowski, 1994). The development of particular types of sexual self-schemas may be related to the nature of emotional attachment individuals experience with their parents early in life. Another line of research has focused on six types of sexual self-conceptions: sexual experience, sexual deviance, sexual attitudes, sexual attractiveness, sexual responsiveness, and romanticism (Garcia, 1999; Garcia & Carrigan, 1998).

Sexual identity is an individual's overall understanding of his sexual nature, which includes one's sexual desires, wishes, fantasies, attitudes, traits, and typical patterns of behavior, as well as the types of individuals he or she finds attractive. Sexual orientation is the tendency to experience emotional, romantic, or sexual attraction toward one sex or the other, or both sexes. However, one's understanding of his or her sexual orientation is likely to be an important influence on behavior because of the relationship of awareness to the choices that individuals make. One's understanding of his or her sexual identity is called sexual orientation identity, one aspect of overall sexual identity.

The most recent theories of sexual orientation identity propose that identity is fluid and has the potential to change throughout the life span, even returning to earlier steps or phases. The steps or phases are (a) awareness, (b) exploration, (c) exiting heterosexual identity, (d) deepening/commitment and developing an LGB personal identity status, (e) developing an LGB social identity, (f) becoming an LGB offspring, (g) developing an LGB intimacy status, (h) entering an LGB community, and (i) internalization/synthesis. An integrated identity provides coherent meaning and direction to one's life.

With respect to heterosexual sexual identity, a recent model proposed by Worthington and colleagues (2002) maintains that individuals may move into five different statuses: (a) unexplored commitment, (b) active exploration, (c) diffusion, (d) deepening and commitment, and (e) synthesis. These theorists also assume that individuals may transition between statuses at different points throughout their lives, as is assumed in the previous nonheterosexual identity models. The models are all recent enough that very little research has been conducted to test them, and in the case of the heterosexual identity model, apparently no research to date has been conducted.

## Chapter 7 Critical Thinking Exercises

1. Sexual self-schemas

   What specific experiences and processes do you think are involved in the differences that were found in the nature of sexual self-schemas for men in comparison to women? Specifically, what factors would contribute to the fact that the positive dimension for men includes not only being passionate and romantic, but also warm and loving, whereas this is not the case for women? What factors are involved in men varying along a dimension of powerful–aggressive, whereas this is not a dimension that is relevant to the self-schemas of women?

2. Sexual identity

   What would you say are differences in typical sexual identity development of heterosexual individuals in comparison to lesbian, gay, and bisexual individuals? What are possible similarities?

**Visit www.sagepub.com/hillhsstudy.com for online activities, sample tests, and other helpful resources. Select "Chapter 7: The Sexual Self and Sexual Identity" for chapter-specific activities.**

# Chapter 8

## SEXUAL MOTIVATION, AROUSAL, AND ATTRACTION

Why do we engage in sexual behavior? The answer seems obvious enough—because we experience physical pleasure when our bodies are stimulated through sexual expression. Even young people begin to experience this type of pleasure at a fairly early age during puberty. Discovery of the potential for physical pleasure may even happen unexpectedly, when individuals are not seeking out the experience. Consider the following description by one woman when she recognized for the first time that she was experiencing sexual arousal as a young adolescent:

My father owned a diner and one day six of us were sitting in a booth and I dropped something on the floor. One of my boy classmates bent down to pick it up for me and accidentally his hand touched my leg. I felt so aroused and it was the first time even though I had crushes on boys since first grade and was preoccupied with men of all ages, and thought about kissing them, I never felt the feeling of aching between my legs or the wetness. He must have had some reaction because he almost ran into the men's room. From then on I wanted to have that feeling and soon found out I could have it through kissing. Touching too but I was too shy to let a boy touch me so kissing was something I loved. In fact it turned me into a tease. I loved being aroused and the

Sexual arousal may sometimes occur unintentionally in unexpected situations.

more I ached the more I liked it. (The Experience of Desire, On-line forum, retrieved July 22, 2006, from The-clitoris.com. Reprinted with permission of The-clitoris.com.)

This woman discovered the physical component of sexual pleasure through an initially nonsexual incident. However, she had actually already developed the potential to respond to the physically stimulating event when it happened. She reveals that she had been having crushes on boys and a fascination with men for several years before feeling sensations in her genitals. This fact suggests that sexual interest involves more than the desire for genital stimulation, or possibly even more than the desire for physical stimulation. Apparently other types of pleasure are also intricately involved in sexual feelings and experiences.

The experience of personal pleasure, whether in the form of physical stimulation or interpersonal gratification, is essential to motivation for sexual expression. Sexual behavior may occasionally occur for reasons unrelated to pleasure. Yet it is not likely to continue very long or to be pursued with much enthusiasm as when sexual activity provides some type of pleasure. In fact, if pain or negative feelings are expected to result from sexual experiences, individuals tend to avoid sexual expression. This is illustrated in an explanation by a woman who identified herself as Rachael regarding why she avoided engaging in her first ever sexual behavior with a partner:

> For six years I was terrified of sexual intercourse. Most of it originated from the nightmarish recounts my friends had divulged about their own sexual encounters. They told me about instances of pain, abuse, rape and/or boredom that had resulted from highly disappointing sexual episodes. Many of the stories were repetitive and I started to wonder if I, too, would suffer the same fate. (Women's Sexual Experiences, On-line forum, retrieved July 22, 2006, from The-clitoris.com. Reprinted with permission of The-clitoris.com.)

She eventually decided to experience sex with her boyfriend after he sent her a link to the Web site, www.the-clitoris.com. She read the entries of numerous women who had contributed their personal experiences, many of them relating tales of pleasure, ecstasy, and joy, even while dealing with difficulties and unhappiness. Eventually, Rachael engaged in sex with her boyfriend with quite positive outcomes. She describes the reason for her experience,

> Most importantly, the Web site reminds its readers that communication between sexual partners is vital to experiencing any sort of sexual gratification. This piece of advice was directly responsible for my joyful memory regarding my first time. I encountered minimal pain during intercourse that day, which vanished the moment I told Steven to stop and allow my body to adapt to him. I feel fortunate and proud that my first experiences with sex are happy ones .... (Women's Sexual Experiences, On-line forum, retrieved July 22, 2006, from The-clitoris.com. Reprinted with permission of The-clitoris.com.)

These various personal stories give insight into the nature of sexual desire and sexual motivation. They also reveal in a very rich way how complex human sexual motivation actually is, a far cry from a mindless quest for simple physical pleasure, tension, or release. Emotional and social types of fulfillment and concerns are at least as important as physical pleasure for humans, if not more so in many cases.

## Sexual Motivation

Lust, the true kind of lust that makes itself known in groin, head, heart, and every atom in between, encourages a holographic view of the body; the whole is implicit in each of its parts. Thus, to brush your lips against a lover's nipple, to inhale his scent and feel his heat, is to intuitively learn more about his essence than would seem to be inherent in any one of those fragments. Lust, far from being demeaning, is a humanizing thing; it is empathy at its deepest level. (Hall, 2000, p. 164)

An important concept in psychology for understanding the causes of behavior is that of motivation. In simple terms, motivation is the desire to attain or accomplish a goal. Within psychological theory, **motivation** is a state of increased interest in a specific goal; accompanying this heightened interest is a process of initiating, energizing, maintaining, and directing behavior intended to attain the goal (Buck, 1988; Heckhausen, 1991). In the case of sexuality, the goal is the experience of satisfaction that results from sexual behavior, fantasy, feelings, thoughts, and relationships (Hill, 1997; Hill & Preston, 1996). Very simply, it is the pleasure and joy individuals experience when they engage in sexual expression. Terms and concepts commonly used to talk about sexual motivation include *sexual desire, sex drive,* and *libido,* although these terms do not capture the full meaning of the concept of sexual motivation. The same is true with informal, slang words used to refer to increased sexual interest, such as feeling "horny," "turned on," or "sexy."

## Incentive Theory of Sexual Motivation

*I love my girlfriend. For the first time in my life I've considered marriage. I could see myself with her forever. But, I can't curb my desire for random sex. Ours is great but the need for the hunt/kill is huge. Whenever I'm out, and I see some hottie across the bar, all I can think about is how bad I wanna get her. To try to get her, to get her home. . . . I'm afraid I'll either be a cheater or alone forever, chasing every beautiful girl I see. I can't stop hunting no matter how much is on the line. (Confession Junkie, 2006b)*

As discussed previously, the factors involved in the experience of sexual pleasure are not as simple as they may seem at first glance. So, what are the factors related to sexual pleasure that lead individuals to want to engage in sexual behavior? Scientific evidence indicates that different individuals may enjoy different aspects of sexual experience, such as feeling valued by one's partner, making one feel better, feeling powerful, and experiencing physical stimulation and excitement (Hill, 1997; Hill & Preston, 1996). Psychological theorists refer to the particular aspects of sexual experience that provide pleasure as **incentives.** Yet for individuals to actually initiate behavior aimed at experiencing these incentives, they must also believe that they have a reasonable chance of actually being successful at obtaining the pleasure (Heckhausen, 1991).

Several recent theoretical models of sexual motivation (Everaerd, Laan, Both, & Spiering, 2001; Hill & Preston, 1996) combine an emphasis on specific incentives with a factor that is also important to consider in human sexuality: processes within the person. These models propose that an accurate and complete understanding of the causes of sexual behavior must

Most individuals only approach others with whom they believe they have a reasonable chance of success at having pleasurable experiences.

**FIGURE 8.1**    The Incentive-Motivation Perspective

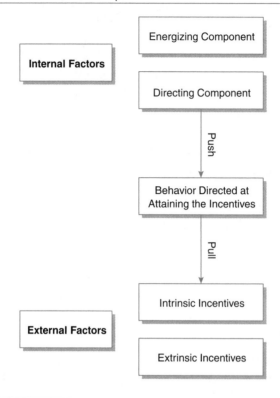

take into account factors both within the individual and outside of the individual in the environment, as presented in Figure 8.1.

Incentive-motivation models (Singer & Toates, 1987) in particular incorporate both types of factors (Atkinson, 1966; Bindra, 1968, 1974; Heckhausen, 1991). Within these models, internal factors interact with external factors to affect behavior; this means that internal and external factors influence, or depend on, one another in the effects they exert on behavior.

Internal factors consist of both an **energizing component** of motivation, as well as a **directing component**. These aspects of motivation are thought to provide the force that *pushes* an individual (the energizing function) toward a specific aspect of the environment that will provide pleasure and gratification (the directing function). Internal factors include structures and processes occurring within the brain and nervous system. In humans, they also involve complex psychological motives such as the long-standing desire for emotional intimacy or the desire for thrill and excitement (Hill, 1997; Hill & Preston, 1996), as discussed in chapter 5 on personality.

External factors are the incentives existing in the immediate situation that produce pleasure on experiencing them. Incentives are also referred to as the **situational aspect** of motivation. They are conceived of as *pulling* individuals toward them, causing the individuals to engage in behavior that will allow them to experience the incentives (Everaerd et al., 2001). Furthermore, sexual motivation involves interest in attaining a general *class* of incentives, not just one specific instance of incentive. Therefore, incentives encompass a range of experiences that provide sexual pleasure (Atkinson, 1966; Heckhausen, 1991); examples include the expression of intense emotional intimacy and tenderness that may occur during sexual interaction, or the profound sensual stimulation and excitement that may result from physical sexual contact.

Intrinsic incentives are outcomes of behaviors that produce pleasure or gratification through the act of engaging in the behaviors themselves. Consequently, the behaviors are engaged in largely, if not solely, to experience the pleasure, not to achieve some other, ulterior goal. Engaging in the behaviors is rewarding in itself (Leiblum & Rosen, 1988).

*What kinds of incentives do you think this type of setting offers for engaging in sensual or sexual behavior? What particular types of sexual expression are most likely to occur?*

For example, only sexual interaction with a partner provides the special sense of being valued by, and attractive to, that person in such a way that the partner wants to be physically close and experience one's body. Feeling valued by one's partner may be experienced through nonsexual behaviors such as discussing one's hopes and fears with him or her; however, feeling valued the way one does through sexual intimacy is a relatively distinct type of emotional intimacy (Hill, 1997; Hill & Preston, 1996).

Other behaviors do not produce the same type of gratification as intrinsic incentives. For an individual who obtains gratification out of feeling valued through sexual interaction, the other ways of being made to feel valued may not provide the kind of intimacy he or she desires. Such an individual is likely to feel unfulfilled, neglected, or unhappy if one's partner does not communicate a special warmth and attachment to him or her through sexual interaction, even if valuing is expressed in other ways as well in the relationship. The specific kind of pleasure is relatively distinctive to sexual intimacy, and therefore is intrinsic to sexual interaction.

Eight types of intrinsic sexual incentives have been identified by Hill and Preston (1996): (a) physical pleasure, stimulation, and excitement; (b) reproduction; (c) feeling valued by one's partner through sexual interaction; (d) expressing value for one's partner through sexual interaction; (e) experiencing relief from stress; (f) providing relief to one's partner; (g) exerting power over one's partner through sexual interaction; and (h) experiencing the power of one's partner.

Yet, individuals may engage in sexual behavior for a variety of reasons that have nothing to do with experiencing sexual pleasure (Leiblum & Rosen, 1988). Such reasons are called **extrinsic incentives**. These include participating in sexual interaction with a partner out of a sense of duty or obligation because of involvement in a romantic relationship with the partner. In fact, an individual may have sex with a partner because she feels obliged, even though she feels she is not really attracted to the person after all. The individual engaging in sex out of a sense of duty is not participating to obtain sexual pleasure, and may even find the experience dull, unexciting, irritating, or unpleasant.

*Do you think this person is engaging in sexual behavior to enjoy some aspect of the sexual interaction with her partner? What might be some reasons she is involved in this sexual relationship?*

Another individual may engage in sexual behavior to receive money from the sexual partner, or because the partner provides other types of material support. In this case, the pleasure associated with money received for sex may be experienced through performing other nonsexual behaviors; it is not specific to engaging in sex. If the individual does not engage in sexual behavior primarily to experience sexual pleasure, the incentive for sexual behavior is *extrinsic* to sexuality. Therefore, such factors as fulfilling obligations and receiving money or material goods are **extrinsic incentives** for sexual behavior.

Factors within the person and in the environment influence one another in very specific ways. Internal factors may involve physiological changes in the brain or nervous system, or thoughts or fantasies that lead to sexual excitement. Such internal factors heighten attention to, and awareness of, aspects of the environment that will provide the desired pleasure or stimulation; again, these aspects of the environment are incentives. The heightening of interest in specific incentives will lead the individual to be more sensitive to their availability in the environment, or even to seek the incentives out to experience them. In turn, aspects of the environment likewise influence internal factors. Encountering sexual incentives, such as a physically attractive person or a person with whom one has become extremely close emotionally, may result in the activation of internal processes in the nervous system and in psychological systems. Exposure to incentives therefore is likely to increase the level of motivation the person feels.

## Sequence Models of Sexual Behavior

Everaerd, Laan, Both, and Spiering (2001) proposed a model of sexual motivation to explain the process through which sexual motivation arises and produces sexual behavior. The model is extremely similar to that developed by Donn Byrne (1977, 1982; Byrne & Schulte, 1990) called the Sexual Behavior Sequence, presented in Figure 8.2. Within the Everaerd and colleagues model, sexual motivation is proposed to energize the sexual system, which includes the nervous system, the body, and psychological processes. The activation may eventually result in overt (observable) sexual behavior.

The Byrne model (1977, 1982; Byrne & Schulte, 1990) does not explicitly include a concept of sexual motivation, which is actually an important concept because it includes the directing function; the directing function guides behavior purposefully toward very specific goals and outcomes. That is, sexual behavior is not aimless and mindless, but occurs for very particular reasons. Byrne does, however, briefly allude to factors that produce arousal as motivational factors. A strength of the Sexual Behavior Sequence model proposed by Byrne is that it provides a highly detailed, well-organized understanding of the many factors that are involved in determining

---

**FIGURE 8.2** The Sexual Behavior Sequence

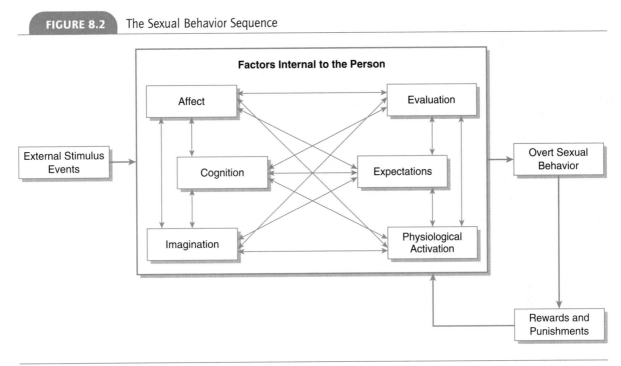

Adapted from Byrne, 1982, and Byrne & Schulte, 1990. Used with permission.

---

sexual behavior. It also includes variables that are essential to sexual motivation, most especially emotions and feelings. The initial phase of the sexual behavior sequence in the Byrne model is called arousal.

## Sexual Arousal

*Sexual arousal* is a state of heightened activation that provides the impetus for sexual behavior in general, rather than for specific types of sexual behavior (Byrne, 1977, 1982; Byrne & Schulte, 1990). Similarly, Everaerd and his colleagues (Everaerd et al., 2001) identified the energizing or activating of the sexual system as **sexual arousal**. A fundamental assumption of Byrne's model is that the likelihood of overt sexual behavior increases with increasing levels of arousal. Everaerd and his colleagues called this increasing likelihood of sexual behavior the **action tendency**. The degree to which the sexual system is energized is determined by the attractiveness of the stimulus, the aspect of the environment that inspires arousal, such as another person. Factors influencing attractiveness of romantic and sexual partners are considered in a later section. The degree of arousal is also affected by the ability of the psychological system to inhibit other thoughts or feelings that may interfere with the sexual system, such as sexual anxiety or guilt, or worrying about some other aspect of one's life (e.g., a problem at work).

According to the model, increasing sexual arousal produces a growing awareness of **sexual desire** after arousal intensity exceeds a minimum level or threshold. Sexual desire is the conscious feeling that one is sexually aroused (Everaerd et al., 2001). The heightened sexual action tendencies activate **motor systems**, aspects of the nervous system and body that produce movement and responding. This may include muscle contractions and increased blood flow in the genital area, which contribute to the subjective experience of desire. Subjective feelings that are typically associated with increased arousal and motivation include "'intense interest,' 'engaged curiosity,' and 'eager anticipation'" (Panksepp, 1998, p. 149).

*What do you think are the conditions that are essential to experiencing sexual arousal and sexual desire?*

According to Byrne, arousal is determined by three interacting components: (a) **external stimuli**, (b) **imagination**, and (c) **physiological activation** (see Figure 8.3). The arousal process may start as a result of any of the three factors.

### External Stimulus Events

External stimulus events are the aspects of the environment that serve as incentives, as discussed with respect to incentive theory. There are three types of external stimuli: (a) unconditioned stimuli, (b) conditioned stimuli, and (c) observing the sexual behavior of others. The terms, *unconditioned* and *conditioned,* are based on fundamental concepts within the learning theory account of classical conditioning; this theory was examined in chapter 5 on personality.

**Unconditioned Stimuli.** *Unconditioned stimuli* are aspects of the environment that produce a particular response without any prior experience or training with the stimuli. Recall that within learning theory, preexisting stimulus–response associations are referred to as *unconditioned.* The automatic response that results

---

**FIGURE 8.3**    Arousal as Conceived Within the Sexual Behavior Sequence Model

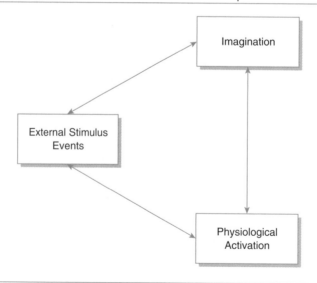

Adapted from Byrne, 1982, and Byrne & Schulte, 1990. Used with permission.

from an unconditioned stimuli is called an **unconditioned response**. The most basic unconditioned stimulus–response associations are those that result from biologically based reflexes, such as the case with the association between food and such automatic responses as increased desire to eat and salivation.

As noted by Byrne (1982), certain sexual stimuli may cause even sexually naive individuals, meaning those with no previous sexual experience at all, to respond sexually. Sexual response may include becoming sexually aroused, seeking contact with the cause of the sexual stimulation (e.g., a particular person), and engaging in sexual behavior. Perhaps the most obvious unconditioned stimulus for sexual arousal is direct touching and stroking of areas of the body sensitive to stimulation, such as the genitals (Byrne, 1982). Yet other parts of the body, such as the face, lips, neck, breasts, thighs, buttocks and abdomen, are also likely to lead to sexual arousal under certain conditions. Sexual arousal may even occur in reaction to brief, accidental brushes of one person's body with that of another person, as was the case in the anonymous example at the beginning of the chapter.

Even this type of stimulation, however, is not purely "reflexive," meaning nonconsciously automatic. Higher-level cognitive and emotional processes involved in understanding the stimulation are almost always involved in reacting. Being touched by someone you do not find attractive, or being caressed in an inappropriate situation (e.g., around others), does not always lead to arousal; in fact, the primary reaction instead is likely to be anger or displeasure. Likewise, some individuals may be less comfortable with the experience of sexual stimulation in general than others, because of religious or emotional inhibitions.

Other unconditioned stimuli may include sexual pheromones, chemical substances produced by the body that activate physiological sexual arousal. Although most research on pheromones has involved lower animals, some evidence suggests that humans may also respond in some ways to their presence (Graham, Janssen, & Sanders, 2000; Thornhill et al., 2003).

Possibly more widely influential for humans are visual cues, the sight of other humans, especially features associated with attractiveness; these factors are discussed later, and include specific attributes of the human body perceived as physically attractive, such as the hourglass shape of the female body and the V-shape of the male torso. Beyond visual stimuli, other types of unconditioned stimuli may include emotionally intimate or nurturant behaviors. Such behaviors signal that another person holds a positive view of an individual, as well as a willingness to maintain an ongoing relationship; these cues may be particularly important to females in producing sexual arousal or interest (Hill, 2002).

Conditioned Stimuli. Conditioned stimuli are aspects of the environment that come to elicit a specific response only after training or experience. Conditioning (or training) consists of combining some aspect of the environment that does not produce a sexual response with a stimulus that does create sexual arousal (i.e., the unconditioned stimulus). For example, a specific song or type of music that is not sexually arousing might be paired with sensual stroking of the body. The unconditioned stimulus, as defined previously, prompts a naturally occurring response, the unconditioned response; in this case, the response is sexual arousal. After a number of pairings of the neutral event (the song) with the unconditioned stimulus (sensual stroking), the song comes to elicit the response of sexual arousal. In this way, with consistent pairing, various aspects of the environment may become capable of producing sexual arousal. After being sexually aroused a number of times while particular music is playing, individuals may eventually find that the music by itself can cause them to become aroused or "feeling sexual."

In fact, seemingly incidental features of the environment, such as music or particular locations (one's bedroom or a nightclub someone frequents), are not the only type capable of producing sexual arousal; specific attributes of other people also often become associated with sexual stimulation. Individuals may develop strong preferences for specific facial features; hair of a certain color or style; smooth, hairless skin or, on the other hand, the presence of body or facial hair; particular types of clothing; particular facial expressions, gestures, or body postures; or specific body shapes. Such attributes are all fairly commonly associated with attractiveness and sexual arousal among people in general. However, an obsession with a single feature to the exclusion of all other features, one that is required to be present for an individual to experience sexual arousal, is a type of psychological disorder called a **fetish**. In fact, classical conditioning has been proposed as a means of explaining the development of fetishes (Byrne, 1982).

Observing the Sexual Behavior of Others. A third type of external stimulus to sexual arousal is observing the sexual behavior of other people either by watching a video recording or watching them in person (Byrne, 1982). This specifically refers to watching others engage in sexual behavior without being directly involved in the sexual behavior or directly stimulating one's own body. Observation produces vicarious arousal, because it involves enjoying the experiences of others and possibly imagining oneself involved in the activity.

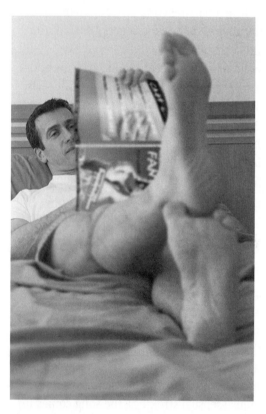

*What psychological functions might viewing erotic images serve for individuals?*

Byrne noted that large numbers of studies have demonstrated that exposure to **erotica**—art, photographs, videos, audio recordings, and written descriptions of sexual activity—produces sexual arousal. Observing sexual behavior in this way has also been shown to increase the likelihood of engaging in sexual behavior. When aroused by viewing erotica, however, an individual is most likely to engage in sexual behavior that is typical for that particular individual, rather than trying to imitate the behavior he or she may have been viewing. Contrary to traditional folk beliefs, viewing erotica does not lead individuals to engage in greater levels of all types of sexual behavior, or unusual sexual behavior.

Several factors have been found to affect the type of response individuals have to erotica. Most typically, erotica is presented in video recordings or in written vignettes describing the sexual behavior. A meta-analysis of 46 studies conducted by Murnen and Stockton (1997) found a gender difference in self-reported arousal to erotica that was small to moderate in size ($d = .31$; refer back to chapter 6 on gender differences for an explanation of the $d$ statistic). Contrary to traditional stereotypes and predictions within evolutionary theory (Symons, 1979), gender differences did not occur for visual types of erotica; Symons had predicted that men would experience greater arousal to visually presented erotica.

Factors related to greater gender differences in sexual arousal to erotica were (a) exposure to erotica in smaller groups of respondents (decreased anonymity leads to increased pressure to conform to gender expectations) and (b) younger age of respondent. Murnen and Stockton (1997) concluded that the results of the meta-analysis in general do not provide support for evolutionary psychology predictions. The disconfirming findings include the relatively small size of the gender differences when they occurred, the lack of a gender difference in visual stimuli, and the fact that gender differences were affected by the social situation, specifically the presence of fewer versus more participants in a research session. Instead, Murnen and Stockton concluded that greater support is provided for a social influence (social constructionist) explanation; in this view, prevailing social roles and expectations are thought to determine the type of reaction that women and men have to erotic stimuli.

**Stimulus Factors Affecting the Amount of Arousal.** Three characteristics of external stimuli—specifically, unconditioned stimuli, conditioned stimuli, and observing sexual behavior—that increase arousal are (a) the attractiveness of the stimulus, (b) the novelty of the stimulus, and (c) the extent to which the stimulus focuses on engaging in overt erotic behavior. Greater attractiveness of the stimulus—in terms of the physical or personality features of a potential partner—has been shown to produce greater arousal, as well as a greater likelihood of experiencing conscious excitement and desire. Novelty refers to the newness of the stimulus; this can result from encountering the same stimulus in different settings (e.g., one's romantic partner at a vacation resort rather than in one's home), the prospect of engaging in different types of sexual behavior, or the potential to engage in sexual behavior with a different partner.

With respect to the focus on overt sexual behavior, research has demonstrated that imagery involving motor expression—that is, engaging in actual behavior—generates greater sexual arousal than imagery not involving motor expression (Dekker & Everaerd, 1988; Dekker, Everaerd, & Verhelst, 1984). This means that simply imagining a desired sexual partner or some feature of his or her body produces less arousal than imagining engaging in some sexual behavior with the partner. In fact, the most popular fantasies for both women and men are about *doing* something with a desired partner, such as engaging in penile–vaginal intercourse, oral–genital sex, or involvement in emotional expression (Leitenberg & Henning, 1995).

### Imagination

**Imagination** involves images and experiences generated within cognitive and emotional systems of the person; these are more commonly known as fantasies, daydreams, and nighttime dreams. **Imaginative processes** are cognitive and emotional activities that produce the fantasies and dreams. Imaginative cues may stimulate sexual arousal and may be critical to maintaining or heightening sexual arousal. As noted by Byrne (1982),

> In all probability, the uniquely human contribution to sexuality is the way in which internal images function to increase or decrease sexual arousal, to provide the opportunity to rehearse acts prior to their actual occurrence, to guide ongoing behavior, and to make it possible to take part imaginatively in activities that are unlikely to occur in real life. (p. 232)

Four types of cognitive activities are critical imaginative processes: (a) imaginative play, (b) anticipatory fantasy, (c) memories, and (d) dreams.

**Imaginative Play.** This process is the creation of erotic ideas, images, and scenarios within one's imagination that serve as stimuli that may increase sexual arousal. The content of these thoughts is likely to be a combination of memories of past erotically stimulating situations and creation of new, imagined situations that might be arousing. The results are specially tailored fantasies that maximize the amount of sexual arousal experienced by each individual. Fantasizing may occur while involved in actual sexual episodes, such as masturbating or engaging in sexual interaction with a partner; it often also occurs, however, at apparently random times throughout the daily routine for many individuals in the form of daydreams (Byrne, 1982; Leitenberg & Henning, 1995).

Why would individuals even concoct imaginary scenarios in their mind at all? Of what value are fantasies that are specifically tailor-made for each person? The significance of personally tailored erotic fantasy is demonstrated in research in which individuals were asked to fantasize in a laboratory setting. Not only are individuals able to conjure up sexual images and scenarios, they also report being more sexually aroused than individuals in another experimental condition who were presented erotic images and stories by the researcher (Byrne, 1982). Fantasies that are designed to tap into a person's most arousing, titillating concepts very likely fulfill his or her wishes more completely than scenarios designed by someone else. Perhaps active engagement in their creation itself involves the person more in the substance of the fantasies, making them more vivid and meaningful as well.

A review of research on sexual fantasy by Leitenberg and Henning (1995) reveals that large proportions of both women and men have engaged in sexual fantasy. The proportions of women and men experiencing sexual fantasies during nonsexual activities are identical; such fantasies take place during the daily routine, rather than specifically in a sexual situation. Likewise, equally high numbers of women and men fantasize during sexual activity, although men are more likely to report fantasizing during masturbation.

The tendency to engage in sexual fantasy has traditionally been viewed as an indication that an individual has been deprived of sufficient sexual satisfaction, and even as an indicator of psychological problems.

Fantasizing about being forceful or submitting to a forceful partner allows individuals to explore the power and energy involved in sexuality, and to allow oneself to feel release from the demands of responsibility.

One of the most prominent advocates of this view was Sigmund Freud (1908/1962), who proposed within psychoanalytic theory that fantasy results from the lack of sufficient satisfaction. Little empirical evidence exists to support such a view, however. In fact, frequency of sexual fantasy is associated with fewer sexual difficulties, less sexual dissatisfaction, greater levels of sexual activity, and more sexual experience. Leitenberg and Henning concluded that people engage in fantasy to increase sexual arousal and enhance sexual enjoyment, rather than to compensate for dissatisfaction. This is consistent with Byrne's proposal that fantasy is one aspect of imaginative processes that may be used to heighten or maintain arousal.

The content of fantasy often differs to some extent by gender. Males frequently generate mental scenarios in which they are the active participant, performing a sexual behavior on a sexual partner. Females typically construct fantasies involving a sexual partner doing something sexual to them. Furthermore, men are more likely in comparison to women to fantasize about sexual behavior with a number of partners (Leitenberg & Henning, 1995). Men also have more sexually explicit fantasies, focusing on specific sexual behavior and body features, whereas women are likely to focus more on emotional expression and romantic feelings. Males tend to imagine themselves in a forceful, dominant role, whereas females are more likely to fantasize about submitting to a partner or even being forced to submit (Byrne, 1982; Leitenberg & Henning, 1995). Leitenberg and Henning concluded that both types of fantasies likely serve the same purpose of affirming sexual power and expressing desire for irresponsibility.

As Byrne (1982) cautions, fantasies do not necessarily relate to the types of experiences individuals wish will occur in real life. Byrne draws the following analogy:

> To believe, for example, that "rape" fantasies among females indicate a widespread desire to become victims of a criminal assault is analogous to assuming that millions of individuals who spent money to view the movie *Jaws* secretly desire to be consumed by a great white shark. (p. 234)

The nature of sexual fantasies of lesbians and gay men tends to be identical to that of heterosexual women and men, with the gender of sexual partner reversed. That is, lesbians fantasize about women as sexual partners and gay men fantasize about men.

Consistent with Byrne's proposal within the Sexual Behavior Sequence model (Byrne, 1977, 1982), conditioning resulting from earlier experiences appears to greatly affect the content of fantasy. Conditioning is the strengthening of a response to an aspect of the environment that previously did not generate the response, such as sexual arousal upon listening to a song that did not cause sexual arousal at one time. With respect to fantasy, conditioning usually results from the pairing of the positive experience of sexual arousal with some unrelated event or experience. As described by Leitenberg and Hanning (1995),

> elements of scenes found to be arousing are repeatedly paired with further pleasurable arousal and orgasm during masturbation and other sexual activity. What one has read and seen as well as directly experienced further influences the content of one's preferred fantasies. (p. 491)

In other words, people and situations that have caused sexual arousal in the past tend to become the subject of a person's fantasies later on.

**Anticipatory Fantasizing.** Anticipatory fantasizing is imagining what the experience of sexual behaviors and interactions will be like before actually engaging in them (Byrne, 1982). This sometimes simply consists of vague, loosely directed curiosity about the nature of the sensations and feelings that will result from erotic activities. On other occasions, individuals create elaborate scenarios and step-by-step scripts in advance of an actual sexual encounter; this may provide a mental framework that helps guide the person's behavior during the encounter.

Anticipatory fantasizing would include the type of fantasy in which individuals engage earlier in their life before actually having engaged in any sexual behavior. Byrne (1982) suggests that this type of fantasy may motivate young people to define themselves sexually, that is, to develop their sexual identity. However, individuals who have already engaged in some types of sexual behavior are also likely to fantasize about erotic situations, partners, and specific sexual behaviors before engaging in them. For some individuals, these musings may actually serve as the basis for developing intentions or strategies to engage in a particular behavior or to experience the situation or partner about which they have fantasized. As described by Byrne, "Quite possibly, repeated exposure to self-created exciting scenes of oral sex, anal sex, group sex, sadism, or whatever would similarly increase the possibility of eventually engaging in such behavior" ( p. 234).

**Memories.** Memories are recollections of events experienced by an individual in the past. Recall of sexual experience is likely to serve as a major source of stimulation contributing to sexual arousal (Byrne, 1982). Research has indicated that, if individuals are asked to describe their most exciting sexual fantasies, past sexual experiences are often a major source of information for the fantasies. For most aspects of life, personal participation in events causes these events to be perceived as especially significant to individuals. Similarly, the sexual encounters an individual experiences himself or herself tend to be especially influential in generating arousal (Kelley, 1979). In fact, memories of previous sexual experiences are often used by individuals to create images and thoughts that enhance arousal leading up to sexual behavior. This type of mental imagery also serves to direct and regulate arousal during sexual behavior (Byrne, 1982).

Dreams. Dreams are images and stories that occur spontaneously and virtually nonconsciously during the rapid-eye-movement (REM) period of sleep. Dreams involving sexual situations typically increase in frequency after the onset of puberty. The increase corresponds with an upsurge in gathering information, thinking about, and possibly experimenting with sexual behavior, including masturbation. Erotic dreaming may coincide with typical physiological arousal during the dreaming process that is virtually identical to the sexual arousal occurring during waking periods. The physiological arousal experienced during dreaming includes erection of the penis for men and, in some cases, even orgasm and ejaculation. The occurrence of ejaculation during sleep in young males is called nocturnal emission, nocturnal orgasm, or in slang terms, "wet dreams" (Byrne, 1982).

### Physiological Activation

The physiological aspect of sexual arousal most obviously involves increased blood flow to the genitals in both males and females. As a result of this increase, as well as restricted outflow, the genitals become engorged with increased quantities of blood, causing them to swell and redden. In females, the labia become larger, and the labia minora—the inner, smaller folds of tissue—may enlarge by as much as two to three times their unaroused size. Moisture also seeps through the walls of the vagina because of the elevated blood pressure, increasing the wetness of the vaginal walls and providing a source of lubrication. In males, the accumulation of blood may result in erection of the penis. Other parts of the body also experience an increased blood flow, causing most notably a flushed appearance to the face and torso (Byrne, 1982).

Another reaction to arousal is a heightening of muscle tension, called **myotonia**, causing various muscular tissue to become more rigid and active; this likewise causes the nipples of the breasts in both genders to become erect. At some point in the process, increasing myotonia results in waves of contraction and expansion of the muscle tissue in the genitals and throughout the body that become involved in the intense physical pleasure of orgasm, and ejaculation of seminal fluid by males (Byrne, 1982).

*Do you think that the experience of sexual pleasure simply involves an increase in muscle tension and waves of contractions? What other types of factors might also be important?*

Some theoretical perspectives have defined sexual arousal entirely in terms of the activation of physiological processes, although it is obvious from the examination of the previous two components of sexual arousal that more is involved than simply activation of body parts. Likewise, another aspect of arousal is the subjective awareness of being sexually interested and experiencing **sexual desire**. This may be measured (e.g., using standardized rating scales as discussed in chapter 5) by asking individuals to report the degree to which they feel sexually aroused or experience sexual feelings. An extremely high level of agreement is typically found between self-reports of arousal and measures of physiological arousal when high-quality measurement procedures are used. Correlations are typically found in the .80 to .90 range or higher, an exceptionally high level indicating close to complete overlap. The correspondence between self-reported arousal and more objective physiological measures is often somewhat higher for men than for women; however, the overlap for women is nonetheless exceptionally great (Byrne, 1982). An example of a self-report questionnaire of sexual arousal is presented in Box 8.1.

---

# BOX 8.1 AN OPPORTUNITY FOR SELF-REFLECTION

### Sexual Excitation Scale

In this questionnaire you will find statements about how you might react to various sexual situations, activities, or behaviors. Obviously, how you react will often depend on the circumstances, but we are interested in what would be the most likely reaction for you. Please read each statement carefully and decide how you would be most likely to react. Then select the number that corresponds with your answer. Please try to respond to every statement. Sometimes you may feel that none of the responses seems completely accurate. Sometimes you may read a statement that you feel is not applicable. In these cases, please select a response that you would choose if it were applicable to you. In many statements you will find words describing reactions such as "sexually aroused," or sometimes just "aroused." With these words we mean to describe feelings of sexual excitement, feeling "sexually stimulated," "horny," "hot," or "turned on." Don't think too long before answering, please give your first reaction. Try to not skip any questions. Try to be as honest as possible. Use the following rating scale: 1 = Strongly agree, 2 = Agree, 3 = Disagree, and 4 = Strongly disagree.

|  |  |  |  |  |
|---|---|---|---|---|
| 1. When I think of a very attractive person, I easily become sexually aroused. | [1] | [2] | [3] | [4] |
| 2. When a sexually attractive stranger looks me straight in the eye, I become aroused. | [1] | [2] | [3] | [4] |
| 3. When I see an attractive person, I start fantasizing about having sex with him or her. | [1] | [2] | [3] | [4] |
| 4. When I talk to someone on the telephone who has a sexy voice, I become sexually aroused. | [1] | [2] | [3] | [4] |
| 5. When I have a quiet candlelight dinner with someone I find sexually attractive, I get aroused. | [1] | [2] | [3] | [4] |
| 6. When an attractive person flirts with me, I easily become sexually aroused. | [1] | [2] | [3] | [4] |
| 7. When I see someone I find attractive dressed in a sexy way, I easily become sexually aroused. | [1] | [2] | [3] | [4] |
| 8. When I think someone sexually attractive wants to have sex with me, I quickly become sexually aroused. | [1] | [2] | [3] | [4] |

*(Continued)*

(Continued)

9. When a sexually attractive stranger accidentally touches me, I easily become aroused.    ☐1  ☐2  ☐3  ☐4

10. When I see others engaged in sexual activities, I feel like having sex myself.    ☐1  ☐2  ☐3  ☐4

11. If I am with a group of people watching an X-rated film, I quickly become sexually aroused.    ☐1  ☐2  ☐3  ☐4

12. If I am on my own watching a sexual scene in a film, I quickly become sexually aroused.    ☐1  ☐2  ☐3  ☐4

13. When I look at erotic pictures, I easily become sexually aroused.    ☐1  ☐2  ☐3  ☐4

14. When I feel sexually aroused, I usually can feel that I am physically aroused or have an erection.    ☐1  ☐2  ☐3  ☐4

15. When I start fantasizing about sex, I quickly become sexually aroused.    ☐1  ☐2  ☐3  ☐4

16. Just thinking about a sexual encounter I have had is enough to turn me on sexually.    ☐1  ☐2  ☐3  ☐4

17. When I feel interested in sex, I usually feel physically aroused or get an erection.    ☐1  ☐2  ☐3  ☐4

18. When I am taking a shower or a bath, I easily become sexually aroused.    ☐1  ☐2  ☐3  ☐4

19. When I wear something I feel attractive in, I am likely to become sexually aroused.    ☐1  ☐2  ☐3  ☐4

20. Sometimes I become sexually aroused just by lying in the sun.    ☐1  ☐2  ☐3  ☐4

To calculate your score for the scale, add together all of the numbers for items. You may want to compare your own scores with the average scores obtained in research by Janssen and his colleagues. The scale was constructed to be used with men only, although the version presented here has been modified to be relevant to both sexes. The average for men was 57.4. The original questionnaire included additional scales, measuring two types of inhibition. Items from all three scales are presented together in random order in that version.

Adapted from Janssen, E., Vorst, H., Finn, P., & Bancroft, J. (2002). The Sexual Inhibition (SIS) and Sexual Excitation (SES) Scales: I. Measuring sexual excitation and sexual inhibition proneness in men. *The Journal of Sex Research, 39*, 114–126. Reprinted with permission from the authors and the Society for the Scientific Study of Sexuality. Please note that the scale has been slightly adapted from the original.

The extent to which physiological arousal is involved in consciously identifying oneself as experiencing sexual desire appears to be different for women in comparison to men, however. This was demonstrated in a study by Chivers, Rieger, Latty, and Bailey (2004). Participants viewed video clips of couples engaged in different types of sexual behavior while physiological arousal was measured. Both heterosexual men and women, and gay men and lesbians, were included. The videos were of (a) two women engaged in oral–genital sex and penetrative sex, with one woman wearing a strap-on dildo that she inserted in the vagina of the other woman; (b) two men engaged in oral–genital sex and penile–anal intercourse; and (c) a man and a woman engaged in oral–genital sex and penile–vaginal intercourse.

A difference was found between women and men in their responses to the various videos. Men experienced heightened sexual arousal only to the videos involving their preferred gender, but did not experience heightened arousal to the videos with only those of the nonpreferred gender. That is, heterosexual men tended to become aroused only to videos portraying women, and gay men became aroused only to videos portraying men. In contrast, two different samples of women were more likely to experience equal or even greater sexual arousal to videos of their nonpreferred gender; specifically for heterosexual women, these were the videos of two women engaged in sex and, for lesbians, they were the videos of two men engaged in sex.

In fact, for the second group of women who were all self-identified heterosexuals, genital arousal was 19% higher for the female–female videos and self-reported arousal was twice as high for the female–female videos compared with the male–male videos. Nonetheless, the women reported being more sexually aroused by the male–female videos than by male–male or female–female videos. As in previous research, this study also found a lower correlation for women between self-reported sexual orientation and genital arousal to the videos than for men; a lower correlation for women was also found between genital arousal and self-reported arousal to the videos.

Chivers and her colleagues (2004) concluded that women tend to have a nonspecific pattern of arousal to sexual stimuli, especially physiological arousal. By this, they meant that sexual stimuli in general produce sexual arousal, rather than only stimuli relevant to their sexual orientation. Yet the results do not support the position that women are inherently bisexual for several reasons. One is that women do not engage in higher rates of same-sex sexual behavior than men. Secondly, the vast majority of women report being sexually attracted exclusively to men. The researchers note that "A self-identified heterosexual woman would be mistaken to question her sexual identity because she became aroused watching female–female erotica; most heterosexual women experience such arousal" (p. 741).

Such a conclusion cannot be drawn about men. Arousal to the same sex in men tends to be associated with a self-identified gay or bisexual orientation. Physiological arousal, especially genital arousal, appears to play a substantially smaller role in the sexual orientation identity of women than it does of men. They suggest that female sexuality may be motivated to a greater extent by factors other than genital arousal, such as by incentives related to emotional intimacy. This proposal finds some support in research on dispositional sexual motives in that, in two out of three studies, women reported stronger

*What conclusions would you draw from the finding that women experience sexual arousal to a range of sexual stimuli, including images not relevant to their sexual orientation?*

tendencies than men for expressing emotional value for their partner as a basis for their sexual interest (Hill & Preston, 1996).

### Mediational Factors

The Byrne model (1977, 1982) proposes that other processes besides arousal influence the specific direction that sexual behavior takes. These factors may be thought of as aspects of the *directing component* in the model advocated by Everaerd and colleagues. On the other hand, sexual arousal is the *energizing component,* the other element of the Everaerd model. The energizing component of motivation provides the activation and impetus for behavior.

The second phase of the Byrne sexual behavior sequence involves mediational factors. Mediational factors are aspects of the directing component in that they move sexual arousal toward particular goals and outcomes. The term *mediational* refers to factors that mediate, or occur in between, arousal and the actions constituting overt sexual behavior. The issue of whether the directing component actually occurs after the arousal component has not been established empirically, and it may be the case that the two components occur simultaneously. Most theories of motivation do not conceive of the energizing and directing components occurring sequentially.

Nonetheless, such factors, whether called mediational factors or the directing component of motivation, are important to account for because they determine the specific types of reactions that individuals have to the arousal that they experience. According to the Byrne model (1977, 1982), **mediational factors** are emotional and cognitive systems within the individual through which a person interprets and reacts to sexual arousal (see Figure 8.4). What are these mediational factors? One classic example is the characteristic of erotophobia–erotophilia presented in chapter 5. As discussed previously, not all individuals respond positively to the experience of sexual stimulation and arousal. Some individuals may feel uncomfortable with the experience, although others may have more positive reactions to sexual arousal. However, Byrne actually proposed four general mediational factors: affect, evaluative responses, informational responses, and expectancies.

**FIGURE 8.4**  Mediational Factors Within the Sexual Behavior Sequence Model

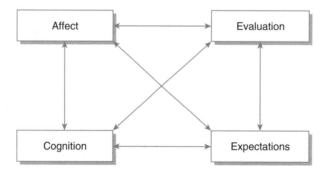

Adapted from Byrne, 1982, and Byrne & Schulte, 1990. Used with permission.

**Affect.** *Affect* refers to emotional reactions to erotic stimuli and the resulting sexual arousal. Some stimuli produce positive feelings, whereas other stimuli result in negative feelings. Moreover, different individuals typically experience more positive or more negative reactions to sexual stimuli, whereas others typically experience a mixture of both positive and negative emotions or little emotional reactions at all. Research has shown that aggressive reactions to sexual stimuli are more likely to occur if negative emotional reactions result from the stimuli (Byrne, 1982).

Evidence also exists for an effect in the reverse direction, with the experience of *negative* emotions leading to *increased* sexual arousal, possibly contrary to what many people might expect. The tendency to experience negative emotions to many aspects of life in general is a personality characteristic discussed in chapter 5 on personality and sexuality. The characteristic is called **neuroticism**, or sometimes **trait anxiety**. Research by Pedro Nobre and his colleagues (Nobre et al., 2004) has demonstrated that men who typically experience high levels of anxiety—those who are high in neuroticism—tend to experience *higher* levels of physiological arousal to viewing erotic videos than those who typically experience more positive emotions; physiological arousal was measured by the extent to which the men's penises became erect while watching the videos.

The researchers interpreted this finding in terms of **arousal transfer** (Barlow, 2002), an effect that occurs in women as well as men, despite the focus on men in this particular study (Barlow, Sakheim, & Beck, 1983; Hoon, Wincze, & Hoon, 1977; Laan, Everaerd, Van-Aanhold, & Rebel, 1993). Arousal transfer is the increase in behavior of one type (i.e., sexual response) caused by arousal associated with a conceptually unrelated type of behavior (i.e., negative emotions, aggressiveness, anger). This can be explained by the fact that increases in physiological sexual arousal heighten activity in the nervous system in general (specifically, the sympathetic nervous system; Meston & Gorzalka, 1996; Palace, 1995; Palace & Gorzalka, 1990). Consequently, other emotions and behaviors unrelated to sexuality cause sexual arousal to become much more likely due to the overall activation.

Contrary to what might be expected, however, men with higher levels of neuroticism reported *lower* levels of subjective arousal to the erotic videos they viewed; they perceived themselves as experiencing less sexual arousal than men who were lower in neuroticism. The tendency to experience negative emotions in general, therefore, may dampen an individual's ability to detect physiological arousal. This is supported by the fact that, in the study by Nobre and his colleagues (2004), highly neurotic men were less accurate in reporting the high levels of physiological arousal occurring, as indicated by greater erection of the penis.

The study (Nobre et al., 2004) additionally demonstrated that men who experienced more positive feelings while watching the videos reported higher levels of subjective sexual arousal. The finding is consistent with other studies (Heiman & Rowland, 1983; Koukounas & McCabe, 2001; Meisler & Carey, 1991; Mitchell, DiBartolo, Brown, & Barlow, 1998; Rowland, Cooper, & Heiman, 1995; Rowland, Cooper, & Slob, 1996) that indicate that it is not high levels of negative feelings that interfere with sexual arousal; rather it is low levels of positive feelings that diminish arousal. Contrary to what many people might believe, positive emotions individuals experience are typically unrelated to the negative emotions they feel; this means that people are capable of experiencing high levels of both positive and negative emotions at the same time.

This is the reason that it was also found that those who reported more positive feelings at the time of viewing the erotic stimuli were somewhat more likely to have greater levels of physiological arousal; however, these men were more accurate in estimating their level of physiological arousal. Mitchell and his colleagues (1998) have proposed that only the type of negative emotions that diminish physiological arousal, such as sadness and depression, interfere with sexual arousal. Negative emotions that increase physiological arousal, such as anxiety and anger, may actually contribute to sexual arousal through the excitation transfer process.

Such research reveals the critical role that cognitive and emotional processes play in sexual behavior in humans (Everaerd et al., 2001). The experience of sexual arousal therefore is only part of the picture in producing sexual behavior. Emotional reactions to stimuli are also critical. The arousal process, including the early nonconscious aspect, interacts with cognitive and emotional processes to determine the specific types of responses and behaviors that will result from the increased motivation.

**Evaluation.** Because it is possible to have both positive and negative feelings about a sexual situation at the same time, this sets up something of a puzzle. Will a person act on his or her positive feelings, or instead will the person respond to the negative feelings? This suggests that individuals go through a process that leads the person toward one particular type of behavior or another. Evaluation is the process that results from the combination of all positive and negative affective responses into one single reaction; the reaction may range from extreme liking for the arousal-producing stimuli to extreme dislike of the stimuli (Byrne, 1982).

Relatively stable individual differences have been found with respect to this type of like–dislike dimension in the form of the trait of erotophobia–erotophilia. Individuals who generally experience largely positive evaluative reactions are more likely to approach arousing stimuli and indulge in sexual behavior related to the stimuli. Those with largely negative evaluative reactions tend to avoid sexually arousing stimuli and related sexual behavior (Byrne, 1982).

**Cognition and Expectations.** Cognition involves knowledge or beliefs about sexual issues. This component of the Byrne model concerns the type of information that individuals possess about sexuality (Byrne, 1982). It includes knowledge of sexual anatomy and physiology. Knowledge also involves understanding social rules and customs related to expected or appropriate behavior, as well as strategies for effectively initiating sexual behavior or attracting partners. Expectations are beliefs about the probability that particular outcomes will result from particular actions. For example, a person may believe that dressing in a sexually provocative way will increase chances of engaging in sexual behavior. That person may be more likely to wear such clothing to attract sexual partners.

### Overt Sexual Behavior

The final component of Byrne's Sexual Behavior Sequence model (Byrne, 1977, 1982) is a set of factors called **overt sexual behavior**. This refers to the types of overt sexual behaviors that result from the internal, less directly observable processes of *arousal* and *mediational factors*. Overt behaviors include **arousal-related behavior**, such as viewing erotic videos and generating sexual fantasies; however, presumably in some situations or characteristically for some people who have negative views of sexuality, arousal-related behavior could involve attempts to avoid erotic stimulation or to inhibit sexual arousal. Another type of overt behavior is **instrumental behavior**, meaning behavior in service of advancing a person toward his or her sexual goals. A person's goals may be to engage in sexual behavior, or they may be to avoid sexual behavior or sexual issues. Examples of these are talking about sex, flirting with one's spouse or partner to entice him or her, and purchasing contraceptives in advance of a sexual encounter. A third kind of overt behavior is **goal behavior**, or engaging in sexual stimulation and sexual expression, or avoiding it; this might involve masturbation, sensually stroking the body or genitals of a partner, oral–genital behavior, penile–vaginal intercourse, or penile–anal intercourse.

Depending on the outcomes that result, overt behavior may increase in frequency over time, or they may decrease. Some behaviors may be followed by positive outcomes, such as when instrumental behaviors succeed in initiating sexual behavior; another positive outcome would be the experience of pleasure and positive feelings during sexual behavior. If such outcomes cause the behavior to increase in the future, they are **reinforcers** (rewards), as discussed in chapter 5 concerning learning theory. Other behaviors may result in negative outcomes, such as failure to initiate sexual interaction, not experiencing arousal or orgasm, or discomfort or negative emotional reactions. Such outcomes may lead an individual to avoid engaging in them again in the future to avoid the outcomes; in this case, the outcome is a **punisher**—outcomes that decrease behavior.

Goal behavior involves engaging in sexual stimulation or sexual expression, including sensually stroking and kissing the body of one's partner.

## Factors Affecting Attractiveness of Partners

As noted in the section on arousal, the attractiveness of a stimulus is one of the three general factors that affect the intensity of sexual arousal an individual experiences. The physical features of a potential partner, his or her face and body, are certainly factors that play into attractiveness and therefore the degree of arousal an individual might experience. However, physical features may not be the strongest influence, particularly for some individuals. What a person is like in terms of his or her personality—the way he or she typically behaves—is also an important element in attractiveness and the potential for sexual arousal. Table 8.1 presents the characteristics that women and men of various cultures around the world consider to be important in selecting a mate.

### Social and Emotional Partner Attributes

Three general types of ideal partner characteristics have been consistently found across a series of studies by Fletcher and Simpson and their colleagues (Fletcher, Simpson, & Thomas, 2000; Fletcher, Simpson, Thomas, & Giles, 1999): (a) **warmth–trustworthiness**, (b) **vitality–attractiveness**, and (c) **status–resources**. The characteristics associated with ideal relationships were also examined. Two sets of characteristics are involved in individuals' conceptions of ideal relationships, which correspond very closely to the first two ideal partner attributes; these are **intimacy–loyalty** and **passion**. Ideal partner and relationship characteristics are more than hypothetical views that have nothing to do with actual real-world outcomes. Research has demonstrated that the overlap of such ideals with perceptions of one's actual partner and relationship is related to greater relationship quality and greater likelihood of the relationship continuing.

The only gender differences were that partner warmth–trustworthiness and relationship intimacy–loyalty were somewhat less important for women than for men. Fletcher and his colleagues (1999) hypothesized that, because women assume that men typically display less commitment and intimacy, women may

**TABLE 8.1**  Characteristics Considered Important in Mates in 37 Cultures Around the World

| Ranking of Characteristics by Women | Ranking of Characteristics by Men |
|---|---|
| 1. Mutual attraction—love | 1. Mutual attraction—love |
| 2. Dependable character | 2. Dependable character |
| 3. Emotional stability and maturity | 3. Emotional stability and maturity |
| 4. Pleasing disposition | 4. Pleasing disposition |
| 5. Education and intelligence | 5. Good health |
| 6. Sociability | 6. Education and intelligence |
| 7. Good health | 7. Sociability |
| 8. Desire for home and children | 8. Desire for home and children |
| 9. Ambition and industriousness | 9. Refinement, neatness |
| 10. Refinement, neatness | 10. Good looks |
| 11. Similar education | 11. Ambition and industriousness |
| 12. Good financial prospects | 12. Good cook and housekeeper |
| 13. Good looks | 13. Good financial prospects |
| 14. Favorable social status | 14. Similar education |
| 15. Good cook and housekeeper | 15. Favorable social status |
| 16. Similar religious background | 16. No prior sexual experience |
| 17. Similar political background | 17. Similar religious background |
| 18. No prior sexual experience | 18. Similar political background |

From Buss, D. M., Abbott, M., Angleitner, A., Asherian, A., et al., International preferences in selecting mates: A study of 37 cultures. *Journal of Cross-Cultural Psychology, 21*, 5–47. Copyright © 1990 SAGE Publications, Inc. Reprinted with permission.

develop lower standards for these attributes. Other research has additionally indicated that women are most attracted to men who exhibit characteristics of not only warmth and benevolence, but also dominance. However, high levels of dominance without substantial levels of warmth and compassion in men are not at all as attractive (Jensen-Campbell, Graziano, & West, 1995); this is apparently because dominance without concern for others suggests that such men are capable of taking advantage of and harming others.

In fact, partner attributes similar to those identified by Fletcher and his colleagues have been shown to correlate with theoretically relevant dispositional sexual motives (Hill, 1997). Ratings of the importance of a romantic partner remaining in love with a person (romantically committed) were correlated with the dispositional sexual motive of *desire to express value for one's partner* independently of all other motives. The romantic commitment dimension is directly analogous to the ideal partner attribute of warmth–trustworthiness and the ideal relationship characteristic of intimacy–loyalty. Furthermore, ratings of the importance of a romantic partner being physically attractive in the Hill study were associated with the dispositional sexual motive of *desire for pleasure and excitement* independently of all other motives. Physical attractiveness is directly relevant to the ideal partner attributes of vitality–attractiveness and the ideal relationship attribute of passion.

Ratings of the importance of a romantic partner being respected by one's friends were correlated in the Hill study with the dispositional sexual motive of *desire to be valued by one's partner*; ratings of the importance of a romantic partner's financial potential were related to *desire to exert power over a sexual partner* and *desire to experience the power of one's sexual partner*. Both of these ratings—respect by one's friends and financial potential—are explicitly relevant to the ideal partner characteristic of status–resources.

Such correlations between partner characteristics and interest in sexual incentives provide empirical evidence for a relationship between desirable partner characteristics and sexual attraction. Partner characteristics related to experiencing emotional closeness, psychological comfort, power, and physical and psychological pleasure are therefore likely to be factors that are attractive and lead to sexual arousal. In fact, all of these factors have been shown to relate to increased sexual attraction (Hill, 1997).

## Physical Attractiveness

A fundamental issue in the examination of attraction involves physical attractiveness. The question regards the extent to which physical attractiveness is actually involved in perceptions of the desirability of individuals. Despite the common belief that physical appearance should not be a criterion for judging individuals in some people's minds, research indicates that physical attractiveness is in fact rated as the most important factor in arousing sexual desire for both women and men (Graziano, Jensen-Campbell, Shebilske, & Lundgren, 1993; Regan & Berscheid, 1995). Although men tend to give higher value to physical attractiveness than women in some studies of self-reported attitudes, research on actual behavior demonstrates that it has as much of an effect on women's reactions as it does on men's (Feingold, 1990).

One of the earliest demonstrations of the importance of physical attractiveness is a classic study by Walster, Aronson, Abrahams, and Rottman (1966). College students were randomly assigned as dates at a dance during the first week of school. After being allowed to dance and interact with one another for several hours, individuals filled out questionnaires about their liking for their partner and their desire to date the person again. The single most influential factor affecting attraction and their intention to date the person, for both women and men, was the partner's physical attractiveness. Physical attractiveness was determined objectively by ratings made independently by the researchers at the beginning of the study. Measures of personality, aptitude, and background characteristics were vastly overshadowed by physical attractiveness. The same results have been obtained as well for gay men (Sergios & Cody, 1985).

One distinction that has been found to affect judgments about the importance of physical attractiveness is the nature of the relationship individuals are considering. When evaluating the desirable characteristics of a partner for a short-term, uncommitted sexual relationship, both women and men list physical attractiveness as the most important of 23 possible characteristics

*Why do you think that physical attractiveness is such an important factor in initial attraction and the desire to become involved in relationships?*

presented to them. Physical attractiveness, however, is more important to men than women when considering desirable traits for a spouse, although even for men it was not one of the most important attributes (Regan & Berscheid, 1997).

## Advantages Afforded by Physical Attractiveness

Based on meta-analyses of a number of studies on perceptions of physical attractiveness (Eagly, Ashmore, Makhijani, & Longo, 1991; Feingold, 1992), research has consistently found that people believe that physically attractive individuals are more likely to be socially competent, sociable, outgoing, and popular. Moreover, they are thought to be happier, more intelligent, and more successful, as well as sexually warmer. Ratings of before and after pictures of individuals who underwent plastic surgery likewise demonstrate that others' impressions of these individuals change in the expected direction; they were seen as more likeable, sensitive, kinder, and sexually warmer after the surgery (Kalick, 1977). Extremely similar kinds of effects for physical attractiveness are found in other cultures as well (Chen, Shaffer, & Wu, 1997; Wheeler & Kim, 1997).

Research actually provides support for the legitimacy of these stereotyped beliefs to some extent. Physically attractive individuals are in fact likely to be more socially skilled and to indicate that they have more satisfying interactions with others than do less attractive individuals (Feingold, 1992; Langlois et al., 2000; Reis, Nezlek, & Wheeler, 1980; Reis, Wheeler, Speigal, Nezlek, & Perri, 1982).

The effect of physical attractiveness may partially result from the self-fulfilling prophecy; people expect attractive individuals to be warmer, more likeable, and more sensitive, and therefore treat them in that way. The physically attractive individuals are therefore set up and enabled to respond with socially positive behavior. Research has demonstrated such an effect in actual interactions in which participants talked with a person of the other sex on the phone. Physical attractiveness was manipulated by showing the interaction partner a picture that was supposedly of the participants, but was actually an attractive or unattractive model. Both women and men whose interaction partners believed them to be more physically attractive were actually rated as more attractive and socially skilled by independent raters listening to the conversation (Andersen & Bem, 1981; Snyder, Tanke, & Berscheid, 1977).

Meta-analyses have confirmed the positive effects of physical attractiveness on both attitudes and behavior across hundreds of studies, as well as generally finding no differences between women and men. That is, physical attractiveness influences both sexes in exactly the same way (Eagly et al., 1991; Feingold, 1992; Langlois et al., 2000).

## Features Contributing to Physical Attractiveness

### Facial Attractiveness

Although standards for deciding facial attractiveness vary to a great extent across culture, time, and individuals (Morse & Gruzen, 1976), certain core features appear to be common to judgments of attractiveness (Berscheid & Reis, 1998; Cunningham, Roberts, Barbee, Druen, & Wu, 1995; Langlois et al., 2000); ratings of faces across different raters are highly correlated with one another, even across different cultures (Langlois & Roggman, 1990). With respect to female facial features, Cunningham (1986) demonstrated that men's ratings of the physical attractiveness of photographs of various women were correlated with (a) larger eyes and larger pupils; (b) high eyebrows; (c) more prominent cheekbones, but narrower cheeks; (d) smaller nose and chin;

and (e) a bigger smile. In addition, an underlying feature of attractiveness is **symmetry**, meaning that both sides of the face or the body have essentially identical appearances.

A later study of male facial features (Cunningham, Barbee, & Pike, 1990) found that larger eyes, stronger cheekbones, a broader chin, and a larger smile were associated with physical attractiveness. The larger eyes and smaller nose are called **babyface features**, because they are characteristic of infants. Such features tend to evoke a sense of warmth and a desire to provide caregiving, a typical first reaction when individuals encounter baby animals and young children (Berry, 1995; Zebrowitz, 1997). The larger cheekbones are associated with sexual maturity and dominance, attributes central to conceptions of masculinity (Sadalla, Kenrick, & Vershure, 1987).

Celebrities known for their attractiveness possess many of the features that research has identified as contributing to facial attractiveness.

However, the most attractive male face is actually a combination of features related to warmth and masculinity. In a study of faces of African American men depicted through line drawings, the head shape rated most attractive and socially competent possessed only a moderate degree of masculine features (Wade, Dyckman, & Cooper, 2004). The authors of the study concluded that masculine features in men are attractive to an extent; however, extreme masculinity may also be associated with negative aspects of masculinity, such as strong aggressiveness and excessive dominance.

### Body Features

Substantially more research has been conducted on the attractiveness of body features and physique for women than for men. Several methods of determining the attractiveness of the body have been proposed, most notably the waist-to-hip ratio (WHR) method and the body mass index (BMI). The WHR is calculated by determining the circumference of the waist at its narrowest point (e.g., the number of inches around) and dividing it by the circumference of the hip at its widest point. This provides an indication of the amount of fat around the middle part of the body, a feature associated with greater health risk (Bjorntorp, 1988), lowered reproductive success (De Ridder et al., 1990; Kaye, Folsum, Princeas, Potter, & Gapstur, 1990; Rebuffe-Scrive, Cullberg, Lundberg, Lindatedt, & Bjorntorp, 1989), and advancing age (Kirschner & Samojilik, 1991). The body mass index is a measure of the proportion of fat relative to muscle tissue in the body.

The guiding hypothesis of most research on the relationship of body shape and size to perceptions of attractiveness is that males are more attracted to females with lower WHR values; lower WHR values result from smaller waists and less fat around the middle of the body relative to the hips. The range of WHR values that are found for the typical woman prior to menopause, when fertility declines and then ends, is 0.67 to 0.80. The typical range for men is between 0.85 and 0.95. A number of studies (Singh, 1993a, 1993b, 1994) using line drawings of female figures have demonstrated that lower WHR (specifically a value of 0.70) is associated with perceptions of greater attractiveness and healthiness; this relationship has also been found in non-U.S.

**FIGURE 8.5**    Line Drawings Portraying Female and Male Physiques of Various Proportions

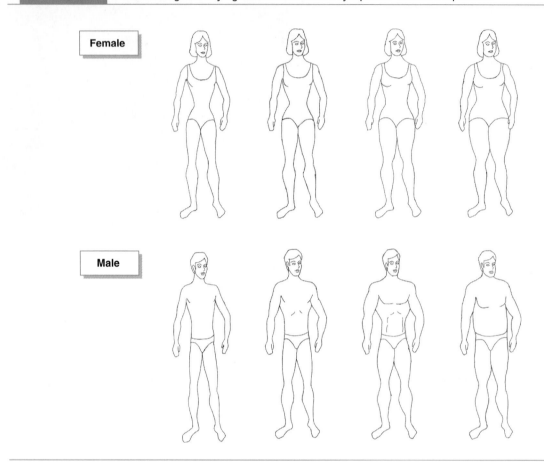

cultures as well (Furnham, McClelland, & Omer, 2003; Furnham, Moutafi, & Baguma, 2000). These types of female figures have waists that are 30% narrower than their hips.

High WHR values, whether due to being overweight or underweight, are perceived as less attractive. Even overweight figures in which the waist is narrower than the hips are viewed as more attractive than overweight figures with bigger midriff areas. Although not exactly the ones used in the cited studies, the line drawings in Figure 8.5 provide an idea of the type of stimuli used in such research. The relationship between WHR and attractiveness has likewise been replicated using photographs of individuals digitally altered to produce figures of different WHR values (Furnham, Mistry, & McClelland, 2004).

Some research indicates that body size has similar effects on attractiveness for both Black and White individuals (Meshreki & Hansen, 2004). However, other research has found that African American men consider the ideal size to be somewhat larger than European American men (Jackson & McGill, 1996; Rosenfeld, Stewart, Stinnett, & Jackson, 1999). In these two studies, both African American women and European American women perceived a slightly thin male body as more attractive than heavier bodies.

## How Do Men and Women Feel About Their Bodies?

In one of the few studies concerning the attractiveness of the male body, Lynch and Zellner (1999) examined perceptions of college women (18–23 years old) compared with older women (30–60 years); they also examined the beliefs of college men and older men about the body type that women find attractive. College women preferred a physique that is more muscular than college men typically believe they have, based on self-ratings by college men in this study. However, college men wanted to have a body that is more muscular than college women reported that they most preferred, because college men thought that the more muscular body is the type that everyone finds most attractive. Older women preferred a less muscular type of male body than college women, the type that older men reported that they currently had. Moreover, older men indicated that they preferred having the type of body they currently had. In other words, older men were satisfied with their muscularity, a feeling that matched the preference of older women. Yet, college women preferred a body type that was somewhat more muscular than college men believe they had, but less muscular than the type that men would like to have.

In a study by Barnett, Keel, and Conoscenti (2001), both Asian and Caucasian college women evaluated their current body as somewhat larger than their ideal body type. Asian men on average, however, believed that their bodies were smaller than their ideal body type. Current body type and ideal body type were virtually identical for Caucasian college men. Increasing pressures for Westernization may be partially responsible for the dissatisfaction expressed by Asian women, even in Asian countries; however, Barnett and her colleagues note that traditional values in Asian societies likewise promote a desire for thinness. Asian men may be even more susceptible to pressures for Westernization, which increases their desire to achieve the Western ideal of a larger, muscular body type. Other research indicates that Asian men who have adopted U.S. values to a greater extent are more driven toward perfectionism than are Asian women (Davis & Katzman, 1999).

### References

Barnett, H. L., Keel, P. K., & Conoscenti, L. M. (2001). Body type preferences in Asian and Caucasian college students. *Sex Roles, 45,* 867–878.

Davis, C., & Katzman, M. A. (1999). Perfection as acculturation: Psychological correlates of eating problems in Chinese male and female students living in the United States. *International Journal of Eating Disorders, 25,* 65–70.

Lynch, S. M., & Zellner, D. A. (1999). Figure preferences in two generations of men: The use of figure drawings illustrating differences in muscle mass. *Sex Roles, 40,* 833–843.

*Genital Features*

Virtually no empirical research exists on perceptions of the attractiveness of female and male external genitals. In fact, it appears that no empirical research has been conducted on perceptions of the attractiveness of female genitals at all. Little thought apparently has been devoted to the nature of female genitals in general, likely accounting for the reason that most people use incorrect terms when referring to female external genitals. The term typically used to talk about female genitals is *vagina,* which is actually an internal sexual structure, the muscular passageway leading outside from the uterus. The correct term for female external genitals is *vulva,* as discussed in chapter 6, which includes the clitoris, labia majora, and labia minora. Most people are essentially unaware of the existence or nature of the clitoris and believe that the inner portion of the vagina is the most sensitive area of the sexual organs, an inaccurate belief. Women tend to report the experience of less pleasure resulting from sexual intercourse than men, a finding that may be accounted for partially by lack of knowledge about the role of the clitoris in sexual pleasure (Ogletree & Ginsburg, 2000).

Only a few studies exist on perceptions of the penis. One study examined perceptions of penis size as it was described in written scenarios about a sexual encounter between a man and a woman (Fisher, Branscombe, & Lemery, 1983). Some participants in this study read a description in which the man was portrayed as having a three-inch penis (small); another version portrayed the man as having a five-inch penis (medium), whereas a third scenario described the man's penis as eight inches long (large). The descriptions were all significantly arousing to both females and males, regardless of penis size, even though the researchers verified that participants were aware of the size of the penises described. Nonetheless, penis size was unrelated to reported sexual arousal for both females and males, with two exceptions.

The first exception involved erotophilia, an aspect of personality involving positive attitudes toward sexuality as discussed in chapter 5. Greater arousal to the scenarios describing the medium or large penis was reported by men who were more erotophilic. Erotophilic women reported greater arousal to the description of the man with the large penis, but no differences were found among women for the other two sizes. The second exception involved men with greater numbers of past sexual partners. Such men reported less arousal to the scenarios of the man with either a small or large penis than did those with fewer sexual partners. Rather, men with greater numbers of past sexual partners experienced more arousal to the depiction of the man with a medium penis.

All of the relationships between variables were fairly small, although statistically significant. Therefore, Fisher and his colleagues concluded that, in general, penis size is not very important to either women or men in terms of sexual arousal. The researchers speculated that, for erotophilic women and men, penis size may serve somewhat as a cue related to sexual pleasure. The cue possibly causes them to become more aroused through positive associations with sexual pleasure they have developed. In contrast, those who are erotophobic experience negative reactions to sexual stimulation, as well as to many issues related to sexuality.

With respect to the greater arousal to the story describing the medium penis by men with more sexual partners, it is likely that men with greater sexual experience feel more confident in their sexual natures. With less concern about sexual adequacy, they may have come to value their own penis attributes to a greater extent than with fewer sexual partners. Because more men possess, by definition, a penis closer to average size, they may have identified more with the man described as having the medium penis, leading to greater arousal.

# Summary

Incentive theory of motivation focuses on incentives, the specific features of sexual experience that provide pleasure intrinsic to sexuality. The availability of sexual incentives in the environment and stronger dispositional sexual motives of the person heighten sensitivity to the incentives and increase the inclination to seek out the incentives to experience them.

Two theoretical models of sexual motivation attempt to account for the process through which sexual motivation produces sexual behavior, one advanced by Byrne (1977, 1982) and the other by Everaerd, Laan, Both, and Spiering (2001). Sexual arousal is the first phase for the two models; as sexual arousal increases, the probability of sexual behavior is proposed to increase as well. In Byrne's Sexual Behavior Sequence model, sexual arousal is conceived as consisting of three interacting components: (a) external stimuli, (b) imaginative processes, and (c) physiological activation.

The second phase of the Sexual Behavior Sequence model involves mediational factors, affective and cognitive systems involved in interpreting and reacting to sexual arousal. Evaluative responses involve the combination of all positive and negative responses into one single reaction. Informational responses are a third type of mediational factor, consisting of knowledge and beliefs that individuals possess regarding sexuality. The third phase of the Sexual Behavior Sequence model is behavior, the overt sexual behaviors that result from the arousal and mediational phases.

Specific attributes that increase the attractiveness of potential sexual partners may be categorized into two groups, (a) social and emotional attributes and (b) physical attributes. Theory and research have identified three types of ideal partner characteristics that are social and emotional attributes: (a) warmth–trustworthiness, (b) vitality–attractiveness, and (c) status–resources.

Physical attractiveness likewise involves a set of attributes that are extremely important in romantic and sexual attraction for both women and men. It is especially influential when individuals are considering the desirable characteristics of a partner for a short-term, uncommitted sexual relationship. Nonetheless, physical attractiveness is more important to men when considering desirable characteristics of a spouse, although even for men it was not rated as one of the most important attributes.

Particular facial features are associated with physical attractiveness. Symmetry of features is a central aspect of attractiveness, such that both sides of the face and body have essentially identical appearances.

Women's figures with smaller waist-to-hip ratios (WHR), in the 0.67 to 0.80 range, are viewed as most attractive—the classic hourglass shaped figure. These perceptions have been found across different racial groups. The most attractive male physique is that which is somewhat muscular.

Although virtually no research has been conducted on features of female genitalia that are related to attractiveness, a few studies have been conducted regarding the penis. In general, penis size portrayed in written scenarios is unrelated to self-reported sexual arousal for both men and women.

## Chapter 8 Critical Thinking Exercises

1. Incentives for Sexual Expression

   Think of specific events or times when you have engaged in sexual behavior with another person because you wanted to do so, or times you have *wanted* to engage in sexual behavior of some type, but did not. In your own words, what specifically caused you to want sexual behavior? That is, what particular experiences, outcomes, feelings, and sensations did you hope to have as a result of the sexual behavior?

2. Sexual Arousal

   Conditioned stimuli are aspects of the environment that come to elicit a specific response only after training or experience (e.g., the fragrance of roses causing sexual arousal). What nonsexual events or objects might more easily become associated with sexual arousal through repeated pairing with sexual arousal? Can you think of any generally nonsexual situations or objects that have come to make you think of sexual issues, or that arouse you sexually? How do you think this association developed for you in particular? That is, how did the event or object become paired with sexual arousal?

**Visit www.sagepub.com/hillhsstudy.com for online activities, sample tests, and other helpful resources. Select "Chapter 8: Sexual Motivation, Arousal, and Attraction" for chapter-specific activities.**

# Chapter 9

## LOVE, INTIMACY, AND SEXUALITY

Why do people engage in sex with someone for the first time? Is it because of overwhelming lust, a moment of uncontrollable passion? Does it really "just happen" with someone whom you find irresistibly attractive? Could it be that some individuals actually plan to "lose their virginity" as a rite of passage into adulthood, or to establish a sense of independence? Maybe they want to begin engaging in sex so that they will be like other people their age, or to define who they are as a person?

The conscious decision to lose one's virginity was actually a theme of an episode on the television series, *Kyle XY.* One of the main characters, Lori Trager, and her friend decided to engage in sex for the first time, yet neither were involved in a romantic relationship. The two characters are high school students who decide they must lose their virginity before the next school year begins. Lori does succeed in having sex and meets their deadline, but the experience does not turn out like she had hoped. Her friend wanted to hurry the process up and so she put a guy up to asking Lori to a party, rather than the guy asking Lori to the party on his own. She is hurt and embarrassed when she discovers that her friend had actually arranged the sexual encounter.

Actually, such a scenario is probably not extremely common. Most people probably do not decide that they are going to have sex just for the sake of losing their virginity. On the other hand, a phenomenon known as "hooking up" has appeared on college campuses around the United States. Hooking up is the situation in which individuals go out on a particular night with the intention of having sex with someone they may have just met, without any desire to start a long-term relationship with the person.

Yet, for the majority of people, the critical issue is whether they are in love with the person they have sex with, and whether they feel that they are involved in a lasting romantic relationship with that person. In fact, research has reliably found that greater intimacy increases the likelihood of engaging in sexual behavior (Christopher & Cate, 1985; Hill, 2002; Roche, 1986; Sprecher, 1989). It is for this reason that the ways in which romantic relationships begin, develop, and then either thrive or fall apart are so important. The experience of love, and how it is related to sexuality, is a major concern that links the various issues involved in human sexual behavior.

# Romantic Relationships

*What do you suppose are the most effective means of increasing the quality of relational intimacy? Does it have to do with sharing of thoughts and feelings, or are other strategies more effective?*

Romantic relationships are only one of a number of types of intimate relationship. An **intimate relationship** is an ongoing involvement between individuals characterized by substantial knowledge and understanding of one another that has been gathered through talking and sharing time together. Another critical aspect of the definition is that an intimate relationship involves a level of closeness that distinguishes it from casual, or nonintimate, relationships (Prager & Roberts, 2004).

The first characteristic of an intimate relationship, therefore, is that individuals have a considerable history of interacting with each other and revealing what they are like in a range of important ways. Of course, an important means of revealing what they are like is by disclosing personal information to one another. The information gathered during these many interactions accumulates into what Prager and Roberts call a **mutually shared body of knowledge**. This information is stored in mental frameworks, or schemas. Schemas provide the basis for anticipating the nature of future interactions with the relationship partner, and what the results of the interactions will be.

For example, will certain types of soothing words help the loved one to feel better and lift his or her spirits? Or will such words of comfort actually backfire and make the partner feel like you are just feeling sorry for him or her? This characteristic of intimate relationships is a recognition of the fact that individuals involved in intimate relationships typically come to know a great deal about one another.

The second characteristic of an intimate relationship is the number and quality of the interactions within the relationship, or its **relational intimacy** (Prager & Roberts, 2004). A relationship with greater relational intimacy involves more frequent interaction in which the couple reveals a great deal of personal information about themselves. Stronger relational intimacy also involves more intense positive experiences within interactions in which the individuals feel valued and respected by their partner. In general, relational intimacy refers to the fact that intimate relationships for different couples vary in terms of the frequency, intensity, and warmth of interactions; some relationships will on average be characterized by very positive, intimate interactions, whereas others on average will involve moderate or lower levels of relational intimacy. In fact, positive emotional experiences figure prominently in what people really desire in romantic relationships, as shown in Table 9.1.

According to Prager and Roberts (2004), a committed couple relationship is, by definition, an intimate relationship, despite the fact that intimate relationships vary in their level of relational intimacy. The reason that all committed couple relationships may be considered intimate relationships is that the body of shared knowledge about one another will be substantial, regardless of differences in the quality of relational intimacy.

The concept of intimate relationship actually encompasses a range of different relationships. These include close friendships, relationships with family members, and romantic relationships, whether these are dating

| **TABLE 9.1** | What Individuals Desire in a Romantic Relationship |
| --- | --- |

**Emotional Rewards**

- Feeling liked and loved
- Feeling understood
- Feeling accepted
- Feeling appreciated
- Physical affection (being kissed and hugged)
- Sex
- Security (commitment to the relationship)
- Plans and goals for the future (dreaming about the future together)

**Personal Rewards**

- Partner having an attractive appearance
- Partner who is friendly and graceful socially
- Partner who is intelligent and informed

**Day-to-Day Rewards**

- Smoothly running daily routine
- Comfortable finances
- Pleasant interaction and good communication

- Sharing responsibility for making decisions that affect both individuals and then carrying through with them
- Remembering special occasions

**Opportunities Gained and Lost From Being in a Relationship**

*Benefits*

- Opportunity to become a parent
- Being invited as a couple to social events
- Having someone to count on as one ages

*Costs*

- Involvement with other potential partners
- Career
- Money
- Travel
- Sexual freedom

From Hatfield, E., & Sprecher, S., Measuring passionate love in intimate relations. *Journal of Adolescence, 9*, 383–410. Copyright © 1986, Elsevier Science & Technology Journals. Reprinted with permission via Copyright Clearance Center.

*What is it that defines an intimate relationship? Would you say that a married couple who argues frequently and goes through long periods of not talking to one another are involved in an intimate relationship? How about a couple who only stays together for the sake of the children?*

# BOX 9.1  AN OPPORTUNITY FOR SELF-REFLECTION

### What Is Your Relationship Like?

Think of the relationship you are currently involved in, or if you aren't in a relationship right now, think of your most recent relationship.

For each of the stages below identified by Levinger, indicate what your relationship was like at that stage, and what it is like in its current stage. Use each of the rating scales to describe the relationship. Of course, if you have not experienced a particular stage, you will not be able to describe your relationship at that stage.

### Attraction Stage

This is the point at which your partner seemed desirable to you and feelings of romantic interest were beginning. You began to realize you wanted to be around your partner and spend time with him or her. Use the following scale for your ratings: 1 = Not at all, 5 = Moderately, and 9 = Very much.

1. How much did you attempt (have you attempted) to show the person that you were (are) interested in him or her and found (find) him or her attractive?    1 2 3 4 5 6 7 8 9

2. How satisfied were you at the time (or are currently satisfied) with the nature or status of your hoped-for relationship?    1 2 3 4 5 6 7 8 9

3. How much sexual intimacy did (do) you expect at this point in the hoped-for relationship?    1 2 3 4 5 6 7 8 9

4. How committed were (are) you to beginning the hoped-for relationship at this point?    1 2 3 4 5 6 7 8 9

5. How likely did (do) you think it was (is) that the hoped-for relationship wouldn't (will not) happen when you first began to realize you were attracted to this person?    1 2 3 4 5 6 7 8 9

### Beginning Stage

At this point, the relationship has begun in the sense of going on dates or intentionally spending some length of time together (not simply greeting each other in passing).

1. How much did you attempt (or have you attempted) to show your partner that you were (are) interested in his or her feelings and wanted (want) to get to know him or her better?    1 2 3 4 5 6 7 8 9

2. How satisfied were (are) you with the nature or status of your relationship?    1 2 3 4 5 6 7 8 9

3. How much sexual intimacy did (do) you expect at this point in the relationship?    1 2 3 4 5 6 7 8 9

4. How committed were (are) you to staying in the relationship at this point?    ① ② ③ ④ ⑤ ⑥ ⑦ ⑧ ⑨

5. How likely did (do) you think it was (is) that the relationship would (will) not work out and might end?    ① ② ③ ④ ⑤ ⑥ ⑦ ⑧ ⑨

**Continuing Relationship**

This is the point in the relationship when both partners are obviously committed to staying in the relationship for as far as you can see at the time. The two of you spend significant amounts of time together, and your daily lives have come to overlap a great deal.

1. How much did you attempt (or have you attempted) to show your partner that you were (are) interested in his or her feelings and wanted (want) to work through conflicts?    ① ② ③ ④ ⑤ ⑥ ⑦ ⑧ ⑨

2. How satisfied were (are) you with the nature or status of your relationship?    ① ② ③ ④ ⑤ ⑥ ⑦ ⑧ ⑨

3. How much sexual intimacy did (do) you expect at this point in the relationship?    ① ② ③ ④ ⑤ ⑥ ⑦ ⑧ ⑨

4. How committed were (are) you to staying in the relationship at this point?    ① ② ③ ④ ⑤ ⑥ ⑦ ⑧ ⑨

5. How likely did (do) you think it was (is) that the relationship would (will) not work out and might end?    ① ② ③ ④ ⑤ ⑥ ⑦ ⑧ ⑨

**Deterioration Stage**

This is the point in the relationship in which it has become clear that you or your partner may not be compatible, or in which a great deal of conflict and negative feelings are common in the relationship.

1. How much did you attempt (or have you attempted) to show your partner that you were (are) interested in his or her feelings and wanted (want) to work through conflicts?    ① ② ③ ④ ⑤ ⑥ ⑦ ⑧ ⑨

2. How satisfied were (are) you with the nature or status of your relationship?    ① ② ③ ④ ⑤ ⑥ ⑦ ⑧ ⑨

3. How much sexual intimacy did (do) you expect at this point in the relationship?    ① ② ③ ④ ⑤ ⑥ ⑦ ⑧ ⑨

4. How committed were (are) you to staying in the relationship at this point?    ① ② ③ ④ ⑤ ⑥ ⑦ ⑧ ⑨

5. How likely did (do) you think it was (is) that the relationship would (will) not work out and might end?    ① ② ③ ④ ⑤ ⑥ ⑦ ⑧ ⑨

*(Continued)*

(Continued)

Look across the various stages for each of the questions; that is, compare your rating on #1 across the four stages, as far as your relationship has progressed. Do this for rating #2, and each of the others. Did you notice any change in rating across the stages?

Research by Kingsbury and Minda (1988) found that levels of expected commitment, expected maintenance, and expected termination varied predictably across relationship stages. Related to this, they demonstrated that relationship satisfaction, love, and expected sexual intimacy increased across the stages, and then fell in the deterioration stage. On the other hand, disagreement between relationship partners in the stage of the relationship—how the relationship is defined—dropped across the stages.

**Reference**

Kingsbury, N. M., & Minda, R. B. (1988). An analysis of three expected intimate relationship states: Commitment, maintenance, and termination. *Journal of Social and Personal Relationships, 5,* 405–422.

relationships or committed, long-term relationships. A **romantic relationship** is a special type of intimate relationship. The distinguishing feature of romantic relationships is the potential for **passion** (Aron & Westbay, 1996), which is the experience of positive feelings related to physical intimacy and sexual involvement. Romantic relationships therefore are of primary concern with respect to sexuality and sexual behavior, because the majority of sexual expression occurs within the context of romantic relationships.

Of course, not all romantic relationships develop into serious, committed relationships. Instead, some deteriorate and end after a period of time depending on the individuals and circumstances involved. Even long-standing, committed relationships may eventually decline in levels of intimacy and quality, ultimately dissolving for various reasons. This issue will be discussed in a later section.

## The Development of Intimate Relationships

### Levinger's Model of Relationship Progression

Relationship development has been summarized within a theory advanced by Levinger (1980) in terms of the increasing interdependence of individuals and the particular emotions experienced in various stages of relationship progression. Awareness by individuals of their feelings of interest in one another develops during the **attraction stage**, in which they evaluate the extent of their desire for interaction with the potential partner.

As discussed in the previous chapter, a range of factors lead individuals to find one another attractive and eventually begin a relationship. Specific personal characteristics of individuals contribute to attraction; these include being warm, being active and energetic (having vitality), possessing desired resources (such as having social status or wealth), being physically attractive, and having similar attitudes and interests. In addition, situational factors, such as proximity, mere exposure, and familiarity, play an important role in determining attraction and greater likelihood of involvement in a relationship. As we will see with social exchange theory later in the chapter, after individuals first meet, they are more likely to want to talk or date in the future if they have more positive experiences (called rewards) with one another than negative experiences (called costs).

The **beginning stage** consists of assessing the level of rewards relative to costs available within the relationship, with interdependence increasing across the later stages for relationships. After reaching a certain level of interdependence, individuals make a **commitment** to remain in the relationship. Interdependence may grow even further after this point, or level off at a stable level, during the stage of **continuing relationship**. If the individuals do not experience commitment to the relationship, or if a great deal of conflict and strife plague the relationship, it may move into the **deterioration stage** and eventually end.

## The Intertwining of Lives

In most cases, establishing an intimate relationship is typically gradual, as well as fairly complex. As the individuals in a relationship come to rely on one another for the rewards and incentives that only the relationship partner can provide, interdependence develops (Kelley et al., 1983; Rusbult & Van Lange, 1996; Thibaut & Kelley, 1959). **Interdependence** is the situation in which relationship partners are able to obtain highly desired benefits primarily from the other relationship partner; no one else provides the same quality or intensity of rewards (e.g., emotional experiences, sexual satisfaction, and security) that the relationship partner is able to provide. For this reason, most of the needs and desires of both partners' depend on being able to stay in the relationship.

For many relationships, interdependence increases without the two individuals having a completely conscious awareness that it is happening. Their lives become more and more intertwined, and a relationship has begun without ever really making an explicit decision. As described by Fiske (2004),

> High interdependence is closeness. To define **closeness**, the most crucial variables comprise the strength, frequency, and diversity of interdependence. **Strength** refers to how much, how quickly, and how reliably one person influences the other. **Frequency** defines the sheer number of interconnections, and **diversity** describes the span of domains [of interconnections]. (p. 284; words in brackets added)

Eventually, the partner's well-being, as well as the continuation of the relationship, become included in an individual's sense of what is important. Positive outcomes for the partner and the relationship are viewed as **rewards** within social exchange theory. Negative outcomes for the partner and the relationship are viewed as **costs** to the individual. This means, for example, that a person may be thrilled and overjoyed when his partner gets a promotion, and will be devastated when the partner's mother passes away. This change in

As couples come to desire the rewards that only their romantic partner can provide, they become interdependent. Such rewards include the unique intimacy, familiarity, comfort, and respect available only from their partner.

perception is called **transformation**, when the partner becomes included in one's personal calculation (Thibaut & Kelley, 1959). Moreover, as interdependence increases, individuals develop commitment to the relationship. **Commitment** is the desire and intention to remain in the relationship over the long-term.

### How Does Commitment Grow?

*Unless commitment is made, there are only promises and hopes; but no plans.*

Peter F. Drucker (ThinkExist.com)

*Passion can never purchase what true love desires: true intimacy, selfgiving, and commitment.*

Unknown (ThinkExist.com)

In applying the social exchange model to an understanding of romantic relationships (see Figure 9.1), Rusbult (1980, 1983) proposed that commitment is enhanced not only by the experience of greater **satisfaction** resulting from positive outcomes that are available by being in the relationship. Commitment is also strengthened by the level of investments an individual has contributed to the relationship. **Investments** are assets the individual has devoted to the relationship that cannot be easily recovered or replaced if the relationship were to break up. As with costs and rewards, investments may be tangible, such as money spent on the relationship partner's career, the house prized by both, or a shared social network. However, they may also be nontangible factors, such as effort devoted to taking care of the partner and providing emotional comfort to the partner.

Intimacy and emotional investment likewise increase with growing levels of commitment, although they are not always perfectly aligned. Intimacy is most accurately conceived as a process, an ongoing series of events throughout the course of the relationship, rather than an endpoint (Fiske, 2004). This concept of intimacy is identical to that of relational intimacy (Prager & Roberts, 2004) discussed in the previous section. Feeling understood, valued, and appreciated—the essence of intimacy—develops through **self-disclosure**, the process of communicating information about oneself to one's relationship partner. Intimacy is enhanced when an individual reveals some aspect of himself or herself, and the romantic partner reacts with understanding in a way that indicates acceptance or admiration. The positive reaction leads to greater attraction for the empathetic partner, thereby strengthening the relationship further.

Beyond social exchange theory, the factors identified within all of the other theories of love that are presented in the next section are also likely to contribute to attraction and the desire to stay in—or to or end—a relationship. You can begin to get an idea of the reason that relationship formation is so complex—there are just so many factors involved. In addition, a clear set of standards have not yet been identified that are widely used to make the conscious decision to enter into a relationship. This is probably an intuitive, highly idiosyncratic process; in other words, the factors affecting attraction and getting involved in a relationship are probably different for each individual.

## *Theoretical Views of Love and Sexuality*

A valuable theoretical framework for understanding thinking about the role of love and sexuality in relationship formation has been developed by noted researchers Arthur and Elaine Aron (1991). Their framework

**FIGURE 9.1** Rusbult's Investment Model of Relationship Commitment

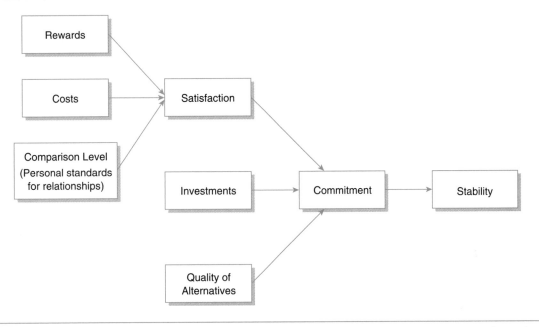

From Rusbult, C.E., A longitudinal test of the investment model: The development (and deterioration) of satisfaction and commitment in heterosexual involvements, in *Journal of Personality and Social Psychology, 45,* copyright © 1983 American Psychological Association. Reprinted with permission.

provides a convenient way to organize the prominent theories of love in social psychology (see Figure 9.2). This model groups theories in terms of the degree to which they focus either on sexuality or on love, although all of them address both love and sexuality in some way. At one extreme of this range of theories are those that concentrate more on sexuality. The other extreme of theories are those that are concerned to a greater extent with the experience of love, with sexuality seen as a form of the fundamental craving for connectedness and meaning. Theories in between the two extremes focus on love and sexuality more or less equally.

## Theories Focusing Primarily on Sexuality

One of the earliest foundations for theories in this group is the biological theory advanced by Charles Darwin. In contemporary times, this thinking gave rise to the areas of sociobiology, and most recently evolutionary psychology. Sociobiology is "the systematic study of the biological basis of all social behavior" (Wilson, 1975, p. 4). The major premise is that the characteristics currently found in humans have been selected throughout time because they enabled later generations to mate and produce offspring. Those with characteristics that did not promote successful reproduction did not produce offspring, such that their characteristics disappeared from the population. Evolutionary psychology built upon the basic foundations of sociobiology, additionally developing detailed explanations of the ways in which specific behaviors and psychological attributes promote successful reproduction.

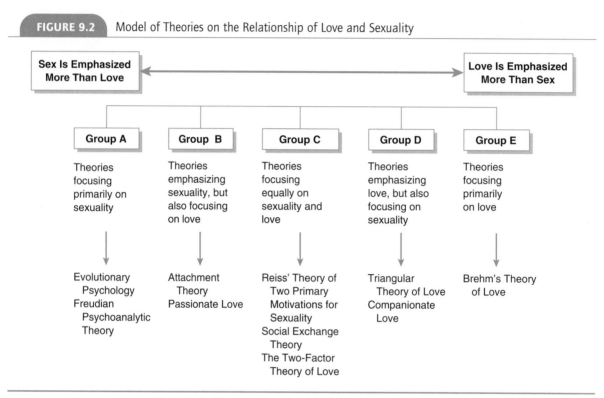

FIGURE 9.2    Model of Theories on the Relationship of Love and Sexuality

Adapted from Aron & Aron, 1991. Reprinted with permission of Lawrence Erlbaum Associates, Inc.

## Evolutionary Psychology

The overarching premise of evolutionary theory is that attraction for particular partner characteristics, and the use of specific mating strategies, have become linked to reproductive fitness over the course of evolution. **Reproductive fitness** is the capability of individuals to bear and raise offspring because of the particular characteristics the individuals possess; the concept of fitness also involves the requirement that offspring inherit these same characteristics that will enable them to produce successful offspring themselves (Russil & Ellis, 2003).

### Parental Investment Theory

According to a widely accepted view within the evolutionary perspective, called **parental investment theory** (Trivers, 1972), the gender (whether the female or the male) that invests more in the survival of offspring within a species is a valuable commodity to the other gender. Among many animals, the female invests more than the male, which includes humans. Because women are capable of producing relatively fewer offspring than men (as illustrated in Figure 9.3), they have developed the strategy of protecting and caring for every offspring they can produce. Women are limited by the fact that they are the ones who carry the developing offspring during 9 months of pregnancy and typically must devote more time to the care of young children. According to this theory, the basic tendency that is common to women is an attraction to potential mates who have good genes and who are willing to commit resources necessary for the survival and care of their offspring. Men, however, could hypothetically produce much larger numbers of offspring by impregnating a number of different women.

According to parental investment theory, as the gender that typically invests less in parenting, males are more prone to engage in sexual behavior with greater numbers of partners, to compete with other males for sexual opportunities with partners, and to be less concerned about the quality of sexual partners. In contrast, women are thought to desire fewer sexual partners and to be much more selective regarding the men with whom they choose to engage in sex. A number of studies have supported these proposals advanced within parental investment theory, in terms of both preferences for mates and actual behavior (Russil & Ellis, 2003).

Within this view, the major concern of women is to find a partner of high social status with a great deal of wealth, or the potential to acquire wealth, who will reciprocate in a loving, monogamous relationship. Moreover, willingness to commit to a long-term relationship is the primary criterion for engaging in sex for women. Because of the limited availability of men with these characteristics, women may adopt an alternate strategy of involvement with several men: one who will provide material resources (e.g., money, property) and another who will provide high-quality genetic input for offspring (that is, they have "good genes"). The theory

**FIGURE 9.3** Evolutionary Theory View of Gender Differences in Reproductive Strategy

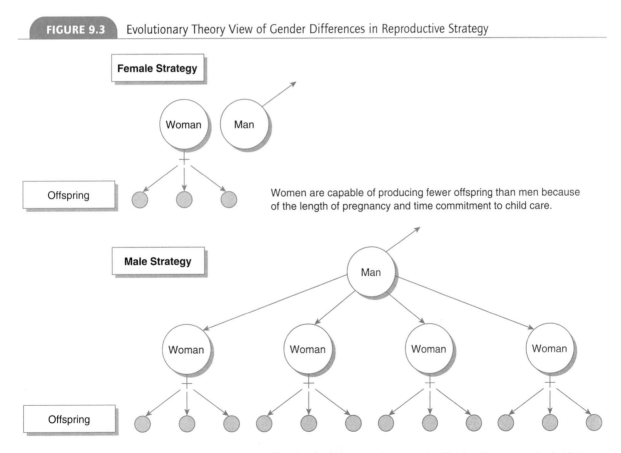

Women are capable of producing fewer offspring than men because of the length of pregnancy and time commitment to child care.

Men are capable of producing more offspring than women by having children with a number of women.

According to evolutionary theories, producing high-quality offspring is at the heart of attraction and mate selection.

proposes that men, at a basic biological level, tend to prefer a mixed type of strategy in general, having an interest in many short-term sexual encounters and a desire for one long-term romantic relationship (Geary, Vigil, & Byrd-Craven, 2004).

### Sexual Strategies Theory

A more recent evolutionary theory, **sexual strategies theory** (Buss & Schmitt, 1993), proposes that both women and men possess not just one type of inclination, or strategy. Rather, both genders possess two strategies. The tendency to become involved in a stable, ongoing relationship with a mate is called a **long-term strategy**. The tendency to become involved in many, short-term sexual involvements is called a **short-term strategy**. Selection pressures have resulted in women developing the long-term strategy to a greater extent than the short-term strategy.

However, this theory maintains that selection forces have also pushed men over time in the direction of greater focus on the long-term strategy, with its emphasis on emotional and romantic attachment (love). This is because of pressure from women to provide signs of commitment to a long-term relationship before agreeing to engage in sex. Moreover, investment in a romantic relationship and family stability assures men of mating with higher-quality women with whom they will have higher quality children; furthermore, men benefit from the pooling of resources in caring for a household that is afforded by a stable romantic relationship. Finally, men have become willing to forgo greater numbers of offspring with a variety of mates for the sake of certainty of paternity, that they are the certain father of a woman's offspring (Buss & Schmitt, 1993).

Women and men differ in the characteristics that they desire in partners, both when considering someone for a short-term affair and for a long-term relationship. Women on average value social status, the ability to obtain resources and wealth, and being generous in sharing these resources to a greater extent than men. Men are more likely to value youthfulness and physical attractiveness—thought to be visible indicators of health and capability of producing offspring—in comparison to women. The size of these differences, based on more than 40 studies, are generally fairly large ($d > .80$). The findings are consistent across many different societies and political systems in both survey studies and data based on real-world data, such as official government data (i.e., regarding age differences in spouses). Lesbian women and gay men express partner preferences that reflect their gender, with lesbians similar to heterosexual women and gay men similar to heterosexual men (Okami & Schackelford, 2001).

In addition, the sexual strategies proposal for gender differences in preferences for short-term and long-term partners has likewise received support in a number of studies, according to a review by Okami and Shackelford (2001). The importance of partner physical attractiveness is greater for women when evaluating desirable characteristics in a short-term partner compared with a long-term partner. Yet, the desirability of social status and possessing resources in short-term partners is as important as it is for long-term partners.

For men, the importance of physical attractiveness is actually lower for short-term compared with long-term partners. Symons (1979) proposed that the reason for this is that it is more likely for men to obtain a high-quality spouse than it is for them to obtain high–quality, short-term partners. In contrast, he argued that it is easier for women to obtain a high–quality, short-term sex partner than it is to obtain a high-quality spouse.

Beyond differences in desirable partner characteristics, research has further demonstrated that men are tremendously more willing to engage in casual sex than are women (Okami & Schackelford, 2001). Casual sex is that in which the partners have no expectations of a subsequent romantically intimate relationship. Differences are found in self-reports of interest in engaging in casual sex across a number of studies. In addition to self-report, two now classic studies assessed reactions to the actual opportunity to engage in casual sex (Clark, 1990; Clark & Hatfield, 1989). These were naturalistic experiments, meaning that they were conducted outside of the laboratory and that conditions were different across different people. Specifically in the Clark and Hatfield study (1989), an attractive male researcher approached women students on a college campus, asking them one of two questions: (a) whether they would be willing to go out on a date with him, or (b) whether they would be willing to have sex with him; the particular question each person was asked was determined randomly. An attractive female researcher approached men students and likewise asked them one of the two questions.

Men were overwhelmingly more likely to agree to casual sex than women. Clark (1990) ruled out fear for safety on the part of women as an explanation for their lower interest in casual sex. Individuals were contacted by good friends at the request of the researcher to let them know about someone who wanted to have sex with them. The friends assured the contacted individuals of the trustworthiness of the person who wanted to have sex with them. Yet, a substantial difference was found between women and men in willingness to have sex with a stranger. Women also reported later that in general it was not concern for safety that influenced their behavior. They were simply less interested in casual sex.

Also consistent with evolutionary psychology predictions, men report substantially greater numbers of sexual partners, as well as greater interest in having more sexual partners. The evolutionary theory explanation of these differences is that, because women do not gain a reproductive advantage from multiple sexual partners, they are less interested. They can only give birth once every 9 months and have a limited number of egg cells that can mature and be released each month. Also, reproduction is "dangerous, time-consuming, painful, and depleting of nutritional resources" (Okami & Schackelford, 2001, pp. 204–205), factors that make sexual intercourse more burdensome if pregnancy results. Men do not experience these types of risks associated with reproduction, making sex with large numbers of partners an effective way of increasing their offspring.

The evolutionary psychology perspective is that reproduction and sexuality for both women and men are the fundamental, driving forces underlying attraction, mate selection, and relationship formation; nonetheless, individuals are often not consciously aware of the influence of these factors. Love develops as a strategy for securing successful reproduction. In women, love is the initial and primary focus, serving as a way of obtaining a committed partner; however, even for women, the basic force driving the mating strategy is successful reproduction. In men, love is a way of assuring that they obtain the benefits of a secure household and are the father of their partner's children.

## Do We Really Know Why We Fall in Love?

Psychoanalytic theory was originally developed by Sigmund Freud in the late 1800s and early 1900s, although the perspective has produced a number of offshoots throughout the 20th century. Freud's theory is

## Box 9.2 Analyze This: Looking at Different Perspectives

### *Biosocial Theory as an Alternative to Evolutionary Theory in Explaining Gender Differences*

A powerful challenge to evolutionary theory has been mounted by theorists who focus on the importance of social roles as opposed to biologically based traits. Alice Eagly (1997), one of the most prominent and outspoken challengers of evolutionary theory in social psychology, has identified a number of weaknesses that limit its usefulness in explaining current human behavior.

Moreover, other theories that do not focus at all on evolution lead to precisely the same predictions for gender differences as does evolutionary theory. Eagly (1997) argues that such alternative explanations have not been satisfactorily rebutted by evolutionary advocates. One prominent example is **biosocial theory** proposed by Wood and Eagly (2002), which maintains that gender differences in behavior result from two factors: (a) biological and physical attributes and related behaviors specific to each gender, and (b) social, economic, technological, and ecological conditions prevailing in a particular culture.

With respect to biological attributes that distinguish women and men, those identified as most significant are women's ability to bear children and nurse infants, and men's larger bodies, greater potential for muscle development, greater speed, and stronger upper bodies. Such physical differences make certain types of activities more easily and efficiently carried out; for example, greater body size and muscle development make it easier to engage in physical aggression or to defend oneself. It has therefore proven useful for women and men to take on duties and roles that are most compatible with their particular physical capabilities. This accounts for the typical role division that is observed across various cultures, in which women take care of children and domestic matters, while men engage in activities outside the home related to resource production.

It is important to note that biosocial theory is different from evolutionary theory in its emphasis on the role of physical differences in the origin of gender differences. Biosocial theory does not propose that the same evolutionary factors that produced differences in male and female bodies cause biological differences in the brain that lead to gender differences in behavior. That is, biological factors do not directly cause behavioral differences. Rather, the physical differences in female and male bodies lead women and men to assume different roles. It is these social roles then that cause women and men to frequently engage in particular behaviors that become associated with each gender. In this way, biosocial theory provides an explanation of how the particular roles come to be assigned to women and men in the first place—because of body differences that make some roles easier, and therefore more practical, for one gender or the other.

To test the ability of biosocial theory to better account for gender differences in comparison to evolutionary theory, Wood and Eagly (2002) examined the available research on variation across cultures with respect to differences between women and men. In less technologically advanced societies, substantial variability exists in the extent to which men are predominantly responsible for obtaining resources. Simpler cultures can be thought of as more likely to reflect the influence of evolved traits that cause gender differences because of fewer factors that make them less relevant (e.g., machinery to do physically demanding chores); simpler cultures therefore provide a better test of evolutionary theory. Such variability across cultures is inconsistent with evolutionary theory proposals that men are endowed with particular behavioral tendencies related to providing for and protecting families.

Furthermore, approximately two-thirds of societies have male-controlled systems, such that male domination is not universal as would be expected by evolutionary theory. Particularly central to evolutionary theory is the proposal that sexual control and power over women by men is universal across cultures. Anthropological evidence indicates, however, that one-third of societies do not place greater restrictions on women's sexuality than they do on men's; that is, the double standard does not exist in a third of human cultures. Also contrary to evolutionary theory, extramarital sexual involvement by women occurs in many societies throughout the world, with 35% of cultures having norms that allow extramarital involvement and even allow wife-sharing.

On the other hand, consistent with biosocial theory, male concern about paternity tends to be greater in societies based on the inheritance of property through male family members. According to biosocial theory, the development of economies and power structures that give advantage to males lead to the perception of greater male status and power, which in turn leads people to engage in behavior patterns that confirm such perceptions. Similarly, differences in sexuality can be explained as resulting from nonreproductive biological factors that lead to greater social power. The greater male physical power and resulting greater status may therefore explain differences in male and female sexuality.

## References

Eagly, A. H. (1997). Sex differences in social behavior: Comparing social role theory and evolutionary theory. *American Psychologist, 52,* 1380–1383.

Wood, W., & Eagly, A. H. (2002). A cross-cultural analysis of the behavior of women and men: Implications for the origins of sex differences. *Psychological Bulletin, 128,* 699–727.

another example of the perspective that love is basically an expression of sexual impulses, although in this case an unconscious expression.

According to Freudian psychoanalytic theory, two primitive unconscious instincts are responsible for all behavior: the pleasure instinct (*Eros,* also called the life instinct) and the aggressive instinct (*Thanatos,* also called the death instinct). The two instincts constitute an aspect of personality called the *id.* Both physical and psychological needs—meaning resources lacked by an individual—cause the instincts to generate psychic energy, called the *libido,* that produces behavior aimed at acquiring the needed resources. The fundamental focus of the pleasure instinct is to provide sensual stimulation, which very early in the developmental process takes the form of a desire for sexual gratification (Funder, 2004).

Through experience with the restraints on self-indulgence demanded by parents and society, a rational component of personality, called the *ego,* develops. The ego constructs unconscious strategies for converting primitive, animalistic needs related to pleasure and sexual gratification into more acceptable forms of behavior; this enables the individual to avoid disapproval and censure from parents and other authority figures. Consequently, a wide array of more acceptable behaviors come to be motivated by the unconscious pleasure-based (sexual) urges, including creativity, desire for closeness and friendship, and love.

Following puberty, the instinctive impulses are transformed into romantic needs and feelings, as well. This leads individuals to enter into a romantic relationship in which the more primitive sexual needs may be more fully expressed, including eventually through explicit sexual behavior. Consequently, within psychoanalytic theory, all love, most especially romantic love, is actually a form of sexual need that has been transformed at an unconscious level by the ego to disguise its true nature.

## Theories Emphasizing Sexuality, but Also Focusing on Love

Theories in this group are those that consider sexuality to be the primary factor underlying the formation of romantic relationships. Love is important as it relates to promoting successful reproduction or as it relates to sexual interest.

### Do Childhood Experiences With Love Color How We Love as Adults?

A prime example of this second group of theories is **attachment theory** (Bowlby, 1969). Actually, attachment theory is another type of evolutionary theory, one that focuses on differences *within* gender in reproductive strategy; in contrast, parental investment theory and sexual strategies theory focus on differences in reproductive strategies *between* genders. In other words, attachment theory proposes that differences exist across individuals in their interest in romantic and sexual partners, regardless of gender, whereas sexual strategies theory is more concerned with differences in romantic and sexual interest for women in comparison to men (Russil & Ellis, 2003).

Within attachment theory, adult relationships are considered to result from three biological systems that function to ensure successful reproduction and to guarantee that offspring will thrive to produce successful offspring themselves (Bowlby, 1969; see Figure 9.4). One system is the sexual system that is directly involved in reproduction. The other two systems are important for humans and other primates because of the extended period of dependence on parents during childhood and adolescence. The second biological system is the emotional attachment that infants develop for parents because of the security and comfort the infants experience through parental caregiving. The third system is that of adult caregiving, not only for offspring, but also one's mate and other adults as well. This system is conceived as a direct extension of the attachment the adult experienced as an infant and child; individuals develop the capacity for attachment that continues into adulthood because of these early caregiving experiences.

Attachment theory places a heavy emphasis on the biological underpinnings of parent–child emotional attachments as a factor that has promoted the survival of human beings. The emotional attachment that

**FIGURE 9.4** The Attachment Theory View of Love

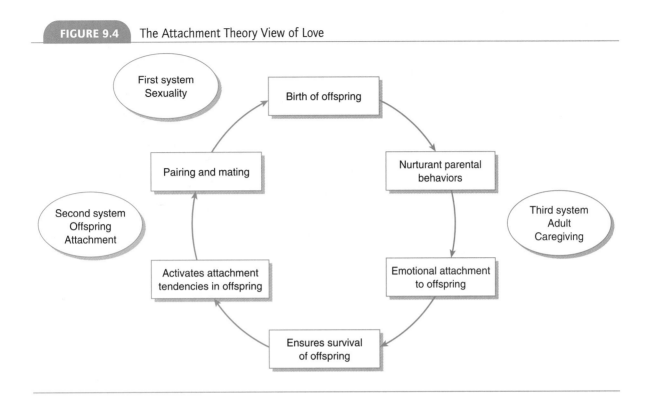

individuals form with their parents during childhood creates what Ainsworth and her colleagues (Ainsworth, Blehar, Waters, & Wall, 1978) called **internal working models**; these are cognitive and emotional templates of relationships that influence the way that individuals understand relationships and react to them emotionally throughout life.

A later version of attachment theory advanced by Hazan and Shaver (1987) has recently integrated views of the origins of parent–child attachments with reproduction, sexuality, and survival of offspring. The focus of this theory is on the effect of the early parent–child attachments on the formation of romantic and sexual relationships in adolescence and adulthood. Hazan and Shaver originally measured the orientation individuals have toward others reflecting early parent–child attachment through a three-item questionnaire. Each item represents one type of infant–parent attachment style proposed by Ainsworth and her colleagues (see Table 9.2). Respondents are asked to indicate which description most accurately describes them, and this is assumed to identify the nature of the attachment that developed with their parents.

**Secure attachment** involves comfort with getting close to and depending on others and an absence of insecurity about being abandoned. In childhood, those with secure attachments are likely to feel comfortable exploring their environment and playing with other children, particularly for young children if their parent is close by. Later in life, individuals with secure attachments are more likely to feel comfortable approaching and interacting with others. They also tend to experience greater intimacy and feel comfortable with closeness when they are involved in a romantic relationship.

**Anxious–ambivalent attachment** consists of intense, obsessive desire to be loved, but substantial insecurity about being abandoned. Children with this type of attachment tend to become easily upset if they are

**TABLE 9.2**   Attachment Questionnaire

Which of the following best describes your feelings?

1. I find it relatively easy to get close to others and am comfortable depending on them and having them depend on me. I don't often worry about being abandoned or about someone getting too close to me. (Choosing this description indicates *secure attachment.*)

2. I am somewhat uncomfortable being close to others; I find it difficult to trust them completely, difficult to allow myself to depend on them. I am nervous when anyone gets too close, and often love partners want me to be more intimate than I feel comfortable being. (Choosing this description indicates *avoidant attachment.*)

3. I find that others are reluctant to get as close as I would like. I often worry that my partner doesn't really love me or won't want to stay with me. I want to merge completely with another person, and this desire sometimes scares people away. (Choosing this description indicates *anxious–ambivalent attachment.*)

Reprinted with permission (Hazan & Shaver, 1987).

separated from their parent or caregiver. Yet, when they are reunited with the caregiver, they are not easily comforted by the person and may even seem to resist being held or being close to the person when he or she is trying to provide comfort. The word *ambivalent* means having both positive and negative reactions to caregivers. As adults, those with an anxious–ambivalent attachment tend to be insecure about relationships with others. They want to be involved in a romantic relationship. They tend to be demanding of attention from their partner, constantly seeking assurance of his or her love, but apparently never fully convinced of their devotion. Such individuals may often be described as "clingy" and jealous.

**Avoidant attachment** is that in which a person is uncomfortable with emotional closeness and having to depend on others, as well as harboring a general mistrust of others. As children, such individuals are relatively indifferent to whether their parent remains close by. They appear to receive little comfort when they are upset and the caregiver tries to console them. Later in life, they are typically unconcerned about close friendships or socializing to a great extent. They tend to not be interested in involvement in romantic relationships to any great extent, and are little concerned about putting effort into maintaining closeness with their partner. They may not be very affected emotionally when relationships dissolve.

In an early survey of adults (Shaver, Hazan, & Bradshaw, 1988), 56% identified themselves as having a secure attachment, 25% had an avoidant attachment, and 19% had an anxious–ambivalent attachment. These percentages were virtually identical to the proportions obtained by Ainsworth and her colleagues resulting from their observations of infants.

Actually, later research demonstrated that attachment style is related to two separate dimensions (Brennan, Clark, & Shaver, 1998; see Figure 9.5). One dimension is **anxiety**, fearfulness about being rejected and abandoned; the second dimension is **avoidance**, uneasiness with intimacy and depending on others. Within this framework, secure attachment is conceived as reflecting low levels of both anxiety and avoidance; anxious–ambivalent attachment reflects low avoidance, but high levels of anxiety (this style was renamed **preoccupied attachment**); and avoidant attachment reflects high levels of both anxiety and avoidance (renamed **fearful attachment**). A fourth attachment style was proposed by Bartholomew and Horowitz (1991), called

| FIGURE 9.5 | Dimensions Underlying Attachment Styles (adapted from Fraley & Shaver, 2000) |

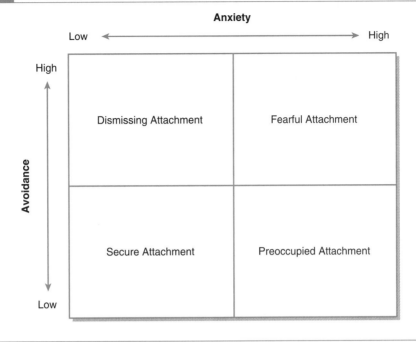

*What do you think it would be like to be involved in a relationship with someone who has an avoidant attachment style? Have you ever been involved with someone like this, or known someone who has?*

**dismissing attachment**. Those with a dismissing style value being independent and not having to rely on others (meaning that they possess high levels of avoidance), but they tend not to be anxious about relationships (low levels of anxiety).

The significance of attachment styles with respect to love is the effect that the styles have on adult romantic relationships (Collins & Sroufe, 1999; Hartup & Laurenson, 1999). Individuals identified as possessing a secure attachment style tend to have satisfying, highly committed romantic relationships that are the most stable and enduring of the various styles. Individuals with the anxious–ambivalent or preoccupied attachment style enter romantic relationships more quickly, which are prone to end more quickly as well. Anxious–ambivalent individuals become extremely angry if those to whom they are attracted are not interested in them. Individuals with avoidant attachment styles tend to avoid involvement in romantic relationships, and report that they are more likely to have never been in love than those with the other styles (Keelan, Dion, & Dion, 1994; Morgan & Shaver, 1999).

Furthermore, dimensions underlying attachment styles have been shown to relate to sexual motivation, including with respect to concern about the breakup of a relationship. Within attachment theory, separation from a desired relationship is especially significant psychologically. This is because relationships are thought to fulfill important needs that affect the security and well-being of individuals with secure and anxious–ambivalent styles. Separation from a relationship partner is thought to threaten the well-being of the individual, particularly anxious–ambivalent individuals because of their lack of self-confidence and emotional hardiness. The ending of a relationship therefore is conceived as increasing the levels of anxiety individuals experience, resulting in the activation of the security-seeking aspects of the attachment system. The desire for sexual intimacy therefore may be related to higher levels of anxiety about the stability of relationships, given that sexual motivation is viewed as an aspect of the attachment system.

In a study by Davis, Shaver, and Vernon (2004), the dimension of attachment anxiety discussed previously was measured to assess concerns individuals felt about the stability of romantic relationships. Attachment anxiety was found to relate to measures of several different types of dispositional sexual motives, which are traits reflecting stable interest in the rewarding aspects of sexual behavior. That is, concern about being involved in a stable relationship is related to desire for rewarding sexual experiences. These include desire for **emotional closeness** (a modification of the desire to express *value for one's partner* discussed in previous chapters), desire to **feel valued by one's partner** (called *reassurance* in the study), desire for **stress reduction**, desire to **express one's power** sexually, desire to **experience the power of one's partner**, desire to provide **nurturance**, and desire for **procreation**. Attachment anxiety was also correlated with the tendency to want sex when feeling insecure and to manipulate one's partner with sex to obtain caregiving or to protect oneself from the partner's negative moods or violence. Finally, attachment avoidance was associated with less-intense feelings of passion for relationship partners and a decline in passion over time.

Davis and her colleagues concluded that the findings reveal the important influence of attachment processes in the development of sexual motivation. Attachment is seen as the primary factor underlying interpersonal behavior in general, a perspective supported by a large number of studies. Their study links attachment to the desire for sexual behavior as well. In fact, Davis and colleagues note that "Our findings support the hypothesis that the sexual system can serve functions similar or identical to those of the attachment and caregiving systems" (p. 1086).

## Love as an Intense Yearning

A classic perspective of the factors involved in romantic love is the theory of **passionate love** (Hatfield & Sprecher, 1986). Passionate love is defined as

> a state of intense longing for union with another. Passionate love is a complex functional whole including appraisals or appreciations, subjective feelings, expressions, patterned physiological processes, action tendencies, and instrumental behaviors. Reciprocated love (union with the other) is associated with fulfillment and ecstasy. Unrequited love (separation) is associated with emptiness, anxiety, or despair. (Hatfield & Rapson, 1993, p. 5)

Other names passionate love is known by include "a crush, obsessive love, lovesickness, head-over-heels in love, infatuation, or being in love" (Hatfield & Rapson, 2005, p. 3).

Because of the very strong correlation between the experience of passionate love and sexual desire for the person who is the focus of the "desire for union," the two sets of feelings are seen as being virtually the same. (Hatfield and Rapson [2005], however, note that longing for union does not include sexual desire in all societies.) Because of the extreme overlap, the concept of passionate love positions sexual attraction, interest, and excitement at the very heart of the experience of passionate love, the most important factors distinguishing "being in love" from "loving another person" (Sprecher & Regan, 1998, 2000).

People who are more passionately in love become more excited when they think about the one with whom they are involved (Hatfield & Sprecher, 1986; Sprecher & Regan, 1998), engage in sexual behavior with their partner more often (Aron & Henkemeyer, 1995), and are more likely to convey their feelings of passion through sexual activity (Marston, Hecht, Menke, McDaniel, & Reeder, 1998). The vast majority of people with whom individuals say they are "in love" are those whom the individuals also identify as people for whom they feel sexual desire (Berscheid & Meyers, 1996). Passionate love therefore is essentially defined by sexual desire (Sprecher & Regan, 2000), at least in a number of cultures.

In addition to desire for physical and sexual contact with the loved one, passionate love is also distinguished from other types of intimate love by the intense devotion and focus on the romantic partner to the exclusion of other people. Typically, romantic love is exceptional in intensity and in its exclusiveness. A measure of passionate love was designed by Hatfield and Sprecher (1986) to assess the intensity of feelings of affection and attraction for a romantic partner, intrusiveness of thoughts about a romantic partner, reactions of jealousy concerning a romantic partner, and extent of being affected by a romantic partner (see Table 9.3).

## Theories Focusing Equally on Sexuality and Love

The set of theories in the middle of the range of theories identified by Aron and Aron (1991) focus on both love and sexuality to about the same extent.

### Love as a Reason for Sex

*Communication leads to community, that is, to understanding, intimacy and mutual valuing.*

Rollo May (ThinkExist.com)

The position advanced by Reiss (1986a, 1986b) proposes two primary motivations for sexuality, the desire for pleasure and the desire for self-disclosure. Reproduction is relevant to sexuality for humans only in the sense that mates stay together to assure that offspring are provided for. The self-disclosure motive involves a desire to experience a highly personal, intimate altered state of consciousness with another person. Although self-disclosure that occurs through sexual interaction is sharing a private aspect of oneself with another person, it is not necessarily affectionate and emotionally intimate. Individuals may show affection for one another without engaging in sexual interaction; likewise, individuals may engage in sexual behavior with one another without feeling or expressing warmth and love. Nonetheless, sexual interaction is one way of increasing intimacy and inspiring feelings of affection and love.

For this reason, Reiss distinguishes the desire for reproduction and desire for pleasure from the desire for intimacy and connectedness, or simply stated, love. Moreover, Reiss ascribes nearly equal status to the desire for intimacy (love) and pleasure (sexual desire), which are seen as more important than the desire for reproduction.

| TABLE 9.3 | The Passionate Love Scale |
| --- | --- |

These items ask you to describe how you feel when you are passionately in love. Think of the person whom you love most passionately right now. If you are not in love right now, think of the last person you loved passionately. If you have never been in love, think of the person you came closest to caring for in that way. Choose your answers remembering how you felt when your feelings were the most intense.

For each of the 15 items, choose the number between 1 and 9 that most accurately describes your feelings. The answer scale ranges from 1, *not at all true*, to 9, *definitely true*. Write the number you choose next to each item.

1. I would feel despair if _____ left me.    [1 2 3 4 5 6 7 8 9]
2. Sometimes I feel I can't control my thoughts: they are obsessively on _____.    [1 2 3 4 5 6 7 8 9]
3. I feel happy when I am doing something to make _____ happy.    [1 2 3 4 5 6 7 8 9]
4. I would rather be with _____ than anyone else.    [1 2 3 4 5 6 7 8 9]
5. I'd get jealous if I thought _____ were falling in love with someone else.    [1 2 3 4 5 6 7 8 9]
6. I yearn to know all about _____.    [1 2 3 4 5 6 7 8 9]
7. I want _____—physically, emotionally, mentally.    [1 2 3 4 5 6 7 8 9]
8. I have an endless appetite for affection from _____.    [1 2 3 4 5 6 7 8 9]
9. For me, _____ is the perfect romantic partner.    [1 2 3 4 5 6 7 8 9]
10. I sense my body responding when _____ touches me.    [1 2 3 4 5 6 7 8 9]
11. _____ always seems to be on my mind.    [1 2 3 4 5 6 7 8 9]
12. I want _____ to know me—my thoughts, my fears, and my hopes.    [1 2 3 4 5 6 7 8 9]
13. I eagerly look for signs indicating _____'s desire for me.    [1 2 3 4 5 6 7 8 9]
14. I possess a powerful attraction for _____.    [1 2 3 4 5 6 7 8 9]
15. I get extremely depressed when things don't go right in my relationship with _____.    [1 2 3 4 5 6 7 8 9]

**Scoring the Passionate Love Scale**

Add together all of the numbers next to each statement.
You may interpret your scores using the following ranges:

106–135 = Wildly, even recklessly, in love
86–105 = Passionate, but less intense
66–85 = Occasional bursts of passion

45–65 = Tepid, infrequent passion
15–44 = No thrill, never was

From Hatfield, E., & Sprecher, S., Measuring passionate love in intimate relations. *Journal of Adolescence,* 9, 383–410. Copyright © 1986, Elsevier Science & Technology Journals. Reprinted with permission via Copyright Clearance Center.

## Are Love and Sex Rewards That Keep Us in Relationships?

Another theoretical perspective that focuses equally on love and sexuality is social exchange theory (Sprecher, 1998; Thibaut & Kelley, 1959). This theory was presented previously in considering factors that contribute to perceptions of attraction and in relationship development. In this perspective, both love and sex are considered to be potential rewards that may be viewed as outcomes one receives in a relationship (Cate, Lloyd, Henton, & Larson, 1982; Foa & Foa, 1974). They therefore have equal standing in this theory, as well. In reality, the two are usually fairly highly related in relationships; the level of love that individuals report typically corresponds to the quantity and quality of sex that characterizes the relationship.

## The View That Arousal + Label = Love (or Sex)

*Love, like fire, cannot subsist without constant impulse; it ceases to live from the moment it ceases to hope or to fear.*

François de la Rochefoucauld (ThinkExist.com)

*We invent what we love, and what we fear.*

John Irving (ThinkExist.com)

A third perspective in which love and sexuality are given equal status includes several approaches that present love and sexuality as resulting from one common underlying motivation; this motivation is the desire to clearly understand the arousal one is experiencing. One of the most prominent of these approaches is the two-factor theory of love advanced by Berscheid and Walster (1974). Based on a more general two-factor theory of emotions (Schachter & Singer, 1962), the theory of love proposes that the experience of love results from two components: **physiological arousal** and a **cognitive label** that identifies the arousal as caused by love or possibly some other emotion (see Figure 9.6). The power of this theory is due to the possibility that the arousal being experienced may actually result from another source other than love, including physical

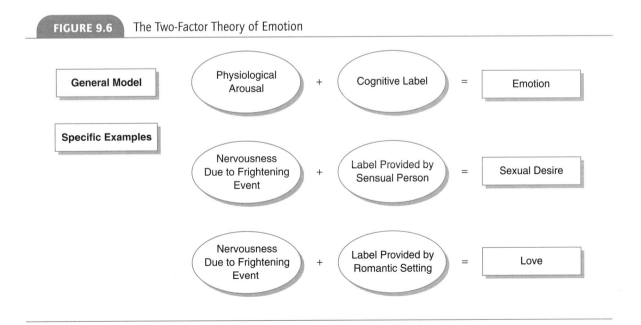

**FIGURE 9.6**   The Two-Factor Theory of Emotion

*Have you ever been in an emergency situation, or one that was fairly stressful, only to find yourself strangely attracted to someone involved in that situation? According to the two-factor theory of love, arousal from other emotions, such as fear and distress, may be relabeled as love or sexual arousal.*

exercise, startle, fear, and anxiety, to name a few. Becoming aware of cues in the environment relevant to love and attraction after experiencing heightened arousal from any source is thought to increase the likelihood that the arousal will be identified as resulting from love. For example, following a frightening event, encountering a loved one, or an individual one finds attractive, may lead people to feel greater love and attraction for that individual (Dutton & Aron, 1974).

In other words, the theory proposes that information from the environment is used as a cue to understand the reason people experience specific emotions such as love. Sexual attraction may be viewed as resulting from the same type of labeling process as love. In addition, arousal resulting from sexual stimulation may be subsequently identified as due to feelings of love, whereas arousal from love-related feelings may be subsequently labeled as sexual attraction and arousal. Therefore, love and sexuality may be thought to originate from the same arousal-label process, having equivalent status and potentially mutually enhancing one another.

## Theories Emphasizing Love, but Also Focusing on Sexuality

The theories in this group are concerned primarily with love, viewing sexuality as one of several aspects, or one type, of love. However, sexuality is not the primary focus.

### The Three Sides of Love

An especially prominent theory within this group is the **triangular theory of love** (Sternberg, 1986, 1997), which proposes that love consists of three separate components, intimacy, passion, and decision/commitment (see Figure 9.7). **Intimacy** refers to feelings of closeness and affection for a person. **Passion** is excitement and arousal felt toward the person, the dimension that includes sexual arousal and interest. **Decision/commitment** is the aspect of love that involves a choice to enter into a relationship with the person before the relationship has formed (decision); it also consists of an ongoing process throughout the relationship in which the individual is determined to remain in and maintain the relationship (commitment).

Sternberg conceived of the components as dimensions that consist of varying levels of intensity. That is, individuals may experience different levels of each dimension for their romantic partner, some experiencing stronger or weaker feelings of intimacy, more or less intense passion, and greater or lesser commitment. The varying levels of each dimension may be assessed by a self-report questionnaire developed by Sternberg (1988). The level of each dimension is represented as aspects of a triangle of a greater or smaller length, resulting in different triangles of different shapes, or different types of love.

**FIGURE 9.7**   The Triangular Theory of Love

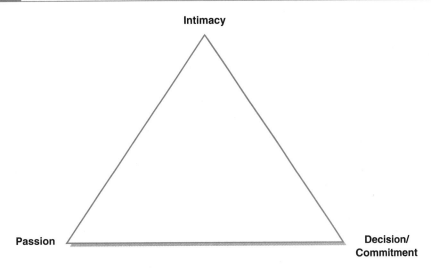

**Romantic Love:** Intimacy and passion

**Companionate Love:** Intimacy and commitment

**Fatuous Love:** Passion and commitment

**Liking:** Intimacy only

**Infatuation:** Passion only

**Empty Love:** Commitment only

**Consummate Love:** Balanced triangle, equal proportions of each component

In the early stages of relationship formation, individuals in U.S. culture typically experience very little commitment because the relationship has not yet developed. Most people experience growing feelings of intimacy as they get to know a potential partner and affection increases; greater levels of intimacy with low levels of passion and commitment characterize **liking**. In other situations, an individual may feel intense sexual attraction to someone they encounter, but not knowing the person well, may have little or no feelings of intimacy and commitment; Sternberg identifies this as **infatuation**. As a romantic relationship develops, individuals typically experience increasing intimacy and passion, even before they make a conscious decision to enter into a relationship or become committed to the relationship. High levels of intimacy and passion constitute **romantic love**.

In some cases after being involved in a romantic relationship for some time, feelings of passion may wane while intimacy and commitment remain at high levels or increase in intensity; this type is **companionate love**. Companionate love is also the kind that exists between family members and friends, emotional closeness and devotion without feelings of physical or sexual attraction. The experience of feelings about a partner that are characterized by high levels of all three dimensions is called **consummate love** by Sternberg, the type of love dreamed of by many people and idealized in romantic novels and movies.

Within this theory, sexuality is merely one of three components that make up the broader experience of love. Sexuality may be present at lower or higher levels within various types of love.

### Passionate Love Versus Companionate Love

*Love is when you take away the feeling, the passion, the romance and you find out you still care for that person.*

Unknown (ThinkExist.com)

An early theoretical position on love distinguished passionate love from companionate love, two types of the more general romantic love (Hatfield & Rapson, 1993; Hatfield & Walster, 1978). The prototypical or idealized expectation for romantic love in U.S. culture is for individuals who have "fallen in love" to be intensely, overwhelmingly preoccupied with a partner, craving constant attention and affection from one another. This is what is meant by the concept of **passionate love**, defined formally as "a state of intense longing for union with another" (Hatfield, 1988, p. 193). As discussed previously, passionate love is strongly associated with intense desire for physical and sexual interaction with the romantic partner (Regan & Berscheid, 1999). For this reason, it was considered in the group of theories emphasizing sexuality.

In contrast to passionate love, another type of love is **companionate love**, which has the same types of feelings of emotional investment, concern, and desire for closeness with one's romantic partner as does passionate love. However, companionate love does not include the same intense physical and sexual attraction as passionate love. Companionate love also does not commonly involve the same level of obsessiveness, preoccupation, and need for constant contact with the romantic partner.

A typical pattern, shown in research conducted in the United States, is for couples to experience passion at the beginning of their romantic relationship, but for the passionate component to wane over time. The romantic relationship therefore changes from being based on passionate love to being grounded in companionate love, although companionate love often subsides as well. For some couples, the experience of companionate love in the later stages of a relationship may be extremely strong and valuable, but it is less likely to involve the obsessiveness and intrusiveness of romantic love, as well as the sexual fascination and passion.

Within this view of companionate love, therefore, sexuality—in the form of physical and sexual attraction to the romantic partner—is somewhat important, but is not central to companionate love in general. Rather, the feelings of devotion, intimacy, and affection are the fundamental aspects of this type of romantic love. They are present in both passionate and companionate love, but for many relationships, the sexual aspect becomes less important, if not secondary, to couples' experience of romantic love in the form of companionate love.

Companionate love may become the predominant form of love in the later years of romantic relationships, although companionate love may decline substantially along with passionate love.

## Theories Focusing Primarily on Love

This theory group focuses largely on love, with sexuality considered in only a relatively minor way.

A prime example of a theory that focuses primarily on love is that by Brehm (1988), who defined passionate love as "the capacity to construct in one's imagination an elaborated vision of a future state of perfect happiness" (p. 253). Aron and Aron (1991) note that Brehm aligns herself with the dualistic philosophy advocated by Plato, a perspective that was examined in chapter 2 in considering religious influences on sexuality. This philosophy distinguishes between two types of love, *eros* (carnal, sensual lust) and *agape* (spiritual appreciation for an individual as a person), that are in opposition to one another.

In ancient dualism, carnal love was considered to detract from a person's capability to experience spritual love for another person; spiritual love was viewed as contributing to humans' quest to elevate themselves to a higher level of existence, closer to God, fulfillment, and immortality. Within Brehm's perspective, sexuality is not critical to the existence of romantic love, but instead is simply one means of enhancing emotional attachment to one's partner. Unlike the sexuality-focused theories above, Brehm's theory deemphasizes sexuality and instead casts love as overwhelmingly more significant, and sexuality as one of many aspects of love.

## Love and Sexuality Around the World

### The Meaning of Love

Views of love among people of the world seem to be remarkably similar in important ways. In other ways, however, various cultures have particular concerns and beliefs that color the associations they have with the experience of love.

As summarized by Hatfield, Rapson, and Martel (in press), reviews of research from a wide range of cultures reveal that conceptions of love are remarkably the same; perceptions were obtained, for example, from the People's Republic of China, Indonesia, and Turkey, as well as the United States. One study by Shaver, Murday, and Fraley (2001) demonstrated that Indonesian women and men make a distinction between passionate love—involving sexual desire and arousal—and companionate love—affection, liking, and fondness—that is identical to the distinction made by U.S. people. The difference between Indonesian and U.S. cultures is that Indonesians appear to cast passionate love more in terms of a yearning and desire, rather than in terms of actual sexual interaction. This may reflect the relatively greater restrictiveness of the Muslim culture of Indonesia, in which sexual expression is even more tightly controlled.

### Are Some Cultures More Likely to Be in Love Than Others?

Because of differences in the value dimension of individualism versus collectivism, Sprecher and colleagues (1994) proposed that Americans are most likely to be in love, Russians next most likely, and Japanese least likely. Individualism is the belief in the importance of independence and pursuing personal goals. Collectivism is the belief in the importance of connection with others and giving lower priority to personal goals than the needs of the community. Individualistic cultures include the United States and countries of northern and western Europe, whereas collectivistic cultures are Asian, African, Latin American, and Pacific Island societies (Markus & Kitayama, 1991; Triandis, McCusker, & Hui, 1990).

Contrary to the expectations of Sprecher and her colleagues, the three groups of student participants were largely similar in the proportion reporting being in love. Specifically, 59% of Americans, 67% of Russians, and 53% of Japanese participants were in love. Women in all three groups were slightly more likely to report that they were in love. Across several studies, a great deal of similarity in proportions of individuals who are in love has been found across ethnic groups (Aron & Rodriguez, 1992; Doherty, Hatfield, Thompson, & Choo, 1994).

Similarly, individuals across various cultures appear to experience the same intensity of passionate love, as measured by the Passionate Love Scale presented previously in the chapter (Doherty et al., 1994; Hatfield & Rapson, 2005).

## Are Love and Sexuality Related to Psychological Well-Being?

Many of us have the sense that both love and sexual satisfaction are very important to us, and have a tremendous impact on our happiness. But what exactly is the psychological reason that they both seem to be so vital to us? Aron and Aron (1991) offer the possibility that it is because they both are caused by a higher-level factor. This factor is a basic type of motivation they call **self-expansion**. According to the self-expansion model (Aron & Aron, 1986), individuals possess a fundamental need to increase their ability to achieve their desired goals and control their own outcomes. This ability to have power and exert control is known as **efficacy**, and is similar to other theories concerning motivation to achieve goals (Bandura, 1982; Deci, 1975; White, 1959).

The self-expansion model maintains that a person's belief that he or she is able to control one's outcomes and to have personal power serves to expand one's sense of self. The expansion of self results in an intensely positive emotional experience. Consequently, the experience of self-expansion is a desired outcome in itself, becoming a goal that people avidly seek to achieve. Self-expansion allows individuals to feel extremely positive about themselves. Experiences that result in a sudden, rapid expansion of self are particularly desirable and sought after. Such experiences include "bursts of creative insights, religious conversions, discoveries, winning lotteries, and the like—and, notably, falling in love and intense sexual experiences" (Aron & Aron, 1991, p. 42).

Therefore, according to self-expansion theory, the experience of both love and sexual passion result in self-expansion, and for this reason are highly desirable experiences. That is, both sexuality and love contribute to a person's sense of their ability to achieve desired goals and to control their outcomes. Simply experiencing the feelings associated with being in love with, or being sexually attracted to, another person may produce the positive feelings of self-expansion. Succeeding in involving the other person in a romantic or sexual relationship may also result in even greater feelings of efficacy and control. Aron and Aron (1991) state that "passion is desired because it is perceived as a moment of limitless potential efficacy, or connection with a source of such limitless power" (p. 42).

In fact, love and sexuality are highly preferred by many as a way of achieving the sense of expanded personal competence and growth. Three reasons are the basis for the special importance of love and sexuality. The first is that they are relatively more available to virtually everyone; this contrasts with the fairly rare experiences of making profound discoveries or accomplishments, of experiencing religious conversion, or of acquiring great wealth. Popular media, in the form of books, television, movies, and music, celebrate the experience of love as well as sexual attraction. Beyond this, popular media promote the idea that the ecstatic joys of success in romance and sexuality are possible for everyone independent of social status, education, and wealth.

The second reason that love and sexuality are so highly valued is that, in U.S. society, they are considered to be most appropriately experienced together. The general belief is that individuals should be in love, ideally in a long-term committed relationship, before sexual interaction occurs for the individual. Because of the joining of sexuality with love, the effect is to combine the intensity of the two experiences, probably multiplying the passion and self-expansion of the experience, rather than simply doubling it by adding the two together.

The third reason suggested by Aron and Aron (1991) is that both love and sexuality may serve the psychological function of allowing individuals to explore aspects of themselves they typically neglect, or even deny. Embracing such hidden aspects may be possible by experiencing them through a romantic or sexual partner who possesses those characteristics or who enables an individual to comfortably express them. The process is similar to that proposed by Carl Jung (1971) in which individuals are proposed to seek wholeness through exploring the various aspects of their personality; this type of exploration is thought to contribute to greater psychological adjustment and greater happiness.

The experience of love and sexuality together within a relationship may amplify the effect of both of them on happiness and well-being in a powerful way.

Jung maintained that all individuals possess both masculine characteristics and feminine characteristics. He advocated the importance of women understanding and integrating into their conscious awareness their masculine qualities, as well as men doing so with their feminine qualities. Beyond this, romance and sexuality permit individuals to explore their less mundane, wilder natures. Experiencing aspects of oneself, and possibly embracing them, is exactly the nature of the process proposed by Aron and Aron in self-expansion theory. Great pleasure and growth are theorized to result from the sense of greater knowledge and control over oneself.

Aron and Aron (1991) ultimately integrate both love and sexuality as aspects of self-expansion with more fundamental issues underlying human psychology:

> We would suggest that the self-expansion motive prods humans to elaborate and expand every element of themselves. Like the bit of sand inside the oyster, secretions are added to that original something—the older the culture, the larger the pearl. The relatively simple communications of other animals become, in humans, language, education, culture, politics, screenplays, poetry, the evening news, and on and on. . . . Mating becomes freighted with fantasies, rites, institutions, medical specialties, . . . and on and on. . . . [W]e may be biologically programmed to find sexuality, attachment, and caregiving rewarding, but these bits of sand also seem to have grown into much, much more. . . . To say a pearl is only a bit of sand plus some stuff around it seems to greatly miss the essence of the pearl. If we want to say something in general about both the bit of sand, which may be biological, and its outer accretions, called culture, perhaps the most interesting commonality is found in the purpose of each—the expansion of human life. (pp. 43–44)

## When Do We First Engage in Sexual Behavior?

*I did promise fidelity to one boyfriend in my rebirth-of-lust period, but he still got very angry with me when other men so much as looked at me. Of course, my appearance had attracted him, but he didn't want anyone else to take notice. . . . His particular attitude is a traditional sexist one, which isn't surprising to find, except that it came from a quiet, highly educated artist with leftist politics and a feminist perspective. He seemed so sweet. I was sad to leave him. A common theme is the good old double standard. These men seemed to be inviting me to share in playful sex, but even if a woman will have casual sex with them, many men convince themselves she wouldn't do it with anyone else. They want to have sex with Sleeping Beauty, who at the moment of a kiss is suddenly transformed into a person with no life, a blank slate upon which the prince writes his desires. (Sullivan, 2000, p. 104)*

Substantial evidence exists that, in popular thinking, love and sexuality are in fact intimately linked. Beyond this, popular views hold that love and sexuality *should* be linked, with strong feelings of love, attachment, and investment needing to be established before a couple engages in most types of sexual behavior. Prior to the late 1960s, engaging in sex prior to marriage was widely considered highly immoral and despicable. Individuals who violated the societal prohibition against sex before marriage were often subjected to profound ridicule and were ostracized within many aspects of society (refer to chapters 2 and 3 for discussion of reasons underlying this issue). Women were especially harshly condemned for engaging in premarital sex because of the *double standard*; this value system allowed men greater tolerance with respect to engaging in sexual behavior outside of marital relationships.

The double standard resulted from a succession of religious and cultural beliefs that cast women as (a) epitomizing morality and spiritual purity during the Middle Ages, (b) then as completely "uncontaminated" by sexual desire in the Victorian Era, and finally (c) as motivated to engage in sexual behavior only when they experience "true love" for one man whom they are fated to marry (who is "meant" only for them). This became the romantic view of love and sexuality, an ethic that prevails into current times. Such values make sexual behavior before marriage much more acceptable in the context of an established, loving romantic relationship.

## Popular Conceptions of the Relationship of Love and Sexuality

### General Beliefs About the Importance of Love

Cognitively, perceptions of sexuality are highly woven into the general understanding of the meaning of romantic love; that is, sexual passion and sexual behavior are conceived as aspects of "being in love," but sexuality is not the most defining or central component. This was determined in research by Luby and Aron (1990) in which conceptions of *loving someone* and *being in love with someone* were compared in an attempt to define the meaning of love.

*Being in love* involved many of the same concepts as *loving someone,* such as caring about a person's wellbeing and feeling closeness, intimacy, and devotion to a person. These are feelings that individuals may associate with many different loved ones beyond a romantic partner, such as one's parents, siblings, and children. However, conceptions of *being in love* included such concepts as *physical attraction, sexual arousal,* and *desire,* indicating that sexuality is conceived as an aspect of romantic love. Yet these qualities were not most central to conceptions of romantic love—indeed they had weaker associations with it than features such as compassion, warmth, and emotional intimacy. In other words, sexual feelings are conceived as subservient to feelings of emotional closeness and are thought to occur within the context of other love-related feelings.

### The Link Between Beliefs and Sexual Behavior

Because of the strong link between love and sexuality in common thinking, it is not surprising that the likelihood of engaging in sexual behavior increases as a function of both (a) the stage of the relationship and

(b) the level of intimacy and emotional attachment, although the two are very highly related to one another. Feelings of mutual love and a sense of commitment are the most important factors that college students report taking into account in their decision to engage in sexual intercourse (Christopher & Cate, 1985). Because women prefer to wait for higher levels of love and commitment, the greatest agreement of couples on the desired level of sexual involvement tends to be in later stages of dating relationships (McCabe & Collins, 1984).

Women and men, in fact, have very different expectations about when sexual behavior should occur in general, however; men typically expect sex to occur substantially earlier than women (Cohen & Shotland, 1996). Specifically, men expect sex to occur after about 10 dates or after 6 weeks of dating. Women, in contrast, expect sex after 17 dates or 13 weeks of dating. The factor that appears to determine when sex actually does occur is the expectation of women; expectations were correlated with actual behavior for women, but not for men, a finding consistent with earlier research on attitudes and behavior (Earle & Perricone, 1986). Other possible explanations offered by Earle and Perricone are that women are more likely to act according to their beliefs, or that women develop an attitude that is consistent with the behavior in which they actually have engaged for the sake of being consistent. However, Cohen and Shotland suggested the possibility that women take on the role of "the gatekeeper" (Peplau, Rubin, & Hill, 1977), controlling when sex occurs based on the more restrictive attitudes associated with the female gender role.

The greater importance of emotional intimacy for women is indicated by the finding that less than two-thirds of women would have sex in a relationship in which the partners were attracted, but did not feel emotionally close; in contrast, essentially all men reported that they would consider engaging in sex under these circumstances (Cohen & Shotland, 1996). In relationships in which partners felt neither attraction nor emotional closeness, approximately 66% of men said they would consider engaging in sex, whereas only approximately 20% of women indicated that they would consider doing so. Actual experience reflected this gender difference. Around 33% of men reported that they had engaged in sex without feeling either attraction or emotional closeness; only 5% of women had engaged in sex under these conditions.

Furthermore, both women and men believe that the average woman or man expects to engage in sexual behavior earlier than they themselves expected. Cohen and Shotland observed that the perception that others have more permissive beliefs than is actually the case is an example of **pluralistic ignorance**. Pluralistic ignorance refers to the widespread inaccurate understanding of the actual beliefs held by the majority of individuals; people are often wrong in the judgments they make about how the majority actually feels or what the majority actually does.

Hardly any research has been conducted on the relationship of love and sexuality among lesbians and gay men. Nonetheless, aspects of love—such as perceptions of attachment and equality—have been found to be important aspects of gay and lesbian relationships. Such feelings affect not only relationship satisfaction, but also the commitment of individuals to the continuation of the relationship (Kurdeck, 1991, 1995). Clearly, love is an important factor, just as it is in heterosexual relationships. Furthermore, research has indicated that lesbians tend to engage in sexual behavior only after substantial intimacy and attachment have developed within their romantic relationship (Leigh, 1989).

## Relationship Stage and Sexual Involvement

Relationship stage has also been explicitly linked to emotional involvement and actual sexual behavior among college students (Roche, 1986). The proportion of both young men and women in this study who engaged in penile–vaginal intercourse increased directly with stage of relationship and emotional involvement. Among women, 4% had engaged in sexual intercourse at stage one (dating with no particular affection), 11% had done so at stage two (dating with affection but not love), 32% had at stage three (dating and in love), 68% had at stage four (dating one person only and in love), and 81% had engaged in penile–vaginal intercourse at stage five (engaged to be married). Similarly, 15% of men had engage in penile–vaginal intercourse at stage one, 18% at stage two, 49% at stage three, 63% at stage four, and 74% at stage five. The lower proportions for women in comparison to men at stages one through three were not found at the two later, more intimate stages; in fact, proportions were greater for women.

The patterns were very similar for other types of sexual behavior, such as "light petting," "heavy petting," and oral–genital sex (*petting* is stroking genitals and breasts with the hands). This is consistent with the finding across a number of studies that being in love and involvement in a serious relationship are more important as a basis for engaging in sexual behavior for women in comparison to men (Carroll, Volk, & Hyde, 1985; Cohen & Shotland, 1996; Hill, 2002; Sprecher, Barbee, & Schwartz, 1995).

### Stoking the Fires of Passion: Behavior Leading Up to Sexual Intimacy

Does it matter what you do or say if you want to set the stage with a partner for sexual intimacy? The short answer is "yes," although the specific way to set the stage depends on whether your partner is a woman or a man. In addition to a general sense of intimacy and attachment within a romantic relationship, the type of specific interactions that occur may play a critical role in the decision to engage in sexual behavior. In a study in which participants imagined themselves in eight hypothetical scenarios (Hill, 2002), different types of partner behaviors were described that strongly suggested the possibility that sexual behavior would occur. Each of the eight types of partner behaviors gave the sense that one of eight sexual incentives, or rewards, was available through sexual behavior with the partner. That is, in the scenario, the partner engaged in behavior suggesting that a specific type of emotional experience would result from engaging in sexual behavior with him or her.

For example, one scenario described an individual feeling stressed by work-related problems after coming home one night, with the partner responding in extremely soothing and affectionate ways to the negative mood. This scenario represented the possibility of engaging in sex to obtain relief from a negative psychological state (stress relief), one of the eight sexual incentives. The other sexual incentives are feeling valued, valuing a partner, providing nurturance to one's partner, feeling powerful, feeling the power of one's partner, experiencing physical pleasure, and attempting to have a child.

*Do you think that you would be more or less likely to experience sexual arousal when being comforted or supported by your romantic partner in comparison to other types of interactions you may have? Does the emotional nature of a situation set the stage for sexual interest?*

Five of the situations were hypothesized to indicate a great degree of **emotional investment** in the partner: specifically, the situations providing the opportunity for stress relief, feeling valued, valuing the partner, providing nurturance, and having a child. The other situations were thought to involve partner behaviors that do *not* convey a sense of emotional investment by the partner: specifically, feeling

**Box 9.3**                                                    **An Eye Toward Research**

### Is There a Link Between Emotional Intimacy and Engaging in Sexual Behavior?

The link between intimacy and engaging in sexual behavior is highlighted in a study by Christopher and Cate (1985). The focus of this study was couples who were involved in a serious, sexually exclusive relationship (meaning that the couples did not engage in sexual behavior with anyone other than their romantic partner). The first goal of the researchers was to determine what the typical patterns of involvement in sexual behavior are for established relationships.

Four patterns of progression to engaging in sexual behavior were identified among 54 dating couples (who were all White). The first pattern was rapid involvement, couples who engaged in high levels of sexual behavior early in their relationship (7.4% of the couples). The second pattern was gradual involvement, those who engaged in only less intimate sexual behavior, such as fondling the woman's breasts while clothed on the first date; however, the couples progressed to more intimate sexual behavior with each relationship stage (31.5% of the couples). The third pattern was delayed involvement, in which couples engaged in less intimate sexual behaviors such as kissing and fondling in the early stages; sexual behavior leading to orgasm did not occur for these couples until the last stage of "becoming a couple" (44.4% of the couples). The last pattern of sexual behavior was low involvement, in which even by the last relationship stage, the most intimate sexual behavior typical of the couples was fondling the woman's genitals to the point of producing vaginal secretions (16.6% of the couples).

Feelings of love experienced by each individual for his or her romantic partner were measured using a self-report questionnaire indicating the degree of closeness and attachment to the partner. Couples who exhibited a pattern of rapid involvement in sexual behavior tended to report having experienced greater feelings of love at earlier stages of the relationship than other types of couples, paralleling the level of sexual intimacy in which they engaged.

Christopher and Cate (1985) noted that two interpretations could account for this relationship. First, it may be that individuals attribute greater feelings of love earlier in the relationship to legitimize the fact that they have engaged in more intimate sexual behavior earlier. Another possibility is that only couples who feel a great deal of love for one another after engaging in sexual behavior continue on to become established romantic couples; given that only established couples were included in the study, it is possible that individuals who did not experience stronger feelings of love did not go on to become established couples so that they could be included in the study.

The important conclusion that can be drawn from this research is that feelings of love and emotional attachment coincide with the likelihood of engaging in sexual behavior. It is not clear from this research whether greater feelings of love cause people to be more motivated to engage in sexual behavior or whether believing that the couple was intensely in love in retrospect provides an after-the-fact justification for it.

### References

Christopher, F. S., & Cate, R. M. (1985). Premarital sexual pathways and relationship development. *Journal of Social and Personal Relationships, 2,* 271–288.

powerful by engaging in sexual behavior, feeling the power of one's partner, and experiencing physical pleasure.

Another factor examined in the study was the type of relationship in which participants imagined that they were involved with the partner: (a) dating one month, and imagining that they could become involved in a serious relationship; (b) dating six months, and imagining a serious relationship was possible; and (c) married or involved in a serious, permanent relationship for six months.

The issue examined in this study was participants' judgments about the likelihood of engaging in sexual behavior with a romantic partner in each situation. The expectation was that women and men would be equally likely to report that they would engage in sexual behavior in situations conveying a sense of emotional investment by the partner (i.e., providing stress relief, feeling valued; see Figure 9.8). However, for both women and men, the likelihood was expected to be greater in more serious, established relationships. In contrast, women were expected to report being less likely to engage in sexual behavior when the partner's behavior did not explicitly convey emotional investment (i.e., expressing power, experiencing the partner's power, and experiencing physical pleasure). Only in the more serious, long-term relationships were women expected to report being equally likely as men to engage in such behavior because emotional attachment is assumed to already exist substantially in these types of relationships.

In large part, these expectations were confirmed by the results of the study. Both women and men reported being more likely to engage in sexual behavior in more serious relationships. Also, women indicated that they

**FIGURE 9.8**    Proposed Likelihood of Sexual Behavior as a Function of Sexual Incentives, Gender, and Type of Relationship

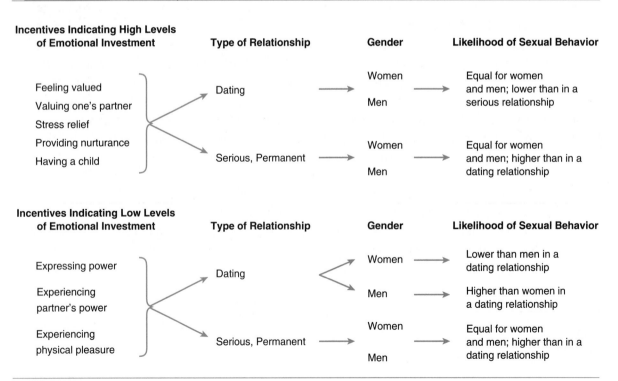

would be more likely to engage in sexual behavior when their partners' behavior communicated greater emotional investment in them, such that gender differences did not occur even in the early dating relationship (dating 1 month). That is, women were as likely as men to say they would engage in sexual behavior very early in a relationship if they felt emotional investment by their partner.

Actually, two notable exceptions to these results were found. First, women indicated being *more* likely to engage in sexual behavior, regardless of level of relationship, when they felt a need for comfort and relief, or their partner felt such a need. Women reported being especially likely to engage in sexual behavior when they needed comfort while in a serious relationship; men reported being equally likely regardless of type of relationship, but substantially less likely than women in a serious relationship.

The second exception was that women reported being dramatically less likely to engage in sexual behavior when the partner conveyed a desire to exert power over them sexually, regardless of the type of relationship. Apparently, men's desire to exert power over women sexually is perceived by women as intimidating and not sexually arousing. It may be that such behavior activates a schema, a cognitive interpretation, of the male gender role as aggressive and potentially unpleasant, if not dangerous. Such a finding is additionally consistent with the view that emotional warmth, intimacy, and attachment are especially important to women in order to experience sexual desire and interest.

## Summary

An intimate relationship is an ongoing involvement between individuals characterized by substantial knowledge and understanding of one another that has been gathered through talking and sharing time together. Another critical aspect of the definition is that an intimate relationship involves a level of closeness in interaction that distinguishes it from casual, or nonintimate, relationships. Relational intimacy involves greater frequency and quality of interactions. A romantic relationship is a type of intimate relationship involving the potential to experience passion: the desire for, and positive emotions, related to physical intimacy and sexual involvement.

Intimate relationships develop through increasing interdependence, the condition of partners being able to obtain highly desired rewards and incentives more and more only from one another. Increasing interdependence contributes to growing commitment to the relationship, the desire and intention to remain in the relationship over the long-term.

Various formal psychological theories of the relationship of love and sexuality have spanned the entire range of possibilities, as noted in Aron and Aron's (1991) theoretical model. The first group of theories focuses primarily on sexuality without focusing on love to any great extent. The second group of theories emphasizes sexuality, but also focuses

*(Continued)*

(Continued)

on love to some extent. The third group of theories focuses equally on sexuality and love. The fourth group of theories emphasizes love, but also focuses on sexuality to some extent. The final group of theories emphasizes the importance of love without really focusing much on sexuality. Aron and Aron suggest that, beyond all of the theories included in the their theoretical continuum, the relationship between love and sexuality may in fact be due to another, higher-order factor, the need for self-expansion.

Sexuality is conceived in the popular mind set as intricately linked to love, as well as involving the belief that sexuality *should* be linked to love. Research has demonstrated that increasing levels of intimacy and emotional attachment, as well as progression to later relationship stages, increases the likelihood of sexual behavior. Nonetheless, substantial gender differences exist in the desired timing of first intercourse because women prefer to wait for higher levels of love and commitment, whereas men are satisfied with lower levels. The expectations of women generally exerts the stronger influence on the actual timing of first intercourse for a couple. Stage of relationship and level of emotional involvement are typically fairly strongly related to the likelihood of sexual behavior for couples.

## Chapter 9 Critical Thinking Exercises

1. The nature of romantic relationships

   Think of at least four relationships with which you are familiar (such as those of family, friends, or acquaintances) or about which you have heard (such as relationships involving a celebrity, movie or TV star, music star, or politician).

   Which relationship is the most intimate, the most sexual, the strongest, the most satisfying, the most argumentative, and the most likely to end?

   Do these dimensions adequately describe romantic relationships? Should other dimensions be included? How important is sexuality to romantic relationships?

2. Initiation of sexual behavior

   Research indicates that women believe they would be more likely to engage in sexual behavior when their partner exhibits behavior that communicates emotional intimacy; this is especially true if either the woman or her partner needs comfort. Women are particularly unlikely to want to engage in sexual behavior when their partner appears to want to exert power and control over them. How important do you think specific partner behaviors are in initiating sexual behavior in relationships?

**Visit www.sagepub.com/hillhsstudy.com for online activities, sample tests, and other helpful resources. Select "Chapter 9: Love, Intimacy, and Sexuality" for chapter-specific activities.**

# Chapter 10

## RELATIONSHIPS AND SEXUALITY

*I'm actually just starting a relationship. So far I'm quite happy with it. Me and [my] boyfriend have agreed that we have plenty of time to experiment sexually during our relationship instead of all at once, and that we're both in no rush to do things. I really enjoy kissing, hugging, and cuddling with him. Eventually we'll do more things when we're both ready and feel it's time. First things first, I'm a virgin, but I don't plan on keeping my virginity until I get married. But I want to at least lose it to someone I love and deserves it. (Emotional Intimacy More Important to Woman? How About the Man? On-line forum, retrieved July 22, 2006, from The-clitoris.com. Reprinted with permission of The-clitoris.com.)*

As the above self-disclosure illustrates, being involved in an intimate relationship is, for many people, a deciding factor in whether they will engage in sexual behavior with someone (Christopher & Cate, 1985; Hill, 2002; Roche, 1986; Sprecher, 1989). Many feel that they must be in a relationship and must be in love first before they will engage in sex. Furthermore, relationship status is important with respect to sexuality because being in a steady relationship also means engaging in sex more often, on average (Laumann, Gagnon, Michael, & Michaels, 1994).

The emotional closeness provided by relationships is therefore a major factor influencing sexuality in a number of ways. Other advantages to sex in established relationships include greater familiarity and comfort, contributing to higher quality communication. Each partner knowing what the other wants can lead to more satisfying sex as well.

Relationships, however, do not always remain at the lofty peak of blissful intimacy and satisfaction that they may soar to early on in the relationship. Instead, many follow a path of growth and change that stretches across the entire duration of individuals' involvement with one another. Aspects of relationships typically shift and evolve as individuals find out more about one another, react to and ponder one another's unfolding behavior, and share feelings with one another. The nature of these changes affect many facets of individuals' lives, including the kinds of sexual behavior in which they engage, their happiness with what they experience, how often they have sex, and the meaning of these sexual encounters with their partner. For this reason, understanding the dynamics underlying relationship change is as critical as understanding the factors that brought individuals together in the first place.

Yet not all sexual behavior occurs within the context of ongoing intimate relationships. Because of the dramatic societal changes that took place throughout the last century, a significant amount of sexual behavior occurs outside of ongoing relationships. An important issue to take into account, therefore, is the nature of factors leading some individuals to engage in sexual behavior of a more casual nature. Behavior of this sort is noteworthy because it occurs despite fairly strong societal norms and values that have succeeded in convincing people in general to restrict sexual expression to ongoing intimate relationships. Because sexual behavior does take place outside of intimate relationships with some frequency, this issue is examined as well. Sex outside of relationships includes that in which neither individual is involved in a relationship at the time; it also includes sexual behavior with a person other than individuals' spouse or romantic relationship partner. If relationship involvement is such an important factor in general, then why do some individuals have sex with others when they are not in a relationship with them? This is one of the issues considered in this chapter.

In the previous chapter, the role of love, intimacy, and emotional attachment in the desire to become involved in romantic and sexual relationships was discussed. The current chapter first considers the ways in which relationships develop and progress over time, a process captured more poetically in a song, as described by the songwriter herself:

> That's why I called it Dangerously in Love [a song she wrote]. It's basically all of the steps in a relationship: from when you first meet a guy, to realizing you're interested, to dancing with him the first night, to thinking that you're in love, to realizing that you're now a little open to making love, to breaking up, to having to love yourself after the breakup. All of that. A celebration of love. (Beyonce Knowles, American pop singer and actress; ThinkExist.com)

Beginning with strategies that individuals typically use to communicate interest in establishing a relationship, the chapter continues with behaviors that increase commitment once a romantic relationship has begun. It also addresses strategies that are involved in coping with conflict and disagreement between individuals involved in a relationship, as well as the process through which relationships deteriorate and come to an end. Following this, factors involved in how sexual activity first begins within relationships are considered. The frequency and types of sexual behavior that are typical are examined, as well as the role of sexual satisfaction in relationship quality and stability. Because not all sexual behavior occurs within relationships, casual sex and sex outside of established relationships (e.g., affairs) are discussed, as well as factors that are associated with their occurrence. Finally, jealousy that results from a concern about sexual involvement outside of a relationship is examined.

## *The Path That Relationships Usually Follow*

### Kindling the Flame: How to Signal Romantic Interest

#### Yea or Nay: What People Do to Show Interest or Lack of Interest

*Flirting is the gentle art of making a man feel pleased with himself.*

Helen Rowland, author (ThinkExist.com)

Expressing feelings of interest and attraction for one another, of course, is an essential process involved in forging new romantic relationships (Taraban, Hendrick, & Hendrick, 1998). Actually, rather than existing as only one single process, however, research suggests that showing interest in becoming involved romantically may occur in a variety of ways (Fichten, Tagalakis, Judd, Wright, & Amsel, 1992). The most common method of expressing interest is that of using **verbal strategies**; these include asking detailed questions, adding to the conversation, complimenting, and requesting the person's phone number or address. A second method is that of using **nonverbal strategies**. The most typical strategies in this group are making eye contact, moving closer, smiling, and looking intently at the other person.

---

### Box 10.1 I Can't Believe You Said That! Those Risky Come-On Lines

Some may believe that a clever come-on line is the best icebreaker, because it shows a sense of humor and wit, maybe a sparkling, fun personality. In fact, belief in the importance of the come-on line rose to extreme prominence during the 1920s. In an era that focused on the importance of personality, rather than character, as was the focus in Victorian times, men believed that it was important to develop their "line" to be able to meet women successfully. Apparently, the contemporary version of this reliance on come-on lines has evolved—some would say, devolved—into raucous, if not humorous, zingers. Some reflexively cause those who hear them to groan.

Advice from the Web site How to Attract Women (2006) warns against using such lines:

Come-ons or "lines" are just plain phony. Women want sincerity from a man. You won't get a date with lines like these:

"What's a nice girl like you doing in a place like this?"

"I'm sure I know you from somewhere."

"You seemed so lonely standing here all by yourself."

If you simply want to talk to a woman, be real. A woman will usually be flattered when you are sincere.

This Web site also advises would-be suitors to avoid making what it calls, the "Biggest Flirting Mistakes." These include:

Playing the little boy routine. This is very annoying to most women.

Being slick, too cool.

Talking negatively.

Acting like a clown to make her laugh will have her laughing at you, not with you.

Whining is an indicator that he is going to be a complainer or nitpicker.

Author Amy Cohen agrees with such advice in her article, *Come On! What's With Those Pick-Up Lines?* She writes:

*(Continued)*

(Continued)

Unfortunately for us, there is no sure-fire way to avoid a Random Act of Sleaziness. By the time a guy approaches and opens his mouth, it is already too late. The key here, I think, is education. The next time a guy comes up to you and asks, "What's your sign?" tell him it's *Stop*, then tell him to just be himself. It's very sexy to see a guy come up to you with the confidence to strike up a conversation without hiding behind some cheesy line you've heard a million times before. And let's face it, we girls all have tired legs— not from running through his mind all night, but from running away from that oh-so-sleazy pick-up line we just can't seem to avoid. (Cohen, 2006)

So, what are other come-on lines to avoid? Although they are called the "Best Come-On Lines" by Wooden Nickel posted on a Web site (Wooden Nickel, 2005, December 23), you might want to steer clear of these:

- You give me a reason to wake up every day.
- I don't know if you are beautiful or not; I haven't gotten past your eyes yet.
- I made a wish on a falling star, and you just made my wish come true!
- Your father must be a weapons specialist because you are the bomb!
- Hey, haven't I seen you before? Oh, yeah, it was in my dreams!
- I'm not like all the other guys.
- What planet are you from? 'Cause I've never seen anyone like you before!
- They say milk does the body good, but darn, how much have you been drinking?
- Your name must be Campbell 'cause you're Mmm! Mmm! Good.
- Out of all the fish in the sea, you're the one I got hooked on.
- You must have been a Girl Scout because you have my heart all tied up in knots.
- Wanna see some pictures of my kids?
- Do you have a map? I'm lost in your eyes.
- Baby, you make me melt like an M & M in your mouth.
- You're the best-looking girl I've seen in a while.
- I only thought about you once today—I just never stopped.
- OK, I'm here, what's your next wish?
- Your smile is as sweet as the sunlight.
- My friend wants to know if you think I'm cute.

### References

Cohen, A. *Come on! Pick-up lines.* Retrieved March 2, 2007, from http://www.newfaces.com/magazine/pickup-lines.php

Wooden Nickel. (2005, December 23). *Best come-on lines.* Retrieved March 2, 2007, from http://www.unsolved mysteries.com/usm438177.html

*How to attract women.* Lines and come-on's. Retrieved March 2, 2007, from http://www.how-to-attract-women .com/lines-come-ons.html

A third means of conveying interest in another person is **touch**, which includes not only simply touching the person, but also putting one's arm around him or her, or kissing. A fourth way of communicating interest is what Fichten and colleagues call **intangible strategies**; these involve behaviors such as paying attention to the other person, acting in a friendly way, flirting, and appearing relaxed. Some strategies are not easily labeled, and were grouped by the researchers into a class called **unclassifiable strategies**. These include such tactics as simply hanging around the other person, performing courteous acts for the person, and phoning often.

Strategies for indicating disinterest likewise fall into the six categories. **Verbal strategies** include informing the other person that one has a romantic partner, lying or making excuses, ending the conversation, and refusing an invitation. Examples of **nonverbal strategies** are looking away from the other person, staying far away from the person, looking bored, and turning away. **Intangible strategies** include being unfriendly and shying away from the person. **Unclassifiable behaviors** are avoiding the other person, distracting oneself while talking with the person, ignoring the person, and avoiding performing courteous acts for the person. None of the strategies for conveying disinterest involved the category of **touch** in their study. This is probably because touch in itself is an intimate experience and could conceivably be misinterpreted as interest in the person. One method of showing disinterest that is not used to express interest is **paralinguistic behavior**; this includes keeping one's statements and responses as short as possible and remaining as silent as possible.

### Reactions to Rejection

*A sad thing in life is that sometimes you meet someone who means a lot to you only to find out in the end that it was never bound to be and you just have to let go.*

Unknown (ThinkExist.com)

In general, most people are quite capable of detecting interpersonal cues that indicate both romantic interest and disinterest. Nonetheless, many of us have probably felt attraction at least once in our lives toward someone who we come to realize does not feel attraction for us. This is referred to as **unrequited love**, the experience of feeling attraction for someone who does not feel a similar attraction in return (Baumeister & Wotman, 1992). However, some individuals report having experienced especially intense feelings of attraction and profound infatuation for another person who was not attracted to them. They therefore felt like they had suffered a severe loss after it became clear that a relationship would not develop.

Have you ever been pursued by someone whom you were not interested in romantically or sexually? Have you ever tried to show interest for someone who you found out was not interested in you? What feelings did you experience in these situations?

Actually, the emotional reactions of both individuals involved in this type of experience—the pursued and the pursuer—are often a mix of negative and positive feelings. The positive emotions reported by those who are attracted to the other person include the feeling that their attraction had provided them with a reason for living; they also report periods of intense happiness when it seemed like the other person might also be interested in them. Individuals who are the object of attraction indicate that they thought they were friends with the person whom they later found out was romantically or sexually attracted to them. They also tend to have felt flattered by the other's attraction for them upon realizing the attraction existed (Baumeister & Wotman, 1992).

However, negative reactions also occur as the pursuer begins to understand that a relationship is not going to happen. The person who is rejected typically feels upset, angry, disappointed, and jealous. Many of the rejected believe that the one they found attractive had led them on and had actually signaled interest in them as well. Often the person who was pursued feels that the pursuer persisted with attempts to begin a relationship even after being given an outright expression of disinterest in him or her. According to Baumeister and Wotman's research, the disinterested person often experienced guilt and anger as a result of the conflict. Unrequited love therefore results in the experience of negative emotions for both individuals, although the one who was pursued reports feeling more negative than positive about the situation (Baumeister & Wotman, 1992).

## Increasing Commitment in a Romantic Relationship

*I learned that you cannot put the relationship second. Because love is not enough.*

Stephan Jenkins (ThinkExist.com)

### Ways to Strengthen Commitment

Once a relationship has begun, what do individuals do to keep the relationship going? What strategies will help them solidify the commitment of their partner? The most common means of clarifying the feelings of one's partner is called a **direct definitional bid** (Tolhuizen, 1989); this is an outright request to the partner for a definite commitment. If the partner who has received such a bid also wants to strengthen the relationship, not surprisingly he or she most commonly uses a strategy called **accept definitional bid**; this is responding affirmatively to the partner's direct definitional bid. No differences among partners' strategies exist if both are equally interested in promoting commitment to the relationship.

Overall, the most frequent strategies for intensifying relationships in general are (a) increasing contact, (b) relationship negotiation, and (c) requesting social support. The strategy of **increasing contact** is arranging to be with the partner or calling the partner more frequently. **Relationship negotiation** is explicitly engaging the partner in discussing their feelings for one another. **Requesting social support** is asking the partner for advice. Women report a greater frequency of using relationship negotiation and acceptance of definitional bid. Men are more likely to use a direct definitional bid, as well as another strategy, **verbal expressions of affection**, such as saying the words "I love you" (Tolhuizen, 1989).

The greater tendency of men to offer such a strong statement of commitment as "I love you" has been confirmed in other research as well (Owen, 1987). The reason for this may be that men are more impulsive with respect to certain types of emotional expression; that is, they are less able to inhibit and control particular emotional reactions. Gender differences are supported as well in research by Hendrick, Hendrick, Foote, and Slapion-Foote (1984), indicating that women are more pragmatic in dealing with romantic feelings; in contrast, men appear to experience especially intense emotions and passion, making it more challenging for them to regulate their strong emotions. Likewise, women tend to be more capable of distinguishing among intimate feelings such as love, caring, and liking (Rubin, 1970). Greater sensitivity to distinctions among emotions might contribute to women being more selective in deciding that they are in love. They may therefore be more guarded in finally offering the explicit sign of commitment, "I love you" (Taraban et al., 1998).

In addition, it is possible that women are less inclined to be the first to verbalize feelings of love because of their traditional role of reacting to events; men are stereotypically expected to take the lead in relationships, such that it is seen as their responsibility to control the course of the relationship. As Taraban and her colleagues note, however, other interpretations of these tendencies are possible.

The use of touch is a powerful signal of greater intimacy within relationships (Taraban et al., 1998). Expressing intimacy through touch conveys a feeling of sensuality and sexual interest, in addition to a sense of warmth and concern. Moreover, touch appears to be a way of expressing intimacy no matter the length of the relationship; it is common in longstanding relationships as well as in the early stages of relationship development. Nonetheless, research by Guerrero and Anderson (1991) indicates that touching increases most dramatically in early stages of a relationship, such that the period of most rapid increase occurs early on. Although frequency of touching may decline over time within enduring relationships, research suggests that touching does not disappear. Instead, it levels off at a frequency close to that of dating couples (Emmers & Dindia, 1995).

Contrary to what some may believe, men are more likely than women to be the first to say those three little, but powerful, words, "I love you."

Other evidence suggests that mutuality of touching increases within stable relationships; mutuality refers to the situation in which individuals come to match one another in the amount of touching one another (Guerrero & Andersen, 1994). Touching in early stages of relationships may serve to intensify intimacy and advance the relationship, whereas in later stages it may reflect already existing affection, emotional investment, and comfort with intimacy (Taraban et al., 1998).

### Giving Your Heart and Soul: What Is Involved in Commitment?

The way that a couple grows to be more and more committed to their relationship is most effectively captured in the concept of **interdependence** or **closeness**; this is the degree to which the fate of individuals in a relationship depend on the relationship partner. One of the most influential theoretical views concerning commitment is the **investment model** (Rusbult, 1980). This model is a version of social exchange theory discussed in the previous chapter, in which greater commitment is proposed to result from (a) high levels of satisfaction, (b) the perception that very few alternatives to one's current relationship exist that are more attractive, and (c) a high degree of investing resources in the relationship.

Within social exchange theory, **satisfaction** is an evaluation of the level of benefits resulting from being in the relationship minus the level of costs. Strong satisfaction is the sense a person has that the relationship is pleasing and contributes tremendously to the quality of his or her life. The behaviors discussed previously that strengthen commitment may do so because they provide pleasurable experiences on which partners come to depend. They may therefore increase the satisfaction that a person experiences within the relationship (Rusbult, 1980).

The concept of **alternatives to the relationship** extends directly from that of comparison levels in social exchange theory. The proposal is that individuals compare the outcomes they obtain from the relationship to those they believe they could obtain from relationships with other individuals. Perceiving a greater distance of current outcomes compared with those available from other relationships contributes to greater commitment to the relationship (Rusbult, 1980).

**Investment** refers to the amount of one's own resources an individual has devoted to the relationship. Resources include actual financial contributions and the extent to which property and possessions are shared mutually by the couple. However, this concept also includes the amount of time and energy one has devoted to the relationship. Higher levels of investment likewise contribute to one's sense of commitment to the relationship (Rusbult, 1980).

Overall then, greater satisfaction, fewer high-quality alternatives to the relationship, and greater investment produce stronger commitment. Research also has revealed that individuals who are committed to their relationship tend to develop ways of thinking that cast their relationship and their partner in a very favorable light; for heterosexuals, individuals of the other sex are judged to be less attractive, both physically and sexually, by those in dating relationships compared with those not in a committed relationship (Simpson, Gangestad, & Lerma, 2000).

## Keeping the Relationship Strong: Dealing With Conflict

Because the lives of individuals involved in a romantic relationship become very interconnected with increasing involvement and commitment, conflict is virtually unavoidable. Even individuals involved in an intimate relationship who care deeply for one another do not have exactly the same needs and goals. If the needs of romantic partners clash, frustration and unhappiness will typically result, especially for important needs. From the perspective of interdependence theory, interference with goals is the cause of conflict (Fiske, 2004).

Four types of reactions to conflict within a relationship are possible (Rusbult, Verette, Whitney, Slovik, & Lipkus, 1991). The reactions are a function of two distinct factors, the **constructiveness** of the response and whether it consists of an **active or passive type** of behavior (see Figure 10.1). One strategy known as **voice** is a constructive, active strategy; voice involves discussing the conflict, seeking help, making suggestions, and attempting to change the situation. A passive, constructive response is **loyalty**, which includes such behaviors as waiting for conditions to change, being patient, hoping or praying for the best, and being supportive of the partner during the conflict. An active, destructive type of tactic is **exit**, which includes screaming, threatening, intimidating, and even leaving the relationship or seeking divorce. Finally, a passive, destructive reaction is **neglect**, ignoring and avoiding the situation, pouting, being irritable toward the partner, criticizing, and letting the relationship deteriorate.

The act of responding to a partner's destructive behavior with a constructive strategy is called **accommodation**. Couples who respond to conflict with accommodation tend to survive conflict and are more likely to continue in the relationship (Van Lange, Rusbult, et al., 1997). Individuals who accommodate their partners are those who are committed to the relationship, tend to be warm, caring, and compassionate (Van Lange, Agnew, Harinick, & Steemers, 1997), take the perspective of their partner, are socially concerned, and are in mutually dependent relationships (Arriga & Rusbult, 1998). Sacrifice for one's partner is related to the partner's willingness to sacrifice as well (Fiske, 2004). Such a response indicates a type of reciprocal influence, in which behavior by one partner leads to identical behavior by the other partner in response; that is, good will begets good will. Individuals satisfied with their relationship also tend to have positive views of the relationship and their partner, leading them to believe that their partner holds beliefs very similar to their own; couples do, in fact, develop more similar attitudes over the course of a relationship (Davis & Rusbult, 2001). Those who feel loved by their partner tend to deal with difficulties by seeking greater intimacy with their partner, whereas those who do not feel loved become hostile toward their partner (Murray, Belavia, Rose, & Griffin, 2003).

| FIGURE 10.1 | Reactions to Relationship Conflict |

**Level of Activity**

|  | Active | Passive |
|---|---|---|
| **Constructive** | Voice | Loyalty |
| **Destructive** | Exit | Neglect |

*(Vertical axis labeled: Constructiveness — Constructive / Destructive)*

From Rusbult, C. E., Verette, J., Whitney, G. A., Slovik, L. F., & Lipkus, I., Accomodation processes in close relationships: Theory and preliminary empirical evidence, *Journal of Personality and Social Psychology, 60*, 53–78. Copyright © 1991, American Psychological Association. Reprinted with permission.

Highly similar patterns of conflict resolution and relationship quality have been found for same-sex couples and heterosexual couples with respect to four strategies identified by Gottman and Krokoff (1989): (a) positive problem-solving (compromise, negotiation), (b) conflict engagement (personal attacks), (c) withdrawal (refusing to talk any further, ignoring), and (d) compliance (giving in, discontinue arguing). Heterosexual couples were essentially identical to lesbian and gay male couples in the frequency of using the four strategies (Kurdeck, 1994). Similar findings have been found in other research (Metz, Rosser, & Strapko, 1994). Likewise, same-sex and heterosexual couples are extremely similar in various processes linked to relationship functioning and quality; where differences occurred, lesbian and gay male partners functioned at a higher level of quality than heterosexual couples in 78% of the comparisons (Kurdeck, 2004).

*How do you typically handle disagreements and hurt feelings in your relationship?* A basic principle in successfully dealing with relationship problems is "Good will begets good will."

In the way that good will begets further good will, negative reactions likewise tend to generate even more negative feelings, as research by Gottman and Levenson (1992) has demonstrated. The process is called a **conflict cascade**. The progression of conflict occurs as a series of events in which difficulties in the relationship produce negative reactions; the negative reactions lead to further conflict, resulting in a continual backdrop of ill will within the relationship. Under these circumstances, individuals may become exceptionally vigilant of their partner's offenses, dwelling on them and trying to explain them, a process called **negative tracking** (Holtzworth-Munroe & Jacobson, 1985). This process typically results in generating explanations that peg the cause of the couple's problems as being due to the partner's personality characteristics. Blaming the problems on the partner's personality casts the partner as entirely responsible for the negative behaviors in which he or she engages. It also leads to the expectation that the partner will commit the offenses repeatedly in the future and that no hope exists for change.

As a result, couples who fall into such a vicious cycle do not come up with the positive interpretations of one another that help to recover from the negative experiences. These couples are at increased risk for separation and breakup of the relationship (Gottman & Levenson, 1992). In relationships that endure over time, supportive behaviors—such as smiling, caressing, and speaking respectfully—are at least five times more prevalent than hurtful types of behavior, such as ridiculing, making nasty comments, and criticizing. The willingness of at least one of the individuals to respond to the partner's negative behaviors with supportive reactions serves to greatly reduce the risk that the relationship will fall apart (Gottman, 1994, 1998).

## The Dying Embers of Love: How Relationships End

> The happiest times in my life were when my relationships were going well—when I was in love with someone, and someone was loving me. But in my whole life, I haven't met the person I can sustain a relationship with yet. So I'm discontented about that. I'm angry with myself. I have regrets.
>
> Billy Joel, singer and songwriter (ThinkExist.com)

> Ellen [DeGeneres] and I had a three and a half year relationship that ended sadly, not because we were both women, but because we both wanted different things for our lives.
>
> Anne Heche, actress (ThinkExist.com)

### Where Did We Go Wrong?

As discussed previously, relationships that are less likely to end are those in which individuals engage in more constructive strategies for resolving conflict, as opposed to destructive strategies. In addition to a stronger relationship orientation and a desire to persist (Arriaga, 2001; Arriaga & Agnew, 2001), those whose relationships flourish attend less to possible alternative relationships (Miller, 1997). They also believe that ending the relationship will be costlier than do those whose relationships actually end, and they also tend to feel a sense of moral obligation to remain in the relationship (Adams & Jones, 1997).

In some cases, an individual may initially become attracted to a romantic partner because of specific unique, alluring characteristics. Ironically, in approximately 30% of breakups, these very characteristics turn out to be primary factors in the eventual decline of the relationship (Felmlee, 1995). Intriguing or fanciful attributes, such as being mysterious or playful, may eventually become irritating and unbearable as an individual has to deal with the tendencies day after day. "Mysterious" becomes "aloof," "brooding," "moody," and "uncommunicative" after many experiences with the partner withdrawing or not being emotionally available. "Playful" becomes "irresponsible," "frivolous," and "immature" following multiple experiences with the partner being unwilling to take any matters seriously. The situation of being attracted to someone initially because of a quality that later causes dissatisfaction and breakup is called "fatal attraction" (Felmlee, 1995).

A great variety of factors have actually been found to contribute to the decline and breakup of romantic relationship, however. Reasons include (a) partners growing to be different from one another in attitudes and interests; (b) lack of emotional expression and sharing; (c) conflicts associated with careers; (d) financial problems; (e) feeling overly controlled or dominated by one's partner; (f) physical or psychological abuse; and (g) no longer being sexually attracted to one's partner (Sprecher, 1994). However, no one type of factor has been identified as the primary cause of relationship breakup (Berscheid, 1994). Possibly a common element underlying the escalation of conflict into relationship-destroying problems is difficulty in developing a mutual understanding of the conflict and the relationship; another contributor may be the inability to understand that differences in viewpoints even exist (Harvey & Weber, 2002; Harvey, Wells, & Alvarez, 1978; Holtzworth-Munroe & Jacobson, 1985).

According to the **cascade model** of relationship deterioration advanced by Gottman (1994), particular behaviors and emotional experiences set in motion a series of reactions that doom relationships to fall apart. Conflict produces an emotional experience he calls **flooding**: feelings of intense shock, upset, confusion, and incapacitation in reaction to the partner's negative emotions. A series of responses and counter-responses produce this stunning emotional experience, which many times proves to be lethal to the well-being of the relationship; for this reason, Gottman has referred to four types of destructive behaviors as the "Four Horsemen of the Apocalypse." The behaviors are (a) **criticism** and complaining, (b) **defensiveness** (rebutting partner criticism, displaying hurt feelings), (c) **stonewalling** (withdrawing from the partner and refusing to interact, becoming stubbornly resistant to further influence attempts by the partner), and (d) **contempt** for the romantic partner.

Typical reactions to this chain of events are to feel that one is the **innocent victim** of the partner's unfair criticism or to feel **righteous indignation** leading to plans for retaliation. A history of these types of reactions closes off the potential for calling upon the more constructive strategies that were discussed previously. Furthermore, the couple's history leads to attributions that the partner's negative behaviors are caused by stable characteristics that will only produce further negative behavior in the future. Hope for change withers, causing partners to withdraw from one another and become distant. The marriage or relationship is reinterpreted as negative and a mistake, leading to the ending of the relationship (Gottman, 1994).

The primary information available on the frequency of the breakup of long-term relationships are those related to divorce because no systematic registry exists for nonmarital relationships. Consequently, little is reliably known about the frequency of the breakup of heterosexual dating relationships, heterosexual cohabitation relationships, or same-sex relationships. The current statistics that are available indicate that approximately 40–50% of all marriages in the United States ultimately end in divorce (Haskey, 1996; Harvey & Weber, 2002; National Vital Statistics System, 1999–2000).

## How Do You Mend a Broken Heart? What Happens After Relationships End?

Individuals who experience the ending of a significant relationship typically endure a number of agonizing emotional states, initially ruminating about the partner who is no longer available and then suffering intense sadness upon accepting that the relationship is truly over. Most individuals gradually distance themselves emotionally from the loss, returning to a well-adjusted state of mind (Hazan & Shaver, 1994). However, individuals who are the ones responsible for the breakup of a relationship have been found to struggle with emotional distress for extended periods, even years. The distress results from the hurt that the breakup caused their former partner, which is worsened if the partner follows up with repeated attempts to rekindle the relationship (Baumeister & Wotman, 1992).

As a way of characterizing the experience of grief and the return to well-being, John Harvey and his colleagues (Harvey, 1996, 2000; Harvey, Weber, & Orbuch, 1990) have developed a theoretical model describing the process of coping with major losses. This proposal is relevant not only to relationship breakup and divorce, but also loss through death. After a traumatic relationship loss—one involving shock, numbness, and feelings of being overwhelmed—individuals are thought to transition through a sequence of stages. However, not all individuals may experience all of the stages, nor progress through all stages in exactly the order proposed within the sequence. The specific stages are (a) outcry, (b) denial, (c) intrusion, (d) working through, (e) completion, and (f) identity change.

**Outcry** involves initially expressing emotions related to the loss, such as fear, despair, and hopelessness. **Denial** is the stage of the process in which individuals struggle with the reality of the loss by feeling or believing that it has not actually happened; this possibly includes avoiding thinking about the loss, as well as avoiding aspects of life that remind the individual of the loved one. These constitute the early phases of the process, which may last varying amounts of time for different individuals, ranging from weeks to months. Harvey and Weber (2002) suggest that, if the early stages of grieving continue for years, an individual may need to seek professional counseling. The third stage is **intrusion**, a period in which an individual experiences what are called flooded states; these are episodes of intense emotions in which the person is absorbed with reminiscing about the lost loved one. The episodes often occur when the individual is alone, and they tend to be largely private; in fact, individuals may seek solitude so that they can reminisce in private.

The later stages involve eventually coming to terms with, and adjusting to, the absence of the lost partner. The first part of this is the **working-through process**, in which an individual constructs an account of the loss. **Accounts** are personal narratives, or stories, about the events and processes involved in the loss and the coping that followed the loss (Harvey & Weber, 2002). The working-through process may involve **confiding**, sharing the personal account with others. By confronting the loss directly through telling others their personal story, grieving individuals may become more accustomed to the state of loss. In fact, immersing oneself in episodes of remembering the loss may serve to demystify the experience, as well as one's feelings about it (Wegner, 1989). Becoming used to the loss emotionally often allows individuals to integrate it into their self-understanding, and possibly move forward in life more effectively (Harvey & Weber, 2002).

Not all divorces or ended relationships are characterized by bitterness, resentment, and avoidance after the divorce. In fact, Amato and Booth (1997) found that many divorced parents in their study cooperated with one another in fairly civil ways. A major reason for this may be that many U.S. couples decide to end their marriages for reasons other than extreme conflict and contempt for one another. Reasons may include the increasing acceptance of divorce in U.S. society, idealistic beliefs about what they want marriage to be like, and a wide range of factors not related to profound conflict.

Another reason that ending a romantic relationship may not result in grief or a sense of loss is that an individual may instead experience pleasure from getting out of an extremely unsatisfying relationship. Others may experience relief upon escaping from a highly controlling partner, or one that is abusive or even violent. In such cases, the individual may have to cope with the ongoing psychological pain resulting from the suffering that occurred while in the relationship. However, grief itself may not be the primary emotions with which these individuals must cope.

# Sexuality Within Long-Term Committed Relationships

As discussed in the previous chapter, various theoretical approaches view love and sexuality as more or less related to one another. In terms of practical, real-world effects on the course of relationships, love and sexuality affect one another in profound ways. For many couples, significant levels of sex do not occur until their relationship has become fairly intimate and they feel they have strong commitment to the relationship (Christopher & Cate, 1985; Hill, 2002; Roche, 1986; Sprecher, 1989). Moreover, satisfaction with sexual aspects of a relationship overlaps a great deal with satisfaction with the relationship in general; consequently, the quality of sexuality within the relationship may be viewed as an important sign of, if not an important influence on, relationship quality overall.

## How Do Couples Signal Interest in Sex?

How do couples involved in romantic relationships initiate sex with one another? The traditional, stereotyped expectation for initiating sexual behavior at all stages of heterosexual relationships is that the man attempts to initiate sexual interaction; women are expected to respond to the overture with a positive reaction or a refusal (Cupach & Metts, 1991). This script is relevant to established or marital relationships as well as dating and developing relationships. However, women may actually play a more active role in initiating sexual behavior than the traditional stereotype would lead one to believe, particularly as time goes on. Women may signal an interest in sex in subtle ways, such as by talking suggestively, flirting, or creating a romantic situation. For example, they may play a type of music that the couple associates with being romantic or sexual, or watching a certain movie. In fact, the strategies of talking suggestively or behaving romantically probably represent the typical strategy used by men as well.

Little research has been conducted on initiation of sex within same-sex relationships. In one study (Blumstein & Schwartz, 1983), it was found that both partners in lesbian relationships tended to believe that they were the one in the relationship who more frequently refused to engage in sexual behavior. In contrast, both partners in gay male relationships believed that they were the one who *initiated* sex more often. This difference between lesbians and gay men may be related to gender-role issues, according to Rutter and Schwartz (1996). Lesbians tend to feel that initiation is a type of sexual aggression, which runs counter to the ideal of mutuality and equality within relationships that many lesbians embrace. At the same time, refusing to engage in sex is viewed as a woman's prerogative, an option that women have a right to. Both factors potentially contribute to a situation in lesbian relationships of relatively low levels of initiation attempts and high rates of declining the partner's attempts at initiation. In contrast, sexual initiation is strongly associated with the male role, such that both partners in gay male couples are more likely to report making attempts at initiating sex. This may be one factor related to the finding that gay male couples have the highest rates of sexual behavior, compared with heterosexual and lesbian couples.

Are individuals likely to just outright ask their partner for sex, or do they tend to hint around that they are interested in sex? Initiating sexual behavior seldom takes the form of a direct request, often because of concerns about embarrassment and fear of rejection (Cupach & Metts, 1991). Most initiation is likely to be subtle and indirect, to protect one's self-esteem and to recast the behavior as nonsexual in the face of rejection. Common subtle strategies include getting closer physically to one's romantic partner, kissing, hugging, stroking areas of the body that are not explicitly sexual, serving alcohol, and playing alluring music.

*Both partners in gay male relationships tend to report that they are the one who initiates sex more frequently, whereas both partners in lesbian relationships tend to report that they are the one who refuses sex more frequently.*

What about when a person is not interested in sex? Even in romantic relationships characterized by great sexual and relationship satisfaction, individuals will not always feel interested in engaging in sexual interaction precisely at the same time. This creates the situation in which one partner may refuse the other partner's sexual overtures. Yet, not wanting to have sex does not usually cause huge conflict or extremely hurt feelings in long-term relationships (Cupach & Metts, 1991). The reason is that expressing lack of interest on any particular occasion often takes the form of a direct verbal statement; in other words, the partner who is not interested simply states outright that he or she does not want to have sex at that time (Cupach & Metts, 1991).

Usually, however, the rejection includes some type of explanation that lets the partner who wants to have sex know that the refusal is not a lack of interest in general or a rejection of him or her personally. Such explanations may also express a sense of regard for the partner. Examples of such explanations are, "I'm sorry. I'm really too tired tonight. I've had such a rough day," and "I would really like to make love, but I must finish this work before tomorrow." Particularly constructive refusals may include the prospect of engaging in sex in the very near future (Cupach & Metts, 1991).

## The Sex Life of Couples

*It's true that the French have a certain obsession with sex, but it's a particularly adult obsession. France is the thriftiest of all nations; to a Frenchman sex provides the most economical way to have fun.*

Anita Loos, American Hollywood screenwriter and novelist, celebrated for her novel, *Gentlemen Prefer Blondes*, 1893–1981 (ThinkExist.com)

## How Much Sex Do Couples Usually Have?

Married heterosexual couples on average engage in sexual intercourse two to three times a week. A range of difference exists, however, in typical frequency. Approximately one-third of couples engage in sexual intercourse fewer than two times a week, one-third have sex two to three times a week, and another one-third engage in sexual intercourse more than three times a week (Michael, Gagnon, Laumann, & Kolata, 1994). Yet, heterosexual couples who are not married, but who cohabit (live together) engage in sex more frequently, even taking into account other factors such as age (Call, Sprecher, & Schwartz, 1995; Laumann, Gagnon, Michael, & Michaels, 1994; Rao & De Maris, 1995). Race, religion, and education are virtually unrelated to the frequency of sex (Laumann et al., 1994). Gay male couples engage in genital sex most frequently of all couples, whereas lesbian couples engage in genital sex the least frequently. Lesbian couples, however, may be most likely to engage in nongenital sexual behavior, such as caressing, rubbing, kissing, and hugging (Blumstein & Schwartz, 1983).

The amount of sexual behavior decreases with time for all couples. This may be true for at least two reasons: (a) decreases in physical and sexual functioning associated with aging and (b) the negative effects of extreme familiarity and predictability on sexual desire for the partner. The decreasing physical stamina and health-related problems that accompany aging may limit the ability of individuals to engage in some strenuous sexual activities. Moreover, if individuals become overly familiar with one another, and sex becomes routine or mundane, it is not unusual for the passion and allure of sexual behavior with a long-term partner to fade to some extent (Sprecher & Regan, 2000).

This typical decline in passion is the subject of a theoretical model proposed by Baumeister and Bratslavsky (1999), presented in Figure 10.2. The model suggests that passionate love may be explained as the result of sudden, intense *increases* in intimacy between people. If you remember from a previous section, intimacy is the sense that one is understood, respected, and appreciated by one's partner. It may be developed in an especially effective way, of course, through verbal self-disclosure—that is, by discussing feelings and desires with one's partner, particularly concerning very private and sensitive issues. In this way, partners' self-conceptions are likely to become more intertwined, and the partners become more important to one another. Positive feelings often result from such increases in mutual understanding, a highly pleasurable aspect of intimacy. Physical and sexual closeness, of course, are also a means of heightening intimacy between individuals.

As noted within the Baumeister and Bratslavsky model, relationship partners typically get to know one another more completely only very gradually over the course of their long-term relationship. As the couple settles into an exclusive relationship, they come to know each other so well that sudden revelations about the other partner become less frequent, and the intervening periods between such revelations become longer. This means that experiencing sudden increases in intimacy grows rarer over time. According to this model, because passion results from sudden increases in intimacy, the frequency of experiencing passion declines over time as well. In contrast, individuals involved in a relatively new relationship usually experience more frequent and intense episodes of passion early in the relationship. Because the couple is typically unfamiliar with most aspects of one another, partners are therefore likely to discover new information on a more frequent basis, bringing about frequent increases in intimacy. Remember that the Baumeister–Bratslavsky model predicts that sudden, profound increases in intimacy result in heightened levels of passion.

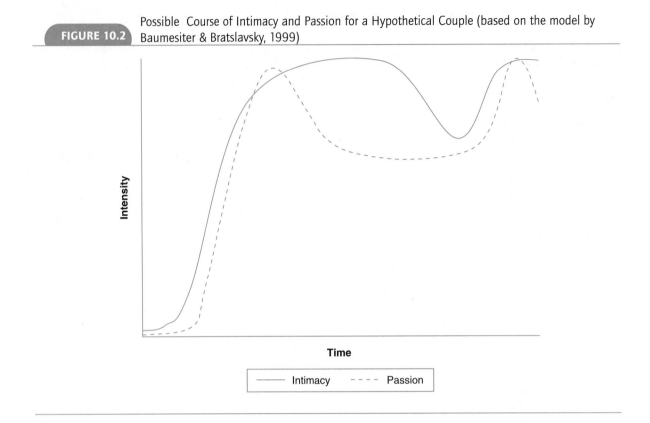

**FIGURE 10.2** Possible Course of Intimacy and Passion for a Hypothetical Couple (based on the model by Baumesiter & Bratslavsky, 1999)

The model therefore explains the reason that intense passion largely occurs early in romantic relationships; it also helps to understand the reason that long-standing, well-established relationships are usually characterized by high levels of intimacy and lower levels of passion. This view is strongly supported by social psychological research on romantic love in general: Passion occurs most frequently earlier in relationships.

Beyond this, the model suggests that couples in long-term relationships are likely to experience dramatically high levels of passion largely at times when they are reunited after being away from one another for a while. Upon returning from a trip, passion may be rekindled as the couple becomes "reacquainted." Even more surprising in a way, the emotional distance created by disagreement or conflict may also set the stage for a reunion of sorts, as long as the conflict is not too extreme. As individuals become reacquainted with one another, intimacy increases markedly, followed by a period of heightened passion. So, the notion that some people may "break up" just so they can "make up" may have a sound psychological basis to it.

### What Do Couples Do Sexually?

Heterosexual couples generally engage in a variety of sexual behaviors, ranging from kissing, exciting one another's bodies and genitals with their hands, oral–genital sex, penile–vaginal sex (inserting the penis in the partner's vagina), and penile–anal sex (inserting the penis in the partner's anus). Lesbians and gays likewise engage in a range of behaviors, including penile–anal sex for gay men.

Box 10.2                                                    **An Eye Toward Research**

### Does Companionate Love Flourish as Passionate Love Wanes?

A common view held by a number of social psychologists is that, for relationships that endure over time, as passionate love fades, companionate love takes its place and fuels emotional intimacy in the later years of the relationship. Consistent with the Baumeister and Bratslavsky (1999) model, feelings of passion and sexual behavior gradually decline over time. But, it is thought that couples stay together in relationships because they become more fulfilling as a couple becomes more like friends and companions; the idea is that they begin to look to one another to spend time together and share activities in the later years.

In fact, Traupmann and Hatfield (1981) conducted a study that looked at the course of both passionate love and companionate love. These researchers interviewed a random sample of dating couples, newlyweds, and older married women (married an average of 33 years, although the longest marriage was 59 years). Traupmann and Hatfield had expected that passionate love would fade over time, but that companionate love would remain strong or possibly grow.

As they expected, passionate love was substantially lower among the older married couples than for the dating and newly married couples. Much to their surprise, companionate love declined to some extent as well. The change was especially prominent for women because their feelings of companionate love was substantially greater among the newlyweds, but they were much lower among the older women. Men's feelings of companionate love were not too much greater among newlywed men compared with dating men and older men (based on the wives' perceptions of their husband's feelings; the older men were not actually interviewed).

This seems to indicate that, even among enduring marriages, companionate love declines along with feelings of passion. The researchers note that the group of older couples does not include individuals whose relationship had deteriorated completely and had separated. The perceptions of love would possibly be even lower if such couples had been included in the sample.

### References

Baumeister, R. F., & Bratslavsky, E. (1999). Passion, intimacy and time: Passionate love as a function of change in intimacy. *Personality and Social Psychology Review, 3,* 49–67.

Traupmann, J., & Hatfield, E. (1981). Love and its effect on mental and physical health. In R. Fogel, E. Hatfield, S. Kiesler, & E. Shanas (Eds.), *Aging: Stability and change in the family* (pp. 253–274). New York: Academic Press.

*What Sexual Behaviors Are Most Appealing?*

> *I prefer intercourse because during intercourse you get the idea that you're both thoroughly involved at the same time.*

> *An anonymous male (Hite, 2005, p. 63)*

Almost all heterosexual women and men, no matter their age, consider penile–vaginal intercourse to be the most appealing type of sexual behavior.

Some of the highest quality information available on sexuality in the United States is that collected in a large study called the National Health and Social Life Survey (Michael et al., 1994). Along with information about the frequency of behavior, data were also obtained regarding the types of sexual behavior considered most appealing to individuals. For both heterosexual women and men of all age groups, the most appealing sexual behavior is penile–vaginal intercourse; over 90% identified it as somewhat appealing or very appealing.

Yet, the meaning of penile–vaginal intercourse differs substantially for women and men. Women perceive vaginal intercourse as involving more of a mutual intimacy than other types of sexual behavior; it is seen as a sexual behavior in which both people are equally involved in the sharing of love and pleasure. Although high proportions of men consider vaginal intercourse to be an appealing type of sexual behavior, for men, vaginal intercourse is only one of a number of very desirable sexual behaviors (Sprecher & McKinney, 1993).

The second most appealing activity among heterosexual individuals for both sexes is watching one's partner undress; at least 67% of individuals rate this as somewhat or very appealing. Following this, receiving and giving oral–genital sex were considered appealing by somewhat lower proportions of heterosexuals. However, larger gender differences were found for oral–genital sex than for the two most appealing behaviors, penile–vaginal intercourse and watching one's partner undress, with men finding oral–genital sex more appealing than women. Similar to the finding for gender, greater variability was found across different age groups for oral–genital sex than the other two types of behavior (Michael et al., 1994).

### Do Many Heterosexuals Engage in Oral–Genital Sex and Penile–Anal Sex?

**Oral–Genital Sex.** Typically, more than 70% of women and men report that they have engaged in oral–genital sex (Billy, Tanfer, Grady, & Klepinger, 1993; Janus & Janus, 1993; Laumann et al., 1994). The proportion of college women and men who have both given and received oral sex is 80% or more (Elliot & Brantley, 1997). Proportions engaging in oral sex are greater among White individuals; 81% of White men say that they have performed oral sex, while 71% of Latino men and 51% of Black men indicate that they have (Laumann et al., 1994). The extent to which individuals have a positive view of their own genitals is very probably a factor underlying differences in comfort with oral–genital sex, and consequently the desire to engage in it (Reinholtz & Muehlenhard, 1995).

**Penile–Anal Intercourse.** Traditional stereotypes cast penile–anal intercourse as a sexual behavior in which only gay males engage. Despite this belief, research actually suggests that a substantial proportion of heterosexual individuals (around 10%) have engaged in penile–anal intercourse in the past year (Laumann et al., 1994). Even greater proportions have engaged in anal intercourse at least once, with several studies revealing that around 20% of both women and men have engaged in anal intercourse (Kotloff et al., 1991; Lottes, 1993; Michael et al., 1994; Reinisch, Hill, Sanders, & Ziemba-Davis, 1995; Reinisch, Sanders, Hill, & Ziemba-Davis, 1992; Reinisch, Sanders, & Ziemba-Davis, 1988). One random probability of heterosexual students at Indiana University revealed that 69% of males and 49% of females who had engaged in penile–anal intercourse at least once had done so in the previous year; furthermore, 25% of males and 16% of females who had engaged in penile–anal intercourse at least once had done so in the previous month (Reinisch et al., 1995).

### Sexual Behavior Among Lesbians, Gay Men, and Bisexual Individuals

For lesbians, stimulation of one another's genitals with fingers and inserting fingers into the vagina are two of the most common types of sexual behavior. Cunnilingus, stimulating the vulva with one's tongue and lips, is the most preferred activity for stimulating a woman to orgasm (Schureurs, 1993). However, a wide range of sexual behaviors are considered extremely enjoyable, including caressing breasts, deep kissing, and cuddling (Lever, 1995). Similar types of behavior are viewed as favorite activities by gay men (Lever, 1994).

In the National Opinion Research Center national survey (Laumann et al., 1994), more than 90% of women who identified as lesbian or bisexual reported both giving and receiving oral–genital sex. The rate was lower for heterosexual women; 67% reported giving oral sex and 73% reported receiving it.

Oral–genital sex is one of the most prevalent types of sexual behavior among gay men, in addition to stroking and caressing the body and genitals; 90% of gay men report engaging in oral–genital sex. Penile–anal intercourse is also a sexual behavior in which substantial proportions of gay men engage, although not at the levels of other types of sexual behavior (Elliot & Brantley, 1997; Kippax & Smith, 2001; Laumann et al., 1994). Among those who identify as gay, 75% of gay men report engaging in anal sex in the insertive role, and 81% report engaging in anal sex in the receiving role (Laumann et al., 1994). Among gay male couples, approximately a third report engaging in anal sex in which partners always take the same role; another third report engaging in both the insertive and receiving roles; and the last third report never engaging in anal sex (Lever, 1994).

*What do you think are the most common types of sexual behaviors in which lesbian couples engage? What about gay male couples?*

## How Often Do Married Heterosexuals Engage in the Various Sexual Behaviors?

One study in particular (Hurlbert, Apt, & Rabehl, 1993) provides insight into the frequency of various sexual behaviors among married heterosexual couples. Information was obtained from 161 married women who recorded all sexual behavior with their husbands in a diary over a 21-day period. The proportion of episodes involving each behavior is presented in Table 10.1. Virtually all of the sexual episodes involved penile–vaginal intercourse (98.5%), whereas other types of sexual behavior occurred in only a minority of the episodes.

**TABLE 10.1** Proportions of Sexual Episodes Involving Various Types of Sexual Behavior for Married Heterosexual Women and Men Over a 21-Day Period

| Sexual behavior | Proportion |
|---|---|
| Penile–vaginal intercourse | 98.5% |
| Fellatio | 46.3% |
| Cunnilingus | 32.2% |
| Woman masturbating herself | 17.4% |
| Man masturbating the woman | 5.3% |
| Penile–anal intercourse | 1.3% |

From Hurlbert, Apt, & Rabehl, 1993

Sexual behavior involving the wife masturbating the husband, as well as sexual behavior in which the man masturbated himself, were both not frequent at all. Giving and receiving oral–genital sex were a distant second and third after penile–vaginal intercourse.

According to reports provided by the wives, men experienced orgasm during penile–vaginal intercourse 96.8% of the time, whereas women experienced orgasm only 25.2% of the time. As noted by the researchers (Hurlbert et al., 1993), lack of orgasm is a typical occurrence for women, given that penile–vaginal intercourse is the most frequent behavior within heterosexual sexuality; penile–vaginal intercourse does not always provide the type of pleasurable stimulation that enables women to climax. This low frequency of orgasm is a finding that is consistent with reports by other researchers as well (Kaplan, 1979; LoPiccolo & Stock, 1986).

In contrast, orgasm was experienced by women 82.6% of the time when their husbands masturbated them, and 81.4% of the time when men engaged in cunnilingus with them. Directly stimulating the vulva, whether orally or by hand, appears to be the primary source of physical pleasure leading to orgasm for women. Importantly, it is not the sheer number of orgasms that women experience over a certain amount of time that relates to sexual satisfaction for women. Rather, it is the proportion of orgasms women have—that is, the consistency of experiencing orgasms when engaging in sexual behavior—that significantly contributes to sexual satisfaction (Hurlbert et al., 1993).

## How Happy With Their Sex Lives Are People in Relationships?

Regardless of the frequency of sexual behavior within relationships, the vast majority of individuals express a great deal of satisfaction with their sexual relationships. Even those having sex relatively infrequently feel very satisfied with the sexual aspects of their relationship. For example, in the National Opinion Research Center survey, 88% percent of married couples report great physical satisfaction and 85% report great emotional satisfaction with the sexual aspects of their relationship (Michael et al., 1994).

### Are People Who Have Sex More Often More Satisfied?

Despite the relatively high level of satisfaction reported by most couples, the frequency of sexual interaction is nonetheless positively associated with satisfaction in general with the relationship (Blumstein & Schwartz,

1983; Call et al., 1995; Donnelly, 1993); this means that more frequent sex is linked to greater happiness in the relationship. Given the lack of studies that follow couples over time, however, it is virtually impossible to determine the causal direction of the link between sexual frequency and satisfaction; that is, it is not possible to tell whether frequent sex leads to greater satisfaction, or whether being satisfied causes individuals to engage in sex more frequently. Not knowing what factors are the causes and which ones are the outcomes is essentially the situation for all factors linked to relationship satisfaction and sexual satisfaction (Sprecher & Regan, 2000).

Actually, it may be that all three factors affect one another mutually, as depicted in Pattern A of Figure 10.3. An alternative possibility is that engaging in frequent sexual behavior produces greater satisfaction, a relationship presented in Pattern B. However, it may also be that couples who are more satisfied are also more interested in engaging in sex with one another and therefore do so more frequently (Pattern C); in contrast, individuals who are unhappy may not be motivated to have sexual contact with their relationship partner as much. Sprecher and Regan (2000) also note that frequency of sex is not as strongly related to relationship satisfaction for lesbian couples as other types of couples (Blumstein & Schwartz, 1983).

Despite the link between frequency of sexual behavior and satisfaction, the *quality* of sexual interaction (i.e., sexual satisfaction) may be more directly associated with general relationship quality (Sprecher & Regan, 2000). Specifically, sexual satisfaction is often more strongly related to general relationship satisfaction than

**FIGURE 10.3**  Possible Patterns of Relationship Among Frequency of Sexual Behavior, Sexual Satisfaction, and Relationship Satisfaction

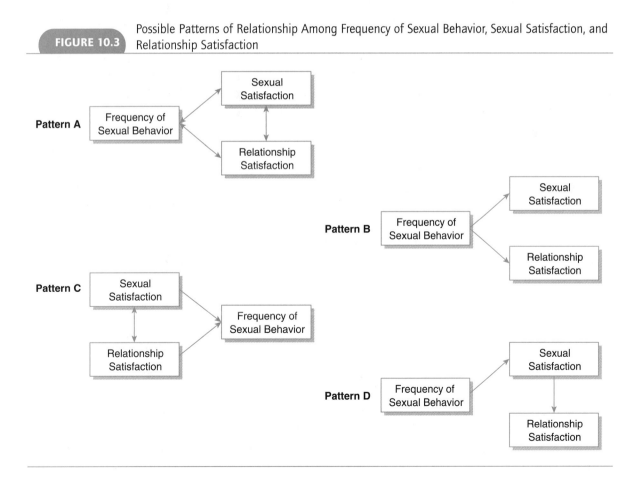

is frequency of sexual behavior (Cupach & Comstock, 1990; Edwards & Booth, 1994; Greeley, 1991; Henderson-King & Veroff, 1994; Kurdeck, 1991; Lawrance & Byers, 1995; Oggins, Leber, & Veroff, 1993). This means that a man or a woman who is happy with his or her relationship will probably feel happy with the sexual aspect of the relationship, even if sex does not happen all that often. In addition, sexual satisfaction appears to be as important to relationship satisfaction for women as for men; actually, marital happiness is related to more aspects of sexual satisfaction for women than men (Henderson-King & Veroff, 1994).

In addition, sexual satisfaction tends to be critical in explaining the link between frequency of sexual behavior and relationship satisfaction; this is demonstrated by the fact that frequency is not significantly related to relationship satisfaction if sexual satisfaction is controlled for statistically (Greeley, 1991). This finding suggests that sexual frequency is only indirectly correlated with relationship satisfaction through its relationship with sexual satisfaction. It is possible, for example, that higher frequency results in greater sexual satisfaction, which in turn increases relationship satisfaction (Figure 10.3 Pattern D). Even so, this explanation is really speculation because, as stated previously, it is not possible to determine the exact direction of causality in most studies.

### Does Sexual Happiness Beget Relationship Happiness—and Vice Versa?

Some theorists have suggested that the most realistic view is that both types of satisfaction—general satisfaction with the relationship and satisfaction with sexual aspects of the relationship—affect each other (consistent with Pattern A in Figure 10.3). Support for this idea comes from comparisons among groups of married couples who varied in terms of relationship satisfaction and sexual satisfaction (Hurlbert & Apt, 1994). Husbands who were both maritally and sexually dissatisfied reported not being as interested in the sexual behavior in which they had engaged in the prior 24 hours in comparison to husbands who were satisfied *either* sexually or maritally. Wives who were maritally dissatisfied, regardless of their sexual satisfaction, reported less initial interest in the sexual behavior they had experienced in the previous 24 hours; furthermore, they reported less arousal during the sexual behavior.

Hulbert and Apt viewed this as pointing to the more pervasive importance of relationship quality in determining sexual satisfaction for women than the actual quality of the sexual behavior itself (this suggests yet another pattern beyond those presented in Figure 10.3). As long as the marriage overall is satisfying, women are more likely to be interested in engaging in sex with their husbands, even if they are not satisfied sexually overall. For men, being satisfied with either the general relationship or with sexual aspects of the relationship leads to interest in engaging in sex with their partner. Despite differences in interest in engaging in sexual behavior, women's relationship and sexual satisfaction levels were unrelated to the frequency of sexual activity within the marriage. This suggests that frequency is more strongly determined by the man in the relationship, given that women's sexual interest is not correlated with frequency.

### Do Some Types of Sexual Behavior Lead to Greater Sexual Satisfaction?

The type of sexual behavior in which heterosexual couples engage is in fact related to relationship and sexual satisfaction. In the Hurlbert and Apt (1994) study, women indicating high levels of sexual satisfaction were more likely to have experienced cunnilingus—stimulating the vulva with the partner's tongue and lips. The most satisfied women were also the least likely to have masturbated their husband to orgasm. The greater sexual satisfaction may reflect the fact that cunnilingus is the most enjoyable method leading to orgasm for women (Hurlbert & Whittaker, 1991); therefore, it is likely that experiencing cunnilingus relatively more frequently contributes to women's greater overall sexual satisfaction. These findings also suggest that a man who is willing to focus more on his partner's stimulation (cunninlingus), and apparently less on his own (being masturbated by the partner), is more likely to have a sexually satisfied partner.

Actually, as stated previously, it is not the absolute number of times women experience orgasm in a particular time period that is important to sexual satisfaction; rather, it is the consistency of experiencing orgasm, or the proportion of times that women experience orgasm when engaging in sexual behavior with a partner (Hurlbert et al., 1993). Timing of orgasm is important to the sexual satisfaction of women, as well; experiencing orgasm before or at the same time as the partner contributes to sexual satisfaction (Darling, Davidson, & Cox, 1991). In fact, women who were either satisfied sexually or with the relationship in general were more likely to experience orgasm during sex with their partner (Hurlbert et al., 1993). In addition, sexually satisfied women were more likely to report adequate levels of foreplay, a finding consistent with other research (Davidson & Darling, 1988; Hurlbert, 1993; Hurlbert et al., 1993).

In the Hurlbert and colleagues (1993) study, women who were more satisfied with their relationship in general were more likely to have performed fellatio—stimulating their husband's penis with their mouth—than those who were not very satis-

A heterosexual man who focuses on his partner's sexual stimulation, such as by orally stimulating her vulva, is more likely to have a sexually satisfied partner.

fied with their relationship. Hurlbert and Apt (1994) speculated that, because of the particularly intimate nature of oral–genital sex, those who feel emotionally intimate and comfortable enough with their partner may be the ones who are largely willing to engage in it.

Perhaps surprisingly, fellatio was considerably less likely to result in orgasm for men in their study conducted over a 21-day period (Hurlbert et al., 1993) —only 23.4% of the time fellatio was performed—compared with the proportion of times orgasm occurred during penile–vaginal intercourse (96.8% of the time). This may reflect the attitude that heterosexual men have regarding oral–genital sex, that it is only one aspect of foreplay leading up to penile–vaginal intercourse. That is, orgasm is "saved" for "real sex." The possibility that most heterosexual men and women view penile–vaginal intercourse as the most desirable behavior in which to orgasm is supported by research on perceptions of sexual behavior. Roughly 60% of both men and women do not consider themselves to have engaged sex if they had experienced oral–genital sex (the question was, "Would you say you 'had sex' if you engaged in oral–genital sex"; Sanders & Reinisch, 1999).

### Do Some People Enjoy the Sex They Have More Than Others?

The answer is definitely *yes*! Even more important to sexual satisfaction than types of sexual behavior appears to be personality and relationship attributes (Hurlbert et al., 1993). The factor most strongly related to sexual satisfaction for women in the study by Hurlbert and his colleagues was the reported closeness of the relationship with their partner (the degree to which one interacts frequently with one's partner and is affected by one's partner). Other factors independently related to sexual satisfaction were the personality characteristics of sexual assertiveness (the tendency to take the initiative in making sure one's sexual needs are fulfilled) and erotophilia (the tendency to have positive emotional reactions to sexual situations and issues).

In fact, erotophilia may play a central role in sexual satisfaction, not only at the level of the individual, but also in terms of the similarity of heterosexual couples with respect to erotophilia. One study by Smith, Becker, Byrne, and Przybyla (1993) found that married couples tend to be very similar in their erotophilia. Greater dissimilarity in erotophilia among couples apparently results in misunderstanding the partner's likes and dislikes sexually, as well as being associated with sexual dissatisfaction and relationship difficulties. In addition, erotophobia (negative reactions to sexual situations and issues) in either partner is related to greater misperception, dissatisfaction, and difficulty, although the erotophobia of the woman is more consistently related to these negative outcomes.

Individuals who are more strongly erotophilic tend to feel positively about their own and their partner's sexual pleasure, as well as having a more accurate understanding of the partner's desires. The greater importance of women's reactions suggested to the researchers that the stereotype of the man as the sexual initiator and women as the regulator, or "gatekeeper" is accurate, even within marriage. If the woman holds negative views of sexuality, the couple tends to have less positive experiences with sexual behavior. Similar results were obtained in a study by Cupach and Metts (1995) related to the attitude of sexual avoidance, a dimension like that of erotophobia.

### What Have You Done for Me Lately? Keep the Good Times Coming

A recent way to conceive of sexual satisfaction is based on an extension of the social exchange model discussed earlier in the chapter. This theoretical view is entitled the Interpersonal Exchange Model of Sexual Satisfaction (Lawrance & Byers, 1995). The model proposes that sexual satisfaction is determined as a function of (a) greater relationship satisfaction; (b) high levels of rewards relative to low levels of costs in one's sexual relationship; (c) the difference between rewards and costs exceeding the rewards that one believes should be obtained in relationships; and, finally, (d) the degree of equality between one's own rewards and those of one's partner, as well as the equality of one's own costs relative to the partner's costs.

Research has demonstrated that each of these components contribute uniquely to sexual satisfaction in short-term heterosexual dating relationships (Byers, Demmons, & Lawrance, 1998), as well as in long-term heterosexual relationships (Lawrance & Byers, 1995). Moreover, a tremendous portion of the differences in sexual satisfaction among couples (79%) was explained by these factors. This model accounts for sexual satisfaction just as well for both women and men. This means that one's own sexual happiness is related not only to having a lot of positive sexual experiences and very few negative experiences oneself, but also that this is true as well for one's sexual partner.

### Do Couples Who Are Sexually Satisfied Stay Together?

As discussed previously, sexual satisfaction has been found to relate strongly to general relationship satisfaction, and to psychological well-being (Edwards & Booth, 1994). Moreover, the strength of the association appears to remain fairly constant over time, at least over the first several years of relationships (Henderson-King & Veroff, 1994). Evidence further indicates that being sexually unhappy predicts marital breakup as much as 8 years later (Edwards & Booth, 1994; Oggins et al., 1993; White & Keith, 1990).

Sexual satisfaction is related to relationship satisfaction, love, and commitment for dating couples as well (Sprecher, 2002), consistent with the finding for married couples. In addition, lower sexual satisfaction increases the chances of breaking up later on, a finding supported by other studies examining the importance of sexual satisfaction (Felmlee, Sprecher, & Bassin, 1990; Simpson, 1987).

However, the relationship between sexual satisfaction and later relationship breakup was not statistically significant for women in the study by Sprecher (2002). Instead, lower levels of *general* relationship satisfaction predicted later relationship breakup for women, which was not the case for men. Sprecher speculated that men may tend to rely on the quality of sexual aspects of a romantic relationship as a basis for judging the entire quality of the relationship. In contrast, it appears that women do not consider sexual satisfaction to any great extent, if at all, in evaluating whether it is worth remaining in the relationship. This type of gender difference has not been found for established or marital relationships; instead, sexual satisfaction tends to be important to both women and men in long-term relationships. The bottom line is that individuals often view sexual incompatibility and sexual difficulties as at least moderately important factors when their marriage or romantic relationships end (Sprecher & Regan, 2000).

## Sexuality Outside of Traditional Relationships

*If a man continually changes the women with whom he has intercourse, the benefit will be great. If in one night he can have intercourse with more than 10 women it is best.*

Yū- fang-pi-chūch, in the writing, *I-shin-fang* ( c. 600, quoted in Cassell Publishers Limited, 1993, p. 200)

*The nude embrace comes to be respected more and more, and finally reverenced, as a pure and beautiful approach to the sacred moment when husband and wife shall melt into one another's genital embrace, so that the twain shall be one flesh, and then, as of old, God will walk with the twain in the garden of bliss "in the cool of the day" when the heat of ill-regulated passion is no more.*

Ida Craddock. *Right Marital Living*, 1899 (quoted in Cassell Publishers Limited, 1993, p. 133)

As we have seen, sexual behavior very frequently occurs within relatively established romantic relationships. The chances of engaging in sex for the first time with a person are greater with increasing emotional intimacy and love. Nonetheless, some proportion of sexual behavior occurs outside of loving, committed relationships, or even outside of any prior relationship at all. An important question, then, is what factors lead people to have sex when they are not involved in an intimate relationship with one another.

### Casual Sex

*One night at the club with my friends, I saw this very sexy girl. I noticed she was eyeing me for a bit. So, I walked up to her. I wanted to start with small talk but instead she pulled me into the bathroom and started stripping. I said, "Wow!" ... Then I stripped. She started rubbing me, and I gave her oral. All I can say is that we had explosive sex. We went to her house and started having explosive sex again! (Brad, 23, Explosive Sex—Brad, Netscape Men's Confessions)*

**Casual sex** is sexual behavior that occurs when individuals do not feel any great emotional intimacy for one another; furthermore, the individuals have no real expectation of becoming involved in a romantic love relationship (Paul, McManus, & Hayes, 2000; Winslow, Franzini, & Hwang, 1992). Hardly any research has been conducted on casual sex, and very little theoretical understanding has been developed for the issue. In fact, researchers have often used different terms to talk about the topic and have examined it in different ways (Herold, Maticka-Tyndale, & Mewhinney, 1998; Paul et al., 2000). In some cases, they have focused on **one-night stands**; these are sexual encounter that take place on only one occasion and never again. Other researchers have focused on a broader array of sexual episodes: from occasional sexual behavior with someone with no special emotional significance ranging to unplanned sexual behavior with an unacquainted person (Winslow et al., 1992).

A relatively new phenomenon popular on U.S. college campuses is the **hookup**. This is "a sexual encounter, usually lasting only one night, between two people who are strangers or brief acquaintances. Some physical sexual interaction is typical, but it may or may not include sexual intercourse" (Paul et al., 2000, p. 76). The specific sexual encounter is usually spontaneous and unplanned; yet, the general desire to hook up with someone on a particular evening exists before the encounter occurs. Also, the individuals intend for the episode to remain fairly anonymous because no further interaction, and certainly not even a dating relationship, is the goal.

In addition to the recent trend in hooking up, another feature of school life contributes to the tendency of a significant minority of students to engage in casual sex. This phenomenon is the annual Spring Break trip taken to beachside vacation spots by a multitude of college students from both the United States and Canada. A similar phenomenon in Australia is the mass migration of thousands of upper-level high school students or graduates to the Australian Gold Coast in late November and early December (Maticka-Tyndale, Herold, & Oppermann, 2003; Rosenthal & Smith, 1997); these vacationing students are known as "schoolies."

Maticka-Tyndale, Herold, and Mewhinney (1998) examined intentions students held prior to the trip related to engaging in sex during Spring Break; they also looked at the actual occurrence of sexual behavior during the vacation. Fifty-five percent of men in a group of Canadian students recruited at a Florida resort area planned to have sex while they were there, whereas only 11% of women planned to do so. In fact, 30% of men had made a pact with their friends to engage in casual sex; merely 5% of women made such a pledge with their friends. In contrast, 21% of the women had made a pact *not* to engage in casual sex, whereas only 5% of men vowed not to have casual sex. In terms of actual behavior, however, only 15% of males and 13% of females actually did engage in casual sex with someone they met on vacation; this means that men and women were not really different in the proportions who had sex. Of those who did engage in casual sex, 68% did so with only one partner, 13% had two partners, and 19% had more than two partners.

The factors that were most strongly related to whether casual sex took place were, for women, the formation of a pact with friends and having others who served as role models related to engaging in sex; social factors were therefore very influential for women. In contrast, peers had no direct effect on the occurrence of sex for men. Rather, peer attitudes only affected having the intention to engage in sex prior to leaving for Spring Break, which was the strongest factor related to casual sex for men.

The phenomenon of 17- and 18- year-old Australian high school students swarming to coastal areas produces similar opportunities for substantial levels of casual sexual behavior. Prior to the "schoolie week" vacation, almost two-thirds of the men and one-third of the women who were sexually experienced in the sample had engaged in sex with a new partner within 24 hours of meeting the individual, one possible definition of

Box 10.3

An Eye Toward Research

## How Common Is Hooking Up?

This question was addressed in a study by Paul and her colleagues (Paul, McManus, & Hayes, 2000). In a random sample of 555 students at an Eastern university, they found that 48% of college students had engaged in at least one hookup that did not involve penile–vaginal intercourse, 30% of the college students had at least one hookup involving penile–vaginal intercourse, and a small minority, 22%, had not engaged in even one hookup. Those who had experienced a hookup either with or without penile–vaginal intercourse had on average 10.8 hookups overall. The number of episodes in a given year ranged from 0–65 hookups, suggesting that some college students hook up on a weekly basis. Women and men were equally likely to engage in hookups overall. However, greater proportions of men (48%) had engaged in penile–vaginal intercourse during the hookup compared with 33% of women.

The majority of students did not see their hookup partner again in the future, and only 12% began a romantic relationship after the episode. The average length of the subsequent relationship was four months, making it clear that casual encounters of this type do not provide a very substantial basis for forging a long-term relationship. The vast majority of these sexual episodes, however, proved to be casual and for all purposes anonymous, given that people generally did not interact with their hookup partners in any meaningful way after they occurred. An overwhelming proportion of those who had engaged in penile–vaginal intercourse reported using a condom (81%), which provides protection from sexually transmitted disease as well as unwanted pregnancy. Other forms of birth control were used by 25% of the college students.

Personality characteristics were related to the tendency to engage in hooking up, indicating that some types of individuals are more likely to engage in casual sex than others. College students who had greater involvement in hooking up were more likely to have the following characteristics: (a) lower self-esteem; (b) greater tendency to engage in dramatic, entertaining behavior and to be the center of attention (a trait called **exhibitionism**); (c) less likely to have a secure attachment style (discussed in the previous chapter on theories of romantic love); and (d) greater levels of some types of the fear of intimacy (Paul et al., 2000).

### Reference

Paul, E. L., McManus, B., & Hayes, A. (2000). "Hookups": Characteristics and correlates of college students' spontaneous and anonymous sexual experiences. *The Journal of Sex Research, 37,* 76–88.

casual sex. During the "schoolie week" vacation itself, 34.5% of the men and 23.6% of the women reported engaging in sexual intercourse. Women were as likely to have engaged in sex with someone they knew or had dated (12.6%) as they were to have engaged in sex with a new or casual partner (11%). Men, however, were much more likely to have sex with a new or casual partner (24.8%) than to have sex with someone they knew or had dated (9.8%).

The two same social factors identified in the Canadian college study were also the major influence on the sexual behavior of women in high school, (a) making a pact not to engage in casual sex and (b) having role models related to sex. The results of this study for men were different from those for Canadian college men, however; in that study, social influences did not have a direct effect on sexual behavior. In the "schoolie study," in contrast, role models did affect the likelihood of engaging in casual sex for the high school men (Maticka-Tyndale et al., 2003).

A common factor is obvious in all of the environments that lead to high rates of casual sex, whether considering hooking up, Spring Break vacations, or holiday trips. The underlying factor is a highly positive attitude toward sexuality, and casual sex in particular. This attitude is promoted by the atmosphere of continual partying, heavy consumption of alcohol, frequent contests promoting partial or complete nudity, and provocative dancing. Hooking up in particular typically takes place in the context of going out to bars and nightclubs, which likewise encourages the more sensual, entertainment-focused environment. The norms prevalent in these uninhibited settings promote the sense that casual sex is not only acceptable, but also very desirable.

## Extradyadic Relationships

*I was working in a bank and there was this sexy coworker whom I always had an eye on. One day, she seemed stressed out over her husband's drinking and wasting money. She wanted to know how to stop him from making long distance calls, which were bringing up a huge bill every month. So, I just asked her out for lunch. During lunch, I made plans for a movie during the weekend and she readily agreed. In the movie, I held her hand and kissed her, and then got a room in a motel. We had sex. She was very satisfied and I was too. This went on for a few months and it was fun while it lasted. (Cole, 30, Affair With a Co-Worker, Netscape Men's Confessions).*

Extradyadic relationships are romantic or sexual involvements with people other than an individual's spouse or primary romantic partner. A dyad is a term referring to two people who are involved in an interaction or a relationship, that is, a couple. The word, *extradyadic,* means *outside of the dyad,* and therefore refers to relationships with individuals other than with one's primary romantic partner. The primary relationship is the one established before one of the partners became involved in a relationship with a third person. The term, *extramarital,* specifically refers to relationships with others besides one's marriage partner. *Extradyadic* includes not only those who are married, but also those who are not married but who are involved in a long-term romantic relationship. Therefore, it is relevant to lesbian and gay couples involved in romantic relationships, as well as heterosexual couples who have not decided to marry, but who are cohabiting, or living together.

A basic assumption underlying views of extradyadic relationships is that couples intend to be "faithful." This means that the individuals in the primary relationship are

*Do you know of someone who has been involved in a sexual affair while also being involved in a romantic relationship or marriage? How common do you think sexual affairs are?*

committed to being emotionally and sexually exclusive—that is, they will be intimate only with one another. The commitment to exclusiveness is usually formalized through legal marriage. However, couples who do not marry, or cannot marry, may have such a commitment, whether by discussing it explicitly or by assuming exclusiveness because it is implied in Western cultures by having intense romantic intimacy. For these reasons, involvement in a relationship with someone other than one's primary relationship partner is considered to be an extremely grave, catastrophic violation of trust and loyalty. Consequently, descriptors such as *unfaithfulness, infidelity,* and *cheating* are typically used to refer to extradyadic relationships (Buunk & Dijkstra, 2000).

The severity of the offense is revealed by the fact that 77% of participants in a U.S. probability study reported that adultery is always wrong (Laumann et al., 1994), although some individuals have more permissive attitudes than others. Furthermore, extradyadic relationships often create a profound danger for the stability of the primary relationship (Buunk & Dijkstra, 2000). Extramarital affairs are a strong factor in divorce across a number of cultures (Betzing, 1989), although they are seldom the most common reason for divorces (Burns, 1984). However, empirical research has not been conducted to establish the exact likelihood that extramarital relationships lead to divorce. Buunk (1987) has proposed that extramarital involvement is more likely to result in divorce if the basis for the affair is unhappiness with the primary relationship.

## The Different Faces of Sexual Affairs

*'Tis the established custom in Vienna for every lady to have two husbands, one that bears the name, and another that performs the duties.*

Lady Mary Wortley Montague, letter to a friend [1716] (Cassell Publishers Limited, 1993, p. 8)

Distinctions have been made among types of extradyadic involvement based on the meaning of the relationship to the individuals (Morgan, 2004). Lawson (1988) identified three types: (a) parallel, (b) traditional, and (c) recreational. The *traditional extradyadic relationship* exists without the knowledge of the primary relationship partner and extends beyond one or two sexual encounters. A *parallel extradyadic relationship* is one that exists relatively openly alongside the primary relationship. A *recreational extradyadic relationship* is one that occurs very briefly for the pleasure and excitement of the sexual affair, possibly enhanced by the danger of discovery.

In a review of what they term *infidelity,* Blow and Hartnett (2005) identify other conceptual frameworks that suggest different types of extradyadic relationships, such as one-night stands, emotional relationships, long-term relationships, and philandering. However, they conclude that insufficient research has been conducted on these various conceptualizations to be confident about their accuracy. They note that some evidence exists for distinctions based on the degree of emotional involvement and sexual involvement (Glass & Wright, 1985; Thompson, 1984). This view suggests that some extradyadic relationships may be largely emotional in nature, some may be largely sexual, and others may be equally emotional and sexual. Blow and Hartnett (2005) also note that each of these types may take the form of more specific types such as Internet or telephone relationships, work-related relationships, sex with sex-workers, and same-sex relationships.

## How Common Are Sexual Affairs?

Fairly reliable data have been collected regarding extradyadic sexual intercourse among heterosexual couples when based on national probability studies (Blow & Hartnett, 2005); these studies include Atkins, Baucom, and Jacobson (2001); Forste and Tanfer (1996); Laumann and colleagues (1994); and Wiederman (1997). According to Forste and Tanfer (1996), at most 25% of men and 20% of women have ever engaged in extradyadic sexual behavior. The lowest proportions of women to have engaged in extradyadic sex are married women (4%), with greater proportions of dating women (18%) and cohabiting women (20%) having done so. Very low proportions of both men and women, approximately 4% or fewer, depending on the particular study, have engaged in extradyadic sex during the previous year in which the study occurred.

However, Harvey and Weber (2002) have noted that "the percentage of women having affairs [is] generally estimated to be between 25 to 50%, and between 50 to 65% for men" (p. 184). The difference in estimates of the frequency of extradyadic sex is probably due to differences in studies on which they are based. The studies differ in the methods used to collect data and the nature of the samples included in the studies.

### Do Men or Women Have Sexual Affairs More Often?

> *I'm glad you like my Catherine. I like her too. She ruled thirty million people and had three thousand lovers. I do the best I can in two hours.*
>
> Mae West in a speech from the stage after her performance in *Catherine the Great*
> (Cassell Publishers Limited, 1993, p. 198)

A simple, straightforward conclusion about whether men or women engage in extradyadic relationships at greater levels is not possible, because of variability of age, primary relationship type, and type of extradyadic relationship for women versus men included in studies. Authors of a number of studies have decisively concluded that more men have engaged in extradyadic sex, have more extradyadic partners, have more permissive attitudes about extradyadic sex, and have greater interest in extradyadic sex. On the basis of a review of the available studies (Blow & Hartnett, 2005), however, other researchers have argued that women and men are fairly similar and are becoming even more similar.

Women have been found to value emotional bonding in extradyadic relationships to a greater extent than men, as well as to experience greater levels of emotional involvement. Women are also more likely to fall in love with their extradyadic partner than men, who view their extradyadic partners more as close friends (Blow & Hartnett, 2005). On average, men are more interested in the sexual experience of extradyadic relationships, and to engage in more physically intimate behavior than women (Glass & Wright, 1985). Lesbians tend to have fewer extradyadic partners than gay men, who seek more sexual variety (Blumstein & Schwartz, 1983).

### What Qualities of Relationships Are Associated With Sexual Affairs

**General Satisfaction With the Primary Relationship.** As identified in the review of research on infidelity by Blow and Hartnett (2005), several studies have found that unhappiness with the primary relationship is linked to greater levels of extradyadic sexual behavior (Atkins et al., 2001; Glass & Wright, 1985), as well as greater interest in extradyadic sex (Prins, Buunk, & Van Yperen, 1993). Women who are dissatisfied with their primary relationship are especially likely to engage in extradyadic sex (Prins et al., 1993; Wiggins & Lederer, 1984). One study found that individuals who became involved in an extradyadic relationship with a coworker were more satisfied with their primary relationship than those who became involved in an extradyadic relationship with someone who was not a coworker. This suggests that coworker relationships may occur because of the opportunity that results from the availability of a desirable coworker, rather than because individuals are seeking outside relationships (Spanier & Margolis, 1983). In fact, statistical analyses have shown that characteristics of the primary relationship only account for approximately 25% of the difference between individuals who engage in extradyadic sex and those who do not (Thompson, 1983).

Sexual Satisfaction With the Primary Relationship. Several large studies indicate that less sexual satisfaction is linked to a greater likelihood of engaging in extradyadic sex (Blow & Hartnett, 2005). Both lower quality and lower frequency of sexual interaction within primary relationships appear to be related (Liu, 2000). This association may be primarily true for men (Liu, 2000), and largely for African Americans and Hispanic men with lower levels of sexual communication ability (Choi, Catania, & Dolcini, 1994).

Duration of the Primary Relationship. The association between the length of time individuals have been in a primary relationship and the likelihood of engaging in extradyadic sex is dramatically different for women and men (Blow & Hartnett, 2005). The probability that married and cohabiting women will engage in extradyadic sex steadily increases with the duration of the primary relationship (Forste & Tanfer, 1996) and peaks at 7 years (Liu, 2000). This association may also be true for women in dating relationships (Forste & Tanfer, 1996), although not all studies have found a correlation (Hansen, 1987). The pattern for married men is reversed, in that duration of the primary relationship is related to less likelihood of engaging in extradyadic sex until about the 18th year of marriage; after this point, the probability rises (Liu, 2000). Men in dating relationships are more likely to engage in extradyadic sex the longer they have been involved in the relationship (Hansen, 1987).

Another relationship factor that is associated with extradyadic sex is the age at which individuals begin a primary relationship. Younger age is related to greater likelihood of extradyadic involvement (Amato & Rogers, 1997; Atkins et al., 2001).

## What Characteristics of the Person Are Associated With Sexual Affairs?

Evidence suggests that stronger interest in sex (Liu, 2000; Treas & Giesen, 2000), greater numbers of sexual partners before the first long-term romantic relationship (Forste & Tanfer, 1996; Treas & Giesen, 2000), and more liberal sexual attitudes for women (Hansen, 1987) are all characteristics related to greater chances of extradyadic sex. Divorce of one's parents (Amato & Rogers, 1997), as well as being divorced (Atkins et al., 2001; Wiederman, 1997), separated (Wiederman, 1997), and remarried (Christopher & Sprecher, 2000) oneself, substantially increases the likelihood that individuals will engage in extradyadic relationships.

Finally, attachment style is linked to greater chances of extradyadic sex (Blow & Hartnett, 2005). Two studies have found that an anxious attachment style (also called preoccupied attachment style) is related to greater levels of extradyadic sex. In one study, this was true for both men and women, but to a greater extent for women (Bogaert & Sadava, 2002). In the other study, the association with anxious attachment style was true only for college women; for college men, the dismissive (or avoidant) attachment style was related to greater extradyadic sex (Allen & Baucom, 2004). This means that women who are extremely needy with respect to feeling valued by their romantic partner and concerned about being abandoned by them are more likely to seek out extradyadic partners; having other partners attracted to them appears to bolster their self-esteem. The motivation for dismissive men—who are not greatly interested in intimate relationships—was to establish an independence from their primary relationship partner.

## Jealousy

*When he is late for dinner and I know he must be either having an affair or lying dead in the street, I always hope he's dead.*

Judith Viorst (ThinkExist.com)

*With many men, possessiveness kicks in shortly after sex, sometimes just after desire. Their sense of entitlement to have what they want from women, simply because they want it, boggles the mind. Their primary desire seems to be to have sex with me, but this is followed closely by a desire to make sure no one else does. The whole can of worms is presented through a smoke screen of romantic symbolism, which makes me suspect they are running a scam. Though they use words such as "commitment," their tone evokes images of control more than love. (Sullivan, 2000, p. 103)*

Although most individuals involved in extradyadic relationships attempt to keep them secret from their primary romantic partner, the primary partner may actually ignore cues that are often available about the affair (Buunk & Dijkstra, 2000). Research based on reports by therapists suggests that almost half of the "deceived" primary partners do not consciously acknowledge the extramarital relationship, in spite of evidence that they really did know. In fact, 58% of the partners were perceived to indicate either open or implied acceptance of the affairs (Charny & Parnass, 1995).

*Are there people who are especially likely to experience jealousy? What do you think might be the reason for this?*

On the other hand, some individuals tend to be highly suspicious and vigilant of any clues concerning their partner's behavior that may hint at extradyadic involvement (Buunk & Dijkstra, 2000). This tendency to be suspicious and worried about a partner's involvement with others is **jealousy**, which in fact may take several forms (Buunk, 1997). **Reactive jealousy** is a negative emotional reaction to a romantic partner's actual extramarital involvement; this is also called *emotional* or *provoked* jealousy. **Anxious jealousy** is fear or worry generated by an individual without necessarily having realistic evidence to suggest the partner's extramarital involvement. The individual becomes obsessively concerned and constantly looks for clues that an affair might occur. This is also called *cognitive* or *neurotic* jealousy.

**Preventive jealousy** involves a mind-set in which an individual is determined to prevent an extramarital affair by his or her partner before it can occur; the individual may have absolutely no evidence to suggest that an affair might occur or is likely to occur, but he or she has the goal of making sure it will never happen. The person monitors all interest of the partner in other individuals, and may do everything possible to limit contact of the partner with others. This type is also called *suspicious* or *unprovoked* jealousy.

### Why Do People Become Jealous?

*He who is consumed by the flame of jealousy turns at last, like the scorpion, the poisoned sting against himself.*

Friedrich Nietzsche *Thus Spake Zarathustra*, 1883–92 (Cassell Publishers Limited, 1993, p. 102)

*Jealousy, the jaundice of the soul.*

John Dryden *The Hind and the Panther,* 1687 (Cassell Publishers Limited, 1993, p. 104).

Men tend to be more concerned about sexual involvement of their partner with another person, whereas women tend to be more threatened by emotional involvement (Buunk & Dijkstra, 2000). Both women and men are most severely distressed by characteristics of another person that most contribute to the person as an attractive competitor; these are called **rival characteristics**. In research based on evolutionary psychological theory, women are most threatened by rivals who are physically attractive; on the other hand, men are most intimidated by rivals with strong status-related attributes (Buss, Shackelford, Choe, Buunk, & Dijkstra, 2000; Dijkstra & Buunk, 1998). This supports the proposal that both women and men will experience the greatest jealousy when their potential rivals have characteristics likely to be most attractive to their partner (Buunk & Dijkstra, 2000). Furthermore, people tend to be most jealous with respect to individuals whom they know and about whom they are envious; in contrast, people are the least jealous of those with whom they were not acquainted (Pines & Aronson, 1983).

In keeping with traditional beliefs about jealous individuals, those with low self-esteem, feelings of personal inadequacy, and negative self-views are more likely to experience jealousy. The personality trait of neuroticism is also related to jealousy; this means that individuals who typically experience higher levels of negative emotions and anxiety tend also to suffer from jealousy more often. Likewise, individuals with an anxious–ambivalent attachment style are the most likely to experience jealousy. Research suggests that individuals with low self-esteem, stronger neuroticism, and more anxious attachments may experience greater jealousy because they feel greater dependency on the romantic relationship to fulfill their needs (Buunk & Dijkstra, 2000).

## Summary

Various strategies are used to promote commitment within romantic relationships. Responses to conflict within relationships have been proposed to take four basic forms: voice, loyalty, exit, and neglect. After a traumatic relationship loss, individuals are thought to transition through a sequence of stages: (a) outcry, (b) denial, (c) intrusion, (d) working through, (e) completion, and (f) identity change.

Initiation of sexual behavior within established heterosexual relationships may tend to follow the traditional script of the man taking the active role, and the woman responding with either a favorable reaction or a refusal. Both partners in lesbian relationships tend to believe that they are the one in the relationship who more frequently refuses to engage in sexual behavior, whereas both partners in gay male relationships tend to believe that they are the one who initiates sex more often.

*(Continued)*

(Continued)

The frequency of sexual behavior for married heterosexual couples is on average two to three times per week, although cohabiting couples engage in sex more frequently. Gay male couples engage in sexual behavior most frequently of all types of couples. Lesbian couples are most likely of all couple types to engage in nongenital sexual behavior, such as caressing, kissing, and hugging. Frequency declines for all couples with time due to aging, and increasing familiarity and predictability.

The most appealing type of sexual behavior for both heterosexual women and men of all ages is penile–vaginal intercourse. Most heterosexual individuals have engaged in oral–genital sex, whereas penile–anal intercourse has been tried at least once by approximately 20% of both women and men. The most common type of sexual behavior for lesbians is stimulating the genitals with hands, although cunnilingus is the preferred behavior to stimulate a woman to orgasm.

The vast majority of individuals report high levels of sexual satisfaction, regardless of the frequency of sexual activity. Greater sexual satisfaction for women is related to the likelihood of experiencing cunnilingus, because of the increased likelihood of experiencing orgasm. Consistency of orgasm is more important in influencing sexual satisfaction for women than the sheer frequency of experiencing orgasm. Personality characteristics of individuals and the nature of a given relationship may be more influential in determining sexual satisfaction than the actual quality of sexual behavior itself. Sexual satisfaction is strongly related not only to relationship satisfaction, but also relationship stability, at least for men. General relationship satisfaction predicts the course of the relationship for women.

A fairly prevalent trend on U.S. college campuses is the hookup, a sexual encounter intended to last only one night with no desire for commitment or further contact. Casual sex is more likely to occur in conducive environments that celebrate sensuality and pleasure-related activities, such as partying, alcohol consumption, dancing, and contests involving nudity. Social factors, such as peer influences on attitudes and others serving as role models, have the largest effect on the occurrence of casual sex in these environments.

Studies indicate that 25–50% of women and 50–65% of men have engaged in extradyadic sex. Dissatisfaction with the primary relationship in general, particularly for women, is associated with greater likelihood of extradyadic involvement. Dissatisfaction with sexual aspects of the primary relationship is also related to involvement in extradyadic relationships, although this may be primarily true for men. Younger age at involvement in a primary relationship, more sexual experience prior to a primary relationship, more liberal sexual attitudes for women, parental divorce, being divorced oneself, having an anxious attachment style (possibly only for women), and having a dismissive attachment style for men all increase the likelihood of extradyadic relationships.

Types of jealousy include reactive jealousy, anxious jealousy, and preventive jealousy. Characteristics of rivals that cause them to be most attractive to one's primary romantic partner produce the greatest levels of jealousy. Individuals with lower self-esteem, greater neuroticism, and those who have anxious attachments tend to experience greater jealousy because they are more dependent on the primary relationship emotionally.

### Chapter 10 Critical Thinking Exercises

1. Sexuality within long-term committed relationships

   What factors do you think are most strongly related to the frequency of sexual behavior in which a couple typically engages? If a couple wished to increase the frequency of sexual behavior in their relationship, what strategies would you recommend as most effective in accomplishing this? What strategies would be most effective in improving the quality of the sexual aspect of their relationship? In what ways are frequency of sexual behavior and sexual satisfaction related for most couples? In what ways are they not related to one another?

2. Sexuality outside of traditional relationships

   Think of examples of extramarital or extra-relationship affairs that you know of or have heard about. What factors contributed to the individuals becoming involved in these extradyadic relationships? What implications does extradyadic involvement have for the primary relationship? Does it always lead to negative consequences?

Visit www.sagepub.com/hillhsstudy.com for online activities, sample tests, and other helpful resources. Select "Chapter 10: Relationships and Sexuality" for chapter-specific activities.

# Chapter 11

## ETHNICITY, RACE, CULTURE, AND SEXUALITY

S uppose you are a scientist who is interested in conducting research on sexuality. You want to find out how important the type of sexual behavior is to the amount of pleasure and satisfaction individuals experience in their sexual relationships. The sexual behaviors you are interested in are stroking and caressing the body, oral–genital sex, and penile–vaginal sex. As is usually the case, the people who are in your study are college students, because they must participate in research as a requirement for their psychology course; therefore, they are very convenient and easy to obtain for your study. All but about 5% of the students are White, middle-class individuals between the ages of 18 and 22 years. You collect your information and then draw conclusions about sexual pleasure that you assume describe what is typical for most people, give or take a few. As a scientist you are trying to discover general principles about sexual behavior that will be relevant to as many people as possible.

Such a strategy of drawing general conclusions on a sample of some aspect of the world has actually been the basis of scientific reasoning from its very beginning. This is the reason that theory and research on sexuality has focused on developing gen-

How relevant to non-White individuals is research on White participants conducted by White researchers?

eral principles that are relevant to as many people as possible. In the very early years of research on sexuality, as in psychology in general, this basic concern led many scientists to think that it was legitimate to conduct their research almost exclusively on White individuals. The feeling has been that knowledge gained in this way is based on human beings who just happen to be White. Yet, because all humans are really very similar in their basic nature, the information is relevant not only to White people, but people of all races and cultures.

Is this really a safe assumption to make about your results? Do you think they really describe the sexual behavior of everyone very well? Is the information about the pleasure related to, for example, oral–genital sex for White college students likely to describe the feelings of individuals who are Black or Latino or Asian American? Recently, some scientists have begun to argue that the answer to these questions is emphatically "no."

Scientists have begun to acknowledge that research needs to include larger numbers of Asian American, African American, Latino/Latina, and Native American individuals on a more frequent basis.

Yet the long-standing assumption that all human beings are essentially the same has been such a strongly held belief that there has been hardly any concern with testing the correctness of the assumption. For this reason, little research has focused on seeing whether scientific data are accurate and describe non-White individuals as well if they are based largely on White people (Lewis & Kertzner, 2003). In recent times, scientists in fact have become more interested in studying issues of sexuality for non-White groups. Even now, however, the focus has not been on basic issues of sexuality, which is traditionally a major concern of research on White populations. Examples of basic issues include the types of sexual behavior that are common, how people feel about their sexuality, its meaning and value to them, how relationships affect sexuality, and sexual satisfaction, among others.

Instead, researchers have been concerned primarily with the sexual behavior of non-White teenagers that puts them at higher risk of pregnancy and sexually transmitted diseases. The subtle message that is conveyed by such a complete focus on problems and disease is that non-White sexuality is dangerous and unhealthy. Satisfying, positive aspects of sexuality have not really been of concern at all (Lewis & Kertzner, 2003).

However, understanding the ways that people are similar and different because of their race and ethnicity is more complicated than you might think at first glance. Differences in people's view of themselves and in their typical sexual behavior have actually been found in scientific research. What is difficult is deciding exactly how to classify people into meaningful groups in the first place (Helms, Jernigan, & Mascher, 2005). Related to this is the difficulty of understanding and explaining the meaning of differences among groups when they are found. A number of highly influential factors—such as social class, income level, and societal privilege—have been different for the various ethnic groups in North America since Europeans began to colonize the continent.

As will be discussed in detail later in the chapter, poverty has proven to be the single most powerful factor that explains differences between African American and European American youth in the early onset of sexual intercourse. For Latinos and Latinas—those whose ancestors originated from Spanish-speaking countries—the factor accounting for early onset of sexual intercourse was a combination of two factors: (a) whether Spanish or English was regularly spoken in the home and (b) the length of time living in or having been born in the United States. Both of these have to do with the influence of culture on sexual expression. In fact, social and cultural factors appear to be the predominant influences that explain differences among groups of people regarding sexual behavior. The overall picture related to sexuality has proven to be fairly complex.

To give an idea of the problems involved, the issue of how the various groups of people were arrived upon in the first place is discussed. Race and ethnicity are traditional categories in the United States, and so these are the focus of this chapter.

## The Concepts of Race and Ethnicity

A widely held assumption is that *race* is a distinction among people that has existed in the same way throughout human history; many probably assume that "race" is an objective "fact" of nature based in biology. However, the concept as we currently know it did not come about until the late 1600s in North America and the Caribbean islands. The highly profitable slave trade that grew during this time was a major reason for the rise of a belief in fundamental differences among groups of people, especially between White people and non-White people (Jackson & Weidman, 2004; Smedley, 1999; Smedley & Smedley, 2005). The concept of race that began during the 1600s and 1700s, however, continued to evolve throughout the 1800s (Augstein, 1996). It became entrenched in the beliefs of European and North American society as an attitude toward people originating from Africa—those whom were being captured and enslaved for labor in the "New World." North American Indians were viewed as inferior to those of European origin, but beliefs about Africans largely account for the development of the concept of race during this time (Smedley, 2001).

### What Evidence Exists for the Notion of Race?

> *As long as there are entrenched social and political distinctions between sexes, races, or classes, there will be forms of science whose main function is to rationalize and legitimize these distinctions.*
>
> Elizabeth Fee (ThinkExist.com)

The concept of race, with a belief in tremendous differences between White and Black people in particular, came about relatively late in the history of humankind. This fact, along with the fact that it has changed in meaning over a relatively short period of time, supports the idea that race is really a culturally constructed notion. The concept of race did not spring out of objective biological research showing that inborn, stable differences exist among groups of people. Instead, scientific thinking about race followed behind the development of folk beliefs about differences. These beliefs were strongly motivated by the cultural need to justify the enslavement and ownership of other human beings. As Smedley observed, "race was, and still is, in North America, a matter of power, prestige, wealth, and privilege. It is about how some Europeans used physical differences among the populations they conquered or enslaved to socially stratify society" (Smedley, 2001, pp. 18–19).

Despite these early beliefs, clear-cut, objective evidence for the existence of distinctions among racial groups do not exist. In fact, modern science has not been able to identify definite, stable genetic or biological factors that distinguish groups of people on the basis of popular notions of "race." The central assumption of the concept of race is the belief that a clear distinction exists among different groups of people in terms of some core set of traits. For example, all members of the White race are presumed to possess basic characteristics, most obviously lighter skin color, that uniquely distinguish them from all members of other races (e.g., Asian, American Indian, or African). In reality, however, substantial variation exists within each "race" for whatever characteristic might traditionally be thought to relate to race; for instance, not all "White" people are absent skin pigmentation to exactly the same extent, and not all "Black" people have high concentrations of pigmentation at the same level (see Figure 11.1). Rather, both White and Black groups have wide ranges of pigmentation.

**FIGURE 11.1**    Hypothetical Range and Prevalence of Skin Pigmentation (Color) in White and Black Groups

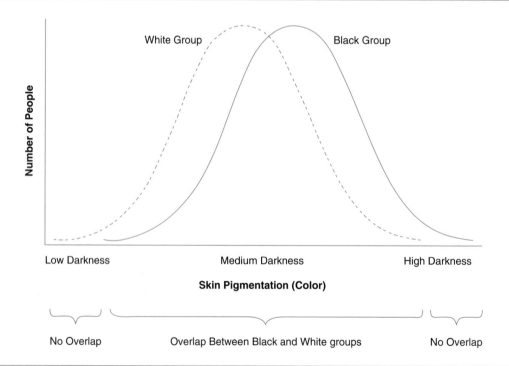

Such a degree of variation exists within races that some members of the White group have the same, or even more, pigmentation in comparison to members of other racial groups, including the Black group. Consequently, no decisive, absolute gap exists between groups, even on supposedly defining, central characteristics. Individuals in the "White" group near the darker end of the "White" spectrum are more similar to members of the "Black" group at the lighter end than they are to most members of their own "White" group. As scientist Alan Goodman (2001) notes, "The division point is arbitrary and up to the whim of the classifier. The continent from which one originates, no less than one's race, is meaningless" (p. 30).

In fact, statistical comparisons of empirical research have supported the conclusion that differences among races on various characteristics are substantially smaller than differences found within races (Appiah, 1999; Goodman, 2001). A related line of research has examined the extent to which racial categories account for genetic variation among individuals. A classic example is research on variation in blood types (A, B, AB, and O; Lewontin, 1972). Only 6.3% of the differences among individuals was explained by the supposed racial group to which individuals belonged. In contrast, a massive 85.4% of the difference in blood type was explained by differences in terms of local group to which individuals belonged; local group refers to the people who live in a particular region or locale. As a matter of fact, the 6.3% of variation that is explained by racial group is actually more satisfactorily explained in terms of geographic closeness, or how closely individuals live to one another (Goodman, 2001).

The lack of distinct physical boundaries among various ethnic groups, as illustrated by light-skinned Black people and dark-skinned White people, exposes the arbitrary, constructed nature of the concept of "race."

Overall, at most, 6% of the 0.2% of genetic material that varies within humans may be attributed to socially defined racial grouping (Zack, 2001). The primary conclusion from this type of genetic research is that the concept of race is not a very powerful or useful explanation of human differences (Goodman, 2001). Instead, evidence supports the view that humans belong to one ancestry, the human race (Zack, 2001).

Another problem with the notion of race exists even at the level of considering a particular set of traits. One of the basic assumptions of the concept of race is that specific, defining characteristics are related to one another, or vary together, in a predictable way to determine racial membership. Skin color is, in fact, reliably correlated with hair and eye color, but not correlated so much with hair texture. The problem with the concept of race is that the characteristics of skin, hair, and eye color are not reliably related to any other theoretically significant biological or bodily feature. Goodman (2001) summarizes evidence for the usefulness of the concept of race in a rather damning way: "We end up with circularities: skin color explains race and race explains skin color, but neither explains much else" (p. 36). For example, with respect to sexuality as discussed later in the chapter, the earlier age of first sexual intercourse found for African American adolescents is actually due to the severity of poverty in which they live, rather than to some characteristic associated with their racial grouping.

The artificial, arbitrary nature of the notion of race is also revealed in the way that racial categories change as a function of the particular situation and historical period in which a judgment is made. An individual who may be thought of as "White" in one locale or setting, may be considered "Latin," "Latina," "Hispanic," "Mexican," or a "person of color" in other settings or times. The "whitening" of various groups considered to be separate races has occurred in a number of instances, such as with Jewish people after World War II (Sacks, 1998) and the Irish and Southern Europeans at other times (Jacobson, 1998). The constructed nature of the concept of race is exposed by the fact that definitions are highly changeable. Sometimes definitions focus on the geographic origin of ancestors (e.g., North America, Europe, Africa, or Asia) that are presumably associated with some set of critically important biological characteristics. Other definitions identify race as a function of what people are like on a set of particular traits (skin and eye color) that are presumed to be based on fundamental biological differences among people. Even the number of races that make up the human species, and the names that should be used, cannot be agreed on (Goodman, 2001).

## The Importance of Culture in Explaining Differences Attributed to Race

*We must recognize that beneath the superficial classifications of sex and race the same potentialities exist, recurring generation after generation, only to perish because society has no place for them.*

Margaret Mead, American anthropologist, 1901–1978 (ThinkExist.com)

In India, the family was the most important institution; it dominated our lives and determined their course. For me, being gay was similar to betraying the family. It wasn't their rejection I feared; it was more whether my father would be able to hold his head high again. What would the neighbors say? Being gay was almost an act of self-ishness—after all your selfless parents did for you, is this their reward in their old age? Coupled with the shame of being gay was an embarrassment about desiring men. Desiring men not for the jobs they had, not for their economic potential, but for their male beauty. It had been branded into our heads that beauty was a word that went with females, sunset, and paintings. Beauty was an "unmanly" thing for men to concern themselves with. (Roy, 2000, p. 29)

Despite the lack of biological evidence for the concept, the effects of a long-standing *belief* in the existence of race are very real and very influential. The distinctions among races thought to be due to biology have been translated into differences in status, power, and privilege within society for the supposed races. Another factor contributing to differences in some dimensions of behavior is that racial groups originally came from different geographic regions of the world. The physical separation resulted in people coming up with different ways of carrying out everyday life and the development of different customs. Adding to original cultural differences, racial groups have historically been separated from one another, initially through formal segregation after the U.S. Civil War. Along with this, because of continuing negative attitudes toward minority groups, communities after the Civil War were arranged such that White people tended to live in areas away from areas in which Black people and other minorities lived. This tendency continues into current times in many places within the United States. Living in separate communities has likewise contributed to the development of somewhat different cultures.

Culture refers to the system of knowledge, beliefs, and values shared by a particular group of people (Goodman, 2001). Culture includes expectations about how to live—how to carry out daily routine, how to interact with one another socially, how to cope with life's challenges, the way of engaging in religious observation, style of clothing, and types of art and entertainment. This system of shared understanding is based on the capability of humans to think symbolically and to create meaning in life (cf., Tylor, 1958).

The variety that exists among groups of people may be most meaningfully explained in terms of differences in culture resulting from being separated geographically. Geographic separation, as discussed previously, is even the reason for the differences that exist in some of the physical characteristics thought to be due to "race." Remember that genetic differences among groups of people have been found to relate to differences in local group membership; local group refers to people living in a particular geographic region. Individuals are genetically more similar to people in their local group; in contrast, racial labels are not highly accurate in explaining people's genetic similarity to one another. This suggests that understanding cultural and sociopolitical issues is much more important than focusing on race in explaining the existence of differences in values and folkways among groups of people (Goodman, 2001).

However, culture has not been an issue of great concern within psychology until very recently. In fact, historically, the view within psychology has been that culture is unlikely to exert any significant influence on important psychological processes and behavior (Goodman, 2001).

## Definitions of Concepts

*However sugarcoated and ambiguous, every form of authoritarianism must start with a belief in some group's greater right to power, whether that right is justified by sex, race, class, religion or all four.*

Gloria Steinem, American writer and social activist (ThinkExist.com)

Dear Emmett Till [an African American 14-year-old adolescent who was murdered in 1955 for whistling at a White woman]: The first time I heard of you, I don't think I was black yet. Let me explain. By "black" I don't mean racially speaking. You might call me "Negro" or "colored" because I am "African American" (as we've decided we want to be called these days).... [W]hat I mean is that I was still the safe and sound kid who moved through the world not knowing that the color of my skin somehow marked me, in some people's eyes, as qualitatively "different." ... I hadn't yet ... been followed around inside a department store, hovered over by the prying eyes of wary security guards and salespeople.... I couldn't drive so I'd never been stopped for a DWB (driving while black). I don't even think I'd yet heard the word "nigger" used without an emphasized "please" behind it. (Poulsson-Bryant, 2005, 1–2)

**Race** may be defined as a socially constructed system of classifying people according to characteristics thought to be important for determining social status and worth. Historically in the United States, the characteristics thought to be important have been the physical attributes of skin, hair, and eye color. The rules for deciding membership in a racial group may be determined either by individuals outside of the group or by those inside of the group (Feagin, 1978; Trimble, Helms, & Root, 2003). Typically, the group with the greatest social, political, and economic power has the largest degree of influence on such definitions, as has been the case in the United States. European settlers who possessed economic and political power established the primary distinctions for determining racial grouping. Ultimately, they positioned themselves as superior to other groups on the basis of characteristics largely associated with lighter skin color. All other people who had darker skin color were designated as inferior and assigned lower social status (Smedley, 2001).

**Ethnicity** is a socially created system of classifying people on the basis of cultural or nationality differences; as with the related concept of race, ethnicity is a means of distinguishing groups of people in terms of social status and worth (Feagin, 1978; Trimble et al., 2003). Sociologist Joanne Nagel (2003) defines ethnicity as the larger category that encompasses race. That is, race is only one specific way of assigning social status and power; with race, the standard for assigning status and power is based on physical characteristics of skin and hair color. Within the concept of ethnicity, a number of other characteristics besides skin color are used

## Box 11.1  Ethnicity and Sexuality

Cultural anthropologists have increasingly viewed ethnicity as more than simply the sharing of a common culture. The concept of ethnicity is additionally recognized as involving a system of actively constructing boundaries between one culture and all others. The system also includes the creation of specific boundary markers that indicate who belongs in an ethnic group and who does not. "According to this view, ethnicity is a matter of who is inside and who is outside an ethnic boundary" (Nagel, 2003, p. 44). In other words, ethnicity serves to maintain separate territories for one group in comparison to others; sometimes, the boundaries partition actual physical space into regions, such as in cases in which ethnic groups tend to be concentrated in particular areas of a city. However, in other cases, the boundaries may involve symbolic segregation of people, as when individuals are distinguished by different styles of clothing or types of music.

Adopting a social constructionist perspective, sociologist Joane Nagel (2003) has concluded that ethnicity and sexuality have been intricately intertwined in human culture throughout history:

> Ethnicity and sexuality join together to form a barrier to hold some people in and keep others out, to define who is pure and who is impure, to shape our view of ourselves and others, to fashion feelings of sexual desire and notions of sexual desirability to provide us with seemingly "natural" sexual preferences for some partners and "intuitive" aversions to others, to leave us with a taste for some ethnic sexual encounters and a distaste for others. (p. 1)

Nagel points to the existence of racial, ethnic, and national boundaries conveyed in the form of ethnic sexual stereotypes, as well as hostility felt by ethnic minorities toward sexual minorities, such as lesbians, gays, bisexuals, and transgendered individuals.

Nagel (2003) created the word, *ethnosexual*, to refer to the ways in which ethnicity and sexuality affect one another in different aspects of life. She documents the various ethnosexual ideologies—systems of beliefs about sexuality—held by various ethnic groups. These ethnosexual ideologies almost always include beliefs about the differences in sexual nature of one's own group and of other ethnic groups, the "Others." The perceived characteristics of the other groups are generally negative and demeaning, conveying a sense of inferiority in comparison to their own group. "Sexual stereotypes commonly depict 'us' as sexually vigorous (usually our men) and pure (usually our women), and depict 'them' as sexually depraved (usually their men) and promiscuous (usually their women)" (p. 10). Cultural conceptions of sexuality affect definitions of ethnicity, rules for avoiding and interacting with members of other ethnic groups, and the types of antagonism that develop. Likewise, definitions surrounding ethnicity influence cultural understandings of sexuality.

### Reference

Nagel, J. (2003). *Race, ethnicity, and sexuality*. New York: Oxford University Press.

as the basis for ascribing status and power. Other criteria for distinguishing groups of people ethnically include language, religion, national origin, and geographic region.

The issue of race is the one that has created the most antagonism and violence in the United States, but in other places in the world, nonracial differences (those not related to skin color) have caused the same levels of strife, discrimination, and violence. You may remember the intense hatred and conflict that occurred in the former Yugoslavia among various groups who made up the country. The groups were different in terms of culture, nationality, and religion (e.g., Serbian Orthodox Christian, Bosnian Catholic, and Bosnian Muslim)—that is, ethnicity rather than skin color. Yet the animosity grounded in cultural differences literally devastated entire regions of the country; moreover, the violent contempt of one ethnic group toward other groups resulted in mass murder, torture, and rape. As Nagel (2003) points out, the similarity of the conflict that results from ethnicity to that which results from race exposes the common nature of race, ethnicity, and nationalism.

A **minority** is a group that has lower status in a society because of the possession of characteristics that are devalued by that society; the characteristics are thought to relate to lesser ability or potential (Wayley & Harris, 1958; Trimble et al., 2003). The concept of *minority groups* in itself involves a racist element because the groups are viewed as possessing negative characteristics and are the targets of discrimination by the majority group. The majority group is the one that possesses desirable characteristics according to societal definitions and have the greatest status, power, and wealth (Trimble et al., 2003). Because they have the greatest power, the majority group typically controls the definition of what are considered desirable and undesirable traits.

For purposes of clarity, it should be pointed out that everyone belongs to an ethnicity, even members of the dominant social group or the majority group. However, it is not unusual for majority people to think of only minority social groups as being ethnic groups, whereas the majority group is not ethnic or does not have ethnicity. Nonetheless, in the United States, White Anglo-Saxon Protestant *is* an ethnic group.

Racial identity is the understanding an individual has of belonging to a particular racial group and the meaning that membership in the group holds for the person. Ethnic identity and cultural identity are highly related in that they both refer to the understanding an individual has of belonging to a particular ethnic or cultural group, as well as the meaning that group membership has for the person (Trimble et al., 2003).

## Racial and Ethnic Composition of the U.S. Population

*We need every human gift and cannot afford to neglect any gift because of artificial barriers of sex or race or class or national origin.*

Margaret Mead, American anthropologist, 1901–1978 (ThinkExist.com)

According to the conventions used by the U.S. Bureau of the Census (2001), seven ethnic groups constitute the primary ethnicities within the United States. The proportion of the population represented by each ethnicity is presented in Figure 11.2. By the year 2050, the Bureau predicts that 47% of the population will be ethnic minority groups, the largest group continuing to be Latino–Latina. Latinos–Latinas are the fastest growing segment of the population, expanding eight times the rate of the White ethnic group (Bernal, Trimble, Burlew, & Leong, 2003).

The terms *Latino, Latina,* and *Hispanic* are used interchangeably to refer to individuals whose ancestors originated from traditionally Spanish-speaking countries such as Mexico, Central and South American countries, and Spain. *Latino* is the term in Spanish for men of Spanish heritage, and *Latina* is the term for women of Spanish heritage.

**FIGURE 11.2** Percentages of Racial/Ethnic Groups in the U.S. Population (U.S. Bureau of Census, 2001)

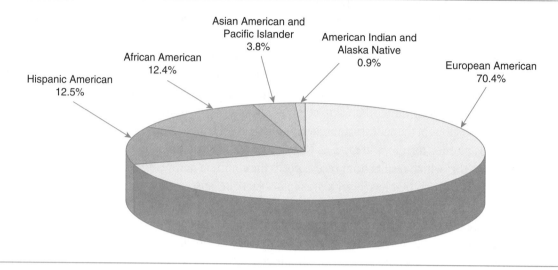

Hispanic American
12.5%

African American
12.4%

Asian American and
Pacific Islander
3.8%

American Indian and
Alaska Native
0.9%

European American
70.4%

Pacific Islanders composed 0.14% of the U.S. population in 2000, whereas American Indians and Alaska Natives composed 0.88%.

# *Sexuality and Ethnicity*

*I remember a little glossy book of photos of a young Indian man on the beach. His name was Arjun, and he emerged from the ocean, wet and glistening and inviting. It was one of the first unabashedly male-erotic images I had seen of an Indian man in an Indian setting. . . . I was quite pleased to see a calendar on Asian men by an Asian photographer. Here at last we were on safe ground; we could unabashedly wallow in our desire without fearing we were playing into the hands of colonists, exploitative, keeping-Asian-boys-as-pets, white men. . . . The foreword explained that this calendar hoped to shatter the stereotype of Asian men as passive, geeky nerds with smudged glasses and hunched shoulders. (Roy, 2000, p. 30)*

Very little research has been conducted on the basic nature of sexuality among racial and ethnic minority populations. In a survey of scientific research published in the two leading sexuality journals between 1971 and 1995, only 26% of the 1,123 articles presented information on the ethnicity of study participants. A mere 4% conducted comparisons among ethnic groups (Wiederman, Maynard, & Fretz, 1996). Yet studies comparing racial and ethnic minority individuals with White individuals frequently suffer from certain limitations. For example, they often are not theoretically based, and therefore frequently do not provide a clear understanding of the reason for the differences that are obtained (Lewis & Kertzner, 2003).

What small amount of research that has been conducted has been from a problem-centered perspective, rather than from a basic knowledge-centered perspective, as discussed briefly in chapter 1 with respect to African Americans (Lewis, 2004; Lewis & Kertzner, 2003). The problem-centered perspective of African American sexuality is consistent with the treatment of African American psychology in general: The tendencies of African Americans are frequently cast as problematic, unhealthy, and dangerous. As noted by Laubscher (2005), theorists and researchers often use the *language of crisis,* conveying the sense that essentially all African Americans are on the path to disease and destruction. The problem-centered perspective of sexuality is concerned entirely with the negative outcomes that may result from sexual behavior. In fact, the vast majority of research on racial minorities has concentrated on factors that place adolescents at risk for early onset of sexual behavior or infection with sexually transmitted diseases.

Virtually no information has been collected on sexuality from the basic knowledge-centered perspective, which traditionally has been a major focus of research on White populations. *Basic issues* are those addressed throughout this book, such as typical reasons for engaging in sexual behavior, feelings about sexuality, and patterns of different kinds of sexual behavior. Because of the tremendous lack of research on race and ethnicity in general, the sexuality of African Americans will be used as a starting point, because much of what little research exists has been conducted with this group.

## Challenges to Accurate Research on Ethnic and Racial Sexuality

The theoretical overview by Lewis and Kertzner (2003) of issues necessary for a more complete understanding of the sexuality of African American men provides a valuable starting point. They suggest that the same issues are likely to be relevant to African American women and other ethnic groups. According to Lewis and Kertzner, the challenges that are uniquely critical to understanding racial and ethnic sexuality are (a) problems associated with the typical assumption that all members of ethnic minority groups are identical, (b) obtaining a superficial understanding of sexuality by focusing on overt behavior rather than the meaning of sexual behavior, and (c) the general absence of theory regarding sexuality.

Hardly any basic research has been conducted on the sexuality of Black, Latino, and Asian groups in the United States. What little that exists has focused on African Americans.

## The Assumption That All Members of Ethnic Minority Groups Are Identical

Terms such as *Black, Asian, White, Hispanic,* and *Native American* lead people to apply what Trimble (1991) calls an "ethnic gloss" to all members of ethnic minorities, as well as to blur distinctions among ethnic minority groups. The ethnic gloss involves using conceptually meaningless—or even inaccurate—categories, such as *Black* and *Hispanic,* on the basis of a superficial understanding of groups of people from various cultural backgrounds. One major reason that researchers continue to use this method of classifying individuals by ethnic group is because they may assume that it has a significant influence on behavior. Identifying individuals by ethnic or racial group also permits comparing these groups with one another on behaviors of interest (Lewis & Kertzner, 2003).

However, this type of convenient shorthand also has the problem of blurring important differences among people who are lumped together in one category. One example is the label *African American,* which has often included people from very different cultural backgrounds. To correct this problem, Lewis and Kertzner (2003) use the term *African Americans* to refer to individuals who self-identify with ancestors who were forced against their wills to migrate to the United States through the system of slavery. This distinguishes them from those of African ancestry emigrating voluntarily from other countries, such as islands in the Caribbean, who originate from a different culture; such individuals may be called *Afro-Caribbean.* This is especially important with respect to sexuality because Afro-Caribbean individuals emphatically distinguish themselves from African Americans, whom they believe to have laxer sexual standards (Kasinitz, Battle, & Miyares, 2001; Waters, 1999).

Another aspect of the problem of the ethnic gloss is that researchers may operate according to the assumption that all "non-White" peoples—African Americans, American Indians, Hispanic Americans, and others—are alike in sharing characteristics that make them highly similar to one another. The attributes that make

---

### Box 11.2  How Common Is Marriage Outside of One's Ethnic Group?

An examination of the intermarriage rates for the various ethnic groups provides an idea of the stability of the ethnosexual boundaries that have been erected, as well as the degree to which excursions occur across the boundaries. The vast majority of Americans marry within their own original ethnic group, although a gradual decline in this tendency has occurred over the past 40 years—from 99.6% in 1960 to 94.6% in 2000. Marriage outside of one's ethnic group was dramatically different across the various groups in 2000: 6.1% for Whites, 10.9% for Blacks, 26.1% for Hispanics, 26.3% for Asian Americans, and 67.0% for Native Americans. Other data indicate that the level of interethnic relationships may be higher than indicated by marriage if the number of individuals involved in cohabitation are included (Nagel, 2003).

Despite some marriage and sexual interaction between individuals of different ethnic groups throughout American history, ethnosexual boundaries have remained fairly stable, not changing or diminishing to any great extent at all. The Black–White boundary has remained the firmest of all, in contrast to the merging of a variety of other ethnic groups into that of the White group. For example, ethnic groups considered to be substantially distinct and separate races only decades ago, such as Irish, Italians, Armenians, and Jewish, are now fairly comfortably identified as White. Nagel (2003) suggests the possibility that a similar type of merging could occur sometime in the future for other ethnic groups, given the degree of intermarriage and interethnic sexual interaction. As Latinos gain in prominence economically and numerically, and with increasing numbers of Asian–White couples, additional merging of categories is not impossible.

#### Reference

Nagel, J. (2003). *Race, ethnicity, and sexuality*. New York: Oxford University Press.

---

them similar are also thought to distinguish them from "White" people in supposedly significant ways (Trimble et al., 2003). Research has really not supported this assumption for any domain of characteristics. Another strategy that creates a distorted view of African Americans in general is the tendency to focus entirely on lower socioeconomic urban African Americans in sexuality research. A primary reason is that researchers have been exclusively concerned about sexual behavior of ethnic minority groups that result in problems; typical concerns are sexual intercourse among adolescents and the risk of pregnancy to unmarried teenagers. The underlying, unspoken assumption may be that such results are relevant as well to middle- and upper-class Blacks, who are much less frequently included in particularly large-scale research projects. Results based entirely on one socioeconomic group, those of the poorest level, tend to confuse factors related to race, cultural background, and financial status (Lewis & Kertzner, 2003).

This, of course, is a tremendous problem because not all African Americans are exactly alike. Research should actually examine other issues that have become confused with race, such as socioeconomic level, because these may offer better explanations of behavior. We will see specific examples of the important influence of socioeconomic factors on sexual behavior in a later section.

### Focusing on Overt Behavior Rather Than the Meaning of Sexual Behavior

The bulk of research on African American sexuality concentrates on overt sexual behavior that is associated with negative outcomes. Consequently, a great deal is known about rates of adolescent sexual behavior, contraception, condom use, pregnancy, and abortion. However, virtually no research has examined the meaning of sexual behavior for adolescents or for African Americans in general. Yet a focus only on what people do sexually does not necessarily reveal *why* people engage in the behavior. It is logical, however, that understanding the reasons motivating behavior is essential to developing strategies for alleviating conditions that promote risky behavior (Lewis & Kertzner, 2003).

### The General Absence of Theory Regarding Sexuality

A survey of articles published in one of the premiere scientific journals devoted to sexuality research, *The Journal of Sex Research,* found very little published research on African American men that was based on formal theory (Lewis & Kertzner, 2003). The absence of theory-guided research probably represents what is true for research on other ethnic groups as well. Focusing largely on describing sexual behavior, rather than targeting the causes underlying behavior, has been a problem for research on sexuality in general, not just for research on African Americans' sexuality. However, the problem of limiting research to only describing sexual behavior is even more common in research on racial and ethnic minority sexuality.

As discussed in chapter 1, using theory to guide research is absolutely essential to developing accurate, unbiased explanations of behavior. Even though research has not focused on the meaning of sexual behavior, some may still assume that a great deal is known about racial and ethnic sexuality. This is simply not the case. Knowledge about minority sexuality is limited entirely to the frequency of risk-related sexual behaviors, and the proportions of individuals engaging in these behaviors. Virtually nothing is known about causes and factors that influence the sexual behavior of minority individuals, and even less is known about nonproblematic behavior.

## Ethnicity and Sexual Behavior in Adulthood

### The Sexual Behavior of African American Women

Until the publication of more contemporary research on African American women by Wyatt, Peters, and Guthrie in 1988, the information obtained by Kinsey, Pomeroy, Martin, and Gebhard (1953) that was collected in the 1930s and 40s stood as the major source of information about African Americans (Wyatt, Peters, & Guthrie, 1988). In fact, the data on African Americans was virtually the only scientific research on non-White populations at all prior to the research by Wyatt and her colleagues. Consequently, the Kinsey research came to be treated as the authoritative source of information on Blacks.

The study conducted by Wyatt and her colleagues in the mid-1980s was intended to compare African American women from the later time period to those in the earlier time period. As noted by Wyatt and her colleagues, the use of the Kinsey data set presented a number of problems because of biases related to how they obtained their sample of people. Approximately half of the more than 700 Black women included in the study had a criminal history, some of whom had been imprisoned for their crimes. Because Wyatt and her colleagues focused on heterosexual African American college women, to make comparisons with those in the Kinsey participants, Black women who were not college-educated or who were not heterosexual were not included in their analyses.

For the later sample collected by the Wyatt team, Black and White women were recruited to participate through a random sampling procedure to ensure that the women were comparable on important characteristics. The Kinsey participants were primarily from the Midwest and Northeast and were simply identified as "Negro" or "colored" (again, the study was conducted in the 1930s and 40s). In contrast, the Wyatt study was based entirely on a representative sample of Los Angeles county women. Moreover, only women who lived fewer than 6 years outside of the United States before the age of 13 years were included in the study to ensure they were socialized according to U.S. cultural standards, and were therefore truly African American (rather than, for example, African Caribbean). This study was ultimately based on 126 African American women. The women in both studies ranged in age between 18 and 36.

Women in the later sample were substantially more likely to have engaged in first penile–vaginal intercourse before the age of 18 (approximately 75%) compared with those in the earlier study (approximately 50%). Moreover, the proportion of women engaging in this type of sexual behavior before the age of 15 years was dramatically greater in the later study, increasing from around 10% in the Kinsey study to 24% in the Wyatt sample. First intercourse was also less likely to be viewed as *not at all enjoyable* among women in the later study; stated another way, first intercourse was more likely to be perceived as somewhat enjoyable among women in the later study. However, the majority of women in both studies did not find their first sexual intercourse enjoyable at all.

In addition, more women in the later study reported engaging in sexual behavior with someone of the same sex during adolescence (9%) compared with those in the earlier study (2%). Greater proportions of women engaging in same-sex behavior did so during adolescence in the later study (45%) than in the earlier study (33%).

The tendency to have greater numbers of sexual partners increased markedly between the two samples, with 26% of those in the Kinsey study reporting six or more partners, compared with 60% of women in the later study. Women were much less likely to have only one sexual partner in the later study (3%) than they were in the earlier study (24%). Considerably more individuals in the later study had ever engaged in cunnilingus, fellatio, and penile–anal intercourse in their lives (70%, 65%, and 21%, respectively) than in the earlier Kinsey study (18%, 15%, and 9%, respectively). Those who had engaged in either type of oral–genital sex (cunnilingus or fellatio) tended to do so regularly. In contrast, penile–anal intercourse occurred on a less-frequent basis.

Wyatt and her colleagues (Wyatt et al., 1988) concluded on the basis of these findings that Black women have expanded their repertoire of acceptable sexual behaviors in more recent times. Marital relationship status was unrelated to preference for type of sexual behavior, particularly in the later study. No difference was found in the proportion of ever-married women who had engaged in extramarital sex (31% of the women in the Kinsey study and 40% of women in the later Wyatt study). No women in the Kinsey study had engaged in prostitution, while 2% of those in the later study had.

*How do you think the sexuality of African American women has changed from the 1930s and 1940s into current times?*

Virtually all women in the later study (98%) had used some form of contraception at least once, compared with women in the earlier study (89%). However, partners of women in the Kinsey study were much more likely to use condoms (80%) than those of women in the later study (46%), suggesting that condoms were used to a great extent for protecting against pregnancy (contraception) rather than against disease. Wyatt and her colleagues concluded that protection methods requiring women to depend on their partner had dropped (which included withdrawal of the penis before ejaculation, as well as condoms). Methods over which women exercise control, such as the oral contraceptive pill, increased. Rather surprisingly, the availability of more effective techniques did not translate into lower levels of unwanted pregnancy, with 20% of women in the later study and 29% of women in the Kinsey study having unwanted pregnancies; these percentages were not statistically different. Wyatt and her colleagues speculated that the reason for little improvement despite the more effective techniques is that the protection methods were not being used appropriately.

Wyatt, Peters, and Guthrie (1988) concluded that some aspects of sexuality had changed for Black women over the decades. These include age of first intercourse, number of partners, earlier first orgasm, and increase in preference for oral–genital sexual behavior. Contraceptive behavior had likewise changed to methods over which women have greater control. They observed that the various aspects of sexuality have not changed as rapidly for Black women as for other ethnic groups; however, the changes nonetheless indicate that African Americans have been assimilated into the mainstream of U.S. culture.

### Comparison of Adult Women of Various Ethnicities at Midlife

A more recent study concerned with ethnicity and sexuality focused on women at midlife, between the ages of 40 and 55 years (Cain et al., 2003). All women were approaching menopause—the time when the monthly cycles of the reproductive system cease—but they had not yet experienced complete menopause. Five ethnic groups were examined: African American (28.2%), Chinese American (7.5%), Hispanic American (8.8%), Japanese American (8.5%), and non-Hispanic European American (White, 47.0%). A major strength of the study included the tremendously large number of participants, 3,262 women selected from seven metropolitan areas in the East, Midwest, and West. Moreover, analyses were statistically adjusted for relevant demographic and socioeconomic factors to eliminate differences on these factors among the groups of women. Such demographic and socioeconomic factors included education and income level.

African American women tended to view sex as more important in their lives than did European American women, whereas Chinese and Japanese American women considered sex to be less important. Among the 22% of the women who had not engaged in sexual behavior with a partner in the previous 6 months, the most common reason was that they did not have a sexual partner (67%). This was true for all ethnic groups except Japanese American women; Japanese American women more frequently cited a lack of interest as the reason for absence of sex, although differences among groups on this reason were not statistically significant. Lack of partner as a reason was least likely to be selected by Japanese American women (44%) and most likely to be selected by African American women (72%). Relatively infrequent reasons were (a) being too tired or too busy on their part or on the part of their partner, (b) their own or their partner's physical problems, and (c) lack of interest by their partner.

For those who had engaged in sexual behavior with a partner in the past 6 months, the two most common reasons for engaging in sex were to express love and to experience pleasure and enjoyment. Approximately 90% of all women identified these two reasons, although European American women were more likely to cite love than African American women; Hispanic American women were the least likely to identify pleasure as a reason. Hispanic and Japanese American women were most likely to report that they engaged in sex because their partner wanted to, whereas African American women were least likely to endorse this as a reason. Hispanic American women were more interested in engaging in sex to get pregnant (roughly 5%) than the other ethnic groups, a proportion that is somewhat surprising given that the women were middle-aged.

Frequency of penile–vaginal intercourse differed according to ethnicity, with greater frequency occurring for African American women compared with European American women, and European American women having greater frequency than Japanese women. Unmarried African American women were more likely to report engaging in sex than unmarried European American women, although no differences existed for married women or women of other ethnic groups. Japanese American women also engaged in sexual touching less frequently than European American women, although no differences in frequency of oral–genital sex were found. European American women engaged in greater levels of masturbation than all other ethnic groups, with women who showed signs of the onset of menopause engaging in masturbation to a greater extent than women who had not begun the initial phases of menopause.

High levels of emotional satisfaction with the sexual relationship and physical pleasure during sexual interaction were reported by all women, which were not different for the various ethnic groups. A large majority of women, 70%, felt aroused during sexual behavior almost always or always, although European American women reported more frequent arousal than other women. The counterpart of this is that European American women experienced pain less frequently during penile–vaginal intercourse than the other ethnic groups. Chinese and Japanese American women reported lower sexual desire than European American women, with the levels for African American and Hispanic American women being similar to European American women.

High percentages of women at midlife engaged in sexual behavior with a partner in the previous 6 months: 78% for all women, which is lower than the 84% obtained by a national representative sample (Laumann, Gagnon, Michael, & Michaels, 1994). Cain and her colleagues suggest that the greater ethnic diversity in their sample of women may account for the slightly lower number. Nonetheless, sex is a substantially important aspect of middle-aged women's lives, with 60% reporting regular sexual behavior and approximately 50% engaging in masturbation in the previous 6 months. Although 40% experienced low frequency of sexual desire, this may be due as much to fatigue or a busy schedule as to a sexual desire disorder, because the majority of women reported high levels of emotional and physical satisfaction in their relationships.

The only factor at all associated with beginning to experience early symptoms of menopause was a greater likelihood of experiencing pain during intercourse. Ethnic differences related to menopause were not found for emotional satisfaction and physical pleasure. Differences were found among women of the various ethnic groups, such as in frequency of intercourse and masturbation and reasons for engaging or not engaging in sexual behavior. Cain and her colleagues (Cain et al., 2003) suggested that these may be due to differences in cultural attitudes about sexuality, although the reasons for the differences were not addressed in the study.

## The Concern About Early Adolescent Sexual Behavior

A long-standing concern dominating virtually all research on ethnic minorities has been risk associated with early onset of sexual behavior among adolescents. As noted by Lewis and Kertzner (2003), this type of focus continues even into current times, although research on adult sexuality and ethnicity has also increased to some extent.

**Box 11.3  The History of Ethnosexual Boundaries of Europeans and Africans**

From the earliest times in Western history, tales of highly sensuous, lusty Africans sparked European fantasy, and Europeans attributed a special sexual capacity to those from the African continent. Beginning with the writings of 17th century authors, Black men have been described as having extremely large penises, whereas Black women were believed to have a sexual appetite that is virtually animalistic in nature. According to Nagel (2003), the dehumanization of Africans through focusing on what were perceived to be almost monstrous genitals and through comparisons with animals served the larger purpose of legitimizing their enslavement, their brutal treatment, confiscation of their lands, and their sexual violation. It would not have been as easy to morally justify such abuses of people who were considered to be intellectual, cultural, and moral equals.

Prior to the U.S. Civil War, Black slaves had virtually no political protection from sexual assault because they were granted no civil rights by the U.S. government. White slave owners had additional incentives beyond sexual gratification for having sex with their slaves. Specifically, slaves who became pregnant provided the owner with yet another slave when they gave birth to a child. Beyond the mere profitability of increasing the number of new slaves, a further reason for a White owner to have sex with slave women was that mixed-race slaves were considered more valuable than purely Black ones. Lighter-skinned slaves were given higher status in the hierarchy, and sold for more money at the slave market, especially if they were women. Lighter slaves were often assigned as servants in the owner's home rather than as workers in the fields; they were also considered much more desirable sexually by White men than darker-skinned slaves.

Power differences created by slavery resulted in an extremely biased response on the part of the legal system to the rape of Black slave women compared with accusations against Black men. From the very outset of slavery in America, Black men accused of rape by White women were almost always prosecuted, and a very high majority of those accused were convicted, which generally resulted in their execution. In contrast, very few claims of rape were even made against White men by Black women, including those who were free (Nagel, 2003).

After the Civil War, the concern of Southern White society became the suppression and control of Black people when they were freed from slavery. Jim Crow laws were enacted to restrict the rights of African Americans in the period after the war, and the Ku Klux Klan (KKK) arose during this time to terrorize them into submission and passiveness. The desire to intimidate Black people in general was probably related to fear of retaliation for the horrors they suffered during the centuries of enslavement and sexual abuse. Fear of sexual reprisal in the form of rape may have often hovered barely below the surface of White fear about their physical safety (Nagel, 2003).

Following the Civil War, White leaders played upon the fear that Black men would relentlessly attack White women sexually if given power. These fears were formally communicated in the testimony they gave before the federal Congress in attempts to limit Black political and economic power. Their argument was that placing Black men in positions of political power would contribute to their demand for equality with Whites, which would lead them to want to have access to White women sexually as well. Numerous documented cases indicate that Black men who achieved too well economically became targets of accusations by White people. Charges were often made that financially successful Black men had raped a White woman, had shown disrespect sexually for White women, or had become too familiar with White women. Lynchings of Black men escalated dramatically after the Civil War, and by the 1890s they had become such a tradition that the events were no longer conducted secretly under the cover of dark. They became organized public spectacles, with advertisements and publicity in advance, taking on the air of festivals or carnivals.

The degree of violence and the intensity of confrontation is no longer as extreme as it was in the last century. However, Nagel (2003) noted that "there remains in U.S. society today no ethnic boundary more sexualized or scrutinized than the color line dividing blacks and whites" (p. 117). For both Black and White groups, the historical schism created by political and economic power differences, as well as the fear and resentment on the part of both groups stemming from slavery and then its abolition, is likely to have reverberations for years to come. The reason for the schism may not be consciously identifiable to those of us who were not alive at the time to remember the chains of slavery, or the lynchings of Black men for largely imagined affronts to White women, or the attack of police dogs and water blasts from fire hoses on Black civil rights protestors. Yet the differences in economic opportunity, political power, and cultural privilege that lie at the root of the schism may take some time to fade before the gulf between the two groups begins to shrink.

### References

Nagel, J. (2003). *Race, ethnicity, and sexuality*. New York: Oxford University Press.

Perhaps one of the most comprehensive projects in terms of the number of factors and individuals examined is the study by Browning, Leventhal, and Brooks-Gunn (2004). These theorists proposed that the factors involved in early adolescent sexual behavior are both numerous and complex. The causes involve more than simply particular characteristics of individuals or even the nature of family life. Features of the neighborhood in which teenagers live were expected to also have an important influence.

Data for their study were obtained during a massive investigation called the Project on Human Development in Chicago Neighborhoods. Young people across age groups ranging from newborns to 18-year-olds were included in the study. They were identified to be in the study using a procedure of randomly selecting

*How do you suppose that neighborhood poverty leads to the early onset of penile–vaginal intercourse among adolescents? Why do you think that other factors, such as the presence of two parents in the household, do not explain ethnic differences in early sexual onset?*

households within each of the 343 neighborhood groups of Chicago. This increased the degree to which study participants accurately represented the population of young Chicagoans. However, the analysis of sexual behavior by Browning and his colleagues focused only on adolescents in the 11- to 16-year-old group. The young people and their parents were interviewed and assessed extensively in their homes at two different time periods, 1995–1996 and 1998–1999.

Ethnic groups differed in substantial ways in terms of family characteristics and social and financial resources. European American adolescents came from families with the highest socioeconomic resources and the smallest families, followed by African American and then Latino youths; socioeconomic resources were measured on the basis of annual household income and the educational level and occupation of the primary caregiver. African American young people were less likely to have two biological parents in the household, more likely to associate with peers who engage in risky or illegal behavior, to have engaged in problem behavior themselves, and to have demonstrated lower academic achievement than Hispanic or European American youths.

African American adolescents also lived in neighborhoods with the highest concentration of poverty, followed by Latinos and European Americans. Poverty was assessed for the neighborhoods by the proportion of incomes below the poverty line, the proportion receiving public assistance, the proportion unemployed, and the proportion of households headed by women. The greater poverty and hardship of African Americans has likewise been found in other research (Haveman & Wolfe, 1994). However, African American adolescents had the highest level of supervision by their primary caregiver, and Latino youths reported the lowest level of risky or illegal behavior.

African American youths were 2.8 times more likely to engage in sexual intercourse than European American youths; European American levels were similar to those of Latinos in likelihood of engaging in sexual intercourse. This finding is consistent with other research that has determined that African American adolescents on average engage in sexual intercourse at an earlier age than other ethnic groups (South & Baumer, 2000). In looking at factors associated with early sexual onset, the presence of two biological parents, smaller household size, and being valued and supported by one's family were related to a lower likelihood of engaging in sexual intercourse earlier. Greater likelihood of early sexual onset was related to four factors: (a) association with friends who engage in risky or illegal behaviors, (b) engaging in this type of behavior oneself, (c) development of secondary sex characteristics, and (d) the personality trait of sociability.

However, taking these influences on early sexual behavior into account did not explain the differences among ethnic groups, because the differences remained even after statistically making these factors equal for all ethnic groups (as shown in Figure 11.3). After making these adjustments, African American youth were still 2.1 times more likely to engage in early sexual intercourse than European American young people. Instead, the remaining differences among ethnic groups were entirely accounted for by the concentration of poverty within a neighborhood (which was assessed using the factors mentioned above). This means that, when poverty was statistically made equivalent for all ethnic groups, African American youth were no more likely to have engaged in early sexual intercourse than the other groups.

A factor of neighborhood collective efficacy independently reduced the likelihood of early sexual intercourse. *Efficacy* is another word for *competence,* and in this study it was measured through a combination of feelings of connection among neighborhood residents and the presence of adults in general who watch over children in the community.

Collective efficacy, however, did not change the influence of concentrated poverty on ethnic differences in sexual behavior. Browning and his colleagues therefore concluded that neighborhood poverty is the primary factor explaining racial differences in early onset of sexual behavior, independent of all other factors that contribute for adolescents in general. Consequently, focusing on individual-level or family-level factors is not sufficient to understand differences among ethnic groups in sexual behavior.

**FIGURE 11.3**    Factors Related to Early Onset of Sexual Intercourse

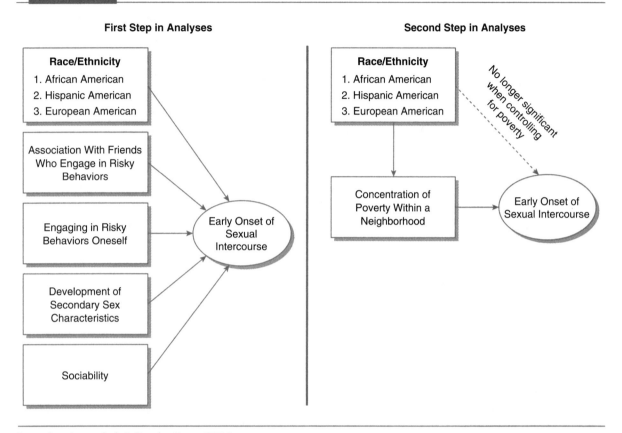

Browning, Leventhal, & Brooks-Gunn, 2004

Similarly, Wallace and his colleagues (Wallace, Fullilove, & Flisher, 1996; Wallace & Fullilove, 1999) have demonstrated that high-risk sexual behavior is associated with living in areas characterized by (a) high population density (large numbers of people concentrated in a small area), (b) poor housing, and (c) neighborhood "renewal" programs imposed by government policy that dislocate individuals and disrupt community cohesion. Racial and ethnic minorities are the primary groups of people affected by these damaging environmental factors. Under such conditions of lack of resources and power, sexual behavior linked to risk factors serve as means of communicating status and popularity; such risk factors include larger numbers of partners and lack of condom use. That is, race and ethnicity in themselves do not cause risk-related tendencies; rather, living under conditions of extreme deprivation and hardship lead individuals to seek means of enhancing their psychological well-being; however, such behaviors endanger their physical well-being.

The overarching conclusion that Lewis and Kertzner (2003) draw based on this research by Wallace and his colleagues is that future research must be directed by theory. They also state that the theory ideally will be derived from the perspective of racial and ethnic minorities themselves, and move away from merely describing sexual behavior. Economic and environmental risk factors are promising candidates for developing theory concerning risky sexual behavior of minority youth.

A view similar to that of Wallace and his colleagues was also proposed by Wyatt (1999), specifically that sexual behavior serves as a means of bolstering psychological well-being. The ethnic minority status experienced by African Americans places them in a position of substantially less power and fewer resources. A common reaction to this vulnerable status for African Americans is to develop a sense of invisibility: the feeling that one's abilities, talents, and characteristics are not valued by society (Franklin & Boyd-Franklin, 2000). The sense of invisibility develops over the course of an individual's life as a result of repeated experiences of blatant prejudice and discrimination. However, it may arise more commonly from the multitude of subtle messages casting African Americans as lesser beings than European Americans; these negative messages are referred to as *microaggressions* by Pierce (1988). The syndrome of invisibility has tremendously detrimental effects. This is especially true for African American males, which Franklin and Boyd-Franklin (2000) suggest may be related to the fact that they have the lowest life expectancy of virtually all groups.

One coping strategy for dealing with this ongoing onslaught against self-worth and self-esteem may be to distance oneself from those characteristics and tendencies of African Americans that the majority culture does not value. This distancing contributes even further to the syndrome of invisibility. One of the many implications of the trauma associated with repeated attacks on self-worth is that individuals may be less likely to take responsibility for protecting themselves against negative sexual outcomes, such as by using condoms. In fact, as a means of boosting self-esteem, African American men may be likely to embrace stereotypes of enormous male genitals and tremendous sexual abilities. Belief in these stereotypes provides the foundation for some African American men's sense of masculinity. Furthermore, having too great of a concern about taking precautions may be seen as unmasculine, which would decrease the desire to take the precautions (Wyatt, 1999).

Wyatt (1999) concluded that these factors contribute to a destructive cycle:

> This proposition develops from clinical observations of males, adolescent and adult. . . . Feelings of invisibility and sexual experiences with multiple partners. The pattern was cyclic—the more partners the individual had, the more isolated, unloved, and unlovable he felt, resulting in his continuing to seek other partners. (p. 807)

No empirical research has yet been conducted to examine exactly how these highly sexualized beliefs about African American men influences sexual attitudes and behaviors for Black male adolescents.

## The Role of Immigration, Second Language, and Acculturation Stress in Sexuality

An issue of tremendous importance when considering the influence of culture on behavior, and sexuality in particular, is the extent to which individuals have been influenced by another culture. This type of concern is especially significant when cultural differences include an entirely different language, as well as when individuals immigrate to a new country in which a different language is spoken. In the United States, the challenges of dealing with a new culture and a new language are extremely common for Latinos and Latinas, the ethnic group that is the fastest growing segment of the U.S. population.

Confronting the new European American majority culture when Hispanic American individuals move to the United States from a Spanish-speaking country is a major challenge for these groups. The issue is particularly important because immigration is a significant reason for the large growth in Hispanic populations in the United States. The stress associated with cultural differences may be a large factor in the fact that Hispanic Americans as a group are at greater risk for HIV infection and AIDS than are European Americans (Guilamo-Ramos, Jaccard, Pena, & Goldberg, 2005). The majority of girls and women in the 13- to 19-year-old group with HIV or AIDS were infected through heterosexual sexual behavior, making it imperative to address early sexual behavior among Hispanic Americans.

Although acculturation stress may increase the tendency to engage in risky behavior, including sexual behavior (Burnham, Hough, Karno, Escobar, & Telles, 1987), much of the research has produced inconsistent results. Guilamo-Ramos and his colleagues (2005) conducted their study to clarify the relationship of acculturation stress to risky sexual behavior. Specifically, they examined the two factors discussed previously that may contribute to acculturation stress; these are immigration to a new country and having Spanish as one's primary language in a country where English is the predominant language.

*Whether due to their family not speaking English or to experience with discrimination, how do you think that stress might play a role in early onset of penile–vaginal intercourse among Latino adolescents?*

Participants were 1,284 Mexican American, 416 Puerto Rican American, and 335 Cuban American males and females. They were brought into the study through a large random sample of students in Grades 7–12 across the United States in 1995. Ultimately 12,105 students were interviewed, and decisions were made about who would be included in the study through a series of steps to ensure the representativeness of the sample and to guarantee large numbers of ethnic minority students. Only those who identified themselves as Mexican, Puerto Rican, or Cuban American were included in the analyses.

The association of primary language with first sexual intercourse was different for those whose family had immigrated to the United States compared with those who had lived in the United States all of their lives. Students whose families had immigrated a longer time before the study were no more likely to engage in sexual intercourse during this early adolescent period than those whose families had immigrated more recently. However, individuals whose family had immigrated to the United States and who usually spoke English in the home were less likely to have engaged in sexual intercourse than those whose family usually spoke Spanish. The relationship of language was opposite for students who had been born in the United States or who had lived most of their lives in the United States. Those whose families usually spoke English in the home were more likely to have engaged in sexual intercourse than those whose family usually spoke Spanish. These effects were true regardless of gender or type of specific Latino heritage (i.e., Mexican, Puerto Rican, or Cuban).

Guilamo-Ramos and his colleagues (2005) speculated that the different role of language based on immigration status may be due to acculturation stress. Individuals whose families had recently immigrated to the United States may experience stress from the challenges of both adapting to the new culture and from the fact that their families do not also attempt to adapt, as indicated by speaking only Spanish at home. Consequently, this may be the reason that such immigrant adolescents engaged in sexual intercourse at a younger age. In contrast, those who have lived most or all of their lives in the United States and whose family speaks English in the home may be those who have had more contact with the majority culture compared with those whose family speaks Spanish. The researchers hypothesized that greater exposure to the majority culture may lead to greater experience with discrimination.

In addition, as discussed with respect to African Americans, Hispanic adolescents probably have had substantial experience with microaggressions, routine messages that minority individuals are not as valued as majority individuals, which contribute to the syndrome of invisibility (Franklin & Boyd-Franklin,

2000). Guilamo-Ramos and his colleagues suggest that such experience may contribute to the tendency to engage in problematic behaviors, including early sexual behavior. Experience with discrimination was not measured directly in the study; therefore, such explanations are completely speculative. The researchers also note that acculturation processes and outcomes were not measured directly either, such as by measuring ethnic identity formation, extent of participating in cultural practices, and endorsement of cultural values. Instead, acculturation was assessed indirectly in terms of duration of living in the United States and the language spoken in the home.

## The Role of Trauma in Native American Sexuality

### Box 11.4  The History of Ethnosexual Boundaries of Europeans and Native Americans

The concept of ethnosexual boundaries proposed by Joane Nagel (2003) was introduced in Box 11.1 as a way of understanding how ethnicity and sexuality affect one another. To illustrate the importance of social and historical context in how we conceive of sexuality, Nagel examined the changes that have taken place in the perceptions and sexual interactions involving Europeans and Native Americans throughout history.

Christopher Columbus and Amerigo Vespucci, two of the first European explorers of North America, actually developed highly different perspectives of the native people they encountered. Despite viewing Native Americans condescendingly as childlike and primitive, Columbus described them in essentially very positive, friendly terms. Vespucci, however, saw Native Americans as immoral creatures, given to cruel aggression, disgusting cannibalism, lewd nakedness, and promiscuous lustfulness.

The only instance of agreement between the two explorers was their opinion that the Native Americans were fairly attractive, particularly light-skinned women. In fact, Vespucci wrote that he and his men, in his own words, indulged the lustiness of the native women by providing them with as much sexual interaction as they requested. Columbus did not record sexual interaction with the Native Americans by his men, although his chronicles indicate that the Native men eventually began to hide their women away from the Europeans because of their intense attraction to the women (Nagel, 2003).

Native Americans were increasingly portrayed as barbaric, lustful, and sexually available in publications about the New World after this time, beginning with the very first brochure about it. Many of these publications adopted a judgmental, morally indignant tenor, but would nonetheless describe in titillating detail the sexual behaviors in which Native Americans supposedly engaged. The accuracy of such accounts is questioned by some scholars because the pervasive motivation of European explorers was the conquest and possession of the new territory. Such accounts of crude, primitive inhabitants likely provided a moral justification for their domination and control, and the eventual removal of them from their territories.

The widespread sexual involvement of Europeans with Native Americans was apparent in the growing population of mixed ethnic individuals after the first waves of settlers and explorers following Columbus and Vespucci. A type of sexual bartering system gradually developed in which goods or services were exchanged for sexual behavior, not only with the Spanish, but also with the English and French.

Evidence suggests that such transactions took place during the historical Lewis and Clark expeditions in the early 1800s as well, in which Western regions of North America were first charted.

Later, a type of legendary horror tale became popular during the frontier days of the United States portraying a type of reverse situation in which White people, usually women, were abducted and ravished by Native Americans; one of the most famous examples is the book *The Last of the Mohicans* by James Fenimore Cooper. Many of these accounts were probably fictitious, written as a type of morality story, in which the victims struggle to make their way back to acceptable, moral society. The concept of the Native American as threatening and dangerous, yet sexual and alluring, wove its way deep into the fabric of White consciousness throughout the 19th century. Gradually, White people who became sexually and romantically involved with Native people were viewed with distrust and considered to be treasonous, as well as immoral and inferior.

According to Nagel (2003), White society eventually attempted to crush or assimilate Native American cultures entirely to eliminate them as a source of competition. Indians were forced onto reservations by the 20th century, their children forced into English-only boarding schools, and many were forced to convert to Christianity. Once Native Americans were imprisoned away on far-removed, desolate reservations, rendered virtually powerless and invisible, the White culture began a process of reinventing the American Indian to suit White needs. White men gradually began to develop an admiration for the Native American symbol of masculine strength, courage, and resourcefulness that evolved out of the "evil villain" representation of the Indian. The Indian or "Redskin" became a symbol of many White organizations, clubs, and sports teams throughout the 20th century.

This idealization of the noble savage Indian continues even today. The glorification of Native Americans include images of handsome, muscular brown savages who overwhelm swooning pale, voluptuous White women on the covers of romance novels, as well as

> Indianized white (or "half-breed") men confronting the feminized forces of repression and threats to their rugged individualism, manly autonomy, and inalienable right to freedom: the *Rambos* and *Billy Jacks* of contemporary American adventure fiction and film. . . . [These] show us that the Indian-white ethnosexual frontier remains an open chapter in the ongoing saga of American culture and identity. (Nagel, 2003, p. 83).

### References

Nagel, J. (2003). *Race, ethnicity, and sexuality*. New York: Oxford University Press.

The history of Native Americans since the appearance of Europeans in North America has been an ongoing, systematic campaign to eliminate American Indian culture through extermination, removal to reservations, and then absorption of Native individuals into European American culture (Choney, Berryhill-Paapke, & Robbins, 1995). Much of the research on American Indian adolescents has therefore focused on problem behavior, "alcohol and drug use, suicide, depression, and their relatively grim economic and scholastic prospects feature prominently" as common problem areas (Kaufman et al., 2004, p. 302). However, virtually no research has been conducted about Native American sexuality, particularly as it is influenced by the inhospitable, and even hostile, environment in which they live.

Kaufman and her colleagues collected information from 289 Northern Plains American Indians ranging in age from 17–25 years to examine the relationship of trauma to sexual behavior. Individuals were selected through random sampling from a registry of the tribes in a way to ensure representativeness for gender and age. Substantial proportions of both women and men, 58% of women and 55% of men, reported having experienced traumas, defined as extremely disturbing events that do not happen to most people. Women were more likely to have been sexually abused or sexually assaulted, whereas men were more likely to have been mugged, robbed, or physically assaulted. Traumas were not consistently associated with the number of partners with whom individuals had been involved in a significant relationship for either women or men. However, for women, the occurrence, the number, and the type of traumas were related to the number of casual sexual partners. In particular, women who had been assaulted by a family member or who had suffered from accidents or natural disasters had greater numbers of casual sexual partners. For men, traumas were not related to any of the aspects of sexuality assessed in the study. Consistency in use of condoms was not affected by traumas at all for women and men.

Clearly, a great deal more research needs to be conducted concerning all aspects of sexuality for all ethnic minority groups. The study discussed above is the only one that was found dealing specifically with Native Americans, and none were located for Asian Americans in the United States. The situation was really not much different for any of the other groups. Consequently, very little is known about the behaviors, feelings, and attitudes of the various ethnic groups outside of European Americans.

## Summary

Little sexuality research has been conducted involving people of ethnic groups other than European Americans. A major reason is the assumption within science that research examines universal principles that are relevant to all individuals. Race as the concept we know today developed during the period of the slave trade as a justification for the permanent enslavement of Africans. However, the concept of race is not based on scientific evidence about biological differences among groups of people. The absence of substantial distinctions among the supposed races leads to the conclusion that the concept of race is not a very useful explanation of variation among humans.

Separation of groups of people geographically and socially has produced very real differences in culture. Culture is the system of knowledge, beliefs, values, expectations for social interaction, and daily routine shared by a particular group of people. Race is a socially constructed system of classifying people according to characteristics thought to be important for determining social status and worth, such as skin and eye color. Ethnicity is a socially constructed system of classifying people on the basis of cultural and nationality differences thought to be important for determining social status and worth.

Very few studies on the sexuality of racial and ethnic minorities have been conducted. The few that exist have tended to assume a problem-centered perspective, in which the sexuality of non-White groups is viewed as problematic, unhealthy, and dangerous. These studies focus on early onset of sexual behavior, early pregnancy, and infection with sexually transmitted diseases of minority adolescents. Limitations of research on ethnic minority sexuality are (a) the typical assumption that all members of ethnic minority groups are identical, (b) obtaining a superficial understanding of sexuality by focusing on overt behavior rather than the meaning of sexual behavior, and (c) the general absence of theory regarding sexuality.

Bias in early theory regarding ethnic minority sexuality resulted in the perpetuation of erroneous and destructive stereotypes of African Americans, Latinos–Latinas, and Asian Americans. Contemporary analysis does not support the accuracy of these stereotypes. Research indicates that adult African American women have engaged in first sexual intercourse at an earlier age, had greater numbers of partners, experienced their first orgasm at an earlier age, and are likely to engage oral–genital behavior on a more regular basis than they did in the early 1900s.

Other research comparing midlife women of various ethnic groups found differences in various aspects of sexuality: the importance of sexual behavior, reasons for engaging and not engaging in sexual behavior, frequency of penile–vaginal intercourse, and emotional satisfaction with the sexual relationship and physical pleasure experienced. Women in general were similar in a number of ways as well.

Regarding sex during early adolescence, African American youth in one study were 2.1 times more likely to engage in sexual intercourse than European American youth, even after controlling for other factors such as risky or illegal behavior, development of secondary sex characteristics, and personality. The differences in ethnicity were entirely due to the concentration of poverty in the neighborhood in which adolescents resided. Engaging in sexual behavior may serve to bolster adolescents' self-esteem in the face of a sense of invisibility that develops among minority populations. Lack of self-esteem may also relate to a decrease in use of protection against sexually transmitted diseases.

Stress due to immigration to the United States from Spanish-speaking countries may also be related to early sexual behavior during adolescence. Adolescents whose families had immigrated and continue to speak Spanish may experience acculturation stress because they must adapt to the new culture while their families do not attempt to adapt. Adolescents born in the United States whose families speak English may have greater exposure to European American culture and therefore have greater experience with discrimination and the resulting stress. Research also demonstrated that experiencing traumas is associated with greater numbers of casual sexual partners for young Native American women. Again, stress appears to be associated with at least one aspect of sexuality for these minority youth.

## Chapter 11 Critical Thinking Exercises

1. Ethnicity and sexuality

   List what you think are stereotypes of the romantic and sexual behaviors of European Americans. How many of the ones you were able to think of are positive? How many are negative? How did these stereotypes develop?

2. Assumptions involved in scientific research

   Think back to the information in chapters 9 and 10 on sexuality, such as related to the different types of sexual behavior and the importance of sexual satisfaction and relationship quality. What aspects of this information are likely to be accurate for the various ethnic groups? What considerations specific to each ethnic group need to be added to this information?

Visit www.sagepub.com/hillhsstudy.com for online activities, sample tests, and other helpful resources. Select "Chapter 11: Ethnicity, Race, Culture, and Sexuality" for chapter-specific activities.

# Chapter 12

## THE BIOPSYCHOLOGY OF SEXUALITY

R esearch on sexuality historically has followed two separate paths, one focusing almost entirely on biological factors and the other concentrating almost exclusively on social and cultural factors. This traditional separation has created two theoretical perspectives that seem to oppose one another in important ways. The result has been to produce a highly incomplete understanding of the nature of human sexuality because each perspective presents only part of the information about sexuality (DeLamater & Hyde, 1998).

The extreme form of the view that biological factors are important has been called the **essentialist perspective**. Social and cultural factors are thought to exert some degree of influence on sexuality. Yet they only begin to shape sexuality after biological factors have laid out the territory and its boundaries. This means that social and cultural factors can only reduce or strengthen the tendencies that have already been established through biological development.

The extreme version of the position that social and cultural factors are responsible for the nature of sexuality is often referred to as the **social constructionist perspective**. This position proposes that sexual tendencies develop out of the expectations and scripts imposed on individuals by social situations and culture. Rather than merely tinkering with the characteristics formed through biological development, social forces are thought to create the very nature of sexuality by defining the meaning of the body and sexual interaction (Tolman & Diamond, 2001).

With its almost exclusive focus on biology, the extreme essentialist perspective has problems explaining the tremendous differences that exist across cultures in the understanding they have of sexuality; it also has difficulty providing a detailed understanding of the way that sexuality is experienced differently by different individuals. Finally, it tends to ignore the significant intentional control and choice that individuals have over their sexual functioning, because the view seems to suggest that sexuality is determined entirely by nonconscious biological forces (Tolman & Diamond, 2001).

On the other hand, the extreme social constructionist perspective cannot explain in sufficient detail the ways in which social expectations are linked to the functioning, psychological makeup, and subjective experience of the individual. That is, the social constructionist perspective is not very precise in terms of what happens at the level of the individual because it focuses almost entirely on social rules that exist outside of individuals (Tolman & Diamond, 2001).

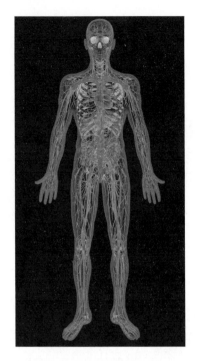

Biological factors are necessarily involved in important ways in human sexuality. Behavior would not be possible without the functioning of the brain and nervous system.

Given the mounting evidence that both types of factors are important, a complete understanding of sexuality must of course include both biological and social factors. In fact, the most accurate and useful view is probably what is called an **interactionist perspective**. According to this approach, biological characteristics of individuals operate together with forces within the environment to create particular tendencies and behaviors (Tolman & Diamond, 2001).

What's more, the debate over whether sexuality is influenced largely by biological or by environmental factors is not really a sensible controversy at all. This is because all behaviors require the operation of the brain at some level—a biological structure—or behavior would not even be possible. Furthermore, much human behavior involves interacting with other humans, such that a good deal of behavior is based on anticipating others and reacting to their behavior. Social influence is therefore definitely a major force acting on human behavior. This means that it really goes without saying that both biological and social factors are involved in behavior (Mustanski, Chivers, & Bailey, 2002).

Up to this point, social factors have been a major concern within this book in providing an understanding of human sexuality. However, because biological factors are also extremely important, it is necessary to consider the ways that biological features are involved in social and sexual interactions as well. This is the focus of the current chapter. Investigation of biological factors involved in sexuality draws upon expertise in the area of psychology called *biopsychology*. **Biopsychology** is the scientific study of the biology of behavior, sometimes also called psychobiology and behavioral neuroscience (Pinel, 2003). To understand the biological issues involved in sexuality, a number of fundamental concepts underlying human anatomy and physiology are addressed first.

The human body is typically conceptualized in terms of various **systems**, an organization of organs and structures that all function to carry out related activities, such as digesting food, circulating blood, and most relevant to sexuality, engaging in behavior and activity. The nervous system and the endocrine system are the two that are most directly involved in the operation of psychological processes and the production of overt behavior. The **nervous system** is the set of organs and structures responsible for sending and receiving of information throughout the body. Sending information from the command centers of the body is necessary to initiate and control all psychological processes and overt behavior. This system will be discussed first.

The **endocrine system** is the set of organs and structures that release chemicals from glands, usually directly into the blood. These chemicals also initiate or end activity in other parts of the body. The ovaries and testicles are examples of organs that release chemicals to influence a wide range of organs and activities in the body. They release sex hormones, such as estrogen and testosterone, that are responsible for the maturation of eggs and sperm. Sex hormones additionally control the development of primary and secondary sex characteristics, as we have already seen in chapter 6 on gender. The endocrine system is examined in the section following the one describing the nervous system.

## The Nervous System

The nervous system is responsible for sending information and governing the activity of the body. The microscopic cells that make up the nervous system are called **neurons**, which send and receive chemical signals. If neurons are sufficiently stimulated by other neurons or by signals from outside the body, they release chemicals, which as a group, are called **neurotransmitters**. A neurotransmitter is the signal that conveys information, in that it activates the receiving neuron, making it more likely that it too will release its neurotransmitter. In other cases, some neurotransmitters inhibit the receiving neuron, decreasing the likelihood that it will release its neurotransmitter.

Chains of neuron pathways sending their information to the same part of the body converge into groups of neuron pathways, or fibers, called **nerves**. The major nerve pathway that channels information between the brain and the body is called the spinal cord. This runs along the back from the hips up the neck to the brain, and is encased in protective bony structures called **vertebrae**. The brain consists of a vast multitude of neuron pathways and structures made up of neurons. Together, the brain and the spinal cord make up the **central nervous system**, which is responsible for monitoring and regulating the activity of the body. All other parts of the nervous system outside of the brain and spinal cord are called the **peripheral nervous system**.

The brain is also, most notably for psychology, the organ in which all higher psychological processes occur, such as affect and cognition. **Affect**, as discussed in chapter 1, refers to emotions, feelings, and mood—the private, subjective experiences of individuals related to pleasure, displeasure, happiness, sadness, love, and hate, to name a few types of emotions. **Cognition** refers to covert (unobservable) intellectual activities, including thinking, understanding, planning, perceiving, interpreting, and problem-solving. The brain is also responsible for initiating and controlling **behavior**, which in psychology refers specifically to overt (observable) actions. These are easily observed movements such as walking, talking, writing, gesturing, facial expressions—and sexual behaviors such as touching, kissing, and genital stimulation.

## The Endocrine System

The **endocrine system** is the set of organs and structures that release chemicals from glands that initiate activity in other parts of the body. **Endocrine glands** are organs that release the chemicals, called **hormones**, into the blood. Hormones are transported throughout the body, where they influence parts of the body that are capable of responding to their chemical properties. Hormones consist of three major types. **Steroid hormones**, those created from cholesterol (a fat molecule), are the type to which sex hormones belong. Steroid hormones are capable of directly affecting the way that genes operate to control body development and functioning; the other two types of hormones do not directly affect genes. Steroid hormones are able to cross through the outer membrane of cells and attach to genetic structures inside cells. This is the way they exert significant effects on development and functioning of the body (Pinel, 2003).

As discussed in chapter 6 on the issue of gender, the gonads are the primary producers of sex hormones. Gonads are the ovaries and testicles, the organs that produce the female and male sex cells involved in reproduction, eggs and sperm. Both the ovaries and testes produce not only **estrogens**, the female sex hormone, but also **androgens**, the male sex hormone; these are both steroid hormones. The most prevalent estrogen is **estradiol**, and the most prevalent androgen is **testosterone**. The ovaries typically produce more estrogens than androgens, and the testicles usually produce more androgens than estrogens.

Both ovaries and testicles manufacture another type of sex hormone, **progestins**, the most common of which is **progesterone**. Progesterone is responsible for building up the inner lining of the uterus in females around the midpoint of the menstrual cycle, readying it for the implantation of a fertilized egg. The adrenal glands that sit on top of each of the kidneys also produce all of the sex hormones, but in smaller quantities than the gonads. Therefore, adrenal glands are not the primary source of sex hormones, and are typically more involved in nonsexual aspects of body functioning.

## Control of Sex Hormone Production by the Brain

Although sex hormones are produced largely in the gonads, control over their production is regulated by several important structures within the brain (Figure 12.1). The **hypothalamus** is centrally important in many aspects of bodily functioning, serving as a monitor of the level of nutrients, fluid, hormones, and temperature within the body. It is positioned in the lower middle area of the brain, near a group of structures in the center of the brain collectively called the **limbic region**. The limbic region is surrounded by the **cerebral cortex**, the outer, highly wrinkled portion that is the largest part of the brain in humans. The cerebral cortex is the area in which the higher intellectual processes, such as thinking, understanding, and reasoning take place.

The hypothalamus measures levels of hormones and other substances as blood passes through it. If the levels are too low or too high, the hypothalamus takes a variety of actions that return the substances to their optimal levels. If estrogens or progestins in women fall below a certain level, the hypothalumus creates a hormone of its own to direct the body to increase output of the sex hormones; this is also true if testosterone dips below a certain level in men. The hormone produced by the hypothalamus in response to low levels of sex hormones is called **gonadotropin-releasing hormone** (abbreviated GnRH). Gonadotropin-releasing hormone is released into a capillary network that travels to a very nearby organ of the brain, the pituitary gland.

In other words, the hypothalamus does not directly cause the increased production of sex hormones. Instead, it operates on the front lobe of the pituitary gland, called the anterior pituitary; pituitary hormones then trigger the production of sex hormones. The **anterior pituitary** is sometimes called *the master gland* because its role in the body is to activate a number of other endocrine glands. The back lobe of the pituitary, called the **posterior pituitary**, actually develops out of tissue from the hypothalamus and serves different functions than those of the anterior pituitary (Pinel, 2003). The pathway through which structures of the brain control hormone production is presented in Figure 12.2.

Gonadotropin-releasing hormone causes the pituitary gland to release two hormones, follicle-stimulating hormone (FSH) and luteinizing hormone (LH), in both women and men. In women, follicle-stimulating hormone and luteinizing hormone travel from the anterior pituitary through the blood stream. When reaching the ovaries, FSH and LH prompt structures in the ovaries, called **follicles**, to produce increased levels of estrogens; follicles are compartments that each contain a single undeveloped egg. Higher levels of estrogen cause a number of eggs to mature during the first 14 days of women's monthly ovulatory cycle.

On approximately Day 14, the midpoint of the 28-day cycle, usually one egg grows so large that it ruptures the wall of the ovary and gushes out into the fluid of the **fallopian tube** (all of these structures were explained in chapter 6). The release of an egg from the ovary is called **ovulation**. The egg is transported down the fallopian tube toward the uterus, where it typically implants in the inner lining if it has been fertilized by a sperm. The follicle that released the matured egg becomes known as the **corpus luteum** (meaning *yellow body* in Latin), and becomes a factory for the production of the hormones, **progesterone** and estrogen. Progesterone

**FIGURE 12.1**  Structures Within the Brain Responsible for Regulating Sex Hormones Production

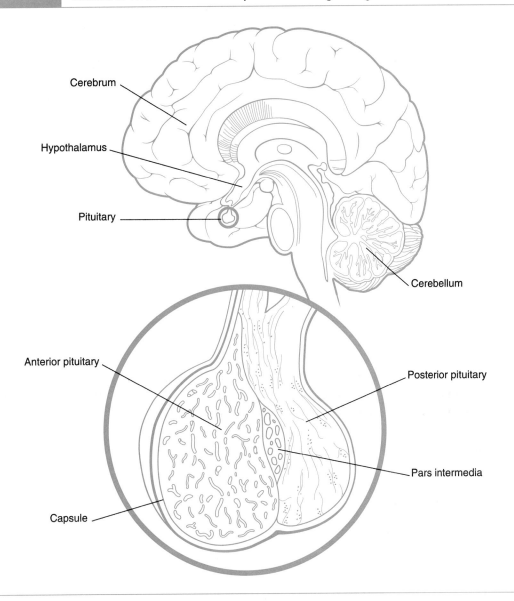

promotes the enriched development of the inner lining of the uterus, the endometrium, in which fertilized eggs typically implant.

In men, when FSH and LH arrive at the testicles, they cause the production of **androgen-binding protein**. This protein causes **Leydig cells** (also called interstitial cells) within the testicles to produce and accumulate testosterone. Higher levels of testosterone then stimulate the growth of primitive sperm cells to mature into viable sperm cells that become capable of fertilizing eggs. This process was likewise addressed in chapter 6.

**FIGURE 12.2**   Control of Sex Hormone Production

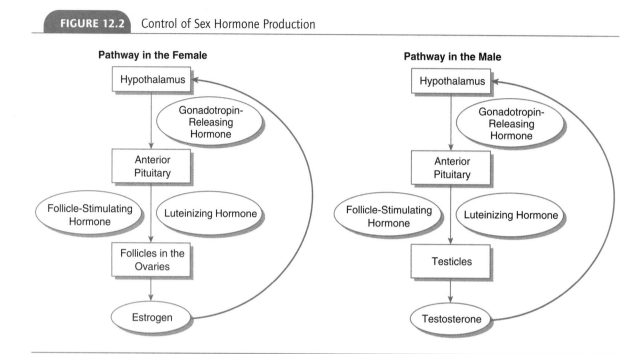

In both women and men, when the sex hormone stimulated by FSH and LH (estrogens for women, testosterone for men) reach elevated levels, the high concentration of the hormone is absorbed into the blood system, transported to the brain, and detected by the hypothalamus. Again, the hypothalamus is the organ in the brain that measures levels of hormones and other substances as blood passes through it, taking a variety of actions to maintain them in appropriate range. In the case of sex hormones, the hypothalamus produces another hormone, called **inhibin**, in response to the heightened sex hormone levels. Inhibin prevents the anterior pituitary from releasing additional FSH and LH, the hormones that stimulate the gonads to manufacture sex hormones. With lower levels of FSH and LH, the creation of sex hormone drops off, ending the maturation of eggs and sperm until the next cycle of increased sex hormone production. The next cycle begins when the hypothalamus detects extremely low levels of sex hormone in the blood system.

Although the overall process of controlling sex hormones is the same for women and men, noticeable differences exist in the pattern of hormone production. Hormone levels increase and decrease in women in a **cyclical pattern**; they occur in 28-day cycles of reaching maximum levels and then declining to minimal levels. This pattern produces the monthly menstrual cycle, in which the endometrium of the uterus builds up before the midpoint of the cycle when the egg is released, and then deteriorates in the last half of the cycle as progesterone levels decline. The next cycle begins with the expulsion of the old endometrium in the menstrual flow. The menstrual flow therefore occurs **at the beginning** of each menstrual cycle.

The male system also operates based on a pattern of increasing sex hormone levels. If the male hormone reaches a maximum level that is detected by the hypothalamus, the result is likewise a subsequent decline in hormone production. However, the fluctuation for males is much less dramatic, changing on a much more frequent and rapid basis. Consequently, the average level of testosterone is fairly constant from day to day, resulting in what is known as a **steady-state pattern**.

# The Role of Sex Hormones in Prenatal Development

## Formation of the Gonads

Much greater levels of sex hormones are produced after puberty than in earlier stages of development (on average, puberty begins at 10.5 years for girls and 11.5 years for boys; Brooks-Gunn & Reiter, 1990). However, sex hormones also play an important role prenatally, that is, before birth. Prior to the sixth week after fertilization, both females and males have exactly the same two primitive organs, called **primordial gonads**, or primitive gonads, that may develop into either ovaries or testicles. Both gonads have an inner layer of tissue, called the **medulla**, which may form into a testicle, as well as an outer layer, called the **cortex**, which may evolve into an ovary.

At six weeks after fertilization, the production of a protein called **H-Y antigen** is initiated by the Y chromosome in genetic males. H-Y antigen stimulates the growth of the medulla, resulting in the formation of a testicle from each primordial gonad. Without the Y chromosome, the H-Y antigen is not synthesized in genetic females, and the cortex of each primordial gonads grows, whereas the medulla does not, resulting in the formation of ovaries (Pinel, 2003).

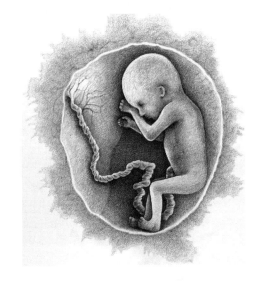

Sex hormones play a crucial role in prenatal development, most noticeably in the formation of the gonads and external genitals.

## Formation of Internal Sexual Organs

### Male Organ Development

In addition to the gonads, both genetic females and genetic males develop two different reproductive tissues, one that has the capacity to form into male internal organs and the other having the potential to develop into female internal organs. One is the **Wolffian system**, which can develop into male ducts, such as the vas deferens and seminal vesicles. The other is the **Müllerian system**, which potentially can develop into female ducts, such as the fallopian tubes, uterus, and upper vagina. At around eight weeks after fertilization, the developing testicles of genetic males typically begin to produce large amounts of testosterone (Hiort, 2000) and **Müllerian-inhibiting substance**. The presence of these two substances result in the development of the male internal reproductive structures. Testosterone causes the Wolffian cells to grow, while the Müllerian-inhibiting substance causes the withering of the Müllerian cells and the migration of the testicles into the scrotum.

### Female Organ Development

In the absence of high levels of testosterone and Müllerian-inhibiting substance, genetic females develop female internal reproductive structures. Formation of the organs results from the growth of the Müllerian cells and the failure of the Wolffian cells to be stimulated to grow. The ovaries remain essentially dormant during the prenatal period, not producing sex hormones at this time. Female sex hormones are not necessary for any of the female sexual organs to develop; the only real requirement is the absence of high levels of male sex hormones (Pinel, 2003).

## Formation of the External Sexual Organs

The external sexual organs for females and males originate from the same tissues, rather than evolving from different tissues as the internal organs do. In the weeks following the surge in testosterone in males and the formation of the internal organs in both sexes, the external sexual organs develop from a set of primitive structures presented in Figure 12.3.

In the typical course of development for females, the body does not produce high levels of a hormone related to testosterone, **dihydrotestosterone**, which is instead produced in males. With the absence of dihydrotestosterone in females, the primitive structure called the **genital tubercle** develops into the female clitoris, the **urogenital folds** grow in size to become the labia minora, the **lateral bodies** form the hood surrounding the clitoris, and the **labioscrotal swellings** become the labia majora. Under the influence of high levels of dihydrotestosterone, the genital tubercle develops into the head of the penis, the urogenital folds fuse and the lateral bodies join together to become the shaft of the penis, and the labioscrotal swellings expand and merge to become the scrotum.

**FIGURE 12.3**   Differentiation and Formation of the External Sexual Organs in Male and Female Fetuses

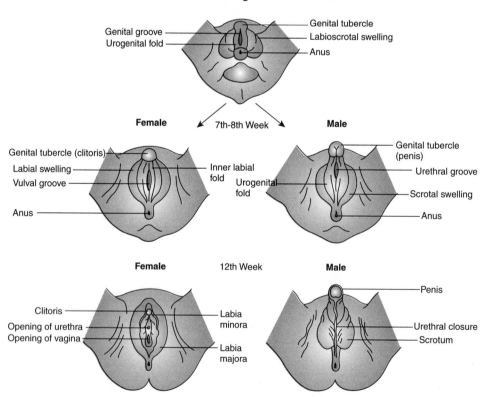

# Biological Factors Involved in Sexuality

## Prenatal Development of the Brain

Because it would be unethical to manipulate biological development in humans, direct examination of the influence of hormones on human embryos is not possible. Consequently, no direct experimental evidence is available regarding the process of gender and sexual development in humans. Although keeping in mind that animals may be different from humans in important ways, biopsychological researchers consider animal studies to provide at least one type of insight into the nature of human development related to gender, sexuality, and sexual orientation.

In early research, testosterone was administered to female guinea pigs prenatally who then had their ovaries removed at birth (a procedure called an ovariectomy). This procedure resulted in genitals that were virtually identical to those of males (Phoenix, Goy, Gerall, & Young, 1959). Even more strikingly, if administered a type of estrogen as adults, the altered females engaged in far less lordosis than females who had not been altered prenatally, but who were also administered estrogen; if given estrogen, normal females typically engage in increased lordosis, which is raising the hindquarters to allow themselves to be mounted for sexual intercourse. The low levels of lordosis behavior in the altered females was equivalent to that of males. The altered females also engaged in more mounting behavior than untreated females. This suggests that the nervous systems of the altered females may have been changed, given that they did not respond to the estrogen injections as normal females do.

A later study established a comparable effect for males (Grady, Phoenix, & Young, 1965). In rats, significant development of the brain and nervous system occurs shortly after birth related to gender and sexuality. Male rats that were castrated soon after birth did not engage in male-typical sexual behaviors as adults, even with testosterone injections. Furthermore, upon injection with estrogen and progesterone, the castrated males engaged in significantly more lordosis than noncastrated males (Pinel, 2003). This indicates that the nervous system of the castrated males had developed in a way typical of females to become sensitive to the female sex hormones.

The evidence for both females and males, therefore, suggests that, at least with respect to lower animals, hormones play a role in organizing the brain in a way that creates female-typical or male-typical tendencies. Actually, the most accurate description of the overall process makes a distinction between those factors that promote female-typical behavior and those that promote male-typical behavior. **Feminization** is the development of tendencies to engage in female-typical behavior, such as lordosis in lower animals. **Masculinization** is the development of tendencies to engage in male-typical behavior; in lower animals, examples of masculine behaviors are mounting, **intromission** (inserting the penis into the vagina), and ejaculation. **Defeminization** is the process of decreasing the tendency to engage in female-typical behavior, whereas **demasculinization** is decreasing the tendency to engage in male-typical behaviors. The presence of testosterone is necessary for masculinization and defeminization to occur (i.e., increasing male-typical behavior and decreasing female-typical behavior).

Interestingly, a widely accepted view in recent times has been that testosterone masculinizes certain structures in the brain by being converted into estradiol, a type of estrogen, the female sex hormone. The existence of this process is supported by (a) the finding that injections of estradiol masculinize the brains of rats prenatally; (b) injections of dihydrotestosterone do not masculinize the brain (dihydrotestosterone is a hormone related to testosterone, but which cannot be converted into estradiol); and (c) chemicals that prevent testosterone from being converted into estradiol block the masculinization of the brain (Pinel, 2003). However, a noted researcher in this area has argued that recent research suggests a direct effect of androgen on structures in the brain that may be related to an attraction to females; this means that androgen, rather than by being converted to estradiol, itself produces an attraction to females (Swaab, 2005).

Females of species in which male brains are masculinized by estradiol are protected from masculinization themselves, because, as discussed previously, female's ovaries are virtually inactive prenatally. Human genetic females are also protected from the estrogen produced by their mother because of the existence of a barrier in the placenta that prevents the hormone from crossing over into the system of the developing female; the placenta is the tissue of the developing embryo that attaches to the uterus, enabling the embryo to receive nutrients and discard wastes through the mother's system. The testes of genetic males however produce testosterone, which is transported to the male's brain, converted into estradiol, and in that form masculinizes the brain.

Some synthetic estrogens, most notably **diethylstilbestrol** (DES), are not stopped by the placental barrier. DES was administered to mothers for two decades starting in the 1940s to maintain pregnancies that were in danger of miscarrying; DES, however, is no longer administered for this purpose because of unexpected side effects. Women who were exposed to diethylstilbestrol before they were born are more likely to exhibit some characteristics that are more typical of males (Pinel, 2003); this finding will be discussed in more detail in a later section.

## The Role of Sex Hormones Following Puberty

As discussed in chapter 6 dealing with issues of gender, sex hormones exert a profound, and perhaps their most observable, effect during puberty, the point at which the body dramatically increases the production of sex hormones. The average age at which puberty begins for girls is 10.5 years and, for boys, 11.5 years (Brooks-Gunn & Reiter, 1990). The surge in sex hormones causes the maturation and growth of the internal and external sexual organs, which are the **primary sex characteristics**. This results eventually in the ability of the individual to produce mature sex cells, eggs or sperm, and to produce offspring. The increase in sex hormone production also results in the development of **secondary sex characteristics**, such as enlarged breasts in women and greater potential for muscle development in men.

An outcome of central importance in sexuality is the development of interest in sexuality and the heightening of sexual desire following the onset of puberty. Sexual desire, of course, is of central importance because heightened sexual desire increases the likelihood an individual will engage in sexual behavior. As discussed in chapter 1, individuals' perception of situations and other people in terms of whether they arouse sexual interest or not is at the heart of the meaning of human sexuality. With respect to biological factors, therefore, an issue of great interest to sexuality researchers is the way in which hormones are related to sexual interest, desire, and behavior.

### Women

The evidence for an association between hormone levels and sexual behavior is far less consistent for women than it is for men. As noted by Bancroft (1988), women do not follow the pattern exhibited by females of many primate species, in which the greatest level of sexual activity occurs around the time of ovulation; the lower primate pattern indicates that sexual behavior is rigidly determined by fluctuations in hormone levels.

**FIGURE 12.4**    Sexual Desire and Androgen Levels Across the Menstrual Cycle

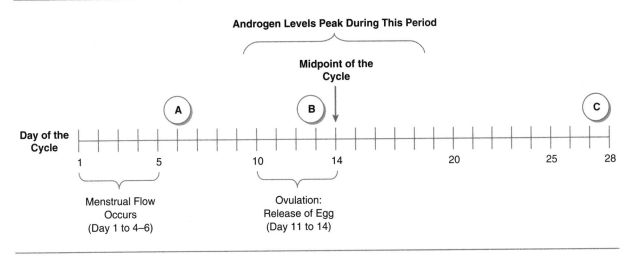

On the basis of available evidence, Bancroft concluded that sexual interest in women appears to reach a maximum immediately before or after menstruation (points A and C in Figure 12.4); menstruation (the discharge of the menstrual flow) occurs at the beginning of the menstrual cycle, and is the period during which hormone levels are at their lowest point. Androgens, the male sex hormones, have been consistently identified as the hormone related to heightened sexual interest in women as well as men. Yet androgen levels are at their highest level during the middle third of the menstrual cycle, creating a puzzling situation if hormones are related to greater sexual desire as hypothesized. Bancroft speculated that androgen may have a 7 to 10 day lag in its influence on sexual interest; this is supported by research on men receiving androgen replacement therapy for low-functioning testicles (Skakkebaek, Bancroft, Davidson, & Warner, 1981). A more recent review of research on the relationship of sexual desire to the menstrual cycle (Regan, 1996), however, indicates that sexual desire and fantasy substantially increase for women around the midpoint of the cycle (point B in Figure 12.4); this is the time at which ovulation occurs and androgen levels are at their peak. Yet other research reviewed by Regan has found that the greatest levels of sexual desire occur several days after menstruation has ended, at the time when hormone levels are on their rise, rather than at their peak (point A in Figure 12.4). Still other studies indicated that the time just before menstruation is the point of greatest sexual desire, the time that was identified by Bancroft (point C in Figure 12.4).

In the final analysis, Regan concluded that no one pattern of heightened sexual desire appears to reliably characterize women. It is also possible that different techniques of collecting data across the different studies make it hard to detect a single pattern if it exists. Moreover, common beliefs about the menstrual cycle may influence feelings of interest in engaging in sexual activity as well. Menstruation, the discharge of the menstrual flow, is often viewed somewhat negatively by both women and men. Moreover, many people believe that changes in the body and in psychological processes occur as a result of the menstrual cycle. Changes in sexual desire, therefore, may be due as much to the emotional reactions of a particular woman to beliefs about the menstrual cycle as they are due to increasing or decreasing hormone levels. Some women might experience more negative emotional states, for example, around the time of the menstrual flow because of cultural expectations that unpleasant physical and psychological changes occur (Regan, 1996). In addition, generally negative views of menstruation or anxieties about becoming pregnant at a particular point of the menstrual cycle may interfere with the experience of sexual desire.

It may also be the case that greater variability exists for women in comparison to men in the influence of hormones on structuring the brain early in development. This may result in a wider range of differences across women in the effect of sex hormones on sexual interest in comparison to men. From an evolutionary perspective, according to Bancroft (1988), rigid control of sexual desire by hormones would not be as necessary among females of higher species, especially humans. This is because males are characteristically more likely to initiate sexual activity than females. Furthermore, Bancroft points out that humans engage in greater levels of sexual behavior than are really necessary to insure sufficient numbers of offspring.

## The Complicating Role of Social Factors in the Influence of Hormones

Social factors appear to play a significant role in determining the influence of hormones on sexual interest for women, as suggested by research on adolescents (Udry, Talbert, & Morris, 1986). Attitudes, beliefs, and behaviors of peers—who are individuals around the age of the adolescent—exert significant influences on sexual desire. Research by Udry (1988) also found that, although levels of testosterone circulating in the body correlated with sexual interest for girls, factors such as the degree of adult feminization of the body (e.g., breast development and development of the hour-glass figure) are also related. In addition, the presence or absence of the father in the home combined with testosterone levels to affect sexual interest. Specifically, for girls whose father was not present in the household, higher levels of testosterone were correlated with greater sexual interest; for girls whose father was present, testosterone levels were not correlated with sexual interest.

The effect of father presence was viewed by Udry as placing greater social control on the sexuality of girls, essentially suppressing the effect of androgen. The role of greater pubertal development on girls' sexual interest may result from the stronger interest of potential sexual partners in girls with more developed, sexually attractive figures. As an aside, in males, religious commitment and involvement tended to reduce the effects of testosterone on sexual interest (although the direction of causality could not be confidently determined). This is a form of social control that apparently restrains male sexual interest or desire.

Some research suggests that women also become more likely to initiate sexual activity in long-term relationships as the relationship progresses (Cupach & Metts, 1991). A variety of factors are likely to account for the increasing sexual interest of women across the life span. One set of factors is greater familiarity and comfort in the relationship, leading to greater comfort with sexual intimacy. Furthermore, relationships may become more egalitarian, meaning equally influenced by both partners, over time. These findings further suggest that social factors may be at least as important as hormonal ones, if not more so, in determining the sexual interest of women.

## Men

The evidence for an association between androgen and sexual functioning in men is overwhelming. Sufficient levels of androgens, most likely testosterone, are necessary for the experience of sexual desire in general, but other influences—in particular environmental, social, and cultural factors—are necessary as well. Androgens also are responsible for the capacity for spontaneous erections during sleep, an indication of normal physiological functioning in adolescent and adult men. In contrast, the experience of erections in response to erotic stimuli, such as pictures and videos, is not at all related to the level of androgens circulating in the male body (Bancroft, 1988).

Studies in which testosterone is administered to sexually well-functioning men indicate that the additional testosterone increases sexual desire and behavior. Yet other studies have examined the relationship of circulating levels of testosterone with sexual interest and behavior; circulating level refers to the amounts that occur naturally and are released into the blood stream where presumably they can affect sexual desire. These studies do not find a clear association in adult men between hormone levels and sexual desire. The reason may be that most men produce levels of testosterone that are far greater than the minimum level necessary for men to experience strong sexual desire (Bancroft, 1988). In other words, testosterone is necessary at a sufficient level to create the ability to experience sexual desire; however, once this minimum threshold is passed, additional levels of testosterone do not produce greater levels of sexual desire.

In fact, men in general may produce such continually high levels of circulating androgens that many may experience a ceiling, or maximum, level of sexual motivation (Udry, 1988). Despite this finding for adult males, differences among boys in levels of circulating testosterone at puberty is the strongest factor related to sexual interest and sexual behavior, often exceeding that of psychological and social influences (Bancroft, 1988). These findings suggest that testosterone is necessary for sexual interest and desire to begin in the first place during puberty. However, once the capacity for desire is launched at puberty, the level of testosterone that is necessary for sexual desire typically does not fall below the minimum; in fact, many men produce sufficient levels of testosterone that they consistently maintain very strong sexual desire.

## A Theoretical View of Sexual Desire

A more recent perspective on the relationship between hormones and sexual desire is that proposed by Tolman and Diamond (2001). This perspective involves two major points: (a) a more complex view of sexual desire is needed for a more complete understanding of the relationship between hormones and sexual desire, and (b) sexual desire for women may be based more on the nature of specific situations and psychological scripts available to them than is the case for men.

With respect to the first point, Tolman and Diamond (2001) find support for the more complex view of sexual desire within a review of research on sexual desire by Wallen (1995). Evidence indicates that sexual desire in the form of **spontaneous sexual urges** is in fact related to hormone levels for both women and men. The term *spontaneous sexual urges* refers to feelings of interest in sexual expression that are unprompted by obvious arousing stimuli in the environment. On the other hand, research suggests that sexual arousal prompted by erotic stimuli is unrelated to hormone levels.

These findings suggest that sexual desire may actually consist of two distinct aspects: (a) **internal sexual motivation**, meaning unprompted interest in sexuality occurring within the individual that causes him or her to seek sexual expression; and (b) **arousability**, the tendency to become sexually aroused by aspects of the environment, such as in response to attractive individuals, sexual overtures, or erotic images and other stimuli (Tolman & Diamond, 2001).

The link between internal sexual motivation and hormone levels has been supported within research, as noted in the review by Wallen (1995). Specifically, changes in estrogen levels during the menstrual cycle have been shown to relate to changes in sexual interest. Estrogen levels, however, are not associated with sexual behavior, which is influenced by social and interpersonal factors. This suggests again that a distinction needs to be made between internal experiences of desire and external factors that affect actual sexual behavior for women.

Considerable evidence also supports a direct relationship between sexual *feelings* and increases in androgen produced by the gonads and adrenal glands. Finally, administering androgens to individuals increases sexual interest in both women and men (Wallen, 1995). Both of these last two findings are related to internal experiences of sexual desire.

In contrast to internal sexual motivation, arousability is unrelated to hormone levels; arousability refers to becoming aroused to stimuli in the environment. Research has found that even men whose testicles produce extremely low levels of testosterone—levels equivalent to having been castrated—are easily sexually aroused by erotic stimuli; this demonstrates that arousability occurs even in the absence of hormones. On the other hand, these men do not tend to seek out sexual stimulation on their own due to low levels of internal motivation (Wallen, 1995).

Furthermore, Wallen concluded, on the basis of research on primates, that arousability may be a more important factor affecting sexual interest and levels of sexual behavior for women than men. This is because daily levels of circulating androgens are lower for women; the primary source of androgens in women is the adrenal glands, whereas consistently high levels of androgens in men result from hormone production by the testicles. Men have been said to generally experience ceiling, or maximum, levels of internal sexual motivation as a result of continually high levels of circulating androgens (Udry, 1988).

Consequently, women on average produce sufficient levels of circulating androgens that they experience arousability on an ongoing basis; that is, they tend to be sexually stimulated by particular events and aspects of the environment when they encounter them. Yet they are most likely to experience periods of greater spontaneous sexual urges—the other aspect of sexual desire—around the time of ovulation. Men, in contrast, experience consistently high levels of both arousability and internal sexual motivation on an ongoing basis (Wallen, 1995). A representation of the proposed differences in sexual desire based on changes in internal sexual motivation and arousability are presented in Figure 12.5.

The difference between women and men in internally generated sexual interest, but not in arousability, provides the basis for the second aspect of Tolman and Diamond's (2001) proposal. The second aspect of their proposal is that sexual desire for women may be based more on what happens in the environment than on internal urges in comparison to men. This means that the nature of specific situations (e.g., seeing a stimulating movie) and psychological scripts available (e.g., being in love with someone means sex is okay) have a larger role in sexual desire. Support for this proposal is that women's sexual interest is more linked to their arousability, the tendency to be stimulated by particular aspects of the environment. Women and men, however, do not differ overall in the *strength* of their interest in initiating sexual activity (Wallen, 1995). Rather, women are more likely to experience such interest in initiating *at particular times,* possibly such as when androgen levels reach a maximum during the menstrual cycle. Consequently, the gender difference is not in terms of *strength* of sex drive nor *interest in initiating* sexual activity, but rather in terms of the frequency within a specific period of time.

The meaning of all of this for women, according to Tolman and Diamond (2001), is that the largest proportion of sexual desire they experience is strongly linked to situational factors; **situational factors** are the stimuli and events that are most prominent in a given setting that influence the behavior of individuals. In other words, the presence or absence of stimuli that are erotically arousing for a particular woman, the interpersonal climate, the social expectations prevailing, and a variety of other factors meaningful to that individual will affect whether she experiences heightened sexual interest. These types of factors that come and go in a person's daily experience can be expected to have a larger impact on women than men; this is because men have a constantly high level of internal sexual desire that keeps their sexual interest strong over time.

The fluctuating nature of women's sexual interest has been called *female sexual plasticity* by Baumeister (2000); the term *plasticity* is related to *plastic,* and means flexible or capable of being shaped and molded. However,

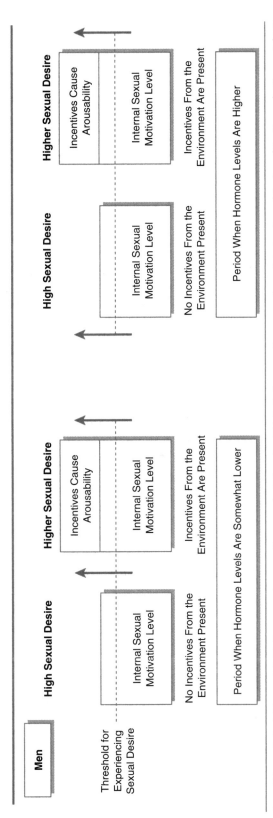

**FIGURE 12.5** The Two Component View of Sexual Desire

From Tolman, D. L., & Diamond, L. M, Desegregating sexuality research: Cultural and biological perspectives on gender and desire. *Annual Review of Sex Research, 12,* copyright © 2001. Reprinted with permission of the authors and the Society for the Scientific Study of Sexuality.

Baumeister viewed the relatively long period during the menstrual cycle in which women experience low levels of internally generated sexual desire as a time in which they are willing to engage in sex even though they have little real sexual desire. In other words, Baumeister assumed that women "put up" with sex during the time of their menstrual cycle in which androgen levels are low (see Figure 12.4, these times are Days 1 through 9 and 19 through 28); Baumeister suggests that women experience little internal sexual desire during this time.

Tolman and Diamond disagree with this view of the changes that occur during the menstrual cycle. From their perspective, it does not take into account the finding that women become sexually interested when they encounter situations they find arousing; this could be a sensual overture, or possibly even an alluring look, by one's romantic partner. Tolman and Diamond (2001) extend the perspective suggested by Wallen (1995) that distinguishes arousability from internally generated sexual motivation. They further propose that biological factors combine with environmental and cultural factors to affect sexual interest. Specifically, they suggest that hormonal factors influence the way that environmental factors are related to sexual desire; at the same time, environmental factors affect the way that hormones relate to sexual desire.

## Biological Factors Involved in Sexual Orientation

Early views of the role of hormones in the development of sexual orientation were based on the animal studies discussed previously in the chapter. In these studies, female rats were given androgens prenatally. The rats were then ovariectomized (had their ovaries removed) around the time of birth and injected with estradiol as mature adults. These female rats were less likely to display female types of sexual behavior and more likely to engage in male-typical mounting behavior. This finding is thought to be relevant to sexual orientation by some scientists based on the assumption that gender-related sexual behavior (i.e., engaging in masculine mounting) is linked to sexual orientation in rats (i.e., preference for sexual behavior with females).

Such a perspective draws upon the inversion hypothesis of sexual orientation that was the predominant early theory of sexual orientation at the beginning of the 20th century (discussed in chapter 3). The inversion hypothesis is that men who are attracted to men have developed feminine tendencies, and women attracted to women have developed masculine tendencies. Yet not all theoretical views buy into the cross-gender assumptions of inversion theory. Other scientists have pointed out that there are significant problems with drawing analogies between lower animal sexual behavior and the complexity of human sexual behavior. Nonetheless, this early research laid the foundation for neurohormonal theories of sexual orientation development.

### Neurohormonal Theories

Neurohormonal theories of sexual orientation development generally propose that exposure to certain types of hormones prenatally leads to greater sexual attraction for women. Most usually these theories suggest that, for humans, androgens structures the brain in a way that leads individuals to find women sexually attractive. The counterpart of this theory is that lack of exposure to androgens results in greater sexual attraction for men.

In terms of research on humans, however, no reliable evidence exists that circulating hormone levels are different for gay men in comparison to heterosexual men (Meyer-Bahlberg, 1984). Inconsistent results have been obtained for research on women, with two studies suggesting that more masculine lesbian women (known within lesbian and gay culture as "butch") tended to have higher levels of salivary testosterone than more feminine lesbian women (known as "femme"). On the other hand, shortcomings in some aspects of the studies weaken the confidence that can be placed in them somewhat (Mustanski et al., 2002).

Scientists have not been able to draw strong conclusions about the relationship of hormones to the development of sexual orientation. A major reason for this is that it is unethical to conduct the types of experimental studies on human beings that are needed to answer questions about the role of hormones. Of course, definitive experiments have not been conducted because of this. One such type of hypothetical experiment, according to Mustanski and his colleagues (2002), would be to randomly select newborns to surgically reconstruct them as the other sex (e.g., boys' sexual organs would be altered to be female sexual organs); in addition, parents would not be told about the surgery and the individuals would be raised as girls. If most of the individuals were attracted to females later in life, this would be strong support for the position that sexual orientation is established in nervous system organization before birth. Once again, it should be strongly emphasized that this type of study would be completely unethical because it violates the human rights of the newborns and their parents.

*Is it likely that "butch" lesbians are more masculine than "femme" lesbians because of higher levels of testosterone?* The scientific jury is still out on this question.

### Evidence From Intersexual Individuals

Although experiments of this sort have not actually been conducted, certain cases have occurred that were not part of an intentional experiment; in a way, these were the result of an "experiment of nature." In these cases, boys have been reassigned as girls through surgery because of the unclear development of their external sexual organs; this means the genitals had not developed into definite male or female organs. The surgery involved reshaping the genitals to be a female vulva. The issue of intersexuality is also relevant to gender and gender identity, and was considered in chapter 6 as well. Although the boys were otherwise healthy at birth, parents were consulted about the condition and were asked for permission for the surgical reassignment. Of 36 individuals examined across two different studies, the overwhelming majority later in life rejected their assigned gender as girls and reported being sexually attracted to women.

It is not possible to draw strong conclusions about the exact cause of these individuals' sexual attraction. The individuals are not typical because they underwent surgical and medical procedures to address the issue of having nontypical sexual organs. Beyond this, the individuals knew about their gender reassignment, that they were males who had been changed into females. Knowing that they were genetic males could have in itself caused them to develop an attraction for females because of the strong expectations that males will be attracted to females. Despite such problems, Mustanski and his colleagues (2002) concluded that the findings are consistent with the position that sexual orientation is greatly influenced by the structuring of the brain during prenatal development.

Other similar studies might also be thought of as experiments of nature. Such studies focus on conditions in which hormonal or genetic factors cause individuals to develop sexual organs that are not typical for their genetic sex. The situation of developing sexual organs different from one's genetic sex is called **intersexuality**.

One such relatively rare condition of intersexuality is **congenital adrenal hyperplasia** (CAH). CAH occurs because of a recessive trait that does not allow the typical production of the hormone cortisol by the adrenal glands. Cortisol is essential to the metabolism of various nutrients that are critical to healthy functioning of the body.

Instead of cortisol, a hormone is produced by the adrenal glands that is converted into testosterone and dihydrotestosterone. Both of these are involved in the masculinization of the body. In genetic females, because of the timing of the release of the testosterone-linked hormone from the adrenal glands, ovaries develop internally. However, the external sexual organs masculinize in a way that ranges from a larger clitoris to a complete penis and empty scrotum. When the situation is correctly identified, surgery may be conducted to construct the vulva in a more typical way and the individual may be raised as a girl. In this type of situation, the effects of high levels of prenatal androgens on genetic females raised as females can be examined (Mustanski et al., 2002).

A second example of intersexuality is **androgen insensitivity syndrome** (AIS). This is a situation resulting from a genetic condition on the X chromosome in which the cells of a genetic XY male are insensitive to androgen. This means the cells are not masculinized, even by the high levels of testosterone that are produced later by the body. Testicles form internally, but the external sexual organs develop fully into a vulva, rather than penis and scrotum. Typically, such individuals are reared as females. This situation permits the assessment of the effects of absence of androgens on sexual orientation in genetic males (Mustanski et al., 2002). The characteristics of two types of conditions resulting in intersexuality are presented in Table 12.1.

With respect to the CAH individuals raised as girls, in one study by Money, Schwartz, and Lewis (1984), 48% experienced fantasies involving the same-sex (females) and 22% had engaged in sexual activity with other women. This compares with 7% experiencing same-sex fantasy and 4% engaging in same-sex sexual activity of the AIS individuals raised as girls. The comparable levels for same-sex fantasy and sexual activity reported by typical women in the early Kinsey study (Kinsey, Pomeroy, Martin, & Gebhard, 1953) were 15% and 10%. Similar levels of same-sex fantasy and activity for CAH females as observed in the Money and Lewis study have been found in later studies as well (Mustanski et al., 2002). All of the androgen insensitivity syndrome females (who are genetically XY) reported attraction to men during adolescence, and 93% were attracted to men in adulthood.

**TABLE 12.1** Characteristics of Three Groups of Intersexual Individuals

| Type of Intersexuality | Cause | Type of Internal Organs | Type of External Organs | Sexual Orientation Tendencies |
|---|---|---|---|---|
| Congenital adrenal hyperplasia (CAH) | A recessive trait produces masculinizing hormones in genetic females | Ovaries and typical female organs | Masculinized, ranging from a larger clitoris to a complete penis and empty scrotum | Greater likelihood of same-sex fantasy and activity, although this is not true for all women |
| Androgen insensitivity syndrome (AIS) | Genetic condition causing cells in genetic males to be unresponsive to androgens | Testicles remain in the abdomen | Vulva develops normally as if the individual is a genetic female | All develop attraction for males |
| Females exposed to diethylstilbestrol (DES) | DES converts into testosterone | Typical female organs | Typical female organs | Greater likelihood of same-sex fantasy |

The results for the CAH women provide the clearest support for the relationship between prenatal andro-gen exposure and sexual attraction to women. This is because they had been raised as girls (Mustanski et al., 2002). The tendency toward same-sex attraction therefore occurred in spite of environmental and social pres-sures for other-sex attraction involved in expectations for women; yet the influence of environmental and social factors promoting same-sex attraction cannot be entirely ruled out. In contrast, the attraction for men expe-rienced by AIS individuals (who are genetically XY) provides less convincing evidence for the role of lack of androgen in attraction toward men. This is because these individuals were in fact raised as females. This means that socialization and cultural forces could also account for the attraction to men; attraction to men is an impor-tant aspect of female gender-role expectations.

### Evidence From Individuals Exposed to Synthetic Estrogen

Yet another line of research is based on the use of diethylstilbestrol (DES) to prevent problem pregnan-cies from miscarrying, a practice that ended in the 1960s. As discussed in a previous section, DES is a syn-thetic estrogen capable of crossing the placental barrier; the barrier protects embryos from a number of factors in the mother's system. DES is converted into testosterone metabolically in developing embryos, which is thought to masculinize females exposed to the hormone. In fact, girls exposed to DES prenatally are more likely to exhibit a number of more male-typical behaviors. Unlike with CAH, however, external sexual organs are not affected because DES is not as powerful a hormone and because it was delivered late in pregnancy after the organs are formed. Nonetheless, women exposed to DES are more likely to report same-sex sexual fantasies. The fact that external sexual organs, as well as internal sexual organs, were not affected by the treatment reduces the pos-sibility that expectations on the part of the women themselves or on the part of others are responsible for the greater likelihood of same-sex fantasies (Mustanski et al., 2002). The characteristics of women exposed to DES are summarized in Table 12.1.

Mustanski and his colleagues (2002) concluded that the pattern of results across the various studies sup-port the influence of androgens on development of sexual orientation. Specifically, individuals exposed to higher levels of androgens tend to experience greater attraction to females. On the other hand, individuals exposed to lower levels of androgens are more likely to have greater attraction to males.

On the other side of the issue, Peplau (2001) notes that the vast majority of women exposed to masculin-izing hormones in fact report that they are heterosexual. For this reason, she concluded that evidence for the influence of prenatal hormones on sexual orientation is not really very convincing. She also notes that sup-porters of the neurohormonal perspective even acknowledge that it does not provide an adequate understand-ing of the range of sexual orientation in most women. Most lesbians have not been exposed to conditions of unusual hormone levels similar to CAH and DES.

### Other Factors Associated With Hormonal Influences

The problem with neurohormonal theories of sexual orientation development is that the largest propor-tion of nonheterosexual individuals have not experienced one of the hormonal conditions discussed in the previous sections. Consequently, researchers have searched for other more commonly occurring factors that indicate exposure to a different hormonal environment prenatally for some individuals in comparison to others. Because research has demonstrated that exposing pregnant rats to stress produces demasculinization and femininization in male offspring, some theorists proposed that maternal stress may affect human males as well. Evidence for humans has been mixed in establishing a link between maternal stress and same-sex orientation. Beyond this, much of the research involves methodological problems that leave in doubt the accuracy of the results (Mustanski et al., 2002).

Other theorists have searched for signs that are thought to be associated with a particular prenatal hormonal environment that may also be linked to nonheterosexual sexual orientation. Handedness, meaning whether an individual is predominantly left-handed or right-handed, was proposed as a possible marker for the influence of sex hormones prenatally; this is because males are more likely to be left-handed or ambidextrous than are females (Mustanski et al., 2002). A meta-analytic review of 20 studies (Lalamière, Blanchard, & Zucker, 2000) found that lesbians were substantially more likely to be nonright-handed than heterosexual women; however, gay men were also somewhat more likely to be nonright-handed than heterosexual men. Neurohormonal theory proposes that lesbians should be more likely to possess male-typical characteristics because of greater exposure to androgens, whereas gay men should be more likely to possess female-typical characteristics because of less exposure to androgens. The results for lesbians supports this proposal. However, the results for gay men argue against the hypothesis, because they are also more likely to be nonright-handed than heterosexual men; being nonright-handed is a male-typical trait (Mustanski et al., 2002).

Another strategy for hunting for factors underlying sexual orientation has been to search for differences in the size and structure of areas of the brain. Primary targets in the brain are those known to be associated with sexual behavior. Other candidates are areas of the brain for which gender differences have been found. Only a small number of studies have been conducted on this issue, and none of these have included lesbian women. In fact, only two studies have investigated the region of the brain for which differences related to sexual orientation have been consistently found (Mustanski et al., 2002). The region for which gender differences and sexual orientation differences have been found is in the anterior hypothalamus. The hypothalamus is the part of the brain discussed earlier that produces the hormone regulating the sex hormones, gonadotropin-releasing hormone (GnRH).

More specifically, brain differences in sexual orientation have been pinpointed to a specific set of neurons in the anterior hypothalamus; this area is called the **third interstitial nuclei of the anterior hypothalamus**, abbreviated **INAH-3**. No sexual orientation differences have been consistently found for the other three interstitial nuclei in the anterior hypothalamus. Heterosexual men tend to have larger INAH-3 than heterosexual women and gay men. The INAH-3 is very similar for heterosexual women and gay men; lesbians have not been included in these studies, such that no comparisons are possible for them. Beyond the fact that only two studies have found evidence for this area, another limitation of this research is that both studies were conducted in a very exploratory fashion. That is, the researchers looked at a number of different areas in a strategy of "fishing" for differences. A method that does not take advantage as much of simple "good luck" is that of examining a very limited number of regions that have been identified as likely candidates in previous research. This strategy attempts to *confirm* the existence of differences (Mustanski et al., 2002).

Gender differences have also been found in a host of other processes or structures of the body, leading researchers to investigate these for differences related to sexual orientation. Lesbians, in comparison to heterosexual women, have been found to exhibit more male-typical responses in their inner ear to short bursts of noise—that is, clicks. Lesbians also exhibit more male-typical brain-wave patterns in response to such clicks.

Gay men, however, were equivalent to heterosexual men in responses in their inner ear to clicks, and in fact exhibited even greater male-typical brain waves related to the clicks than heterosexual men. Moreover, two studies, one of them based on an extremely large sample, have found that gay men tend to have larger penises; differences have been found with respect not only to the length of the erect penis, but to an even greater extent in terms of the circumference (width; Bogaert & Hershberger, 1999; Nedoma & Freund, 1961). The greater level of male-typical characteristics in gay men presents a fairly severe challenge to neurohormonal theories and to the inversion hypothesis, which proposes that gay men have not been exposed to as great masculinizing influences as heterosexual men.

Gender differences have also been found in other characteristics as well: (a) in the length of the index finger relative to the ring finger; (b) in the pattern of skin ridges on the hands and feet; (c) in overall body weight and height; and (d) in age of puberty. Consequently, researchers have examined all of these characteristics as potential markers for differences in sexual orientation. However, research has found mixed or virtually no support for differences in these characteristics hypothesized to relate to sexual orientation (Mustanski et al., 2002).

Mustanski and his colleagues nonetheless concluded that neurohormonal theory is supported by several lines of evidence they reviewed. Such evidence includes the clinical research involving genetic males with conditions that lead to their gender reassignment as females; it also includes the research involving genetic females exposed to androgens and genetic males whose bodies were insensitive to, and therefore not affected by, androgen. As discussed previously, however, Peplau (2001) has maintained that these data do not really provide strong support for the neurohormonal theory for women; this conclusion is based on the fact that the majority of women exposed prenatally to androgens instead identify themselves as heterosexual.

The search for markers of sexual orientation in the brain or the body has produced largely inconsistent support for neurohormonal theory. The bottom line is that much more work needs to be done to test this theoretical perspective. Some support exists, but challenges to the accuracy of the research upon which the evidence is based leave the issue open to question (Mustanski et al., 2002).

## Genetic Factors

Early theorists who focused on genetic factors underlying sexual orientation proposed that gay men are essentially genetically female. However, the discovery of the X and Y chromosomes as the genetic source controlling gender required that this view be discarded (Pare, 1956). As it turns out, nonheterosexual individuals are genetically the same with respect to these chromosomes.

Studies examining the frequency of same-gender orientation among family members of gay men and lesbians typically find a greater rate of same-gender orientation in their families than is true for heterosexual individuals. Across a number of studies on the topic, the median rate for same-gender orientation among brothers of gay men is approximately 9% and the range for sisters of lesbians is between 6 and 25% (Bailey & Pillard, 1995). Yet the higher rate of same-gender orientation cannot be linked only to genetic similarity; this is because family members share both a common environment as well as a common genetic heritage. It could be due as much to family environment as to genetic influence (Mustanski et al., 2002).

*What can identical twins tell us about the role of genetic factors in behavior and sexual orientation?*

*Twin Studies*

An extremely valuable strategy for separating genetic background from environmental factors is the examination of identical twins, who have exactly the same genetic material. Through statistical techniques, it is possible to separate influences on sexual orientation into genetic similarity, shared environmental influence, and nonshared environmental influence. Shared environment consists of those factors that cause siblings (brothers and sisters) to be more similar, and nonshared environment consists of those factors that cause siblings to be less similar. Several studies based on large, random samples provided support for moderate genetic influence on sexual orientation, as well as moderate influence by nonshared aspects of the environment. The genetic influence appears to be somewhat greater for men than for women (Mustanski et al., 2002).

Genetic effects in this type of research are reported in terms of the **concordance rate**, the percent of twin pairs in which both siblings are gay. The rate of same-gender orientation for identical twins is compared with the rate for fraternal twins. Identical twins have exactly the same genes, and therefore may be influenced by essentially the same genetic effects. Fraternal twins are siblings conceived at the same time, but result from two different fertilized eggs; fraternal twins have the same degree of genetic information in common as other brothers and sisters, which is one-quarter of that of identical twins. In contrast, identical twins result when one fertilized egg divides into two identical embryos.

Among the large studies with especially strong methodology, concordance rates for same-gender orientation range between 24–55% for identical twins, whereas the rates range between 10.5–23% for fraternal twins (Hyde, 2005). The higher proportion of twins with same-gender orientation among identical twins than for fraternal twins suggests at least a small genetic effect.

## Fraternal Birth Order

In addition to hormonal and genetic influences on sexual orientation, researchers have discovered other factors that appear to differ for heterosexual and nonheterosexual individuals. Fraternal birth order is one such factor, and refers to the order in which an individual is born into a family relative to the position of his or her brothers. In a review of 14 studies examining the issue (Blanchard, 2001), gay men had significantly greater numbers of older brothers than heterosexual men. After taking into account the number of older brothers, birth order relative to sisters was not related to sexual orientation. The effect appears to be greater for highly feminine gay men. Statistical analyses indicate that the sexual orientation of approximately 15% of gay men is related to the fraternal birth-order effect. Each older brother increases the chances of a same-sex sexual orientation by 33%. However, no relationship to birth order has been found for women, nor to the gender ratio of siblings, the proportion of male siblings to female siblings.

Little evidence is available to test a number of explanations that have been suggested for this effect. However, research has actually disconfirmed some of the explanations. The most accepted hypothesis at this time is that mothers develop an immune response to some substance created by male offspring during pregnancy. The antibodies created by the mother may then increasingly affect the development of each successive son. The number of older brothers has also been found to relate to lower birth weights for gay men, but not for heterosexual men. This indicates that a type of birth-order effect occurs prenatally, which may be related to the birth-order effect for sexual orientation (Mustanski et al., 2002).

## Conclusions About Biological Factors

Mustanski, Chivers, and Bailey (2002) draw four conclusions about research on biological factors involved in sexual orientation. First, biological factors appear to have some degree of effect before birth, as indicated by the studies on gender reassignment and atypical prenatal hormone exposure. Their second conclusion is that genetic factors likewise play some type of role in the development of sexual orientation. However, research so far does not address whether genetic influences operate before or after birth. A third conclusion is that research supports the existence of differences in brain structure and functioning related to sexual orientation. Finally, the sexual orientation of women and men are influenced to some extent by different biological factors. They are likely to develop in somewhat different ways, such that research on men cannot simply be assumed to be applicable to women.

It should be noted that the entire tradition of theory and research on sexual orientation, more specifically on "homosexuality," has been criticized by a number of theorists. This line of criticism is perhaps most clearly and fully presented in a book by De Cecco and Parker (1995). The contributors to this book raise many of the same theoretical issues presented in chapter 1 of the current book concerning sexuality in general, as well as at the beginning of this chapter. Such issues concern the problems and limitations of the position that (a) sexuality is an established part of reality, "out in the world," to be discovered by scientists; (b) sexual orientation is essentially the same for everyone, in a way that all people can be easily and clearly categorized into two or three groups; and (c) sexuality is largely determined by biological factors, such that social and cultural factors seem to be fairly minor or unimportant.

The criticisms as a group are based on the view that many of the biological theories take an extreme essentialist position, as discussed at the beginning of the current chapter. The limitation of this extreme perspective is a lack of concern with social and cultural influences on sexuality, as well as a lack of attention to differences among individuals. The theoretical view presented in the next section addresses these limitations, especially for women, by proposing a truly interactionist approach. The interactionist perspective maintains that biological aspects of individuals and aspects of the environment combine together to influence behavior (Tolman & Diamond, 2001).

## Relationship Orientation Rather Than Sexual Orientation

Evidence for a biological influence on women's sexual orientation is less convincing than for men. For this reason, Peplau (2001) has proposed a modified view of the role of biological factors in women's sexuality. She has suggested that the traditional conception of sexual orientation as an attraction to one gender or the other may not be as appropriate for women as it is for men. A more accurate description for women may be in terms of their relationship orientation, rather than in terms of sexual orientation. Her proposal is based on evidence that women in general tend to hold a relationship or partner-focused orientation to sexuality, in contrast to men who tend to have a recreational or body-focused orientation. The distinction between type of orientation is likely to be relevant to differences between lesbians and gay men, as well as to differences between heterosexual women and men.

To support her proposal, Peplau draws upon the large body of research that has repeatedly found differences between women and men in their feelings, attitudes, desires, and behavior with respect to sexuality. Beginning in adolescence, women on average tend to view sexuality within the context of an increasingly more intimate emotional relationship with one particular partner. Men, in contrast, tend to develop a belief that many women are potential sexual partners, and that sexual involvement occurs for reasons of pleasure, requiring little or no emotional investment (DeLamater, 1987). Men are more likely to view their experience of sexual desire in more sexualized terms in comparison to women. Women in contrast are more likely to interpret their experience of sexual desire in terms of romantic feelings and love (Regan & Berscheid, 1996). Peplau observed that sexual desire and behavior are not the defining attributes of women's relationships with either women or men, although they are highly important. Rather, love, supportiveness, and companionship typically define the focus of women involved in both lesbian and heterosexual relationships.

For these reasons, the traditional conception of "sexual orientation" may not be as meaningful regarding female sexuality:

> Researchers' tendency to accord greater weight to sex acts than to enduring relationships may be an unintended legacy of male-centered thinking. Indeed, if we were to conceptualize sexual orientation on the basis of women's experiences, we might well rename it "relationship orientation." An adequate understanding of women's sexual orientation will require a shift away from focusing on sexual behavior toward studying the formation of close pair bonds. (Peplau, 2001, p. 13)

Peplau proposes that a neurohormonal basis may exist for the gender differences observed in sexuality. Such biological differences might influence women toward more of a relationship emphasis and men toward a more recreational emphasis (Andersen, Cyranowski, & Aarestad, 2000; Panksepp, 1998). Specifically, the hormone **oxytocin** (pronounced OX ee TOH sin) may play a more central role in the functioning of women. Oxytocin stimulates contraction of uterine muscles, such as those involved in the experience of orgasm and related to delivery of offspring (i.e., labor).

Beyond this, research on nonhuman mammals indicates that oxytocin is also involved in greater maternal behavior and caregiving, as well as greater affiliation (friendship behaviors). Higher oxytocin levels may contribute to the tendency to form close pair bonds among adults, that is the formation of intimate relationships with others, as in friendships or romantic relationships. Especially in women, stress appears to trigger the release of oxytocin, increasing the tendency to seek out others, possibly women in particular (Taylor et al., 2000); this has been called the *tend and befriend* reaction that is different from the *fight or flight* reaction more typical of men. Pleasant forms of physical contact, such as touch, massage, and stroking, additionally result in greater levels of the hormone. Finally, oxytocin levels are positively related to sexual arousal and orgasm. Peplau proposes that these lines of research support an association among an orientation toward relationships, nurturing tendencies, and sexuality.

Oxytocin functioning may exert a greater impact on women in terms of relationship orientation and sexuality for a number of reasons. Women have a more elaborate network of neurons in the brain that are involved in the release of the hormone. Moreover, areas of the brain related to sexuality are physically closer in women to areas involved in caregiving and nurturance behaviors; in contrast, the sexuality areas for men are closer to the areas involved in aggression. Furthermore, androgens are associated both with higher levels of sexual arousal and certain types of aggressive tendencies. Androgens additionally tend to diminish the effects of oxytocin, whereas estrogen tends to amplify them (Panksepp, 1998). Such hormonal differences may explain, according to Peplau (2001), the reason that, for lesbians, emotionally intimate friendships often lead to the experience of intense sexual attraction; this is less likely to occur among young gay men (Diamond & Savin-Williams, 2000). Emotionally intimate, supportive behaviors may stimulate oxytocin systems, increasing the likelihood of women experiencing sexual attraction.

Peplau (2001) has further proposed that the available evidence currently justifies focusing more on the many similarities that exist between lesbians and heterosexual women, rather than on the traditional inversion approach typical of neurohormonal theories. As presented in the previous section, the concern of neurohormonal theories is with identifying characteristics that show a masculinizing effect of male sex hormones; consequently, lesbians are assumed to be more similar to heterosexual men, and gay men are assume to be more similar to heterosexual

The release of high levels of oxytocin by women in reaction to stress contributes to their greater tendency to *tend and befriend*, rather than to experience the *fight or flight reaction* typical of men.

women. Moreover, evidence for a significant influence of biological factors on the development of sexual orientation in males is much stronger than for women. Peplau acknowledged that some theorists call on socialization processes and differences in power structures within society to explain gender differences, rather than focusing on hormonal influences. Regardless of whether the particular theory focuses on social or biological factors, Peplau concluded that separate explanations of sexual orientation must be developed for women and men. However, a competing explanation of the development of sexual orientation is presented in Box 12.1, *Analyze This*.

Peplau (2001) additionally emphasizes the significance of women's tendency to respond to features of the environment in the nature of their sexuality. This is consistent with the conclusion drawn by Baumeister (2000) that the sexuality of women is fairly flexible in comparison to that of men. Likewise, Tolman and Diamond (2001) stress the importance of women's greater focus on environmental incentives relative to men. According to Peplau, various cognitive, psychological, and social factors influence women's choice of partners at different times in their lives.

Furthermore, because of the powerful role of environmental conditions in their sexual choices, women are not likely to all develop along one single pathway and may change in their sexual tendencies at different points in their lives. This may explain why women are more likely to move from attraction to one type of partner to another at different times in their lives, changes in what is traditionally called "sexual orientation." Because men are less influenced by environmental factors, this may provide the reason that they are less changeable in their attraction toward one gender or the other.

## Box 12.1   Analyze This: Looking at Different Perspectives

### *How Does Sexual Orientation Develop?*

A comprehensive theory of sexual orientation that integrates biological, social, and environmental factors into a developmental process has been proposed recently by noted social psychologist Daryl Bem (1996, 2001). This perspective is called the **Exotic Becomes Erotic Theory** (EBE Theory).

The fundamental premise of the theory is that sexual attraction develops toward individuals from whom one felt different during childhood regarding gender-related issues. Typically, as children, girls tend to isolate themselves from boys, and boys likewise tend to isolate themselves from girls. This pattern, called **gender segregation**, is virtually universal in cultures around the world and is typically enforced by children themselves; it is usually not imposed on children by adults.

The eventual effect of this social isolation of girls and boys is that the other gender comes to be seen as inherently different and rather mysterious, that is **exotic**. Those whom adolescents view as exotic and unfamiliar along gender-related lines become the most likely focus of newly awakening sexual interest, according to this theory; exotic individuals therefore **become erotic** because of their seemingly mysterious gender-based nature. In this way, girls typically develop an erotic attraction for boys, and boys typically develop an erotic attraction for girls. Such a process is the basis for the development of a heterosexual orientation.

However, the theory is able to account for the formation of same-gender sexual orientation as well. Any of a number of factors may cause individuals to feel more distant or isolated from one's own gender than they feel distant from the other gender; if this happens, individuals of the same gender become exotic and mysterious, rather than individuals of the other gender, as is typically the case. After puberty, members of the individual's own gender then become erotic.

The aspect of the theory that makes it comprehensive is that it integrates the biological influences considered in the current chapter with experiences that individuals have throughout childhood, adolescence, and even adulthood. Figure 12.6 presents the series of processes and events that contribute to the development of sexual orientation across the various periods of early life. Very little research based on predictions from Exotic Becomes Erotic (EBE) theory, and designed specifically to test these predictions, has been conducted. However, Bem has argued that existing research supports a number of the proposals within the theory. Research bearing on other aspects of the theory has simply not yet been conducted.

Bem has also proposed that more than one pathway is possible in the course of forming an individual's sexual orientation. The sequence presented in the main part of the Exotic Becomes Erotic Theory is the path typically occurring for most individuals in a highly gender-polarized society, such as that of the United States. Gender polarization is the practice within a culture of viewing females and males as possessing different abilities and traits, of assigning them different roles and statuses, and generally reacting differently to females and males. Yet even for a person who

THE BIOPSYCHOLOGY OF SEXUALITY

early in life feels similar to others of his or her own sex, events may actually happen that alter the eventual sexual orientation of that individual. The idea is that biological factors operating prenatally and early in childhood provide an initial tendency to develop in a certain way; however, the "push" in a particular direction does not mean that biological factors are inevitable—that is, that these factors are "written in stone."

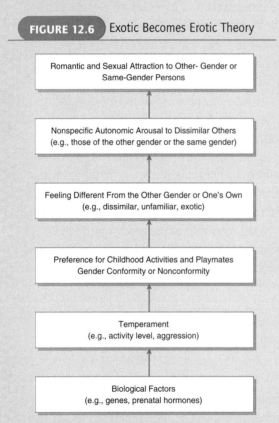

**FIGURE 12.6** Exotic Becomes Erotic Theory

Romantic and Sexual Attraction to Other- Gender or Same-Gender Persons

↑

Nonspecific Autonomic Arousal to Dissimilar Others (e.g., those of the other gender or the same gender)

↑

Feeling Different From the Other Gender or One's Own (e.g., dissimilar, unfamiliar, exotic)

↑

Preference for Childhood Activities and Playmates Gender Conformity or Nonconformity

↑

Temperament (e.g., activity level, aggression)

↑

Biological Factors (e.g., genes, prenatal hormones)

From Bern, D. J., Exotic becomes erotic: A developmental theory of sexual orientation, *Psychological Review*, 103, 320–335, copyright © 1996, American Psychological Association. Reprinted with permission.

Bem offers the example of individuals who exhibit largely, if not entirely, gender typical activity and friendship patterns in childhood. This generally leads people to associate with the same gender, rather than the other sex, and to develop a heterosexual orientation. Yet changes in a person's

life, possibly a move to a new location or some other event, cause the individual to feel different in significant ways from his or her same-sex peers. Evidence from one study found that lesbians and gay men who were typical of their sex in childhood nonetheless felt different from same-sex peers in some way related to gender. For example, lesbians who were gender typical in childhood tended to report that most of their friends in grade school were boys (Bell, Weinberg, & Hammersmith, 1981). Ultimately, it is the sense of *feeling* the same as, or different from, same-sex peers concerning gender-based issues that is a major influence on sexual orientation and identity (Bem, 2001).

The theory is not without its critics, however (Peplau, Garnets, Spalding, Conley, & Veniegas, 1998). EBE theory is a relatively recent explanation of the development of sexual orientation, and no research has yet been conducted to explicitly test its proposals. Likewise, Peplau and other theorists continue to advocate explanations that compete with EBE theory. Consequently, the debate among various theorists is likely to continue for some time.

## References

Bell, A. P., Weinberg, M. S., & Hammersmith, Exotic becomes erotic: A developmental theory of sexual orientation. *Psychological Review, 103,* 320–335.

Bem, D. J. (2001). Exotic becomes erotic: A developmental theory of sexual orientation. *Psychological Review, 103,* 320–335.

Bem, D. J. (2001). Exotic becomes erotic: Integrating biological and experiential antecedents of sexual orientation. In A. R. D'Augelli & C. J. Patterson (Eds.), *Lesbian, gay, and bisexual identities and youth: Psychological perspectives* (pp. 52–68). New York: Oxford University Press.

Peplau, L. A., Garnets, L. D., Spalding, L. R., Conley, T. D., & Veniegas, R. C. (1998). A critique of Bem's "Exotic Becomes Erotic" theory of sexual orientation. *Psychological Review, 105,* 387–394.

# Summary

Production of sex hormones is controlled by the hypothalamus, a structure in the limbic region of the brain. If levels of estrogens in women or levels of androgens in men drop below a certain level, the hypothalamus releases gonadotropin-releasing hormone (GnRH). GnRH causes the anterior pituitary to release two hormones into the blood stream, follicle-stimulating hormone (FSH) and luteinizing hormone (LH). FSH and LH cause the ovaries to produce greater levels of estrogen and the testicles to produce testosterone.

Testicles typically develop in genetic males from primordial gonads because H-Y antigen stimulates the medulla of the primordial gonads to become testicles. In the absence of the H-Y antigen, the cortex of the primordial gonads develop into ovaries. In most genetic males, Wolffian cells grow and the Müllerian cells deteriorate, creating the various internal male sexual organs. In the absence of testosterone and Müllerian-inhibiting substance, the Müllerian cells develop, the Wolffian cells wither, and internal female sexual organs form. Male external sexual organs develop from primitive structures as a result of the male sex hormone, dihydrotestosterone. In the absence of dihydrotestosterone, female external organs develop.

The association between hormone levels after puberty and the experience of sexual desire is not as strong for women as it is for men. No single pattern of relationship between hormones and sexual desire reliably exists across all women. Beliefs and expectations regarding menstruation and fluctuations in hormones may affect the experience of desire. For men, variations in circulating testosterone levels across individuals are not related to differences in sexual interest. Most men produce levels that result in substantial, consistent sexual desire.

A recent view of sexual desire proposed by Tolman and Diamond (2001) is that sexual desire consists of two components: internal sexual motivation and arousability. Women may be more likely to initiate sexual activity at the time when the effect of their sex hormones peaks and they experience higher internal sexual motivation. However, hormone levels are possibly sufficient throughout the monthly cycle to maintain a substantial level of arousability. Consequently, women may be more generally influenced by environmental factors than by internally generated sexual motivation. This perspective holds that women do not have less intense sexual desire, but rather sexual desire that varies in nature across the monthly cycle.

Neurohormonal theories propose that exposure to androgens prenatally causes the brain to be structured in a way that leads to greater attraction toward women. Little evidence has been found for a relationship between hormones and sexual orientation for men, whereas evidence is inconsistent for women.

Mustanski and his colleagues concluded that evidence exists that prenatal hormones affect sexual orientation, genetic factors play some type of role in sexual orientation development, differences in brain structures may be related to sexual orientation, and different biological factors appear to relate to sexual orientation for women in comparison to men. However, Peplau (2001) concluded that evidence for the role of hormones in the development of sexual orientation for women is not extremely convincing.

Because of gender differences in factors related to sexual orientation, Peplau (2001) proposed a modified perspective of the role of biological factors in female sexuality. She maintained that a more accurate characterization for women is relationship orientation, rather than sexual orientation, in part because greater similarity than difference exists among women. Women in general tend to view sexuality within the context of emotional intimacy, love, and supportiveness, rather than in terms of physical pleasure and recreation as is more typical of men. Given the greater flexibility of women's sexuality, they are particularly likely to be influenced by features of the environment that stimulate sexual desire and arousal. Women are not likely to develop along one single pathway and may change at different junctures in their lives. The influence of the environment may account for changes in sexual orientation that are more typical of women than men.

## Chapter 12 Critical Thinking Exercises

1. Hormone levels and sexual desire

   In what ways may interpersonal and social factors affect how adolescent girls and boys understand and experience increases in sexual desire during puberty? For example, research indicates that the presence or absence of the father in the household changes how strongly girls experience sexual interest. How would the presence of the father affect feelings of sexual interest? How can their experiences with sexual desire during puberty affect the way they feel about sexual desire and sexual behavior as they grow older?

2. Sexual orientation

   What conclusions would you draw about the support that exists for a relationship between hormones and sexual orientation? Specifically, what support exists for the view that the presence of androgens is related to attraction for females and the absence of androgens is related to attraction for males? What are the implications if this view is correct? What are the implications if it is not correct?

**Visit www.sagepub.com/hillhsstudy.com for online activities, sample tests, and other helpful resources. Select "Chapter 12: The Biopsychology of Sexuality" for chapter specific activities.**

# Chapter 13

## SEXUALITY IN THE EARLY YEARS AND ADOLESCENCE

*Don't bother discussing sex with small children. They rarely have anything to add.*

Fran Lebowitz, American writer and humorist
(ThinkExist.com)

Of course, the quip by Fran Lebowitz is meant to be funny. However, despite common assumptions about the "innocence" of children, very little that is known about the development of sexuality in the early years of life is based on systematic empirical research. Likewise, virtually no research exists regarding the relationship of extremely early childhood experiences and later sexuality. Much of what exists is concerned with sexual abuse rather than factors involved in the typical development of children (Sandfort & Rademakers, 2000b).

Historically, children have been viewed as completely **devoid of a sexual nature or feelings**. Even more, a child engaging in any type of sexual behavior, or even having a natural response such as a spontaneous erection, was viewed as having an **evil character** (see chapter 3). For this reason, parents may be unwilling to acknowledge sexual responses in their children at all. Because many people do not believe childhood sexuality exists, parents may view such behavior in a nonsexual way; they might simply not notice it, or view it as childish silliness. Furthermore, given the highly negative beliefs about sexuality throughout Western history, especially regarding children, researchers have avoided addressing childhood sexuality at all.

Views of parents about childhood sexuality may affect research even when scientists attempt to collect information on it. Given that parents often do not believe that children have sexual feelings and desires of any kind, many are probably unwilling to allow their children to participate in research at all. A concern may be that exposure to questions about sexuality of any type will contaminate a naive child with ideas and images that damage what is perceived to be a frail, developing mind. This belief about sexuality is based on a **disease perspective**, in which early exposure to anything sexual is thought to corrupt and damage development. Beyond this, interest in the sexuality of youngsters by adults may be thought to signal a morbid personal desire to have sexual contact with children—that is, a tendency for **pedophilia** (Sandfort & Rademakers, 2000b).

Such a concern may have actually influenced participation in a group of studies that are among the few available on sexual behavior in children. Nonetheless, they have provided the highest quality and most comprehensive knowledge available to date (Sandfort & Rademakers, 2000a). The rate of parents' refusal to allow their children to participate was substantial in several studies that reported rates: 60% in a study by Volbert (2000) and 73% in a study by Schurhke (2000). On the other hand, two other studies reported refusal rates of less than 30% (Friedrich, Sandfort, Ostveen, & Cohen-Kettenis, 2000; Meyer-Bahlberg, Dolezal, & Sandberg, 2000), suggesting that under some circumstances parents may have fewer misgivings.

Another reason for the profound absence of research on childhood sexuality is methodological. As discussed in chapter 4, it is extremely difficult to conduct research on sexuality outside of self-report questionnaires or interviews; because of the extreme privacy that many societies demand for sexuality, it is virtually impossible for scientists to observe sexual activities directly. This is particularly true for those occurring in real-world settings outside of the laboratory. However, children are able to communicate about sexuality only in extremely limited ways, just as they are regarding complex motivations and emotions in general. This feature of children's capabilities makes it very difficult to have great confidence in their self-reports about their sexuality. In addition, children may sense that sexual issues occupy a guarded position of extreme sensitivity, secretiveness, and even discomfort for adults. They may therefore feel that it is not acceptable for them to talk openly about such issues; that is, they recognize that sexual issues are **taboo** (Sandfort & Rademakers, 2000b).

---

### BOX 13.1  AN OPPORTUNITY FOR SELF-REFLECTION

**Do You Remember When?**

Obtaining information about childhood sexual behavior is quite challenging, leading some researchers to ask adults about their recollections. These are called retrospective self-reports.

Here's your chance to experience what this is like. Think back into your past and try to remember the first time you engaged in each of these behaviors related to sexuality. Considering only behavior that occurred during childhood (before the age of 11 years), when did you first do the following:

1. Touch your own genitals in an exploratory fashion or because of the pleasurable feeling that resulted.
   a. What was your age?
   b. How did you feel about the behavior?
   c. Did your parents or others observe you engage in the behavior? How did they react?

2. Touch the breasts of an adult woman out of curiosity.
   a. What was your age?
   b. How did you feel about the behavior?
   c. Did your parents or others observe you engage in    the behavior? How did they react?

3. Visually examine or touch the genitals of an adolescent. or adult female
   a. What was your age?
   b. How did you feel about the behavior?
   c. Did your parents or others observe you engage in the behavior? How did they react?

4. Visually examine or touch the genitals of an adolescent   or adult male.
   a. What was your age?
   b. How did you feel about the behavior?
   c. Did your parents or others observe you engage in the behavior? How did they react?

5. Visually examine or touch the genitals of another. child 10 years old or younger.
   a. What was your age?
   b. How did you feel about the behavior?
   c. Did your parents or others observe you engage in the behavior? How did they react?

6. Engage in a game of "I'll show you mine, if you show me yours"—that is, exposing your genitals with another child.
   a. What was your age?
   b. How did you feel about the behavior?
   c. Did your parents or others observe you engage in the behavior? How did they react?

7. Play "doctor" or "house" in which you and another child. explored genitals or played at some kind of sexual intimacy.
   a. What was your age?
   b. How did you feel about the behavior?
   c. Did your parents or others observe you engage in the behavior? How did they react?

8. Masturbate by yourself before the age of 21.
   a. What was your age?
   b. How did you feel about the behavior?
   c. Did your parents or others observe you engage in the behavior? How did they react?

Were you able to remember these kinds of behaviors very easily? If not, do you think it was because you did not engage in such behaviors as a child, or do you think you simply cannot remember the specific times when you did engage in the behaviors? What are your feelings now as an adult about the sexuality-related or exploratory behaviors in which you engaged? Are you comfortable thinking about them now?

Because of such problems with conducting research about childhood, early information on children came primarily from professional observations by physicians and other medical personnel. Although this information was provided by trained professionals, much of it was based on case histories, the observations of one or several individuals, rather than on systematic examination of large numbers of children. Case studies present problems of their own because of their substantial limitations, which were discussed in chapter 4 on research methods.

Another source of information is from the observations of parents who have, in many cases, more contact with their children than anyone else. This provides more detailed information about children in their everyday lives than can be provided by medical professionals, and is the method used in the recent studies that are discussed in later sections. The technique is not without its limitations, however, especially in that it relies on the judgment of parents in defining behavior as sexual. What may be viewed as sexual behavior by parents may not be understood in that way by the children themselves.

Of course, a compelling reason for studying the development of sexuality across the entire life span—including during childhood—is the need for **basic knowledge** about the human experience that is accurate and complete. This is the justification for all basic scientific research about humans—to obtain information on what humans are like. However, for those requiring additional reasons for research on such a sensitive topic beyond basic knowledge, Sandfort and Rademakers (2000b) point out that a convincing practical reason for having information about childhood sexuality does exist. Children who display unusual sexual interests and behavior may have been sexually abused. In order to be more certain about exactly what qualifies as unusual interests and behavior, it is necessary first to establish what is "normal" for children. This should help to reassure parents when they discover certain behaviors or curiosity in their own children. Children will in fact learn about sexuality even if parents attempt to protect their children or pretend that it does not exist. Knowledge therefore will allow parents and professionals to respond in reasonable ways to events in the lives of children.

## *Development During Infancy*

Prenatally, ultrasound recordings have documented the occurrence of erections of the penis in male fetuses; this indicates that, by the second half of the prenatal period, nervous system structures involved in the functioning of the genitals have developed sufficiently to produce a type of reflexive arousal (Money & Musaph, 1977). Ultrasound technology does not permit detection of sexual arousal in female fetuses, although Serbin and Sprafkin (1987) speculate that arousal of the clitoris and other sexual organs is highly likely. In addition, both erections in male newborns and vaginal lubrication in females newborn have been observed, but no systematic research has been conducted to document the frequency of, or specific ages at which, these events have occurred. The implications of these capabilities, however, are not apparent (Serbin & Sprafkin, 1987). Yet they suggest that physiologically the human body develops at a very early age in a way that may lay the foundation for later sexual functioning.

**Infancy** is the period from birth up to 2 years; see Figure 13.1. Because of the negative attitudes about sexuality in children, virtually no systematic research exists regarding infant sexual functioning. However, as noted by Serbin and Sprafkin (1987), "Anyone who has worked with infants can testify that masturbation, manipulation of the genitals, is a common occurrence during the first year" (p. 170). A number of writers in the early to middle part of the 20th century documented that infants and young children touch and stimulate their own genitals. These reports were based on statements by parents and pediatricians about toddlers and preschool children engaging in masturbation, although this behavior was described in nonsexual ways by the

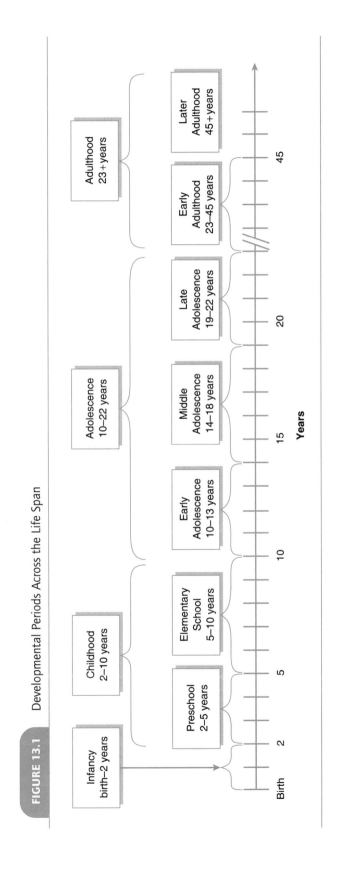

**FIGURE 13.1** Developmental Periods Across the Life Span

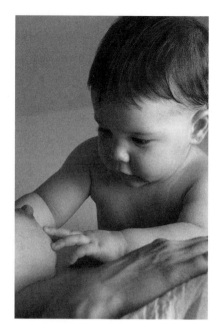

*What role do you think very early experiences play in the later development of sexuality?*

adults. Yet, in some cases, the stimulation resulted in arousal, even to the point of reactions that appeared similar to orgasm-like responses and subsequent release of tension. These reports also indicated that self-stimulation occurred at times when the children were upset or stressed, possibly as a way of obtaining relief; at other times, masturbation occurred when they seemed to be seeking merely pleasure or stimulation (Ryan, 2000).

The nature of the mother–infant social environment that is characteristic for an individual may be viewed as setting the stage for the development of sexuality; this might also be true for other early relationships as well. Serbin and Sprafkin (1987) additionally propose that the foundations for sexuality may develop in early experiences such as breastfeeding. Oral stimulation, such as that resulting from sucking, is highly pleasurable and soothing for infants (De Lora, Warren, & Ellison, 1981). For this reason, breastfeeding very probably is a highly positive experience, not only for infants, but also for mothers. They note that breastfeeding stimulates the nipple and breast of the mother, typically producing general bodily arousal. Such stimulation is even capable of initiating uterine and vaginal contractions that are markedly similar to those involved in orgasm (Masters & Johnson, 1966). The implication is that early pleasurable physical contact may establish the beginning of positive associations related to interpersonal contact for both mother and child. These pleasant experiences are likely to contribute to a tendency to respond positively to physical intimacy in the long run by the child.

Beyond this, the way that parents typically react to infant behavior that is even remotely suggestive of sexuality probably establishes the basis for the child's view of his or her body. Infants frequently touch their genitals and other parts of their body, such as the abdomen or upper legs, in an absentminded way. More obvious situations are those in which children fondle their genitals in a more explicitly conscious way, including

*Is it possible that being cuddled and cared for by parents during infancy lays the foundation for the development of sexuality by making individuals more comfortable with being touched and caressed?*

engaging in masturbation. Different parents may react in different ways to such self-touching. Parents who have more restrictive or negative views of sexuality in general are likely to express disapproval of self-touching (Fisher, Byrne, White, & Kelley, 1988; Lemery, 1983). Parental reactions may range in form from subtle facial expressions (e.g., frowning or wincing) to more explicit prohibitions (e.g., "Don't touch yourself there!") or overt behaviors, such as pushing or slapping the infant's hands away from that part of the body.

Other parents might merely ignore infant self-exploration, possibly out of discomfort with what they interpret as sexuality-associated behavior. Some caregivers may view such self-touching and stimulation as merely exploration and nonsexual. Regardless of the specific reaction when self-touching occurs, many parents probably tend to discourage or try to prevent such behavior. Furthermore, caregivers may view masturbation that continues into the early school years as inappropriate and indicating a type of problem (Ryan, 2000). Whatever the specific form, the reaction of parents in the very early years most likely begins the process of instilling attitudes and values about physical and erotic pleasure, ranging from discomfort and shame to acceptance and pleasure (De Lora et al., 1981; Serbin & Sprafkin, 1987).

Girls may be particularly prone to lack of knowledge and familiarity with their genitals, and possibly develop a resulting discomfort associated with them for several reasons (Serbin & Sprafkin, 1987). Female genitals are not as prominent visually as male genitals—the penis and scrotum extend outside the body, making male genitals more salient. Furthermore, cultural values tend to discourage female sexual expression to an even greater extent than is the case for males.

Serbin and Sprafkin (1987) proposed that, for children, issues highly relevant to sexuality are the formation of gender identity, recognition of gender constancy, mastery of knowledge about gender roles and sexuality, and development of gender-role identity. Many of these concepts were discussed in chapter 6 on issues related to gender. Concepts related to gender and gender roles most likely do contribute to the foundation on which sexuality develops. However, the ways in which gender and self-understanding about gender are involved in sexuality are not necessarily straightforward. For example, gender identity—an individual's sense that they are male or female, or some combination—does not correspond perfectly with the gender of those whom one finds attractive. Individuals who feel that their gender does not match the body into which they were born may elect to have surgery to reconstruct their genitals to be those of the other gender; such individuals are **transsexual**. Transsexual individuals may be attracted to either gender, and this attraction may remain the same after their surgery. Beyond this, little research has directly examined the way that early gender concept formation relates to later sexuality.

# *Development During Childhood*

It is reasonable to assume that gender-related concepts and socialization provide the foundation on which later sexual development builds. Just as importantly, the ways in which children learn to interact with others early in life are likely to affect the way that they behave toward others when explicit sexual feelings do arise. Social competence and involvement in peer networks during childhood may form the basis for the tendencies that adolescents develop regarding sexuality. They will also determine adolescents' ability to deal effectively with attraction, dating, and romantic relationship formation. Consequently, the social development of young children is important to consider in understanding the development of sexuality.

## The Role of Parent–Child Interactions

Temperament exerts a significant effect on the course of children's lives. For example, having an easy or difficult temperament has been found to relate to the way in which individuals later respond to problems. However, parents also have an influence on children above and beyond the tendencies due to children's basic temperament. The importance of childhood **attachment** to parents is highlighted by the finding that attachment quality relates to the quality of relationships that children have later with their peers. A major factor contributing to secure attachment is the sensitivity of the caretaker to the needs and feelings of the child. Related to this is a responsiveness in which the caretaker adjusts his or her behavior to accommodate the child's

Developing a secure attachment to one's parents during infancy and childhood is based on the sensitivity of parents to the needs and feelings of the child.

behavior and feelings (Sroufe, Carlson, & Shulman, 1993). Children developing secure attachments tend to have higher quality relationships and are more effective in relationships with peers (Parke et al., 2002).

In addition, parents influence the social development of their children by providing **direct advice** regarding peer relationships and friendships. In early childhood (e.g., 2–4 years) parents are likely to be involved in promoting smooth interaction and giving children guidance on strategies for developing quality social skills. Parental involvement in this way has been linked to greater social competence and greater acceptance by peers. In later childhood (e.g., 8–10 years), explicit advice by parents regarding routine interaction with peers is seen as less appropriate from the perspective of both children and parents; direct parental involvement may occur primarily when significant difficulties are experienced by children. By middle childhood (e.g., 5–7 years), parents exert influence over peer relationships by controlling the types of opportunities their children have to interact with other children and monitoring their choice of friends. Children of parents who engage in greater levels of monitoring are less likely to be delinquent and to engage in antisocial, harmful types of behaviors. Nonetheless, the nature of peer relationships impacts the social development of children even after taking into account the influence of parents (Parke et al., 2002).

## The Preschool Period

The **preschool period** ranges from 2 to 5 or 6 years of age.

### Are Children Capable of Experiencing Passionate Love?

As noted at the beginning of the chapter, historically children have been viewed as completely incapable of experiencing sexual feelings of any sort. This is a belief that has not been supported by empirical research at all. Elaine Hatfield and her colleagues (Hatfield, Schmitz, Cornelius, & Rapson, 1988) were able to interview young people who ranged in age from 4–18 years about their feelings of passionate love; 114 were male and 122 were female. As defined previously in chapter 9, passionate love is the desire for union with another person, and among adults it is strongly related to the desire for physical and sexual contact with the person.

Actually, the study took more than two years to arrange because of tremendous resistance from various school administrators related to allowing students to participate. The researchers were eventually able to obtain the consent of 96% of parents contacted to permit their children to participate. To measure the experience of passionate love in young people, Hatfield and her colleagues revised the Passionate Love Scale used with adults so that the wording and concepts would be understandable to children and adolescents. The new scale was called the Juvenile Love Scale (JLS), and as with the adult version, it asks individuals to think of one person whom they love. In the case of the JLS, the young people were asked to think of someone whom they would like to have as their boyfriend or girlfriend if they could.

All children understood the concept of boyfriend–girlfriend and were able to identify such a person they would like to have as one. With this person in mind, they were asked to rate on a 9-point scale how much they agreed that each statement or question was true for them. Two children had to have a word explained to them. Examples of statements and questions on the JLS are "Did you ever keep thinking about _____ when you wanted to stop and couldn't?" "If I could, when I grow up I'd like to marry (live with) _____," and "When _____ is around I really want to touch him (her) and be touched."

The youngest and the oldest children actually obtained the highest scores on the passionate love scale, indicating that the experience of passionate love is possible from a very early age. Moreover, the findings reveal that this intense interest in another person may begin at extremely early ages. The results also indicate that passionate love is not driven by hormonal changes around the time of puberty, which occurs in late childhood. Therefore, age is not a factor involved in the tendency to experience passionate love. However, gender was in fact related to passionate love, with girls having higher scores than boys.

The outcomes related to age and gender were also found in a second study (Hatfield, Brinton, & Cornelius, 1989). The follow-up study also demonstrated that the tendency to experience anxiety is associated with passionate love in young people. This is consistent with the arousal transfer hypothesis discussed in chapter 8 and the two-factor theory of love presented in chapter 9. Other research has demonstrated that negative emotions, such as anxiety and fear, can contribute to greater levels of sexual arousal. The answer to the question, "Are children capable of experiencing passionate love?" is definitely *Yes!*

## What Do Children Know About Sexuality?

*The two big subjects that supposedly parents are going to help their children understand—sex and money—are the two things we have the most difficulty talking about.*

Robert Duvall, American actor (ThinkExist.com)

*Parents ought not be afraid to talk to their children early and often about sex, love, and relationships, and to be as specific as they are comfortable being.*

Bill Albert (ThinkExist.com)

As with the issue of sexuality in general, hardly any research exists about children's knowledge of sexual issues, outside of investigations of the development of gender identity and children's understanding of pregnancy and birth. In addition, many of the existing studies were conducted a number of years ago, with virtually no recent information available. Little exists as well regarding children's knowledge of adult sexual behavior or sexual abuse (Volbert, 2000).

### Names of Sexual Organs

Think back to when you were a little toddler of about two or three. What name did you and your family use to refer to sexual organs? Did you have a different name for male parts and female parts? Did you use the accurate names of *vulva* for the female external organs and *penis* and *scrotum* for the male external organs? Or were cute, little nicknames, such as *willie* and *bottom,* the order of the day, or maybe even *down there.* Well, if you are like most people, your family had nicknames for both female and male organs, or your family only vaguely referred to them, if at all.

In general, parents apparently do not even attempt to inform children about the names of the sexual organs. Many preschoolers in one study were able to accurately identify quite a number of nongenital body parts, such as the head, arm, and leg. Yet few were able to say what the correct anatomical names are for the genitals (Wurtele, Kast, & Melzer, 1992). An earlier study by Bem (1989) found that similar proportions of boys and girls (67% and 68%, respectively) in the 3–5 year age range were able to provide a label for male genitals, although almost four times as many girls, a majority, were able to provide a name for female genitals (e.g., vulva) as were boys.

Other studies have not replicated this finding of greater knowledge on the part of girls, but have more generally found that children are given names for male genitals more frequently than they are for female genitals (Gordon, Schroeder, & Abrams, 1990; Moore & Kendall, 1971; Victor, 1980; Volbert, 2000). Girls between the ages of 1 and 4 years are less likely to be given a label for their own genitals by their mothers than for male genitals (Fraley, Nelson, Wolf, & Lozoff, 1991). The name often given to female genitals is *bottom,* which is frequently also used to refer to the buttocks and anus; this is an inaccurate and misleading term that confuses female sexuality with organs involved in the elimination of bodily wastes (Moore & Kendall, 1971).

### *When Are Children Able to Understand Gender?*

In a study of German preschool children aged 2–6 years (Volbert, 2000), all but one 2- year-old youngster was able to accurately classify drawings of clothed and unclothed children and adults in terms of their gender. Most 2-year-olds could not offer an explanation of the reasoning for their grouping, whereas explanations of 3- and 4-year-olds were based on nongenital factors such as the style of hair. Genitals were more likely to be offered as the basis for decisions among 5- and 6-year-olds, although this rationale was often provided only after viewing the pictures of unclothed children.

As indicated in chapter 6, most children have established their gender identity, a sense that they are a girl or a boy, by age 3 years. This was also found in the Volbert study. Only a quarter of 2-year-olds were able to identify their own gender. In contrast, the vast majority of 3-year-olds accurately indicated their own gender, and essentially all children 4 years and older understood their own gender. Yet very few of any of the age groups identified their gender on the basis of the type of genitals they possessed.

## Do Children Associate Sex Organs With Sexuality and Reproduction?

Children between the ages of 2 and 7 years are generally not aware of **sexual functions** associated with the genitals. The study of German preschoolers found that most children aged 2–6 years view genitals entirely in terms of elimination of body wastes (Volbert, 2000). If they are aware of the sexual function, it is typically conceived in terms of pregnancy and birth (Gordon et al., 1990), rather than pleasure and their role in romantic relationships. Only an extremely small proportion of the children in the Volbert study were aware of a sexual function of genitals, with most of the children thinking entirely in terms of the role of gender in giving birth. Even fewer knew that the penis had a sexual function, reporting for example that it is the source of seed involved in producing babies; however, they could not provide any further information (Volbert, 2000).

### *Do Children Know How Babies Are Made?*

Preschool children's limited ability to understand concepts related to time and causality make it unlikely that many will be able to accurately understand the concept of **reproduction**. Children of this age are not easily able to grasp the notion of creation, meaning that what currently exists did not exist at one time. If confronted with the issue of where babies come from, young preschoolers think in terms of a location, such as from a mother's body, rather than thinking in terms of the process of development during pregnancy (Serbin & Sprafkin, 1987).

In one study of 366 children in this age range (4–7 years), only a small proportion were able to state that babies result from an egg that grows inside the mother's abdomen (Bosinski, 1989, cited in Volbert, 2000). The recent study of German preschoolers (Volbert, 2000) revealed that only by 4-years-old were most children able to understand intrauterine (within the uterus) development, whereas all 6-year-olds were aware of the process. Substantial majorities of 2- and 3-year-olds had no knowledge of birth occurring through the vagina, or of cesarean surgery, whereas most children 4 and older were aware of at least one of these methods.

Young children with more advanced cognitive abilities understand a vague notion of babies being made somehow, but seldom understand the concept of a baby developing through a biological process. Children between the ages of 4 and 6 years therefore possess only the most basic understanding of reproduction, which is likely to be somewhat inaccurate. Among young children, the father is seldom seen as having more than a helping role, a type of assistant to the mother in the process of having a baby. German preschool children were virtually unaware of the

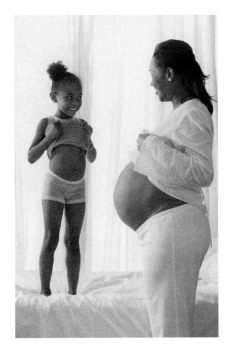

*How much do you think preschool children are able to comprehend about the complex concept of creation through reproduction?*

issue of fertilization or how it occurs, with most 2- to 6-year-olds having no knowledge at all. Only a handful of the older children were able to offer any statements at all concerning sexual behavior, but none linked the behavior to the process of procreation. Most children's understanding of intimate behavior when presented with a picture of a semiclothed or unclothed couple in bed involved simply *kissing* and *hugging*. A mere 3% alluded to any concept that was sexual, such as making a baby, and this was among the oldest children (Volbert, 2000).

One perspective conceives of children's understanding as a progression across three levels of knowledge about the roles of mothers and fathers: (a) nonsexual understanding, (b) transitional sexual understanding, and (c) overtly sexual understanding (Goldman & Goldman, 1982). Children typically think of reproduction in terms of nonsexual female and male roles until around the age of 11 years. Even though a few younger children may have a grasp of some of the facts about procreation, they are still nonetheless thought of in nonsexual ways (specifically, the growth of an egg into a baby is not connected to its fertilization through sex by the parents).

### What Do Children Know About Sex?

Although very little information exists concerning the issue, preschool children rarely have knowledge of penile–vaginal intercourse. Although a few appear to have some knowledge, the information provided by young children is extremely vague and it is not clear that their understanding involves any substantial detail. No research exists about knowledge of other types of sexual behavior. Mothers are typically viewed in a more active role in producing babies by younger children, but fathers are seen in a more active role than mothers by older children (Volbert, 2000).

*What do you think most children would say about a picture of an adult woman touching an unclothed boy?*

In the Volbert (2000) study, when German children were shown a drawing of a girl touching a boy's penis, most responded by simply describing the girl as pointing to, or touching, the boy's "thing." A small proportion expressed beliefs that the behavior was prohibited or wrong. The children were also shown drawings of a woman leaning over an unclothed child and of a woman touching an unclothed boy's penis. Most children interpreted the pictures in terms of parental care of the child; only a few of the children suggested that the behaviors were not related to care, saying that the adult was tickling or playing with the penis. Seven percent of the children indicated that the actions were unacceptable or wrong.

### Are There Differences Among Children in What They Know?

*This whole safety curriculum. It's technically not sex ed, but our issue is that they're introducing what we believe to be deviant sexual scenarios into the minds of these little children.*

John Murphy (ThinkExist.com)

*Before the child ever gets to school it will have received crucial, almost irrevocable sex education, and this will have been taught by the parents, who are not aware of what they are doing.*

Dr. Mary S. Calderone, Adjunct Professor, Program in Human Sexuality, in the New York University Department of Health Education, pioneering advocate for sex education, 1904–1998 (ThinkExist.com)

Education by parents is related to greater sexual knowledge among 2- to 7-year-old children with respect to pregnancy and birth issues, but not knowledge of adult sexual behavior (Gordon et al., 1990). Parents typically restrict the type of information they provide, often to basic issues regarding reproduction (Finkelhor, 1984). Cultural differences among children have also been found, with children from English-speaking countries demonstrating accurate knowledge of the birth process by 11 years of age; in contrast, Swedish children possessed knowledge comparable to that of 11-year-old English-speaking children at 9 years. Furthermore, over a third of Swedish children were able to provide a realistic account of birth at 5 years (Goldman & Goldman, 1983). The earlier knowledge of Swedish children is likely due to differences in timing of parental education of children. Individuals in Scandinavian countries tend to hold less restrictive and less conservative attitudes about sexuality than do individuals in the United States.

In fact, less restrictive sexual attitudes by parents are associated with greater sexual knowledge of their children overall, as well as greater knowledge in specific areas. Parental attitudes are related to socioeconomic level, with mothers in lower socioeconomic levels reporting more restrictive sexual attitudes and providing less information to their children (Gordon et al., 1990).

## Curiosity About One's Own and Others' Genitals

Again, think back to when you were a very young kid. Did you ever try to look at another person's body or to touch their breast or sexual organ? Do you think that most children do that sort of thing? In fact, many sexual scientists have concluded that curiosity about the sexual characteristics of one's own body, as well as those of others, is an important aspect of sexual development. **Curiosity** in general is a fundamental motivation (Schurhke, 2000), an important factor leading children to learn about the world in which they live. It is through curiosity that they acquire substantial amounts of knowledge critical to their survival and development.

Exploration of one's own body, as well as that of others, enables children to formulate a **bodily representation** for both sexes. The representation changes over the course of development as the body changes. In infancy and early childhood, the schema may largely take the form of an understanding of where the body parts and organs are, relative to each other, in a general way. This understanding is crucial to developing a basic coordination with respect to posture and movement, although this is likely not a conscious representation. Specific aspects of the body schema take on increasing levels of meaning as the child encounters reactions and evaluations by caregivers, family, and other members of the culture. These views and feelings then become integrated into children's own body schemas. The basic point here is that a child's understanding of his or her sexual organs evolves in the context of learning about the body in general (Schurhke, 2000).

The process of understanding the nature and meaning of sexual organs nonetheless also includes factors that are not involved in children's understanding of other parts of the body. The genitals are capable of providing much more intense pleasure and joy than other body parts, although parents often discourage children from touching or stimulating them. Genitals often become shrouded in great secrecy, mystery, or even shame and humiliation as adults go to great pains to protect genitals from the sight of others. Yet children also eventually come to realize that the genitals are the fundamental basis for gender stereotypes and gender roles that they are expected to enact effectively. The very organs that are earnestly hidden from view and avoided in most conversation, it is realized, have a tremendous impact on individuals' lives (Fisher, 1989). One of the few studies that has been conducted on childhood sexuality addresses the issue of exactly what young children are curious about; this study is examined in Box 13.2.

Close physical contact is essential for the development of high-quality attachments for children, just as it is infants; attachment provides the basis for the formation of emotional security and trust toward others, as discussed previously. Cuddling and close contact may also cause children to become more aware of their own bodies, as well as those of others; physical contact may additionally lead to heightened feelings of sensuality and possibly sexual interest (Schurhke, 2000).

Research reveals that the greater frequency of 2- to 10-year-old children bathing with their parents is related to a greater tendency of children to touch their parents' genitals or breasts (Rosenfeld, Bailey, Siegel, & Bailey, 1986). Yet research also reveals that, if parents begin to feel that their children's curiosity is overtly sexual, they cease bathing with them or discontinue the practice of allowing siblings to bathe together (Rosenfeld, Siegel, & Bailey, 1987). All of these experiences contribute to children's accumulating knowledge about the body, physical pleasure, and sensuality that eventually become a part of their understanding of sexuality.

The impact of physical closeness and exposure to nudity on sexuality is shown in a number of studies on the relationship of these experiences to later behavior. College students reporting retrospectively on their childhood experiences provide evidence that greater exposure to nudity and sleeping with their parents during childhood was positively associated with higher levels of sexual activity, greater comfort with physical closeness and affection, and greater self-esteem (Lewis & Janda, 1988). Sexual activity during childhood was likewise correlated with greater nudity within a family (Friedrich, Grambsch, Broughton, Kuiper, & Beilke, 1991).

**Box 13.2**                                                    **An Eye Toward Research**

### Just Exactly What Are Young Children Curious About?

A recent study of 26 German children during the second year of life and again during the sixth year focused on curiosity about others' genitals; 15 of the children were boys and 11 were girls (Schurhke, 2000). Around age 2, more than half of the boys, as reported by their parents, had visually examined both female and male genitals, as well as touching male genitals of family members. Just fewer than half of the boys were interested in naming male genitals. Over half of the girls were concerned about naming female and male genitals, looking at male genitals, and had expressed some type of interest in them. Somewhat fewer than half of the girls had touched male genitals. The boys in this study were largely interested in penises, rather than the scrotum or pubic hair, whereas girls were mainly interested in pubic hair or the genital area in general.

Parents were usually the individuals about whom the children were first interested, before being interested in siblings or other children. Interest in others' genitals typically occurred when the others were using the toilet, washing or taking a shower or bath, or walking around the house nude. Children exhibited no signs of sexual arousal during these behaviors, but displayed a range of emotions, as reported by the parents; these included (a) positive emotions, such as joy or enthusiasm; (b) neutral reactions, such as surprise or curiosity; and (c) negative emotions, such as upset, discomfort, and embarrassment.

In terms of the number of behaviors that children directed at their parents, girls and boys were equally interested in the genitals of their own sex. However, boys were less interested in the genitals of the other sex than were girls, as well as being more interested in same-sex genitals than in other-sex genitals. Girls were equally interested in the genitals of both sexes. Finally, girls were more likely to be interested in the genitals of other-sex children than were boys (Schurhke, 2000).

Mothers were interviewed again when the children entered their sixth year. Interest in mothers' genitals did not decline from the second year to the sixth year of life for both boys and girls; however, boys' interest in their father's genitals diminished, whereas girls' interest did not. Children were more interested in the genitals of children outside of the family during the later phase of the study than they were in the first phase. At this age, the children were less likely to observe their fathers when they were using the toilet in comparison to when they were younger; no change occurred in the incidence of observing mothers while using the toilet. Likewise, no change occurred with respect to children taking a shower or bath with their parents; those who did so during their second year were just as likely to do so during their sixth year. Also, all children tended to take baths or showers with their siblings at both ages (Schurhke, 2000).

What does this all mean? Both boys and girls in general display a degree of curiosity about others' genitals. Very young boys appear to be particularly interested in finding out about male genitals, whereas girls seem to be interested in both female and male genitals, as well as understanding names for them. The focus changed for 6-year-old boys in terms of less interest in male genitals. Early interest is focused on parents, which is probably related as much to the greater opportunity to see parents as they undress or use the toilet in comparison to others. Older children become more interested in the genitals of others. It can be said that curiosity about genitals is a fairly typical interest of children.

### References

Schurhke, B. (2000). Young children's curiosity about other people's genitals. In T. G. M. Sandfort & J. Rademakers (Eds.), *Childhood sexuality: Normal sexual behavior and development* (pp. 27–48). New York: Haworth.

## Sexual Behavior

We have just seen that, yes, many children are curious about their own and others' bodies from a very early age. What about sexual behavior? Do children engage in actual behavior that might be considered at least related to sexuality? Noting the lack of research on the issue, Serbin and Sprafkin (1987) have speculated that preschool children engage in masturbation and sex play with peers. Yet virtually nothing is known about the proportion of U.S. children who engage in such activity, its frequency, or its meaning. Because the few studies that exist are based on children from different countries, it is important to be aware of differences that might exist among children of various cultures; this issue is considered in more detail in Box 13.3, An Eye Toward Research.

---

**Box 13.3**                                    **An Eye Toward Research**

### Are U.S. and Dutch Children Similar in Sexual Behavior?

We have an answer to the question of whether children engage in some kinds of sexual behavior. Many children actually do, although the behavior probably does not have the sexual meanings for the children that adults might attach to it. The information was based on reports by mothers of Dutch children, which for many of us leads to the question of how U.S. children compare.

In fact, research indicates that culture does play a role in reports of sexual behavior. In general, Dutch individuals have less restrictive sexual attitudes than people in the United States (Friedrich, Sandfort, Ostveen, & Cohen-Kettenis, 2000). Four value-related dimensions have been used by sociologists to compare different cultures, one of which accounts for the different views of sexuality by U.S. and Dutch cultures. The two societies are similar on three cultural dimensions: power distance (unequal versus equal), individualism–collectivism (independent of others versus concerned about others), and uncertainty avoidance (rigid versus flexible; Hofstede, 1991). However, Dutch and U.S. culture differ on the fourth cultural dimension, masculinity–femininity (tough versus tender), with Dutch society more tender-minded than U.S. society. Tender-minded societies are likely to be more permissive regarding sexuality (Hofstede, 1998), with the Netherlands generally embracing a less restrictive position on sexuality than the United States (Van den Akker, Halman, & de Moor, 1994)

In a study that compared U.S. children with Dutch children on a variety of sexual behaviors (Friedrich et al., 2000), the average age of U.S. children was 4.2 years, whereas the average age in two Dutch samples was 3.5 years and 5.4 years; the age range was from 2–6 years old. A major strength of this study is that the number of children on whom mothers reported was very large, more than 100 girls and 100 boys for each Dutch sample and more than 200 girls and 200 boys for the U.S. sample.

The proportion of Dutch mothers reporting that their daughters had engaged in particular sexual behaviors was more than five percentage points different from the reports of U.S. mothers on 20 of 25 sexual behaviors. Those sexual behaviors involving the largest overall proportions of daughters were *touches sexual parts at home* (Dutch girls = 96.0% and 84.6% [there were two Dutch samples] versus U.S. girls = 54.4%); *touches breasts* (Dutch girls = 80.3% and 78.3% versus U.S. girls = 48.4%); *interested in the other gender* (Dutch girls = 63.7% and 66.5% versus U.S. girls = 20.6%); and *tries to look at people undressing* (Dutch girls = 43.9% and 44.8% versus U.S. girls = 33.3%).

---

*(Continued)*

(Continued)

Dutch mothers also reported that greater proportions of their sons engaged in 22 of the 25 sexual behaviors compared with U.S. mothers' reports of their sons. The sexual behaviors on which the largest overall proportions of Dutch boys were greater than U.S. boys by at least five percentage points were *touches sexual parts at home* (Dutch boys = 96.6% and 91.8% versus U.S. boys = 64.1%); *touches breasts* (Dutch boys = 73.8% and 59.7% versus U.S. boys = 43.5%); *interested in the other gender* (Dutch boys = 64.1% and 54.0% versus U.S. boys = 21.0%); *tries to look at people undressing* (Dutch boys = 43.9% and 40.2% versus U.S. boys = 33.9%); and *masturbates with hand* (Dutch boys = 57.4% and 45.3% versus U.S. boys = 22.6%).

Differences between girls and boys were largely similar for the two countries. Greater proportions of girls *talked flirtatiously* in both countries than boys, whereas more boys *showed their sexual parts to other children*, *showed their sexual parts to adults*, *touched their sexual parts at home*, and *masturbated with their hand*.

Differences in the procedure through which data were obtained from people in the two countries may partly underlie the differences that were found. However, that greater proportions of Dutch children engaged in some of the behaviors is also consistent with other research indicating that attitudes may account for the differences as well. Parents who do not feel that childhood sexuality is normal tend to report that their child engages in fewer sexual behaviors (Friedrich, Fisher, Broughton, Houston, & Shafran, 1998).

Friedrich and his colleagues (2000) concluded that it is unlikely that Dutch children are inherently more sexually motivated than U.S. children. Rather, because of differences in parental attitudes between the two cultures, it is more probable that childrearing practices and socialization experiences are different for Dutch and U.S. children. U.S. parents may tend to discourage and punish the expression of behaviors they perceive to be sexual. It is also possible that children engage in sexual behaviors when parents are not present because of concern that they will react negatively to them. For this reason, U.S. parents may actually underreport the level of their children's sexual behavior because they are not aware of all of it.

## References

Friedrich, W. N., Fisher, J., Broughton, D., Houston, M., & Shafran, C. (1998). Normative sexual behavior in children: A contemporary sample. *Pediatrics, 101*(4), 9.

Friedrich, W. N., Sandfort, T. G. M., Ostveen, J., & Cohen-Kettenis, P. T. (2000). Cultural differences in sexual behavior: 2–6 year old Dutch and American Children. In T. G. M. Sandfort & J. Rademakers (Eds.), *Childhood sexuality: Normal sexual behavior and development* (pp. 117–129). New York: Haworth.

Hofstede, G. (1991). *Cultures and organizations: Software of the mind.* London: McGraw-Hill.

Hofstede, G. (1998). Comparative studies of sexual behavior: Sex as achievement or as relationship? In G. Hofstede (Ed.), *Masculinity and femininity: The taboo dimension of national cultures* (pp. 153–178). Thousand Oaks, CA: Sage Publications.

Van den Akker, P., Halman, L., & de Moor, R. (1994). Primary relations in Western society. In P. Ester, L. Halman, & R. de Moor (Eds.), *The individualizing society: Value change in Europe and North America* (pp. 97–127). Tilburg, the Netherlands: Tilburg University Press.

In contrast, a recent study of Dutch and Belgian children provided some of the first empirical information on sexuality-related behavior in children (Sandfort & Cohen-Kettenis, 2000). The research is based on reports by 670 mothers who responded to a questionnaire published in a Dutch magazine, *Parents Today*. The mothers indicated the frequency of 22 behaviors they had observed their 313 daughters and 351 sons engage in; these behaviors are presented in Table 13.1. Each mother reported on only their oldest child. The vast

**TABLE 13.1** Sexual Behaviors of 2- to 6-Year-Old Dutch Children as Reported by Their Mothers

| Behavior | Girls | Boys |
|---|:---:|:---:|
| Touches own sexual parts | 96 | 98 |
| Touches breasts | 79 | 74 |
| Interested in the other sex | 66 | 65 |
| Plays doctor | 65 | 55 |
| Asks questions about sexuality | 56 | 51 |
| Masturbates with hand | 39 | 59 |
| Tries to look at people undressing | 44 | 43 |
| Touches others' sexual parts | 36 | 30 |
| Undresses other people | 28 | 22 |
| Shows sexual parts to adults | 17 | 25 |
| Shows sexual parts to children | 18 | 24 |
| Masturbates with object | 20 | 12 |
| Looks at nude pictures | 13 | 18 |
| French kissing | 14 | 15 |
| Hugs unfamiliar adults | 13 | 17 |
| Draws sexual parts | 16 | 11 |
| Uses sexual words | 11 | 11 |
| Rubs body against people | 10 | 11 |
| Talks flirtatiously | 12 | 8 |
| Talks about sexual acts | 8 | 9 |
| Inserts objects in vagina or anus | 7 | 1 |
| Makes sexual sounds | 4 | 3 |
| Asks to engage in sexual acts | 3 | 3 |
| Imitates sexual behavior with dolls | 4 | 1 |
| Asks to watch explicit TV | 2 | 1 |

*Note:* Numbers are the percent of girls or boys who had engaged in each behavior.

From Sandfort, T. G. M., & Cohen-Kettenis, P. T., Sexual behavior in Dutch and Belgian children as observed by their mothers. In T. G. M. Sandfort & J. Rademakers (Eds.), *Childhood sexuality: Normal sexual behavior and development* (pp. 105–115). Copyright © 2000. Reprinted with permission of Haworth Press, Inc.

majority of children were between the ages of 2 and 6 years, for an average age of 4. The behaviors reported for the greatest proportion of children were *touches own sexual parts, touches breasts, interested in the other gender, plays doctor, asks questions about sexuality,* and *masturbates with hand.* Girls were more likely to play doctor and ask about sexuality, whereas greater proportions of boys touched their own genitals and masturbated with their hand.

Hardly any children engaged in certain behaviors: (a) ask to watch explicit TV, (b) imitate sexual behavior with dolls, (c) ask to engage in sex acts, (d) make sexual sounds, (e) insert objects into vagina or anus, or (f) talk about sex acts. A number of behaviors, however, were more likely to be observed in older children, such as playing doctor, asking questions about sexuality, looking at nude pictures, drawing sexual parts, and using sexual words. The overall frequency of the behaviors was somewhat related to increasing age. Only a very small relationship was found between the tendency to show physical intimacy (e.g., hug, snuggle) and higher levels of sexual behavior; a similarly small relationship was found with greater openness about nudity (Sandfort & Cohen-Kettenis, 2000).

As noted by Sandfort and Cohen-Kettenis (2000), the results demonstrate that large proportions of children, even fairly young children, engage in certain types of sexual behavior. Other research has likewise revealed that a range of behaviors are not entirely uncommon for preschool and elementary school children; these behaviors include incidental touching of parents' breasts and genitals (Rosenfeld et al., 1986), and even children placing their mouths on sexual organs, masturbating with an object, and inserting objects in their vagina or rectum (Friedrich et al., 1991).

Given that many of the children in the study did touch their own sexual organs, even masturbate, and asked questions related to sexuality, what do you suppose that it meant to them? Do you think they were focused on sexual stimulation similar to what adults seek out? As the authors of the study conclude, it is not likely at all for children of this age. Despite the fact that mothers viewed the behaviors reported in the study as sexual, it is unlikely that the children themselves understand many concepts involved in sexuality and may not perceive their own behaviors in a sexual way. Only as children mature will they begin to realize the meaning and significance of behaviors that are labeled as sexual by adults. If they recognize the importance attributed to such behaviors, that realization may actually alter the frequency or nature of the behavior. Beyond this, parents may react differently toward the child upon discovering sexual behavior (Sandfort & Cohen-Kettenis, 2000), further serving to reduce the frequency of the behavior in children. They may get the idea that parents are uncomfortable with their behavior, or even disapproving.

It must be kept in mind that the information provided within this study is based on a self-selected group of women. Observations were reported primarily by highly educated mothers in the Netherlands and Belgium who were interested in sending in a magazine questionnaire. The mothers and children are therefore likely to be a very select group (Sandfort & Cohen-Kettenis, 2000). As indicated in a previous section, lower socioeconomic status is related to more restrictive parental sexual attitudes. Educational level likewise is typically associated with greater socioeconomic level, such that the results of the study might not be relevant to those with lower educational and socioeconomic levels. Mothers with more permissive attitudes will be more accepting of, and therefore more attuned to, the occurrence of sexual behavior in their children, making it likely that they will report greater levels of sexual behavior. It could also be the case, however, that children of less restrictive mothers actually do engage in more sexual behavior because the mothers do not discourage it to the same extent as more restrictive mothers.

Moreover, as children grow older, they realize that most sexual behavior is viewed negatively by parents, such that they often hide sexual activity from parents to avoid disapproval or punishment (Sandfort & Cohen-Kettenis, 2000). The reports of children's sexual behavior are therefore very probably underestimates of their actual frequency for this reason. These two factors, mothers' educational level and children's concern about disapproval, may actually have opposing effects in this particular study.

## The Elementary School Period

For the purposes of thinking about psychological development, the elementary school period may be thought to extend from 5- to 10-years-old, encompassing a time when tremendous cognitive, emotional, and social development occurs. The trend of an increasing importance and influence of peers surges during this time, although parents and family continue to have tremendous impact on the lives of children as well.

> *There were 4 or 5 boys in my neighborhood around my age that I was good friends with. We more or less formed a jack-off club of sorts and would often get together for masturbating and fun. This is where I learned how to masturbate another cock, and how good it felt to have someone else masturbate you. In the summer time we would go out into the nearby woods where there was a swimming hole. We would strip and go skinny dipping, and play and stroke each other under the water. I liked to masturbate by rubbing the head of my penis against the head of another boy's, god that felt good. I was initiated into boy–girl sex at age 15, and with this new found fun I drifted away from my boyhood friends. (Male Masturbation Reality, 2006)*

According to a review of the little research that exists on the topic, most adults recall that their first experience of sexual attraction was on average between the ages of 10 and 10.5 years (McClintock & Herdt, 1996). One of the few studies on the topic (Ryan, Miyoshi, & Krugman, 1988) was based on retrospective accounts by adults—that is, adults remembering events and behaviors that occurred when they were children. Furthermore, the adults were professionals concerned with child sexual abuse and juvenile sexual offenders, which makes it very probable that the survey respondents were not typical of the general adult population. Given the extreme lack of any empirical research, however, the data provide valuable information about a highly under-studied topic.

A majority of adults (56.1%) reported that, by age 12 years, they had engaged in touching and exploration of one another's genitals with other children in a way that they perceived as sexual. However, sexual behavior beyond fondling occurred for less than 5% of the study participants. Such behavior included oral–genital contact, insertion of fingers in the vagina or rectum, and anal penetration;

*What do you think is the most likely setting for sexual play and experimentation among young children?*

penile–vaginal intercourse with same-age relatives and peers did not occur at all before age 12 for these individuals. The majority viewed the sexual behavior as consensual—that is, desired by both children—whereas merely a fraction engaged in the behavior because they were offered bribes or were threatened. Only a very small minority viewed the sexual behavior as exploitive of the other children or exploitive of themselves. Likewise, only about one-fifth felt that the sexual activity was scary, whereas almost a third viewed it as exciting.

More sexual behavior involved older childhood peers, rather than siblings, cousins, or younger friends, although the older peers did not include teenagers. A majority of the sexual activity took place while engaged in fantasy play, such as pretending that the friends were married or while "playing doctor."

Most were not caught while engaged in the sexual behavior. Of those who were caught, nearly half were punished. Yet the vast majority of the adults felt that their childhood sexual activity was normal, and indicated that they had experienced sexual arousal prior to puberty. Despite this context, the adult study participants tended to think their childhood behaviors were not really sexually motivated. Ryan (2000) suggested that the discrepancy between participants' overall perception of the behavior as not sexually motivated and what they reported in terms of specific behavior and feelings may result from the widespread denial of childhood sexuality.

A group of professionals convened by the Kempe Children's Center of the University of Colorado School of Medicine drew a number of conclusions about childhood sexuality on the basis of this study. First, more sexual activity occurs during the elementary school period than would be expected if children enter a latency period in which sexuality is dormant, as proposed within psychoanalytic theory. The evidence provided by this study, therefore, refutes the position that children become uninterested in sexual issues during this time. Secondly, a variety of sexual behavior occurs, likewise arguing against the notion of a latency period. Third, the preponderance of sexual arousal, exploration of other children's bodies, and sexual behavior involves children outside of the family. Fourth, children engage in sexual exploration in situations that avoid discovery and observation by adults. Finally, children evaluate their sexual behavior based on the emotions they experience and the beliefs they have developed (Ryan, 2000). The fact that individuals reported that they hid their sexual experiences from adults strongly indicates that reports provided by parents and caregivers are probably extremely unreliable for elementary school children.

## *Adolescence*

*Mother nature is providential. She gives us twelve years to develop a love for our children before turning them into teenagers.*

William Galvin (Boloji.com, August 10, 2006)

**Adolescence** is the period generally viewed within psychology as extending from approximately 10 years through the early 20s. Actually, the boundaries for the period of adolescence have been a source of considerable controversy among developmental psychologists. This is because different theorists have emphasized different aspects of development in deciding upon a particular range of years to call *adolescence*. Possible issues

*What was adolescence like for you? Was it challenging and interesting, stormy and tumultuous, or fun and adventurous?*

to consider are biological, emotional, cognitive, interpersonal, social, educational, legal, and cultural factors. The period is divided further into three smaller periods. **Early adolescence** is from around 10–13 years, **middle adolescence** is from 14–18 years, and **late adolescence** is from 19–22 years (Steinberg, 2002). These periods are identified in Figure 13.2.

This phase of development typically consists of quite a number of changes that may, for some characteristics, be dramatic and very fast paced. The changes involve not only biological processes, but also psychological and social aspects of the individual. Nonetheless, developmental psychologists have documented that substantial continuity also characterizes the period of adolescence, rather than being entirely a break from the psychological processes emerging during childhood. For example, core values (such as the importance of education), the structure of cognitive abilities, and factors related to problem behaviors all remain relatively stable from childhood into adolescence. Therefore, both continuity and change are involved in this time of life (Lerner et al., 1996).

## Puberty

**Puberty** is the physical maturation of the reproductive and sexual organs that leads to changes in a wide range of bodily features and enables the individual to produce offspring. Although the overwhelming perception is that puberty begins around the time of adolescence, it is actually an ongoing process with origins in developments that occur prenatally. During the prenatal period, as discussed in chapter 12, hormones called **androgens** are produced at increasing levels, particularly in genetic males. Androgens structure the reproductive system in a specific way, setting them up to produce even greater levels of hormones. However, the hormones are subsequently suppressed after birth throughout early childhood, until the reproductive organs are awakened. Androgen suppression ends, resulting in the initiation of puberty in late childhood (Archibald, Graber, & Brooks-Gunn, 2003).

## How Does the Body Change During Puberty?

*When I was about 12, I remember sitting up in my bed with a ruler, trying to see how long my penis was. It wasn't very long when erect, I would be excited for it to even be close to four inches. Nonetheless, I tried all the time and would get precum—I didn't really know it at the time. But I would do what I could to get horny and one way included the campfire sticks method. One time I kept doing it and suddenly felt like I had to pee. So I ran to the bathroom and stood over the toilet as I had my first orgasm. At the time I had no idea what it was, but soon enough it made sense. I continued to masturbate that same way until I realized I could do it the normal way just by rubbing up and down. (Male Masturbation Reality, 2006)*

The physical changes that occur at puberty can be identified in terms of five overarching categories (Marshall & Tanner, 1974). The first set of changes, as discussed above, are those in the endocrine system that begin the production of **greater levels of hormones**, specifically androgens; the hormones subsequently initiate changes in other areas of the body. The increased androgen production begins in the adrenal glands that sit atop the kidneys at approximately 6 years of age in girls and 8 years in boys; the beginning of this increase in androgen production is called **adrenarche**, which occurs before other hormonal and physical changes (Cutler & Loriaux, 1980). The effects of pubertal hormones initially are not directly observable, but at a later point are noticeable with respect to external features of the body (Archibald et al., 2003). The time line of significant developmental events for girls and boys at puberty is presented in Figure 13.2.

The second set of pubertal changes is the maturation of **primary and secondary sex characteristics**. **Primary sex characteristics** are the genitals and internal reproductive organs. **Secondary sex characteristics** are attributes not directly involved in reproduction, but that develop because of higher levels of sex hormones. These include maturation of the breasts in girls, growth of facial hair on boys, and growth of pubic and body hair in both girls and boys. **Breast budding** is usually the first observable sex characteristic in girls, although androgen from the adrenal glands has also been effecting changes in other parts of the body, such as the ovaries, as well. The noticeable maturation of breasts begins between the ages of 8 and 13 years; the average age for Black girls is 8.87 and for White girls 9.96 (Herman-Giddens et al., 1997; Kaplowitz et al., 1999).

Marshall and Tanner (1969) formulated a rating system for describing the continuous process of development consisting of five stages. Stage 1 is that in which breast development has not occurred; Stage 2 is breast budding; Stage 3 involves the breasts becoming more distinct but no real separation between the two of them exists; in Stage 4, distinction between the two breasts is noticeable and the areola forms a definite mound on each breast. Stage 5 is the mature stage, in which the breasts are completely developed and larger, although they vary in size across women at this stage; the areola recedes back into the general contour of each breast (Brooks-Gunn & Reiter, 1990).

For boys, the first observable development of sexual characteristics is the **enlargement of the testicles**, beginning typically between the ages of 11 and 11.5 years. At the lower extreme, some boys may exhibit this growth beginning at 9.5 years. Most of the size increase results from the growth in number of tubules (small tubes) that produce sperm, rather than cells that produce androgens. The penis and scrotum start the maturation process at the earliest about 10.5 years, although in some boys this can occur as late as 14.5 years. The process typically ends between 12.5 and 16.5 years. A system describing the changes in the male external genitals analogous to that developed to describe breast development has also been proposed (Marshall & Tanner, 1969; Morris & Udry, 1980). Stage 1 is the period in which pubertal maturation has not begun, and genitals

**FIGURE 13.2**    Physical Changes During Puberty

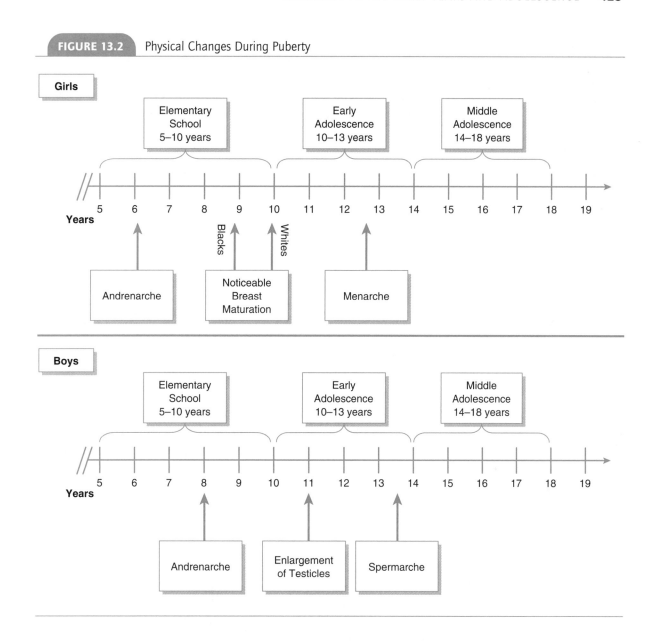

are in a small, undeveloped condition. Stage 2 is that in which the scrotum enlarges, reddens, and changes in texture. In Stage 3, the scrotum continues to enlarge, with the penis beginning to lengthen, as well as to widen to some extent. Stage 4 consists of the penis growing in both length and width, with the glans (the tip) enlarging and the scrotum still increasing in size and darkening. Stage 5 is the end state of adult maturity and size.

Pubic hair usually appears after the beginning of the growth of breasts in girls or testicles in boys. For girls, pubic hair growth starts shortly after breast budding around age 9 or 10; for boys, onset is around age 12 (Archibald et al., 2003).

Another outward indication of the maturation of the reproductive system for girls is **menarche**, the occurrence of the first menses, or menstrual flow. The average age for African American girls is 12.16 years and for

European American girls is 12.88 years. For boys, a comparable sign of gonadal maturation is **spermarche**, the first ejaculation of fluid from the penis; the typical age of spermarche is between 13 and 14 years.

The third set of changes related to puberty is actually the very first observable indication of the beginning of puberty, the **growth spurt**; this is the rapid increase in growth of bones that result in dramatic jumps in height and size. The growth spurt is followed by a slowing down of the growth process that ends in early adulthood. The age range for this aspect of puberty is 9.5 to 14.5 years for girls; for boys, the growth spurt can begin anywhere between 10.5 and 16 years and end anywhere between 13.5 and 17.5 years (Tanner, 1962). The average age of the onset of this period of rapid growth is usually very close to the time that breast maturation begins, which on average is 8.87 years for Black girls and 9.96 years for White girls; the average of the growth spurt for boys is 11.7.

The fourth set of pubertal changes is that of increasing fat or muscle tissue, as well as a redistribution of fat throughout the body. Before puberty, fat and muscle composition are very similar in girls and boys. However, after puberty, boys have 1.5 times the lean body mass and skeletal mass of girls, whereas girls have two times the amount of body fat that boys have (Grumbach & Styne, 1998). The difference is caused by greater numbers of muscle cells in male bodies, such that by the end of puberty more than half of body weight is typically muscle mass. Female bodies increase in fat to a greater extent, although the size of most girls' waists does not change much. Rather, fat is deposited on the hips and legs to produce a pear-shaped body, or in both the lower and upper body, resulting in the hour-glass shape. Increased levels of fat appear to be necessary to enable adequate reproductive functioning, given that increases occur around the time of menarche (Archibald et al., 2003).

The fifth set of bodily changes resulting from puberty is increased circulatory and respiratory capacity, providing greater strength and endurance. Other physical changes that are often of great concern to adolescents are the onset of acne in both girls and boys. In some girls, acne is in fact the first visible sign of the onset of puberty. In addition, the growth of hair under the arms and on other parts of the body during late puberty may be of psychological significance to some individuals (Archibald et al., 2003).

*What physical changes first come to mind when you think of puberty?*

## Psychological Processes During Puberty

Do you remember feeling moody or edgy or touchy as you were moving into the early years of adolescence? Maybe you have noticed mood swings or touchiness in your own children around this age. Well, there may be somewhat of a biological basis for at least part of these emotional changes.

Initial increases in hormone levels early in puberty have been found to relate to a slight tendency in girls to experience negative emotions. Higher levels of luteinizing hormone (LH) relative to follicle stimulating hormone (FSH) are related to greater levels of anger in preadolescent girls (see chapters 6 and 12 for an explanation of these hormones). This is true even after taking into account noticeable signs of puberty onset with respect to secondary sex characteristics; by controlling for the development in secondary sex characteristics, self-perceptions and perceptions of the individual by others cannot explain the more intense anger (Archibald et al., 2003).

Concerning boys, greater levels of androgens are associated with problem behaviors. In addition, a greater proportion of testosterone to estradiol in boys is related to less sadness and problem-behavior (Archibald et al., 2003).

## How Do Adolescents Feel About Changes in Their Body at Puberty?

### Perceptions of Secondary Sex Characteristics

Initial reactions of girls in fifth and sixth grade to the development of breasts and pubic hair are that breast development is more important than the growth of pubic hair. This is because breasts are more noticeable to others than is pubic hair (Archibald et al., 2003). Apparently, the status provided by recognition of their greater maturity is valuable to many girls. Breasts are generally a source of pride and excitement during this time. However, as breasts mature to an even greater extent, girls are more likely to experience teasing and harassment from family and boys. Archibald and her colleagues (2003) suggest that girls' feelings about breast development may become less positive as a result of reactions by others during middle school. No research has been conducted specifically concerning boys' feelings about the maturation of their bodies.

### Perceptions of Menarche and Spermarche

Prior to menarche—the onset of menstruation—girls believe that they will tell their girlfriends about the event sooner than they actually do when they experience menarche. Pre-menarche girls also believe that they will experience greater pain, water retention, and negative mood associated with menstruation than they actually have when they experience menstruation.

After menarche, girls report both positive and negative reactions to the experience of menstruation. Girls interviewed 2 to 3 months after their first menstruation reported a variety of feelings; 20% indicated that they experienced only positive reactions, 20% indicated only negative feelings, 20% reported mixed types of feelings (such as feeling "funny"), and 40% indicated they had both positive and negative reactions (Brooks-Gunn & Ruble, 1982).

Initially, girls are secretive about beginning menstruation with everyone except their mothers, although by 6 months they begin talking about the issue with their girlfriends. They seldom discuss their experiences with boys or their fathers, reporting that they would be very uncomfortable talking about it with their fathers (Archibald et al., 2003).

Very few studies have been conducted concerning boys reactions to spermarche, their first ejaculation (Archibald et al., 2003). In one small study (Gaddis & Brooks-Gunn, 1985), boys typically had more positive reactions to their first ejaculation than girls did to their first menstruation, although none of them had told their friends about it; rather, they had just joked about it in a general way. Many boys experience their first ejaculation during masturbation, which may account for their complete silence about its occurrence. Other studies based on older adolescents (Stein & Reiser, 1994) and retrospective accounts by adult men (Downs & Fuller, 1991) obtained similar findings.

### Perceptions of Physique Changes

Boys generally have very positive feelings about increases in height and weight, most likely because Western cultures place greater value on size and strength in men. Girls are more likely to have negative perceptions of increases in height and weight in their bodies, again probably due to the importance placed on slenderness and petiteness in Western cultures (Archibald et al., 2003). Girls often report a desire to be thinner than they are after the onset of weight gain resulting from puberty. Greater body mass gain during puberty was related to an elevated probability of developing eating problems among middle- and late-adolescent girls who were followed over a period of time (Attie & Brooks-Gunn, 1989; Graber, Brooks-Gunn, Paikoff, & Warren, 1994). As noted by Archibald and her colleagues (2003), the majority of girls in these studies had bodies that were in the normal weight range, rather than being obese.

Again, little research has been conducted on the relationship of boys' body image perceptions to damaging behavior patterns. It is often assumed that the danger of body image problems is far greater for girls. However, Archibald and her colleagues (2003) suggest that, because societal expectations of male bodies have become unrealistically extreme in the focus on muscularity, problems may increase for boys as well. It is possible that some proportion of boys will become obsessive about weight training and quick methods of building muscle, such as through steroid use.

### Reactions to the Rate of Pubertal Changes

Little evidence exists regarding adolescents' feelings about the speed of changes that occur in their bodies. One study conducted indicates that girls experience initial declines in positive feelings and increases in negative feelings. However, after a period of time, positive feelings rebound and negative feelings decrease. Those who changed in body features fairly gradually over time were more likely to maintain stable, positive feelings throughout the period. In contrast, girls with more rapid body changes were more likely to undergo greater declines in mood (Archibald et al., 2003).

## Is It More of an Advantage to go Through Puberty Earlier, About the Same Time, or Later Than Most Adolescents?

A number of studies have consistently demonstrated that early onset of puberty for girls is related to a host of mental health and behavioral problems (Archibald et al., 2003). This relationship may be largely true for European American girls, in that at least one study did not find greater levels of problems for African American and Hispanic American girls (Hayward, Gotlib, Schraedley, & Litt, 1999). Most studies include too few non-European American girls to draw definitive conclusions about this issue. Early maturation is associated with greater lifetime experience of depression, problem behavior, substance abuse, and suicide risk. In addition, early-maturing girls are more likely to engage in sexual behavior at a younger age. Late-maturing girls, in comparison to girls in the typical range of onset, also appear to be at greater risk for depression, self-consciousness, and conflict with parents (Archibald et al., 2003).

Possible reasons for the greater problems among early-maturing girls include (a) feeling different from, and more conspicuous than, peers; (b) deviation from societal ideals of beauty because of early weight gain associated with puberty; (c) overlap of pubertal body changes with other life transitions at the time, such as switching schools; and, finally, (d) greater pressures for early dating and sexual behavior. Girls who attend all-girl schools are less likely to experience problems related to early maturation. Interaction with boys appears to be a factor involved in difficulties, particularly interaction with older boys. Early-maturing girls are more likely to associate with older boys, as well as being at greater risk for problem behaviors if they do (Archibald et al., 2003).

Women in one study who had matured early had completed less education by age 30 and had lower-level careers than typically maturing women, despite exhibiting no differences in academic achievement prior to puberty (Stattin & Magnusson, 1990). Other evidence, however, suggests that it may be largely girls who display signs of behavior problems in middle childhood who are likely to experience greater problems as a result of early puberty (Archibald et al., 2003).

*Why do you suppose that early maturation of the body presents such a substantial challenge to adolescents, at least for some girls?*

Early-maturing boys may also be at greater risk for problems, although these appear to be less severe in nature than those that occur for girls; somewhat increased levels of depression and greater tobacco use, for example, are the types of problems seen in such boys. Late-maturing boys suffer from problems with school-work and self-consciousness. Boys who do not experience puberty during the typical time period, whether early or late, were found in one study to be more likely to engage in greater alcohol use and have greater alcohol-related problems (Andersson & Magnusson, 1990). However, much less research has been conducted on the effects of puberty timing with respect to boys (Archibald et al., 2003).

## Sexual Expression

According to a model proposed by Hill (1983), sexuality is one of five major psychosocial issues confronting individuals as they progress into adolescence. Sexuality represents one of a number of challenges faced by youth that are relatively unique to adolescence because of the sudden, rapid increase in complexity and intensity they experience. During a surprisingly short period of time relative to the entire life span, individuals must come to terms with a dramatically changing body, both with respect to its appearance and the way that it functions.

Beyond this, young people must learn to recognize and understand sexual desires. They must also accustom themselves to the experience of sexual stimulation and the emotional reactions associated with sexual arousal. In addition, adolescents must come to understand the attention they receive from others because of their increased sexual attractiveness and integrate it into their self-concept and value system. They must also explore and crystallize their attitudes about sexual behavior and relationships. Finally, they must deal with the meaning of physical and emotional intimacy, and the vulnerability involved in these types of interactions (Crockett, Raffaelli, & Moilanen, 2003).

As was noted in chapter 11, much of the research on racial and ethnic groups not based on European American populations has been concerned with the risks and dangers of early sexual behavior among racial and ethnic minority adolescents. Such a focus tends to reduce all racial and ethnic minority sexuality entirely to the behavior of adolescents; moreover, it conveys the sense that the sexuality of minorities is largely about irresponsibility and danger. In the same way, adolescent sexuality is treated as if all early sexual expression is necessarily risky or destructive. In addition, similar to research on racial and ethnic minority sexuality, much of the research on adolescent sexuality focuses on objective description of the type and frequency of various sexual behaviors, contraception use, and pregnancy and abortion.

Little is known about the meaning and emotional significance of dealing with sexual issues, engaging or not engaging in sexual behavior, and involvement in relationships. This lack of concern about the deeper psychological aspects of adolescent sexuality is most definitely related to the cultural view prevailing in the United States that adolescent sexuality is almost always unacceptable and damaging. In turn, this ethic is grounded in religious moral beliefs that sex outside of marriage is evil (Crockett et al., 2003). These beliefs about sexual morality target adolescent sexual behavior especially intensely because the majority of such behavior necessarily occurs outside of marriage, because marriage is generally not viewed as acceptable in early adolescence in U.S. culture.

In fact, the negative outcomes assumed to be linked to early sexual behavior have received some support in empirical research, providing a degree of justification for the concern. Yet, by ignoring the psychological underpinnings and motivations of adolescent sexuality, important factors that might explain why early sexual behavior occurs are excluded (Crockett et al., 2003). It also leaves a massive gap in the basic knowledge on human sexuality.

### Formation of Sexual Identity

*Sexual identity* is one's overall understanding of *all* aspects of his or her sexuality—that is, what the person is like in terms of sexual feelings, attitudes, and behaviors. Sexual identity also includes one's *sexual orientation identity,* the understanding a person has of being sexually and romantically attracted to males, females, or both (Mohr, 2002; Worthington, Savoy, Dillon, & Vernaglia, 2002). However, it is more than feelings about one's sexual orientation. The formation of sexual identity intensifies around the time of puberty as secondary sex characteristics begin to develop and the individual begins to experience increased levels of sexual feelings and desires. Relationships with parents and peers likewise change in light of expectations that adolescents will eventually take on adult roles and responsibilities.

The sexual identity of adolescents has been proposed to vary in terms of three major dimensions: sexual self-esteem, sexual self-efficacy (self-confidence and assertiveness), and sexual attitudes (e.g., feelings about arousal, interests in exploring sexual behaviors, desire for commitment; Buzwell & Rosenthal, 1996). Adolescents have been found to form five different types of sexual identities based on these three dimensions. Those with a **sexually competent** sexual identity tend to have some sexual experience, are higher in sexual self-esteem and self-efficacy, hold moderate sexual attitudes, and tend to be older. **Idealistic** and **unassured** adolescence are less likely to have had sexual experience and tend to be younger. Those with an **adventurous** sexual identity have high sexual self-esteem, self-efficacy, more positive attitudes about arousal and sexual exploration, and are more likely to be older males. Individuals with a **sexually driven** sexual identity tend to be males, have the most positive attitudes about sexual arousal and exploration, the lowest levels of anxiety and desire for commitment, and to express difficulty in refusing unwanted sexual behavior; this was the least frequent type of sexual identity.

All of the groups of sexual identities include adolescents who are not certain about their sexual orientation, although most adolescents identify as heterosexual. Those with adventurous sexual identities are the most likely to have engaged in same-sex sexual behavior; 14% in the Buzwell and Rosenthal study (1996) had same-sex experience. However, adolescents who self-identified as lesbian or gay had only a sexually competent sexual identity or a sexually unassured identity.

The distinction between actual sexual behavior and the sexual orientation identity that an individual embraces is further illustrated in other research on adolescent sexual behavior (Graber & Archibald, 2001). Research on 35,000 adolescents in grades 7–12 (Remafedi, Resnick, Blum, & Harris, 1992) found that the proportion of youth identifying themselves as lesbian or gay was relatively consistent across the age groups. Only a small fraction of the adolescents described themselves as lesbian or gay (1.1%) or bisexual (0.9%), although an additional 11% labeled themselves as *unsure.* Students were more likely to use this last label in the earlier grades than in later grades.

However, more adolescents reported that they had engaged in same-gender sexual behavior than labeled themselves as unsure, lesbian, or gay. The proportion of individuals who engaged in same-gender sexual behavior increased from 1% in seventh grade to 3% in twelfth grade; yet only 27% of such adolescents identified themselves as lesbian, gay, or bisexual. Even greater proportions indicated that they experienced same-gender attraction, 2% in seventh grade and 6% in twelfth grade; 3% overall reported same-gender fantasies. Despite feeling same-gender *attraction,* only 5% of such adolescents identified themselves as lesbian, gay, or bisexual, and only 30% of those experiencing same-gender *fantasies* labeled themselves as lesbian, gay, or bisexual.

Very little information exists on the proportion of adolescents under the age of 21 who identify as gay, lesbian, or bisexual. One study based on 34,196 high school students found that 0.8% identified as bisexual, whereas 0.34% identified as lesbian or gay (French, Story, Remafedi, Resnick, & Blum, 1996). In another study involving 4,159 high school students, 2.5% identified as lesbian, gay, or bisexual (Garofalo, Wolf, Kessel, Palfrey, & DuRant, 1998). However, a number of lesbians, gay men, and bisexual individuals report that they were not aware of, or did not reveal to others, their sexual orientation until early adulthood.

Nonetheless, many lesbian, gay, and bisexual individuals develop at least a beginning awareness of their attraction to the same sex in early adolescence (Graber & Archibald, 2001). A portion of these individuals engage in same-gender behavior during their youth, although many lesbians, gays, and bisexuals recall that they largely experienced feelings of "being different" rather than actually engaging in same-gender behavior (D'Augelli, 1998; Savin-Williams, 1990; Troiden, 1990). This is also the period during which many adolescents who are attracted to the other sex begin to experience sexual attraction and fantasy as well, and engage in sexual behavior. The increase in sexual interest and behavior is likely due to the onset of puberty.

## Fantasy

Fantasizing about sexual issues is the most prevalent form of sexual behavior among adolescents (Crockett et al., 2003). According to one of the few studies on the topic, a substantial majority (72%) of adolescents report experiencing sexual fantasies (Coles & Stokes, 1985). According to Katchadourian (1990), fantasy enables young people to explore the nature of their sexual desires and to anticipate how to behave during sexual experiences.

## Masturbation

Masturbation is the stimulation of erotic areas of one's own body, especially the genitals, by an individual. This self-stimulation may include such behaviors as touching, caressing, stroking, and fondling the body to produce pleasurable sensations. Masturbation may or may not always result in orgasm or ejaculation. Approximately one-third of girls have masturbated by the ages of between 13 and 15 years. In contrast, as many as two-thirds of boys have masturbated by this age. However, by 19 or 20, 75% of women and 90% of men have masturbated. Girls masturbate less frequently than boys, although quite a range of differences exist (Chilman, 1983; Leitenberg, Detzer, & Srebnik, 1993).

As is true for adults, masturbation is not a substitute for other types of sexual behavior. Adolescents who have engaged in sexual intercourse engage in greater levels of masturbation than those who have not experienced sexual intercourse (Chilman, 1983). Despite its high prevalence, masturbation is not openly discussed to any great extent in the United States, continuing to be a forbidden and embarrassing topic to many (Crockett et al., 2003).

## Physically Intimate Behavior With Others

One type of sexual behavior that does not involve penile–vaginal intercourse or oral–genital sex is touching, caressing, stroking, fondling, and kissing the body of a sexual partner. This has been called *necking, petting,* and *making out* at various points across U.S. history. *Necking* is behavior in which individuals kiss and touch one another in sensuous, erotic ways. *Petting* is caressing another person, and *heavy petting* is caressing the person's genitals, but stopping just short of penile–vaginal intercourse (the Concise Oxford English Dictionary, 2004). Among European American individuals, a widely held cognitive script maintains that physically intimate behaviors must progress from kissing and necking, to touching above the waist, to touching genitals, culminating eventually in penile–vaginal intercourse (Miller, Norton, Fan, & Chistopherson, 1998; Smith & Udry, 1985). African American adolescents however do not tend to subscribe to this type of script, with penile–vaginal intercourse just as likely to occur before heavy petting as after (Smith & Udry, 1985).

Very little research has been conducted on the prevalence of kissing, caressing, and fondling among adolescents (Arnett, 2001). Of a sample of 14- to 17-year-old ethnic minority individuals who had not engaged in penile–vaginal intercourse, 86% reported kissing someone, 47% indicated they had rubbed their body against another person, and 16% had touched someone's genitals (Miller, Clark, et al., 1997). In another study, 73% of 13-year-old girls and 60% of 13-year-old boys had kissed at least once; 35% of these girls reported that a boy had touched their breasts, and 20% of the boys said that they had touched a girl's breast. Of 16-year-olds in this study, 60% of both girls and boys had experienced fondling of the vulva, with 77% of girls and boys indicating that they had experienced fondling of the penis (Coles & Stokes, 1985). These studies indicate that touching another person's body, and especially kissing, are relatively common among adolescents.

## Penile–Vaginal Intercourse

*By the time I was 18, I was very curious about what it would be like to be in a sexual relationship with a girl.... Honestly, I guess I really didn't like her much but I was very curious about girls.... I bought condoms at a gas station and we parked in a lower-class neighborhood hoping for some privacy.... I had no idea what I was doing the first time. I just know*

*I was really ecstatic afterwards. I was just happy I actually got aroused and had an orgasm from a girl. I guess I had been concerned for quite some time about proving that I was a real "straight guy" since I heard my other friends talking about sex. I thought I was certain that I did like the way a woman could make me feel. (Male Masturbation Reality, 2006)*

A review of three national surveys indicates that the proportion of adolescence who have engaged in sexual intercourse has dropped from 54% in 1991 to 47% in 1997 (Lindberg, Boggs, Porter, & Williams, 2000). In such national surveys, 50% of adolescents between the ages of 14 and 18 reported that they had engaged in penile–vaginal intercourse (Blum et al., 2000; Centers for Disease Control and Prevention, 2000), with around two-thirds doing so by the 12th grade (Centers for Disease Control and Prevention, 2000). Crockett and her colleagues (2003) note that this is very likely an underestimate of the proportion that have engaged in penile–vaginal intercourse because they are school-based surveys; such studies do not include dropouts and students enrolled in alternative schools, who tend to be more sexually active.

Substantial majorities of both adolescent girls and boys report that they have kissed someone, and significant proportions indicate that they have fondled the genitals of another person.

The prevalence of penile–vaginal intercourse varies in terms of racial and ethnic group. Just under half of European American (46%) and Hispanic American (47%) high school students indicated in one study that they had engaged in this type of sex; however, 67% of African American high school students reported doing so (Blum et al., 2000). Another study found that 88% of African American boys between the ages of 17 and 19 had engaged in penile–vaginal intercourse, whereas 64% of non-African American boys had (Ku et al., 1998). Slightly smaller differences have been found for 15- to 19-year-old girls: 60% for African Americans, 56% for Hispanic Americans, and 51% for European Americans (Singh & Darroch, 1999).

By ninth grade, boys engaged in penile–vaginal intercourse for the first time at an earlier age than girls; 45% of boys and 33% of girls had engaged in intercourse by this time (Centers for Disease Control and Prevention, 2000). Most adolescent girls (67%) and half of adolescent boys have fewer than two sexual partners (Crockett et al., 2003), although 13% of girls and 19% of boys have four or more sexual partners (Centers for Disease Control and Prevention, 2000). This is probably due in general to adolescents becoming involved in a series of monogamous relationships, in which one relationship ends and another one begins some time after that; this is known as **serial monogamy**. Number of partners therefore increases with age (Crockett et al., 2003).

### Sexual Behavior of Gay, Lesbian, and Bisexual Youth

Information about the sexual behavior of lesbian, gay, and bisexual (LGB) adolescents is sparse and is often based on small, volunteer samples, rather than large, random samples. As with research on adolescent sexuality in general, as well as racial and ethnic minority adolescent sexuality, research on LGB youth is focused largely on risk-related sexual behaviors. Many of the small studies find that LGB adolescents engage in high levels of risky behavior, such as unprotected penile–anal intercourse. However, when lesbian, gay, bisexual, and heterosexual adolescents are obtained from the same types of settings, such as a social service office or homeless shelter, similar levels of risk-related sexual behavior are found for the adolescent groups. Yet gay males and bisexual women who engage in sex with men are more likely to use condoms than heterosexual individuals from these settings (Rotheram-Borus & Langabeer, 2001).

Despite assumptions that individuals only engage in sexual behavior with one gender once they have identified as lesbian or gay, a number of studies have found that a proportion of lesbians engage in sex with men. Lesbian adolescents may be more likely to engage in sex with the other sex than gay men. However, approximately a third of the male sexual partners of lesbians are gay men (Rotheram-Borus & Langabeer, 2001). Yet in one study, half of gay male adolescents had engaged in sex with a woman after they had identified as gay. Especially problematic is that these gay youth were less likely to use condoms with their female partners than they were with male partners (Rotheram-Borus et al., 1994).

### Sexual Coercion

> As I grew older, I found that directing a gaze, never mind an admiring gaze, could instantly attract attention that I didn't know how to handle. No one taught me how to say "No" or that I had at least a 50 percent . . . [stake] in what might happen between me and a man sexually, never mind how to physically protect myself in case I attracted the wrong kind of attention. Not only were men stronger and more comfortable being pushy, but it seemed their lust came on so fast, furiously, and insistently that I generally didn't have the time or space to find my own desire, or to even know that slowing down was what I needed. On top of this, it felt as though men were trained to be sexually intimate by "stealing" something from us. . . . I felt my job was to protect my vulnerability and sex from male lust until I was sure I was safe. (Zandi, 2000, p. 74; word in brackets added)

**Sexual coercion** is being forced to engage in sexual behavior against one's will through intimidation, threat, or physical force. Seven percent of 17- to 23-year-old women reported in a national survey that they had engaged in sex due to sexual coercion or had been raped (Miller, Monson, & Norton, 1995). First penile–vaginal intercourse was not voluntary for 7% of 15- to 19-year-old girls, and it was voluntary but not wanted for an additional 24%. Sexual coercion was more likely for girls who first engaged in sexual intercourse before 13 (SEICUS, 1997). Although a much lower rate than for girls and women, a proportion of males also are coerced into sex, usually through psychological intimidation. Estimates across various studies suggest roughly between 15% and 25% of males have engaged in unwanted sexual behavior (Christopher, 2001).

Two forms of sexual coercion are suggested by research on the topic: physical sexual coercion and psychological sexual coercion (Christopher, 2001; Christopher actually uses different terms to label the two types). **Physical sexual coercion** involves the use of physical force and bodily harm, or threats of physical force or bodily harm, to attempt to engage in sex with a person against his or her will. Force can include physically restraining someone, slapping, hitting, kicking, or use of a weapon. Physical coercion occurs even if sex does not actually occur. **Psychological sexual coercion** is the use of verbal statements, nonverbal actions, psychological intimidation, and manipulation (trickery) to pressure a person to engage in sex against his or her will. Again, psychological sexual coercion occurs even if sex does not actually occur.

What could possibly lead individuals to force or pressure another person to engage in unwanted sexual behavior? Christopher (2001) reviewed research that points to a number of factors that contribute to the likelihood of sexual coercion: (a) gender-based dating roles, (b) societal sanctioning of sexual coercion, (c) peer endorsement of sexual aggression, (d) situations conducive to sexual aggression, (d) relationship factors, and (e) personal characteristics.

### Gender-Based Dating Roles

With respect to the first factor, Christopher draws upon the thinking of Lloyd and Emery (Lloyd, 1991; Lloyd & Emery, 1999) to identify three aspects of dating roles that contribute to sexual coercion. To begin with, tradition places men in the role of **controlling relationship progression**, such that the wishes of women may be seen as secondary, whether conscious or not, to those of men, or they may not be considered at all. Men may therefore be in a position of power that causes them to be more concerned with their own desires than those of the woman. Second, women are traditionally placed in a role of **caretaker of relationships**, such that they feel they must maintain the good quality of the relationship, even in light of forceful acts by the man. Women may feel that the relationship success falls largely on their shoulders, so that they must do whatever is needed to ensure its well-being. A third factor is **romanticism**, the idealistic belief in the extreme value of passionate desire as the basis for dating relationships. The great value placed on passionate love may result in forced sex being perceived as normal, even positive, because passion indicates the intensity of one's feelings for the partner. A common reaction by women who are raped by their date is to blame themselves and to excuse their partner, even forgiving the person.

### Societal Sanctioning of Sexual Coercion

Societal sanctioning of sexual coercion refers to common beliefs endorsed within a culture, called **rape myths**, that place the responsibility for the occurrence of sexual coercion on women (Burt, 1980, 1983). The basis for such highly sexist myths is the belief (a) that women secretly or unconsciously desire to be raped, (b) that women should not allow any type of physical intimacy to occur and therefore deserve the negative consequences if they do allow it to occur, and (c) that women should be able to fend off the advances of men if they really want to do so.

### Peer Endorsement of Sexual Coercion

Peer endorsement of sexual coercion is based on aspects of the male gender role. Male friends may tend to lend credence to the belief that women are naturally and legitimately sexual objects, available to men for their own personal sexual gratification. Other males may even award higher social status to sexually forceful men for living up to and fulfilling the ideal of masculinity and dominance. This belief system is related to the notion of sex as conquest or accomplishment (DeKeseredy & Kelly, 1995; Kanin, 1970; Koss & Dinero, 1988).

### Situations Conducive to Sexual Aggression

Situations contributing to the likelihood of sexual coercion, not surprisingly, are those that involve isolation or remoteness from others (Amick & Calhoun, 1987). If an individual is alone with another person, he or she is more likely to be attacked sexually because others are not around to witness it or to protect the victim. Use of alcohol and drugs also contribute to the likelihood of being sexually attacked (Koss & Dinero, 1988; Muehlenhard & Linton, 1987; Small & Kerns, 1991).

*Relationship Characteristics*

One relationship factor contributing to sexual coercion is a sense of greater control in a relationship in general (Muehlenhard & Linton, 1987). Greater control may lead to the perception that an individual has the right to demand sexual behavior from one's partner. The belief that one's partner is inferior due to some defining characteristic (e.g., religion, educational achievement, age, or socioeconomic background) may contribute to sexually coercive tendencies (Kanin, 1970). This may be because the lower status leads a person to devalue the wishes and rights of the partner.

Yet another factor is prior sexual intimacy (Kanin & Parcell, 1977). If a couple has already engaged in sexual behaviors such as kissing and fondling of breasts and genitals, men may interpret the behaviors as general consent to sexual intimacy, or even encouragement for additional sexual behavior. Furthermore, individuals involved in more committed and monogamous relationships, and who desire greater sexual involvement, may also view their committed status as license to pursue and demand further sex (Christopher, 2001). Finally, previous experience in a poor-quality relationship is also related to sexual coercion (Christopher, McQuaid, & Updegraff, 1998; Christopher, Owens, & Stecker, 1993). Individuals who have had bad experiences in the past may reinforce the desire to have greater control in the relationship, such that forcing a partner to engage in sexual behavior is a means of asserting that control.

*Why do you think that involvement in a committed and monogamous relationship would contribute to the likelihood of sexual coercion?*

*Personal Characteristics*

Personal characteristics that contribute to the tendency to engage in sexual coercion are stronger belief in the rape myths discussed previously; lack of inhibition and inability to control one's impulses; possessing antisocial attributes, which involve a reduced tendency to empathize with others; being socially dominant and powerful; and belief in traditional gender-roles for women and men, which places men in higher status and control than women (Christopher, 2001). Sexual attitudes and motivations appear also to be key factors. Those who are more strongly interested in engaging in sex may be more likely to pursue sexual involvement with greater earnestness; this may cause them to be more motivated to overcome partner resistance to engaging in sexual behavior.

Summarizing the results of various studies, Christopher (2001) noted that " . . . single sexually aggressive men [have] an almost predatory approach to their sexuality. They are easily aroused, seek novel and frequent sexual interactions with a number of partners, prefer to have little commitment with their sexual partners, but often find their sexual encounters less than satisfying. This dissatisfaction may motivate them to seek their next sexual conquest" (p. 149).

## Factors Related to Adolescent Sexuality

### Biological Factors

Can the rise in sexual interest and behavior in adolescence be explained by changes in the body that take place around this time? Very definitely, although other factors are involved as well. Pubertal development and the timing of puberty onset are both associated with an increase in sexual interest and a greater likelihood of beginning to engage in sexual behavior. For both girls and boys, increases in pubertal development are related to increases in sexual fantasy and with beginning to engage in sexual behavior, including penile–vaginal intercourse. Earlier pubertal onset, and for girls early menarche, has been found to relate to younger age of first penile–vaginal intercourse (Crockett et al., 2003).

Studies that have examined differences in androgen levels across young adolescents have found an association of androgen levels with sexual motivation and sexual behavior. However, research that has followed the same individuals over time does not support the proposal that changes in androgen levels produce changes in sexual behavior. At the start of one study, initial differences in testosterone among boys were related to differences in sexual behavior. Yet changes over time did not predict changes in sexual fantasy or behavior (Halpern, Udry, Campbell, & Suchindran, 1993). Degree of pubertal development among girls who had already started menstruation predicted the extent of a number of types of sexual behavior at a later time, although testosterone levels did not (Udry & Campbell, 1994). Hormones do not appear to affect sexual motivation and behavior directly during adolescence, but rather through their effect on maturation of the body and the resulting increase in sexual attractiveness (Crockett et al., 2003).

## Psychological Factors

As we have seen in the previous section, the maturation of the body plays a tremendous role during adolescence in heightening sexual desire and increasing sexual behavior. Does this mean that there is no room for the influence of emotional, cognitive, and social factors? Absolutely not. Research has supported the significant role of a number of psychological factors that are examined in this section: attitudes, academic goals, risk-taking tendencies, psychological adjustment, and characteristics of the family.

### Attitudes

Personal attitudes about the acceptability of premarital sexual behavior predict the likelihood that adolescents will engage in sexual behavior, as well as predicting the level of sexual experience (Treboux & Busch-Rossnagel, 1990; Whitbeck, Yoder, Hoyt, & Conger, 1999). Various aspects of religious beliefs and participation in religion are associated with less sexual expression as well. For example, young people who are not affiliated with a particular religion are more likely to engage in sexual behavior during adolescence. On the other hand, greater frequency of attending church, belonging to a church that promotes abstinence, and placing greater importance on religious beliefs are all related to lower likelihood of sexual behavior among teenagers (Crockett et al., 2003).

### Academic Orientation

Young people who have goals for greater educational attainment and who have higher academic performance are more likely to delay sexual behavior and, after they start, to engage in less sexual behavior. Likewise, those who participate to a greater extent in academic activities are less likely to engage in early sexual behavior, which is especially true for girls (Crockett et al., 2003).

### Risk-Taking Orientation

A propensity to engage in risky behavior in general is related to engaging in sexual behavior during adolescence. In contrast, boys who exhibited a greater ability for self-restraint had fewer sexual partners and were less likely to engage in problem behaviors over a 4-year period (Crockett et al., 2003).

*Psychological Adjustment*

Psychological depression increases the likelihood that girls will engage in sexual behavior. Greater levels of problem behaviors, such as criminal and unethical activity, are associated with increased probability of engaging in early sexual behavior (Crockett et al., 2003).

*Family-Related Factors*

*Why do you suppose that a good adolescent–parent relationship tends to decrease the likelihood of adolescent sexual behavior?*

Parent–Adolescent Relationship Quality. Higher quality of relationships between adolescents and their parents is related to decreased likelihood of engaging in early sexual behavior, lower frequency of sexual behavior, and lower number of sexual partners (Miller, Benson, & Galbraith, 2001). The quality of relationship with the mother is important for both girls and boys (Jaccard, Dittus, & Gordon, 1998), and the relationship with the father is significant for boys only (Feldman & Brown, 1993). Parent–child relationship quality has been shown to relate to sexual behavior for both African American and European American adolescents (Crockett et al., 2003).

Low-quality parental relationships may affect sexuality by causing adolescents to turn to peers for the satisfaction of emotional and social needs, possibly leading them to forge relationships with those more likely to engage in problem behavior (Whitbeck, Conger, & Kao, 1993). Girls may be more likely to engage in early sexual behavior if they have low-quality relationships with their parents because they are at increased risk for depression. Research additionally indicates that low quality parental relationships increase the likelihood of alcohol consumption among boys, which increases chances of early sexual behavior (Whitbeck, Hoyt, Miller, & Kao, 1992).

Parental Monitoring and Supervision. Parental monitoring of adolescents is associated with delayed onset of sexual behavior and lower frequency of sexual behavior. The reason for this is most likely that parental involvement decreases the opportunity to engage in sexual behavior, although it may have a detrimental effect if the monitoring is extreme or intrusive. Parental communication regarding sexuality may likewise have the effect of delaying sexual involvement (Crockett et al., 2003). However, this is largely true if the communication is open and clearly about sexual issues, if the parent–child relationship is high quality, and if the parent communicates particular types of values (Miller et al., 2001). Parental disapproval of sex is associated with the delay of sexual involvement (Crockett et al., 2003).

Family Structure. Living in a single-parent household—that is, with only one parent in the home—has been found across a number of studies to relate to early onset of sexual behavior (Miller et al., 1997). This association is true across a number of demographic factors, such as race and ethnicity, socioeconomic level, and age. Single parents usually become involved in romantic relationships themselves, which may serve as a modeling for their children. The amount of sexual experience by sons of recently divorced mothers was directly related to whether the mother dated, whereas permissive sexual attitudes of daughters was a mediating factor determining sexual experience if their mother dated; that is, permissive daughters were more likely to engage in sexual behavior if their mother dated (Whitbeck, Simons, & Kao, 1994).

Adolescents whose mothers engaged in sexual behavior and had children at a young age are also more likely to engage in sexual behavior and begin sexual behavior at an earlier age. Having older siblings who have begun to engage in sexual behavior is associated with a greater likelihood of younger siblings likewise initiating sexual involvement, as well as with starting at an earlier age and a greater risk of becoming pregnant; this is particularly true for individuals with adolescent sisters who are pregnant or have had children (Crockett et al., 2003). Dating parents and sexually active siblings may serve as models for adolescents, conveying the message that sexual behavior is appropriate and possibly rewarding. However, the associations may also be explained in terms of a genetically transmitted tendency toward early puberty (Newcomer & Udry, 1984).

Factors related to socioeconomic level, such as lower family income (Upchurch, Aneshensel, Sucoff, & Levy-Storms, 1999) and less parental education (Brewster, 1994; Sieving, McNeely, & Blum, 2000), have been consistently been found to relate to an increased probability of adolescent sexual behavior. Differences in expectations regarding professional and economic opportunities may account for such socioeconomic differences (Crockett et al., 2003).

## Peer-Related Factors

Friends. Although a prevalent belief is that peers and friends exert a profound influence on adolescent sexual behavior, a recent study that examined a range of factors found only a small effect of other adolescents; moreover, the influence was primarily with respect to friends with similar sexual experience (Jaccard, Blanton, & Dodge, 2005). A number of factors that were controlled for in this study may be the reason that relationships have been found with peer sexual attitudes and behavior in previous research that did not control for them. Such factors included inaccuracy in adolescents' understanding of the behavior in which peers were engaging, the type of friends focused on (or not focused on), and the extent of similar experiences (such as the rate of pubertal development). It appears that adolescents' perception of what their friends are doing sexually, rather than what their friends are actually doing, may be the most important influence on sexual behavior (Crockett et al., 2003).

Romantic Partners. Adolescence is the period of dramatic increase in involvement in romantic relationships. This was documented in one study, in which approximately 33% of 13-year-olds, 50% of 15-year-olds, and 70% of 17-year-olds were involved in a serious romantic relationship in the previous 18-month period (Crockett et al., 2003). Involvement in romantic relationships is a powerful factor in the likelihood of engaging in sexual behavior during adolescence (Dittus & Jaccard, 2000; Miller et al., 1997; Thornton, 1990). Approximately 75% of women who reported engaging in voluntary sexual behavior for the first time before age 18 were going steady or engaged (Manning, Longmore, & Giordano, 2000).

### Neighborhood Factors

Adolescent boys who live in lower-income neighborhoods tend to engage in sexual behavior more frequently than those in higher-income neighborhoods (Ku, Sonenstein, & Pleck, 1993). Greater proportions of girls are also likely to become pregnant (Hogan & Kitagawa, 1985). Clearly, neighborhood socioeconomic factors are involved in adolescent sexual behavior patterns (Crockett et al., 2003).

As discussed in chapter 11, neighborhood poverty has been demonstrated to account for differences in rates of adolescent sexual behavior that were not explained by such factors as the tendency for oneself and friends to become involved in problem behaviors, level of pubertal development, and dispositional sociability (Browning, Leventhal, & Brooks-Gunn, 2004). After making adjustments for these factors, African American youth were still 2.1 times more likely to engage in early sexual intercourse than European American young people. The differences among ethnic groups, however, were entirely accounted for by the **concentration of poverty within a neighborhood** (assessed by the proportion of incomes below the poverty line, the proportion receiving public assistance, the proportion unemployed, and the proportion of households headed by women). Neighborhood poverty therefore can be seen as the primary factor explaining racial differences in early onset of sexual behavior, independent of all other factors that contribute to adolescent sexual behavior in general.

High-risk sexual behavior is also associated with living in areas characterized by (a) high population density (large numbers of people concentrated in a small area), (b) poor housing, and (c) neighborhood "renewal" programs imposed by government policy that dislocate individuals and disrupt community cohesion (Wallace, Fullilove, & Flisher, 1996; Wallace & Fullilove, 1999). Racial and ethnic minorities are the primary groups of people affected by these damaging environmental factors. This research indicates that race and ethnicity in themselves do not cause risk-related tendencies; rather, living under conditions of extreme deprivation and hardship leads people to attempt to enhance their psychological well-being in a way that unwittingly endangers their physical well-being.

## Box 13.4 Analyze This: Looking at Different Perspectives

### *Do the Media Lead Young People to Engage in Sex?*

"Media is a powerful sex educator, but not always in the best interest of children. "Desperate Housewives" could use condoms. Why not? On reality programs, let's get real. People do use condoms. What's missing in the media are the three Cs. Rarely is there a commitment, contraceptives, or consequences." Jane Brown, (ThinkExist.com)

"I honestly don't understand the big fuss made over nudity and sex in films. It's silly. On TV, the children can watch people murdering each other, which is a very unnatural thing, but they can't watch two people in the very natural process of making love. Now, really, that doesn't make any sense, does it?" (Sharon Tate Polanski, American actress, pregnant at the time of becoming a victim in the "Manson Family" mass murder, 1943–1969, ThinkExist.com)

Despite the pervasive belief that music, cinema, television, and magazines cause adolescents to be more likely to engage in sexual behavior, the issue has not been examined to an extent that permits confident conclusions (Crockett, Raffaelli, & Moilanen, 2003). An association between media exposure and adolescent sexual behavior has not been substantiated because of this lack of research (Huston, Wartella, & Donnerstein, 1998).

Other theorists reviewing the research offer a slightly different conclusion:

Under some conditions, exposure to sexual content in the media is likely to affect some young people's judgments and attitudes regarding sexual behaviors . . . and possibly influence their sexual behaviors. We feel justified in reaching this conclusion even though there are only a few studies in this area specifically studying children and adolescents (Malamuth & Impett, 2001, p. 282).

In the same volume on the effects of media on children and adolescents, however, Donnerstein and Smith (2001) reiterate the warning that little is actually known about the effect of viewing sexual content on actual sexual behavior patterns.

One recent study, however, found a modest relationship between viewing or listening to media containing sexual content and aspects of sexuality among a large number of adolescents in the seventh and eighth grade; media viewing was somewhat associated with levels of sexual behavior, as well as the intention to engage in sexual behavior (Pardun, L'Engle, & Brown, 2005). The types of media that were related to "light" sexual experience (e.g., having a crush, light kissing, French kissing) were movies and music. The media that were related to "heavy" sexual activity (e.g., touching of breasts, the vulva, or penis; oral–genital sex; penile–vaginal sex) were movies, music, and magazines. Finally, four of the types of media that were examined— television, movies, music, and magazines—were correlated with intention to engage in sexual behavior.

This was not a longitudinal study—one that followed the students over time—and so it is not possible to say that exposure to the media *caused* the adolescents to engage in sexual behavior or

*(Continued)*

(Continued)

caused them to intend to engage in sexual behavior. A plausible alternative explanation is that adolescents who are sexually experienced are more interested in viewing or listening to media with sexual content than those who have not engaged in sexual behavior. Past experience could lead to greater interest. Another possibility is that adolescents with stronger interest in sexuality beforehand are more likely to partake of sexually related media, to engage in sexual behavior, and to intend to engage in sexual behavior in the future.

### References

Crockett, L. J., Raffaelli, M., & Moilanen, K. L. (2003). Adolescent sexuality: Behavior and meaning. In G. R. Adams & M. D. Berzonsky (Eds.), *Blackwell handbook of adolescence* (pp. 371–392). Malden, MA: Blackwell Publishing.

Donnerstein, E., & Smith, S. (2001). Sex in the media: Theory, influences, and solutions. In D. G. Singer & J. L. Singer (Eds.), *Handbook of children and the media* (pp. 289–307). Thousand Oaks, CA: Sage Publications.

Huston, A. C., Wartella, E., & Donnerstein, E. (1998). *Measuring effects of sexual content in the media: A report to the Kaiser Family Foundation*. Washington, DC: Kaiser Family Foundation.

Malamuth, N. M., & Impett, E. A. (2001). Research on sex in the media: What do we know about effects on children and adolescents? In D. G. Singer & J. L. Singer (Eds.), *Handbook of children and the media* (pp. 269–287). Thousand Oaks, CA: Sage Publications.

Pardun, C. J., L'Engle, K. L., & Brown, J. D. (2005). Linking exposure to outcomes: Early adolescents' consumption of sexual content in six media. *Mass Communication & Society, 8*(2), 75–91.

ThinkExist.com. *Jane Brown quote*. Retrieved August 10, 2006, from http://en.thinkexist.com/search/searchquotation.asp?search=child%20sex&page=6

ThinkExist.com. *Sharon Tate Polanski quote*. Retrieved August 10, 2006, from http://en.thinkexist.com/search/searchquotation.asp?search=child%20sex&page=10

## Summary

Parents do not provide much information to their children about sexuality, not even the names of sexual organs. Children have a limited conception of the process of reproduction and cesarean or vaginal birth before the age of 4 or 5. Preschool children are likely to engage in certain types of sexually related behaviors. The most common behaviors include touching their own sexual organs, touching breasts, playing doctor, asking questions about sexuality, and masturbating themselves. The majority of children engage in touching and fondling one another's genitals with other children by the age of 12.

Girls have a greater tendency to experience negative emotions, including anger, after puberty. Boys have an increased likelihood of problem behaviors, although greater levels of testosterone relative to estradiol may decrease problem behavior and sadness. The development of breasts initially is very important to many girls, because they are visible to others, as opposed to pubic hair. However, because of teasing and commenting by boys and family, feelings about larger breasts may become less positive during middle school.

Girls have different reactions to menarche, divided among various combinations of positive and negative feelings. Boys generally have very positive reactions to the growth in height and weight because of societal value placed on size for males. Early onset of puberty places girls at risk for a variety of mental health and behavioral problems, although primarily for European American girls. Late maturation in girls increases the probability of depression, self-consciousness, and parental conflict. Late maturation in boys is related to greater alcohol use and alcohol-related problems.

Large majorities of girls and boys engage in sexual fantasizing, as well as masturbation, by late adolescence. Large majorities of young adolescents also engage in kissing, although only a minority fondle breasts or genitals. Substantial majorities of older adolescents fondle genitals or have had their genitals fondled. Several large national surveys have found that 50% of adolescents between the ages of 14 and 18 have engaged in penile–vaginal intercourse. Most girls and about half of boys have fewer than two sexual partners. Seven percent of late adolescent girls have been coerced into having sex, raped, or have not engaged in sex voluntarily.

Early pubertal development is associated with engaging in penile–vaginal intercourse at an earlier age. Androgen levels do not predict changes in sexual fantasy and behavior over time. The effect of hormones on sexual behavior patterns is likely through their effect on maturation of the body and sexual attractiveness.

Attitudes about the acceptability of premarital sexual behavior are related to the likelihood that adolescents will engage in sexual behavior and the frequency of sexual behavior. Having a higher quality relationship with parents delays the onset of sexual behavior among adolescents, as well as decreasing the frequency of sexual behavior and the number of sexual partners.

Living in a single-parent home is associated with early onset of sexual behavior across a range of demographic characteristics. Perception of the level of sexual activity of peers is more important than the actual level of sexual activity by peers. Living in impoverished neighborhoods is associated with greater levels of sexual behavior, the single most important factor accounting for differences among racial and ethnic groups.

Not enough empirical research has been conducted to conclusively determine whether exposure to various types of media with sexual content is related to greater likelihood of adolescent sexual involvement. A recent study found a modest relationship between exposure to various media and specific types of sexual behavior.

## Chapter 13 Critical Thinking Exercises

1. Conducting research on childhood and adolescent sexuality

   Devise a study that you believe would provide the highest quality information about childhood sexuality. What would your hypotheses be; that is, what would you set out to find out? What background and family factors would you examine in your study? What specific behaviors would you measure? How would you measure each of these factors? Who would you include in your study? How would you recruit them?

2. Children and sexuality

   Think of incidents you are aware of in which children engaged in the types of behaviors presented in the chapter, such as touching his or her own sexual parts, touching an adult's breasts, being interested in the other gender, playing doctor, asking questions about sexuality, and masturbating. Are you aware of many instances of such behaviors? How did their parents react to such behaviors? How should parents handle these types of behaviors?

3. Adolescence and sexuality

   Very little research has been conducted on kissing and fondling during adolescence, whereas much more research has focused on penile–vaginal intercourse. Likewise, hardly any research has been conducted concerning penile–anal intercourse in adolescence. What factors might account for the typical focus in studies on young people? What does this say about U.S. culture in terms of societal values regarding sexuality?

**Visit www.sagepub.com/hillhsstudy.com for online activities, sample tests, and other helpful resources. Select "Chapter 13: Sexuality in the Early Years and Adolescence" for chapter-specific activities.**

# Chapter 14

## ADULTHOOD
### Challenges and Decisions

*Adults are obsolete children and the hell with them.*

Dr. Seuss, American writer and cartoonist best known for
his collection of children's books, 1904–1991 (ThinkExist.com)

A dulthood is not a point in life at which all issues suddenly become dazzlingly clear, the correct decisions are entirely obvious, and we instantly have all of the answers. Instead, a great range of challenges confront young adults that we may have had little prior experience with, and new issues continuously crop up throughout our entire adult life. As young adults, we continue to wrestle with the kind of person we are and who we want to be, what type of job we want or can get, and what kind of romantic partner and relationship we desire. Do we want children, how many, how will we raise them, and will we be able to support them? During our teenage years, we may contemplate and worry about such questions, but usually in more general, abstract ways. However, in the early adult years, the issues are not future possibilities.

In middle adulthood, most of us have dealt with the issues and stresses of the early years, but new issues continue to arise. If we have children, at this time in our lives they are often in their late adolescent period, wrestling with issues we confronted ourselves earlier in our lives concerning relationships, education, and career. This may be a demanding challenge for us, too, as we advise and help them with their problems and challenges. Providing such support can siphon attention and energy away from our own career and romantic relationship, affecting relationship quality and sexual satisfaction as well. In our later years, we must confront physical changes that may limit our capabilities and activities to some extent. However, as you will see in the later sections, for a number of people sexual activity continues well into their senior years, and sexual satisfaction continues to be very important to them.

The challenges and decisions that individuals typically confront during each of the phases of adulthood is the focus of the current chapter. In early adulthood, individuals often deal with three major issues related to sexuality: (a) forging a sexual identity, most notably sexual orientation identity; (b) establishing a romantic relationship; and (c) making decisions about the type of family they desire. Consequently, the development of sexual orientation and sexual identity are considered first. Second, factors affecting involvement in relationships are considered, as well as how the relationship is integrated with other aspects of individuals' lives. Next, decisions about having children are considered, including whether a couple wants to have children or not; relevant to this issue, methods of contraception are presented as a means of controlling the number of children in a family based on one's personal choices. For those who have children, issues related to pregnancy and the effects of having children on sexuality are discussed. Finally, issues related to aging and sexuality are addressed.

Adulthood is a developmental period that does not necessarily have a definite beginning, at least in U.S. society; no specific event formally marks the transition from adolescence into adulthood (Schaie & Willis, 2002). However, the end of adolescence was defined in the previous chapter as 22 years (Steinberg, 2002), and so 23 can be viewed as the beginning of the adult period. Adulthood is divided into three periods: **early adulthood**, from 23–44 years; **middle adulthood**, from 45–64 years; and **late adulthood**, 65 years and older (adapted from Levinson, 1986). According to Lerner (1995), five landmarks signal the start of adulthood. These events are (a) **the completion of formal education**, (b) employment that provides **fiscal independence**, (c) maintaining a **residence** separate from one's birth family, (d) involvement in a **long-term romantic relationship**, and (e) **being a parent**.

Pursuing a higher education has been established as the one goal that is central to the other adult goals; this is because giving priority to higher education determines the timing of many of the other goals for a substantial number of people in the United States. Individuals seeking a higher education tend to postpone the other four while pursuing what is prevalently viewed as the path to creating a higher quality life. Education is especially influential in determining the timing of relationships and parenting for many women (Schaie & Willis, 2002).

## *Challenges of Young Adulthood*

*A boy becomes an adult three years before his parents think he does, and about two years after he thinks he does.*

Lewis B. Hershey, American soldier, 1893–1977 (ThinkExist.com)

*The average, healthy, well-adjusted adult gets up at seven-thirty in the morning feeling just plain terrible.*

Jean Kerr, American writer, 1923–2003 (ThinkExist.com)

In addition to basic concerns of adulthood, such as education, career, and relationship development, women have increasingly faced the additional issue of integrating a full-time career along with primary responsibility for family care and household duties. From 1975 to 1996, the rate of women participating in the workforce has increased from 45.9% to 58.8%. The rate for women with children under the age of 18 has soared from 47.3% to 70.2% (U.S. Bureau of Labor Statistics, 1997). This suggests that large numbers of young women have essentially two full-time occupations; one of them—family care—is a 24-hour, 7-day-a-week job. Furthermore, 9.8 million women are single mothers, and 2.1 million men are single fathers, which means that these individuals have total responsibility as income-earner and parent (Work/life today, 1999).

When women first began to move into the paid workforce in increasing numbers, mental health professionals were initially concerned that women might suffer greatly from the burdens of such multiple roles and demands. Instead, for the most part, women have successfully blended full-time employment and family life into a fairly positive, rewarding experience (Albino Gilbert & Rader, 2001). It is true that research has found that men benefit from marriage to a greater extent than women in terms of its effect on their overall health and well-being (Steil, 1997). However, women who are employed are in fact in better physical and psychological health than those who are not (Barnett & Rivers, 1996), despite feeling very busy and often stressed (Albino Gilbert & Rader, 2001).

With respect to sexuality, noted theorists Gagnon and Simon (1973) maintain that young adults must confront three major challenges: (a) **establishing sexual orientation**, (b) **forging intimacy and making commitments**, and (c) and **integrating love and sex**. Of course, these three concerns do not suddenly arise out of nowhere in the early 20s. Instead, issues related to intimacy, relationships, and even sexuality have their origins in events occurring earlier in life and continuing into adulthood, as noted in previous chapters. Interactions with parents, other caregivers, and family members in infancy and childhood are building blocks for later relationships. They establish the foundations for the emotional reactions and views that individuals will have toward others throughout life, as shown within research on attachment theory. Likewise, curiosity about one's body typically starts in early childhood, with large proportions of children exploring issues related to sexuality. Individuals gather information about love, romance, and sexuality throughout adolescence, and sizable numbers of young people engage in some type of sexual behavior during this time.

Yet it is in the late adolescent and early adult years that one's needs, desires, goals, and plans often come together in a stable, meaningful understanding. This understanding, or identity, typically takes a form that guides the individual's behavior in a more consistent fashion than was true during earlier periods of the individual's life. **Identity** is a psychologically important factor in terms of influencing behavior, in understanding events in one's life, and in perceptions of personal well-being. As a matter of fact, research has demonstrated that individuals who have fashioned a stable sense of self by early adulthood are more likely to have positive, satisfying relationships at midlife (Kahn, Zimmerman, Csikzentmihalyi, & Getzels, 1985). In the following section, the emergence of adult identity is considered with respect to sexual orientation.

## *Establishing Sexual Orientation*

I don't know how girls can stand it. If I had breasts, I'd be playing with myself all day. . . . Back in the land of reality, of course, we knew that we would never have our own female breasts to play with. If we wanted to get lost in the ecstatic wonder of soft, smooth, round breasts, they would have to be someone else's breasts. And so, those of us who were heterosexually inclined gained new motivation to venture across the gender divide, to learn about girls and what made them tick—to find our way, awkwardly or gracefully, reliably or haphazardly, to the first of what would be many related erotic Holy Grails. Getting to play with breasts was, of course, not the only reason to be interested in girls, even in junior high school. But it was definitely up there on the list. (D. Steinberg, 2000, June 30)

My wife was out of town, and I had the guys over for poker. Three guys spent the night, so Tom got into our bed. I don't know why I did, but I put my hand on his privates. He was excited, and we had oral sex two times that night. We did it the second time while he watched a sex tape of my wife and I. (Al, 40, Netscape Men's Confessions)

Sexual experiences we have when we are young may contribute to our sexual identity, but often probably in more complex ways than is typically expected. Sexual orientation identity is more than simply the accumulation of behavioral experiences, or even feelings and desires.

*Why do you think that engaging in certain sexual behavior does not always figure into the sexual orientation identity people develop?*

As discussed in chapter 7, **sexual identity** is the *understanding* that an individual has developed concerning his or her sexual needs, desire, and attributes. The concept includes issues far greater than simply sexual orientation; this is despite the fact that sexual orientation has historically been the subject of much greater theorizing and research than other aspects relevant to sexual identity. *Sexual orientation* must be distinguished from sexual identity because sexual orientation is typically treated as the actual feelings that the person experiences; *sexual identity* is the *understanding* that the individual has of his or her sexual behavior and sexual nature. It is important as well to note that sexual orientation identity is one aspect of overall sexual identity; **sexual orientation identity** refers to the individual's *understanding* of whether he or she is attracted to women or to men, or both (Mohr, 2002; Worthington, Savoy, Dillon, & Vernaglia, 2002).

As illustrated in the personal report above, individuals may engage in sexual behavior that does not seem to be consistent with their sexual orientation identity; these individuals engaged in same-gender behavior, but continued to view themselves as heterosexual. Their sexual orientation identity remained stable, regardless of one or two incidents, or even occasional incidents, of same-gender behavior. Likewise, empirical research has formally documented that some men engage in sexual behavior with other men, but do not consider themselves to be gay or bisexual (Peterson & Marin, 1988); rather, they steadfastly maintain to themselves, and other people, that they are really heterosexual.

Figure 14.1 illustrates the relationship among sexual orientation, sexual identity, and sexual orientation identity. Sexual orientation is the attraction and possibly behavior that an individual actually experiences, whereas identity is the person's awareness, acknowledgment, and understanding of the behavior and what he or she is like. Behavior and feelings strongly influence identity and self-understanding, which is what the arrow in the diagram is intended to reflect. However, self-understanding does not always overlap perfectly with what one actually does.

The tendency to engage in sexual behavior that does not match one's sexual orientation identity may be especially likely during adolescence. In one study discussed in the previous chapter (Buzwell & Rosenthal, 1996), adolescents classified as having *adventurous*

---

**FIGURE 14.1** Sexual Orientation, Sexual Identity, and Sexual Orientation Identity

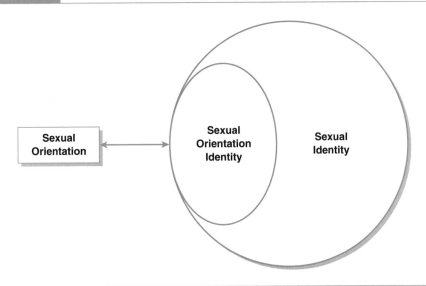

---

*sexual identities* were also those who were most likely to have engaged in same-gender sexual behavior. However, adolescents who identified themselves as lesbian, gay, or bisexual all had *sexually competent sexual identities* or *sexually unassured sexual identities.* These findings make the point that not all young people who engage in same-gender sexual behavior think of themselves as being lesbian or gay. In the same way, a number of adolescents who viewed themselves as lesbian or gay had not yet engaged in same-gender sexual behavior, further illustrating identity–behavior discrepancy.

In addition to supporting the distinction between behavior and identity (that is, self-labeling), these data also support another point. Specifically, they indicate that a number of individuals do not establish a sense of their own sexual orientation until late adolescence or early adulthood. A fundamental challenge of early adulthood for many individuals therefore is sorting out their feelings about sexual orientation and establishing at least a tentative identity.

Some may question Gagnon and Simon's position that the development of sexual orientation is a significant aspect of adult development. This skepticism may stem from the fact that many heterosexual individuals consider their sexual orientation to be largely an effortless awareness of a "natural" aspect of their constitution. Such a perspective results from the tendency of people in a majority group (e.g., heterosexual) to view their own situation or outcome as occurring naturally, and therefore of no need of explanation or examination. However, scientists have recently begun to realize the danger of such a sweeping assumption that heterosexuality is "normal" and therefore "just naturally develops." The effect of such an assumption is that many issues remain ignored and unexamined, because researchers believe an explanation already exists. In particular, factors involved in the development of heterosexuality would never be investigated empirically and never fully understood if the assumption that it just naturally develops were treated as the explanation.

**Box 14.1**

**An Eye Toward Research**

## Proportions of Individuals Identifying With Sexual Orientation Groups

According to early studies, estimates of the proportion of the population that identifies as lesbian or gay vary from 4% to 17% (Gonsiorek & Weinrich, 1991). Following the earlier estimates, a survey based on a very large, nationally representative sample of the U.S. population placed the percentages at 1.4% of women and 2.8% of men who identify as same-gender orientation or bisexual (Laumann, Gagnon, Michael, & Michaels, 1994).

This may in fact represent a minimum estimate, in that nonheterosexual orientations are viewed negatively in general; for this reason, lesbians, gay men, and bisexual individuals might be reluctant to acknowledge their sexual orientation in some research situations. The differences in estimates are also due to variations in sampling, the way that people were recruited to be in the study. Sampling is affected to a great extent by the fact that the sexual orientation of individuals cannot be known based on easily observable characteristics and so it is not easy to identify potential study participants (Gonsiorek & Weinrich, 1991). It is much easier to see what the gender or race and ethnicity of an individual is and make sure enough women are included, for example. Instead, researchers must rely on study participants to identify themselves as associated with a particular sexual orientation. Based on these data, anywhere from 83% to 98% of adults identify themselves as heterosexual.

Although the sexual orientation identity of the individuals was not assessed in any of the studies, one review of research examined the prevalence of male–male sexual behavior occurring in adulthood. The minimum proportion of adult men who have had sex with other men is between 5% and 7% (Rogers & Turner, 1991). Early data from the Kinsey research in the 1930s and 1940s suggests that between 20% and 37% of adolescent and adult males have experienced orgasm while engaged in sexual behavior with other men; 10% of the males were largely involved in same-gender sexual behavior for at least 3 years of their lives, and 4% were involved in same-gender behavior across their entire life (Kinsey, Pomeroy, & Martin, 1948). Other research has found that approximately 13% of women have experienced orgasm while engaging in sex with other women, despite the fact that between 1% and 3% identified as lesbian (Kinsey, Pomeroy, Martin, & Gebhard, 1953; Laumann et al., 1994).

### Reference

Gonsiorek, J., & Weinrich, J. (1991). The definition and scope of sexual orientation. In J. Gonsiorek & J. Weinrich (Eds.), *Homosexuality: Research implications for public policy* (pp. 1–12). Newbury Park, CA: Sage Publications.

Kinsey, A. C., Pomeroy, W. B., & Martin, C. E. (1948). *Sexual behavior in the human male*. Philadelphia: W. B. Saunders.

Kinsey, A. C., Pomeroy, W. B., Martin, C. E., & Gebhard, P. H. (1953). *Sexual behavior in the human female*. Philadelphia: W. B. Saunders.

Laumann, E. O., Gagnon, J. H., Michael, R. T., & Michaels, S. (1994). *The social organization of sexuality*. Chicago: University of Chicago Press.

Rogers, S. M., & Turner, C. F. (1991). Male–male sexual contact in the U.S.A.: Findings from five sample surveys, 1970–1990. *The Journal of Sex Research, 28,* 491–519.

# *Romantic Relationships*

The above section dealt with one of the three challenges that Gagnon and Simon (1973) proposed confront individuals in adulthood, that is, establishing one's sexual orientation. The other two challenges are forging intimacy and making commitments and integrating love and sex.

## Intimacy and Commitment in Romantic Relationships

*The distinction between children and adults, while probably useful for some purposes, is at bottom a specious one, I feel. There are only individual egos, crazy for love.*

Niccolo Machiavelli, Italian writer and statesman,
author of *The Prince*, 1469–1527 (ThinkExist.com)

A **romantic relationship** is type of intimate relationship, which is an ongoing involvement between individuals characterized by substantial knowledge and understanding of one another. It also involves a level of closeness that distinguishes it from casual, or nonintimate, relationships. The factor that distinguishes romantic relationships from other intimate relationships is the experience of **passion**—the desire for, and positive emotions related to, physical intimacy and sexual involvement. **Intimacy** is feeling understood and validated by the partner's responses to one's self-disclosures and behaviors.

Close relationships develop through increasing **interdependence**, the condition of partners being able to obtain highly desired rewards only from one another. Increasing interdependence contributes to growing **commitment** to the relationship, the desire and intention to remain in the relationship over the long-term.

Being involved in a long-term romantic relationship—whether formally sanctioned or not—means that a couple is involved in an intimate relationship. This is because such couples have a shared body of knowledge about one another that is unique to them.

**Long-term romantic relationships** are by definition intimate relationships, despite variations in **relational intimacy** (Prager & Roberts, 2004). Relationships with greater relational intimacy are ones in which the partners interact frequently in a way in which they reveal personal information about themselves; they also have more intense positive experiences in interacting with one another.

Even though couples differ from one another in terms of relational intimacy (Prager & Roberts, 2004), relationships that are characterized by greater intimacy are more satisfying to individuals and are more stable (Talmadge & Dabbs, 1990). What types of intimate behavior contribute to the greater quality of relationships? Important intimate behaviors are those in which individuals reveal themselves to one another (Haas & Stafford, 1998; Lippert & Prager, 2001), respond emotionally to one another rather than avoiding sharing emotions (Gottman & Krokoff, 1989; Roberts & Krokoff, 1990; Smith, Vivian, & O'Leary, 1990), develop an accurate (Swann, De La Ronde, & Hixon, 1994) and positive (Murray, Holmes, & Griffin, 1996) understanding of one another, and engage in more frequent and gratifying sexual interaction (Prager & Buhrmester, 1998). Furthermore, distressed couples seeking counseling typically experience conflict regarding intimacy (Christensen & Shenk, 1991).

In heterosexual relationships, both women and men value intimacy, sexual exclusivity, and commitment, a value dimension called **dyadic attachment** by Cochran and Peplau (1985). This value is also important in lesbian and gay male relationships (Peplau & Cochran, 1981; Peplau, Cochran, Rook, & Padesky, 1978). Yet women experience greater dissatisfaction regarding some aspects of marital relationships than men, which is due somewhat to the level of intimacy they desire with their husbands and the degree of intimacy they feel they are experiencing. The unhappiness may also be due to the greater parenting responsibility women bear (Dion & Dion, 2001).

One explanation of the gender differences in satisfaction is that the different ways women and men express intimacy may lead women to be dissatisfied with men's ways of showing intimacy (Wood, 1997). However, recent research by Vangelitisi and Daly indicate that women and men value the same types of relationship qualities, but women were more likely to feel that their expectations for the relationship had not been fulfilled (Vangelitisi & Daly, 1997).

## The Relationship of Love and Sexuality in Romantic Relationships

*What a pleasure to share this joy with your husband or the one you love.... I absolutely love sex and it is my wish that ALL women learn to enjoy sex too! Sex is to enjoy. Personally, I don't think I would continue to have sex if I was not reaching orgasm.... I love my husband, and I love having sex with him. We have a great relationship.... I feel that perhaps I have been blessed to have had such a wonderful experience with sex in my life. (Kristi, age 31; Women's Sexual Experiences, On-line forum, retrieved July 22, 2006, from The-clitoris.com. Reprinted with permission of The-clitoris.com.)*

The third challenge for adulthood according to Gagnon and Simon (1973) is integrating love and sex. In the thinking of lay people (those who are not scientists), sexuality is intimately linked to love, but more than this, it involves the belief that sexuality *should* be linked to love. Recent research on the cognitive representations of "being in love" held by everyday people include a sexual component, such as physical attraction, sexual

| Box 14.2 | An Eye Toward Research |

**Prevalence of Types of Relationships**

As individuals move into their early 20s, a little more than 25% of women and just under 20% of men are married. By the end of the 20s, the proportion of individuals who are in a marital relationship skyrockets dramatically; at this point, 42% of men and 48% of women are married. Between the ages of 30 and 39, about 67% of both women and men have married. Yet, at the same time, 16% of women in this age group are divorced, separated, or widowed, a proportion almost two times that of men. After age 40, the marriage rate reverses for women and men, with 78% of men and 69% of women married at this time. Moreover, women continue to have much higher rates of divorce, separation, or widowhood in their 40s in comparison to men (Alan Guttmacher Institute, 2005).

According to the 2000 U.S. Census (Simmons & O'Connell, 2003), of the 105.5 million U.S. households, 56.8% consisted of coupled households, meaning households headed by two individuals involved in a partnered relationship; 90.9% of these were legally married couples. An increasing number of coupled households are those who are living together but who are not married: 5.5 million couples in recent years, compared with 3.2 million in 1990. Male–female couples accounted for the vast bulk of unmarried couples (4.9 million), although over a half of a million were households with same-gender partners.

**References**

Alan Guttmacher Institute. (2005). *Sexual and reproductive health: Women and men.* Retrieved September 12, 2005, from http://www.guttmacher.org/pubs/fb_10-02.html

Simmons, T., & O'Connell, M. (2003). *Married-couple and unmarried partner households: 2000.* Washington, DC: U.S. Bureau of the Census.

arousal, and desire. Other research has found that the initial stages of developing romantic relationships are in fact characterized by what social psychologists call **passionate love**; this is based to a great extent on sexual attraction and desire. Furthermore, increasing levels of intimacy and emotional attachment that lead to later relationship stages tend to also increase the likelihood of sexual behavior.

## Establishing a Family

One of the decisions faced by many young adults, as well as many adolescents, is whether to have children, and how many children they would like in their family. Of course, a number of pregnancies happen unintentionally. However, with the general availability of various methods of contraception, having children has become a matter of choice to a greater extent than at any previous time in history.

*Why do you think that in recent times couples have been having fewer children—on average, currently about two? What might account for the fact that African Americans are less likely to delay having children than are European Americans?*

Most heterosexual couples eventually have at least one child, whether by giving birth to offspring themselves or by adopting children. Prior to the last quarter of the 20th century, couples usually had their first child within the second year of marriage (Schaie & Willis, 2002). However, in general European American couples have been delaying the start of their families much more frequently, with greater proportions of women giving birth in their early 30s in the United States. In contrast, African Americans have been much less likely to put off having children (Dion, 1995). U.S. couples are also having fewer children. According to the 2002 Current Population Survey conducted by the U.S. Census Bureau (Downs, 2002), women are likely to end their reproductive years with on average 1.9 children (based on statistics for women in the 40–49 age group); this is more than one child less than that of women of the same age group in 1976.

## Couples Who Decide Not to Have Children

Not all couples in long-term relationships decide that they want to have children. Instead, they may decide to focus on other important goals in their lives.

### The Proportion of Couples Deciding Not to Have Children

An increasing proportion of legally married couples are deciding to remain childless voluntarily. In 2002, 44% of women of childbearing age (27 million) did not have children; childbearing age is defined as between 15 and 44 years. Of women in the 40–44 year age group (who are approaching the end of childbearing years), 18% did not have any children, two times as many as in 1976 (10%; Downs, 2002). The proportion of women of this age group who want to remain childless is increasing, according to the National Center of Health Statistics; whereas the proportion was 2.4% in 1982, in 1995 it was 6.6 percent (4.1 million).

The desire to remain childless has been found to relate to giving greater priority in life to self-fulfillment through enjoying leisure time or enhancing romantic relationship quality (Neal, Groat, & Wicks, 1989), or to pursuing greater financial wealth (Schoen, Kim, Nathonson, Fields, & Astone, 1997).

### Preventing Pregnancy: Birth Control and Contraception

Reasons for desiring to prevent pregnancy can range from deciding not to have children at all, desiring to postpone having children until after finishing formal education or establishing a career, or wishing to control the number of children in one's family. The risk of pregnancy on any single occasion of unprotected penile–vaginal intercourse depends on the point in a woman's menstrual cycle at which the intercourse occurred (see chapter 5 for information on the menstrual cycle and fertilization); *unprotected* means using no technique to

**FIGURE 14.2**  The Most Fertile Time During the Menstrual Cycle and the Natural Family Planning Method

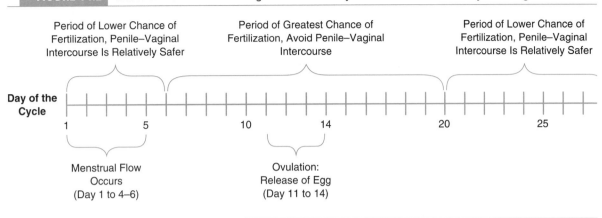

prevent pregnancy. In the day or so just before the midpoint of the menstrual cycle when ovulation occurs (Day 14), the likelihood of the egg being fertilized is as much as 30% (see Figure 14.2). The chances become lower in the days following ovulation prior to menstruation (Barnard College Student Health Services, 2005). For heterosexual couples who do not want to have children or who want to control the number of children in their family, the issue of what preventative techniques to use is a very important one.

The general name for methods of preventing pregnancy is **birth control**, which is any method of preventing birth from occurring. One general technique is that of preventing conception, that is, fertilization of the egg. Birth control also includes methods that prevent a fertilized egg from implanting in the uterus or that remove an implanted embryo. The primary examples of the latter type are administering the drug, RU-486, and surgical abortion.

**Contraception** (meaning "against conception") is any method of preventing conception. Contraceptive methods include withdrawal, natural family planning techniques, male and female condoms, other female barrier methods, contraceptive hormone administration, the intrauterine device (IUD), emergency contraception, and surgical sterilization. The various contraceptive methods available in current times are actually extremely effective (with the exception of withdrawal); in fact, 47% of all unintended pregnancies are the result of a tiny percentage of women not using any contraception at all (Alan Guttmacher Institute, 2004).

### Withdrawal

**Withdrawal** involves the man removing his penis from the woman's vagina before ejaculation and expelling his semen outside her body away from the vaginal opening. Historically, this method has been called *coitus interruptus,* and it is the oldest form of contraception given that it is mentioned in the Hebrew Torah (Christian Old Testament) and the Qur'an (Everett, 2004). The effectiveness of withdrawal in preventing fertilization under conditions of **perfect use** is 96% (i.e., using withdrawal prevents fertilization 96% of the time); perfect use is using the technique without the occurrence of human error. However, under conditions of **typical use** (that is, the way that the average person actually uses the withdrawal method), effectiveness is 73% (Alan Guttmacher Institute, 2004). The effectiveness for the various types of contraception is also presented in Table 14.1.

**TABLE 14.1**     Perfect Use and Typical Use Effectiveness of Contraceptive Methods

| Method | Perfect use effectiveness | Typical use effectiveness |
| --- | --- | --- |
| Withdrawal | 96% | 73% |
| Natural family planning | 91% | 75% |
| Male condom | 97% | 85% |
| Female condom | 98% | 85% |
| Diaphragm | 94% | 84% |
| Cervical cap | 82% | 72% |
| Spermicide | 94% | 71% |
| Oral pill | 99.9% | 92% |
| Hormone injection | 99.97% | 97% |
| Hormone implant | 99.95% | 99% |
| Intrauterine device | 99.4% | 99% |
| Tubal ligation | 99.5% | 99.3% |
| Vasectomy | 99.9% | 99.8% |

*Note*: Effectiveness rates are obtained from the Alan Guttmacher Institute (2004), with the exception of the female condom which is obtained from Trussell, Sturgen, Stickler, and Dominik (1994).

A substantial difficulty with this technique is that sperm is often present in the fluid that is released into the urethra of the man's penis *before* ejaculation; this fluid is called *pre-ejaculate.* Even these few sperm may be released into the woman's vagina and travel through the uterus and fallopian tubes to fertilize an egg. Moreover, it does not provide any protection at all from sexually transmitted diseases (Everett, 2004). The method also requires concentration and self-control on the part of the male to keep from ejaculating in the vagina. Overall, this is one of the least effective methods of contraception.

### Natural Family Planning Methods

**Natural family planning methods** actually consist of a group of techniques that have also been referred to as *fertility awareness* and the *rhythm method.* Although four different techniques have been developed, the common element of all of them is collecting information about the woman's menstrual cycle to predict when ovulation will occur; the purpose of the information is to avoid penile–vaginal intercourse during the time when fertilization is most likely. This time is between 12 and 16 days before the next menstrual period, which is the several days around ovulation. The various methods involve (a) measuring body temperature, and comparing it to typical body temperature, looking for changes that are related to the ovulatory cycle; (b) looking for a change in mucus released from the cervix of the uterus; (c) tracking a woman's menstrual cycle over a 6–12 month period and calculating the range of days around ovulation; and (d) a combination of the various natural family planning methods (Everett, 2004).

These techniques require a great deal of dedication to accurate recording of information about the woman's body over an extended period of time. Body temperature can also fluctuate due to illness, sleep pattern changes, stress, medication, and alcohol consumption. The methods also require abstinence (refraining from penile–vaginal intercourse) for substantial periods of time (Everett, 2004). Finally, the techniques do not provide any protection at all from sexually transmitted diseases.

### Male and Female Condoms

Both the male and the female condoms are barrier methods; that is, they block sperm from entering the female reproductive tract. The **male condom** is a latex sheath that is rolled down over the top of the penis to its base. The latex material captures the semen ejaculated from the penis, keeping it from being transmitted into the vagina. After ejaculation, the male withdraws his penis, and removes the condom after he has moved away from the genital area of the female, carefully avoiding spilling any seminal fluid on the vulva. In this way, sperm are not able to travel through the female reproductive system to fertilize any egg that has been released during ovulation. The male condom has the drawback of interrupting the spontaneity of sexual intercourse, seeming messy, requiring planning to make sure a condom is available, diminishing sensitivity for the male, and requiring use of non-oil-based lubricants (oil degrades latex condoms, making them prone to break). Condom use is one of the most effective methods available, and additionally provides substantial protection from sexually transmitted diseases (Everett, 2004).

*What factors do you think affect whether couples use the male condom for protection or not?*

The **female condom** is a lubricated polyurethane sheath that is inserted in the vagina, with rings at both ends to hold it in place. The end that is inserted inside the vagina is sealed to prevent sperm from having actual contact with the woman's reproductive system; the outer ring presses against the vulva when the man's penis is inserted inside (Everett, 2004). The female condom has virtually the same disadvantages as the male condom. As for advantages, in addition to protecting from sexu-

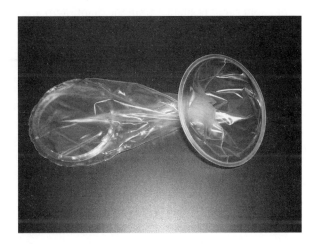

*What do you think might be the advantages of using the female condom in comparison to other types of protection techniques?*

ally transmitted diseases, it is used by the woman, giving her greater control over her body (Everett, 2004). It is also less likely to interfere with spontaneity, because the woman can put it in place before sexual activity begins.

A diaphragm.

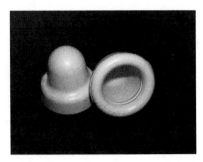

Cervical caps.

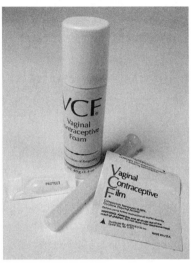

Spermicides include vaginal inserts, foam, and film.

### Female Barrier Methods

The **female barrier methods** are similar to the female condom, in that they block sperm from progressing past the vagina into the uterus. The **diaphragm** is a latex dome positioned inside the vagina near the top at the front wall so that it covers the opening to the cervix. A second method is the **cervical cap**, a dome made of rubber that is smaller than the diaphragm and covers only the cervix rather than the surrounding vaginal walls as well. **Spermicides** are chemicals placed inside the vagina that inactivate sperm by changing the nature of their cell membrane. They may be administered in the form of creams, foams, gels, and solids. These are used in conjunction with the diaphragm and the cervical cap (Everett, 2004).

The diaphragm and cervical cap may provide some protection against some sexually transmitted diseases, except for HIV infection. Spermicides may provide protection from both. Women must learn to insert the diaphragm and cervical cap properly for them to be effective, and because they are used with spermicides they may be perceived as messy. However, they give women control over protection from unwanted pregnancy (Everett, 2004).

### Contraceptive Hormone Administration

**Contraceptive hormone administration** involves women receiving doses of female sex hormones that block the maturation and release of eggs. A combination of estrogen and progesterone, or progesterone by itself, may be administered in a variety of ways. The methods of administration are (a) the oral pill, (b) a patch attached to an area of the body, (c) a ring inserted within the vagina (the NuvaRing®), (d) through injection into the blood system (e.g., Deproprovera), and (e) capsules implanted under the skin (Norplant). The hormones, estrogen and progesterone, are administered at sufficiently high levels that they are similar to those occurring during pregnancy. The hypothalamus registers the high levels and therefore does not send a signal (in the form of the hormone GnRH) to begin the process of maturing a new egg in the ovaries (see chapter 6 for a discussion of the process of ovulation). Consequently, eggs do not mature and are not released, so that fertilization is not possible even if sperm are deposited in the vagina during penile–vaginal intercourse (Everett, 2004).

Oral contraceptive pills contained in a compact dispenser.

*What might be some of the advantages of the contraceptive patch over contraceptive pills? Can you think of any disadvantages?*

The NuvaRing® is a thin, clear, flexible ring that dispenses estrogen and progestin to prevent ovulation. The ring is inserted in the vagina, where it remains for 4 weeks, after which it must be replaced with a new ring.

The oral pill has the disadvantage that a woman must remember to take the pill every day during the phase in which she is taking the pill; the procedure involves 1 week out of the month when the hormone or hormones are not taken. This problem is avoided by the other techniques—the patch, ring, injection, and implant—because the hormone is delivered automatically by these devices. A potential danger of the estrogen–progesterone combination pill is increased risk of cardiovascular disease and hypertension. The progesterone-only regimens entail some increased risk of other health diseases as well, but not at the level found with the combination pill (see Everett, 2004, for details about the risks). Health-related advantages associated with taking these contraceptive hormones may also occur. The contraceptive hormone administration technique provides no protection from sexually transmitted diseases.

### The Intrauterine Device (IUD)

The **intrauterine device** is a small solid structure of various shapes (such as a T shape or wing-shaped) with copper wire coiled around the center trunk of the T shape. Another shape is that of a small single rod. The device is inserted through the cervix into the inner cavity of the uterus. A string

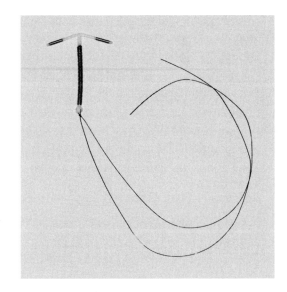

An IUD prevents fertilization of eggs by changing the uterine environment so that both the egg and sperm are damaged.

dangles from the end of the center trunk or rod into the vagina to indicate the IUD is still in place. It prevents pregnancy by changing the chemical composition of the fluid in the uterus and fallopian tubes so that it is not hospitable to the eggs and sperm. The presence of the IUD causes an immune-type reaction that creates the inhospitable environment, along with the copper having a toxic effect on the eggs and sperm. Because they are not viable, the sperm cannot fertilize the egg and pregnancy does not occur (Everett, 2004).

### Emergency Contraception

This technique is called **emergency contraception** because it is administered in the event of problems with other contraceptive methods (such as a condom is used improperly or a woman forgets to insert her diaphragm). Of course, individuals may want to use emergency contraception after engaging in unprotected sex, meaning that no contraception was used at all during the sex. The strategy involves taking a huge amount of the type of hormone used in the oral contraceptive, patch, injection, and implant. Specifically, the hormone in the method that has the least side effects, called **Plan B**, is progestin levonorgestrel. The dose must be given within 72 hours of the episode of penile–vaginal intercourse of concern. Another dose is administered 12 hours later. Ideally, the first round of the hormone should be given within 12 hours of penile–vaginal intercourse.

Depending on the point in the ovulatory cycle in which Plan B is given, the large dose of hormone prevents ovulation, or it will impede fertilization or implantation. It does not interfere with a fertilized egg that has already implanted in the endometrium, and therefore is *not* the "abortion pill," which is RU-486 (Everett, 2004).

### Surgical Sterilization

**Surgical sterilization** for women involves blocking the fallopian tubes, or cutting them and then tying each of the cut ends; this latter technique is called **tubal ligation**. These techniques prevent sperm from traveling through the woman's reproductive system to reach eggs that are released from the ovaries; both eggs and sperm cannot get past the obstruction. Consequently, fertilization cannot occur (Everett, 2004).

Surgical sterilization for men—called a **vasectomy**—consists of cutting and tying the severed ends of each vas deferens, the duct that transports sperm from the testicles to the urethra during ejaculation. The separation and blockage prevent sperm from being transported out of the body during ejaculation (Everett, 2004).

The perfect use effectiveness of tubal ligation is 99.5% and for vasectomy it is 99.9%. The typical-use effectiveness of tubal ligation is 99.3%; for vasectomy it is 99.8% (Alan Guttmacher Institute, 2004). These techniques also do not protect against sexually transmitted disease. Please note that "perfect use" in the case of surgical procedures such as these refers to situations involving high-quality surgical techniques and other optimal conditions. The figures for "typical use" include the likelihood of lower-quality surgical technique, as well as other unusual outcomes such as spontaneous reconnection of separated fallopian tubes or vas deferens.

### Abortion as Birth Control

**Abortion as birth control**, or induced abortion, is the method of ending a pregnancy using one of several procedures. Abortions occur in a certain proportion of pregnancies without medical intervention. Rather, such abortions occur because of health-related problems, either on the part of the woman or the developing embryo; these are called **spontaneous abortions**, or more commonly, miscarriages. Methods of medically inducing abortion are the use of a chemical substance called RU-486 (Mifeprex) and surgical procedures. Surgical procedures include vacuum aspiration and dilation and evacuation.

**RU-486** is given to a woman in the form of a pill, which blocks the effect of progesterone on the uterus. Without progesterone to maintain the quality of the endometrium, it degenerates and no longer supports the implanted fertilized egg (blastocyst) or embryo. A second drug is then administered several days later that causes the muscles of the uterus to contract and expel the degenerated material.

Box 14.3 Analyze This: Looking at Different Perspectives

## *Abortion: Its History and Politics in the United States*

Attempts to end pregnancies as a means of controlling the number of children in a family have occurred for thousands of years, dating back to various ancient civilizations. Beginning in the 1820s, laws were enacted in the United States against not only abortion, but also all other birth control techniques as well; it became illegal for physicians even to talk to couples about birth control. Nonetheless, women continued to seek abortions because, particularly in the lower classes, families would have large numbers of children that they simply did not have the financial means to take care of.

The dire situation of many impoverished families was championed between 1912 and 1916 by Margaret Sanger, a public health nurse, after the agonizing death of one of her clients resulting from a botched abortion she performed on herself. Sanger vowed to do whatever she could to prevent the endless cycle of pregnancy, poverty, and death. Eventually, she succeeded in having a number of laws overturned, such that it became legal in some places in the United States to market condoms and diaphragms (D'Emilio & Freedman, 1997; Petersen, 1999).

Nonetheless, many states continued to retain laws against not only abortion, but birth control techniques. Laws against abortions, however, were stricken down in the 1973 *Roe v. Wade* U.S. Supreme Court decision that restrictions on abortion are unconstitutional during the first 3 months of pregnancy. In addition, the ruling asserted that only a woman and her physician had the right to decide whether an abortion would be performed during the second 3 months. Anti-abortion groups began forming shortly after the decision was handed down, with Christian conservatives adding great force to the movement in the last half of the 1970s. As a result of strong, skillful political organizing, anti-abortion groups have succeeded in placing substantial restrictions on the availability of abortions, federally and at the state level.

The controversy over the Supreme Court decision reached a fevered pitch in the 1980s. Anti-abortion activists came to label their point of view "pro-life," some taking the position that termination of pregnancy at any point is intolerable because it ends a life and is, therefore, murder. Radical pro-life activists used extreme tactics such as displaying bloody pictures of aborted fetuses or harassing doctors and clinics involved in abortion services. Less extreme pro-life activists picketed abortion clinics and doctors' homes, as well as publicizing information about political candidates' views about abortion.

Politicians also took on the cause, introducing legislation in an attempt to undercut or neutralize the effects of the Supreme Court decision. The failure of such attempts likely served as one factor in the onset of violent attacks on birth-control clinics in the early 1980s by frustrated and angry pro-life extremists. Clinics were bombed or set afire in various locations across the United States, with 24 bombings occurring in 1984 alone (Petersen, 1999).

*(Continued)*

(Continued)

Despite the lack of success at passing a constitutional amendment to prohibit abortions or legislation to undermine the court ruling entirely, in 1976, the Hyde Amendment to a funding bill was passed that prohibited federal financial support for abortions for women who could not afford them personally; the constitutionality of the legislation was affirmed by the U.S. Supreme Court in 1980. The effect was to reduce abortions by 7,500%—to 4,000 a year by 1980 (Marty, 1997).

Beyond this, state laws and Supreme Court decisions upholding them gradually limited the ability to receive abortions. Utah required physicians to notify the parents of minors who asked for an abortion, which the Court ruled was constitutional. In 1990, the Court reaffirmed the constitutionality of other state laws requiring parental notification in cases in which unmarried minors were seeking abortions (Marty, 1997).

On the other side of the issue, the attacks on the availability of abortions and abortion clinics caused those who were defenders of the right to have an abortion to organize formally into groups; these organizations called their position "pro-choice." Attitudes on the issue have polarized dramatically from that point on into current times, with advocates of both sides unwilling to acknowledge the legitimacy of any aspect of the other point of view (Marty, 1997).

The issue may move to the forefront of American politics again in the near future, with further attempts by pro-life groups to overturn the *Roe v. Wade* Supreme Court decisions. Efforts have not been successful up to this point because a majority of Supreme Court justices have not hailed from the conservative side of the issue. With the appointment of conservative Chief Justice John Roberts and Associate Justice Samuel Alito, the court has moved closer to a consensus that might support a change in the *Roe v. Wade* decision. The next Supreme Court appointment will be the deciding factor in whether abortion remains legal in the U.S. or is prohibited.

## References

D'Emilio, J., & Freedman, E. B. (1997). *Intimate matters: A history of sexuality in America* (2nd ed.). Chicago: University of Chicago Press.

Marty, M. A. (1997). *Daily life in the United States, 1960–1990: Decades of discord*. Westport, CT: Greenwood.

Petersen, J. R. (1999). *The century of sex: Playboy's history of the sexual revolution, 1900–1999*. New York: Grove.

The surgical procedure of **vacuum aspiration** is used during the first trimester of pregnancy (the first 3 months). This involves inserting a small tube through the cervix into the interior of the uterus; the vacuum tube draws out the embryo, along with the endometrium. **Dilation and evacuation** is the method that is used during the second trimester (the second 3 months). **Dilation** refers to the process of slowly opening up the cervix of the uterus, so that a curette—a small, spoon-like instrument—can be inserted into the uterus to remove the embryo (**evacuation** is the removal of the embryo). This is somewhat more of an involved procedure and is somewhat riskier than vacuum aspiration.

The Physical Safety of Abortions. In 2002, 1.29 million abortions occurred in the United States. The overwhelming majority—approximately 88%—are conducted within the first trimester (12 weeks) of pregnancy;

59.1% of abortions occur before the 9$^{th}$ week of pregnancy. Very little risk is associated with the procedure in that fewer than 1% of women undergoing them experience major complications. The risk of death is one in one million for abortions conducted 8 weeks or sooner after conception; in fact, the risk of death from childbirth is 11 times higher than that for abortion. No evidence exists that having an abortion affects the woman's ability to have children (Alan Guttmacher Institute, 2005).

The majority of women receiving abortions, 54%, reported using contraception in the month that they became pregnant. Pregnancy largely results from inconsistent use of contraception; 76% of oral contraceptive users and 49% of condom users used the method inconsistently. Only 8% of women having abortions have never used a method of birth control; many of these women are young, poor, African American, Hispanic, or poorly educated (Alan Guttmacher Institute, 2005). In fact, women receiving abortions in general tend to be young, poor, and unmarried (Crawford & Unger, 2000).

**The Psychological Safety of Abortions.** Critics of abortion have claimed that women tend to suffer from a postabortion syndrome. To address this concern, the American Psychological Association sponsored a review of the empirical research on the issue (Public Interest Directorate, 1987). The conclusion based on this review was that women in general do not experience major negative effects after having an abortion. Distress declines sharply immediately following an abortion, with no increase in the low levels of distress in follow-up measurements over the next several weeks (Crawford & Unger, 2000).

The primary factor related to psychological difficulties among the few women who experience them (ranging from 0.5–15% of women having an abortion) is their psychological adjustment prior to the abortion. Greater proportions of women who seek abortions have experienced prior physical, emotional, and sexual abuse than women who do not seek abortions (Russo, 2000). In other words, such women are at greater risk for psychological problems even before receiving the abortion.

Factors that are related to psychological distress following an abortion, in addition to the presence of prior psychological problems are (a) lack of support from family or friends, (b) perception of having been pressured into having the abortion, (c) strong religious beliefs about the immorality of abortions, and (d) belief that one would have problems dealing with the abortion (Public Interest Directorate, 1987). Ironically, the level of depression after an abortion is also associated with the strength of protests encountered when entering the clinic to obtain an abortion (Cozzarelli & Major, 1998). As noted by Crawford and Unger (2000),

> Although our society expects women to accept most of the responsibility for caring for children, it has been less willing to entrust them with the freedom to make responsible reproductive choices. Steeped in the motherhood mystique, many people still view reproductive rights as unnatural and maternal sacrifice as women's lot in life. (p. 329)

## Motivations for Establishing a Family With Children

*Who of us is mature enough for offspring before the offspring themselves arrive? The value of marriage is not that adults produce children but that children produce adults.*

Peter De Vries, American comic visionary, novelist, and linguist, 1910–1993 (ThinkExist.com)

*Creativity is not merely the innocent spontaneity of our youth and childhood; it must also be married to the passion of the adult human being, which is a passion to live beyond one's death.*

Dr. Rollo May (ThinkExist.com)

It is probably the case that many heterosexual couples have discussed and generally planned to have children because they want to start a family; that is, many pregnancies are probably welcome, if not each one intentionally planned. Planning to have a family will often lead to the decision to maintain a pregnancy, rather than end it. In fact, evidence indicates that half of all unintended pregnancies are ended by abortion (Alan Guttmacher Institute, 1999). Consequently, the desire to have children appears to be an important factor in continuing a pregnancy and starting a family with children.

## Rewards of Parenthood

Early research on the issue of the motivation to have children focused on the specific value that children are perceived to have for prospective parents. This research found that interest in having children was associated with the stronger belief that they provide important benefits. The most notable benefits were related to their economic value and to psychological rewards such as receiving love, experiencing stability, and feeling socially connected (Lawson, 2004).

*What might account for the differences in beliefs among individuals about the costs and benefits of having children? How important to your life goals is having children?*

Research on the types of outcomes individuals believed they would experience by parenting children revealed six categories of outcomes (Lawson, 2004). The first is **enrichment**, the belief that raising children provides happiness, results in feeling proud, and enables the experience of fun and enjoyment. The second expectation is **isolation**, feeling that having children results in a lack of time for friendship, for other activities parents find enjoyable, and for time with one's spouse. **Commitment** is a set of expectations that children need to be cared for the rest of their lives and represent a 24-hour-a-day responsibility. The expectation of **instrumental costs** is the belief that raising children is financially expensive, and emotionally and physically exhausting. **Continuity** is the expectation of receiving substantial benefits over the years by having grandchildren, a close relationship with adult children, financial security in old age, and carrying on the family line. The final expectation is **perceived support**, the belief that other family members will help take care of their children and the community will provide support as well.

For a group of non-college-student adults, the importance of parenting children in one's lifetime was found to be independently related to the *enrichment* and *commitment* expectations. That is, individuals who indicated that it was important for them personally to have children expected that children would enrich their lives and would require continued care for the rest of their lives. In addition, individuals who felt that it was important for them to have children tended to believe that they would experience less isolation from friends and less restriction of social activities (i.e., they had lower *isolation* expectations) than individuals for whom having children was not as important. Those for whom becoming a parent was more important also thought that having children would be less financially expensive, and less emotionally and physically exhausting (i.e., they had lower *instrumental cost* expectations) than those for whom having children was not important. Similarly, individuals who were in fact parents actually expressed lower *isolation* and *instrumental cost* expectations than those who intended not to have children (Lawson, 2004).

### Cultural Beliefs About the Importance of Motherhood

A significant reason that many women may desire to have children is because most cultures cast motherhood as a defining feature of adult women's identities—that is, their sense of who they are and what they are like. Motherhood is considered to be a major aspect of the development of women, essential to their health, happiness, and life satisfaction. The central position that motherhood occupies in conceptions of women is indicated by comparison with views of fatherhood. Being a father is considered to be an important aspect of men's lives, because fatherhood is also thought to provide immense joy and gratification. Yet, for men, fatherhood is only one of many equally or more important goals (Woollett & Marshall, 2001).

Imagine others' perceptions of a man whose only significant accomplishment was raising children, but who did not want to work, or did not have a job; compare that with a woman whose major accomplishment in life was raising her children, but never worked at paid employment. The woman would nonetheless be generally held in great esteem, whereas the man would be viewed as unmotivated, strange, and possibly unmanly. Western societies, particularly in the past, have maintained motherhood as the ultimate goal of women, worthy of tremendous personal sacrifice in other aspects of their lives for the sake of raising high quality children (Woollett & Marshall, 2001). The belief that parenthood is the primary, if not the greatest, source of fulfillment and accomplishment is very likely a major factor in the motivation for women to having children.

## Families With Children

### Giving Birth to Children

Traditional homemakers and happily married couples are those most likely to give birth to children (Myers, 1997). Higher levels of education are related to later age of having children, or not having children at all, whereas greater income is associated with having children intentionally. Concern about the stability of the marital relationship increases the chances of not having children. Greater career aspirations, as well as issues related to having the time and energy for a career, are not associated with reduced interest in having children (Dion, 1995; Heaton, Jacobson, & Holland, 1999). As noted previously, approximately half of all pregnancies in the United States are not specifically planned, but rather simply result from engaging in penile–vaginal intercourse and pregnancy unintentionally occurs (Alan Guttmacher Institute, 1999).

### Having Children Through Alternative Insemination

Historically, the process of impregnating a woman through technical procedures, rather than through penile–vaginal intercourse, has been referred to as *artificial insemination*. However, the procedure has also been called *alternative insemination* (Mallon, 2004), which avoids the connotations of "artificial," "unnatural," "false," and "not real." Women may seek alternative insemination for a variety of reasons, such as with respect to heterosexual women whose male partner has fertility problems, or women who are not partnered and desire children. Lesbian women, whether partnered or single, may seek alternative insemination because of a desire to have children in their family as well. In such cases, individuals may obtain sperm from a friend or family member, a paid donor, or from a sperm bank in which sperm from donors is frozen for storage until it is needed.

Likewise, gay men and couples may choose alternative insemination with a woman who is a friend or family member. In other cases, they may employ a woman as a **surrogate**, someone with whom they were not acquainted previously, who becomes pregnant with the semen of the gay men. The motivations for surrogate mothers can include a desire to help others, enjoyment at bringing children into the world, and payment (Mallon, 2004).

As noted by Woollette and Marshall (2001), reproductive technologies in general (as well as adoption of children) are usually perceived as the strategy of last resort. This is because of the intense value placed on biological relatedness to children because of the desire for continuity; moreover, a pervasive concern exists about the quality of care provided to unrelated children, due to the belief that biological parents feel greater commitment to their biological children out of a sense of connection to oneself. Woollett and Marshall (2001) have also observed that some feminists express misgivings about the use of reproductive technologies; they argue that the technologies increase control over women's reproduction by people other than the women themselves.

A number of techniques are available to assist in accomplishing alternative insemination. **Intrauterine insemination** involves injecting semen into the reproductive tract of a woman. **In vitro fertilization** is the technique of fertilizing an egg outside of a woman's body in a laboratory container and then positioning the fertilized egg in the endometrium of the woman's uterus.

## Adoption

Adoption is the legal process in which "the parental rights of the birth parents are terminated and the adopting parent becomes the legal parent" (Mallon, 2004, p. 45). Although adoption has been romanticized and conceived in a highly sentimental way, in fact the process can be grueling for everyone involved. For individuals or couples hoping to adopt a child, the experience may be difficult and challenging for a number of reasons, such as with respect to finding a child they can adopt and navigating the complex and often immense legal network. Reuniting children with their birth families remains the primary concern of authorities and the legal system, reducing the availability of children for adoption (Mallon, 2004).

*Why do you think that lesbians and gay men would choose to go through the extremely challenging, grueling process of adopting children? What does this say about the role of offspring in individuals' identity and well-being?*

Heterosexual couples typically pursue adoption only after a long process of dealing with problems related to fertility; the term **fertility problems** refers to the situation in which the reproductive system of one or both members of the couple is not functioning in a way that allows them to give birth to their own children. This process may involve various medical procedures to attempt to correct fertility problems, attending infertility workshops and, in some cases, then dealing with lack of success, disappointment, and grief. In these cases, adoption is an alternate plan for creating a family if all else has failed, a strategy to which they must adjust and cope.

For gay men and lesbians, adoption may be the primary pathway, if not the only way, to creating a family. However, in a number of U.S. states, the government and legal system are not extremely friendly, if friendly at all, to gay men and lesbians adopting children. Even where adoption is legal, social workers may have feelings against such adoptions and work against the adoption. For example, in one study, "a constant theme in the interviews was that social workers assigned to their cases were biased against and lacked information about gay people" (Mallon, 2004, p. 43).

According to Mallon (2004), couples and individuals who wish to adopt often have the typical fantasies that birth parents do about what the experience of having children will be like. People may hope that the child will look like them, behave perfectly, and have a bright, accomplished future. Reality, however, is the same as it is for birth parents. The experiences of gay and lesbian couples are extremely similar to those of heterosexual couples, having little to do with sexual orientation or identity. The quality of the transition into becoming a family after not having any children depends on the particular circumstances of each family, as well as each individual's ability to adjust to changes and stress.

Martin (1993) recommends that prospective parents ask themselves the following questions as they consider whether to adopt children or not: "How well do we adapt to change in general? How quickly do we recover from disruption? How high is our tolerance for chaos, noise, sleep deprivation, intrusion, lack of solitude" (Mallon, 2004, p. 67). According to Mallon, most parents are shocked when the adopted child moves in with them; the level of adjustment was simply more extreme than what they had imagined. Moreover, gay men find that they do not fit into the "mommy-driven culture" (i.e., tailored for women) as the parent who assumes primary care for children; nor do they conform to the male role of father who is the income-earner, but who has the option of less involvement in his children's lives. Gay men tend to find themselves "not just involved in their child's life, but . . . in the words of one dad, superparents: 'the president of the parents' association, the head of Scouts, and the neighborhood's day care center—and . . . still don't feel like [they] do enough'" (Mallon, 2004, p. 71).

## Pregnancy

Pregnancy produces monumental changes in a woman's body, as a result of dramatically higher levels of progesterone and estrogen. Negative symptoms that may be experienced include breast tenderness, fatigue, and nausea. Pregnancy also involves significant changes in weight and the shape of the body. Women tend to experience both positive and negative emotional reactions to such changes; these include joy and pleasure, as well as fear, frustration, and unhappiness (Crawford & Unger, 2000).

Pregnant women typically experience decreases in sexual desire as well. However, the levels of desire can change over the course of the pregnancy and vary quite widely across different women. The decline in sexual desire is also related to less frequency of sexual intercourse. By the last trimester (beginning at the 7$^{th}$ month), more than 75% of pregnant women experience decreased sexual desire; likewise, more than 80% report a drop in the frequency of intercourse. The lower levels of desire, sexual intercourse, and sexual satisfaction continue after the birth of the child (De Judicibus & McCabe, 2002), a time known as the **postpartum period**. The experience of pleasure during sexual intercourse rebounds only fairly gradually over time (Hyde, DeLamater, Plant, & Byrd, 1996).

However, the extent of diminished sexual interest may not be extremely dramatic. In a recent study (De Judicibus & McCabe, 2002), hardly any women experienced a complete loss of sexual desire and satisfaction, or a complete absence of sexual intercourse during the last trimester. Relationship satisfaction actually increased for women in this study across their pregnancy. This may be due to anticipation and excitement about the upcoming birth. As is typically found in research on relationships in general, greater sexual satisfaction was related to greater relationship satisfaction.

Many women had begun engaging in sexual intercourse again within 3 months after the birth of their child. However, many of them reported sexual problems, most notably dyspareunia (disruptive pain during intercourse) and lower sexual desire. By this time, relationship satisfaction was lower than expressed before childbirth, although most women were still at least moderately satisfied with their relationship. By 6 months, sexual desire, intercourse, and satisfaction remained at a lower level in comparison to levels before becoming pregnant. Dyspareunia likewise continued as a problem, although it had lessened in comparison to the 3-month point.

## Effects of Children on Relationships and Sexuality

In the study by De Judicibus and McCabe (2002), the nature of the mother's relationship with her newborn baby was a significant factor affecting the quality of sexual interaction with her husband at 6 months after birth. Higher levels of satisfaction by women with their **mother role** were associated with greater sexual desire, satisfaction, and levels of sexual intercourse, as well as greater relationship satisfaction. Moreover, women with higher-quality mother-role perceptions experienced less depression and fatigue. The mother-role ratings very likely reflect the nature of the mother's interactions with her young infant. Specifically, having better-quality interactions with the infant is the major factor contributing to greater satisfaction and enjoyment with the mother role. Quality of mother–infant interaction is at least partially due to the temperament of the infant, in terms of whether he or she has a difficult or an easy temperament.

Other research on first-time parents indicates that a potential source of difficulty in marital relationships is that fathers often have stronger sexual desire than mothers. This research found that relationship satisfaction was greater among couples who communicated with one another about their sexual desires, as well as relating to each other in emotionally intimate and sensual ways (Ahlborg, Strandmark, & Dahlöf, 2000). Both fathers and mothers characteristically express relative dissatisfaction with their sexual relationship around 6 months after the birth of their child, compared with the period before childbirth. Mothers in one study more frequently reported that they felt too tired for sex in comparison to fathers. Not surprisingly, fatigue was related to lower levels of sensual interaction for the couples in this study. In addition, breastfeeding was related to reductions in sexual desire, satisfaction, and intercourse. Nonetheless, most parents indicated that they were very happy as new parents, with the child apparently providing a sense of increased purpose and meaning in their lives (Ahlborg, Dahlöf, & Hallberg, 2005).

*Do you think that most people have a realistic understanding of the demands involved in being a parent? Do you think that the pleasures and benefits live up to the expectations individuals hold prior to having children?*

The birth of children actually appears to lower the probability of divorce, although it ironically also decreases relationship satisfaction (Belsky, 1990; Kalmijn, 1999). Moreover, lower levels of satisfaction linger for at least several years after the birth of children (Belsky, 1990). The presence of children in a family most likely creates a sense of responsibility and commitment to maintaining the relationship for the benefit of the children; other barriers probably include the financial cost of raising children and the effort involved in caring for them alone. Little evidence regarding the effect of children on marital relationships exists beyond the early childhood years. However, some research indicates that the presence of adolescents in the family does not affect marital satisfaction directly. Rather, the quality of parent–adolescent relationships and the extent of the adolescent's push for independence influence the nature of the marital relationship; lower-quality relationships with adolescents and their greater demand for independence are related to lower-quality marital relationships (Schaie & Willis, 2002).

Factors involved in the decline in romantic relationship quality related to having children are likely (a) changes in communication patterns and (b) the effort involved in caring for the children (Schaie & Willis, 2002). Communication drops off among couples with children in comparison to those without children, especially with respect to issues related to the romantic or marital relationship itself. In addition, couples less frequently engage in activities focused on simply enjoying time together or involving pursuits of mutual interest; these types of interactions are known as *companionate activities*. The situation does not change until after the children grow up and leave home, allowing the couple more time alone together (Anderson, Russell, & Schumm, 1983).

Furthermore, issues related to childrearing may lead to conflict, which reduces the quality of the couple's relationship. The presence of children additionally compounds the domestic workload because of the new demands of child care and extra household chores (Schaie & Willis, 2002). Increasingly, this additional household workload comes on top of a full-time career for both parents. Yet the demand is generally greater for women; their domestic work level during weekdays increases with increasing age of the children, until it begins to drop off as children move into adolescence and early adulthood (Moen, 1999). These extra demands contribute to fatigue and interfere with time that can be devoted to romantic and sexual interactions for couples.

## *Midlife and Beyond*

*Graduation day is tough for adults. They go to the ceremony as parents. They come home as contemporaries. After twenty-two years of child-raising, they are unemployed.*

Erma Bombeck, U.S. humorist, 1927–1996 (ThinkExist.com)

*A child-like man is not a man whose development has been arrested; on the contrary, he is a man who has given himself a chance of continuing to develop long after most adults have muffled themselves in the cocoon of middle-aged habit and convention.*

Aldous Huxley, English novelist and critic, 1894–1963 (ThinkExist.com)

Thoroughly unprepared we take the step into the afternoon of life; worse still, we take this step with the false presupposition that our truths and ideals will serve us as hitherto. But, we cannot live the afternoon of life according to the program of life's morning—for what was great in the morning will be little at evening, and what in the morning was true will at evening have become a lie. (Jung, 1933, p. 108)

Change continues throughout life, including into later adulthood. According to a review of research on midlife by Lachman (2004), some evidence exists to support Jung's contention that the experiences and beliefs developed during adolescence and early adulthood do not serve us well in midlife. On the other hand, research paints a picture of a substantial degree of continuity with earlier years regarding some aspects of life. The development of a consistent sense of self additionally provides a good foundation to help us weather the challenges we face in our later years.

Furthermore, the belief that adults inevitably face a "midlife crisis" is not supported by research. Only 26% of individuals report experiencing a crisis of any sort after the age of 40. However, the majority of crises that people report ever having occur before age 40 or after age 50. When crises do occur, a third of the time they are brought about by serious events such as job loss, financial difficulties, or illness; these events can occur at any time in a person's adult years. Evidence indicates that personality characteristics, such as anxiety-proneness and neuroticism, are important in causing people to react to stress with great turmoil and distress (Lachman, 2004).

With respect to psychological functioning, research likewise does not support the view that decline in intellect, cognitive abilities, and memory occurs in a dramatic way during the middle years (Lachman, 2004). In fact, verbal abilities and skills based on knowledge and experience appear to peak during this time. Memory declines typically occur much later in life, if they occur at all (Willis & Schaie, 1999).

The period during the 50s is an important turning point for personality, with people often becoming much more self-reflective and analytical. Individuals who have developed a sense of mastery and self-control over their lives are able to adapt to the challenges and solve problems in a way that minimizes distress (Lachman & Firth, 2004). It is the case that midlife adults, along with young adults, experience greater numbers of daily stressors than older adults, often because of problems with children and financial difficulties (Almeida & Horn, 2004). Moreover, many people at midlife report that they have little time for leisure because of work-related demands and family responsibilities (AARP, 2002). Despite these challenges, evidence indicates that the middle years are a period of greater well-being and happiness compared with other periods, although this may be less the case for individuals with fewer social and economic resources (Markus, Ryff, Curhan, & Palmersheim, 2004).

On the basis of people's own assessments, a major factor related to well-being in the middle years is having developed positive relationships with loved ones, especially with one's romantic partner, children, and parents (Markus et al., 2004). A great deal of variety exists in the type of relationships middle-aged adults have with their children depending on their social class, the age of the children, and how close they live to them geographically. Some still have children living with them, others have children who live on their own, and others have children return to live with them following their divorce or graduation from college. Many people with children also become grandparents during this period. One issue that is as inevitable as it is difficult is dealing with the declining abilities and health of one's parents. Although a number of individuals begin their middle years with both parents alive, by the time they move into late adulthood, the vast majority have lost both parents (Lachman, 2004).

## Physical Changes Related to Sexuality

Various theories of aging have been proposed to account for changes in the body and psychological processes characteristic of the last half of life (Schaie & Willis, 2002). Such theories have pointed to genetic factors that cause aging at the cellular level. Proposals include a currently prominent theory maintaining that advanced aging results from damage to genetic material over the course of experience; cell replication gradually is based on genetic commands that are different from what they were earlier in life (Schneider, 1993).

Other theories propose that tissue or body parts suffer gradual damage and eventually change in structure as a result, or that they simply wear out. Changes in the endocrine system may also be involved. Various abilities and functions of the body gradually decline, such as the ability to understand speech, as well as vision, hearing, and other senses. Neuron loss also occurs over time (neurons are the cells that make up the nervous system). In addition, disease becomes more likely to afflict individuals as they age.

### Women

Physical changes likewise occur beginning in midlife related to sexuality. Women experience **menopause**, the gradual decline in the functioning of the ovaries, eventually resulting in a complete end to the production of sex hormones and release of eggs. The process begins around 40, and continues for a period of time that varies across women. Menopause occurs because follicles in the ovaries degenerate more quickly at this time, such that they cannot respond to the hormones, follicle-stimulating hormone (FSH) and luteinizing hormone (LH), released by the pituitary gland (refer to chapter 6 for more information about ovarian cycles). Specifically, because of the decline of the follicles, they are not able to manufacture the sex hormones, estrogen and progestin in reaction to the FSH and LH. Eventually, none of the follicles are able to function, and eggs no longer mature to be released into the fallopian tubes; the possibility for the woman's eggs to be fertilized during sexual intercourse, therefore, ends.

During the time of menopause, hormone levels may vary to some degree; for some women, the fluctuation is wide-ranging. Not all women experience changes in the body and psychological processes as a result of the hormone shifts, although others do experience the symptoms stereotypically associated with menopause. These may include variability in the menstrual cycle; dramatic increases in body temperature and sweating, called *hot flashes;* irritability; changes in appetite and eating habits, with either weight gain or weight loss; mood swings; and possibly depression.

*How much of an impact do you think that menopause-related declines in vaginal lubrication play in women's sexual relationships? What other factors do you think might be important?*

Of direct significance to sexuality, women often experience a reduction in the amount of moisture produced in the vagina during sexual excitement and arousal; it also often takes longer for the lubrication to begin once a woman becomes sexually aroused. Women may be placed on hormone replacement therapy, which involves being given doses of estrogen to substitute for the declines in estrogen produced by the ovaries; this often relieves the symptoms that do occur. Vaginal lubrication is improved by the replacement estrogen, in addition to alleviating the other types of symptoms.

Changes associated with menopause, however, have not been found to be the primary factors influencing the quality and frequency of women's sexual relationships. Increasing age accounts for decreases in sexual satisfaction and frequency of behavior to a greater extent than menopausal symptoms. On the other hand, how far along women are in the menopausal process is related to declines in sexual interest and decreasing likelihood of experiencing orgasms. Changes in the structure and functioning of the sexual organs and the body in general may account for difficulties related to sexuality. These include thinning, shrinking, and loss of elasticity in the vaginal walls, as well as less fullness of the labia (Decks & McCabe, 2001). Women remain capable of experiencing orgasms, although muscle contractions may become less intense and less frequent during middle age (Masters & Johnson, 1966).

The gradual changes that take place physically, however, do not mean that middle age is necessarily a period of great sexual difficulty for women. In looking at the frequency of sexual problems in the previous 12 months, data from the National Health and Social Life Survey (Laumann, Palk, & Rosen, 2001) indicate that women between the ages of 50 and 59 were less likely to experience sexual problems than women in the youngest age group; the exception was difficulties related to the lower levels of vaginal lubrication typical of the middle years. Moreover, women's sexual anxieties tend to diminish with age, whereas men become more likely to experience sexual problems over time.

## Men

As individuals age, they are increasingly likely to experience a number of health problems such as cardiovascular diseases (e.g., high cholesterol leading to blockages that reduces blood flow, high blood pressure) and diabetes. Such problems can lead to difficulties for men in being able to experience erection of the penis, or in maintaining the erection during sexual behavior. This type of difficulty is called **erectile dysfunction (ED)** more recently, as well as *impotence* in the past.

Within psychology, problems maintaining an erection that occur on an ongoing basis or happen frequently, and that interfere with sexual activity, are formally known as **male erectile disorder**. In addition, to be considered a formal disorder, the problem must result in significant distress or relationship difficulties. If erection problems are caused specifically by a medical condition such as diabetes or vascular disease, a diagnosis is made as **male erectile disorder due to …**, and the specific medical condition is included in the diagnosis. Erectile disorder may be caused by other factors as well, for example a psychological disorder such as mood disorders (e.g., depression) or by consumption of substances such as tobacco and some medications (American Psychiatric Association, 1994).

Despite the increased likelihood of sexual difficulties as men age, little evidence exists for what some have called "male menopause." Changes that occur are fairly gradual, and may begin in the 30s, rather than occurring as a sudden, dramatic decline during middle age (Metz & Miner, 1995, 1998). As is true with women, midlife physical changes decrease the muscular contractions involved in orgasm, making the experience less intense and shorter lasting. In addition to a decline in the rigidity of the penis during erection and the lower likelihood of experiencing and maintaining erections, smaller, thinner amounts of seminal fluid are produced during ejaculation, which is also typically less forceful (Laumann et al., 2001; McKinlay & Feldman, 1994; Theinhaus, Conter, & Bosmann, 1986).

Given that variability can always be found among people in how they develop, a useful question is whether specific factors can be identified that make a difference in sexual functioning later in life. One valuable source of information comes from a large-scale study that examined the physical and mental health of men between the ages of 40 and 70 (McKinlay & Feldman, 1994). Being in better physical health in general, as indicated through medical examinations and records, was found to be related to greater levels of sexual activity and sexual satisfaction. That is, men who were in better shape overall were more likely to engage in more sexual behavior and to enjoy it more.

What about the development of sexual difficulties? The only physical factor related to problems with sexual functioning was having prostate surgery. This is because one of the unfortunate side effects of surgery on the prostate gland, which is a major producer of seminal fluid, is sometimes problems with the ability to have erections. An important nonphysical factor associated with sexual difficulties in this study was poorer psychological functioning, most notably greater levels of anger and depression (McKinlay & Feldman, 1994). Psychological well-being therefore is important to sexual functioning, above and beyond the role of physical health.

### How Does the Aging Process Affect the Well-Being of the Couple?

Yet another important issue is the type of effect that physical aging has on the sexual well-being of couples, not just the individual, during middle age. Knowing what to expect in the later years will very likely help individuals to adjust to these developments. Couples who are caught by surprise as the changes occur may react negatively to the sexual difficulties they experience, feeling substantial embarrassment and anxiety. If this happens, couples may avoid talking about the situation, withdraw from one another, and possibly shy away from sexual contact. Moreover, the negative stereotypes held within U.S. society about aging bodies may contribute further to problems with self-esteem (Burgess, 2004).

Another potential problem is that the two individuals involved in a relationship may experience sexual difficulties at different times due to differences in the aging process (Burgess, 2004). Because one person is going through problems and the other one is not, the person with the difficulties may feel that the spouse or partner will not understand. It may also be that the healthy partner serves as an embarrassing comparison that intensifies feelings of inadequacy on the part of the one experiencing problems. Men are especially likely to be affected by this type of situation because research has found that men tend to react more negatively to their physical changes than do women (Edwards & Booth, 1994; Laumann et al., 2001).

Yet the effects of physical changes are not entirely negative (Burgess, 2004). Some individuals tend to shift their focus away from goals that were important in earlier years of the relationship, such as ensuring that they achieve orgasm for themselves or making sure that they "give an orgasm" to their partner. Instead, they may become more interested in simply experiencing greater intimacy as part of their sexual relationship and worry less about "performance" (Brecher, 1984).

A number of older people actually feel that the later years are the highest quality of their lives. The privacy provided by children leaving home and the increase in leisure time resulting from retirement permits greater personal control over sexuality and allows it to take place in a more relaxed setting (Brecher, 1984). Age may also bring greater self-acceptance and less concern about getting approval from family regarding sexual issues (Burgess, 2004). This is true for gay men as well, who feel less anxious about their sexual orientation than younger men (Berger, 1996). Likewise, in one study (Sang, 1993), 50% of older lesbians believed that their sexual relationships were better because they were more open and communicated to a greater extent and also because they personally felt less pressure to have orgasms.

## Sexual Attitudes and Behavior

> *Being 68-yrs-old I find I am becoming more sexually active and use a vibrator at least once a week. I use the Dr Ruth vibrator. I also am searching to see if there are other women my age who are experiencing the same feelings. I am becoming more open in telling my husband what I like and for him to research my body more. It is interesting how men of our generation do not have the vaguest idea of where the clitoris is and the G-Spot. He is becoming more attentive to my desires and not just a wham bam thank you ma'am time. With all that I am having more orgasms than before and am enjoying sex a lot more, but then again I always did enjoy sex. (Sandra; Women's Sexual Experiences, On-line forum, retrieved July 22, 2006, from The-clitoris.com. Reprinted with permission of The-clitoris.com.)*

The above passage by a woman in her senior years is, of course, an anecdotal report or case history. It was provided by an individual visiting a Web site devoted to sexuality, and therefore cannot be assumed to be similar to women in general. Yet it does indicate that some portion of women in their later years are very much interested in sexual expression and engage in regular sexual behavior.

Relatively little empirical research, however, has been conducted on sexuality in later life. The most prominent study was that commissioned by AARP in 1999; AARP is an organization devoted to advocacy for the well-being of seniors. This study is noteworthy for its focus on people 45 years and older, as well as because of the size of its sample, its high participation rate, and the fact that it was a nationally representative sample. AARP commissioned a follow-up study in 2004 (AARP, 2005) to compare the findings with those of the 1999 study; a second major reason for the second study was to include large enough numbers of Asian, African, and Hispanic Americans in order to obtain a better understanding of these groups.

As with all research on sexuality, the results are based on people who agree to participate, which means that participants may be different from those in the general population. Again, however, the fact that people were selected on the basis of sophisticated probability sampling procedures and contacted to be in the study, and a high number of them agreed to participate, makes this possibility much less likely. In fact, earlier studies had dramatically lower participation rates (meaning many people refused to participate; Starr & Weiner, 1981) or were based entirely on people who contacted the researcher themselves because they were interested in participating (Brecher, 1984).

In the AARP study, individuals were contacted initially by telephone to recruit their participation in the study. They were then mailed self-report questionnaires, along with an incentive for completing the survey. Additional numbers of Hispanic Americans, African Americans, and Asian Americans above their proportion in the population were recruited so that large enough numbers would be available for reliable comparisons. The final group of respondents consisted of 1,682 people from the general population sample and, in addition, 1,248 individuals recruited to increase the representation of non-European Americans. Many of the results in the 2004 study were very similar to those obtained in the 1999 study, indicating that the results are very reliable and stable.

In addition to measures of sexual behavior, the survey obtained information about sexual attitudes and beliefs. Midlife and older adults overwhelmingly believe that they would not be happy if they never had sex again (70%), indicate that they enjoy sex (71%), and disagree with the position that sex is only for younger people (84%). They also feel that sexual activity is a critical part of a good relationship (60%). These beliefs indicate that, in general, sex is a relatively important aspect of life for older adults. Having a regular sexual partner is related to more strongly endorsing these sexual attitudes, such that those who have a partner feel that sexuality is more important to them and to the quality of their relationship.

Consistent with research on adolescents and young adults, the AARP study documented that men and women across all age groups have different attitudes toward sexuality and have engaged in different levels of sexual behavior. Men reported more positive attitudes than women with respect to every issue dealing with the importance of sexuality.

About half of respondents (51%) reported that they experienced erotic thoughts, fantasies, or dreams once a week or more frequently. Men were dramatically more likely to report this (76% of men) in comparison to women (29%), Greater proportions of both men and women in the oldest age groups reported less frequent erotic thoughts, fantasies, or dreams. Approximately 20% of individuals in the study indicated that they did not experience sexual thoughts, feelings, or dreams at all.

Extremely large majorities of both women and men indicated that they had engaged in at least one of five sexual activities once a week or more frequently within the previous 6-month period (78% of women and 95% of men). Considering only those with a regular sexual partner, the proportions were 99% for both women and

*Why do you think researchers conducting the AARP study recruited higher numbers of Hispanic American, African American, and Asian American individuals than would be expected from their proportions in the population?*

men; that is, virtually all individuals engaged in some type of sexual behavior fairly frequently over the 6-month period. Table 14.2 presents the percentages for the various sexual behaviors for individuals overall, whereas Table 14.3 presents percentages for only those with a regular sexual partner. The proportions are very similar for women and men across the age groups among those with regular sexual partners.

However, when looking at all study participants, substantial gender differences exist. Having a regular sexual partner appears to be a more influential factor in the frequency of sexual behavior for women than men (AARP, 2005); the important role of being in an ongoing relationship has been documented in other studies as well (Laumann, Gagnon, Michael, & Michaels, 1994; Marsiglio & Donnelly, 1991). In addition, the proportion of people engaging in sexual activity decreased with age for both women and men in the AARP study (AARP, 2005). Other studies have likewise found similar declines related to age (Edwards & Booth, 1994; Marsiglio & Donnelly, 1991; Matthias, Lubben, Atchison, & Schweitzer, 1997).

How much of a decrease in sexual behavior is typical? Another high-quality study conducted by Call, Sprecher, and Schwartz (1995) provides a bird's-eye view of the issue in examining over 7,500 married and cohabiting individuals over the age of 19. The information was based on the 1988 National Survey of Families

| TABLE 14.2 | Proportions of Individuals 45 Years and Older Overall Engaging in Five Sexual Behaviors Once a Week or More in the Past 6 Months |
| --- | --- |

|  | Gender | | Female | | | | Male | | | |
|  | | | Age in years | | | | Age in years | | | |
| Type of behavior | Female | Male | 45-49 | 50-59 | 60-69 | 70+ | 45-49 | 50-59 | 60-69 | 70+ |
| --- | --- | --- | --- | --- | --- | --- | --- | --- | --- | --- |
| Kissing or hugging | 62 | 76 | 73 | 69 | 58 | 49 | 83 | 83 | 73 | 64 |
| Sexual touching or caressing | 46 | 61 | 60 | 57 | 41 | 27 | 68 | 67 | 54 | 54 |
| Sexual intercourse | 31 | 41 | 46 | 43 | 24 | 14 | 54 | 49 | 36 | 22 |
| Self-stimulation | 8 | 34 | 16 | 11 | 3 | 3 | 55 | 36 | 28 | 15 |
| Oral sex | 10 | 19 | 23 | 10 | 7 | 2 | 24 | 26 | 15 | 8 |

Note: The numbers for the sexual behaviors are percentages. The overall number of respondents was 1,554, with 809 women and 743 men.

From Montenegro, X. P., Sexuality at midlife and beyond: 2004 update of attitudes and behaviors. Retrieved September 15, 2005, from http://www.aarp.org/research/family/lifestyles/2004_sexuality.html. Reprinted with permission.

| TABLE 14.3 | Proportions of Individuals 45 Years and Older With a Regular Sexual Partner Engaging in Five Sexual Behaviors Once a Week or More in the Past 6 Months |
| --- | --- |

|  | Gender | | Female | | | | Male | | | |
|  | | | Age in years | | | | Age in years | | | |
| Type of behavior | Female | Male | 45-49 | 50-59 | 60-69 | 70+ | 45-49 | 50-59 | 60-69 | 70+ |
| --- | --- | --- | --- | --- | --- | --- | --- | --- | --- | --- |
| Kissing or hugging | 86 | 89 | 84 | 88 | 83 | 89 | 90 | 91 | 87 | 85 |
| Sexual touching or caressing | 70 | 74 | 71 | 76 | 63 | 63 | 75 | 74 | 71 | 77 |
| Sexual intercourse | 48 | 50 | 54 | 57 | 38 | 34 | 59 | 54 | 46 | 34 |
| Self-stimulation | 9 | 34 | 14 | 10 | 4 | 5 | 57 | 32 | 26 | 14 |
| Oral sex | 15 | 23 | 29 | 14 | 11 | 5 | 25 | 28 | 19 | 12 |

Note: The numbers for the sexual behaviors are percentages. The overall number of respondents was 1,068, with 498 women and 568 men.

From Montenegro, X. P., Sexuality at midlife and beyond: 2004 update of attitudes and behaviors. Retrieved September 15, 2005, from http://www.aarp.org/research/family/lifestyles/2004_sexuality.html. Reprinted with permission.

and Households. The frequency of sexual behavior was around 12 times a month for couples in the 19- to 24-year-old group, 5 times a month for those in the 50–54 group, and 2 times a month in the 65–69 group. Taking into account the independent effect of various factors that might relate to sexual frequency, only the age of the individual emerged as the single significant characteristic accounting for how frequently couples engaged in sex.

Physical health appears to be an important factor determining whether sexual interaction occurs at all for couples, but a connection between health and how *frequently* couples engage in sex has not been consistently found across studies. It may be that, for heterosexual couples, the health of the man is fairly important in determining the frequency of sexual behavior, specifically because problems of getting and maintaining erections are likely to limit sexual behavior for the couple (Burgess, 2004).

Kissing, hugging, and sexual touching are the most common behaviors engaged in very frequently (once a week or more often), according to the AARP study (AARP, 2005). Sexual intercourse occurs frequently for moderate proportions of the respondents (more than 50%), particularly for those in the two younger age groups and those with regular sexual partners (see Tables 14.2 and 14.3). The percentages of women engaging in self-stimulation (masturbation) once a week or more are fairly low at all age groups (16% or less), regardless of having a regular sexual partner or not. This is generally true for men as well, except for those in the 40- to 49-year-old group; the percentage engaging in masturbation once a week or more was around 55% for men in the youngest group, whereas it was 36% or less in the oldest groups. The proportions of individuals engaging in oral sex once a week or more were fairly similar for women and men (30% or lower), regardless of having a regular sexual partner or not; however, the percentages declined with age.

Of those individuals engaging in penile–vaginal intercourse in the previous 6 months, the majority always or usually experienced an orgasm. For men at all age groups, 85% usually or always experienced an orgasm; for women at the two younger age groups, the proportions were greater than 70%, and somewhat smaller for the two older groups. Approximately half of both women and men indicated that they are extremely or somewhat satisfied with their sex life. However, the proportions are somewhat higher for individuals in the three youngest groups, and 40% for both women and men in the over 70 group. Other research has likewise shown that middle-aged and older adults are generally sexually satisfied,

*What factors do you think are significant in affecting the frequency of sexual behavior among middle-age and senior individuals? How important to their life satisfaction do you think sexuality is?*

Few recent studies exist regarding the sexuality of older lesbians. Research on older gay men indicates that, for the most part, sexual patterns are similar to those found for older heterosexual men.

even to some extent with relatively low levels of sexual frequency (Burgess, 2004). However, higher levels of sexual activity and better mental health are both related to greater sexual satisfaction.

Virtually no studies have been conducted on older lesbian, gay male, or bisexual individuals, certainly none based on large numbers of people. The research that does exist tends to address issues of sexual identity and coping with the negative social climate for lesbians, gay men, and bisexuals. Furthermore, research concerning lesbians is less likely to focus on actual sexual behavior, often more concerned instead with relationship issues rather than sexuality itself (Burgess, 2004).

One of the few studies providing information about sexual behavior is a national sample of 100 lesbians over the age of 60, although it was conducted almost two decades ago (Kehoe, 1988). Trends may have changed somewhat for lesbian women since that time. In this study, only 18% of the women reported having sex in the past week, and only 21% said that they had sex once a month or more. Moreover, more than 50% of the women had not engaged in sex with another woman in the previous year (in a later study, far fewer lesbians—26%—reported that they were celibate; Sang, 1993). Despite this low level of sexual activity, 33% indicated that they were somewhat or very satisfied with the sex they had had over the previous year. The lack of correlation between sexual frequency and satisfaction is consistent with findings found for heterosexuals in other studies, particularly heterosexual women.

Several studies have examined sexuality patterns of midlife and older gay men. In a study of 112 men who were 40 and older (Berger, 1996), 61% engaged in sexual behavior once a week or more, a rate substantially higher than that for heterosexual men. Around 50% of the men reported satisfaction with their sex lives, which was further associated with greater life satisfaction in general. Nonetheless, sexual frequency declines with age for gay men as well. For example, in a study of older Chicago gay men (Pope & Schulz, 1990), 81% of those between 40 and 49 engaged in sex once a week or more, whereas 43% of men older than 60 had sex that frequently. The percentage is similar to that found in the AARP study (AARP, 2005) for heterosexual men between 60 and 69 regarding penile–vaginal sex, specifically 36%. The proportion of 70- to 79-year-old heterosexual men engaging in penile–vaginal intercourse once a week or more, however, was much smaller (22%). With respect to gay men involved in relationships in particular, Dutch couples who had been together longer engaged in sex less frequently than those who had been together for a shorter time (Deenen, Gijs, & van Naerssen, 1994).

These various studies indicate that, despite traditional stereotypes of the senior years as a period of virtual absence of sexual pleasure, sexuality is in fact a relatively important aspect of the lives of individuals in their middle to advanced years. Some decline does occur. Yet individuals engage in a variety of sexual behaviors and obtain substantial pleasure and gratification from their sexual relationships. Quality of health has a noticeable impact on aspects of sexuality in the middle to later years. However, overall people see themselves in a sexually vibrant way during this period, and generally continue to enjoy sexuality into their senior years as well.

In fact, it is very likely that being sexually active is a positive influence on individuals' psychological and physical well-being. Sexual involvement may actually protect against declines usually associated with increasing age (Bortz & Wallace, 1999; Burgess, 2004; Edwards & Booth, 1994; Trudel, Turgeon, & Piche, 2000). Greater sexual activity has been found to be associated with longer life for individuals between 45 and 90 years old (Palmore, 1982; Smith, Frankel, & Yarnell, 1997). Likewise, at least for women, greater frequency of orgasm over the course of their married lives is associated with living longer (Seldin, Friedman, & Martin, 2002). All in all, the outlook for sexuality throughout one's adult life is very good.

# *Summary*

Three challenges involving sexuality critical to adulthood are (a) establishing sexual orientation, (b) forging intimacy and making commitments, and (c) integrating love and sex. Estimates of the proportion of the population that identifies as lesbian or gay vary from 4% to 17% in early research. More recent representative research places the proportion identifying as lesbian as 1.4% and identifying as gay as 2.8%. Somewhere between 83% and 98% of people in various studies identify themselves as having a heterosexual orientation.

In terms of establishing a family, most heterosexual couples eventually have at least one child. A larger proportion of legally married couples are intentionally remaining childless. Birth control is any method of preventing birth from occurring, which includes techniques for preventing conception (fertilization of an egg) and techniques for preventing or ending pregnancy once conception has occurred. Contraception is any method of preventing conception, with most currently available methods proving extremely effective. Most abortions (88%) are conducted within the first trimester, 59% before the first 9 weeks. Very little risk is associated with abortion, with fewer than 1% of women experiencing major complications. The vast majority of women do not experience the psychological difficulties proposed to occur by critics, with only 0.5% to 15% suffering problems.

The primary motivations to have children are the perceived benefits, and lack of costs, associated with having children. About half of all pregnancies are not specifically planned. Alternative insemination (artificial insemination) is the process of impregnating a woman through technical procedures rather than through penile–vaginal intercourse. Adoption is a legal process in which the legal rights of birth parents are ended so that the adopting parents obtain complete legal responsibility for a child or children. Heterosexual couples typically adopt only after pursuing strategies to conceive their own children. Gay men and lesbians may perceive adoption as their primary or only means of creating a family, despite legal systems and social workers that are biased against such adoptions.

By the last trimester, more than 75% of pregnant women feel decreased sexual desire, and more than 80% report a decline in frequency of penile–vaginal intercourse. These lower levels of desire and intercourse continue after the birth of the child, with pleasure and desire rebounding only gradually. After birth, relationship satisfaction, sexual desire, intercourse frequency, and sexual satisfaction all remain at lower levels than before pregnancy for a period of time. Diminished relationship satisfaction continues for at least several years after childbirth, although ironically the probability of divorce decreases during this time. Evidence suggests that conflict in the parent–adolescent relationship adversely affects the quality of marital relationships. Challenges to the relationship continue until the children grow up and leave home.

Two monumental studies focused exclusively on individuals 45 and older have been conducted by AARP in 1999 and 2004. Participants overwhelmingly indicated that sexuality is important to their happiness, that they enjoy sex, and that they believe that sex is not only for younger people. A large majority of women and virtually all men indicated that they engaged in at least one of five sexual activities once a week or more frequently in the previous six months; these sexual activities are kissing or hugging, sexual touching, sexual intercourse, oral sex, and masturbation. Across all participants, approximately half indicated that they are extremely or somewhat satisfied with their sex life.

## Chapter 14 Critical Thinking Exercises

1. Sexual orientation identity

   The idea that heterosexual individuals have a sexual orientation identity may be quite difficult for many to understand or accept. This may be because many heterosexuals are often not confronted with challenges to their sexual orientation. Society at large and those who are heterosexual simply assume that virtually everyone is heterosexual. Most people are given the benefit of the doubt and many departures from expectations about heterosexuality are dismissed as unimportant. What do you think are the most critical characteristics and roles that define heterosexuality for individuals as their sexual orientation identity is developing?

2. Family

   Becoming pregnant and giving birth substantially reduces sexual desire and satisfaction, as well as relationship satisfaction, for a period of months following birth. What factors do you think might contribute to, or worsen, this decline in sexual and relationship satisfaction? What factors might reduce the problems and improve the quality of the couple's relationship and life?

3. Midlife and beyond

   Research indicates that sexuality remains an important aspect of individuals' lives in older adulthood, relatively more so for those who have a regular sexual partner. Why do you suppose that importance is related to having a regular sexual partner? Would you draw the conclusion that having a partner increases the importance of sexuality, or would you say that importance increases the likelihood of having a regular sexual partner? Why would having a regular sexual partner have a greater effect on frequency of sexual behavior for women than men?

Visit www.sagepub.com/hillhsstudy.com for online activities, sample tests, and other helpful resources. Select "Chapter 14: Adulthood: Challenges and Decisions" for chapter-specific activities.

# References

AARP. (2002). *Tracking study of the baby boomers in midlife.* Washington, DC: Author.

AARP. (2005). *Sexuality at midlife and beyond: 2004 update of attitudes and behaviors.* Retrieved February 13, 2007, from http://www.aarp.org/research/family/lifestyles/2004_sexuality.html

Adams, J. M., & Jones, W. H. (1997). The conceptualization of marital commitment: An integrative analysis. *Journal of Personality and Social Psychology, 72,* 1177–1196.

Adorno, T. W., Frenkel-Brunswick, E., Levison, D. J., & Sanford, R. N. (1950). *The authoritarian personality.* New York: Harper & Row.

Ågmo, A. (2003). Unconditioned sexual incentive motivation in the male Norway rat (Rattus norvegicus). *Journal of Comparative Psychology, 117,* 3–14.

Ågmo, A., & Ellingsen, E. (2003). Relevance of non-human animal studies to the understanding of human sexuality. *Scandinavian Journal of Psychology, 44,* 293–301.

Ahlborg, T., Dahlöf, L., & Hallberg, L. R.-M. (2005). Quality of the intimate and sexual relationship in first-time parents six months after delivery. *The Journal of Sex Research, 42,* 167–174.

Ahlborg, T., Strandmark, M., & Dahlöf, L. (2000). First-time parents' sexual relationships. *Scandinavian Journal of Sexology, 3,* 127–139.

Ainsworth, M. D. S., Blehar, M. C., Waters, E., & Wall, S. (1978). *Patterns of attachment: A psychological study of the strange situation.* Hillsdale, NJ: Erlbaum.

Alan Guttmacher Institute. (1999). *Sharing responsibility: Women, society and abortion worldwide.* New York: Author.

Alan Guttmacher Institute. (2004). *Get "in the know": 20 questions about pregnancy, contraception and abortion.* Retrieved March 12, 2007, from http://www.guttmacher.org/in-the-know/index.html

Alan Guttmacher Institute. (2006). *Facts on induced abortion in the United States.* Retrieved March 12, 2007, from http://www.guttmacher.org/pubs/fb_induced_abortion.pdf

Albino Gilbert, L., & Rader, J. (2001). Current perspectives on women's adult roles: Work, family, and life. In R. K. Unger (Ed.), *Handbook of the psychology of women and gender* (pp. 156–169). New York: Wiley.

Alexander, M. G., & Fisher, T. D. (2003). Truth and consequences: Using the bogus pipeline to examine sex differences in self-reported sexuality. *The Journal of Sex Research, 40,* 27–35.

Allen, E. S., & Baucom, D. H. (2004). Adult attachment and patterns of extradyadic involvement. *Family Process, 43,* 467–488.

Allport, G. W. (1937). *Personality: A psychological interpretation.* New York: Holt, Rinehart, & Winston.

Allyn, D. (2000). *The sexual revolution: An unfettered history.* Boston: Little, Brown.

Almeida, D., & Horn, M. (2004). Is daily life more stressful during middle adulthood? In O. G. Brim, C. D. Ryff, & R. Kessler (Eds.), *How healthy are we: A national study of wellbeing in midlife* (pp. 425–451). Chicago: University of Chicago Press.

Amato, P. R., & Rogers, S. J. (1997). A longitudinal study of marital problems and subsequent divorce. *Journal of Marriage and the Family, 59,* 612–624.

American Psychiatric Association. (1994). *Diagnostic and statistical manual of mental disorders: DSM-IV* (4th ed.). Washington, DC: Author.

American Psychological Association. (1992). Ethical principles of psychologists and code of conduct. *American Psychologist, 47,* 1597–1611.

American Psychological Association (1998). *Answers to your questions about sexual orientation and homosexuality* [Brochure]. Washington, DC: Author.

Amick, A. E., & Calhoun, K. S. (1987). Resistance to sexual aggression: Personality, attitudinal, and situational factors. *Archives of Sexual Behavior, 16,* 153–163.

Andersen, B. L., & Cyranowski, J. M. (1994). Women's sexual self-schema. *Journal of Personality and Social Psychology, 67,* 1079–1100.

Andersen, B. L., Cyranowski, J. M., & Aarestad, S. (2000). Beyond artificial, sex-linked distinctions to conceptualize female sexuality: Comment on Baumester (2000). *Psychological Bulletin, 126,* 380–384.

Andersen, B. L., Cyranowski, J. M., & Espindle, D. (1999). Men's sexual self-schema. *Journal of Personality and Social Psychology, 76,* 645–661.

Andersen, S. M. (1984). Self-knowledge and social inference: II. The diagnosticity of cognitive/affective and behavioral data. *Journal of Personality and Social Psychology, 46,* 294–307.

Andersen, S. M., & Bem, S. L. (1981). Sex typing and androgyny in dyadic interaction: Individual differences in responsiveness to physical attractiveness. *Journal of Personality and Social Psychology, 41,* 74–86.

Andersen, S. M., & Ross, L. D. (1984). Self-knowledge and social inference: I. The impact of cognitive/affective and behavioral data. *Journal of Personality and Social Psychology, 46,* 280–293.

Anderson, A., Russell, C., & Schumm, W. (1983). Perceived marital quality and family life cycle categories: A further analysis. *Journal of Marriage and the Family, 45,* 127–139.

Andersson, T., & Magnusson, D. (1990). Biological maturation in adolescence and the development of drinking habits and alcohol abuse among young males: A prospective longitudinal study. *Journal of Youth and Adolescence, 19,* 33–41.

Appiah, K. A. (1999). Why there are no races. In L. Harris (Ed.), *Racism: Key concepts in critical theory* (pp. 267–277). Amherst, NY: Humanity Books.

Archibald, A. B., Graber, J. A., & Brooks-Gunn, J. (2003). Pubertal processes and physiological growth in adolescence. In G. R. Adams & M. D. Berzonsky (Eds.), *Blackwell handbook of adolescence* (pp. 24–47). Malden, MA: Blackwell Publishing.

Armor, D. A., & Taylor, S. E. (1998). Situated optimism: Specific outcome expectancies and self-regulation. In M. P. Zanna (Ed.), *Advances in experimental social psychology* (Vol. 30, pp. 309–379). San Diego, CA: Academic Press.

Arnett, J. J. (2001). *Adolescence and emerging adulthood: A cultural approach.* Upper Saddle River, NJ: Prentice Hall.

Aron, A., & Aron, E. (1991). Love and sexuality. In K. McKinney & S. Sprecher (Eds.), *Sexuality in close relationships* (pp. 25–48). Hillsdale, NJ: Erlbaum.

Aron, A., & Aron, E. N. (1986). *Love and the expansion of self: Understanding attraction and satisfaction.* New York: Hemisphere.

Aron, A., & Henkemeyer, L. (1995). Marital satisfaction and passionate love. *Journal of Social and Personal Relationships, 12,* 139–146.

Aron, A., & Rodriguez, G. (1992, July 25). *Scenarios of falling in love among Mexican-, Chinese-, and Anglo-Americans.* Paper presented at the Sixth International Conference on Personal Relationships, Orono, ME.

Aron, A., & Westbay, L. (1996). Dimensions of the prototype of love. *Journal of Personality and Social Psychology, 70,* 535–551.

Aronson, E., Wilson, T. D., & Akert, R. M. (2005). *Social psychology.* Upper Saddle River, NJ: Pearson Education.

Arriaga, X. B. (2001). The ups and downs of dating: Fluctuations in satisfaction in newly formed romantic relationships. *Journal of Personality and Social Psychology, 80,* 754–765.

Arriaga, X. B., & Agnew, C. R. (2001). Being committed: Affective, cognitive, and conative components of relationship commitment. *Personality and Social Psychology Bulletin, 27,* 1190–1203.

Arriga, X. B., & Rusbult, C. E. (1998). Standing in my partner's shoes: Partner perspective taking and reactions to accommodative dilemmas. *Personality and Social Psychology Bulletin, 24,* 927–948.

Atkins, D. C., Baucom, D. H., & Jacobson, N. S. (2001). Understanding infidelity: Correlates in a national random sample. *Journal of Family Psychology, 15,* 735–749.

Atkinson, J. W. (1966). Motivational determinants of risk-taking behavior. In J. W. Atkinson & N. T. Feather (Eds.), *A theory of achievement motivation* (pp. 11–29). New York: Wiley.

Attie, I., & Brooks-Gunn, J. (1989). Development of eating problems in adolescent girls: A longitudinal study. *Developmental Psychology, 25,* 70–79.

Augstein, H. F. (1996). Introduction. In H. F. Augstein (Ed.), *Race: The origins of an idea, 1760–1850* (pp. ix–xxxiii). Bristol, England: Thoemmes Press.

Bailey, J. M., & Pillard, R. C. (1995). Genetics of human sexual orientation. *Archives of General Psychiatry, 48,* 1089–1096.

Bancroft, J. (1988). Sexual desire and the brain. *Sexual and Marital Therapy, 3,* 11–27.

Bandura, A. (1971). *Social learning theory.* New York: General Learning Press.

Bandura, A. (1977). *Social learning theory.* Englewood Cliffs, NJ: Prentice Hall.

Bandura, A. (1982). Self-efficacy mechanism in human agency. *American Psychologist, 37,* 122–147.

Barlow, D. H. (2002). *Anxiety and its disorders: The nature and treatment of anxiety and panic* (2nd ed.) New York: Guilford.

Barlow, D. H., Sakheim, D. K., & Beck, J. G. (1983). Anxiety increases sexual arousal. *Journal of Abnormal Psychology, 92,* 49–54.

Barnard College Student Health Services. (2005). *Emergency contraception: What can I do if I had unprotected intercourse?* Retrieved February 14, 2007, from http://www.barnard.edu/health/morningafterpill.htm#pregrisk

Barnes, G. E., Malamuth, N. M., & Check, J. V. P. (1984). Personality and sexuality. *Personality and Individual Differences, 5,* 159–172.

Barnett, R. C., & Rivers, C. (1996). *She works/He works: How two-income families are happier, healthier, and better off.* New York: HarperCollins.

Bartell, G. D. (1971). *Group sex: A scientist's eyewitness report on the American way of swinging.* New York: P. H. Wyden.

Barth, R. P., Fetro, J. V., Leland, N., & Volkan, K. (1992). Preventing adolescent pregnancy with social and cognitive skills. *Journal of Adolescent Research, 7,* 208–232.

Bartholomew, K., & Horowitz, L. M. (1991). Attachment styles among young adults: A test of a four category model. *Journal of Personality and Social Psychology, 61,* 226–244.

Basow, S. A. (1992). Gender stereotypes and roles. (3rd ed.) Pacific Grove, CA: Brooks/Cole

Baumeister, R. F. (2000). Gender differences in erotic plasticity: The female sex drive as socially flexible and responsive. *Psychological Bulletin, 126,* 347–374.

Baumeister, R. F., & Bratslavsky, E. (1999). Passion, intimacy and time: Passionate love as a function of change in intimacy. *Personality and Social Psychology Review, 3,* 49–67.

Baumeister, R. F., & Wotman, S. R. (1992). *Breaking hearts: The two sides of unrequited love.* New York: Guilford.

Bauserman, R., & Davis, C. (1996). Perceptions of early sexual experiences and adult sexual adjustment. *Journal of Psychology & Human Sexuality, 8,* 37–58.

Becker, M. A., & Byrne, D. (1985). Self-regulated exposure to erotica, recall errors, and subjective reactions as a function of erotophobia and type A coronary-prone behavior. *Journal of Personality and Social Psychology, 48,* 135–151.

Belsky, J. (1990). Children and marriage. In J. Fincham & T. Bradsury (Eds.), *The psychology of marriage: Basic issues and applications* (pp. 172–200). New York: Guilford.

Bem, D. J. (1972). Self-perception theory. In L. Berkowitz (Ed.), *Advances in experimental social psychology* (Vol. 6, pp. 1–62). New York: Academic Press.

Bem, S. L. (1989). Genital knowledge and gender constancy in preschool children. *Child Development, 60,* 649–662.

Benda, B. B., & DiBlasio, F. A. (1994). An integration of theory: Adolescent sexual contacts. *Journal of Youth and Adolescence, 23,* 403–420.

Berger, R. M. (1996). *Gay and gray: The older homosexual man* (2nd ed.). New York: Haworth.

Bernal, G., Trimble, J. E., Burlew, A. K., & Leong, F. T. L. (2003). Introduction: The psychological study of racial and ethnic minority psychology. In G. Bernal, J. E. Trimble, A. K. Burlew, & F. T. L. Leong (Eds.), *Handbook of racial and ethnic minority psychology* (pp. 1–12). Thousand Oaks, CA: Sage Publications.

Berry, D. S. (1995). Beyond beauty and after affect: An event perception approach to perceiving faces. In R. A. Eder (Ed.), *Craniofacial anomalies: Psychological perspectives* (pp. 14–29). New York: Springer-Verlag.

Berscheid, E. (1994). Interpersonal relationships. *Annual Review of Psychology, 45,* 79–129.

Berscheid, E., & Meyers, S. A. (1996). A social categorical approach to a question about love. *Personal Relationships, 3,* 19–43.

Berscheid, E., & Reis, H. T. (1998). Attraction and close relationships. In D. T. Gilbert, S. T. Fiske, & G. Lindzey (Eds.), *The handbook of social psychology* (4th ed., Vol. 2, pp. 193–281). New York: McGraw-Hill.

Berscheid, E., & Walster, E. (1974). A little bit about love. In T. L. Huston (Ed.), *Foundations of interpersonal attraction* (pp. 355–381). New York: Academic Press.

Betzing, L. (1989). Causes of conjugal dissolution: A cross-cultural study. *Cultural Anthropology, 30,* 676–694.

Billy, J. O., Tanfer, K., Grady, W. R., & Klepinger, D. H. (1993). The sexual behavior of men in the United States. *Family Planning Perspectives, 25,* 52–60.

Bindra, D. (1968). Neuropsychological interpretation of the effects of drive and incentive-motivation on general activity and instrumental behavior. *Psychological Review, 75,* 1–22.

Bindra, D. (1974). A motivational view of learning, performance, and behavior modification. *Psychological Review 81,* 199–213.

Bjorntorp, P. (1988). The association between obesity, adipose tissue distribution and disease. *Acta Medica Scandinavica, 723,* 121–134 (supplement).

Blanchard, R. (2001). Fraternal birth order and the maternal immune hypothesis of male homosexuality. *Hormones and Behavior, 40,* 105–114.

Block, J. (1971). *Lives through time.* Berkeley, CA: Bancroft Books.

Blow, A. J., & Hartnett, K. (2005). Infidelity in committed relationships II: A substantive review. *Journal of Marital and Family Therapy, 31,* 217–233.

Blum, R. W., Beuhring, T., Shew, M. L., Bearinger, L. H., Sieving, R. E., & Resnick, M. D. (2000). The effects of race/ethnicity, income, and family structure on adolescent risk behaviors. *American Journal of Public Health, 90,* 1879–1884.

Blumstein, P., & Schwartz, P. (1983). *American couples: Money, work, sex.* New York: William Morrow.

Bogaert, A. F., & Hershberger, S. (1999). The relation between sexual orientation and penile size. *Archives of Sexual Behavior, 28,* 213–221.

Bogaert, A. F., & Sadava, S. (2002). Adult attachment and sexual behavior. *Personal Relationships, 9,* 191–204.

Bolin, A. (1998). Transcending and transgendering: Male-to-female transsexuals, dichotomy, and diversity. In D. Denny (Ed.), *Current concepts in transgender identity* (pp. 63–96). New York: Garland Publishing.

Boloji.com. (2006). *Help! My child has become a teenager.* Retrieved February 14, 2007, from http://www.boloji.com/parenting/00227.htm

Bortz, W. M., & Wallace, D. H. (1999). Physical fitness, aging, and sexuality. *Western Journal of Medicine, 170,* 167–169.

Bowlby, J. (1969). *Attachment and loss. Vol. 1, Attachment.* New York: Basic Books.

Bowlby, J. (1973). *Attachment and loss, Vol. 2, Separation: Anxiety and anger.* New York: Basic Books.

Branje, S. J. T., van Lieshout, C. F. M., & van Aken, M. A. G. (2004). Relations between Big Five personality characteristics and perceived support in adolescents' families. *Journal of Personality and Social Psychology, 86,* 615–628.

Breakwell, G. M., & Millward, L. J. (1997). Sexual self-concept and sexual risk-taking. *Journal of Adolescence, 20,* 29–41.

Brecher, E. L. (1984). *Sex and aging: A Consumers' Union report.* Boston: Little, Brown.

Brehm, S. (1988). Passionate love. In R. J. Sternberg & M. Barnes (Eds.), *The psychology of love* (pp. 232–263). New Haven, CT: Yale University Press.

Brennan, K. A., Clark, C. L., & Shaver, P. R. (1998). Self-report measurement of adult attachment: An integrative view. In J. Simpson & W. S. Rholes (Eds.), *Attachment theory and close relationships* (pp. 46–76). New York: Guilford.

Brewster, K. L. (1994). Race differences in sexual activity among adolescent women: The role of neighborhood characteristics. *American Sociological Review, 59,* 408–424.

Bristow, J. (1997). *Sexuality.* London New York: Routledge.

Brooks-Gunn, J., & Reiter, E. O. (1990). The role of pubertal processes. In S. S. Feldman & G. R. Elliott (Eds.), *At the threshold: The developing adolescent* (pp. 16–53). Cambridge, MA: Harvard University Press.

Brooks-Gunn, J., & Ruble, D. (1982). The development of menstrual related beliefs and behaviors during early-adolescence. *Child Development, 53,* 1567–1577.

Brown, S. E. (2000). Movie stars and sensuous scars. In K. Kay, J. Nagle, & B. Gould (Eds.), *Male lust: Pleasure, power, and transformation* (pp. 37–42). New York: Harrington Park Press.

Browning, C. R., Leventhal, T., & Brooks-Gunn, J. (2004). Neighborhood context and racial differences in early adolescent sexual activity. *Demography, 41,* 697–720.

Buck, R. (1988). *Human motivation and emotion.* New York: Wiley.

Bullough, B., & Bullough, V. (1997). Are transvestites necessarily heterosexual? *Archives of Sexual Behavior, 26,* 1–12.

Bullough, V. L., & Brundage, J. A. (1994). *Sexual practices and the medieval church.* Amherst, NY: Prometheus Books.

Bullough, V. L., & Bullough, B. (1977). *Sin, sickness, and sanity.* New York: Garland Publishing.

Bullough, V. L., & Bullough, B. (1995). *Sexual attitudes: Myths and realities.* Amherst, NY: Prometheus Books.

Burgess, E. O. (2004). Sexuality in midlife and later life couples. In J. H. Harvey, A. Wenzel, & S. Sprecher (Eds.), *The handbook of sexuality in close relationships* (pp. 437–454). Mahwah, NJ: Erlbaum.

Burnham, M. R., Hough, R. L., Karno, M., Escobar, J. I., & Telles, C. A. (1987). Acculturation and lifetime prevalence of psychiatric disorders among Mexican Americans in Los Angeles. *Journal of Health and Social Behavior, 28,* 89–102.

Burns, A. (1984). Perceived causes of marriage breakdown and conditions of life. *Journal of Marriage and the Family, 46,* 551–562.

Burt, M. R. (1980). Cultural myths and supports for rape. *Journal of Personality and Social Psychology, 38,* 217–230.

Burt, M. R. (1983). Justifying personal violence: A comparison of rapists and the general public. *Victimology, 8,* 131–150.

Buss, D. M., Abbott, M., Angleitner, A., Asherian, A., Biaggio, A., Blanco-Villasenor, A., et al. (1990). International preferences in selecting mates: A study of 37 cultures. *Journal of Cross-Cultural Psychology, 21,* 5–47.

Buss, D. M., & Schmitt, D. P. (1993). Sexual strategies theory: An evolutionary perspective on human mating. *Psychological Review, 100,* 204–232.

Buss, D. M., Shackelford, T. K., Choe, J., Buunk, B. P., & Dijkstra, P. (2000). Distress about mating rivals. *Personal Relationships, 7,* 235–243.

Buunk, B. P. (1987). Conditions that promote breakups as a consequence of extradyadic involvements. *Journal of Social and Clinical Psychology, 5,* 271–284.

Buunk, B. P. (1997). Personality, birth order, and attachment styles as related to various types of jealousy. *Personality and Individual Differences, 23,* 997–1006.

Buunk, B. P., & Dijkstra, P. (2000). Extradyadic relationships and jealousy. In C. Hendrick & S. S. Hendrick (Eds.), *Close relationships: A sourcebook* (pp. 317–329). Thousand Oaks, CA: Sage Publications.

Buzwell, S., & Rosenthal, D. (1996). Constructing a sexual self: Adolescents' sexual self-perceptions and sexual risk-taking. *Journal of Research in Adolescence, 6,* 489–513.

Byers, E. S., Demmons, S., & Lawrance, K. (1998). Sexual satisfaction within dating relationships: A test of the interpersonal exchange model of sexual satisfaction. *Journal of Social and Personal Relationships, 15,* 257–267.

Byrne, D. (1977). Social psychology and the study of sexual behavior. *Personality and Social Psychology Bulletin, 1,* 3–30.

Byrne, D. (1982). Predicting human sexual behavior. In A. G. Kraut (Ed.), *The G. Stanley Hall lecture series* (Vol. 2, pp. 211–254). Washington, DC: American Psychological Association.

Byrne, D. (1983a). The antecedents, correlates, and consequents of erotophobia–erotophilia. In C. Davis (Ed.), *Challenges in sexual science: Current theoretical issues and research advances* (pp. 53–75). Philadelphia: Society for the Scientific Study of Sex.

Byrne, D. (1983b). Sex without contraception. In D. Byrne & W. A. Fisher (Eds.), *Adolescents, sex, and contraception* (pp. 3–30). Hillsdale, NJ: Erlbaum.

Byrne, D., & Schulte, L. (1990). Personality dispositions as mediators of sexual responses. *Annual Review of Sex Research, 1,* 93–117.

Cain, V. S., Johannes, C. B., Avis, N. E., Mohr, B., Schocken, M., Skurnick, J., et al. (2003). Sexual functioning and practices in a multi-ethnic study of midlife women: Baseline results from SWAN. *The Journal of Sex Research, 40,* 266–276.

Call, V., Sprecher, S., & Schwartz, P. (1995). The incidence and frequency of marital sex in a national sample. *Journal of Marriage and the Family, 57,* 639–652.

Canary, D. J., & Hause, K. S. (1993). Is there any reason to research sex differences in communication? *Communication Quarterly, 41,* 129–144.

Cantwell, C., & Kawanami, H. (2002). Buddhism. In L. Woodhead, P. Fletcher, H. Kawanami, & D. Smith (Eds.), *Religions in the modern world: Traditions and transformations* (pp. 41–69). New York: Routledge.

Carroll, J. L., Volk, K. D., & Hyde, J. S. (1985). Differences between males and females in motives for engaging in sexual intercourse. *Archives of Sexual Behavior, 14,* 131–139.

Carver, C. S., & Scheier, M. F. (2000). *Perspectives on personality* (4th ed.). Boston: Allyn & Bacon.

Caspi, A. (1987). Personality in the life course. *Journal of Personality and Social Psychology, 6,* 1203–1213.

Cassell Publishers Limited. (1993). *Sex and sexuality: A thematic dictionary of quotations.* London: Author.

Cate, R. M., Lloyd, S. A., Henton, J. M., & Larson, J. H. (1982). Fairness and reward level as predictors of relationship satisfaction. *Social Psychology Quarterly, 45,* 177–181.

Centers for Disease Control and Prevention. (1996, February). *Condoms and their use in preventing HIV infection and other STDs.* Retrieved March 12, 2007, from http://www.aegis.org/files/cdc/FactSheets/1996/condoms.pdf

Centers for Disease Control and Prevention. (2000). Youth risk behavior surveillance—United States, 1999. *Morbidity and Mortality Weekly Report, 49* (No. SS-5). Retrieved March 12, 2007, from http://www.cdc.gov/mmwR/preview/mmwrhtml/ss4905a1.htm#top

Centers for Disease Control and Prevention. (2005). *Trends in reportable sexually transmitted diseases in the United States, 2005.* Retrieved February 18, 2007, from http://www.cdc.gov/std/stats/trends2005.htm

Chapman, B. E., & Brannock, J. C. (1987). Proposed model of lesbian identity development: An empirical examination. *Journal of Homosexuality, 14,* 69–80.

Charny, I. W., & Parnass, S. (1995). The impact of extramarital relationships on the continuation of marriages. *Journal of Sex & Marital Therapy, 21,* 101–115.

Chen, N. Y., Shaffer, D. R., & Wu, C. (1997). On physical attractiveness stereotyping in Taiwan: A revised sociocultural perspective. *Journal of Social Psychology, 137,* 117–124.

Cherry, F., & Byrne, D. (1977). Authoritarianism. In T. Blass (Ed.), *Personality variables in social behavior* (pp. 109–133). Hillsdale, NJ: Erlbaum.

Chilman, C. S. (1983). *Adolescent sexuality in a changing American society* (2nd ed.). New York: Wiley.

Chivers, M. L., Rieger, G., Latty, E., & Bailey, J. M. (2004). A sex difference in the specificity of sexual arousal. *Psychological Science, 15,* 736–744.

Choi, K. H., Catania, J. A., & Dolcini, M. M. (1994). Extramarital sex and HIV risk behavior among U.S. adults: Results from the National AIDS Behavioral Survey. *American Journal of Public Health, 84,* 2003–2007.

Choney, S. K., Berryhill-Paapke, E., & Robbins, R. R. (1995). The acculturation of American Indians: Developing frameworks for research and practice. In J. G. Ponterotto, J. M. Casas, L. A. Suzuki, & C. M. Alexander (Eds.), 1995 (pp. 73–92). Thousand Oaks, CA: Sage Publications.

Christensen, A., & Shenk, J. L. (1991). Communication, conflict, and psychological distance in nondistressed, clinic, and divorcing couples. *Journal of Consulting and Clinical Psychology, 59,* 458–463.

Christopher, C. F., & Sprecher, S. (2000). Sexuality in marriage, dating, and other relationships: A decade review. *Journal of Marriage and the Family, 62,* 999–1017.

Christopher, F. S. (2001). *To dance the dance: A symbolic interactional exploration of premarital sexuality.* Mahwah, NJ: Erlbaum.

Christopher, F. S., & Cate, R. M. (1985). Premarital sexual pathways and relationship development. *Journal of Social and Personal Relationships, 2,* 271–288.

Christopher, F. S., McQuaid, S., & Updegraff, K. (1998, June). *Dating relationships and men's sexual aggression: A test of a relationship-based model.* Paper presented at the biennial meeting of the International Society for the Study of Personal Relationships, Saratoga Springs, NY.

Christopher, F. S., Owens, L. A., & Stecker, H. L. (1993). Exploring the darkside of courtship: A test of a model of male premarital sexual aggressiveness. *Journal of Marriage and the Family, 55,* 469–479.

Clark, R. D. (1990). The impact of AIDS on gender differences in willingness to engage in casual sex. *Journal of Applied Social Psychology, 20,* 771–782.

Clark, R. D., & Hatfield, E. (1989). Gender differences in receptivity to sexual offers. *Journal of Psychology and Human Sexuality, 2,* 39–55.

Cochran, S. D., & Peplau, L. A. (1985). Value orientations in heterosexual relationships. *Psychology of Women Quarterly, 9,* 477–488.

Cohen, E. S., & Fromme, K. (2002). Differential determinants of young adult substance use and high-risk sexual behavior. *Journal of Applied Social Psychology, 32,* 1124–1150.

Cohen, J. (1977). *Statistical power analysis for the behavioral sciences.* San Diego, CA: Academic Press.

Cohen, L. L., & Shotland, R. L. (1996). Timing of first sexual intercourse in a relationship: Expectations, experiences, and perceptions of others. *The Journal of Sex Research, 33,* 291–299.

Coles, R., & Stokes, G. (1985). *Sex and the American teenager.* New York: Harper & Row.

Collins, W. A., & Sroufe, L. A. (1999). Capacity for intimate relationships: A developmental construction. In W. Furman, C. Feiring, & B. B. Brown (Eds.), *Contemporary perspectives on adolescent romantic relationships.* New York: Cambridge University Press.

Confession Junkie. (2006a). Retrieved February 14, 2007, from http://www.confessionjunkie.com/CA/conf.cfm/html/id=10770/Confession_10770.htm

Confession Junkie. (2006b). Retrieved February 14, 2007, from http://www.confessionjunkie.com/CA/conf.cfm/html/id=10787/Confession_10787.htm

Cooley, C. H. (1902). *Human nature and the social order.* New York: Scribner.

Coria, G. A., Haley, J. M., Manzo, J., Pacheco, P., & Pfaus, J. (2001, November). *Olfactory conditioned partner preference in the female rat.* Paper presented at the annual meeting of the Society for Neuroscience, San Diego, CA.

Cozzarelli, C., & Major, B. (1998). The impact of antiabortion activities on women seeking abortion. In L. J. Beckman & S. M. Harvey (Eds.), *The new civil war: The psychology, culture, and politics of abortion* (pp. 81–104). Washington, DC: American Psychological Association.

Crawford, M., & Unger, R. (2000). *Women and gender: A feminist psychology.* Boston: McGraw-Hill.

Crockett, L. J., Raffaelli, M., & Moilanen, K. L. (2003). Adolescent sexuality: Behavior and meaning. In G. R. Adams & M. D. Berzonsky (Eds.), *Blackwell handbook of adolescence* (pp. 371–392). Malden, MA: Blackwell.

Cronbach, L. J., & Meehl, P. E. (1955). Construct validity in psychological tests. *Psychological Bulletin, 52,* 281–302.

Cross, W. E., Jr. (1978). The Thomas and Cross models of psychological Nigrescence: A literature review. *Journal of Black Psychology, 4,* 13–31.

Cunningham, M. R. (1986). Measuring the physical in physical attractiveness: Quasi-experiments on the sociobiology of female facial beauty. *Journal of Personality and Social Psychology, 50,* 925–935.

Cunningham, M. R., Barbee, A. P., & Pike, C. L. (1990). What do women want? Facialmetric assessment of multiple motives in the perception of male facial physical attractiveness. *Journal of Personality and Social Psychology, 59,* 61–72.

Cunningham, M. R., Roberts, A. R., Barbee, A. P., Druen, P. B., & Wu, C. (1995). "Their ideas of beauty are, on the whole, the same as ours": Consistency and variability in the cross-cultural perception of female physical attractiveness. *Journal of Personality and Social Psychology, 68,* 261–279.

Cupach, W. R., & Comstock, J. (1990). Satisfaction with sexual communication in marriage: Links to sexual satisfaction and dyadic adjustment. *Journal of Social and Personal Relationships, 7,* 179–186.

Cupach, W. R., & Metts, S. (1991). Sexuality and communication in close relationships. In K. McKinney & S. Sprecher (Eds.), *Sexuality in close relationships* (pp. 93–110). Hillsdale, NJ: Erlbaum.

Cupach, W. R., & Metts, S. (1995). The role of sexual attitude similarity in romantic heterosexual relationships. *Personal Relationships, 2,* 287–300.

Cutler, G., & Loriaux, D. L. (1980). Adrenarche and its relationship to the onset of puberty. *Federation Proceedings, 39,* 2384–2390.

Cyranowski, J. M., & Andersen, B. L. (1998). Schemas, sexuality, and romantic attachment. *Journal of Personality and Social Psychology, 74,* 1364–1379.

D'Augelli, A. R. (1994). Lesbian and gay male development: Steps toward an analysis of lesbians' and gay men's lives. In B. Greene & G. M. Herek (Eds.), *Lesbian and gay psychology: Theory, research, and clinical applications. Psychological perspectives on lesbian and gay issues* (pp. 118–132). Thousand Oaks, CA: Sage Publications.

D'Augelli, A. R. (1998). Enhancing the development of lesbian, gay, and bisexual youths. In E. D. Rothblum & L. A. Bond (Eds.), *Preventing heterosexism and homophobia* (pp. 124–150). Thousand Oaks, CA: Sage Publications.

D'Emilio, J., & Freedman, E. B. (1997). *Intimate matters: A history of sexuality in America* (2nd ed.). Chicago: University of Chicago Press.

Darling, C. A., Davidson, J. K., Sr., & Cox, R. P. (1991). Female sexual response and the timing of partner orgasm. *Journal of Sex & Marital Therapy, 17,* 3–21.

Davidson, J. K. (1985). The utilization of sexual fantasies by sexually experienced university students. *Journal of American College Health, 34,* 24–32.

Davidson, J. K., Sr., & Darling, C. A. (1988). The sexually experienced woman: Multiple sex partners and sexual satisfaction. *The Journal of Sex Research, 24,* 141–154.

Davis, D., Shaver, P. R., & Vernon, M. L. (2004). Attachment style and subjective motivations for sex. *Personality and Social Psychology Bulletin, 30,* 1076–1090.

Davis, J. L., & Rusbult, C. E. (2001). Attitude alignment in close relationships. *Journal of Personality and Social Psychology, 81,* 65–84.

De Cecco, J. P., & Parker, D. A. (Eds.). (1995). *Sex, cells, and same-sex desire: The biology of sexual preference.* Binghamton, NY: Harrington Park Press.

De Judicibus, M. A., & McCabe, M. P. (2002). Psychological factors and the sexuality of pregnant and postpartum women. *The Journal of Sex Research, 39,* 94–103.

De Lora, J. S., Warren, C. A. B., & Ellison, C. R. (1981). *Understanding sexual interaction* (2nd ed.). Boston: Houghton Mifflin.

De Ridder, C. M., Bruning, P. F., Zonderland, M. L., Thijssen, J. H. H., Bonfrer, J. M. G., Blankenstein, M. A., et al. (1990). Body fat mass, body fat distribution and plasma hormones in early puberty in females. *Journal of Clinical and Endocrinological Metabolism, 70,* 888–893.

Deaux, K. (1987). Psychological constructions of masculinity and femininity. In J. M. Reinisch, L. A. Rosenblum, & S. A. Sanders (Eds.), *Masculinity/femininity: Basic perspectives* (pp. 289–303). New York: Oxford University Press.

Deaux, K., & Stewart, A. J. (2001). Framing gendered identities. In R. Unger (Ed.), *Handbook of the psychology of women and gender* (pp. 84–97). New York: Wiley.

Deci, E. L. (1975). *Intrinsic motivation.* New York: Plenum Press.

Decks, A. A., & McCabe, M. P. (2001). Sexual function and the menopausal woman: The importance of age and partner's sexual functioning. *Journal of Sex Research, 38,* 219–225.

Deenen, A. A., Gijs, L., & van Naerssen, A. X. (1994). Intimacy and sexuality in gay male couples. *Archives of Sexual Behavior, 23,* 159–179.

DeKeseredy, W. S., & Kelly, K. (1995). Sexual abuse in Canadian university and college dating relationships: The contribution of male peer support. *Journal of Family Violence, 10,* 41–53.

Dekker, J., & Everaerd, W. (1988). Attention effects on sexual arousal. *Psychophysiology, 25,* 45–54.

Dekker, J., Everaerd, W., & Verhelst, N. (1984). Attending to stimuli or to images of sexual feelings: Effects on sexual arousal. *Behaviour Research and Therapy, 23,* 139–149.

DeLamater, J. D. (1987). Gender differences in sexual scenarios. In K. Kelley (Ed.), *Females, males, and sexuality: Theories and research* (pp. 127–129). Albany: State University of New York Press.

DeLamater, J. D., & Hyde, J. S. (1998). Essentialism vs. social constructionism in the study of human sexuality. *The Journal of Sex Research, 35,* 10–18.

Denney, N. W., Field, J. K., & Quadagno, D. (1984). Sex differences in sexual needs and desires. *Archives of Sexual Behavior, 13,* 233–245.

Diamond, L. M. (1998). Development of sexual orientation among adolescent and young adult women. *Developmental Psychology, 34,* 1085–1095.

Diamond, L. M., & Savin-Williams, R. C. (2000). Explaining diversity in the development of same-sex sexuality among young women. *Journal of Social Issues, 56,* 297–313.

Diamond, M. (1996). Intersexuality: Recommendations for management. *Archives of Sexual Behavior, 27,* 634–641.

Diamond, M. (2002). Sex and gender are different: Sexual identity and gender identity are different. *Clinical Child Psychology and Psychiatry, 7*(3), 320–334.

DiBlasio, F. A., & Benda, B. B. (1990). Adolescent sexual behavior: Multivariate analysis of a social learning model. *Journal of Adolescent Research, 5,* 449–466.

Dijkstra, P., & Buunk, B. P. (1998). Jealousy as a function of rival characteristics: An evolutionary perspective. *Personality and Social Psychology Bulletin, 24,* 1158–1166.

Dion, K. K. (1995). Delayed parenthood and women's expectations about the transition to parenthood. *International Journal of Behavioral Development, 18,* 315–333.

Dion, K. K., & Dion, K. L. (2001). Gender and relationships. In R. K. Unger (Ed.), *Handbook of the psychology of women and gender* (pp. 256–271). New York: Wiley.

Dittus, P. J., & Jaccard, J. (2000). Adolescents' perceptions of maternal disapproval of sex: Relationship to sexual outcomes. *Journal of Adolescent Health, 26,* 268–278.

Doctor, R., & Prince, V. (1997). Transvestism: A survey of 1,032 cross-dressers. *Archives of Sexual Behavior, 26,* 589–605.

Doherty, R. W., Hatfield, E., Thompson, K., & Choo, P. (1994). Cultural and ethnic influences on love and attachment. *Personal Relationships, 1,* 391–398.

Donnelly, D. A. (1993). Sexually inactive marriages. *The Journal of Sex Research, 30,* 171–179.

Downs, A. C., & Fuller, M. J. (1991). Recollections of spermarche: An exploratory investigation. *Current Psychology: Research & Reviews, 10,* 93–102.

Downs, B. (June 2002). Fertility of American women. In *Current Population Reports, P20–548.* Washington, DC: U.S. Census Bureau.

Duling, D. C., Perrin, N., & Ferm, R. L. (1994). *The New Testament: Proclamation and paranesis, myth and history* (3rd ed.). Fort Worth, TX: Harcourt Brace.

Dunn, C. W., & Woodard, J. D. (1996). *The conservative tradition in America.* Lanham, MD: Rowman & Littlefield Publishers.

Durant, L. E., & Carey, M. P. (2000). Self-administered questionnaires versus face-to-face interviews in assessing sexual behavior in young women. *Archives of Sexual Behavior, 29,* 309–322.

Dutton, D. G., & Aron, A. P. (1974). Some evidence for heightened sexual attraction under conditions of high anxiety. *Journal of Personality and Social Psychology, 30,* 510–517.

Eagly, A. H., Ashmore, R. D., Makhijani, M. G., & Longo, L. C. (1991). What is beautiful is good, but . . . : A meta-analytic review of research on the physical attractiveness stereotype. *Psychological Bulletin, 110,* 109–128.

Eagly, A. H., Wood, W., & Diekman, A. B. (2000). Social role theory of sex differences and similarities: A current appraisal. In T. Eckes & H. M. Trautner (Eds.), *The developmental social psychology of gender* (pp. 123–174). Mahwah, NJ: Erlbaum.

Earle, J. R., & Perricone, P. J. (1986). Premarital sexuality: A ten-year study of attitudes and behavior on a small university campus. *The Journal of Sex Research, 22,* 304–310.

Eckes, T., & Trautner, H. M. (2000). Developmental social psychology of gender: An integrative framework. In T. Eckes & H. M. Trautner (Eds.), *The developmental social psychology of gender* (pp. 3–32). Mahwah, NJ: Erlbaum.

Eder, F. X., Hall, L. A., & Hekma, G. (1999). Introduction. In F. X. Eder, L. A. Hall, & G. Hekma (Eds.), *Sexual cultures in Europe: National histories.* New York: Manchester University Press.

Edwards, J. N., & Booth, A. (1994). Sexuality, marriage, and well-being: The middle years. In A. S. Rossi (Ed.), *Sexuality across the life course* (pp. 233–259). Chicago: University of Chicago Press.

Eliason, M. J. (1995). Accounts of sexual identity formation in heterosexual students. *Sex Roles, 32,* 821–834.

Elliot, L., & Brantley, C. (1997). *Sex on campus: The naked truth about the real sex lives of college students.* New York: Random House.

Emmers, T. M., & Dindia, K. (1995). The effect of relational stage and intimacy on touch: An extension of Guerrero and Andersen. *Personal Relationships, 2,* 225–236.

Epley, N., & Huff, C. (1998). Suspicion, affective response, and educational benefit as a result of deception in psychology research. *Personality and Social Psychology Bulletin, 24,* 759–768.

Everaerd, W., Laan, E., Both, S., & Spiering, M. (2001). Sexual motivation and desire. In W. Everaerd, E. Laan, & S. Both (Eds.), *Sexual appetite, desire and motivation: Energetics of the sexual system* (pp. 95–110). Amsterdam: Royal Netherlands Academy of Arts and Sciences.

Everett, S. (2004). *Handbook of contraception and reproductive sexual health.* Edinburgh, Scotland: Bailliere Tindall.

Eysenck, H. J. (1947). *Dimensions of personality.* London: Routledge & Kegan Paul.

Eysenck, H. J. (1976). *Sex and personality.* Austin: University of Texas Press.

Faderman, L. (1984). The "new gay" lesbians. *Journal of Homosexuality, 10,* 85–95.

Fassinger, R. E., & Miller, B. A. (1996). Validation of an inclusive model of sexual minority identity formation on a sample of gay men. *Journal of Homosexuality, 32,* 53–78.

Feagin, J. R. (1978). *Racial and ethnic relations.* Englewood Cliffs, NJ: Prentice Hall.

Feingold, A. (1990). Gender differences in effects of physical attractiveness on romantic attraction: A comparison across five research paradigms. *Journal of Personality and Social Psychology, 59,* 981–993.

Feingold, A. (1992). Good-looking people are not what we think. *Psychological Bulletin, 111,* 304–341.

Feldman, S. S., & Brown, N. (1993). Family influences on adolescent male sexuality: The mediational role of self-restraint. *Social Development, 2,* 16–35.

Felmlee, D., Sprecher, S., & Bassin, E. (1990). The dissolution of intimate relationships: A hazard model. *Social Psychology Quarterly, 53,* 13–30.

Felmlee, D. H. (1995). Fatal attractions: Affection and disaffection in intimate relationships. *Journal of Social and Personal Relationships, 12,* 295–311.

Festinger, L. (1954). A theory of social comparison processes. *Human Relations, 7,* 117–140.

Feuchtwang, S. (2002). Chinese religions. In L. Woodhead, P. Fletcher, H. Kawanami, & D. Smith (Eds.), *Religions in the modern world: Traditions and transformations* (pp. 86–107). New York: Routledge.

Fichten, C. S., Tagalakis, V., Judd, D., Wright, J., & Amsel, R. (1992). Verbal and nonverbal communication cues in daily conversations and dating. *The Journal of Social Psychology, 132,* 751–769.

Finkelhor, D. (1984). *Child sexual abuse: New theory and research.* New York: The Free Press.

Fisher, J. D. (1984). *Revising the Sexual Opinion Survey.* Unpublished manuscript, London, Ontario.

Fisher, J. D., Byrne, D., & White, L. A. (1983). Emotional barriers to contraception. In D. Byrne & W. A. Fisher (Eds.), *Adolescents, sex, and contraception* (pp. 207–239). Hillsdale, NJ: Erlbaum.

Fisher, J. D., & Misovich, S. J. (1990). Social influence and AIDS-preventive behavior. In J. Edwards, R. S. Tindale, L. Heath, & E. J. Posavac (Eds.), *Social influence processes and prevention* (pp. 39–70). New York: Plenum Press.

Fisher, S. (1989). *Sexual images of the self: The psychology of erotic sensation and illusions.* Hillsdale, NJ: Erlbaum.

Fisher, W. A. (1980). *Erotophobia–erotophilia and performance in a human sexuality course.* Unpublished manuscript, University of Western Ontario, London, Ontario.

Fisher, W. A., Branscombe, N. R., & Lemery, C. R. (1983). The bigger the better? Arousal and attributional responses to erotic stimuli that depict different size penises. *The Journal of Sex Research, 19,* 377–396.

Fisher, W. A., Byrne, D., Edmunds, M., Miller, C. T., Kelley, K., & White, L. A. (1979). Psychological and situation-specific correlates of contraceptive behavior among university women. *The Journal of Sex Research, 15,* 38–55.

Fisher, W. A., Byrne, D., White, L. A., & Kelley, K. (1988). Erotophobia–erotophilia as a dimension of personality. *The Journal of Sex Research, 25,* 123–151.

Fisher, W. A., Fisher, J. D., & Byrne, D. (1977). Consumer reactions to contraceptive purchasing. *Personality and Social Psychology Bulletin, 3,* 293–296.

Fisher, W. A., & Gray, J. (1988). Erotophobia–erotophilia and sexual behavior during pregnancy and postpartum. *The Journal of Sex Research, 25,* 379–396.

Fiske, S. T. (2004). *Social beings: A core motives approach to social psychology.* Hoboken, NJ: Wiley.

Fletcher, G. J. O., Simpson, J. A., & Thomas, G. (2000). The measurement of perceived relationship quality components: A confirmatory factor analytic approach. *Personality and Social Psychology Bulletin, 26,* 340–354.

Fletcher, G. J. O., Simpson, J. A., Thomas, G., & Giles, L. (1999). Ideals in intimate relationships. *Journal of Personality and Social Psychology, 76,* 72–89.

Flory, K., Lynam, D., Milich, R., Leukefeld, C., & Clayton, R. (2002). The relations among personality, symptoms of alcohol and marijuana abuse, and symptoms of comorbid psychopathology. *Experimental and Clinical Psychopharmacology, 10,* 425–434.

Foa, U. G., & Foa, E. B. (1974). *Societal structures of the mind.* Springfield, IL: Charles C. Thomas.

Forbes, G. B., Adams-Curtis, L. E., Hamm, N. R., & White, K. B. (2003). Perceptions of the woman who breastfeeds: The role of erotophobia, sexism, and attitudinal variables. *Sex Roles, 49,* 379–388.

Forste, R., & Tanfer, K. (1996). Sexual exclusivity among dating, cohabiting, and married women. *Journal of Marriage and the Family, 58,* 33–47.

Fraley, M. C., Nelson, E. C., Wolf, A. W., & Lozoff, B. (1991). Early genital naming. *Developmental and Behavioral Pediatrics, 12,* 301–305.

Franklin, A. J., & Boyd-Franklin, N. (2000). Invisibility syndrome: A clinical model of the effects of racism on African-American males. *American Journal of Orthopsychiatry, 70,* 33–41.

French, S. A., Story, M., Remafedi, G., Resnick, M. D., & Blum, R. W. (1996). Sexual orientation and prevalence of body dissatisfaction and eating disordered behaviors. *International Journal of Eating Disorders, 19,* 119–126.

Freud, S. (1962). Creative writers and daydreaming. In J. Strachy (Ed.), *The standard edition of the complete psychological works of Sigmund Freud* (Vol. 9, pp. 142–152). London: Hogarth. (Original work published 1908)

Friedrich, W. N., Grambsch, P., Broughton, D., Kuiper, J., & Beilke, R. L. (1991). Normative sexual behavior in children. *Pediatrics, 88,* 456–464.

Friedrich, W. N., Sandfort, T. G. M., Ostveen, J., & Cohen-Kettenis, P. T. (2000). Cultural differences in sexual behavior: 2–6 year old Dutch and American children. In T. G. M. Sandfort & J. Rademakers (Eds.), *Childhood sexuality: Normal sexual behavior and development* (pp. 117–129). New York: Haworth.

Frymer-Kensky, T. (1995). Law and philosophy: The case of sex in the Bible. In J. Magonet (Ed.), *Jewish explorations of sexuality* (pp. 3–16). Providence, RI: Berghahn Books.

Funder, D. C. (1993). Judgments as data for personality and developmental psychology: Error versus accuracy. In D. C. Funder, R. D. Parke, C. Tomlinson-Keasey, & K. Widaman (Eds.), *Studying lives through time: Personality and development* (pp. 121–146). Washington, DC: American Psychological Association.

Funder, D. C. (1999). *Personality judgment: A realistic approach to person perception.* San Diego, CA: Academic Press.

Funder, D. C. (2004). *The personality puzzle* (3rd ed.). New York: W. W. Norton.

Funder, D. C., & Block, J. (1989). The role of ego-control, ego-resiliency, and IQ in delay of gratification in adolescence. *Journal of Personality and Social Psychology, 57,* 1041–1050.

Furnham, A., McClelland, A., & Omer, L. (2003). A cross-cultural comparison of ratings of perceived fecundity and sexual attractiveness as a function of body weight and waist-to-hip ratio. *Psychology, Health & Medicine, 8,* 219–230.

Furnham, A., Mistry, D., & McClelland, A. (2004). The influence of age of the face and the waist to hip ratio on judgments of female attractiveness and traits. *Personality and Individual Differences, 36,* 1171–1185.

Furnham, A., Moutafi, J., & Baguma, P. (2000). A cross-cultural study of weight and waist-to-hip ratio and female attractiveness. *Personality and Individual Differences, 32,* 729–745.

Gaddis, A., & Brooks-Gunn, J. (1985). The male experience of pubertal change. *Journal of Youth and Adolescence, 14,* 61–69.

Gagnon, J. H., & Simon, W. (1973). *Sexual conduct.* Chicago: Aldine.

Garcia, L. T. (1999). The certainty of the sexual self-concept. *Canadian Journal of Human Sexuality, 8,* 263–270.

Garcia, L. T., & Carrigan, D. (1998). Individual and gender differences in sexual self-perceptions. *Journal of Psychology & Human Sexuality, 10,* 59–70.

Garofalo, R., Wolf, R. C., Kessel, S., Palfrey, J., & DuRant, R. H. (1998). The association between health risk behaviors and sexual orientation among a school-based sample of adolescents. *Pediatrics, 101,* 895–902.

Geary, D. C., Vigil, J., & Byrd-Craven, J. (2004). Evolution of human mate choice. *Journal of Sex Research, 41,* 27–42.

Geen, R. G. (1997). Psychophysiological approaches to personality. In J. Hogan, J. Johnson, & S. Briggs (Eds.), *Handbook of personality psychology.* San Diego, CA: Academic Press.

Geer, J. H., & O'Donohue, W. T. (1987). Introduction and overview. In J. H. Geer & W. T. O'Donohue (Eds.), *Theories of human sexuality* (pp. 1–19). New York: Plenum Press.

Geis, B. D., & Gerrard, M. (1984). Predicting male and female contraceptive behavior: A discriminant analysis of groups high, moderate, and low in contraceptive effectiveness. *Journal of Personality and Social Psychology, 46,* 669–680.

Gerhard, J. F. (2001). *Desiring revolution: Second-wave feminism and the rewriting of American sexual thought, 1920 to 1982.* New York: Columbia University Press.

Gerrard, M. (1987). Sex, sex guilt, and contraceptive use revisited: Trends in the 1980s. *Journal of Personality and Social Psychology, 52,* 975–980.

Gerrard, M., Gibbons, F. X., & McCoy, S. B. (1993). Emotional inhibition of effective contraception. *Anxiety, Stress, and Coping, 6,* 73–88.

Gerrard, M., Kurylo, M., & Reis, T. (1991). Self-esteem, erotophobia, and retention of contraceptive and AIDS information in the classroom. *Journal of Applied Social Psychology, 21,* 368–379.

Glass, S. P., & Wright, T. L. (1985). Sex differences in type of extramarital involvement and marital dissatisfaction. *Sex Roles, 12,* 1101–1120.

Goldberg, L. R. (2001). Analyses of Digman's child-personality data: Derivation of Big-Five factor scores from each of six samples. *Journal of Personality, 69,* 709–743.

Goldberg, L. R., & Rosolack, T. K. (1994). The Big Five factor structure as an integrative framework: An empirical comparison with Eysenck's P-E-N model. In C. F. Halverson, Jr., G. A. Kohnstamm, & R. P. Martin (Eds.), *The developing structure of temperament and personality from infancy to adulthood* (pp. 7–35). Hillsdale, NJ: Erlbaum.

Goldfarb, L., Gerrard, M., Gibbons, F. X., & Plante, T. (1988). Attitudes toward sex, arousal, and the retention of contraceptive information. *Journal of Personality and Social Psychology, 55,* 634–641.

Goldman, R., & Goldman, J. (1982). *Children's sexual thinking.* London: Routledge and Kegan Paul.

Goldman, R., & Goldman, J. (1983). Children's perceptions of sex differences in babies and adolescents: A cross-national study. *Archives of Sexual Behavior, 12,* 277–294.

Goodman, A. H. (2001). Six wrongs of racial science. In C. Stokes, T. Melendez, & G. Rhodes-Reed (Eds.), *Race in 21st century America* (pp. 25–47). East Lansing: Michigan State University Press.

Gordon, B. N., Schroeder, C. S., & Abrams, M. (1990). Age and social-class difference in children's knowledge of sexuality. *Journal of Clinical Child Psychology, 19,* 33–43.

Gottman, J. M. (1994). *What predicts divorce: The relationship between marital processes and marital outcomes.* Hillsdale, NJ: Erlbaum.

Gottman, J. M. (1998). Psychology and the study of the marital processes. *Annual Review of Psychology, 49,* 169–197.

Gottman, J. M., & Krokoff, L. J. (1989). Marital interaction and satisfaction: A longitudinal view. *Journal of Consulting and Clinical Psychology, 57,* 47–52.

Gottman, J. M., & Levenson, R. W. (1992). Marital processes predictive of later dissolution: Behavior, physiology, and health. *Journal of Personality and Social Psychology, 63,* 221–233.

Gould, S. J. (1995). Sexualized aspects of consumer behavior: An empirical investigation of consumer lovemaps. *Psychology and Marketing, 12,* 395–413.

Graber, J. A., & Archibald, A. B. (2001). Psychosocial change at puberty and beyond: Understanding adolescent sexuality and sexual orientation. In A. R. D'Augelli & C. Patterson (Eds.), *Lesbian, gay, and bisexual identities and youth: Psychological perspectives* (pp. 3–26). New York: Oxford University Press.

Graber, J. A., Brooks-Gunn, J., Paikoff, R. L., & Warren, M. P. (1994). Prediction of eating problems: An eight year study of adolescent girls. *Developmental Psychology, 30,* 823–834.

Grady, K. L., Phoenix, C. H., & Young, W. C. (1965). Role of the developing rat testis in differentiation of the neural tissues mediating mating behavior. *Journal of Comparative and Physiological Psychology, 59,* 176–182.

Graham, C. A., Janssen, E., & Sanders, S. A. (2000). Effects of fragrance on female sexual arousal and mood across the menstrual cycle. *Psychophysiology, 37,* 76–84.

Graziano, W. G., & Eisenberg, N. (1997). Agreeableness: A dimension of personality. In R. Hogan, J. Johnson, & S. Briggs (Eds.), *Handbook of personality psychology* (pp. 795–824). San Diego, CA: Academic Press.

Graziano, W. G., Jensen-Campbell, L. A., Shebilske, L. J., & Lundgren, S. R. (1993). Social influence, sex differences, and judgments of beauty: Putting the interpersonal back in interpersonal attraction. *Journal of Personality and Social Psychology, 65*(3), 522–531.

Greeley, A. M. (1991). *Faithful attraction: Discovering intimacy, love, and fidelity in American marriage.* New York: St. Martin's.

Grumbach, M. M., & Styne, D. M. (1998). Puberty: Ontogeny, neuroendocrinology, physiology, and disorders. In J. D. Wilson, D. W. Foster, & H. M. Kronenberg (Eds.), *Williams textbook of endocrinology* (pp. 1509–1625). Philadelphia: W. B. Saunders.

Guerrero, L. K., & Andersen, P. A. (1991). The waxing and waning of relational intimacy: Touch as a function of relational stage, gender and touch avoidance. *Journal of Social and Personal Relationships, 8,* 147–165.

Guerrero, L. K., & Andersen, P. A. (1994). Patterns of matching and initiation: Touch behavior and touch avoidance across romantic relationship stages. *Journal of Nonverbal Behavior, 18,* 137–153.

Guilamo-Ramos, V., Jaccard, J., Pena, J., & Goldberg, V. (2005). Acculturation-related variables, sexual initiation, and subsequent sexual behavior among Puerto Rican, Mexican, and Cuban youth. *Health Psychology, 24,* 88–95.

Gutierrez, G., & Domjan, M. (1997). Differences in the sexual conditioned behavior of male and female Japanese quail. *Journal of Comparative Psychology, 111,* 135–142.

Haas, S. M., & Stafford, L. (1998). An initial examination of maintenance behavior in gay and lesbian relationships. *Journal of Social and Personal Relationships, 15,* 846–855.

Hall, C. (2000). God is a bullet. In K. Kay, J. Nagle, & B. Gould (Eds.), *Male lust: Pleasure, power, and transformation* (pp. 159–165). New York: Harrington Park Press.

Hall, J. (1998). How big are nonverbal sex differences? The case of smiling and sensitivity to nonverbal cues. In D. J. Canary & K. Dindia (Eds.), *Sex differences and similarities in communication: Critical essays and empirical investigations of sex and gender in interaction. LEA's communication series* (pp. 155–177). Mahwah, NJ: Erlbaum.

Hall, J. A. (1984). *Nonverbal sex differences: Communication accuracy and expressive style.* Baltimore: Johns Hopkins University Press.

Hall, J. A., & Halberstadt, A. G. (1986). Smiling and gazing. In J. S. Hyde & M. C. Inn (Eds.), *The psychology of gender: Advances through meta-analysis* (pp. 136–185). Baltimore: Johns Hopkins University Press.

Halperin, D. M. (1990). *One hundred years of homosexuality: And other essays on Greek love.* New York: Routledge.

Halpern, C. T., Udry, J. R., Campbell, B., & Suchindran, C. (1993). Testosterone and pubertal development as predictors of sexual activity: A panel analysis of adolescent males. *Psychosomatic Medicine, 55,* 436–447.

Hansen, G. L. (1987). Extradyadic relations during courtship. *The Journal of Sex Research, 23,* 382–390.

Harrison, J. B., & Sullivan, R. E. (1971). *A short history of Western civilization* (3rd ed.). New York: Knopf.

Hartup, W. W., & Laurenson, B. (1999). Relationships as developmental contexts: Retrospective themes and contemporary issues. In W. A. Collins & B. Laurenson (Eds.), *Relationships as developmental contexts: Minnesota symposia on child psychology* (Vol. 30, pp. 13–35). Mahwah, NJ: Erlbaum.

Harvey, J. H. (1996). *Embracing their memory: Loss and the social psychology of story-telling.* Needham Heights, MA: Allyn & Bacon.

Harvey, J. H. (2000). *Give sorrow words: Perspectives on loss and trauma.* Philadelphia: Brunner/Mazel.

Harvey, J. H., & Weber, A. L. (2002). *Odyssey of the heart: Close relationships in the 21st century* (2nd ed.). Mahwah, NJ: Erlbaum.

Harvey, J. H., Weber, A. L., & Orbuch, T. L. (1990). *Interpersonal accounts: A social psychological perspective.* Oxford: Blackwell.

Harvey, J. H., Wells, G. L., & Alvarez, M. D. (1978). Attribution in the context of conflict and separation in close relationships. In J. H. Harvey, W. J. Ickes, & R. F. Kidd (Eds.), *New directions in attribution research* (Vol. 2, pp. 235–259). Hillsdale, NJ: Erlbaum.

Haskey, J. (1996). The proportion of married couples who divorce: Past patterns and current prospects. *Population Trends, 83,* 25–36.

Hatfield, E. (1988). Passionate and companionate love. In R. J. Sternberg & M. I. Barnes (Eds.), *The psychology of love* (pp. 191–217). New Haven, CT: Yale University Press.

Hatfield, E., & Rapson, R. I. (1993). *Love, sex, and intimacy: Their psychology, biology, and history.* New York: HarperCollins.

Hatfield, E., & Rapson, R. L. (2005). *Love and sex: Cross-cultural perspectives.* Lanham, MD: University Press of America.

Hatfield, E., & Sprecher, S. (1986). Measuring passionate love in intimate relations. *Journal of Adolescence, 9,* 383–410.

Hatfield, E., & Walster, G. W. (1978). *A new look at love.* Reading, MA: Addison-Wesley.

Hatfield, E., Brinton, C., & Cornelius, J. (1989). Passionate love and anxiety in young adolescents. *Motivation and Emotion, 13,* 271–289.

Hatfield, E., Rapson, R. L., & Martel, L. D. (in press). Passionate love and sexual desire. In S. Kitayama & D. Cohen (Eds.), *Handbook of cultural psychology.* New York: Guilford Press.

Hatfield, E., Schmitz, E., Cornelius, J., & Rapson, R. L. (1988). Passionate love: How early does it begin? *Journal of Psychology & Human Sexuality, 1,* 35–51.

Hause, S. C., & Maltby, W. S. (1999). *Western civilization: A history of European society.* Belmont, CA: West/Wadsworth.

Haveman, R., & Wolfe, B. (1994). *Succeeding generations: On the effects of investments in children.* New York: Russell Sage Foundation.

Hayward, C., Gotlib, I. H., Schraedley, P. K., & Litt, I. F. (1999). Ethnic differences in the association between pubertal status and symptoms of depression in adolescent girls. *Journal of Adolescent Health, 25,* 143–149.

Hazan, C., & Shaver, P. (1987). Romantic love conceptualized as an attachment process. *Journal of Personality and Social Psychology, 52,* 511–524.

Hazan, C., & Shaver, P. (1994). Attachment as an organizational framework for research on close relationships. *Psychological Inquiry, 5,* 1–22.

Heaton, T. B., Jacobson, C. K., & Holland, K. (1999). Persistence and change in decisions to remain childless. *Journal of Marriage & the Family, 61,* 531–539.

Heckhausen, H. (1991). *Motivation and action.* Berlin: Springer-Verlag.

Heiman, J. R., & Rowland, D. L. (1983). Affective and physiological sexual response patterns: The effects of instructions on sexually functional and dysfunctional men. *Journal of Psychosomatic Research, 27,* 105–116.

Helminiak, D. A. (2000). *What the Bible really says about homosexuality* (Millennium ed.). Tajique, NM: Alamo Square Press.

Helms, J. E. (1995). An update of Helms' White and people of color racial identity models. In J. G. Ponterotto, J. M. Casas, L. A. Suzuki, & C. M. Alexander (Eds.), *Handbook of multicultural counseling* (pp. 181–198). Thousand Oaks, CA: Sage Publications.

Helms, J. E., Jernigan, M., & Mascher, J. (2005). The meaning of race in psychology and how to change it: A methodological perspective. *American Psychologist, 60,* 27–36.

Helweg-Larsen, M., & Howell, C. (2000). Effects of erotophobia on the persuasiveness of condom advertisements containing strong or weak arguments. *Basic and Applied Social Psychology, 22,* 111–117.

Henderson-King, D. H., & Veroff, J. (1994). Sexual satisfaction and marital well-being in the first years of marriage. *Journal of Social and Personal Relationships, 11,* 509–534.

Hendrick, C., Hendrick, S. S., & Reich, D. A. (2006). The Brief Sexual Attitudes Scale. *Journal of Sex Research, 43,* 76–86.

Hendrick, C., Hendrick, S., Foote, F. H., & Slapion-Foote, M. J. (1984). Do men and women love differently? *Journal of Social and Personal Relationships, 1,* 177–195.

Henshaw, S. K. (1998). Unintended pregnancy in the United States. *Family Planning Perspectives, 30,* 24–29, 46.

Herman-Giddens, M. E., Slora, E. J., Wasserman, R. C., Bourdony, C. J., Bhapkar, M. V., Koch, G. G., et al. (1997). Secondary sexual characteristics and menses in young girls seen in office practice: A study from the pediatric research in office settings network. *Pediatrics, 99,* 505–511.

Herold, E. S., Maticka-Tyndale, E., & Mewhinney, D. (1998). Predicting intentions to engage in casual sex. *Journal of Social and Personal Relationships, 15,* 502–516.

Hill, C. A. (1997). The distinctiveness of sexual motives in relation to sexual desire and desirable partner attributes. *The Journal of Sex Research, 34,* 139–153.

Hill, C. A. (2002). Gender, relationships stage, and sexual behavior: The importance of partner emotional investment within specific situations. *The Journal of Sex Research, 39,* 228–240.

Hill, C. A., & Preston, L. K. (1996). Individual differences in the experience of sexual motivation: Theory and measurement of dispositional sexual motives. *The Journal of Sex Research, 33,* 27–45.

Hill, J. (1983). Early adolescence: A framework. *Journal of Early Adolescence, 3,* 1–21.

Hiort, O. (2000). Neonatal endocrinology of abnormal male sexual differentiation: Molecular aspects. *Hormone Research, 53,* 38–41.

Hite, S. (1976). *The Hite report: A nationwide study of female sexuality.* New York: Dell Publishing.

Hite, S. (2005). *Oedipus revisited: Sexual behaviour in the human male today.* London: Arcadia Books.

Hoffman, H., Janssen, E., & Turner, S. L. (2004). Classical conditioning of sexual arousal in women and men: Effects of varying awareness and biological relevance of the conditioned stimulus. *Archives of Sexual Behavior, 33,* 45–53.

Hogan, D., P., & Kitagawa, E. M. (1985). The impact of social status, family structure, and neighborhood on the fertility of black adolescents. *American Journal of Sociology, 90,* 825–855.

Hogan, J., & Ones, D. S. (1997). Conscientiousness and integrity at work. In R. Hogan, J. Johnson, & S. Briggs (Eds.), *Handbook of personality psychology* (pp. 849–870). San Diego, CA: Academic Press.

Hogben, M., & Byrne, D. (1998). Using social learning theory to explain individual differences in human sexuality. *The Journal of Sex Research, 35,* 58–71.

Holmes, M. (2002). Rethinking the meaning and management of intersexuality. *Sexualities, 5,* 159–180.

Holtzworth-Munroe, A., & Jacobson, N. S. (1985). Causal attributions of married couples: When do they search for causes? What do they conclude when they do? *Journal of Personality and Social Psychology, 48,* 1398–1412.

Hoon, P., Wincze, J. P., & Hoon, E. (1977). A test of reciprocal inhibition: Are anxiety and sexual arousal in women mutually inhibitory? *Journal of Abnormal Psychology, 86,* 65–74.

Hoyle, R. H., Fejfar, M. C., & Miller, J. D. (2000). Personality and sexual risk taking: A quantitative review. *Journal of Personality, 68,* 1203–1231.

Hurlbert, D. F. (1993). A comparative study using orgasm consistency training in the treatment of women reporting hypoactive sexual desire. *Journal of Sex & Marital Therapy, 19,* 41–55.

Hurlbert, D. F., & Apt, C. (1994). Female sexual desire, response, and behavior. *Behavior Modification, 18,* 488–504.

Hurlbert, D. F., Apt, C., & Rabehl, S. M. (1993). Key variables to understanding female sexual satisfaction: An examination of women in nondistressed marriages. *Journal of Sex & Marital Therapy, 19,* 154–165.

Hurlbert, D. F., & Whittaker, K. E. (1991). The role of masturbation in marital and sexual satisfaction: A comparative study of female masturbators and nonmasturbators. *Journal of Sex Education & Therapy, 17,* 272–282.

Husted, J. R., & Edwards, A. E. (1976). Personality correlates of male sexual arousal and behavior. *Archives of Sexual Behavior, 5,* 149–156.

Huston, A. C. (1983). Sex-typing. In E. M. Heatherington (Ed.), *Handbook of child psychology: Socialization, personality, and social development* (Vol. 4, pp. 388–467). New York: Wiley.

Hyde, J. S. (2005). The genetics of sexual orientation. In J. S. Hyde (Ed.), *Biological substrates of human sexuality* (pp. 9–20). Washington, DC: American Psychological Association.

Hyde, J. S., DeLamater, J. D., Plant, E. A., & Byrd, J. M. (1996). Sexuality during pregnancy and the year postpartum. *The Journal of Sex Research, 33,* 143–151.

Irvine, J. (1990). *Disorders of desire: Sex and gender in modern American sexology.* Philadelphia: Temple University Press.

Jaccard, J., Blanton, H., & Dodge, T. (2005). Peer influences on risk behavior: An analysis of the effects of a close friend. *Developmental Psychology, 41,* 135–147.

Jaccard, J., Dittus, P. J., & Gordon, V. V. (1998). Parent-adolescent congruency in reports of adolescent sexual behavior and in communication about sexual behavior. *Child Development, 69,* 247–261.

Jackson, J. P., Jr., & Weidman, N. M. (2004). *Race, racism, and science: Social impact and interaction.* Santa Barbara, CA: ABC-CLIO.

Jackson, L. A., & McGill, O. D. (1996). Body type preferences and body characteristics associated with attractive and unattractive bodies by African Americans and Anglo Americans. *Sex Roles, 35,* 295–307.

Jacobson, M. (1998). *Whiteness of a different color.* Cambridge, MA: Harvard University Press.

Janus, S., & Janus, C. (1993). *The Janus report on sexual behavior.* New York: Wiley.

Jensen-Campbell, L. A., Graziano, W. G., & West, S. G. (1995). Dominance, prosocial orientation, and female preferences: Do nice guys really finish last? *Journal of Personality and Social Psychology, 68,* 427–440.

*John Geddes Lawrence and Tyrone Garner v. Texas* (U.S. Supreme Court 2003).

Jones, J. C., & Barlow, D. H. (1990). Self-reported frequency of sexual urges, fantasies, and masturbatory fantasies in heterosexual males and females. *Archives of Sexual Behavior, 19,* 269–279.

Judge, T. A., Bono, J. E., Ilies, R., & Gerhardt, M. W. (2002). Personality and leadership: A qualitative and quantitative review. *Journal of Applied Psychology, 87,* 765–780.

Judge, T. A., Heller, D., & Mount, M. K. (2002). Five-Factor model of personality and job satisfaction: A meta-analysis. *Journal of Applied Psychology, 87,* 530–541.

Jung, C. G. (1933). *Modern man in search of a soul.* New York: Harcourt, Brace & World.

Jung, C. G. (1971). *The portable Jung.* New York: Viking.

Kahn, S., Zimmerman, G., Csikzentmihalyi, M., & Getzels, J. W. (1985). Relations between identity in young adulthood and intimacy at midlife. *Journal of Personality and Social Psychology, 49,* 1316–1322.

Kalichman, S. C., Heckman, T., & Kelly, J. A. (1996). Sensation seeking as an explanation for the association between substance use and HIV-related risky sexual behavior. *Archives of Sexual Behavior, 25,* 141–154.

Kalichman, S. C., Kelly, J. A., & Stevenson, L. Y. (1997). Priming effects of HIV risk assessments on related perceptions and behavior: An experimental field study. *AIDS Behavior, 1,* 3–8.

Kalick, S. M. (1977). *Plastic surgery, physical appearance, and person perception.* Unpublished doctoral dissertation, Harvard University, Cambridge, MA. Cited by E. Berscheid in, An overview of the psychological effects of physical attractiveness and some comments upon the psychological effects of knowledge of the effects of physical attractiveness. In W. Lucker, K. Ribbens, & J. A. McNamera (Eds.), *Logical aspects of facial form.* Ann Arbor: University of Michigan Press, 1981.

Kalmijn, M. (1999). Father involvement in childrearing and the perceived stability of marriage. *Journal of Marriage and the Family, 61,* 409–421.

Kanin, E. J. (1970). Sexual aggression by college men. *Medical Aspects of Human Sexuality, 4,* 28–40.

Kanin, E. J., & Parcell, S. R. (1977). Sexual aggression: A second look at the offended female. *Archives of Sexual Behavior, 6,* 67–76.

Kantorowitz, D. A. (1978). An experimental investigation of preorgasmic reconditioning and postorgasmic deconditioning. *Journal of Applied Behavior Analysis, 11,* 23–34.

Kaplan, H. S. (1979). *Disorders of sexual desire.* New York: Brunner-Mazel.

Kaplowitz, P. B., Oberfield, S. E., & the Drug and Therapeutics and Executive Committees of the Lawson Wilkins Pediatric Endocrine Society. (1999). Reexamination of the age limit for defining when puberty is precocious in girls in the United States: Implications for evaluation and treatment. *Pediatrics, 104,* 936–941.

Kasinitz, P., Battle, J., & Miyares, I. (2001). Fade to black? The children of West Indian immigrants in southern Florida. In R. G. Rumbaut & A. Portes (Eds.), *Ethnicities: Children of immigrants in America* (pp. 267–300). Berkeley: University of California Press.

Katchadourian, H. (1990). Sexuality. In S. S. Feldman & G. R. Elliott (Eds.), *At the threshold: The developing adolescent* (pp. 330–351). Cambridge, MA: Harvard University Press.

Kaufman, C. E., Beals, J., Mitchell, C. M., LeMaster, P., Pickenscher, A., & The Pathways of Choice and Healthy Ways Project Teams. (2004). Stress, trauma, and risky sexual behaviour among American Indians in young adulthood. *Culture, Health & Sexuality, 6,* 301–318.

Kaye, S. A., Folsum, A. R., Princeas, R. J., Potter, J. P., & Gapstur, S. M. (1990). The association of body fat distribution with lifestyle and reproductive factors in a population study of post menopausal women. *International Journal of Obesity, 14,* 583–591.

Keelan, J. P. R., Dion, K. I., & Dion, K. K. (1994). Attachment style and heterosexual relationships among young adults: A short-term panel study. *Journal of Social and Personal Relationships, 11,* 201–214.

Kehoe, M. (1988). Lesbians over 60 speak for themselves. *Journal of Homosexuality, 16,* 1–11.

Kelley, H. H., Berscheid, E., Christensen, A., Harvey, J. H., Huston, T. L., Levinger, G., et al. (1983). *Close relationships.* New York: Freeman.

Kelley, K. (1979). Socialization factors in contraceptive attitudes: Roles of affective responses, parental attitudes, and sexual experience. *The Journal of Sex Research, 15*(1), 6–20.

Kelley, K. (1985a). The effects of sexual and/or aggressive film exposure on helping, hostility, and attitudes toward women and men. *The Journal of Research in Personality, 19,* 472–483.

Kelley, K. (1985b). Sex, sex guilt, and authoritarianism: Differences in responses to explicit heterosexual and masturbatory slides. *Journal of Sex Research, 21,* 68–85.

Kelley, K., Byrne, D., Greendlinger, V., & Murnen, S. (1997). Content, sex of viewer, and dispositional variables as predictors of affective and evaluative responses to sexually explicit films. *Journal of Psychology & Human Sexuality, 9,* 53–71.

Kelley, K., Smeaton, G., Byrne, D., Przybyla, D. P., & Fisher, W. A. (1987). Sexual attitudes and contraception among females across five college samples. *Human Relations, 40,* 237–254.

Kenrick, D. T., & Funder, D. C. (1988). Profiting from controversy: Lessons from the person-situation debate. *American Psychologist, 43*(1), 23–34.

Kessler, S. (1998). *Lessons from the intersexed.* New Brunswick, NJ: Rutgers University Press.

Kimmel, A. J. (1998). In defense of deception. *American Psychologist, 53,* 803–805.

King, J. L. (2004). *On the down low: A journey into the lives of "straight" Black men who sleep with men.* New York: Broadway Books.

Kinsey, A. C., Pomeroy, W. B., & Martin, C. E. (1948). *Sexual behavior in the human male.* Philadelphia: W. B. Saunders.

Kinsey, A. C., Pomeroy, W. B., Martin, C. E., & Gebhard, P. H. (1953). *Sexual behavior in the human female.* Philadelphia: W. B. Saunders.

Kippax, S., & Smith, G. (2001). Anal intercourse and power in sex between men. *Sexualities, 4,* 413–434.

Kirschner, M. A., & Samojilik, E. (1991). Sex hormone metabolism in upper and lower body obesity. *International Journal of Obesity, 15,* 101–108.

Kling, K. C., Ryff, C. D., Love, G., & Essex, M. (2003). Exploring the influence of personality on depressive symptoms and self-esteem across a significant life transition. *Journal of Personality and Social Psychology, 85,* 922–932.

Knafo, D., & Jaffe, Y. (1984). Sexual fantasizing in males and females. *Journal of Research in Personality, 18,* 451–462.

Kochanska, G., Friesenborg, A. E., Lange, L. A., & Martel, M. M. (2004). Parents' personality and infants' temperament as contributors to their emerging relationship. *Journal of Personality and Social Psychology, 86,* 744–759.

Koss, M. P., & Dinero, T. E. (1988). Predictors of sexual aggression among a national sample of male college students. In R. A. Prentky & V. L. Quinsey (Eds.), *Human sexual aggression: Current perspectives. Annals of the New York Academy of Sciences* (Vol. 528, pp. 133–146). New York: New York Academy of Sciences.

Kotloff, K. L., Tacket, C. O., Wasserman, S. S., Bridwell, M. W., Cowan, J. E., Clemens, J. D., et al. (1991). A voluntary serosurvey and behavioral risk assessment for human immunodeficiency virus infection among college students. *Sexually Transmitted Diseases, 18,* 223–227.

Koukounas, E., & McCabe, M. P. (2001). Sexual and emotional variables influencing sexual response to erotica: A psychophysiological investigation. *Archives of Sexual Behavior, 30*(4), 393–408.

Krafft-Ebing, R. V. (1937). *Psychopathia sexualis with reference to the antipathic sexual instinct: A medico-forensic study.* Brooklyn, NY: Physicians and Surgeons Book Company. (Original work published 1906)

Ku, L., Sonenstein, F. L., & Pleck, J. H. (1993). Neighborhood, family and work: Influences on the premarital behaviors of adolescent males. *Social Forces, 72,* 479–503.

Ku, L., Sonenstein, F. L., Lindberg, L. D., Bradner, C. H., Boggess, S., & Pleck, J. H. (1998). Understanding changes in sexual activity among young metropolitan men: 1979–1995. *Family Planning Perspectives, 30,* 256–262.

Kunda, Z., Fong, G. T., Sanitioso, R., & Reber, E. (1993). Directional questions about self-conceptions. *Journal of Experimental Social Psychology, 29,* 63–86.

Kurdeck, L. A. (1991). Correlates of relationship satisfaction in cohabiting gay and lesbian couples. *Journal of Personality and Social Psychology, 61,* 910–922.

Kurdeck, L. A. (1994). Conflict resolution styles in gay, lesbian, heterosexual nonparent, and heterosexual parent couples. *Journal of Marriage and the Family, 56,* 705–722.

Kurdeck, L. A. (1995). Developmental changes in relationship quality in gay and lesbian cohabiting couples. *Developmental Psychology, 31,* 86–94.

Kurdeck, L. A. (2004). Are gay and lesbian cohabiting couples *really* different from heterosexual married couples? *Journal of Marriage and the Family, 66,* 880–900.

Kyvig, D. E. (2002). *Daily life in the United States, 1920–1939: Decades of promise and pain.* Westport, CT: Greenwood Press.

Laan, E., Everaerd, W., Van-Aanhold, M. & Rebel, M. (1993). Performance demand and sexual arousal in women. *Behaviour Research and Therapy, 31,* 25–35.

Labranche, E. R., Helweg-Larsen, M., Byrd, C. E., & Choquette, R. A., Jr. (1997). To picture or not to picture: Levels of erotophobia and breast self-examination brochure techniques. *Journal of Applied Social Psychology, 27,* 2200–2212.

Lachman, M. E. (2004). Development in midlife. *Annual Review of Psychology, 55,* 305–331.

Lachman, M. E., & Firth, K. (2004). The adaptive value of feeling in control during midlife. In O. G. Brim, C. D. Ryff, & R. Kessler (Eds.), *How healthy are we: A national study of wellbeing in midlife* (pp. 320–349). Chicago: University of Chicago Press.

LaFrance, M., Hecht, M. A., & Paluck, E. L. (2003). The contingent smile: A meta-analysis of sex differences in smiling. *Psychological Bulletin, 129,* 305–334.

Lalamière, M. L., Blanchard, R., & Zucker, K. J. (2000). Sexual orientation and handedness in men and women: A meta-analysis. *Psychological Bulletin, 126,* 575–592.

Langlois, J. H., Kalakanis, L., Rubenstein, A. J., Larson, A., Hallam, M., & Smoot, M. (2000). Maxims or myths of beauty? A meta-analytic and theoretical review. *Psychological Bulletin, 126,* 390–423.

Langlois, J. H., & Roggman, L. A. (1990). Attractive faces are only average. *Psychological Science, 1,* 115–121.

Laubscher, L. (2005). Toward a (de)constructive psychology of African American men. *Journal of Black Psychology, 31,* 111–129.

Laumann, E. O., Gagnon, J. H., Michael, R. T., & Michaels, S. (1994). *The social organization of sexuality.* Chicago: University of Chicago Press.

Laumann, E. O., Palk, A., & Rosen, R. C. (2001). Sexual dysfunction in the United States: Prevalence and predictors. In E. O. Laumann & R. T. Michael (Eds.), *Sex, love, and health in America: Private choices and public policies* (pp. 352–376). Chicago: University of Chicago Press.

Lawrance, K., & Byers, E. S. (1995). Sexual satisfaction in long-term heterosexual relationships: The interpersonal exchange model of sexual satisfaction. *Personal Relationships, 2,* 267–285.

Lawson, A. (1988). *Adultery.* New York: Basic Books.

Lawson, K. L. (2004). Development and psychometric properties of the perceptions of parenting inventory. *The Journal of Psychology, 138,* 433–455.

Leiblum, S. R., & Rosen, R. C. (1988). Introduction: Changing perspectives on sexual desire. In S. R. Lieblum & R. C. Rosen (Eds.), *Sexual desire disorders* (pp. 1–17). New York: Guilford Press.

Leigh, B. C. (1989). Reasons for having and avoiding sex: Gender, sexual orientation, and relationship to sexual behavior. *The Journal of Sex Research, 26,* 199–209.

Leitenberg, H., Detzer, M. J., & Srebnik, D. (1993). Gender differences in masturbation and the relation of masturbation experience in preadolescence and/or early adolescence to sexual behavior and sexual adjustment in young adulthood. *Archives of Sexual Behavior, 22,* 87–98.

Leitenberg, H., & Henning, K. (1995). Sexual fantasy. *Psychological Bulletin, 117,* 469–496.

Lemery, C. R. (1983). *Children's sexual knowledge as a function of parent's affective orientation to sexuality and parent–child communication about sex: A causal analysis.* Unpublished masters thesis, University of Western Ontario, London, Ontario.

Lerner, R. M. (1995). Developing individuals within changing contexts: Implications of developmental contextualism for human development research. In T. A. Kindermann & J. Valsiner (Eds.), *Development of person-context relations* (pp. 13–37). Hillsdale, NJ: Erlbaum.

Lerner, R. M., Lerner, J. V., von Eye, A., Ostrom, C. W., Nitz, K., Talwar-Soni, R., et al. (1996). Continuity and discontinuity across the transition of early adolescence: A developmental contextual perspective. In J. A. Graber, J. Brooks-Gunn, & A. C. Petersen (Eds.), *Transitions through adolescence: Interpersonal domains and context* (pp. 3–22). Mahwah, NJ: Erlbaum.

Letourneau, E. J., & O'Donohue, W. (1997). Classical conditioning of female sexual arousal. *Archives of Sexual Behavior, 26,* 63–78.

Lever, J. (1994, August 23). Sexual revelations. *The Advocate,* 17–24.

Lever, J. (1995, August 22). Lesbian sex survey. *The Advocate,* 21–30.

Levinger, G. (1980). Toward the analysis of close relationships. *Journal of Experimental Social Psychology, 16,* 510–544.

Levinson, D. J. (1986). A conception of adult development. *American Psychologist, 41,* 3–13.

Lewin, K. (1999). Psychology and the process of group living. In M. Gold (Ed.), *The complete social scientist: A Kurt Lewin reader* (pp. 333–345). Washington, DC: American Psychological Association.

Lewis, L. J. (2004). Examining sexual health discourses in a racial/ethnic context. *Archives of Sexual Behavior, 33,* 223–234.

Lewis, L. J., & Kertzner, R. M. (2003). Toward improved interpretation and theory building of African American male sexualities. *The Journal of Sex Research, 40,* 383–395.

Lewis, R. J., Gibbons, F. X., & Gerrard, M. (1986). Sexual experience and recall of sexual vs. nonsexual information. *Journal of Personality, 54,* 676–692.

Lewis, R. J., & Janda, L. H. (1988). The relationship between sexual adjustment and childhood experiences regarding exposure to nudity, sleeping in the parental bed, and parental attitudes toward sexuality. *Archives of Sexual Behavior, 17,* 349–362.

Lewontin, R. C. (1972). The apportionment of human diversity. *Evolutionary Biology, 6,* 381–398.

Lindberg, L. D., Boggs, S., Porter, L., & Williams, S. (2000). *Teen risk-taking: A statistical report.* Washington, DC: Urban Institute.

Lippa, R. A. (2002). *Gender, nature, and nurture.* Mahwah, NJ: Erlbaum.

Lippert, T., & Prager, K. J. (2001). Daily experiences of intimacy: A study of couples. *Personal Relationships, 8,* 283–298.

Liu, C. (2000). A theory of marital sexual life. *Journal of Marriage and the Family, 62,* 363–374.

Lloyd, S. A. (1991). The darkside of courtship: Violence and sexual exploitation. *Family Relations, 40,* 14–20.

Lloyd, S. A., & Emery, B. C. (1999). *The darkside of dating: Physical and sexual violence.* Thousand Oaks, CA: Sage Publications.

LoPiccolo, J., & Stock, W. E. (1986). Treatment of sexual dysfunction. *Journal of Consulting and Clinical Psychology, 54,* 158–167.

Lottes, I. L. (1993). Nontraditional gender roles and the sexual experiences of heterosexual college students. *Sex Roles, 29,* 645–669.

Luby, V., & Aron, A. (1990, July). *A prototype structuring of love, like, and being in love.* Paper presented at the International Conference on Personal Relationships, Oxford.

Male masturbation reality. (2006). Retrieved February 14, 2007, from http://sexeditorials.com/masturbation/male/index.html

Mallon, G. P. (2004). *Gay men choosing parenthood.* New York: Columbia University Press.

Manning, W. D., Longmore, M. A., & Giordano, P. C. (2000). The relationship context of contraceptive use at first intercourse. *Family Planning Perspectives, 32*(3), 104–110.

Marcia, J. E. (1987). Identity in adolescence. In J. Adelson (Ed.), *Handbook of adolescent psychology.* New York: John Wiley.

Markus, H. R. (1977). Self-schemata and processing information about the self. *Journal of Personality and Social Psychology, 35,* 63–78.

Markus, H. R., & Kitayama, S. (1991). Culture and self: Implications for cognition, emotion, and motivation. *Psychological Review, 98,* 224–253.

Markus, H. R., Ryff, C. D., Curhan, K., & Palmersheim, K. (2004). In their own words: Well-being at midlife among high school and college-educated adults. In O. G. Brim, C. D. Ryff, & R. Kessler (Eds.), *How healthy are we: A national study of well-being in midlife* (pp. 273–319). Chicago: University of Chicago Press.

Marshall, W. A., & Tanner, J. M. (1969). Variations in the pattern of pubertal changes in girls. *Archives of Disease in Childhood, 44,* 291–303.

Marshall, W. A., & Tanner, J. M. (1974). Puberty. In J. D. Douvis & J. Drobeing (Eds.), *Scientific foundations of pediatrics* (pp. 124–151). London: Heinemann.

Marsiglio, W., & Donnelly, D. (1991). Sexual relations in later life: A national study of married persons. *Journal of Gerontology: Social Sciences, 46,* 338–344.

Marston, P. J., Hecht, M. L., Menke, M. L., McDaniel, S., & Reeder, H. (1998). The subjective experience of intimacy, passion, and commitment in heterosexual love relationships. *Personal Relationships, 5,* 15–30.

Martin, A. (1993). *The lesbian and gay parenting handbook: Creating and raising our families.* New York: HarperPerennial.

Marty, M. A. (1997). *Daily life in the United States, 1960–1990: Decades of discord.* Westport, CT: Greenwood Press.

Masters, W. H., & Johnson, V. E. (1966). *Human sexual response.* Boston: Little Brown.

Masters, W. H., Johnson, V. E., & Kolodny, R. C. (1995). *Human sexuality* (5th ed.). New York: HarperCollins.

Maticka-Tyndale, E., Herold, E. S., & Mewhinney, D. (1998). Casual sex on spring break: Intentions and behaviors of Canadian students. *The Journal of Sex Research, 35,* 254–264.

Maticka-Tyndale, E., Herold, E. S., & Oppermann, M. (2003). Casual sex among Australian schoolies. *The Journal of Sex Research, 43,* 158–169.

Matthias, R. E., Lubben, J. E., Atchison, K. A., & Schweitzer, S. O. (1997). Sexual activity and satisfaction among very old adults: Results from a community-dwelling Medicare population survey. *The Gerontologist, 37,* 6–14.

McAdams, D. P. (1997). A conceptual history of personality psychology. In R. Hogan, J. Johnson, & S. Briggs (Eds.), *Handbook of personality psychology* (pp. 3–39). San Diego, CA: Academic Press.

McCabe, M. P., & Collins, J. K. (1984). Measurement of depth of desired and experienced sexual involvement at different stages of dating. *The Journal of Sex Research, 20,* 377–390.

McCarn, S. R., & Fassinger, R. E. (1996). Revisioning sexual minority identity formation: A new model of lesbian identity and its implications for counseling and research. *The Counseling Psychologist, 24,* 508–534.

McClintock, M. K., & Herdt, G. (1996). Rethinking puberty: The development of sexual attraction. *Current Directions in Psychological Science, 5,* 178–183.

McConaghy, N. (1970). Subjective and penile plethysmograph responses to aversion therapy for homosexuality: A follow-up study. *British Journal of Psychiatry, 17,* 555–560.

McConaghy, N. (1974). Penile volume responses to moving and still pictures of male and female nudes. *Archives of Sexual Behavior, 3,* 565–570.

McConnell, J. V. (1985). Psychology of the scientist: LII. John B. Watson: Man and myth. *Psychological Reports, 56,* 683–705.

McCoul, M. D., & Haslam, N. (2001). Predicting high risk sexual behaviour in heterosexual and homosexual men: The roles of impulsivity and sensation seeking. *Personality and Individual Differences, 31,* 1303–1310.

McCown, W. (1993). Personality factors predicting failure to practice safer sex by HIV positive males. *Personality and Individual Differences, 14,* 613–615.

McCrae, R. R. (1982). Consensual validation of personality traits: Evidence from self-reports and ratings. *Journal of Personality and Social Psychology, 43*(2), 293–303.

McCrae, R. R. (1989). Why I advocate the Five Factor model of personality: Joint factor analysis of the NEO-PI with other instruments. In D. M. Buss & N. Cantor (Eds.), *Personality psychology: Recent trends and emerging directions* (pp. 237–345). New York: Springer-Verlag.

McCrae, R. R., & Costa, P. C., Jr. (1984). *Emerging lives, enduring dispositions.* Boston: Little & Brown.

McCrae, R. R., & Costa, P. C., Jr. (1987). Validation of the Five-Factor model of personality across instruments and observers. *Journal of Personality and Social Psychology, 52,* 81–90.

McCrae, R. R., & Costa, P. C., Jr. (1997). Conceptions and correlates of openness to experience. In R. Hogan, J. Johnson, & S. Briggs (Eds.), *Handbook of personality psychology* (pp. 825–847). San Diego, CA: Academic Press.

McGirr, L. (2001). Conservative politics in a liberal age: A history of the right in the 1960s. In J. Heideking, J. Helbig, & A. Ortlepp (Eds.), *The sixties revisited: Culture, society, politics* (pp. 451–468). Heidelberg, Germany: Universitätsverlag.

McGuire, W. J., & McGuire, C. V. (1988). Content and process in the experience of self. In L. Berkowitz (Ed.), *Advances in experimental social psychology* (Vol. 21, pp. 97–144). New York: Academic Press.

McKinlay, J. B., & Feldman, H. A. (1994). Age-related variation in sexual activity and interest in normal men: Results from the Massachusetts male aging study. In A. S. Rossi (Ed.), *Sexuality across the life course* (pp. 261–285). Chicago: University of Chicago Press.

McLaren, A. (1999). *Twentieth-century sexuality: A history.* Malden, MA: Blackwell.

Mead, G. H. (1934). *Mind, self, and society.* Chicago: University of Chicago Press.

Meisler, A. W., & Carey, M. P. (1991). Depressed affect and male sexual arousal. *Archives of Sexual Behavior, 20,* 541–554.

Merriam-Webster. (2004). *Merriam-Webster online dictionary* (10th ed.). Springfield, MA: Author.

Meshreki, L. M., & Hansen, C. E. (2004). African American men's female body size preferences based on racial identity and environment. *Journal of Black Psychology, 30,* 451–476.

Meston, C. M., & Gorzalka, B. B. (1996). Differential effects of sympathetic activation on sexual arousal in sexually dysfunctional and functional women. *Journal of Abnormal Psychology, 105,* 582–591.

Meston, C. M., Heiman, J. R., Trapnell, P. D., & Paulhus, D. L. (1998). Socially desirable responding and sexuality self-reports. *Journal of Sex Research, 35*(2), 148–157.

Metz, M. E., & Miner, M. H. (1995). Male "menopause," aging, and sexual function: A review. *Sexuality and Disability, 13,* 287–307.

Metz, M. E., & Miner, M. H. (1998). Psychosexual and psychosocial aspects of male aging and sexual health. *The Canadian Journal of Human Sexuality, 7,* 245–259.

Metz, M. E., Rosser, B. R. S., & Strapko, N. (1994). Differences in conflict-resolution styles among heterosexual, gay, and lesbian couples. *Journal of Sex Research, 31,* 293–308.

Meuwissen, I., & Over, R. (1990). Habituation and dishabituation of female sexual arousal. *Behavioral Research and Therapy, 28,* 217–226.

Meyer-Bahlberg, H. F. L. (1984). Psychoendocrine research on sexual orientation: Current status and future options. In G. J. DeVries, J. P. C. D. Bruin, H. M. B. Uylings, & M. A. Corner (Eds.), *Progress in brain research* (Vol. 61, pp. 375–398). Amsterdam: Elsevier.

Meyer-Bahlberg, H. F. L., Dolezal, C., & Sandberg, D. E. (2000). The association of sexual behavior with externalizing behaviors in a community sample of prepubertal children. In T. G. M. Sandfort & J. Rademakers (Eds.), *Childhood sexuality: Normal sexual behavior and development* (pp. 61–79). New York: Haworth.

Michael, R., Gagnon, J., Laumann, E., & Kolata, G. (1994). *Sex in America: A definitive survey.* Boston: Little, Brown.

Miller, B. C., Benson, B., & Galbraith, K. A. (2001). Family relationships and adolescent pregnancy risk: A research synthesis. *Developmental Review, 21,* 1–38.

Miller, B. C., Monson, B. H., & Norton, M. C. (1995). The effects of forced sexual intercourse on White female adolescents. *Child Abuse and Neglect, 19,* 1289–1301.

Miller, B. C., Norton, M. C., Curtis, T., Hill, E. J., Schvaneveldt, P., & Young, M. H. (1997). The timing of sexual intercourse among adolescents: Family, peer, and other antecedents. *Youth and Society, 29,* 54–83.

Miller, B. C., Norton, M. C., Fan, X., & Chistopherson, C. R. (1998). Pubertal development, parental communication, and sexual values in relation to adolescent sexual behaviors. *Journal of Early Adolescence, 18,* 27–52.

Miller, J. D., Lynam, D., Zimmerman, R. S., Logan, T. K., Leukefeld, C., & Clayton, R. (2004). The utility of the Five Factor model in understanding risky sexual behavior. *Personality and Individual Differences, 36,* 1611–1626.

Miller, K. S., Clark, L. F., Wendell, D. A., Levin, M. L., Gray-Ray, P., Velez, C. N., et al. (1997). Adolescent heterosexual experience: A new typology. *Journal of Adolescent Health, 20,* 179–186.

Miller, R. S. (1997). Inattentive and contented: Relationship commitment and attention to alternatives. *Journal of Personality and Social Psychology, 73,* 758–766.

Mischel, W. (1999). Personality coherence and dispositions in a cognitive-affective personality system (CAPS) approach. In D. Cervone & Y. Shoda (Eds.), *The coherence of personality: Social-cognitive bases of consistency, variability and organization* (pp. 37–60). New York: Guilford.

Mitchell, W. B., DiBartolo, P. M., Brown, T. A., & Barlow, D. H. (1998). Effects of positive and negative mood on sexual arousal in sexually functional males. *Archives of Sexual Behavior, 27,* 197–207.

Moen, P. (1999). *The Cornell couples and careers study.* Ithaca, NY: Cornell University Press.

Mohr, J. J. (2002). Heterosexual identity and the heterosexual therapist: An identity perspective on sexual orientation dynamics in psychotherapy. *The Counseling Psychologist, 30,* 532–566.

Money, J., & Musaph, H. (Eds.). (1977). *Handbook of sexology: Vol. 3.* New York: Elsevier.

Money, J., Schwartz, M., & Lewis, V. G. (1984). Adult erotosexual status and fetal hormonal masculinization and demasculinization: 46, XX congenital virilizing adrenal hyperplasia and 46, XY androgen insensitivity syndrome compared. *Psychoneuroendocrinology, 9,* 405–414.

Moore, J. E., & Kendall, D. C. (1971). Children's concepts of reproduction. *The Journal of Sex Research, 7,* 42–61.

Morgan, D. H. J. (2004). The sociological significance of affairs. In J. Duncombe, K. Harrison, G. Allan, & D. Marsden (Eds.), *The state of affairs: Explorations in infidelity and commitment* (pp. 15–34). Mahwah, NJ: Erlbaum.

Morgan, H. J., & Shaver, P. R. (1999). Attachment processes and commitment to romantic relationships. In J. M. Adams & W. H. Jones (Eds.), *Handbook of interpersonal commitment and relationship stability* (pp. 109–124). New York: Kluwer.

Morris, N. M., & Udry, J. R. (1980). Validation of a self-administered instrument to assess stage of adolescent development. *Journal of Youth and Adolescence, 9,* 275–276.

Morse, S. J., & Gruzen, J. (1976). The eye of the beholder: A neglected variable in the study of physical attractiveness? *Journal of Personality, 44,* 209–225.

Mosher, D. L., & Cross, H. J. (1971). Sex, guilt, and premarital sexual experiences of college students. *Journal of Consulting and Clincial Psychology, 36,* 27–32.

Muehlenhard, C. L., & Linton, M. A. (1987). Date rape and sexual aggression in dating situations: Incidence and risk factors. *Journal of Counseling Psychology, 34,* 186–196.

Murnen, S. K., & Stockton, M. (1997). Gender and self-reported sexual arousal in response to sexual stimuli: A meta-analytic review. *Sex Roles, 37,* 135–153.

Murray, H. A. (1938). *Explorations in personality.* New York: Oxford University Press.

Murray, S. L., Belavia, G. M., Rose, P., & Griffin, D. (2003). Once hurt, twice hurtful: How perceived regard regulates daily marital interactions. *Journal of Personality and Social Psychology, 84,* 126–147.

Murray, S., Holmes, J., & Griffin, D. (1996). The benefits of positive illusions: Idealization and the construction of satisfaction in close relationships. *Journal of Personality and Social Psychology, 70,* 79–98.

Mustanski, B. S., Chivers, M. L., & Bailey, J. M. (2002). A critical review of recent biological research on human sexual orientation. *Annual Review of Sex Research, 13,* 89–140.

Myers, S. M. (1997). Marital uncertainty and childbearing. *Social Forces, 75,* 1271–1289.

Nagel, J. (2003). *Race, ethnicity, and sexuality.* New York: Oxford University Press.

National Institute of Business Management. (1999). *Work/life today.* (Available from 1750 Old Meadow Road, McLean, VA 22102).

National Vital Statistics System. (1999–2000). Divorce rates and marriage rates: What happened. *Monthly Vital Statistics Report, 49.*

Neal, A., Groat, H. T., & Wicks, J. (1989). Attitudes about having children: A study of 600 couples in the early years of marriage. *Journal of Marriage and the Family, 51,* 313–328.

Nedoma, K., & Freund, K. (1961). Somatosexual findings in homosexual men. *Ceskoslovenska Psychiatre, 57,* 100–103.

Netscape Men's Confessions. *Affair With a Co-Worker.* Retrieved February 14, 2007, from http://webcenters.netscape .compuserve.com/men/confession.jsp?confession=116

Netscape Men's Confessions. *Al, 40.* Retrieved February 14, 2007, from http://webcenters.netscape.compuserve.com/ men/confession.jsp?confession=932

Netscape Men's Confessions. *Explosive Sex—Brad.* Retrieved February 14, 2007, from http://webcenters.netscape .compuserve.com/men/confession.jsp?confession=965

Netscape Love & Personals. *My best friend.* Retrieved February 19, 2007, from http://channels.isp.netscape.com/ love/confession.jsp?confession=791

Newcomer, S. F., & Udry, J. R. (1984). Mothers' influence on the sexual behavior of their teenage children. *Journal of Marriage and the Family, 46,* 477–485.

Nisbett, R. E., & Ross, L. (1980). *Human inference: Strategies and shortcomings of human judgment.* Englewood Cliffs, NJ: Prentice Hall.

Nobre, P. J., Wiegel, M., Bach, A. K., Weisberg, R. B., Brown, T. A., Wincze, J. P., et al. (2004). Determinants of sexual arousal and the accuracy of its self-estimation in sexually functional males. *The Journal of Sex Research, 41,* 363–371.

O'Donohue, W., & Plaud, J. J. (1991). The long-term habituation of sexual arousal in the human male. *Journal of Behavioral Therapy and Experimental Psychiatry, 22,* 87–96.

O'Donohue, W. T., & Geer, J. H. (1985). The habituation of sexual arousal. *Archives of Sexual Behavior, 14,* 233–246.

Oggins, J., Leber, D., & Veroff, J. (1993). Race and gender differences in Black and White newlyweds' perceptions of sexual and marital relationships. *The Journal of Sex Research, 30,* 152–160.

Ogletree, S. M., & Ginsburg, H. J. (2000). Kept under the hood: Neglect of the clitoris in common vernacular. *Sex Roles, 43,* 917–926.

Okami, P., & Schackelford, T. K. (2001). Human sex differences in sexual psychology and behavior. *Annual Review of Sex Research, 12,* 186–241.

Oliver, M. B., & Hyde, J. S. (1993). Gender differences in sexuality: A meta-analysis. *Psychological Bulletin, 114,* 29–51.

Owen, W. E. (1987). The verbal expression of love by women and men as a critical communication event in personal relationships. *Women's Studies in Communication, 10,* 15–24.

Palace, E. M. (1995). Modification of dysfunctional patterns of sexual response through autonomic arousal and false physiological feedback. *Journal of Consulting and Clinical Psychology, 63,* 604–615.

Palace, E. M., & Gorzalka, B. B. (1990). The enhancing effects of anxiety on arousal in sexually functional and dysfunctional women. *Journal of Abnormal Psychology, 99,* 403–411.

Palmore, E. B. (1982). Predictors of the longevity difference: A 25-year follow-up. *Gerontologist, 22,* 513–518.

Panksepp, J. (1998). *Affective neuroscience.* New York: Oxford University Press.

Pare, C. M. B. (1956). Homosexuality and chromosomal sex. *Journal of Psychosomatic Research, 1,* 247–251.

Parke, R. D., Simpkins, S. D., McDowell, D. J., Kim, M., Killian, C., Dennis, J., et al. (2002). Relative contributions of families and peers to children's social development. In P. K. Smith & C. H. Hart (Eds.), *Blackwell handbook of childhood social development* (pp. 156–177). Malden, MA: Blackwell.

Paul, E. L., McManus, B., & Hayes, A. (2000). "Hookups": Characteristics and correlates of college students' spontaneous and anonymous sexual experiences. *The Journal of Sex Research, 37,* 76–88.

Paunonen, S. V. (2003). Big Five factors of personality and replicated predictions of behavior. *Journal of Personality and Social Psychology, 84,* 411–424.

Pavlov, I. P. (1927). *Conditioned reflexes.* Oxford: Oxford University Press.

Peplau, L. A. (2001). Rethinking women's sexual orientation: An interdisciplinary, relationship-focused approach. *Personal Relationships, 8,* 1–19.

Peplau, L. A., & Cochran, S. D. (1981). Value orientations in intimate relationships of gay men. *Journal of Homosexuality, 6,* 1–19.

Peplau, L. A., Cochran, S. D., Rook, K., & Padesky, C. (1978). Loving women: Attachment and autonomy in lesbian relationships. *Journal of Social Issues, 34,* 7–27.

Peplau, L. A., Rubin, Z., & Hill, C. T. (1977). Sexual intimacy in dating relationships. *Journal of Social Issues, 33,* 86–109.

Petersen, J. R. (1999). *The century of sex: Playboy's history of the sexual revolution, 1900–1999.* New York: Grove Press.

Peterson, J., & Marin, G. (1988). Issues in the prevention of AIDS among Black and Hispanic men. *American Psychologist, 43,* 871–877.

Pfaus, J. G., Kippin, T. E., & Centeno, S. (2001). Conditioning and sexual behavior: A review. *Hormones and Behavior, 40,* 291–321.

Phoenix, C. H., Goy, R. W., Gerall, A. A., & Young, W. C. (1959). Organizing action of prenatally administered testosterone propionate on the tissues mediating mating behavior in the female guinea pig. *Endocrinology, 65,* 369–382.

Pierce, C. (1988). Stress in the workplace. In A. F. Coner-Edwards & J. Spurlock (Eds.), *Black families in crisis: The middle class* (pp. 27–34). New York: Brunner/Mazel.

Pinel, J. P. J. (2003). *Biopsychology* (5th ed.). Boston: Allyn & Bacon.

Pines, A., & Aronson, E. (1983). Antecedents, correlates, and consequences of sexual jealousy. *Journal of Personality, 51,* 108–136.

Pope, M., & Schulz, P. (1990). Sexual attitudes and behavior in midlife and aging homosexual males. *Journal of Homosexuality, 20,* 169–177.

Porter, R. (1982). *English society in the eighteenth century.* London: Allen Lane.

Poulsson-Bryant, S. (2005). *Hung: A meditation on the measure of Black men in America.* New York: Doubleday.

Prager, K. J., & Buhrmester, D. (1998). Intimacy and need fulfillment in couple relationships. *Journal of Social and Personal Relationships, 15,* 435–469.

Prager, K. J., & Roberts, L. J. (2004). Deep intimate connection: Self and Intimacy in couple relationships. In D. J. Mashek & A. Aron (Eds.), *Handbook of closeness and intimacy* (pp. 43–60). Mahwah, NJ: Erlbaum.

Prins, K. S., Buunk, B. P., & Van Yperen, N. W. (1993). Equity, normative disapproval, and extramarital relationships. *Journal of Social and Personal Relationships, 10,* 39–53.

Public Interest Directorate, American Psychological Association. (1987). *Follow-up report to oral presentation of December 2, 1987. Psychological sequelae of abortion.* Washington, DC: American Psychological Association.

Rachman, S. (1966). Sexual fetishism: An experimental analogue. *Psychological Record, 16,* 293–296.

Rachman, S., & Hodgson, R. J. (1968). Experimentally-induced "sexual fetishism": Replication and development. *Psychological Record, 18,* 25–27.

Rao, K. V., & De Maris, A. (1995). Coital frequency among married and cohabiting couples in the U.S. *Journal of Biosocial Science, 27,* 135–150.

Rebuffe-Scrive, M., Cullberg, G., Lundberg, P. A., Lindatedt, G., & Bjorntorp, P. (1989). Anthropometric variables and metabolism in polycystic ovarian disease. *Human Metabolic Research, 21,* 391–397.

Regan, P. C. (1996). Rhythms of desire: The association between menstrual cycle phases and female sexual desire. *The Canadian Journal of Human Sexuality, 5,* 145–156.

Regan, P. C., & Berscheid, E. (1995). Gender differences in beliefs about the causes of male and female desire. *Personal Relationships, 2,* 345–358.

Regan, P. C., & Berscheid, E. (1996). Beliefs about the state, goals, and objects of sexual desire. *Journal of Sex & Marital Therapy, 22,* 110–120.

Regan, P. C., & Berscheid, E. (1997). Gender differences in characteristics desired in a potential sexual and marriage partner. *Journal of Psychology & Human Sexuality, 9,* 25–37.

Regan, P. C., & Berscheid, E. (1999). *Lust: What we know about human sexual desire.* Thousand Oaks, CA: Sage Publications.

Reinholtz, R. K., & Muehlenhard, C. L. (1995). Genital perceptions and sexual activity in a college population. *The Journal of Sex Research, 32,* 155–165.

Reinisch, J. M., Hill, C. A., Sanders, S. A., & Ziemba-Davis. (1995). High-risk sexual behavior at a midwestern university: A confirmatory survey. *Family Planning Perspectives, 27,* 79–82.

Reinisch, J. M., Sanders, S. A., Hill, C. A., & Ziemba-Davis, M. (1992). High-risk sexual behavior among heterosexual undergraduates at a midwestern university. *Family Planning Perspectives, 24,* 116–121.

Reinisch, J. M., Sanders, S. A., & Ziemba-Davis, M. (1988). The study of sexual behavior in relation to the transmission of human immunodeficiency virus: Caveats and recommendations. *American Psychologist, 43,* 921–927.

Reis, H. T., Nezlek, J., & Wheeler, L. (1980). Physical attractiveness in social interaction. *Journal of Personality and Social Psychology, 38,* 604–617.

Reis, H. T., Wheeler, L., Speigal, N., Nezlek, J., & Perri, M. (1982). Physical attractiveness in social interaction: 2. Why does appearance affect social experience? *Journal of Personality and Social Psychology, 43,* 979–996.

Reiss, I. L. (1967). *The social context of premarital sexual permissiveness.* New York: Holt Rinehart and Winston.

Reiss, I. L. (1986a). *Journey into sexuality: An exploratory voyage.* Englewood Cliffs, NJ: Prentice Hall.

Reiss, I. L. (1986b). A sociological journey into sexuality. *Journal of Marriage and the Family, 48,* 233–242.

Remafedi, G., Resnick, M., Blum, R., & Harris, L. (1992). Demography of sexual orientation in adolescents. *Pediatrics, 89,* 714–721.

Rich, A. (1980). Compulsory heterosexuality and lesbian existence. *Signs: Journal of Women in Culture and Society, 5,* 631–660.

Ripa, C. P. L., Hansen, H. S., Mortensen, E. L., Sanders, S. A., & Reinisch, J. M. (2001). A Danish version of the Sensation Seeking Scale and its relation to a broad spectrum of behavioral and psychological characteristics. *Personality and Individual Differences, 30,* 1371–1386.

Roberts, L. J., & Krokoff, L. J. (1990). A time-series analysis of withdrawal, hostility, and displeasure in satisfied and dissatisfied marriages. *Journal of Marriage and the Family, 52,* 95–105.

Robinson, M. D., & Ryff, C. D. (1999). The role of self-deception in perceptions of past, present, and future happiness. *Personality and Social Psychology Bulletin, 25,* 595–606.

Roche, J. P. (1986). Premarital sex: Attitudes and behavior by dating stage. *Adolescence, 21,* 107–121.

Roscoe, W. (1998). *Changing ones: Third and fourth genders in Native North America.* New York: St. Martin's.

Rosenfeld, A. A., Bailey, R., Siegel, B., & Bailey, G. (1986). Determining incestuous contact between parent and child: Frequency of children touching parents' genitals in a nonclinical population. *Journal of the American Academy of Child Psychiatry, 25,* 481–484.

Rosenfeld, A. A., Siegel, B., & Bailey, R. (1987). Familial bathing patterns: Implications for cases of alleged molestation and for pediatric practice. *Pediatrics, 79,* 224–229.

Rosenfeld, L. B., Stewart, S. C., Stinnett, H. J., & Jackson, L. A. (1999). Preferences for body type and body characteristics associated with attractive and unattractive bodies: Jackson and McGill revisited. *Perceptual & Motor Skills, 89,* 459–470.

Rosenthal, D. A., & Smith, A. M. A. (1997). Adolescent sexual timetable. *Journal of Youth and Adolescence, 26,* 619–636.

Rotheram-Borus, M. J., & Langabeer, K. A. (2001). Developmental trajectories of gay, lesbian, and bisexual youths. In A. R. D'Augelli & C. Patterson (Eds.), *Lesbian, gay, and bisexual identities and youth: Psychological perspectives* (pp. 97–128). New York: Oxford University Press.

Rotheram-Borus, M. J., Rosoario, M., Meyer-Bahlberg, H., Koopman, C., Dopkins, S., & Davies, M. (1994). Sexual and substance use acts among gay and bisexual male adolescents in New York City. *Journal of Sex Research, 31,* 47–57.

Rotter, J. B. (1954). *Social learning and clinical psychology.* Englewood Cliffs, NJ: Prentice-Hall.

Rowe, W., Bennett, S. K., & Atkinson, D. R. (1994). White racial identity models: A critique and alternative proposal. *The Counseling Psychologist, 22,* 129–146.

Rowland, D. L., Cooper, S. E., & Heiman, J. R. (1995). A preliminary investigation of affective and cognitive response to erotic stimulation in men before and after sex therapy. *Journal of Sex & Marital Therapy, 21,* 3–20.

Rowland, D. L., Cooper, S. E., & Slob, A. K. (1996). Genital and psychoaffective response to erotic stimulation in sexually functional and dysfunctional men. *Journal of Abnormal Psychology, 105,* 194–203.

Roy, S. (2000). Mapping my desire. In K. Kay, J. Nagle, & B. Gould (Eds.), *Male lust: Pleasure, power, and transformation* (pp. 23–31). New York: Harrington Park.

Rubin, Z. (1970). Measurement of romantic love. *Journal of Personality and Social Psychology, 16,* 265–273.

Ruble, D. N., & Martin, C. L. (1998). Gender development. In W. Damon & N. Eisenberg (Eds.), *Handbook of child psychology: Vol. 3. Social, emotional, and personality development* (5th ed., pp. 933–1016). New York: Wiley.

Ruggiero, G. (1993). *Binding passions: Tales of magic, marriage, and power at the end of the Renaissance.* New York: Oxford University Press.

Rusbult, C. E. (1980). Commitment and satisfaction in romantic associations: A test of the investment model. *Journal of Experimental Social Psychology, 16,* 172–186.

Rusbult, C. E. (1983). A longitudinal test of the investment model: The development (and deterioration) of satisfaction and commitment in heterosexual involvements. *Journal of Personality and Social Psychology, 45,* 101–117.

Rusbult, C. E., & Van Lange, P. A. M. (1996). Interdependence processes. In E. T. Higgins & A. Kruglanski (Eds.), *Social psychology: Handbook of basic principles* (pp. 564–596). New York: Guilford.

Rusbult, C. E., Verette, J., Whitney, G. A., Slovik, L. F., & Lipkus, I. (1991). Accommodation processes in close relationships: Theory and preliminary empirical evidence. *Journal of Personality and Social Psychology, 60,* 53–78.

Russil, D., & Ellis, B. J. (2003). Evolutionary psychology. In M. Gallagher & R. J. Nelson (Eds.), *Handbook of psychology: Vol. 3. Biological psychology* (pp. 1–33). Hoboken, NJ: Wiley.

Russo, N. F. (2000). Understanding emotional responses after abortion. In J. C. Chrisler, C. Golden, & P. D. Rozee (Eds.), *Lectures on the psychology of women* (pp. 113–128). Boston: McGraw-Hill.

Rust, P. C. (1993). "Coming out" in the age of social constructionism: Sexual identity formation among lesbian and bisexual women. *Gender & Society, 7,* 50–77.

Rutter, V., & Schwartz, P. (1996). Same-sex couples: Courtship, commitment, context. In A. E. Auhagen & M. von Salisch (Eds.), *The diversity of human relationships* (pp. 197–226). New York: Cambridge University Press.

Ryan, G. (2000). Childhood sexuality: A decade of study. Part I—Research and curriculum development. *Child Abuse & Neglect, 24,* 33–48.

Ryan, G., Miyoshi, T., & Krugman, R. (1988). *Early childhood experience of professionals working in child abuse.* Paper presented at the Seventeenth Annual Symposium on Child Abuse and Neglect, Keystone, CO.

Sacks, K. (1998). *How Jews became white folks.* New Brunswick, NJ: Rutgers University Press.

Sadalla, E. K., Kenrick, D. T., & Vershure, B. (1987). Dominance and heterosexual attraction. *Journal of Personality and Social Psychology, 52,* 730–738.

Sanders, S. A., & Reinisch, J. M. (1999). Would you say you "had sex" if . . . ? *Journal of the American Medical Association, 28,* 275–277.

Sandfort, T. G. M., & Cohen-Kettenis, P. T. (2000). Sexual behavior in Dutch and Belgian children as observed by their mothers. In T. G. M. Sandfort & J. Rademakers (Eds.), *Childhood sexuality: Normal sexual behavior and development* (pp. 105–115). New York: Haworth.

Sandfort, T. G. M., & Rademakers, J. (2000a). *Childhood sexuality: Normal sexual behavior and development.* New York: Haworth.

Sandfort, T. G. M., & Rademakers, J. (2000b). Introduction. In T. G. M. Sandfort & J. Rademakers (Eds.), *Childhood sexuality: Normal sexual behavior and development* (pp. 1–3). New York: Haworth.

Sandmel, S. (1978). *Judaism and Christian beginnings.* New York: Oxford University Press.

Sang, B. E. (1993). Existential issues of midlife lesbians. In L. D. Garnets & D. C. Kimmel (Eds.), *Psychological perspectives on lesbian and gay male experiences* (pp. 500–516). New York: Columbia University Press.

Savin-Williams, R. C. (1990). *Gay and lesbian youth: Expressions of identity.* Washington, DC: Hemisphere.

Schachter, S., & Singer, J. (1962). Cognitive, social and physiological determinants of emotional state. *Psychological Review, 68,* 379–399.

Schaie, K. W., & Willis, S. L. (2002). *Adult development and aging.* Upper Saddle River, NJ: Prentice Hall.

Schmalhausen, S. (1931). The war of the sexes. In V. F. Calverton (Ed.), *Women's coming of age* (pp. 260–297). New York: Liveright.

Schmitt, D. P., & Buss, D. M. (2000). Sexual dimensions of person description: Beyond or subsumed by the Big Five? *Journal of Research in Personality, 34,* 141–177.

Schneider, E. L. (1993). Biological theories of aging. In R. L. Sprott, R. W. Huber, & T. F. Williams (Eds.), *The biology of aging.* New York: Springer.

Schneider, M. S. (2001). Toward a reconceptualization of the coming-out process for adolescent females. In A. R. D'Augelli & C. Patterson (Eds.), *Lesbian, gay, and bisexual identities and youth: Psychological perspectives*, 71–96. New York: Oxford University Press.

Schoen, R., Kim, Y. J., Nathonson, C. A., Fields, J., & Astone, N. M. (1997). Why do Americans want children? *Population and Development Review, 23,* 333–358.

Schureurs, K. M. (1993). Sexuality in lesbian couples: The importance of gender. *Annual Review of Sex Research, 4,* 49–66.

Schurhke, B. (2000). Young children's curiosity about other people's genitals. In T. G. M. Sandfort & J. Rademakers (Eds.), *Childhood sexuality: Normal sexual behavior and development* (pp. 27–48). New York: Haworth.

Seaman, L. C. B. (1973). *Victorian England: Aspects of English and imperial history, 1837–1901.* London: Methuen.

SEICUS. (1997). Male involvement in teen pregnancy. *SHOP Talk (School Health Opportunities and Progress) Bulletin, 2.*

Seldin, D. R., Friedman, H. S., & Martin, L. R. (2002). Sexual activity as a predictor of life-span mortality risk. *Personality and Individual Differences, 33,* 409–425.

Semph, M. E. (1979). *Emotional orientation toward sexuality: Its relation to expecting and perceiving contraceptive side effects.* Unpublished honors thesis, University of Western Ontario, London, Ontario.

Serbin, L. A., & Sprafkin, C. H. (1987). A developmental approach: Sexuality from infancy through adolescence. In J. H. Geer & W. T. O'Donohue (Eds.), *Theories of human sexuality* (pp. 163–195). New York: Plenum.

Sergios, P. A., & Cody, J. (1985). Physical attractiveness and social assertiveness skills in male homosexual dating behavior and partner selection. *Journal of Social Psychology, 125,* 505–514.

Shafer, A. B. (2001). The Big Five and sexuality trait terms as predictors of relationships and sex. *Journal of Research in Personality, 35,* 313–338.

Sharot, S. (2001). *A comparative sociology of world religions: Virtuosos, priests, and popular religion.* New York : New York University Press.

Shaver, P. R., Murdaya, U., & Fraley, R. C. (2001). Structure of the Indonesian emotion lexicon. *Asian Journal of Social Psychology, 4,* 201–224.

Shaver, P., Hazan, C., & Bradshaw, D. (1988). Love as attachment: The integration of three behavioral systems. In R. Sternberg & M. Barnes (Eds.), *The psychology of love* (pp. 68–99). New Haven, CT: Yale University Press.

Siegler, I. C., & Brummett, B. H. (2000). Associations among NEO personality assessments and well-being at mid-life: Facet-level analyses. *Psychology and Aging, 15,* 710–714.

Sieving, R., McNeely, C., & Blum, R. (2000). Maternal expectations, mother–child connectedness, and adolescent sexual debut. *Archives of Pediatrics and Adolescent Medicine, 154,* 809–816.

Simon, W. (1996). *Postmodern sexualities.* New York: Routledge.

Simpson, J. A. (1987). The dissolution of romantic relationships: Factors involved in relationship stability and emotional distress. *Journal of Personality and Social Psychology, 53,* 683–692.

Simpson, J. A., Gangestad, S. W., & Lerma, M. (2000). Perception of physical attractiveness: Mechanisms involved in the maintenance of romantic relationships. *Journal of Personality and Social Psychology, 59,* 1192–1201.

Singer, B., & Toates, F. M. (1987). Sexual motivation. *The Journal of Sex Research, 23,* 481–501.

Singh, D. (1993a). Adaptive significance of female physical attractiveness: Role of waist-to-hip ratio. *Journal of Personality and Social Psychology, 65,* 293–307.

Singh, D. (1993b). Body shape and women's attractiveness: The critical role of waist-to-hip ratio. *Human Nature, 4,* 297–321.

Singh, D. (1994). Is thin really beautiful and good? Relationship between waist-to-hip ratio (WHR) and female attractiveness. *Personality and Individual Differences, 16*, 123–132.

Singh, S., & Darroch, J. E. (1999). Trends in sexual activity among adolescent American women: 1982–1995. *Family Planning Perspectives, 31*, 212–219.

Skakkebaek, N. E., Bancroft, J., Davidson, D. W., & Warner, P. (1981). Androgen replacement with oral testosterone undecanoate in hypogonadal men: A double-blind controlled study. *Clinical Endocrinology, 14*, 49–67.

Skinner, B. F. (1938). *The behavior of organisms: An experimental analysis.* New York: Macmillan.

Small, S. A., & Kerns, D. (1991, November). *Sexual coercion in adolescent relationships.* Paper presented at the annual meeting of the National Council on Family Relations, Denver, CO.

Smedley, A. (1999). *Race in North America: Origin and evolution of a worldview* (2nd ed.). Boulder, CO: Westview.

Smedley, A. (2001). Social origins of the idea of race. In C. Stokes, T. Melendez, & G. Rhodes-Reed (Eds.), *Race in 21st century America* (pp. 3–23). East Lansing: Michigan State University Press.

Smedley, A., & Smedley, B. D. (2005). Race as biology is fiction, racism as a social problem is real: Anthropological and historical perspectives on the social construction of race. *American Psychologist, 60*, 16–26.

Smigel, E. O., & Seiden, R. (1968). The decline and fall of the double standard. *Annals of the American Academy of Political and Social Science, 376*, 6–17.

Smith, D. (2002). Hinduism. In L. Woodhead, P. Fletcher, H. Kawanami, & D. Smith (Eds.), *Religions in the modern world: Traditions and transformations* (pp. 15–40). New York: Routledge.

Smith, D. A., Vivian, D., & O'Leary, K. D. (1990). Longitudinal prediction of marital discord from premarital expressions of affect. *Journal of Consulting and Clinical Psychology, 58*, 790–798.

Smith, E. A., & Udry, J. R. (1985). Coital and non-coital sexual behaviors of white and black adolescents. *American Journal of Public Health, 75*, 1200–1203.

Smith, E. R., Becker, M. A., Byrne, D., & Przybyla, D. P. J. (1993). Sexual attitudes of males and females as predictors of interpersonal attraction and marital compatibility. *Journal of Applied Social Psychology, 23*, 1011–1034.

Smith, G. D., Frankel, S., & Yarnell, J. (1997). Sex and death: Are they related? Findings from the Caerphilly cohort study. *British Medical Journal, 315*, 20–27.

Smith, G. E., Eggleston, T. J., Gerrard, M., & Gibbons, F. X. (1996). Sexual attitudes, cognitive associative networks, and perceived vulnerability to unplanned pregnancy. *Journal of Research in Personality, 30*, 88–102.

Snyder, M., Tanke, E. D., & Berscheid, E. (1977). Social perception and interpersonal behavior: On the self-fulfilling nature of social stereotypes. *Journal of Personality and Social Psychology, 35*, 656–666.

Sophie, J. (1985–1986). A critical examination of stage theories of lesbian identity development. *Journal of Homosexuality, 12*, 39–51.

South, S. J., & Baumer, E. (2000). Deciphering community and race effects on adolescent premarital childbearing. *Social Forces, 78*, 1379–1408.

Spanier, G. B., & Margolis, R. L. (1983). Marital separation and extramarital sexual behavior. *The Journal of Sex Research, 19*, 23–48.

Spence, J. T. (1983). Commenting on Lubinski, Tellegen, and Butcher's "Masculinity, femininity, and androgyny viewed and assessed as distinct concepts." *Journal of Personality and Social Psychology, 44*, 440–446.

Spence, J. T. (1985). Gender identification and its implications for masculinity and femininity. In T. B. Sonderegger (Ed.), *Nebraska symposium on motivation and achievement: Psychology and gender* (Vol. 32, pp. 59–95). Lincoln: University of Nebraska Press.

Spence, J. T. (1993). Gender-related traits and gender ideology: Evidence for a multifactorial theory. *Journal of Personality and Social Psychology, 64*, 624–635.

Sprecher, S. (1989). Influences on choice of a partner and on sexual decision making in the relationship. In K. McKinney & S. Sprecher (Eds.), *Human sexuality: The societal and interpersonal context* (pp. 438–462). Norwood, NJ: Ablex.

Sprecher, S. (1994). Two sides to the breakup of dating relationships. *Personal Relationships, 1*, 199–222.

Sprecher, S. (1998). Social exchange theories and sexuality. *Journal of Sex Research, 35*, 32–43.

Sprecher, S. (2002). Sexual satisfaction in premarital relationships: Associations with satisfaction, love, commitment, and stability. *The Journal of Sex Research, 39,* 190–196.

Sprecher, S., & McKinney, K. (1993). *Sexuality.* Newbury Park, CA: Sage Publications.

Sprecher, S., & Regan, P. C. (1998). Passionate and companionate love in courting and young married couples. *Sociological Inquiry, 68,* 163–185.

Sprecher, S., & Regan, P. C. (2000). Sexuality in a relational context. In C. Hendrick & S. S. Hendrick (Eds.), *Close relationships: A sourcebook* (pp. 217–227). Thousand Oaks, CA: Sage Publications.

Sprecher, S., Aron, A., Hatfield, E., Cortese, A., Potapova, E., & Levitskaya, A. (1994). Love: American style, Russian style, and Japanese style. *Personal Relationships, 1,* 349–369.

Sprecher, S., Barbee, A., & Schwartz, P. (1995). "Was it good for you, too?": Gender differences in first sexual intercourse experiences. *The Journal of Sex Research, 32,* 3–15.

Sroufe, L. A., Carlson, E., & Shulman, S. (1993). Individuals in relationships: Development from infancy through adolescence. In D. C. Funder, R. D. Parke, C. Tomlinson-Keasey, & K. Widaman (Eds.), *Studying lives through time: Personality and development* (pp. 315–342). Washington, DC: American Psychological Association.

Stacy, A. W., Newcomb, M. D., & Ames, S. L. (2000). Implicit cognition and HIV risk behavior. *Journal of Behavioral Medicine, 23,* 475–499.

Stanovich, K. E. (2004). *How to think straight about psychology* (7th ed.). Boston: Pearson/Allyn & Bacon.

Starr, B. D., & Weiner, M. B. (1981). *The Starr-Weiner report on sex and sexuality in the mature years.* Manor, NY: Stein & Day.

Stattin, H., & Magnusson, D. (1990). *Paths through life: Vol. 2. Pubertal maturation in female development.* Hillsdale, NJ: Erlbaum.

Steil, J. M. (1997). *Marital equality: Its relationship to the well-being of husbands and wives.* Thousand Oaks, CA: Sage Publications.

Stein, J. A., & Reiser, L. W. (1994). A study of white middle-class adolescent boys' responses to "semenarche" (the first ejaculation). *Journal of Youth and Adolescence, 23,* 373–384.

Steinberg, D. (2000, June 30). *Where I leave off, where you begin.* Retrieved February 15, 2007, from http://www.nearbycafe.com/loveandlust/steinberg/erotic/cn/cn98.html#anchor

Steinberg, L. (2002). *Adolescence* (6th ed.). Boston: McGraw-Hill.

Sternberg, R. J. (1986). A triangular theory of love. *Psychological Review, 93,* 119–135.

Sternberg, R. J. (1988). *The triangle of love.* New York: Basic Books.

Sternberg, R. J. (1997). Construct validation of a triangular love scale. *European Journal of Social Psychology, 27,* 313–335.

Stipp, J. L., Hollister, C. W., & Dirrim, A. W. (1972). *The rise and development of Western civilization* (2nd ed.). New York: Wiley.

Sullivan, P. (1998). Sexual identity development: The importance of target or dominant group membership. In R. L. Sanlo (Ed.), *Working with lesbian, gay, bisexual, and transgender college students: A handbook for faculty and administrators* (pp. 3–12). Westport, CT: Greenwood.

Sullivan, S. (2000). What the fuck? In K. Kay, J. Nagle, & B. Gould (Eds.), *Male lust: Pleasure, power, and transformation* (pp. 101–106). New York: Harrington Park Press.

Surrey, J. (1991). The "self-in-relation": A theory of women's development. In J. Jordan, A. Kaplan, J. B. Miller, I. Stiver, & J. Surrey (Eds.), *Women's growth in connection: Writings from the Stone Center* (pp. 51–66). New York: Guilford.

Swaab, D. F. (2005). The role of hypothalamus and endocrine system in sexuality. In J. S. Hyde (Ed.), *Biological substrates of human sexuality* (pp. 21–74). Washington, DC: American Psychological Association.

Swann, W. B. (1987). Identity negotiation: Where two roads meet. *Journal of Personality and Social Psychology, 53,* 1038–1051.

Swann, W. B., Jr., De La Ronde, C., & Hixon, G. (1994). Authenticity and positivity strivings in marriage and courtship. *Journal of Personality and Social Psychology, 66,* 857–869.

Symons, D. (1979). *The evolution of human sexuality.* New York: Oxford University Press.

Talmadge, L. D., & Dabbs, J. M. (1990). Intimacy, conversational patterns, and concomitant cognitive/emotional processes in couples. *Journal of Social and Clinical Psychology, 9,* 473–488.

Tannahill, R. (1992). *Sex in history.* Chelsea, MI: Scarborough House.

Tanner, J. M. (1962). *Growth at adolescence.* New York: Lippincott.

Taraban, C. B., Hendrick, S. S., & Hendrick, C. (1998). Loving and liking. In P. A. Andersen & L. K. Guerrero (Eds.), *Handbook of communication and emotion: Research, theory, applications, and contexts* (pp. 331–351). San Diego, CA: Academic Press.

Taylor, S. E., Klein, L. C., Lewis, B. P., Gruenwald, T. L., Gurung, R. A. R., & Updegraff, J. A. (2000). Biobehavioral responses to stress in females: Tend-and-befriend, not fight-or-flight. *Psychological Review, 107,* 411–429.

The Concise Oxford English Dictionary. (2004). *The Concise Oxford English Dictionary:* Oxford University Press.

Theinhaus, O. J., Conter, E. A., & Bosmann, H. B. (1986). Sexuality and aging. *Aging and Society, 6,* 39–54.

Thibaut, J. W., & Kelley, H. H. (1959). *The social psychology of groups.* Oxford: Wiley.

ThinkExist.com. *Aldous Huxley quote.* Retrieved February 17, 2007, from http://thinkexist.com/quotes/aldous_huxley/

ThinkExist.com. *Anita Loos quote.* Retrieved February 17, 2007, from http://thinkexist.com/quotes/anita_loos/

ThinkExist.com. *Beyonce quote.* Retrieved February 17, 2007, from http://thinkexist.com/quotes/beyonce_knowles/

ThinkExist.com. *Bill Albert quote.* Retrieved February 17, 2007, from http://thinkexist.com/quotes/bill_albert/

ThinkExist.com. *Billy Joel quote.* Retrieved February 17, 2007, from http://thinkexist.com/quotes/billy_joel/

ThinkExist.com. *Dr. Mary S. Calderone quote.* Retrieved February 17, 2007, from http://thinkexist.com/quotes/Dr._Mary_S._Calderone/

ThinkExist.com. *Dr. Seuss quote.* Retrieved February 17, 2007, from http://en.thinkexist.com/quotes/dr._seuss/

ThinkExist.com. *Elizabeth Fee quote.* Retrieved February 17, 2007, from http://thinkexist.com/quotes/elizabeth_fee/

ThinkExist.com. *Erma Bombeck quotes.* Retrieved February 17, 2007, from http://thinkexist.com/quotes/erma_bombeck/

ThinkExist.com. *Fran Lebowitz quote.* Retrieved February 17, 2007, from http://thinkexist.com/quotes/fran_lebowitz/

ThinkExist.com. *Gloria Steinem quote.* Retrieved February 17, 2007, from http://thinkexist.com/quotes/gloria_steinem/

ThinkExist.com. *Helen Rowland quote.* Retrieved February 17, 2007, from http://thinkexist.com/quotes/helen_rowland/

ThinkExist.com. *Jean Kerr quote.* Retrieved February 17, 2007, from http://thinkexist.com/quotes/jean_kerr/

ThinkExist.com. *John Murphy quote.* Retrieved February 17, 2007, from http://thinkexist.com/quotes/john_murphy/

ThinkExist.com. *Judith Viorst quote.* Retrieved February 17, 2007, from http://thinkexist.com/quotes/judith_viorst/

ThinkExist.com. *Lewis B Hershey quote.* Retrieved February 17, 2007, from http://en.thinkexist.com/quotes/lewis_b._hershey/

ThinkExist.com. *Love and fear quotes.* Retrieved February 17, 2007, from http://en.thinkexist.com/quotes/john_irving/

ThinkExist.com. *Love quotes.* Retrieved February 17, 2007, from http://thinkexist.com/quotation/passion_can_never_purchase_what_true_love_desires/173150.html

ThinkExist.com. *Margaret Mead quote.* Retrieved February 17, 2007, from http://en.thinkexist.com/quotes/margaret_mead/

ThinkExist.com. *Niccolo Machiavelli quotes.* Retrieved February 17, 2007, from http://en.thinkexist.com/quotes/niccolo_machiavelli/

ThinkExist.com. *Passion quotes.* Retrieved February 17, 2007, from http://thinkexist.com/quotation/love_is_when_you_take_away_the_feeling-the/161463.html

ThinkExist.com. *Peter De Vries quote.* Retrieved February 17, 2007, from http://en.thinkexist.com/quotes/peter_de_vries/

ThinkExist.com. *Rejection quote.* Retrieved February 17, 2007, from http://en.thinkexist.com/quotation/ever_had_a_relationship_end_in_such_a_way_that/8709.html

ThinkExist.com. *Relationship ending quote.* Retrieved February 17, 2007, from http://en.thinkexist.com/search/searchquotation.asp?search=relationship+end

ThinkExist.com. *Robert Duvall quote.* Retrieved February 17, 2007, from http://en.thinkexist.com/quotes/robert_duvall/

ThinkExist.com. *Peter F. Drucker quotes.* Retrieved February 17, 2007, from http://thinkexist.com/quotes/peter_f._drucker/

ThinkExist.com. *Rollo May quote.* Retrieved February 17, 2007, from http://en.thinkexist.com/quotes/rollo_may/

ThinkExist.com. *Rollo May quotes.* Retrieved February 17, 2007, from http://en.thinkexist.com/search/searchquotation.asp?search=intimacy

ThinkExist.com. *Stephan Jenkins quote.* Retrieved February 17, 2007, from http://en.thinkexist.com/quotes/stephan_jenkins/

Thompson, A. P. (1983). Extramarital sex: A review of the research literature. *The Journal of Sex Research, 19,* 1–22.

Thompson, A. P. (1984). Emotional and sexual components of extramarital relations. *Journal of Marriage and the Family, 46,* 35–42.

Thorndike, E. L. (1911). *Animal intelligence.* New York: Macmillan.

Thornhill, R., Gangestad, S. W., Miller, R., Scheyd, G., McCollough, J. K., & Franklin, M. (2003). Major histocompatibility complex genes, symmetry, and body scent attractiveness in men and women. *Behavioral Ecology, 14,* 668–678.

Thornton, A. (1990). The courtship process and adolescent sexuality. *Journal of Family Issues, 11,* 239–273.

Tiefer, L. (2000). The social construction and social effects of sex research: The sexological model of sexuality. In C. B. Travis & J. W. White (Eds.), *Sexuality, society, and feminism.* Washington, DC: American Psychological Association.

Tiefer, L. (2001). A new view of women's sexual problems: Why new? Why now? *The Journal of Sex Research, 38,* 89–96.

Tobin, R. M., Graziano, W. G., Vanman, E. J., & Tassinary, L. G. (2000). Personality, emotional experience, and efforts to control emotions. *Journal of Personality and Social Psychology, 79,* 656–669.

Tolhuizen, J. H. (1989). Communication strategies for intensifying dating relationships: Identification, use, and structure. *Journal of Social and Personal Relationships, 6,* 413–434.

Tolman, D. L., & Diamond, L. M. (2001). Desegregating sexuality research: Cultural and biological perspectives on gender and desire. *Annual Review of Sex Research, 12,* 33–74.

Treas, J., & Giesen, D. (2000). Sexual infidelity among married and cohabiting Americans. *Journal of Marriage and the Family, 62,* 48–60.

Treboux, D., & Busch-Rossnagel, N. A. (1990). Social network influences on adolescent sexual attitudes and behaviors. *Journal of Adolescent Research, 5,* 175–189.

Triandis, H. C., McCusker, C., & Hui, C. H. (1990). Multimethod probes of individualism and collectivism. *Journal of Personality and Social Psychology, 59,* 1006–1020.

Trimble, J. (1991). Ethnic specification, validation prospects and the future of drug abuse research. *International Journal of the Addictions, 25,* 149–169.

Trimble, J. E., Helms, J. E., & Root, M. P. P. (2003). Social and psychological perspectives on ethnic and racial identity. In G. Bernal, J. E. Trimble, A. K. Burlew, & F. T. L. Leong (Eds.), *Handbook of racial and ethnic minority psychology* (pp. 239–275). Thousand Oaks, CA: Sage Publications.

Trivers, R. L. (1972). Parental investment and sexual selection. In B. Campbell (Ed.), *Sexual selection and the descent of man: 1871–1971* (pp. 136–179). Chicago: Aldine.

Trobst, K. K., Herbst, J. H., Masters, H. L., III, & Costa, P. C., Jr. (2002). Personality pathways to unsafe sex: Personality, condom use, and HIV risk behaviors. *Journal of Research in Personality, 36,* 117–133.

Troiden, R. R. (1990). Homosexual identity development. *Journal of Adolescent Health Care, 9,* 105–113.

Trudel, G., Turgeon, L., & Piche, L. (2000). Marital and sexual aspects of old age. *Sexual and Relationship Therapy, 15,* 381–406.

Trussell, J., Sturgen, K., Stickler, J., & Dominik, R. (1994). Comparative contraceptive efficacy of the female condom and other barrier methods. *Family Planning Perspectives, 26,* 66–72.

Tylor, E. B. (1958). *Primitive culture.* New York: Harper & Row (Original work published 1871)

U.S. Bureau of Labor Statistics. (1997, September). *Monthly Labor Review Online 120(9).* Retrieved from http://stats.bls.gov/opub/mlr/1997/09/contents.htm

U. S. Census Bureau. (2001). *Overview of race and Hispanic origin.* Washington, DC: U.S. Department of Commerce, Economics and Statistical Administration.

Udry, J. R. (1988). Biological predispositions and social control in adolescent sexual behavior. *American Sociological Review, 53,* 709–722.

Udry, J. R., & Campbell, B. C. (1994). Getting started on sexual behavior. In A. S. Rossi (Ed.), *Sexuality across the life course* (pp. 187–207). Chicago: University of Chicago Press.

Udry, J. R., Talbert, L. M., & Morris, N. M. (1986). Biosocial foundations for adolescent female sexuality. *Demography, 23,* 217–229.

Unger, R. K. (1979). Toward a redefinition of sex and gender. *American Psychologist, 34,* 1085–1094.

Upchurch, D. M., Aneshensel, C. S., Sucoff, C. A., & Levy-Storms, L. (1999). Neighborhood and family contexts of adolescent sexual activity. *Journal of Marriage and the Family, 61,* 920–933.

Van Lange, P. A. M., Agnew, C. R., Harinick, F., & Steemers, G. E. M. (1997). From game theory to real life: How social value orientation affects willingness to sacrifice in ongoing close relationships. *Journal of Personality and Social Psychology, 73,* 1330–1344.

Van Lange, P. A. M., Rusbult, C. E., Drigotas, S. M., Arriga, X. B., Witcher, B. S., & Cox, C. L. (1997). Willingness to sacrifice in close relationships. *Journal of Personality and Social Psychology, 72,* 1373–1395.

Vance, C. S. (1991). Anthropology rediscovers sexuality: A theoretical comment. *Social Science and Medicine, 33,* 875–884.

Vangelitisi, A. L., & Daly, J. A. (1997). Gender differences in standards for romantic relationships. *Personal Relationships, 4,* 203–219.

Victor, J. S. (1980). *Human sexuality: A social psychological approach.* Englewood Cliffs, NJ: Prentice Hall.

Volbert, R. (2000). Sexual knowledge of preschool children. In T. G. M. Sandfort & J. Rademakers (Eds.), *Childhood sexuality: Normal sexual behavior and development* (pp. 5–26). New York: Haworth.

Wade, T. J., Dyckman, K. A., & Cooper, M. (2004). Invisible men: Evolutionary theory and attractiveness and personality evaluations of 10 African American male facial shapes. *Journal of Black Psychology, 30,* 477–488.

Waines, D. (2002). Islam. In L. Woodhead, P. Fletcher, H. Kawanami, & D. Smith (Eds.), *Religions in the modern world: Traditions and transformations* (pp. 182–203). New York: Routledge.

Wallace, R., & Fullilove, M. T. (1999). Why simple regression models work so well describing "risk behaviors" in the U.S.A. *Environment and Planning A, 31,* 719–734.

Wallace, R., Fullilove, M. T., & Flisher, A. J. (1996). AIDS, violence, and behavioral coding: Information theory, risk behavior and dynamic process on core-group sociogeographic networks. *Social Science and Medicine, 43,* 339–352.

Wallen, K. (1995). The evolution of female sexual desire. In P. R. Abramson & S. D. Pinkerton (Eds.), *Sexual nature/sexual culture* (pp. 57–79). Chicago: University of Chicago Press.

Walster, E., Aronson, V., Abrahams, D., & Rottmann, L. (1966). Importance of physical attractiveness in dating behavior. *Journal of Personality and Social Psychology, 4,* 508–516.

Waters, M. C. (1999). *Black identities: West Indian immigrant dreams and American realities.* Cambridge, MA: Harvard University Press.

Watson, D., & Clark, L. A. (1984). Negative affectivity: The disposition to experience aversive emotional states. *Psychological Bulletin, 96,* 465–490.

Watson, D., & Clark, L. A. (1997). Extraversion and its positive emotional core. In R. Hogan, J. Johnson, & S. Briggs (Eds.), *Handbook of personality psychology* (pp. 767–793). San Diego, CA: Academic Press.

Watson, J. B. (1930). *Behaviorism* (rev. ed.). Chicago: University of Chicago Press.

Wayley, C., & Harris, M. (1958). *Minorities in the new world: Six case studies.* New York: Columbia University Press.

Weeks, J. (1986). *Sexuality.* New York: Tavistock Publications.

Wegner, D. M. (1989). *White bears & other unwanted thoughts: Suppression, obsession, and the psychology of mental control.* New York: Penguin Books.

Weis, D. L. (1998). The use of theory in sexuality research. *The Journal of Sex Research, 35,* 1–9.

Weisner-Hanks, M. E. (2000). *Christianity and sexuality in the early modern world.* New York: Routledge.

Wheeler, L., & Kim, Y. (1997). What is beautiful is culturally good: The physical attractiveness stereotype has different content in collectivistic cultures. *Personality and Social Psychology Bulletin, 23,* 795–800.

Whitbeck, J. W., Conger, R., & Kao, M. (1993). The influence of parental support, depressed affect, and peers on the sexual behaviors of adolescent girls. *Journal of Family Issues, 14,* 261–278.

Whitbeck, J. W., Hoyt, D., Miller, M., & Kao, M. (1992). Parental support, depressed affect, and sexual experiences among adolescents. *Youth and society, 24,* 166–177.

Whitbeck, J. W., Yoder, K. A., Hoyt, D. R., & Conger, R. D. (1999). Early adolescent sexual activity: A developmental study. *Journal of Marriage and the Family, 61,* 934–946.

Whitbeck, L. B., Simons, R. L., & Kao, M. Y. (1994). The effects of divorced mothers' dating behavior and sexual attitudes on the sexual attitudes and behavior of their adolescent children. *Journal of Marriage and the Family, 56,* 615–621.

White, J. W., Bondurant, B., & Travis, C. B. (2000). Social constructions of sexuality: Unpacking hidden meanings. In C. B. Travis & J. W. White (Eds.), *Sexuality, society, and feminism* (pp. 11–33). Washington, DC: American Psychological Association.

White, K. (1993). *The first sexual revolution: The emergence of male heterosexuality in modern America.* New York: New York University Press.

White, L., & Keith, B. (1990). The effect of shift work on the quality and stability of marital relations. *Journal of Marriage and the Family, 52,* 453–462.

White, L. A., Fisher, W. A., Byrne, D., & Kingma, R. (1977, May). *Development and validation of a measure of affective orientation to erotic stimuli: The sexual opinion survey.* Paper presented at the Midwestern Psychological Association, Chicago.

White, R. W. (1959). Motivation reconsidered: The concept of competence. *Psychological Review, 66,* 297–333.

Wiederman, M. W. (1997). Extramarital sex: Prevalence and correlates in a national survey. *The Journal of Sex Research, 34,* 167–174.

Wiederman, M. W., Maynard, C., & Fretz, A. (1996). Ethnicity in 25 years of published sexuality research: 1971–1995. *The Journal of Sex Research, 33,* 339–342.

Wiggins, J. D., & Lederer, D. A. (1984). Differential antecedents of infidelity in marriage. *American Mental Health Counselors, 6,* 152–161.

Willis, S. L., & Schaie, K. W. (1999). Intellectual functioning in midlife. In S. L. Willis & J. D. Reid (Eds.), *Life in the middle: Psychological and social development in middle age* (pp. 233–247). San Diego, CA: Academic.

Wilson, E. O. (1975). *Sociobiology: The new synthesis.* Cambridge, MA: Harvard University Press.

Wilson, T. D. (2002). *Strangers to ourselves: Discovering the adaptive unconscious.* Cambridge, MA: Harvard University Press.

Winslow, R. W., Franzini, L. R., & Hwang, J. (1992). Perceived peer norms, casual sex, and AIDS risk prevention. *Journal of Applied Social Psychology, 22,* 1809–1827.

Wood, J. T. (1997). Clarifying the issues. *Personal Relationships, 4,* 221–228.

Woolf, H. B., Artin, E., Crawford, F. S., Gilman, E. W, Kay, M. W., Pease, R. W., Jr., et al. (Eds.). (1973). *Webster's New Collegiate Dictionary.* Springfield, MA: G. & C. Merriam.

Woollett, A., & Marshall, H. (2001). Motherhood and mothering. In R. K. Unger (Ed.), *Handbook of the psychology of women and gender* (pp. 170–182). New York: Wiley.

Worthington, R. L., Savoy, H. B., Dillon, F. R., & Vernaglia, E. R. (2002). Heterosexual identity development: A multidimensional model of individual and social identity. *The Counseling Psychologist, 30,* 496–531.

Wurtele, S. K., Kast, L. A., & Melzer, A. M. (1992). Sexual abuse prevention education for young children: A comparison of teachers and parents as instructors. *Child Abuse & Neglect, 16,* 865–876.

Wyatt, G. E. (1999). Beyond invisibility of African American males: The effects on women and families. *The Counseling Psychologist, 27,* 802–809.

Wyatt, G. E., Peters, S. D., & Guthrie, D. (1988). Kinsey revisited: Part II. Comparisons of the sexual socialization and sexual behavior of Black women over 33 years. *Archives of Sexual Behavior, 17,* 289–232.

Young, W. A. (2002). *Quest for harmony: Native American spiritual traditions.* New York: Seven Bridges Press.

Zack, N. (2001). Different forms of mixed race: Microdiversity and destabilization. In C. Stokes, T. Melendez, & G. Rhodes-Reed (Eds.), *Race in 21st century America* (pp. 49–58). East Lansing: Michigan State University Press.

Zandi, J. (2000). Finding my "Yes!" In K. Kay, J. Nagle, & B. Gould (Eds.), *Male lust: Pleasure, power, and transformation* (pp. 73–76). New York: Harrington Park Press.

Zebrowitz, L. A. (1997). *Reading faces: Window to the soul?* Boulder, CO: Westview.

Zucker, K. J. (2001). Biological influences on psychosexual differentiation. In R. Unger (Ed.), *Handbook of the psychology of women and gender* (pp. 101–115). New York: Wiley.

Zuckerman, M., Eysenck, S. B. G., & Eysenck, H. J. (1978). Sensation seeking in England and America: Cross-cultural, age, and sex comparisons. *Journal of Consulting and Clinical Psychology, 46,* 139–149.

Zuckerman, M., Tushup, R., & Finner, S. (1976). Sexual attitudes and experience: Attitudes and personality correlates and changes produced by a course in sexuality. *Journal of Consulting and Clinical Psychology, 44,* 7–19.

# Index

Note: In page references, f indicates figures and t indicates tables.

# Author Biography

**Craig A. Hill** earned his PhD in social psychology from the University of Texas at Austin in 1984, with dissertation research examining personality traits related to affiliation motivation. Following a postdoctoral position at the University of Utah in social-personality and organizational psychology, he taught at several universities before becoming a research scientist at The Kinsey Institute for Sex, Gender, and Reproduction at Indiana University in 1987. In 1991, he joined the Psychology Department at Indiana University—Purdue University Fort Wayne (IPFW), where he began his own research program on personality and sexual motivation. He is currently an associate professor of psychology.

Dr. Hill has published a number of articles in such scientific journals as the *Journal of Personality and Social Psychology,* the *Journal of Research in Personality,* and *The Journal of Sex Research.* The courses he teaches are human sexuality, social psychology, personality theory, elementary psychology, and undergraduate teaching assistant experience. He typically has at least several undergraduate students involved in his research on sexual motivation each semester. He is adviser for the IPFW chapter of Psi Chi The National Honor Society in Psychology and the Psychology Club.